Natural Language Semantics

B

This book is dedicated to my parents
John and Molly Allan
and to my wife
Wendy Allen

Natural Language Semantics

Keith Allan

BLACKWELL
Publishers

First published 2001

2 4 6 8 10 9 7 5 3 1

Blackwell Publishers Ltd
108 Cowley Road
Oxford OX4 1JF
UK

Blackwell Publishers Inc.
350 Main Street
Malden, Massachusetts 02148
USA

British Library Cataloguing in Publication Data
A CIP catalogue record for this book is available from the British Library.

Library of Congress Cataloging-in-Publication Data has been applied for

ISBN 0-631-19296-4 (hardback); 0-631-19297-2 (paperback)

Typeset by the author

Printed in Great Britain by M.P.G. Books Ltd, Bodmin, Cornwall

This book is printed on acid-free paper.

Contents

4 Morphology and listemes   107

5 The power of words: connotation and jargon   147

6 Semantic relations between sentences   181

Preface

Natural Language Semantics discusses fundamental concepts for linguistic semantics, combining theoretical exegesis of several methods of inquiry with some detailed semantic analysis. It aims to equip the reader with the basic tools and skills needed to progress to original research in semantics. The intended readership is undergraduate and graduate students of linguistics and relevant areas of psychology, philosophy, anthropology, sociology, communications, language studies, and education. Pilot usage has shown that students find the material challenging but manageable. Basic familiarity with linguistics is assumed, because terms such as *syntax, morphology, phoneme, sentence, noun phrase, NP, verb, VP* are used but not explained. "Symbols and conventions" (p. xv) lists all symbols used in the book. In every chapter, definitions of terms and concepts, and also important assumptions, are highlighted and numbered for ready reference. Key words (words that refer to key concepts) are presented in SMALL CAPITALS when introduced, and then listed at the end of the chapter along with a summary of the main points made. Most sections end with exercises to aid, complement, and test learning and understanding to that point. Answers to many exercises are available on-line by application to the author; email keith.allan@arts.monash.edu.au. Suggestions for further reading are indicated in the text by a superscript number in square brackets: [0]. The book's "Index" identifies in bold font the location of definitions and explications of terms.

The underlying philosophy of *Natural Language Semantics* is that semantics is about meaning in human languages and linguistic meaning is cognitively and functionally motivated. Human language is not a code in which auditory or visual signals are converted on a one-to-one basis into cognitive structures – or vice versa. Instead, when used normally, language provides a set of underspecified clues that need to be expanded by semantic and pragmatic inferences based on knowledge of the lexicon and grammar but heavily reliant upon encyclopedic knowledge and awareness of the conventions for language use. Human beings use language as an essential means of cementing social bonding and displaying it to others, at both individual and community levels. Expressing meaning through language is deeply influenced by the social-interactive functions of language – demonstrated in the pervasive importance of the cooperative principle, common ground, and implicature. Semantic theory must explain how this is achieved by giving a demonstrably rational account of the structure of the meaningful categories and constructions of human language, their properties, interrelations, and motivations. *Natural Language Semantics* takes up the challenge to elucidate paths to that goal.

Chapters 1–2 introduce fundamental assumptions about meaning in language. Chapter 1 explains compositionality, inference, the functions of a theory, and criteria for choosing a metalanguage to use in semantic analysis. The importance of context in fixing meaning is briefly examined, leading to discussion of the speech event and the conventions of cooperative behaviour in language interaction. The most significant category of context is a model of the world-and-time spoken of, through which the speaker refers to things outside of language. In order to understand language, a hearer must be able to reconstruct this model from his or her own resources. Speaker meaning and hearer meaning is examined in Chapter 2 which focuses on the relating of 'dictionary meanings' to the world-and-time spoken of.

Chapters 3–5 are on lexicological semantics. Listemes – the words and other language expressions listed in the lexicon (= dictionary) are the principal building blocks for meaning. Chapter 3 argues that whereas information about listemes is listed in the lexicon, information about the things a listeme denotes is entered into the encyclopedia of which the lexicon is a part. The sources and stylistic characteristics of listemes and the effects of form on word meaning are the topics of Chapters 4–5. Chapter 4 identifies which kinds of morphological items are listemes; it also explains the various types of sound symbolism. Chapter 5 focuses on the semantic significance of connotation, a topic that receives minimal attention in most books on semantics.

Chapters 6–7 explain formal semantic tools in the course of beginning a semantics for clauses and sentences. Chapter 6 introduces propositional logic as a mechanical procedure for evaluating truth. This naturally leads first to discussion of entailment, then to conventional and conversational implicature: all are used extensively in the rest of the book. Conversational implicature is pragmatic inference, important in the interpretation of utterance meaning and to recognizing the speaker's presuppositions – also examined in this chapter. Chapter 7 adopts the language of mathematics in assembling tools such as predicate logic, meaning postulates, set theory, functions, and lambda expressions as rigorous means for analysing the internal semantic composition of clauses and sentences. These tools are necessary for the formal semantic specification of a lexicon entry – left aside in Chapter 3 for want of such instruments. They are extensively used in subsequent chapters.

Chapters 8–10 review cognitive and functional approaches to semantics, and lexical semantics in particular. Chapter 8 examines semantic frames, semantic fields, and analysis in terms of semantic components or primitives. It appraises semantic primitives, what a semantic description is meant to achieve, and who or what a semantic specification is designed for. An important finding in Chapter 8, amply confirmed later in the book, is that the semantic specifications for a listeme are sometimes incomplete without an accompanying statement of the standard conversational implicature. It is evident that semantic properties and relations are constrained and informed by the categories and relations that we humans experience in the world around us, and conceive of in abstract fields such as knowledge and moral or ethical behaviour. In short, semantic categories depend on human cognitive awareness. In Chapter 9, the relation between word, percept, and thing spoken of is explored within a language and across languages to reveal the influence of human perceptions and experience in determining semantic categories, properties, and relations. Chapter 10 evaluates prototype and stereotype semantics, and defines the links between linguistic labels, the things they can be used to refer to, and how reference is achieved.

Although ill-advised, the pressured teacher could end here. The last four chapters of *Natural Language Semantics* demonstrate the application of formal methods of semantic analysis to an extensive corpus of data that confirms the cognitive and functional motivations for semantic composition.

Chapters 11–12 investigate the internal semantics of clauses. Chapter 11 addresses the semantics of mood, tense, modality, and thematic roles in the semantic frames of clause predicates. Pursuing a rigorous componential analysis of clause predicates, Chapter 12 reviews and compares Jackendoff's 'lexical conceptual structures' of verbs, and the 'logical structures' of predicates in Van Valin's role and reference grammar.

Chapter 13 turns from the semantics of predicates to the internal semantics of NPs, focusing on countability, quantifiers, and (in)definiteness in English. These NP categories, together with extensionality and anaphora (Chapter 2), naming (Chapter 3), gender marking and nominal classification (Chapter 9), are what help the hearer determine whether to update the information on some entity already spoken of or to detect a new one (Chapter 13). The book ends with a section that uses insights from earlier chapters to make an exhaustive analysis of all the constituents of a simple classificatory sentence.

Natural Language Semantics ends with an "Epilogue" that looks back on what has been achieved and forward to the future of linguistic semantics.

No introductory book on semantics can encompass everything that an author would like to include. There is hardly a topic touched upon which has not given rise to an extensive literature and almost as many points of view as there are authors. References cited in the text or as "Notes on further reading" can fill out the semantic sketches given here. There are also annotations in "References". Handy sources of summary information are to be found in encyclopedias such as the *Encyclopedia of Languages and Linguistics* 1994 and the *International Encyclopaedia of Linguistics* 2001 [1992]. The most recent views are to be found in scholarly journals such as *Cognition, Cognitive Linguistics, Journal of Linguistics, Journal of Pragmatics, Journal of Semantics, Language, Language Sciences, Linguistics and Philosophy, Linguistic Inquiry, Natural Language Semantics, Pragmatics and Cognition*, to mention just a few. No topic in semantics is self-contained, and the sequence of chapters in this book is largely determined by the need to know about one topic in order to understand the next. Even so, in the interests of continuity and easing the learning burden, some new concepts have to be mentioned before being properly examined. In general, the later chapters contain more reliable information on a given topic than the earlier ones do.

Thanks are due to Wendy Allen for spousely support through thick and thin, Peter Barclay (for the Western Dani), Francis Bond, Ronnie Cann, Richard Holton, Lloyd Humberstone, Ray Jackendoff, Sakarepe Kamene (for the Zia), Peter Kipka, Adrienne Lehrer, Robert MacLaury, Sally McConnell-Ginet, Dick Oehrle, Bert Peeters, Hideo Sawada, Andy Smith, Jae Song (for the Korean and more), Humphrey van Polanen Petel, Robert D. Van Valin Jr, Natalia Vyshnevy (for the Ukrainian), Debra Ziegeler, and several anonymous reviewers for their help on this or that topic. Kate Burridge deserves special thanks for suggesting ways to make the text more readable. No one but me is in any way to blame for the infelicities that remain.

Keith Allan
Monash University, Vic 3800. Australia
keith.allan@arts.monash.edu.au
http://www.monash.edu.au/ling/ka.shtml

Symbols and conventions

Typographical conventions

- Ch.1 refers to Chapter 1
- §7.3 refers to Chapter 7 section 7.3.
- Examples are numbered within chapters.
- 'Single quotes' indicate quotations from other texts or from examples in this text. Also so-called 'scare quotes'.
- "Double quotes" give meanings (senses). Also they enclose headings for parts of this part, e.g.. "References".

Different fonts indicate statuses of parts of the text. Certain symbols (see below) have specified fonts but otherwise:
- *Italic script* is used for words and sentences cited within the text. It is also used for focus within examples.
- SMALL CAPITALS are used to focus on terms in the text.
- **Bold** is sometimes used for focus in the text and within examples. Semantic representations are often bolded and followed by a prime; words within them are separated by underline, e.g. **be_the_wife_of′**.
- **SMALL BOLD CAPITALS** mark primary stress e.g. *UMpire*
- In morph-by-morph translations components of a morph are tied by dots, e.g.

Co   mama   robi?
what   mother   3.s.do   ['3.s.do' translates the "third person singular of *do*"]
"What are you doing mother?"

Selected phonetic and prosodic symbols

V	any vowel
VV *or* V:	long vowel
V•	half long vowel
v́	stressed vowel

Vowels with IPA values:
i, ɪ, e, ɛ, æ, a, ɑ, ɒ, ɔ, o, u, ə

Additional vowels in non-rhotic (e.g. British) English phonemic transcriptions:

ʌ	low-mid central vowel, e.g. *butt*
ei	diphthong in *bate*
eə	diphthong in *air*
ai	diphthong in *bite*
aiə	triphthong in *fire*
ou	diphthong in *boat*

Consonants

C	any consonant
C:	geminate (long) consonant
p, b, t, d, c, k, g, kp, q, ʔ	stops
ȼ, č, ǰ	affricates
f, v, θ, ð, s, z, š, x	fricatives
w, ɹ, j, h	glides
m, ṇ, n, ŋ	nasals
r	alveolar trill
l	alveolar lateral
ṭ	voiceless alveolar retroflex
t'	voiceless alveolar ejective
kʰ	aspirated voiceless velar stop
pꟷ	unreleased voiceless bilabial stop

Miscellaneous prosodic and phonological symbols

[kʰæt]	phonetic *cat*
/ræm/	phonemic *ram*, [ɹæm]
'	primary stress in phonetic and phonemic transcriptions, e.g. / 'ʌmpaiə/
/	pause (disjuncture), e.g. *John, / come here!*
yès	simple fall tone
yês	rise-fall tone
yés	simple rise tone
yɛ̌s	fall-rise tone
yɛ̄s	level tone
/ mid $^{high}_{low}$ /	Relative pitch levels. Typically, mid is normal and displays a neutral attitude; high indicates excitement and enthusiasm; low is for parenthetical, perfunctory, uninterested, or resigned remarks; also, for tailing off a topic to hand over the floor.

Other symbols

∅	(a) zero morphological form; (b) the null (empty) set or ensemble
1,2,3	(in morph-by-morph interpretations) first, second, third person
Adj	adjective
Adv	adverb
Adv$_{dyn}$	dynamic adverb
Adv$_{stat}$	stative adverb
AP	adjective phrase
Aux	auxiliary verb
A'	the complement set of A, A'={x:x∉A}
ben	beneficiary/benefactive
c	(a) conclusion from premises; (b) constant term (name)
[c/v]Φ	an instruction to replace every variable, v, in Φ by the constant, c.
C	connective, truth functor
Conj	conjunction

Det	determiner
e_{OL}	any expression in the object language
"e_M"	metalanguage expression giving the sense of an object language
F	(SMALL CAPITAL) feminine gender
F	false (in propositional logic)
F	(**bold**) future tense
iff	if and only if (biconditional)
L	landmark (cognitive grammar)
λ	lambda, the set abstraction operator
L_P	the predicate calculus
loc	locative
M	(SMALL CAPITAL) masculine gender
M	a model
$M^{w,t}$	model of the world(s) and time(s) spoken of
Man.Adv	manner adverb
N	(SMALL CAPITAL) neuter gender
N	noun
N	(**bold**) present tense
N_0	noun unmarked for number
NEG	negation
NP	noun phrase
$[NP_A]$	NP is actor
$[NP_U]$	NP is undergoer
NSM	natural semantic metalanguage (Wierzbicka, Chapter 8)
O1	first or direct object
p	(**bold**) present participle
p, q	variables for propositions
P	(**bold**) past tense
P, Q	variables for predicates
Φ, Ψ	variables for well-formed formulae
PL	(SMALL CAPITALS) plural
poss	possessive
Pp	(**bold**) past participle
PP	prepositional phrase
Pred	predicate
$Pred_n$	n-place predicate
Prep	preposition
Q	quantifier
Q.Adv	quantifying adverb
Qx	quantifier, e.g. ∀x, [*few* x: Fx], [*a(n)* x: Fx], [*the* x: Fx]
RRG	role and reference grammar (Chapter 12)
S	(SMALL CAPITAL) singular
S	sentence
t	(a) time (b) term (constant or variable)
⟦e⟧	the denotation of e
$⟦t⟧^{M,g}$	the denotation of term t in model M under assignment g
T	(a) true (propositional logic); (b) trajector (cognitive grammar)

$t_i < t_j$	time t_i precedes time instant t_j
$t_i \leq t_j$	t_i precedes or is simultaneous with t_j
$t_i > t_j$	t_i follows t_j
v	variable, e.g. x
V	verb
VP	verb phrase
vPrt	verb particle (in phrasal verb)
wff	a well-formed formula
<w,t>	world–time pair, an index
x, y	(a) variables for individuals; (b, Chapter 13) variables for ensembles
∴	therefore
∵	because
*X	X is unattested, unacceptable, ungrammatical
*?X	X is most probably unacceptable
??X	X is highly dubious
?X	X is somewhat doubtful
#X	X is inappropriate in the relevant sense
⇒	(a) meaning derives from, "X"⇒"Y" "sense Y derives from sense X"; (b) translates into, A⇒B "A translates into B"
(a)	sense is copied or semantically extended to, A⇨B "the sense of A is copied or extended to B"
⊢p	turnstile p, p is valid from the premises
⊬p	invalid inference, p is not valid from the premises
∧	conjunction ("and"), $p \land q$ "p and q"
∨	inclusive disjunction ("and/or"), $p \lor q$ "p and/or q"
⊻	exclusive disjunction ("or else"), $p \veebar q$ "only one of either p or q"
→	(a) conditional (semantic implication), $p \rightarrow q$ "if p then q"; (b) syntactic expansion symbol or rewrite arrow, S→NP VP "S expands to NP and VP"
↛	not a logical implication, $p \nrightarrow q$ "q is not a logical implication from p"
↔	biconditional (semantic equivalence), $p \leftrightarrow q$ "p if and only if (=iff) q"
=	identity, x=y "x is identical to y"
≠	not identical to, x≠y "x is not identical to y"
¬p	not-p, it is not the case that p (negation)
⊩	entails, A⊩B "A entails B"
⊮	not entail, A⊮B "A does not entail B"
⊪	synonymous with, A⊪B "A and B are synonymous"
⫴	not synonymous, A⫴B "A and B are not synonymous"
▶	conventionally implicates, A▶B "A conventionally implicates B"
↯	not conventionally implicate, A ↯ B "A does not conventionally implicate B"
▷	conversationally implicates, A▷B "A conversationally implicates B"
(b)	(a) precedes chronologically; (b) takes precedence over. A<B (a) "A precedes B"; (b) "A takes precedence over B when choosing between them"
➤	is a better exemplar than, A➤B "A is a better exemplar than B"
⌢	concatenates with, A⌢B "A is concatenated with B and precedes it"

»	presupposes, A»B "A presupposes B"
⊢[Φ]	(**bold** ⊢) declarative mood
?[Φ]	(**bold ?**) interrogative mood
![Φ]	(**bold !**) imperative mood
X[Φ]	(**bold X**) expressive mood
¡[Φ]	(**bold ¡**) (declarative) subjunctive mood
?[¡[Φ]]	(**bold ?** and **¡**) interrogative subjunctive mood
◇Φ	it is possible that Φ is true
□Φ	Φ is necessarily true, Φ must be so
∃x	there is some (at least one) x (existential quantifier)
∃!x	there is exactly one x
∀x	for all x (universal quantifier)
∈	member (element) of, x∈F "x is a member of set F"
∉	not a member of, x∉G "x is not a member of set G"
{x:Px}=F	every member of set F has the property P
{x,y,z}=F	set F has the members x, y, and z (taken in any sequence)
⊆	(a) subset of, A⊆B "A is a subset of B"; (b, Chapter 13) subensemble of, x⊆y "ensemble x is a part of ensemble y"
⊄	(a) not a subset of, A⊄B "A is not a subset of B"; (b, Chapter 13) not a part of, x⊄y "ensemble x is not a part of ensemble y"
⊂	(a) proper subset of, A⊂B "A is a proper subset of B"; (b, Chapter 13) proper part (subensemble) of, x⊂y "ensemble x is a proper part of ensemble y"
∩	(a) overlap (intersection), F∩G "sets F and G overlap"; (b, Chapter 13) overlap, x∩y "the overlap of ensembles x and y"
∪	(a) merge (union), F∪G "the merge of sets F and G"; (b, Chapter 13) merge, x∪y "the merge of ensembles x and y"
⌈x:x Fx⌉=f	f is the ensemble of parts that are f
∪x:x⊆u	the merge of all subensembles of u
[Qx: Fx]	restricted quantifier, quantification is restricted to x that are F
<x,y>	a two-tuple or ordered pair
$<x_1,x_2,...x_n>$	n-tuple
|x|	measure function on x, the quantity of x
≪	very much less than
≈	approximately equal to, about the same as
≪	much less than
<	less than
≤	(a) less than or equal to; (b) is a meronym of
≥	greater than or equal to
>	greater than
≯	not greater than
≫	much greater than
≫	very much greater than
≫̸	not very much greater than

1 Some fundamental concepts for semantics

All science, all significant inquiry, is a web with indefinite frontiers.
(Justus Buchler 'Introduction' to Peirce 1940:xii)

> It is advisable to read the "Preface" before starting on this chapter.

1.1 Where we are heading

This chapter outlines some fundamental concepts for semantics, concepts that will be referred to either explicitly or implicitly throughout the rest of the book. Here, and throughout the book, KEY words and concepts are introduced in SMALL CAPITALS and also listed in the summary section.

In doing semantics it is essential to define the terms used in discussion. For instance:

Definition 1.1 SEMANTICS is the study of meaning in human languages.

To begin with, interpret the word *meaning* as anyone who knows English might reasonably do; this whole book is about the meaning of *meaning*. Note that within the discipline of linguistics the term *semantics* is not in the least bit pejorative as it is in the colloquial accusation *That's just semantics!* which means "You're just quibbling and prevaricating." The definition of semantics refers to human languages – also referred to throughout the book as 'natural languages' – and we discuss them in §1.2.

> *killed, crocodile, hunter, the, the*

Textbox 1

If I ask you to construct a meaningful sentence using all the words in Textbox 1, you can do so because meaning is compositional. The compositionality of meaning is examined in §1.3. It raises the distinction between the language we are describing, the OBJECT LANGUAGE, and the language (and formulae) we use when describing it, the METALANGUAGE. Because semantics is about meaning in human languages, the object language will be a human language. But what form does the language of semantic theory (the metalanguage) take? §1.4 discusses the options and also the functions of a THEORY. Like any theory, a semantic theory is developed by applying the analyst's experience and intuitions to inferences drawn from occurrences of actual speech events. INFERENCE is defined and examined in §1.5.

Meaning in language is significantly underspecified. For a simple demonstration, consider 1.

1 Last night the King of France fell off her bike while playing polo.

I expect you to be surprised by 1 and to recognize it as nonsense. This does not depend on what is explicit in 1 but on knowledge that I expect you to have, namely: that there is no longer a King of France; that polo is played on horseback not bikes; and that 'her' cannot normally refer to a king. Every language user relies on nonlinguistic as well as linguistic knowledge when speaking and understanding language. In §§1.6–8 we consider aspects of the speech situation and the conventions of language use that facilitate the underspecification of meaning. In §1.6 we define speaker, speech act, hearer, and indexicality. §1.7 is on context and common ground. §1.8 explains the semantic expectations that arise from the conventions for cooperative behaviour in language interaction. §1.9 summarizes the chapter and looks ahead to the next.

1.2 Human language and semantics

Human languages are important because of the meanings they convey. It is a bonus that the sound of a human voice is comforting, or that beautiful calligraphy delights us: these are by-products of the main function. Therefore, semantics studies the essential property of language.

Human language can be investigated from at least four different perspectives.

(a)   Language is manifest as a PHYSICAL object or physical event. Right now, you can see language in the print before your eyes. You see people signing in ASL, Auslan and other languages for the deaf; you hear language spoken, even feel the air pressure changing if you are close enough to someone's mouth when they speak. Language as a physical object or physical event is language uttered at a particular time in a particular place – giving it spatio-temporal coordinates.

> *Definition 1.2* In the CANONICAL SPEECH EVENT, Speaker makes an utterance to Hearer at a certain time and place.

The physical attributes of language are only relevant to semantics with respect to forms and modulations on them which give rise to meaningful effects, e.g. the sound symbolism (Chapter 4) which links the meanings of *bash, crash, flash, smash, splash*, etc.; the stress differences between 2 and 3 (where **BOLD SMALL CAPITALS** identify the stressed syllable); and the tone differences that distinguish the statement in 4 (final fall tone) from the question in 5 (final rise tone).

2   Maisie didn't **SHOOT** her husband, she **KNIFED** him.
3   Maisie didn't shoot her **HUS**band, it was her ex-**LOV**er.
4   Maisie spoke to Jòe.
5   Maisie spoke to Jóe?

(b)   Ask yourself what the physical manifestations of language are manifestations of. The answer: something ABSTRACT and intangible. English, for instance, is not just all that is written and spoken in English; it is also something abstracted from people and times and places, it is something that speakers of English are able to use in order to say something that has never ever been said before – consequently it must exist independently of any particular speakers. Most semantic analysis approaches language as something abstracted from the spoken and written texts that people like you and I actually produce when communicating with others.

(c)   To use a language, you must know it: so language is also a COGNITIVE or psychological entity. Exemplified and discussed in terms of functional, conceptual, and cognitive semantics from Chapter 8 onwards is lots of evidence that the cognitive aspects of language are of immense importance to the construction of meaning. This gives rise to:

> *Assumption 1.1* Meaning in natural languages is very responsive to, and often a reflex of, human perception and conception.

(d)   Language exists as a vehicle for communication between people; in other words, language is a manifestation of SOCIAL INTERACTIVE behaviour. Social interaction includes flirting and passing the time of day, but also the exchange of information and the expression of arguments. It involves the use of language for entertainment in factual historical anecdotes as well as in fictional narrative. Social interaction is of primary importance within human communities, and language is the principal means of social interaction; cf. Clark 1996. Whether or not language was motivated and developed for this purpose, its grammar is certainly influenced by the fact that it is a means of social interaction, a means of revealing one's thoughts and perceptions to others.

This book is a general introduction to the field of semantics that attempts to give fair treatment to a number of differing perspectives on semantics. Nevertheless, an underlying philosophy will be apparent:

> *Assumption 1.2* The expression of meaning through language is an essential means of cementing human bonding and of displaying it to others, both at the individual and the community level.

Assumption 1.2 does not conflict with the view that language is a system for the expression of thought.[1] Some people think in visual images, so language is not a prerequisite for solipsistic thinking. But, beyond the simplest level, it is absolutely essential for the expression of thought to others. Whether and how one expresses a particular thought to a particular other is determined, more often than not, by a judgment of the desired effect on the hearer or reader. Because of the dominant social interactive function of language, we shall find that it is impracticable (if not impossible) to discuss semantics without making frequent reference to aspects of pragmatics.

> *Definition 1.3* PRAGMATICS is the context-dependent assignment of meaning to language expressions used in acts of speaking and writing.

We discuss context in §§1.6–7. Time and again you will see that semantics is determined by the needs of human beings when seeking to communicate with one another.

> *Assumption 1.3* At the simplest level of analysis, any language is a system of forms paired with meanings.

This is most obvious in dictionaries where forms are listed and their meanings given, e.g.

bonza/bonzer
> excellent; terrific; very good
> (*The Dinkum Dictionary: A Ripper Guide to Aussie English* 1988)

For reasons discussed in Chapter 3, most dictionaries do more. The forms are sometimes referred to as *signs* and sometimes *symbols* (see Lyons 1977 Ch. 4 for discussion). Natural signs are referred to in nostrums like those in 6.

6 (a)   Where there's smoke, there's fire.
   (b)   Those clouds mean rain.
   (c)   Red sky at night, shepherds' delight; red sky in the morning, shepherds' warning.

Natural signs needn't involve language at all: a wet pathway outside your house means that it has been raining. The study of non-natural signs is SEMIOTICS. Within human society, the kind of food you eat, the clothes you wear, the things people know that you own, your religion and ideology are components of cultural expression that communicate information to others about you and are therefore of potential interest to semioticians.[2] We speak of 'natural language' because human language has evolved with the species and not been consciously constructed. Nevertheless, natural language uses non-natural signs in the sense that there is no natural connection between form and meaning (see Chapter 4 for discussion). For example, none of the translation equivalents *ájá* (Yoruba), *cane* (Italian), *dog* (English), *Hund* (German), *kare* (Hausa), *mbwa* (Swahili), *pies* (Polish) is naturally representative of dogs or of their distinctive properties. Thus Grice 1957 refers to language meaning as 'non-natural meaning' or 'meaning$_{NN}$'. Many people believe that linguistics is a part of semiotics (presumably Chomsky and many of his followers would either disagree or regard the point as trivial; cf. Chomsky 1975:57). This book assumes that language is an aspect of culture and cultural transmission. On many occasions it is also best interpreted in the context of the speaker's (or writer's) cultural background, i.e. in the light of his or her belief system and probable assumptions.[3] The physical and social distance maintained between interlocutors, where their gaze is directed, the management of terms of address and reference to others, notions of appropriate discourse, the perception of silence, the indicators of intention to speak, voice quality – all these are (sub)culturally conditioned and vary between speech communities even within one society (cf. Chapter 5, Tannen 1990). The cultural norms guide behaviour, and so a speaker's observation or modification of them contribute to meaning in human languages.

In this section we have discussed different perspectives on human language that affect the assumptions we make about what semantics should investigate and the scope of that investigation. In §1.3 we look at the way that meaning is structured in a human language.

Exercises

1.2.1 Identify some languages that are not natural human languages.

1.2.2 Can you think of any supporting evidence for the assumption that meaning in natural languages is very responsive to, and often a reflex of, human perception and conception?

1.2.3 A whistle is used in different semiotic systems by a football referee, a policeman directing traffic, the doorman at a five-star hotel, and once upon a time by a workman on a building site when a young woman walks by. Comment on what all these systems have in common and yet how in each one the whistle has a distinct purpose. What is/are the language counterparts to the whistle?

1.2.4 Discuss why it is that human languages are regularly referred to as 'natural languages' yet Grice referred to their meanings as 'meaning$_{NN}$'.

1.2.5 Just what difference can you detect between language as an abstract entity on the one hand, and language as either a physical or psychological object?

1.3 Meaning is compositional

[E]very sentence, no matter how complicated, can be seen as the result of a systematic construction process which adds logical words one by one.

(Frege's principle of compositionality, Gamut 1991 I:15)

Most people in our community hold two true beliefs:

(a)   Meanings are a property of words.
(b)   Word meanings are stored in dictionaries.

As a review of this book's Contents and Preface shows, there is much more to semantics than this. We need to expand Definition 1.1 as follows.

Definition 1.1 (expanded) Semantics is the study of meaning in human languages. More precisely, it is the study and representation of the meaning of every kind of constituent and expression in language, and also of the meaning relationships between them.

The popular notion that words (the vocabulary of the language) are the basic building blocks for language construction is not precise enough. The defining characteristic of the basic building blocks is that they are form–meaning pairs (Assumption 1.3) but their meaning is not determinable from any meaning that can be assigned to their constituent forms – e.g. the meaning of *paddle* cannot be correctly computed from the meaning of *pad-* and the meaning of *-dle*. So, the language user must memorize each basic building block individually, as a form paired with its meaning. All that a grammar can do is list them in the lexicon (= dictionary). For that reason, Di Sciullo and Williams 1987 dubbed them LISTEMES.

> *Definition 1.4* A LISTEME is a language expression whose meaning is not determinable from the meanings (if any) of its constituent forms and which, therefore, a language user must memorize as a combination of form and meaning.

We language users combine listemes into words, phrases, sentences, and longer texts. At each level we construct meanings. The meaning of the word *bachelors* is composed from at least the listemes *bachelor* and *-s* and also the morphosyntactic relationship between the two listemes. The semantics of the combination of the listemes is just as important as the semantics of the listemes themselves and is part of the reason that dictionaries usually specify the morphosyntactic class (also referred to as 'lexical class') of each entry (Chapter 3). The noun phrase *young bachelors* is composed from the meaning of the adjective listeme *young*, the compound meaning of the word *bachelors*, and the syntactic relationship between the two words that is roughly captured by saying that *young* restricts the reference (Chapter 2) of the head noun *bachelors* to a subset (Chapter 7) of bachelors. A clause such as *young bachelors are often irresponsible* is composed of the meaning of *young bachelors* and the meaning of the other phrases, words, and listemes in the clause, as well as the various relationships between the constituent listemes and their combinations indicated by the syntactic structure. In case the importance of structural meaning is not already obvious to you, look at the difference in meaning between two sentences containing identical listemes but different structural relations:

7   Everyone loves someone.
8   Someone loves everyone.

In Chapter 7 we shall discuss the structural difference and the fact that it indicates a difference in the interpretation of 'someone' in the two sentences.

The principle we have been describing is 'compositionality'. Many semanticists believe that the meanings of listemes can themselves be decomposed into SEMANTIC COMPONENTS (Chapter 8) – e.g. that *kill* has *cause* and *die* as semantic components.

> *Definition 1.5* COMPOSITIONALITY: any complex language expression can be analysed in terms of simpler constituent expressions down to the semantic

components of listemes and the structures that combine them (cf. Kamp and Partee 1995:135).

The flip-side of compositionality is generativity.

Definition 1.6 GENERATIVITY: language has a structure that permits boundless meanings to be created from a finite set of listemes.

Compositionality is a guiding principle for all kinds of semantics. The program for semantic theory includes:

(a)   Specify the rules for translating sentences of the object language into a metalanguage that captures their proper semantic components.
(b)   Identify the rules for combining these components in such a way as to interpret the input sentences of the object language.

In the course of this book we review hypotheses about what counts as a semantic component, and ways in which the systematic construction process is to be represented. In doing so, bear the following in mind:

> If you asked me how a motor car worked you would think me somewhat pompous if I answered in terms of Newton's laws and the laws of thermodynamics, and downright obscurantist if I answered in terms of fundamental particles. It is doubtless true that at bottom the behaviour of a motor car is to be explained in terms of interactions between fundamental particles. But it is much more useful to explain it in terms of interactions between pistons, cylinders and sparking plugs.
>
> (Richard Dawkins *The Blind Watchmaker* 1988:12)

It is important to recognize that any explanation is directed to an audience; thus, presentation of the theory and its components should make the commonplace assumptions about the level of knowledge and understanding of its anticipated audience – i.e. build on common ground (§1.7). For reasons discussed in the next section, formalisms within a theory are no excuse for obscurity.

Exercises

1.3.1 How does the difference between (a) and (b) show the contribution of syntactic relations to the meanings of the sentences?
   (a) The old woman chased the young man.
   (b) The old man chased the young woman.

1.3.2 What is the difference in interpretation between 'someone' in 7 and the same word in 8?

1.4   The metalanguage: the language of the semantic theory

Human languages are the objects that we study in semantics. For that reason, the language under investigation is known as the OBJECT LANGUAGE. The language which a linguist uses to describe and analyse the object language is called the METALANGUAGE. The basic requirement for a metalanguage is to satisfactorily communicate the meaning of item e_{OL} – that is, any expression in the object language, whether it is a word, a phrase, or a sentence – in terms of an expression "e_M" in the metalanguage. A metalanguage is just another language, often an artificial and not a natural one.

One important practical constraint on a metalanguage is that (mostly) it needs to be understood by human beings who normally communicate in a natural language of which they have fluent command. If you understood neither Polish nor Swahili there is little point in my using Swahili as a metalanguage for the semantic analysis of Polish (or vice versa): e.g. to say *To jest pies* means "Ni mbwa" will not help you at all. Readers of this book must, perforce, know English, so we can use English as a metalanguage and say *To jest pies* (in Polish) means "It's a dog"; or we can say *To jest pies* means "Ni mbwa" in Swahili, which means "It's a dog" (here using English as a meta-metalanguage). To ensure that readers understand the semantic metalanguage used in this book, it is often translated into English – i.e. English is used as either a metalanguage or a meta-metalanguage. In practice, every scholar does exactly this either by explicitly providing natural language glosses for exotic metalanguage expressions, or by assuming that the reader has some existing knowledge of the semantics of the symbols and expressions being used: e.g. that '∀' means "for all", '↔' means "if and only if", '∧' means "logical and" (as you will be expected to do by the time you've finished Chapter 7).

> INFORMAL: *dog* means "canine animal"
> FORMAL: $\forall x[\textbf{dog}'(x) \longleftrightarrow \textbf{animal}'(x) \wedge \textbf{canine}'(x)]$

Textbox 2

Ideally, a semantic metalanguage would be a FORMAL LANGUAGE. A clue to the difference between a formal and an informal metalanguage is given in Textbox 2. Strictly, a formal language has a fully defined vocabulary and syntax (the vocabulary and syntax of the formal example in Textbox 2 will be explained later in the book). Ideally, the vocabulary would be a specified set of symbols whose forms and correlated meanings are fully defined; all possible combinations of vocabulary items in the metalanguage would be generated from fully specified syntactic axioms and rules of syntax; and the meanings of syntactically well formed structures would be fully specified by semantic axioms and rules for the metalanguage.

All systems of FORMAL SEMANTICS attempt to create exactly such formal languages whether they be couched in terms of propositional logic, predicate logic, truth-conditional semantics, possible worlds semantics, intensional logic, model theoretic semantics, situation semantics, dynamic semantics and discourse representation theory, or whatever.[4]

However, defining a formal metalanguage for natural language semantics requires that it have the same expressive power as a natural language because:

(a)   The metalanguage is in effect a translation of the object language (cf. Carnap 1937:228), and the object language is a natural language.
(b)   In order for the metalanguage to be understood and used by human beings it must be communicable, and hence translate into a natural language.

The ideal formal semantic metalanguage would have to be at least as comprehensive as a natural language (and to date no formal system achieves this goal). In other words, it would be a deliberately contrived artificial language of the same notational class as a natural language and, like a natural language, would reflect genuine properties of human perceptions of the real world as well as other aspects of human cognition. Contriving such a metalanguage would be a triumph for human ingenuity and might, as a by-product, reveal something about the nature of human languages. However, it will not in other respects be superior to a natural language used as a semantic metalanguage. We must conclude:

> *Assumption 1.4* A metalanguage expression "e_M" used in the semantic definition of a natural language expression e_{OL} will always be equivalent to the natural language expression through which it is interpreted.

The advantages of a formal semantic metalanguage are the explicit definition of primitives and standards of rigour and exactitude that tend to be ignored when using an informal metalanguage such as a natural language. Furthermore, proper formalization of the metalanguage should permit proofs of particular conclusions about semantic structure and so prevent mistaken conclusions derived from faulty assumptions and/or inference procedures. However, none of these advantages of a formal system is necessarily unobtainable using an informal system like a natural language metalanguage for semantics. Given two metalanguages which apparently have the same descriptive and explanatory capacities, the only way to choose between them is to be guided by your gut feeling: favour the one you are happier with. Never forget that a metalanguage is the product of an analyst's mind; the analyst not being God, every metalanguage is limited by the beliefs, perspectives, and purposes of its creator.

The metalanguage is the language of the semantic theory. The principal function of the theory is to explain data (words, sentences) from natural language. The goal of the theory is to explain all the data that it was constructed to explain; therefore, limitations on its range need to be clearly stated. A theory should have predictive power insofar as it raises expectations about data that have not yet come to light. It is absolutely necessary that a theory be internally consistent. But what about its external relations?

No theory of semantics can completely ignore syntax and phonology, and the ideal semantic theory will integrate with theories of both these components of a grammar. Semantic theory should also integrate with theories of pragmatics which seek to explain meaning in social and cultural contexts[5] and with theories of discourse structure.[6] A semantic theory should not only make useful revelations about the nature of human language but also about human cognition because, as stated in Assumption 1.1, meaning is often a reflex of human perception and conception. All theories, without exception, are abstractions from reality; so the relation of theory to reality 'is not analogous to that of soup to beef but rather of check number and overcoat' (Einstein 1973:294). Like any other kind of theory, semantic theory is developed by applying the analyst's experience and intuitions to inferences drawn from occurrences of actual speech events to create a demonstrably rational account of their structures and causes.[7] What, exactly, are inferences? They are defined and examined in the next section.

Exercises

1.4.1   What is meant by 'all possible combinations of vocabulary items in the metalanguage would be generated from fully specified syntactic axioms and rules of syntax; and the meanings of syntactically well formed structures would be fully specified by semantic rules and axioms for the metalanguage'?

1.4.2   Sometimes, in kin term semantics for example, we find the symbols "♀" and "♂" used in the metalanguage expression. What do you understand by them? Are they equivalent in meaning to some natural language expression? Do you think they can be understood without reference to a natural language?

1.4.3   To get a machine to understand human language and to respond with human language as another person would, is it necessary for the semantic metalanguage to be equivalent to a natural language?

1.4.4   What is the difference between knowing a language and knowing about a language?

1.5   Three kinds of inference

Logic, *n.* The art of thinking and reasoning in strict accordance with the limitations and incapacities of the human misunderstanding. The basic of logic is the syllogism, consisting of a major and a minor premise and a conclusion – thus:
  Major premise: Sixty men can do a piece of work sixty times as quickly as one man.
  Minor premise: One man can dig a post hole in sixty seconds; therefore –
  Conclusion: Sixty men can dig a post hole in one second.
This may be called the syllogism arithmetical, in which, by combining logic and mathematics, we obtain a double certainty and are twice blessed.
                                                                    (Bierce 1971:211f)

Definition 1.7 A logic is a system of valid inference from assumptions (= premises).

Roughly speaking, an inference is a conclusion drawn from one or more assumptions. ABDUCTIVE REASONING was championed by the early pragmatist Charles Peirce as an empirically focused procedure for the construction of classes and categories from observed data. He defined it as follows:

The surprising fact, C, is observed;
But if A were true, C would be a matter of course,
Hence, there is reason to suspect that A is true.   (Peirce 1940:151)

Abduction does not really require that the fact observed be surprising. Peirce's definition of abductive reasoning is presented as a syllogism (a form of argumentation developed by Aristotle in the 4th century BCE). We use (a1), (a2), etc. to mark assumptions, '∧' is logical conjunction (Chapter 6) which, for the present, may be interpreted by English "and", '⊢' (named 'turnstile') means "is valid from the assumptions" and '(c)' is the conclusion.

9   (a1)   Fact C is observed;
  ∧   (a2)   If A were true, C would be a matter of course;
  ───
  ⊢   (c) There is a reason to suspect that A is true.

Abductive inferences lead to testable hypotheses about the way things are. Data are correlated on the basis of their similarity or by analogy with some known system, usually with an eye to their apparent function or relevance within the emerging general description. An example of abductive reasoning in historical linguistics is 10.

10   (a1)   In the ancient Indic language Sanskrit, words for numbers 2–7 are *dva, tri, catur, pañca, ṣaṣ, sapta*. These are similar to number words in European languages known to be related to one another: e.g Slovak *dva*, Latin *duo* "2"; Slovak *tri*, Italian *tre* "3"; Latin *quattuor* "4"; Welsh *pump*, German *fünf* "5"; Spanish *seis*, English *six* "6"; Latin *septem* "7".
  ∧   (a2)   If Sanskrit were related to these European languages (i.e. they all have a common ancestor), the similarity would be a matter of course.
  ───
  ⊢   (c) There is a reason to suspect that Sanskrit is related to European languages.

10 (a1) collapses several similar observations. We could deconstruct (a1) and (a2) into a series of syllogisms like the following:

Sanskrit *dva* means "2"   ⎫
Slovak *dva* and Latin *duo* also mean "2" ⎬ cf. (a1)
                                     ⎭
  ───
Perhaps Sanskrit is related to Slovak and Latin (already
    known to be related to each other) [cf.(a2)]

(a2) is an imaginative leap because Sanskrit is separated by time and thousands of kilometres from the European languages, and it was spoken by a different race. (a2) expresses the intuition underlying the creation of the hypothesis in 10(c).[8] The abduced hypothesis (c) can be inductively confirmed by finding additional systematic correspondences (including all those given in 10(a1)) leading to the recognition of an Indo-European language family. Once a part of the system is recognized and predictions about the whole system begin to be made, the investigator moves from abduction – hypothesizing – to hypothesis testing and inductive reasoning.

An example of INDUCTIVE inference is 11.

11   (a1)   Every day till now the sun has risen in the east.

⊢   (c)   If we check tomorrow, the sun will have risen in the east.

The inductive inference (c) is a prediction based on sampling. If the sampling technique is good, the prediction will probably be verified: in 11, (c) is highly probable given the assumption (a1), but it is not necessarily going to be the case. Inductive inference is used in linguistics: for instance, if you are told that almost all French nouns ending in -*ion* are feminine then you can inductively infer that the next French noun you encounter that ends in -*ion* will most probably be feminine. Induction uncovers tendencies, but not certainties, and so is open to dispute; so, the problem with inductive reasoning is exactly that it identifies conclusions in which we have some degree of confidence (given the assumptions) but not the kind of confidence that is given to deductions.

In formal semantics DEDUCTIVE reasoning is required because, provided the assumptions and the reasoning process are correct, a valid conclusion is guaranteed. For instance, from any proposition p we can validly deduce p.

12   (a)   Max weighs 250 pounds.

(c)   Max weighs 250 pounds.

Definition 1.8 A PROPOSITION is (roughly speaking) the meaning of a declarative clause.

More interesting deductions involve more than one assumption, e.g. from (a1) *A bachelor is a man who has never married* and (a2) *Max is married*, we can deduce that (c) *Max is not a bachelor*. The steps to the conclusion in this case are given in 13; they are given informally i.e. they rely on your common sense, because we have not specified the deductive system – in fact this is one of the tasks for semantics.

13   (a1)   A bachelor is a man who has never married

⊢   (c1)   A man who has married is no longer a bachelor

(a2)   Max is a man
∧   (a3)   Max is married

⊢   (c2)   Max is a man who has married

```
     (a4)=(c1)  A man who has married is no longer a bachelor
∧   (a5)=(c2)  Max is a man who has married
    ──────────────────────────────────────
⊢    (c3)       Max is no longer a bachelor


    (c3=a6)   Max is no longer a bachelor
    ──────────────────────────────────────
⊢    (c4)       Max is not a bachelor
```

In 14, the conclusion validly follows from assumptions (a1, a2) because the reasoning is sound.

```
14     (a1)    Snow is black
  ∧   (a2)    Snow is hot and dry
      ─────────────────────────────
⊢   (c)     Snow is hot, dry, and black.
```

What this clearly demonstrates is that false assumptions will lead to valid but probably (see exercise 1.5.3) false conclusions. It follows that we must get our assumptions right if we are to use deductive inference in natural language semantics to seek true as well as valid conclusions.

Deductive inference is used all the time in ordinary language understanding; e.g. we readily interpret from *Max is married* that *Max is not a bachelor*. One of the functions of linguistic semantics is to account for such valid inferences by establishing the steps that validate them. Take another example: from *Francis killed Xavier* we can validly infer all of the following (and more).

15 (a) Xavier was killed by Francis.
   (b) Xavier was alive until he was killed by Francis.
   (c) Xavier is dead.
   (d) Francis caused Xavier's death.
   (e) Xavier's death came about as the result of something Francis did.
   (f) Francis killed someone.
   (g) Francis killed something.
   (h) Francis has killed.
   (i) There was a killing.
   (j) There is someone called Francis.
   (k) There was someone called Xavier (now deceased).

We can also infer that if the above are true, the following (among other propositions) are false:

16 (a) Xavier is alive.
   (b) Francis never killed anyone.

All these facts arise from the nature of semantic relations and must be accounted for within a semantic theory.

We have looked at three different kinds of inference. Abductive reasoning is used in figuring out classes, categories, and functions of observed phenomena – i.e. arriving at a hypothesis. With abductive reasoning the conclusions are based on a best guess; once predictions are built on the results of abduction, we have induction (market research is one practical use of induction). Deductive inference is the move from assumptions to valid conclusions by observing strict rules of procedure (identified in systems of logic) that guarantee a valid conclusion from the assumptions; the assumptions must be correct if the conclusions are to accord with the facts. Any thorough account of natural language understanding uses all three kinds of inference. As Peirce (1940:154) says:

> These distinctions [between abductive, inductive, and deductive reasoning] are perfectly clear in principle, which is all that is necessary, although it might sometimes be a nice question to say to which class a given inference belongs.

Exercises

1.5.1 We deduced from *Max is no longer a bachelor* that *Max is not (now) a bachelor*. Is this due to the fact that the meaning of *not* is contained within the meaning of *no longer*?

1.5.2 In what way is compositionality relevant to the deduction from (a1) and (a2) to (c)?
        (a1)   All semantics students are smart
∧ (a2)   Harry is a semantics student

⊢ (c)   Harry is smart

1.5.3 What kind of inference leads to conclusion (c) from assumption (a):
    (a)   Emma is drinking champagne and dancing

    (c)   Emma is dancing

1.5.4 Construct one valid and one invalid argument using (in each case) three out of the four following propositions: (a) *A dentist is a tooth-doctor*. (b) *Harry was a policeman*. (c) *Harry is a tooth-doctor*. (d) *Harry is a dentist*.

1.5.5 Comment on the following syllogism:
        (a1)   Women are cats
∧ (a2)   Cats are human

⊢ (c)   Women are human

1.5.6 In English there is a distinction between singular and plural NPs: *one sheep, three sheep*; *one stone, two stones*; etc. What sort of reasoning leads people who were not brought up to speak native standard English to say things like *a trouser, two equipments, some furnitures*?

1.5.7 Swahili (Bantu, E. Africa), like other Bantu languages, has many noun classes. Human beings (in singular number) mostly go into class one, e.g. *mtu* "person", *mwanamke* "woman", *mtoto* "child", *mzee* "old person", *mgonjwa* "sick person", *mgeni* "traditional doctor", *mwalimu* "teacher", *mpishi* "a cook". But the following singular nouns go into class seven (typically the class for artifacts, diseases, and diminutives): *kibogoyo* "toothless person", *kidurango* or *kibete* "dwarf", *kikaramba* "old crone/old fart", *kinukamito* "unstable, unsettled person", *kipofu* "blind person", *kisiki* "prostitute", *kiwete* "a cripple", *kiziwi* "deaf person". Suggest a reason for this and and for deciding whether your reasoning is abductive, inductive, or deductive.

1.5.8 Use deductive reasoning to show that *the stone died* is anomalous (is nonsense) whereas *the cat died* is not.

1.6 Speakers, speech acts, hearers and overhearers

> Communication is successful not when hearers recognize the linguistic meaning of the utterance, but when they infer the speaker's "meaning" from it.
>
> (Sperber and Wilson 1986:23)

This book adopts the social-interactionist view that language results from acts of speaking or writing when someone (Speaker) says (or writes) something to someone else (Hearer) at a certain time in a certain place (Definition 1.2) – often as part of a longer discourse or interchange. Normal utterance involves a hierarchy of SPEECH ACTS.[9] To begin with, there is the ACT OF UTTERANCE. This is recognizable even in an unknown language in which we cannot distinguish the sentences used, and what Speaker's message is. Utterance is recognized by brute perception: hearing the utterance spoken, seeing it signed or written, or feeling it impressed in braille. Linguistics is concerned with utterances in which Speaker uses a language expression and thereby performs a locutionary act (and more).

Definition 1.9 In performing a LOCUTIONARY ACT Speaker uses an identifiable sentence or sentence fragment from a language L.

Producing the locution demands that Speaker has knowledge of the grammar, lexicon, semantics, and phonology of L; recognizing it, that Hearer has comparable knowledge. Speaker uses the locution to REFER to things, i.e. talk about them (Chapter 2, Definition 2.5). Different Speakers using different locutionary and utterance acts can refer to the same thing. For instance, at a gathering in which there are speakers of English (17), Swahili (18), and Tohono O'odham (19), 17–19 could all be referring to the same dog.

17 The dog's barking!
18 Mbwa anabweka!
19 Hi:nk o g gogs!

Austin 1962 alerted us to the fact that Speaker DOES something when making an utterance. Some examples are: Speaker

states a fact or an opinion	*Semantics can be difficult.*
confirms or denies something	*It's not true that Marilyn Monroe committed suicide.*
makes a prediction	*It'll rain tonight.*
makes a promise	*I'll be with you in five minutes.*
makes a request	*What's the time?*
offers thanks or an invitation	*Can you come to dinner next Saturday?*
issues an order or an umpire's decision	*Out!*
gives advice or permission	*Yes, of course you can leave early today.*
names a child or a ship	*I name this ship "QE3".*
swears an oath	*I swear allegiance to the King.*

Definition 1.10 In making an utterance, Speaker performs an ILLOCUTIONARY ACT by using a particular locution with the ILLOCUTIONARY FORCE of a statement, a confirmation, a denial, a prediction, a promise, a request, etc.

Assumption 1.5 Although an utterance has more than one illocutionary force (Allan 1994g), it will usually have only one message to convey; the illocutionary force that carries this message is said to be the ILLOCUTIONARY POINT of the utterance.

20 I'll make the tea.

In 20, the locution is what you see following the example number. Context of utterance will determine the reference of 'I' and 'the tea' (§1.7, Chapter 2). The primary illocutionary force is a statement about a future act. It may be used with a second illocutionary force: to make a promise. If this promise is Speaker's illocutionary intention, 20 has the illocutionary point "Speaker is promising to make the tea."

Typically, the illocutionary point of 21 is to have Hearer recognize that Speaker is offering a bet. The acceptance or refusal of the challenge is the PERLOCUTIONARY EFFECT of the utterance.

21 I bet you a dollar you can jump that puddle.

Definition 1.11 Speaker's PERLOCUTIONARY ACT is act of achieving a particular perlocutionary effect on Hearer as a result of Hearer recognizing (what s/he takes to be) the locution and illocutionary forces in Speaker's utterance.

A perlocution is Hearer's behavioural response to the utterance – not necessarily a physical or verbal response, perhaps merely a mental or emotional response of some kind. Other perlocutions are such things as:

alerting Hearer by warning Hearer of danger;
persuading Hearer to an opinion by stating supporting facts;
intimidating Hearer by threatening;
getting Hearer to do something by means of a suggestion, a hint, a request, or a
    command;

and so forth. (Responding to a raised voice or an angry look does not result from Hearer recognizing a locution and illocutionary point and therefore does not count as a perlocutionary effect. It is instead a gestural effect.) Perlocutions are extremely significant within a theory of communication because the normal reason for speaking is to cause an effect in Hearer, and Speaker typically strives to achieve this by any means s/he can. However,

Assumption 1.6 Perlocutionary effects fall beyond the boundary of linguistics because they are not part of language but behavioural and/or cognitive and/or emotional responses to the illocutions (= illocutionary forces) in utterances.

Linguists can properly look at Speaker's illocutionary intention:

Definition 1.12 Speaker's ILLOCUTIONARY INTENTION is have Hearer recognize the illocutionary point of Speaker's utterance in order to achieve a particular perlocutionary effect.

In the canonical speech event (Definition 1.2), there is an assumption that Speaker intends to communicate with Hearer (cf. Definition 1.27). As recognized by Grice, the intention is reflexive: it is Speaker's intention to have a person in earshot recognize that Speaker wants him or her to accept the role of Hearer and therefore be an (or the) intended recipient of Speaker's message and consequently react to it.

Definition 1.13 Speaker's REFLEXIVE INTENTION towards Hearer is the intention to have Hearer recognize that when uttering U in context C, Speaker intends U to have a certain effect on Hearer partly caused by Hearer recognizing that Speaker has the intention to communicate with him or her by means of U.[10]

So, when Joe hears Sue talking in her sleep, he will not assume she has a reflexive intention towards him, and therefore not expect that she intends her utterance to have any effect on him – though she might unintentionally keep him awake. There are innumerable mental, emotional, and physical effects that speakers might wish to produce, e.g.

persuading Hearer to an opinion, intimidating Hearer, alerting Hearer of danger, getting
Hearer to do something by means of a suggestion, a hint, a request, or a command.

In the spoken medium there is never more than one speaker per utterance; however, two
speakers may utter identical utterances in unison, or Speaker may speak on someone else's
behalf. Co-authors generally take joint responsibility for what is written but, normally,
each writes only a part of the text. This starkly contrasts with the number of hearers or
readers Speaker may have for an audience. (A1.6 refers to Assumption 1.6.)

> *Definition 1.14* HEARER is anyone who, at the time of utterance, Speaker
> reflexively intends should recognize the illocutionary point (A1.6) of the
> utterance (= Speaker's message).

Speaker tailors the utterance to suit Hearer, taking into account the presumed common
ground (§1.7) and what s/he knows or guesses about Hearer's ability to understand the
message s/he wants to convey.

Clark and Carlson 1982 distinguish between Hearer as 'direct addressee' and Hearer
as 'ratified participant', the latter being a member of the audience participating in the
speech act (cf. Goffman 1981:131). The notion of face (§1.8, Brown and Levinson 1987)
is useful in distinguishing between two kinds each of hearers and overhearers.

> *Definition 1.15* An ADDRESSEE is someone who cannot reject the role of
> Hearer without serious affront to Speaker.

Direct address is determined contextually – by direction of gaze, pointing a finger,
touching an arm, using a name, or on the basis of who spoke last; less commonly, the
nature of the message will determine who is the intended addressee. Note the change of
addressee in 22:

22 *Joan*, Max bought me this beautiful ring for our anniversary, didn't you *Max*, you
   sweetie!

And the nonspecific addressee in 23:

23 Congratulations, *whoever* came first!

> *Definition 1.16* A RATIFIED PARTICIPANT is a Hearer, but not directly or
> personally addressed. So s/he can reject the Hearer role more freely than an
> addressee and with less of an affront to Speaker.

When Speaker is speaking, all those who can reasonably consider themselves ratified
participants are expected, as part of the cooperative endeavour, to keep tabs on what is
said, so that if called upon to participate they may do so appropriately.

Any other person hearing the utterance, U, is an OVERHEARER: either a bystander or an
eavesdropper. People in earshot are expected to overhear, though not necessarily to listen;
only hearers are properly expected to listen. It can happen that U is overheard by someone
when there was no original specific intention on Speaker's part that this should happen; to

put it more precisely, Speaker has a reflexive intention towards Hearer but not towards an overhearer. An overhearer may perchance understand the message the same way Hearer does because they share common ground; but, because s/he is not necessarily party to the appropriate contextual information relevant to the correct interpretation of the utterance, it is possible that s/he may seriously misinterpret it.

> *Definition 1.17* A BYSTANDER within earshot was not originally intended as a Hearer and may, depending on circumstances, accept or reject the role of Hearer without loss of face.

Consider an occasion where X is arguing with Y within earshot of Z.

24

[*X to Y as addressee*]	Shut up or I'll lay one on you.
[*Y to Z as ratified participant*]	You heard him threaten to hit me, didn't you?
[*X to Z as bystander*]	You mind your own business.
[*Z to X and Y, rejecting the role of Hearer*]	I wasn't listening.

> *Definition 1.18* An EAVESDROPPER can only admit to listening at the risk of looking bad, and perhaps also affronting Speaker.

The speech event defines a context for the utterance. This is further specified in the next section.

Exercises

1.6.1 Why use Speaker and Hearer to include "writer" and "reader" respectively, rather than Writer to include "speaker", Reader to include "Hearer"?

1.6.2 Discuss the locution, reference, apparent illocutionary point, and possible perlocutionary effect of *I'm hungry*.

1.6.3 Exactly why is Speaker's intention described as 'reflexive'?

1.6.4 How does a messenger fit into the scheme of hearers and overhearers? E.g. Cleopatra addresses Caesar's messenger, Thidias as follows;
> Most kind messenger,
> Say to great Caesar this in deputation,
> I kiss his conquering hand: tell him, I am prompt
> To lay my Crown at's feet, and there to kneel.
> Tell him, from his all-obeying breath, I hear
> The doom of Egypt.
>
> (Shakespeare *Antony and Cleopatra* III.xiii.88–93)

1.7   Context and common ground

The term CONTEXT denotes any or all of four things: the world and time spoken of; the co-text, i.e. the text that precedes and succeeds a given language expression; and the situations of utterance and interpretation. We discuss them in turn.

In the course of interpreting any text a hearer or reader must construct a MODEL of THE WORLD AND TIME SPOKEN OR WRITTEN OF in the text. The technical terms *model* and *world and time spoken of* (used as an abbreviation for "world and time spoken or written of") are sometimes called the discourse world or discourse model. They refer to the mental model of the world which a cognitivist believes that we all construct in order to be able to produce or understand a phrase, a sentence, or a much longer text. For instance, to interpret a declarative sentence such as 25, Hearer models a world in which it is day-time and the sun is (mostly) shining and there is (at least) one person mowing a lawn.

25 It's a sunny day and someone is mowing a lawn

Typically, the world and time spoken of contain people and things Hearer knows or knows of; thus it is a contextualization of the states of affairs referred to by the text producer in terms of place, objects, and participants, etc. It can be (a reconstruction of) the real world, or some other possible world that can be imagined, desired, or supposed. A world that can be spoken of is referred to in this book as an (ADMISSIBLE) POSSIBLE WORLD defined as one that is known (factual), imagined, desired, or supposed (all nonfactual). Worlds that can be spoken of overlap with logically possible worlds.[11] Occasionally people speak of logical impossibilities such as *the largest prime number*; and there may be logically possible worlds no speaker conceives of.

It is often the case that a single utterance evokes more than one world and/or time.

26 If Max owned a Rolls Royce, he'd be a lucky man.
27 Nimoy plays Spock in "Star Trek".
28 President Clinton was a baby in 1946.

26 evokes an actual world where Speaker presupposes (Chapter 6) that Max does not own a Rolls, but imagines a hypothetical world in which he does (this sentence is further discussed in Chapter 2). In 27 Speaker refers to the fictional world of "Star Trek" in which Spock exists and which is to be found within the actual world in which Leonard Nimoy exists. In 28 the person who was the baby in 1946 became the US president in 1993. The same individual may occupy different worlds;[12] two worlds that include the same people and places may exist at different times (28) or in different realities (26–27). Models are therefore defined as world–time pairs (Chapter 2). In fact only a part of a world is focused upon in any text, nevertheless the rest of the world (and the universe that contains it) is accessible and can be elaborated upon if need be.[13]

Speaker and Hearer are mutually aware that, normally, their interlocutor is an intelligent being. Speaker does not need to spell out those things which are

(a)   obvious to the sensory receptors of Hearer, or
(b)   which Hearer can very easily reason out on the basis of

(i)   knowing the language and the conventions for its use, and
(ii) using the knowledge that each of us develops from birth as we experience the world around us.

These constitute what is called 'common ground'.[14] Much of our understanding rests on an assumption of common ground: e.g. pointing to something and saying *Isn't that nice?* on the assumption that Hearer understands English and can also see it; or saying *Let's go to Paris* on the assumption that 'Paris' will be understood as referring to a certain city. Some common ground is universal e.g. knowledge of sun, rain, the physiological differences between the sexes; some common ground is very restricted, e.g. between a couple who use *the Hobgoblin* to refer to the man's first wife. Speaker can usually readily assess the probable common ground with Hearer, and choose his or her words accordingly. A simplified definition of common ground is:

> *Definition 1.19* COMMON GROUND for any community K of two or more people is that:
>   (a) every member, or almost every member, of K knows or believes some fact or set of facts F; and
>   (b) a member is presumed to know or believe F by (almost) every other member of K; and
>   (c) a member of K knows that both (a) and (b) are true.
> When a member of K applies knowledge of F in order to interpret P, a state of affairs or something said, s/he can presume that others in the community will also apply knowledge of F in order to interpret P. The existence of F, P, and the application of knowledge of F to interpreting P is common ground for members of the community K. Once attended to, P becomes part of F, incrementing the common ground.

(c) is similar to Lewis's 1969:78 definition of CONVENTION. Roughly speaking, a convention is a regularity of behaviour to which, in a given situation almost everyone within a population conforms and expects almost everyone else to conform. Moreover, almost everyone prefers this state of affairs to an alternative. This is not say that the convention is immutable: if people cease to conform to a particular regularity and prefer to cease to conform to it, it will cease to remain a convention; and if they gradually adopt another regularity in behaviour, this will become a convention when almost everyone in the population conforms to it and almost everyone prefers this state of affairs to the alternative. In my definition of common ground, F includes not only behaviours but also manifest facts such as what can be seen and heard, etc. by the interlocutors.

Common ground allows meaning to be underspecified by Speaker, so that language understanding is a constructive process in which a lot of inferencing is expected from Hearer. Take, for example, the following interchange:

29   [*The doorbell to Maggie and Frank's apartment rings*]
                MAGGIE [*voice off*]: Did you hear the doorbell, dear? I'm in the bathroom.
                        FRANK: I'll get it.

(a)   First of all Maggie draws to Frank's attention to P_1, the fact that the doorbell has been rung, by asking whether Frank has heard it.

(b)   By asking the question of him, P_2, she demonstrates that she assumes that Frank is not deaf: this is a GENERALIZED IMPLICATURE attached to all spoken questions (part of F; 'implicature' is defined in Chapter 6).

(c)   It also suggests that she thinks that he possibly heard the doorbell himself (P_1 becomes part of F): this is a PARTICULARIZED implicature relevant to this particular context.

(d)   Maggie could, in principle, justify these implicatures on the basis of what she assumes to be common ground with Frank: he speaks English and knows the conventions for using it (part of F); the doorbell to their apartment has rung (P_1) and it is sufficiently noisy that they both have sufficiently good perceptual and cognitive abilities to recognize that if one of them has heard it the other one will have done (part of F).

(e)   It follows that Maggie expects Frank to infer (as we do) that she is implying that the caller (part of F recognized from P_1) needs to be attended to (more of F). This is another generalized implicature, that would usually be described as the illocutionary point (Assumption 1.5) of this part of the utterance.

(f)   Secondly, Maggie announces she is in the bathroom, thereby implying that she is unable to open the door herself (more of F).

(g)   Frank takes the hint (P_3). Again by a process of implication, we, along with Maggie, recognize the statement 'I'll get it' as a promise (yet more F). If Frank's promise is sincere – which is our normal expectation (§1.8 and §6.5) – he will act upon it.

Note the amount of inferencing that Maggie expects from Frank. This is typical of normal language interchange (cf. Sperber and Wilson 1995), and it is a constant refrain in this book. We have to conclude:

> *Assumption 1.7* Speaker expects Hearer to make constructive inferences and produces his or her text accordingly.

Additional evidence for the constructive nature of text understanding includes:

(a)   Inference and speculation enables Hearer to predict what might happen next, allowing a sentence begun by one participant in conversation to be completed by another.

(b)   Titles and headings set up expectations about the text which follows, and so facilitate understanding.

(c)   Tests on eyewitness testimony and experiments with scrambled stories confirm that we tend to reformulate what we see, hear, and read in terms of what we expect to see, hear, and read.[15]

PRACTICAL REASONING is used in calculating the meaning of an utterance. It uses assumptions in which Hearer has a certain confidence, but which are not necessarily held to be true; the degree of confidence in the conclusion will be the same as that of its weakest assumption. Practical reasoning uses all three kinds of inference: abduction, induction, and deduction (§1.5); e.g.

30 I am waiting for the bus to go to work. The ride is scheduled to take ten minutes, and
    I can make it if the bus arrives on time. I don't know if the bus will arrive when it
    should. Even if the bus arrives on time, it may be delayed at the roadworks. It looks as
    though I could be late.

In (the model of) the world and time spoken of, states of affairs exist and/or events
occur that Hearer is expected to be able to understand or imagine.

*Assumption 1.8 A text is judged coherent where the world at the time spoken of
is internally consistent and generally accords with accepted human knowledge.*[16]

Even an imaginary world is necessarily interpreted in terms of the world of our experience.
Decide which of 31–33 seems best to you and why.

31 Tracy had first aroused before daylight when the dog barked at something, then turned
    over for another half hour. Cosmetic surgery would have to wait, cosmetic application
    was urgent. The shower refreshed her; the mirror depressed her with red eyes returning
    her gaze. She had been studying till the early hours and slept in later than usual. Just
    before eight she dragged herself into consciousness and out of bed. She set about it.
32 Cosmetic surgery would have to wait, cosmetic application was urgent. Just before
    eight Tracy dragged herself into consciousness and out of bed. She had been studying
    till the early hours and slept in later than usual. She set about it. She had first aroused
    before daylight when the dog barked at something, then turned over for another half
    hour. The shower refreshed her; the mirror depressed her with red eyes returning her
    gaze.

33 Tracy had been studying till the early hours and slept in later than usual. She had first
    aroused before daylight when the dog barked at something, then turned over for another
    half hour. Just before eight she dragged herself into consciousness and out of bed. The
    shower refreshed her; the mirror depressed her with red eyes returning her gaze.
    Cosmetic surgery would have to wait, cosmetic application was urgent. She set about
    it.

Chronological coherence is an important aspect of texts; so is coherent unfolding of a
story-line. 33 has these characteristics, 31–32 do not.
    The world and time spoken of form the most crucial category of context. Co-text is only
significant for identifying the world and time spoken of or something within the world.

Definition 1.20 Co-TEXT is the text that precedes and succeeds a given
language expression.

A sentence fragment like *By taxi* sends us to the co-text to discover who or what is
travelling by taxi. The interpretation of pronouns and other anaphoric expressions (Chapter
2) usually requires that they be correlated with names or full noun phrases in their co-text,
e.g. the co-indexed (subscripted) NPs in 29.

34 When he_i did at last get home, Eddy_i fell asleep.

The co-text provides information necessary to the proper interpretation of ambiguous forms: e.g. the word *bank* can be a noun (*a bank*) or a verb (*to bank money*); as a noun it can denote a financial institution (*Citibank*) or its buildings (*the bank on High Street*), a raised earthwork (*river bank*). The co-text will ordinarily disambiguate by permitting only one interpretation to make sense 'in context'. Language expressions not only take from their co-text, they also give to it: what we say or write at any point most often has an important bearing on how a text will continue. The reason that titles and headings facilitate communication is their co-textual function of identifying the topic of the narrative.

In face-to-face interaction the situation of utterance and the situation of interpretation are practically indistinguishable in time, though the locations of Speaker and Hearer are distinct. For some telephone conversations across great distances, and for nearly all written texts there is an obvious time difference between the two situations.

Definition 1.21 The SITUATION OF UTTERANCE identifies the place at and the time in which Speaker makes the utterance.

Definition 1.22 The SITUATION OF INTERPRETATION identifies the place at and time in which the utterance is heard, seen, and/or read.

The situation of utterance could be described as the world and time spoken IN. It is most significant to language understanding when it is spoken of: the exception is in those matters of politeness which are determined by relationships between participants irrespective of the world (and time) being spoken of (Chapter 5); this is less important in English than in the languages of such cultures as Japanese and Javanese.[17] The situations of utterance and interpretation provide anchors for DEICTIC or INDEXICAL categories such as tense (Chapter 11), personal pronouns, deictic locatives and demonstratives; see Table 1.1. In personal pronoun systems, Speaker is first person, Hearer is second person, all others are third person. Many languages, including some English dialects, have corresponding locatives meaning roughly "near Speaker", "near Hearer", "not-near either Speaker or Hearer". Standard English has two: "near Speaker" and "not-near Speaker".

Situation of Utterance	Situation of Interpretation	Neither
present tense = time of utterance		
Speaker = 1st person	Hearer = 2nd person	3rd person
here, this place Japanese *kono*	*there, that place* Japanese *sono*	*there, yonder* Japanese *ano*

Table 1.1 Sketch of some deictic categories, the situations of utterance and interpretation

The situations of utterance and interpretation may determine choices of adverbials and directional verbs relative to the location of Speaker and Hearer; e.g. the choice among the verbs *come, go, bring, come up, come down, come over*, etc. Situation of utterance and assumptions about Hearer also play a role in determining the topic and the linguistic register or jargon – that is, the variety of language associated with a particular occupational, institutional, or recreational group: for instance, legalese, medicalese, cricketese, linguisticalese, and so forth (Chapter 5).[18] They influence politeness factors such as terms of address and reference to others; and are where and when paralanguage occurs such as gesture, facial expression, and the positions and postures of interlocutors (cf. Argyle 1988, Clark 1996).

In this section we have seen that language understanding is a constructive process, and that Speaker underspecifies meaning knowing that s/he can rely on Hearer's ability to correctly infer Speaker's meaning without every scrap of it having to be made explicit. The fact that people have the ability to use language at all makes it a cognitive entity, and this constructive aspect of understanding exploits human cognitive abilities to the full.

The facts that

(a)   language is used to talk about things in the real and imaginary worlds and times and
(b)   Hearer must model (construct) the worlds and times spoken of in order to understand an utterance

indicate the crucial significance of context in semantic analysis. If Hearer is to properly understand Speaker's text, Speaker needs to ensure that s/he makes the most accurate assumptions possible about Hearer and the situation of interpretation. Likewise, Hearer needs to take account of what is known about the situation of utterance (see the discussion of utterance meaning in Chapter 2). Context includes the world and time spoken of, i.e. the content of some mental space; this is normally linked directly to the world and time spoken in, which is defined on the spatio-temporal characteristics of situation of utterance. In fictional and imaginative works, however, the association with the world and time spoken in may be much less substantial – though Speaker's assumptions and beliefs will undoubtedly be influenced by them. The word *context* is often used to refer to the co-text of a given word or longer expression; this is principally because the co-text reveals information about the world and time spoken of.

What we have been discussing in §§1.6–7 confirms that human language is primarily a form of social interaction. Like other social activities, language interchange requires participants to mutually recognize certain conventions. These are the topic of the next section.

Exercises

1.7.1 Here is a demonstration that language understanding is a constructive process. Read the following two introductory paragraphs from a story and then try answering the questions below it.

The Maasai Clans

The Maasai people are divided into two moieties, the one called the Odomong'i (people of the red oxen) and the other the Orok-kiteng' (people of the black cow). These moieties are further subdivided into five, this latter subdivision being the origin of the Maasai clans. This is how the division came about.

  Long ago, at the beginning of time, lived a demigod called Naiterukop, Beginner-of-the-Earth. Naiterukop married two wives. Now, as for the first wife, he gave her red cattle and she was given the bridal name Nadomong'i, She-of-the-red-oxen. It was allowed that she build her house by the gatepost on the righthand side of the gate into the compound.

Now answer the following questions and discuss the basis for your answer, commenting on what it shows about the way we understand language. Where relevant refer to common ground (and/or the lack of it).

    (a)   Guess what colour cattle the second wife got.
    (b)   Guess what her married name was.
    (c)   Guess which side of the gateway the second wife built her hut.
    (d)   If the two wives gave rise to the Maasai moieties, where would you guess that the five clans come from?
    (e)   What does the title help you to do?

[The rest of the story is given in "Answers to Selected Exercises" (see "Preface")]

1.7.2 Our tendency to speculate about (predict) what is likely to happen next in a narrative occasionally leads to 'garden-pathing' (cf. Clark and Clark 1977:80–2) as in *A horse raced towards the gate fell* where many a Hearer pulls up short at the apparent ungrammaticality of 'fell' and has to reprocess the sentence to make sense of it. Explain how you can be 'led up the garden path' by each of (a–c).

(a) A horse raced towards the gate fell.
(b) Our astronomer gazed transfixed at the star racing towards him with her arms outstretched.
(c) Mary is afraid her mother saw her duck behind the curtain. (Her mother hates her to take the bird into the house.)

1.7.3 What does model (world and time) construction have to do with the comprehending of one (or both) of the following:

(a) The major problem is quite simply one of grammar, and the main work to consult in this matter is Dr Dan Streetmentioner's *Time Traveller's Handbook of 1001 Tense Formations*. It will tell you for instance how to describe something that was about to happen to you in the past before you avoided it by time-jumping forward two days in order to avoid it. The event will be described differently according to whether you are talking about it from the standpoint of your own natural time, from a time in the further future, or a time in the further past and is further complicated by the possibility of conducting conversations whilst you are actually travelling from one time to another with the intention of becoming your own mother or father.   (Adams 1992:216)

(b) It is the moment of non-construction, disclosing the absentation of actuality from the concept in part through its invitation to emphasize, in reading, the helplessness – rather than the will to power – of its fall into conceptuality.   (Paul Fry *A Defense of Poetry* 1995)

1.7.4 In what way does the interpretation of the word *morphology* differ in (a), and *lamb* in (b); and what are the clues to the difference?
(a₁) the morphology of the Basque language   (a₂) the morphology of the whale
(b₁) the lamb frolicked in the field   (b₂) the lamb tasted delicious

1.7.5 Discuss the fact that language treats Speaker and Hearer as being in different locational zones (different places) but not in different time zones. What does this tell you about the differences between speech and writing?

1.7.6 Ilocano (Austronesian, Philippines) has the personal pronouns listed below. Show how their semantics systematically represents components of person deixis in terms of Speaker, Hearer, and third persons.

> *co* "I/me"; *mo* "you singular"; *ta* = *co* and *mo* (together); *na* "he/him, she/ her, it"; *da* "them"; *mi* = *co* and *na/da* (together); *yo* = *mo* and *na/da* (together); *tayo* = *co* and *mo* and *na/da* (together)

1.7.7 Which categories of context seem to be used to interpret the italicized pronouns in (a–d)?
(a) When Harry and Sally first met *she* didn't like *him* at all.
(b) *I* want *you* to bring *that* – whatever *it* is – *here*, and put it *there*.
(c) Anna beat Sandra at chess because *she* was the better player.
(d) Anna beat Sandra at chess because *she* was an incompetent player.

1.7.8 How do evaluations of 'talking to oneself' square with our view that language is primarily a vehicle for social interaction among human beings?

1.7.9 Discuss the fact that Frank's pronoun 'it' in 29 (the doorbell interchange) has no antecedent.

1.8 Maxims of the cooperative principle, and the principle of relevance

Make your conversational contribution such as is required, at the stage at which it occurs, by the accepted purpose or direction of the talk exchange in which you are engaged. One might label this the COOPERATIVE PRINCIPLE.

(Grice 1975:45)

In this section we establish some basic assumptions about the cooperative principle, and its competitor, relevance theory (Sperber and Wilson 1995). Both are pragmatic rather than semantic, and so we do not give them the attention they would merit in a book on pragmatics. As we shall see, however, the cooperative maxims are fundamental to a proper account of meaning in natural language; to build a semantic theory that makes no reference to the implicatures that arise from cooperative maxims would be like building a car with square wheels.

Grice 1975 described the cooperative principle in terms of four categories of maxims given in the original as follows.

Quantity:
  1   Make your contribution as informative as is required (for the current purposes of the exchange).
  2   Do not make your contribution more informative than is required.
Quality:
  Try to make your contribution one that is true.
  1   Do not say what you believe to be false.
  2   Do not say that for which you lack adequate evidence.
Relation:
  Be relevant
Manner:
  Be perspicuous.
  1   Avoid obscurity of expression.
  2   Avoid ambiguity.
  3   Be brief (avoid unnecessary prolixity).
  4   Be orderly.   (Adapted from Grice 1975:45f)

Such maxims are not laws to be obeyed, but reference points for language interchange – much as the points of the compass are conventional reference points for identifying locations on the surface of the earth. The perceptiveness of Grice's observations cannot be denied; much criticism has been levelled against various maxims but it fails if we interpret Grice charitably. One frequent objection is that Grice mistook the conventions of his own society to be universal; this is a common enough mistake and not fatal to the theory, as we shall see.

The Grice quantity maxims can be usefully augmented with Atlas and Levinson's (1981:40–50) informativeness principle, paraphrased in Levinson 1983:146f, 'read as much into the utterance as is consistent with what you know about the world.' For the purpose of this book, the augmented Grice maxims are revamped as follows:

Definition 1.23 The maxims of QUANTITY. Quantity1 enjoins Speaker to make the strongest claim possible consistent with his/her perception of the facts. Quantity 2 enjoins Speaker to give no more and no less information than is required to make his/her message clear to Hearer.[19]

Complementing these is a principle of interpretation by Hearer:

Assumption 1.9 Given the semantic content of the utterance and Hearer's perception of the contextually relevant facts, the strongest inference possible is to be drawn from the utterance.

We shall see evidence for this when we discuss implicature in Chapter 6. We do not normally say things like 35 because it contains an unnecessary relative clause:

35 My neighbour, who is a woman, is pregnant.

We know that if the neighbour is pregnant, it MUST be a woman (notwithstanding the De Vito/Schwarzenegger film "Junior").

Definition 1.24 The maxim of QUALITY. Speaker should be genuine and sincere.

That is, Speaker should state as facts only what s/he believes to be facts; make offers and promises only if s/he intends carrying them out; pronounce judgments only if s/he is in a position to judge etc. For example it would violate the maxim of quality to assert 36.

36 The book in which this sentence occurs is suitable for five-year-olds.

Our definition of the maxim of quality significantly differs from Grice's original, which – perhaps because Grice was a philosopher and not a linguist or sociologist – referred to truth instead of sincerity (cf. Lewis's 1969:178 'regularity of truthfulness'). Truth is something independent of human action and belief (Chapters 6, 10), though beliefs about what constitutes truth are not; cf. Shapin 1994. From a cognitivist or functionalist viewpoint, language, and particularly meaning in language, is closely bound to human action and belief (Chapter 9). There are many kinds of utterance (= kinds of speech act) for which the evaluation of truth is either inapplicable or of secondary consideration to aspects of Speaker credibility and sincerity, for example, when giving advice, apologizing, thanking, or congratulating someone. In human communication it is not sufficient to utter a truth, the truth also needs to be credible and it is often important to modify the truth in order to preserve social harmony (see the discussion of lying in Chapter 10). Thus, we emphasize cooperation in social interaction in having the maxim of quality recommend that Speaker ensure his or her credibility by being genuine and sincere. The maxim of quality can be identified with Speaker's sincerity in believing that the preconditions on the utterance hold good (Chapter 6): e.g. Speaker believes the facts are as stated, believes there is reason to apologize or congratulate Hearer, believes s/he will carry out the promise being made, believes that Hearer can accomplish the request being made of him or her, and so forth. Thus, if requested to do so, Speaker is under an obligation to provide justification for whatever kind of speech act is used (cf. Habermas 1979:65).

Definition 1.25 The maxim of RELATION ("be relevant"). In general, an utterance should not be irrelevant to the context in which it is uttered, because that makes it difficult for Hearer to comprehend.

We shall presume that Speaker has some reason for making the particular utterance U in context C, in the particular form which s/he uses, rather than maintaining silence or uttering something different.

> *Definition 1.26* The maxim of MANNER. Where possible, Speaker's meaning should be presented in a clear, concise manner that avoids ambiguity, and avoids misleading or confusing Hearer through stylistic ineptitude.

Thus one should ordinarily avoid saying things like 37:

37 There is a male adult human being in an upright stance using his legs as a means of locomotion to propel himself up a series of flat-topped structures some fifteen centimetres high.

(What do we say instead?)

We will augment Grice's original cooperative principle by requiring that the cooperative principle holds whenever Speaker and Hearer mutually recognize Speaker's observance of three things.

> *Definition 1.27* The COMMUNICATIVE PRESUMPTION: When Hearer perceives Speaker's utterance to be linguistic, Hearer presumes that Speaker has made the utterance with the intention of communicating some message using the conventions of natural language.

> *Definition 1.28* The REASONABLENESS CONDITION: The communicative presumption presupposes that Speaker is acting reasonably, i.e. Speaker has some reason for making that particular utterance U_a, at that time t_a, in that place w_a, rather than maintaining silence or uttering something different (Sperber and Wilson 1995 describe this as Speaker observing the principle of relevance).

The communicative presumption and reasonableness condition explain why a reader will make the effort to understand 38.

38 Wants pawn term dare worsted ladle gull hoe lift wetter murder inner ladle cordage honour itch offer lodge dock florist. Disc ladle gull orphan worry ladle cluck wetter putty ladle rat hut, end fur disc raisin pimple caulder Ladle Rat Rotten Hut.

Furthermore, Speaker does not randomly choose the forms and style (Chapter 5) to use in making the utterance: s/he normally has some reason for selecting the particular ones used – a reason sought by Hearer (not necessarily consciously) when interpreting Speaker's utterance.

The final component of cooperation in language interaction is observance of the NORMAL CONVENTIONS PERTAINING TO FACE EFFECTS (politeness phenomena) of their community. Scholars who have criticized Grice's statement of the maxims for not being universally applicable overlook the possibility that the cooperative principle is motivated by conventions pertaining to face effects: conventions that vary between situations and communities (Leech 1983 even differentiates a 'Politeness Principle' from the cooperative principle). Face (Brown and Levinson 1987, Brown and Gilman 1989) has two aspects:

> *Definition 1.29* Positive face is the want of a person to have their attributes, achievements, ideas, possessions, goals, etc. well regarded by others.

> *Definition 1.30* Negative (or impositive) face is the want of a person not to be imposed upon by others.

Brown and Levinson's definition of negative face has been criticized for being Anglo-centric (e.g. in Watts, Ide, and Ehlich (eds) 1992) and there is no doubt that many cultures give community wants and needs priority over individual wants and needs with the consequence that the original Brown and Levinson definition of face needs adjusting to cultural differences (cf. Lee-Wong 2000, Scollon and Scollon 1995:134). Nonetheless, face concerns offer the most feasible explanation for the maxims of the cooperative principle. Face can be lost (affronted), gained (enhanced), or just maintained. In virtually every utterance, Speaker needs to take care that what is said will maintain, enhance, or affront Hearer's face in just the way s/he intends to affect it, while at the same time maintaining or enhancing Speaker's own face. There is a general presumption that Speaker will be polite except when intending to affront Hearer's positive face; and Speaker will not normally impose on Hearer without good reason, lest Hearer's negative face be affronted. The meaningful effects of an utterance (and longer texts) which result from the Gricean maxims and other face effects are CONVERSATIONAL IMPLICATURES (referred to earlier simply as 'implicatures').

> *Assumption 1.10* A theory of meaning must take account of normal conventions pertaining to face effects within a language community because utterance meaning is partly determined by reference to them; they form part of the common ground.

The cooperative principle governs one category of positive face effects – making Hearer feel good – and five categories of negative face effects. One is a nonverbal category governing such matters as eye contact; the rest are verbal categories. In the interests of social harmony, Speaker normally avoids the following four modes of behaviour unless s/he intends to affront Hearer's negative face.

(a)   Attacks on Hearer's positive face, e.g. with imprecations or abusive epithets.
(b)   Impositions on Hearer's person, possessions, time, and the like, e.g. requiring Hearer to do something, asking for the use of Hearer's possessions or ideas, etc. where these are not sanctioned as social obligations.
(c)   Wittingly misleading Hearer into erroneous beliefs and assumptions (governed by the maxim of quality).
(d)   Requiring Hearer to expend unreasonable effort in order to understand what Speaker means by making the utterance because it is: uncomfortably loud, inaudible, incoherent,

irrelevant, abstruse, or otherwise unreasonable. The maxims of quantity, relation, and manner govern different aspects of this final category of impositives.

> *Assumption 1.11*   Were there no cooperative principle (no communicative presumption, no reasonableness condition, nor conventions pertaining to face effects) systematic communication would be impossible. There would be no ground rules for deciding whether or not an utterance – or longer text – makes sense nor what value should be put on it. Conversely, Speaker would have no ground rules for getting her or his message across to Hearer. It is these ground rules that we shall have cause to refer to when identifying conversational implicatures. They are crucial to the understanding of ordinary language.

Sperber and Wilson's 1995 RELEVANCE THEORY seeks to replace the Gricean maxims with just one principle of relevance.[20] Some scholars think it succeeds, but others find that the individual Gricean and neo-Gricean maxims are incorporated under relevance – in other words, relevance theory does exactly the same thing using different terminology but without demonstrating any reason to abandon Grice. One difference we can point to is that relevance theory has a purely cognitive basis, whereas the cooperative principle as described in this book is social-interactive. Grice himself probably regarded his cooperative principle as a pragmatic complement to truth-conditional semantics (Chapter 6). The cognitive basis for relevance theory can be seen in Sperber and Wilson's 1995 observations on 'context'. In relevance theory, context is the set of assumptions manifest to Speaker and Hearer on the basis of common ground. Each 'assumption' is a structured set of concepts. A fact is 'manifest' (i.e. perceptible or inferable) to an individual at a given time only if s/he is capable of representing it mentally and accepting its representation as credible. The set of facts that are manifest to an individual is his or her cognitive environment. Two people who share the same cognitive environment are capable of making the same assumptions because they are cognizant of the same context and potentially share the same common ground (however, they do not necessarily do so). What we are calling the 'model' and the 'world and time spoken of' are networks of such assumptions.

In relevance theory, optimal relevance for Hearer is to recover as many contextual effects as possible for the least cost in cognitive processing. Contextual effects reveal or create something novel in a given context. To achieve this, Hearer joins new assumptions with existing assumptions, sometimes to derive further assumptions, and hence model the world and time spoken of. An assumption is relevant to an individual at a given time only if it is relevant in one or more of the contexts accessible to that individual at that time. It is relevant to an extent determined by its contextual effects weighted against the effort required to process it. Thus relevance theory goes beyond language to give us an explanation for the way in which our knowledge develops and changes in response to what we see and hear in our immediate environment. In this book, which assumes a social-interactive basis for the cooperative principle (whose motivation was not accounted for by Grice), there is frequent reference to maxims of the cooperative principle. This does not entail a rejection of the cognitive approach of relevance theorists, but it does reflect on their failure to sufficiently specify the cognitive conditions that underlie each of the maxims we have defined in this section.

This section has sketched the cooperative principle in language interaction. The conventions for cooperative language behaviour are expected to be known within a language community and both observance and violation of them have meaningful implications. Speakers exploit them to persuade, to curry favour, to insult, and every other kind of effect that language can produce. We shall constantly refer to them in the course of this book.

Exercises

1.8.1 Suppose that Ed, a logician who has five children, is in conversation with Nancy:
  NANCY: Do you have any children?
  ED: I have two.
Ed did not misunderstand the question. Why is it that although Ed can claim to be telling the truth his answer is misleading?

1.8.2 What cooperative maxims do you believe might be referred to when accounting for the following interchange; the context is that a car is for sale.
  BUYER: How much do you want?
  SELLER: Three thousand.
  BUYER: I'll give you two.

1.8.3 What do you make of 38 in the main text? (Wants pawn term dare worsted ladle gull hoe lift wetter murder inner ladle cordage honour itch offer lodge dock florist. Disc ladle gull orphan worry ladle cluck wetter putty ladle rat hut, end fur disc raisin pimple caulder Ladle Rat Rotten Hut.) Try translating it into ordinary English and explain the reasons for being able to do so.

1.8.4 What maxim(s) can be referred to in accounting for B's response in
  A: What happened to those sausages I left to thaw?
  B: The dog's looking very pleased with herself.

1.8.5 Here are some examples of the violation of the manner maxim. Try glossing them and say how you would describe them.
  (a) The cognitive-affective state characterized by intrusive and obsessive fantasizing concerning the reciprocity of amorant feelings by the object of the amorance.
  (b) A manual earth-restructuring implement.
  (c) Localized capacity deficiency inhibiting vehicular ingress and egress.
  (d) Ballistically-induced aperture in the subcutaneous environment
  (e) Nutritional avoidance therapy.
  (f) An outlet for reutilization marketing.

1.9 Summary

This chapter introduced concepts fundamental to semantics, the study of meaning in human languages. The primary function of language is to be a medium for social interaction, and this imposes constraints on its systems and structures. In due course, we shall attest the influence of human perception and experience on the categories of meaning, because language is a product of the mind. Language is produced by speakers, but it also exists independent of them; so, when doing semantics we also address language as an abstract entity. Broadly speaking, language is used most efficiently when Speaker utters as little as possible and relies on Hearer to read between the lines. Hearer constructs meaning from what is said by adding inferences based on context and experience. This chapter has given some pointers to these fundamentals of language understanding. Already we have begun to answer some of the research questions for semantics. In the course of this book we seek to answer all of the following:

❶ What are the tools of semantic analysis?
❷ How do we account for the relationships between words and things?
❸ How do we account for the meaning relationships between language expressions?
❹ What is the relationship between a lexicon and an encyclopedia?
❺ Where do listemes come from?
❻ What are the components of listeme meaning?
❼ What relationships hold between the form and meaning of listemes?
❽ How do we account for the meanings of phrases, sentences, and larger structures?
❾ What kinds of meaningful effects result from the use of particular listemes and sentences?
❿ What are the cognitive and functional bases for meaning in language?

Chapter 2 builds on Chapter 1 to look at dictionary meaning, sentence meaning, utterance meaning, speaker meaning, and hearer meaning. It offers an account of the terms *sense, denotation, reference, intension, extension,* and *specificity*; and there are brief reviews of generic NPs and aspects of anaphora.

● Key words and phrases whose meanings and import you should know, or know better, after reading this chapter – in some cases there will be more information given later in the book. (In what follows, A1.1 refers to Assumption 1.1 and D1.2 refers to Definition 1.2.)

abduction	context
addressee (D1.15)	convention
assumption (premise)	conversational implicature
bystander (D1.18)	cooperative principle
canonical speech event (D1.2)	deduction
co-text (D1.20)	deictic (indexical) category
coherence	eavesdropper (D1.18)
common ground (D1.19)	face effects (politeness phenomena)
communicative presumption (D1.27)	generalized implicature
compositionality (D1.5)	generativity (D1.6)

Hearer (D1.14)
illocutionary act (D1.10)
illocutionary force (D1.10)
illocutionary intention (D1.12)
illocutionary point (A1.5)
induction
inference
listeme (D1.4)
locutionary act (D1.9)
logic (D1.7)
maxim of quality (D1.24)
maxim of quantity (D1.23)
maxim of manner (D1.26)
maxim of relation (relevance) (D1.25)
metalanguage
model (of the world(s) and time(s)
    spoken of)
negative (Impositive) face (D1.30)
non-natural meaning
object language
overhearer
particularized implicature
perlocutionary act (D1.11)

perlocutionary effect (A1.6)
positive face (D1.29)
possible world
practical reasoning
proposition (D1.8)
pragmatics (D1.3)
ratified participant (D1.16)
reasonableness condition (D1.28)
reflexive intention (D1.13)
relevance theory
semantic component
semantics (D1.1)
semiotics
situation of interpretation (D1.22)
situation of utterance (D1.21)
Speaker
speech act
utterance act
valid inference (symbolized by ⊢
    'turnstile')
world and time spoken of
world-time pair

● Many linguists believe that semantics is a part of semiotics, but semiotics additionally studies the meanings of many nonlinguistic signs and symbols.
● Meaning in natural languages is very responsive to, and often a reflex of, human perception and conception (A1.1).
● Language is an abstract entity that has physical manifestations in spoken and written utterances.
● The canonical speech event is an instance of social-interactive behaviour.
● The expression of meaning through language is an essential means of cementing human bonding and of displaying it to others, both at the individual and the community level (A1.2).
● Speaker's and Hearer's knowledge of language and how to use it reflects a cognitive ability and indicates that language is a psychologically real entity.
● At the simplest level of analysis, any language is a system of forms paired with meanings (A1.3).
● The object language is the one whose semantics is being described, and the metalanguage is the language or symbolic system used in describing it.
● Ideally a metalanguage would be a formal language with a fully defined vocabulary, syntax and (paradoxically) semantics. The advantage of a formal metalanguage is (or should be) its explicitness and rigour.
● The problem for any metalanguage for natural language semantics is that it must have the expressive power of a natural language because, in effect, it translates the object

language; and then in order to communicate in an illuminating fashion it has to be translatable back into a natural language (cf. A1.4).

● Abductive reasoning is used in figuring out classes, categories, and functions of observed phenomena – i.e. creating hypotheses.

● Inductive inference is a prediction based on sampling. If the sampling technique is good, the prediction will be verified.

● Deductive inference requires one or more assumptions from which a conclusion is derived by well established rules of rules of inference. Provided the assumptions are correct and the reasoning process accurate, a valid conclusion is guaranteed.

● Much linguistic categorization and theorizing is inductive; but formal semantics is deductive.

● A proposition is the content of a (declarative) clause; it is often referred to as a sentence or a statement because these are what express the proposition.

● With very few exceptions, the purpose of speaking or writing is to cause an effect on the audience.

● An utterance act occurs when Speaker makes an utterance in whatever medium. No knowledge of the particular language used is required to recognize an utterance act.

● A locution is the form of words produced and then recognized by someone who has knowledge of the grammar, lexicon, semantics, and phonology of the language used. In considering the locution no regard is paid to the things Speaker is talking about, nor why the Speaker should be saying it.

● In the locution is to be found Speaker's message. The message is the illocutionary point of the utterance, which is one of the illocutionary forces in the utterance.

● Speaker has an illocutionary intention to create a perlocutionary effect by means of a reflexive intention to have Hearer recognize this intention via an understanding of the locution and illocutionary point of the utterance. A perlocutionary effect is the behavioural and/or cognitive and/or emotional response. Most of what human beings say is aimed towards a perlocutionary effect.

● There are two kinds of Hearer: addressees and ratified participants. Overhearers are divided into bystanders and eavesdroppers. The acceptance and rejection of these roles has implications for face maintenance.

● There are four categories of context: the world(s) and time(s) spoken of, the co-text, and the situations of utterance and interpretation.

● Situations of utterance and interpretation define deictic (= indexical) categories.

● A model of the world and time spoken of is the content of a mental space which can be readily associated in a variety of ways with other worlds and times occupying other mental spaces (see Chapter 2). Because worlds spoken of are revealed through language, they all have some association with the world Speaker inhabits. You will see the effect of this if you compare, e.g., the science fiction of H.G. Wells with one of today's SF writers.

● We speak of ideas and of things that don't exist (Chapter 2); but mostly we speak of things that exist in some world or other. To recognize the things spoken about, to mentally model the world and time spoken of, we look to context.

● Meaning is underspecified by Speaker and language understanding is a constructive process in which a lot of inferencing is expected from Hearer (A1.7).

● We tend to reformulate what we see, hear, and read in terms of what we expect to see, hear, and read.

● A text is judged coherent where the world at the time spoken of is internally consistent and generally accords with accepted human knowledge (A1.8).
● Grice's cooperative principle is characterized by four categories of maxims: quantity (make the strongest claim possible without giving too much or too little information); quality (be sincere); relation (be relevant); and manner (don't mislead or confuse through stylistic ineptitude).
● Relevance theory seeks to replace the Gricean maxims with just one principle of relevance.
● The strongest inference possible is drawn from the utterance, given its semantic content and Hearer's perception of the contextually relevant facts (A1.9).
● The cooperative principle holds whenever Speaker and Hearer mutually recognize Speaker's observance of the communicative presumption, the reasonableness condition, and the normal conventions pertaining to face effects (politeness phenomena) of their community.
● The cooperative principle is motivated by conventions pertaining to face effects – which are culturally (and subculturally) determined.
● A theory of meaning must take account of normal conventions pertaining to positive and negative face effects within a language community because utterance meaning is partly determined by reference to them. They form part of the common ground (A1.10).
● The cooperative principle comprises a set of conventions guiding social behaviour, a system of ground rules or conditions for communicating with others. Certain identifiable systematic inferences, called 'conversational implicatures', will be drawn from both compliance and violation of the cooperative principle. Awareness of the cooperative conventions is crucial to the understanding of ordinary language. (Cf. A1.11.)

10   Notes on further reading

[1] On language as a system of thought: Heraclitus 'although the word is common to all, most people live as if each had a private understanding of their own' (Kahn 1979:28); Chomsky 'Language, it is argued, is "essentially" a system for the expression of thought' (1975:57).

[2] On semiotics see Eco 1976, 1984, Hodge and Kress 1988, Sebeok 1994.

[3] On the influence of culture on language, see Humboldt 1836, Boas 1911, Sapir 1921, 1929, Whorf 1956.

[4] See Gamut 1991, McCawley 1993 for overviews of formal semantics; Tarski 1956, Davidson 1971 on truth-conditional semantics; Carnap 1956, Kripke 1963, Montague 1974, Lewis 1970, Cresswell 1973, Benthem 1988 on intensional model theoretic semantics; Barwise and Perry 1983 on situation semantics; Kamp and Reyle 1993 on discourse representation theory.

[5] On pragmatics see Stalnaker 1978, Gazdar 1979, Cole (ed.) 1978, 1981, Leech 1983, Levinson 1983, Blommaert (ed.) 1995.

[6] On discourse structure see Labov and Fanshel 1977, Brown and Yule 1983, Dijk and Kintsch 1983, Seuren 1985, Kamp and Reyle 1993, Schiffrin 1994, Givón (ed.) 1997

[7] On the importance of intuition in creating theories and logic in stating them, see Poincaré 1946:214f, 219, Einstein 1973:221, 334, Bronowski 1978 Ch. 4, Katz 1981 Ch.6, Kuhn 1970:122f, Pirsig 1976.

[8] The essential contribution of intuition to scientific theory is widely recognized among philosophers of science.

> Pure logic could never lead us to anything but tautologies; it could create nothing new; not from it alone can any science issue. [...T]o make arithmetic, as to make geometry, or to make any science, something else than pure logic is necessary. To designate this something else we have no word other than *intuition*. [... L]ogic and intuition have each their necessary role. Each is indispensable. Logic, which alone can give certainty, is the instrument of demonstration; intuition is the instrument of invention.
>
> (Poincaré 1946:214f, 219)

> The supreme task of the physicist is to arrive at those elementary laws from which the cosmos can be built up by pure deduction. There is no logical path to these laws, only intuition resting on sympathetic understanding of experience can reach them.
>
> (Einstein 'Principles of research' 1973:221)

Similar conclusions were reached by Bronowski 1978 Ch. 4, Katz 1981 Ch. 6, Kuhn 1970:122f, Pirsig 1976.

[9] On speech acts see Austin 1962, Searle 1969, 1979, Labov and Fanshel 1977, Bach and Harnish 1979, Edmondson 1981, Recanati 1987, Allan 1994e,f.

[10] Reflexive intention was first recognized by Grice (1957, 1968, 1969) and the notion has been revised by others, notably Recanati 1987.

[11] On logically possible worlds, see Bradley and Swartz 1979 for an easy-to-read introduction. There are more challenging accounts in Kripke 1963, Lewis 1973, 1986, Cresswell 1988, Gamut 1991.

[12] The same individual may occupy different worlds; see Lewis 1973, 1986, Bradley and Swartz 1979, Cresswell 1988, Fauconnier 1985.

[13] As described here, worlds spoken of are roughly equivalent to the 'situations' of Barwise and Perry 1983 and the content of the 'mental spaces' of Fauconnier 1985.

[14] On common ground see Stalnaker 1973, 1974, Clark 1996.

[15] On the use of inferences and speculations, see Allan 1981, Charniak 1976, 1977, Clark 1977, Graesser and Clark 1985, Johnson-Laird 1983, Schank and Abelson 1977, Sperber and Wilson 1995, Thorndyke 1976, Dijk and Kintsch 1983 and many others. On the effect of titles and headings see Bransford and Johnson 1972, Kozminsky 1977. On the ability to predict what happens next see Coates 1997, Gernsbacher and Givón (eds) 1995, Linell and Korolija 1997, Uyl and Oostendorp 1980. On eyewitness testimony see Loftus 1979. On the replacement of

abnormal by normal events but not vice versa in recall situations see Schank and Abelson 1977, Dijk and Kintsch 1983. On experimental evidence for the realignment of scrambled stories in both summaries and recall see Kintsch et al. 1977, Thorndyke 1977.

[16] On coherence and accepted knowledge, see Thorndyke 1976, Reinhart 1980, Gernsbacher and Givón (eds) 1995.

[17] On politeness and honorifics, see Brown and Gilman 1960, Brown and Ford 1961, Geertz 1972, Ervin-Tripp 1972, Ervin-Tripp et al. 1984, Loveday 1981, Moedjanto 1986, Sanada 1993, Shibatani 1994.

[18] On jargons (registers) see Chapter 5, Wardhaugh 1986, Allan and Burridge 1991.

[19] There is more on quantity in Chapter 6 and thereafter. See also Allan 1999, Atlas and Levinson 1981, Horn 1984, Levinson 1995.

[20] On relevance theory, see Sperber and Wilson 1995.

2 Words and worlds and reference

Semantics is the theory concerning the fundamental relations between words and things.

(Bealer 1982:157)

2.1 Where we are heading

Loosely speaking, this chapter examines some meanings of *meaning*. We build on Chapter 1 by establishing ways for relating dictionary meaning to the world and time spoken of. In order to do so it is necessary to define and differentiate the terms *sense, denotation, reference, intension*, and *extension*. This chapter offers a new look at these terms, which are used with overlapping meanings by a shamefully large number of people. §2.2 defines SENSE (roughly, dictionary meaning). §2.3 distinguishes SENTENCE MEANING from UTTERANCE MEANING and SPEAKER MEANING.[1] §2.4 unravels the differences between REFERRING (which is something Speaker does), and two kinds of DENOTING: INTENSION and EXTENSION (which define different kinds of relation between words and worlds). §2.5 takes up the difficult question of how we understand reference to what does (or might) not exist. §2.6 is on GENERICS (making law-like observations). §2.7 addresses the topic of ANAPHORA (multiple references to something). §2.8 summarizes the chapter.

2.2 Dictionary meaning

A dictionary relates words to words when it gives the sense or senses of a listeme (D1.4); e.g.

[1]**canine** ... *adj* [L *caninus*. fr. *canis* dog] **1:** of or relating to dogs or the family (Canidae) including the dogs, wolves, jackals, and foxes **2:** of, relating to, or resembling a dog
[2]**canine** *n* **1:** a conical pointed tooth; *esp*: one situated between the lateral incisor and the first premolar **2:** dog

(Webster's New Collegiate Dictionary 1977)

Here we find two HOMONYMS (words with the same form), [1]**canine** and [2]**canine**, each of which is two ways POLYSEMOUS because each has two senses numbered **1** and **2**.

Definition 2.1 A listeme is POLYSEMOUS if it has more than one meaning given within a single lexicon entry.

Definition 2.2 Two listemes of the same form are HOMONYMOUS if they warrant separate lexicon entries because the identity of form is coincidental.

It is left to you as a dictionary user to decide which of the senses given is relevant to a particular context in which the word is used. This is because:

Definition 2.3 SENSE is decontextualized meaning, abstracted from innumerable occurrences of the listeme (or combination of listemes) in texts.

Generalizing, a language expression such as [2]**canine** is an instance of e_{OL} – an expression e in the object language (being described), indicated by the subscript $_{OL}$. Its sense is given in a metalanguage by expression "e_M".

Assumption 2.1 The sense of a language expression, e_{OL}, is a description of its informational content in terms of some other language expression "e_M".

In a monolingual dictionary such as *Webster's* or the *OED*, "e_M" will be in the same language as e_{OL}. In a bilingual dictionary, "e_M" will be in some other language. For example, it is identity of sense that defines the words in 1 as translation equivalents independently of any particular context of use.

1   *ájá* (Yoruba), *cane* (Italian), *dog, canine quadruped* (English), *Hund* (German), *kare* (Hausa), *mbwa* (Kiswahili), *pies* (Polish)

Exercises

2.2.1   Homonyms can be divided into HOMOPHONES – listemes that sound alike, and HOMOGRAPHS – listemes that are written alike. Can you find examples of homophony and homography in the following?
   (a)   Police chase winds through three towns.   (Beaugrande 1994:172)
   (b)   'Mine is a long and sad tale!' said the Mouse, turning to Alice, and sighing.
         'It *is* a long tail, certainly,' said Alice, looking down with wonder at the Mouse's tail; 'but why do you call it sad?'   (Carroll 1965:39)

2.2.2   Give two more examples each of homonymy and polysemy.

2.3   Sentence meaning, utterance meaning, and speaker meaning

"No" often subsequently means "Yes".
> (Justice Bland in a rape case, *R v Donald* Morwell County Court
> 15 April 1993, 34–5, quoted in Moses 1993:291)

The **sense** of the one-word sentence *No* is uncontroversially negative. Yet Justice Bland opined that when a woman says *No* to sexual advances she often means "yes". If you think that the judge's claim is absurd, it is because you believe that the woman's utterance meaning and speaker meaning are the same as the sentence meaning. For Justice Bland, the utterance and speaker meaning are "yes" on the ground that Speaker is presumed to be teasing; consequently, the sentence meaning, "no", is not to be understood literally.

> *Assumption 2.2* SENTENCE MEANING is an abstract entity, a property of the language itself; it is the sense of the sentence.

Detaching sentence meaning from utterance and speaker meaning is not always inappropriate. For instance, lots of people have said *It killed me* and immediately been recognized as speaking nonliterally. We saw something similar in the doorbell interchange of 29 in Chapter 1: Maggie's 'I'm in the bathroom' was literally meant but underspecified the utterance and speaker meaning, forming the basis for the further inference "so I am unable to attend to the caller". Perceived discrepancies between sentence meaning and utterance meaning give rise to the frequently asked question *What did s/he mean when s/he said that?*
     Sentence 2 has at least the three senses listed below it.

2   He stood by the bank.

(a)   "A male person (or perhaps an animal) was in a bipedal (quadrupedal) stance beside the building of an institution for the custody of money."
(b)   "A male person (or perhaps an animal) was in a bipedal (quadrupedal) stance beside the raised body of earth."
(c)   "A male person remained a supporter of the troubled institution for the custody of money when it was in trouble."

Because 2 has these three meanings, we say it is three ways AMBIGUOUS (polysemy is ambiguity in a listeme).[2] Speakers use the senses of language expressions (such as sentences) in order to communicate particular messages about particular things and events on particular occasions in particular contexts. It is a conventional discourse requirement that Speaker should not be ambiguous without good cause (Chapter 1); so when uttering 2 under normal circumstances, a speaker would be referring to a particular individual, one or the other kind of action, and one type of bank.
     It is Speaker's use of sentence meaning within a particular utterance that gives rise to utterance meaning.

Definition 2.4 The UTTERANCE MEANING of utterance U is the meaning that any reasonable Hearer would assign to U, given the sentence meaning in U, and Hearer's judgment of Speaker's presumed purpose in using that particular sentence when uttering U in the prevailing context.

Because utterance meaning is arrived at by inference and appeal to context (Chapter 1), interpretation is open to the following vicissitudes:

(a)   Different interpretations by different Hearers[3] give rise to disputes over what someone 'said', the interpretation of legal documents, the meaning of literary texts, etc. Utterance meaning, like sentence meaning, is in the public domain; ideally, it would be a consensus of hearer-meanings.

(b)   Interpretation goes astray because Speaker presumes Hearer has certain information to hand that Hearer does not in fact have.

(c)   Hearer has made some mistake in interpreting.

(d)   Speaker mis-spoke in some way or other.

When Hearer reveals his or her interpretation, it may lead Speaker to claim *That is not what I meant*, thus distinguishing speaker meaning from utterance meaning. Speaker meaning is private, and therefore Hearer can only make presumptions of speaker meaning on the basis of utterance meaning; if Speaker is misinterpreted s/he must repair the damage by making another utterance using more carefully chosen words. For practical purposes of everyday language usage, therefore, utterance meaning is presumed to reveal speaker meaning unless Speaker makes it apparent this is not the case.

    In this section, sentence meaning, which is the abstract, decontextualized sense of a sentence, was distinguished from utterance meaning, which is the interpretation that Hearer may be expected to put on an utterance, given the context in which Speaker made it. There is a vast literature on various kinds of nonliteral language, from irony and indirect speech acts to metaphor.[4] Though utterance meaning can be distinguished from speaker meaning, on most occasions the utterance meaning is presumed to be what Speaker meant. Recall that the context-dependent assignment of meaning to language expressions used in acts of speaking and writing is studied in pragmatics (D1.3): therefore pragmatics studies utterance and/or speaker meaning. If the term 'semantics' is understood very restrictedly and contrasted with 'pragmatics', then semantics is restricted to the study of senses and sense-relations; but the term 'semantics' is also used for the whole field of meaning in natural language, and thus properly includes pragmatics. The most important reason for this is that it is impracticable (if not impossible) to discuss semantics without making frequent reference to aspects of pragmatics. Time and again we shall see the truth of

Assumption 2.3 Semantics is determined by the needs of human beings when seeking to communicate with one another.

Exercises

2.3.1 In legal philosophy there is a difference of opinion over whether the proper interpretation of legal statutes should be based on the words of a statute or on the presumed intention of law-makers based on external material such as parliamentary reports. How can this difference of opinion be framed in terms of the various types of meaning identified here?

2.3.2 Discuss the following (quoted in Beaugrande 1994:172): *Actor sent to jail for not finishing sentence.*

2.3.3 Give an example of deliberate purposeful ambiguity and say what justifies it.

2.3.4 Give at least one example each of irony or sarcasm and figurative use of language to demonstrate divergence of sentence meaning from utterance or speaker meaning.

2.4 An informal description of reference, denotation, extension, and intension

People talk about things (physical objects, abstract entities, places, states, events) that have existed (happened) in the past, things that exist (are happening) at present, and things that they predict will exist (happen) in the future. They also talk about things that could be or could have been if the world were different than it was, is, or is expected to be. They talk about things in fictional worlds and times of books and films; about things represented in paintings and photographs; about things that they deny exist; even about impossible things such as *the largest prime number* or *My brother is an only child.* We need to consider how semantic theories meet the challenge of connecting the language expressions used to talk about all these different kinds of things to the very things spoken about. In short, we shall be looking at the way language connects to things in the worlds and times spoken of. A word of warning: some of the concepts described in this section are particularly difficult to understand and often misunderstood.

Reference and denotation are relations between expressions in the language and worlds and times spoken of. Unfortunately, there is inconsistency among scholars in their use of the terms *reference* and *denotation.* The meaning ascribed to them here is determined by the need to have names for each kind of relationship between 'words and things'. I said in §2.2 that the sense of e_{OL} (any language expression e in the object language) is a description of its informational content in terms of some other language expression "e_M" and that each sense of e_{OL} is independent of the context on any particular occasion of e_{OL}'s use. For example, the sense of 3 is 4:

3   I totalled my car yesterday.
4   "Speaker did irreparable damage to his or her car the day before this sentence was uttered."

The reference will depend on:

(a)   Who utters 3 – which determines between 'his' or 'her' car.
(b)   When 3 was uttered – which dates 'yesterday'.

> *Definition 2.5* The REFERENCE of a language expression *e* in utterance U is "what Speaker is talking about when using *e* in U"; e.g. Speaker refers to particular entities, events, places, and times within the world and time s/he is speaking of. Thus, referring is something that Speaker does, and it is intimately connected with speaker meaning.

Speaker refers in U to things that the constituents of U denote. We need to distinguish reference from denotation for those occasions when Speaker errs and, for instance, refers to your husband as 'your father' – i.e. Speaker intends to refer to Hearer's husband, but the formal constituents of U denote Hearer's father. In 5, B points out an anomaly (D3.7) in A_1, which interlocutor A repairs in A_2.

5   A_1:   I saw your father at the library, and he says you guys are just back from a
                    holiday in Spain.

      B: But my father lives in Spain!?!

      A_2:   Did I say father? I meant husband.

Frege 1892 distinguished between *Sinn* and *Bedeutung*, that is between "sense" and what we have called "denotation". Within intensional logic and model theoretic semantics Frege's *Sinn* and *Bedeutung* have been reconstructed into 'intension' and 'extension', two terms that we can also make good use of.[5] A great deal of terminological confusion arises from the fact that, irrespective of any particular semantic theory, *intension* (distinct from the homophonous *intention*, "something intended") is sometimes assumed to be identical in meaning to *sense*, and *reference* to *extension*. What is absolutely essential to semantic theory is observance of Principle 2.1:

> *Principle 2.1* Any of the terms 'denotation', 'extension', 'intension', 'reference', and 'sense', used in semantic theory, must be defined by the theorist such that any particular use of the term is theory-bound.

Ideally, Principle 2.1 should extend to all terminology. All five terms listed in it are used in this book; I have already discussed the meanings given to *sense* and *reference*, and now turn to the others.

> *Definition 2.6* DENOTATION is the relation between language expressions and things or events in worlds – not just the world we live in, but any world and time that may be spoken of.

Denotation is a convenient cover term for intension and extension when we have no need to distinguish between them. Extension is easier to grasp than intension, so we'll tackle that first.

> *Definition 2.7* To say that a language expression *e* has EXTENSION in a world w_i at time t_i is equivalent to saying *e* denotes something that exists in the world w_i at time t_i.

The world spoken of is a mental model of an actual or recalled or imagined world in which it is important to identify what there is and what there isn't. Speaker refers differently to things which have extension in the world spoken of and to things which do not. It is sometimes said that 'referring expressions' identify things that exist, and 'nonreferring expressions' identify things which don't; but this book stipulates that Speaker refers by using the intensions of language expressions (we'll talk about them in a minute). Some language expressions that Speaker uses have extensions in the world spoken of and others do not. In 6, the extension of *a dog* would be some dog, for instance, my dog Zelda:

6   We have a dog at home; her name is Zelda.

Yes, as I write, I do have a dog named Zelda, but no cat; so

7   We have a dog at home; her name is Zelda. But we have no cat.

The relation of *no* to *a(n)* is discussed in Chapter 13, but it is clear that 'no cat' in 7 indicates that there is no extension for '[a] cat' in this particular world spoken of. Whether or not an expression has extension in a world spoken of can usually be checked by locating the expression within the complement noun phrase of an affirmative indicative existential clause of the type *There was/were ..., There is/are..., There will be ...* etc. The negation of this indicates NON-EXTENSION. For example, from 7 we can infer 8.

8   *There is* a dog at our house, but *there isn't* a cat.

We will consider other markers of non-extension in §2.5.

Many semanticists think that the purpose of semantic theory is provide an account of how Speaker has the ability to recognize the truth conditions on statements.

> *Definition 2.8* A TRUTH CONDITION on a statement or proposition is the condition that must be met for it to be assigned one of the TRUTH VALUES from the range {true, false}.

We shall look at some methods for doing this in Chapter 6; in the meantime we rely on a common-sense understanding of what it means for a statement to be either true or else false. In order to understand and evaluate the meaning of *It is raining* or *Kangaroos are marsupials* or *De Gaulle was taller than Napoleon* you need to know the conditions under which these statements would be true. Knowing these conditions allows you to make inferences such as that you will get wet if you go out into the rain and that female kangaroos have pouches. One problem is connecting the language used to the world being spoken of. A greater problem is providing an acceptable semantics for non-truth-functional sentences like *Be quiet!* or *What's your name?* or *Thank you*, or an expressive such as *Shit!*

Extension in a world links with the notion of truth in a world at a certain time because, for instance, if Zelda exists then I can truly predicate this of her in the sentence *Zelda exists* or I can presuppose her existence (i.e. take it for granted, D6.14) and predicate of her *Zelda is a good-natured dog.* This leads to the question: What does it mean for a proposition to be true? The truth of *My brother Bill wasn't bald when he married Cynthia* depends on (at least) the following facts – according to Speaker:

(a)   Speaker has (or once had) a brother Bill.
(b)   At the time Bill married Cynthia he was not bald (he had a full head of hair).
(c)   At a later time, Bill is or was bald, or it has been implied that he is or was bald (even though he may not be).

> *Definition 2.9* TRUTH AT AN INDEX: Truth, the extension for a proposition, is tied to a world at a certain time. Extensionality is existence or nonexistence in a world w paired with a time t (D2.7). This pair, <w,t>, is usually referred to as an INDEX.

It is just such a spatio-temporal index that gives rise to the deictic categories, also called 'indexicals', sketched in Chapter 1.

● Let's represent Speaker's and Hearer's model M of the world w and time t spoken of by the symbols $M^{w,t}$.

Every language expression that has extension in M^{w_i,t_i} (a particular world w_i at time t_i) also has intension. As we shall see in 13–15, two language expressions with different intensions can have the same extension. A language expression that has no extension in M^{w_i,t_i} can have extension in another world, and this gives rise to the notion of its intension (§2.5 discusses problems with negatives and words like *noone*, which we ignore for now). Look at the two pictures below.

Picture 1   **Picture 2**

We can truly say of them

9   There is an illustration of a dinosaur in Picture 1

and

10 There isn't an illustration of a dinosaur in Picture 2.

In 9 and 10 'Picture 1' and 'Picture 2' both have extension in our world and time (there they are before your eyes) '[A]n illustration of a dinosaur' has extension in Picture 1 of our world, and no extension in Picture 2. Sometimes, as in these examples, we can point to the extension of a language expression; this is never possible with an intension, because it is an abstract notion. The way you understand the words 'an illustration of a dinosaur' in 10 is through the intension alone.

Neither *a dog* nor *a canine quadruped* denote Fig.2.1:

Figure 2.1 A dog

Fig.2.1 is a picture of a dog, not the denotation of *a dog*.

What makes a particular entity worthy of being called *a dog* is the essential property we might call its "dogginess". Dogginess is the abstract property that is the intension of the noun *dog*. The intension of the NP *a dog* would be (the property of being) one individual from the genus of dogs. Compare this with the sense of *a dog*, which is "a single canine quadruped" or "one individual from the class of dogs". Notice that sense can be expressed in more than one way in the metalanguage: discovering the optimum form for the "e_M" (quotes are a reminder that we are referring to sense) is one task for semantics. To be of value, "e_M" needs to point the way out of language towards the things that language is used to talk about; the way it does this is to pick out salient characteristics of the typical DENOTATUM (= "that which is denoted") for the object-language expression, e_{OL}.

> *Definition 2.10 (preliminary)* The INTENSION of expression e_{OL} in the object language is the characteristic property or set of properties that a typical denotatum must perforce have for e_{OL} to be used in a conventional manner within the (object) language.

This seems to favour a checklist of properties to be satisfied for correct use of an expression; cf. Fillmore 1975. For example, the denotatum of *a bird* might be expected to be bipedal, have feathers, and be capable of flight. But there are several species of flightless birds. A downy chick and a plucked chicken are featherless, but nonetheless birds. A one-legged bird and even a mutant three-legged bird are also birds. So the notion of a checklist of essential properties is problematical. We shall discuss this matter further in Chapter 10 and revise the definition of intension accordingly.

> *Definition 2.11* A metalanguage expression "e_M" is an expression that describes the intension of expression e_{OL} in the object language.

A consequence of this state of affairs is a seeming redundancy because to spell out the sense we put quotes around a description of the intension, e.g.

11 The intension of *red* is a colour prototypically that of blood, an electromagnetic wave between 590–700 nanometres, and focally around 695 nanometres.

12 The sense of *red* is "colour prototypically that of blood, an electromagnetic wave between 590–700 nanometres, and focally around 695 nanometres".

The redundancy arises because in order to talk and write about semantics we have to use language; we must therefore resort to typographical ploys to distinguish distinct concepts.

(a)   Sense is presented in a metalanguage expression "e_M", it IS LANGUAGE.
(b)   Intension IS OUTSIDE OF LANGUAGE – even though it is intangible.

Senses are no more than translations or paraphrases. Intensions provide the nonlanguage bases for them.

> *Assumption 2.4* Intensions are the content of concepts.

For instance in 11, the words attempt to capture the concept 'red'. Intensions are sometimes described as concepts, e.g. by Gamut 1991, Cann 1993. This might be helpful in coming to understand what intensions are, but not if Partee 1979:8 is right when she says: 'the psychological semantic representation of a word is often very different from its intension.' Concepts are cognitive entities, and intensions are what the concepts are concepts of: intensions are abstract entities.[6] This allows for a further assumption:

> *Assumption 2.5* Intension is not tied to a particular world or time.

Speaker uses the intension of language expressions in speaking about M^{w_i,t_i}, that is, a particular world at a particular time.[1]

Two language expressions that have the same extension do not necessarily have the same intension. For instance, according to Frege 1892, the brightest astral body in the evening sky is the planet Venus, known to the ancients as *the evening star*. The brightest astral body just before the sun rises was known as *the morning star*; its extension is Venus also. In other words, the thing called *the evening star* is the thing also called *the morning star*. This situation is illustrated (but not defined) in Fig. 2.2 where the left diagram depicts the situation for the observer who does not know the identity between the morning star 'ms' and the evening star 'es', i.e. $M^{w_i,t_i}m \neq M^{w_i,t_i}e$. Each oval represents a world-time pair that, in this example, corresponds to an event. The solid line indicates identity across

---

1. In intensional logic (IL), intension is defined as a function (Chapter 7) from possible worlds to extensions in a particular world (or worlds) – roughly speaking, a concept (in the IL view) is mapped to a particular world. This identifies what intension does, but not what its content is. Compare the IL definition of a verb (e.g. *smiles*) as a function from entities (e.g. *Sheila*) to truth values: the idea is that the verb predicates the NP to produce *Sheila smiles* which is either true or false in the world. This identifies what *smiles* does but not its content (what smiling is); cf. Johnson-Laird 1983:172f.

indices. In the right-hand diagram, the observer does recognize the identity of 'ms' and 'es'; i.e. $M^{w_i t}{}_m = M^{w_i t}{}_e$. The figure as a whole represents Frege's model.

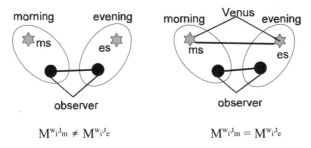

Figure 2.2 Different models

13 is true from an earthly perspective, but 14 is false because *morning* and *evening* do not mean the same.

13 The evening star is the morning star.
14 *The evening star* means "the morning star".

15 identifies the intension of *the evening star*, and through the intension, its sense also.

15 *The evening star* means "the star that can be seen in the evening sky".

The intension of *the evening star* is the star that can be seen in the evening sky in all possible worlds – not just from earth..

> *Assumption 2.6* Two language expressions differ in intension when it is possible for them to differ in extension.

For instance, one can imagine a planet in some distant galaxy from which the morning star is an entity as distinct from the evening star as Venus is from Mars. Nullities and impossibilities pose a problem for A2.6. *Noone* and *nothing* both have a null extension, yet they have different meanings. An impossible object like *a round square* also has a null extension. A solution is to say that the component parts *a round thing* (or *roundness*) and *a square* do have extension in possible worlds, but they can never have the same extension in any world or time (i.e. no possible world contains an entity which is both a square and at the same time round). Negatives such as *Noone lives here* and *God does not exist* can also be understood in terms of their components, see §2.5. Some listemes, e.g. *the*, have no independent intension, but they too participate in the intensions of constructions into which they enter; cf. Chapter 13.

Suppose that I have a sister called Jackie and that my friend Harry speaks the words *I love your sister*. In these circumstances, 16 is true but 17 false.

16 Harry told me he loved Jackie.
17 Harry spoke the words 'I love Jackie.'

Reports like 16 can use extensional equivalence. But direct quotation like 17 requires the use of the same words with the same intensions as the original speaker; extensional equivalents are unacceptable.

 The proposition in 18 is true in ALL possible worlds and times.

18 A bachelor is a man who has never married.

This is a linguistic TAUTOLOGY. One sense of bachelor is "a man who has never married", and this sense is included in the predicate 'is a man who has never married'. In other words, 18 is equivalent to the painfully explicit tautology *A man who has never married is a man who has never married*.

> *Definition 2.12* A linguistic tautology results when the meaning of one major clause constituent is included within (or identical to) the meaning of some other major clause constituent (including the clause itself) within a sentence.

19 7 is between 2 and 9.
20 A cat is an animal.
21 He sold it for money.
22 If Emma smiled and waved, then Emma smiled.
23 Bill is happy or Bill is not happy.

Example 19 is tautologous because the set of numbers between 2 and 9 necessarily includes 7. Example 20 is tautologous because the meaning of *animal* is included within the meaning of *cat* (see Chapters 7–8). 21 contains a tautology because *sell* means "exchange for money" (Chapter 12). In 22, 'Emma smiled' is one of the conjuncts in the *if*-clause (Chapter 6). In the disjunction (Chapter 6) of 23, 'Bill is happy' is a semantic constituent of 'it is not the case that Bill is happy' (not everyone would agree with this, but see 26 below for the semantic structure). Looking at the intensions: in every world and time, if a man, B, is a bachelor, then B is a man who has never married. In every world and time, 7 is between 2 and 9. In every world and time, a cat is an animal (though see the discussion in Chapter 3). In every world and time, selling is a transaction in which goods are exchanged for money. In every world and time a proposition is identical to itself (*Emma smiled = Emma smiled*; *Bill is happy = Bill is happy*). In short, tautologies hold true for all possible worlds and times. Truths that are not tautological are CONTINGENT on at least one possible world (e.g. the real world), but not all.

 In this section we have differentiated and defined reference, denotation, extension, and intension, and begun to demonstrate what it means to say that people speak of different worlds and times.

Exercises

2.4.1 Distinguish between the sense and reference of *You get out of here by tomorrow*.

2.4.2 John says to Jane *I love you!* He refers to himself as 'I'. What does *I* denote? How does John refer to Jane?

2.4.3 What has extension in the following scene (excluding the background enclosed between square brackets), and what is identified as having none:

[*The Chief of Control (Edward Platt) is taking Agent 86, Maxwell Smart (Don Adams), through photos of KAOS agents to see if he can identify a suspect.*]

MAX: Wait a minute Chief, that's him!

CHIEF: Impossible!

MAX: Why? Isn't he a KAOS agent?

CHIEF: Well yes. But ...

MAX: Well give me one good reason why it couldn't be him!

CHIEF: Because that man is dead.

MAX: I asked you for a good reason, not a terrific one.

(*Get Smart* was created by Mel Brooks with Buck Henry; this 1965 episode was written by Arne Sultan and Chris Hayward.)

2.4.4 Suppose you were asked to discover the name of the first child born in the year 2000. You search the records and report *The first child born in 2000 was Zaphod Beeblebrox*. Whether or not this is true depends WHERE you looked. The international date line runs longitudinally through the western Pacific, so a child born at 2 a.m. on January 1, 2000 in, say, Fiji, was born 23 hours before a child born at 2 a.m. on January 1, 2000 in Samoa. What does this tell you about conditions on truth?

2.4.5 Assuming normal conditions of ordinary language use, identify the extensions of expressions in:
(a) My brother is a dentist.
(b) Napoleon was short.
(c) Harriet carried the can.

2.4.6 The sense of *water* is "a colourless, tasteless liquid consisting of H_2O"; its intension is a colourless, tasteless liquid consisting of H_2O; its extension in the utterance *My petrol tank has water in it* is a quantity of H_2O in my petrol tank (if the assertion of its presence is correct). Give a sense, intension, and extension for *muesli* and for *a cat*.

2.4.7 Have you ever been called by someone else's name, but answered nonetheless? Is it ALWAYS necessary to correct a mistaken reference?

2.4.8 What does it mean to claim that *a bachelor* and *a man who has never married* are logically equivalent?

2.4.9 Which of the following are tautologies, and which are contingently true?
(a) A daughter is a female kinsperson.
(b) Hitler became the Fuehrer.
(c) To kill is to cause something to die.
(d) The star we call *the sun* is hot.

2.4.10 Russell Hines holds two portfolios in the State parliament: he is both Minster for Mining and Minister for the Environment. In these circumstances do *Minister for Mining* and *Minister for the Environment* have the same (a) intension, (b) extension?

2.4.11 When the President's daughter says *Daddy* she is referring to the President; but does her utterance also denote the President?

2.4.12 NPs denoting impossible objects such as *a round square* and *the largest prime number* present a problem for the claim that 'two language expressions differ in intension when it is possible for them to differ in extension.' What is the problem?

2.4.13 What is peculiar about *I'm sitting here completely surrounded by no beer!* (Onslow complaining to Daisy and Rose in the BBC sitcom "Keeping Up Appearances".)

2.5 When there is no extension or extension is uncertain

'Who did you pass on the road?' the King went on, holding out his hand to the Messenger for some hay.
'Nobody,' said the Messenger.
'Quite right,' said the King: 'this young lady saw him too. So of course Nobody walks slower than you.'
'I do my best,' the Messenger said in a sullen tone. 'I'm sure nobody walks faster than I do!'
'He can't do that,' said the King, 'or else he'd have been here first.'
(Lewis Carroll *Through the Looking-Glass* [1871] 1965:182)

Suppose my brother-in-law, a dentist, is on his way to a fancy-dress party and stops by my New Year's party in clerical garb. A guest, Mervyn, asks me *Who's the priest?* Strictly speaking there is no priest and so no extension for 'the priest'; but I understand to whom Mervyn is attributing the description and answer *That's my brother-in-law*. Now, if I don't correct Mervyn, he will mistakenly believe that my brother-in-law is a priest and might one day embarrass us all by calling on him to perform the last rites for his mother, so it would be cooperative for me to add *But he's not a priest, he's a dentist. He's dressed like that because he's going to a fancy-dress party.* This is because

Assumption 2.7. The important thing about denotation is its function of making manifest to each participant in language interaction the existential status of phenomena within $M^{w,t}$.

Speakers regularly make what Donnellan 1966 described as ATTRIBUTIVE REFERENCE. Examples are the italicized NPs in 24–25.

24 How *they* built Stonehenge is a mystery.
25 The forest and several homes have been destroyed by fire, which police are saying was
   deliberately lit. *Whoever* did this (if anyone did) must be most severely punished.

We don't know who built Stonehenge, though we assume that someone did. In 25,
'whoever' refers to the presumed firebug. However, it could be that the police are wrong
and there was no such person. Either way, Speaker successfully refers. Note that default
attributive reference is made by *whoever, whatever,* or *whichever*; thus a paraphrase of 24
is *How whoever built Stonehenge did it is a mystery.*
   We mostly talk about things that exist, so the denotation of any NP or sentence
ordinarily has extension unless otherwise indicated. Imagine one person uttering 26 to
another who answers with 27.

26 God is good.
27 God does not exist.

The fact that we can speak of nothing has led to much discussion among philosophers.[7]
In 26 Speaker makes it apparent to Hearer that s/he presupposes (= takes it for granted) that
the NP 'God' has extension. By parity of argument, we should say that 'God' in 27 has
extension, yet it doesn't. We make the following pragmatic assumption with respect to
sentences like 27; cf. Gazdar 1979:67f.

> **Assumption 2.8** Speaker does not deny the existence of X unless X's existence
> is normally taken for granted, and/or there has been some earlier assertion of
> X's existence.

You could test this claim by truthfully announcing 28 to some friend and observing the
response.

28 There is no eagle digging under the sea-bed six nautical miles west of Gibraltar.

Perhaps the reason for this constraint is that the number of NON-ENTITIES that can be
spoken of at any given world and time is infinitely larger than the number of ENTITIES that
can be spoken of. With their finite resources, language users can only attend to those non-
entities purported to be entities. If you suppose 26 and 27 to be a discourse between A and
B respectively, in 27 B presupposes that God may have extension in A's and other people's
belief worlds and asserts that this is contrary to fact (in B's opinion). The situation is
sketched in Fig. 2.3 where the rectangle represents A's world and the ellipse B's. G[od]
exists in A's world along with A and B, but for B, G[od] exists only within A's world.

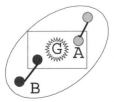

Figure 2.3 God as a
nonexistent within B's
model (ellipse), except
as an entity within A's
model (rectangle)

In natural language semantics we have to represent as factual or nonfactual what Speaker or Hearer take to be factual or counterfactual – not what God, some scientist, sectarian, or philosopher thinks is the case (unless this person is a participant in the speech event). Thus, in 27, the opinion contrary to Speaker's is taken to be nonfactual. It is surely no accident that in all semantic theories, a representation for 27 would place the proposition *God exists* within the scope (cf. Chapter 7) of a negative in a manner analogous to 29 – which can be glossed "It is not the case that God exists".

29

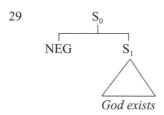

Negation of sentences and NPs (the latter marked by *no* or *any*, Chapter 13) indicates nonextension for certain constituents within the SCOPE of negation. For the time being, we define scope in terms of C-COMMAND (cf. Reinhart 1976):

> *Definition 2.13* A category α c-commands category β only if the first branching node dominating α also dominates β, and neither α nor β dominates the other. The scope of a node α is the set of nodes that α c-commands.[2]

Look at the tree in 29. NEG corresponds to α. S_0 is the first branching node that dominates NEG; and S_0 also dominates S_1 (= β). Neither NEG nor S_1 dominates the other. Therefore S_1 is negated. Both *there is no God* and *God does not exist* deny an extension for 'God'. *I didn't go* and *I never went* deny extension for 'my going on some past occasion'. *John isn't happy* denies extension for 'John's happiness'. *Noone* denies extension for 'a person' . *Nothing* denies extension for 'a thing'.

SUBJUNCTIVES (Chapter 11) indicate nonextension in one world (usually the world spoken in) but hypothesize extension in some supposed or nonfactual world. Compare 30 with 31:

30 If Max owned a Rolls, he was a lucky man.
31 *If* Max own*ed* a Rolls, he*'d be* a lucky man.

In 31 nonfactuality is indicated by the italicized initial *if* plus the subjunctive verb forms. 30 should be interpreted something like "If indeed it is the case (as you claim) that Max

---

2. In case you don't already know: 'α' is the Greek letter *alpha* and 'β' is *beta*. Government Binding theory has renamed c-command 'm-command', and substituted the words *maximal projection* for 'branching node': A category α m-commands category β only if the first maximal projection dominating α also dominates β, and neither α nor β dominates the other. A maximal projection is the highest projection of a lexical head in a given structure – NP, AP, PP, VP, IP, CP.

owned a Rolls, then he was a lucky man" in which Speaker maintains a degree of scepticism, but nevertheless accepts Max's Rolls-Royce ownership as a fact – at least for the sake of argument. The important point here is that the model consists of just one world that contains Max and the Rolls; cf. Fig. 2.4.

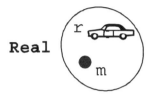

Figure 2.4 The co-extension of Max (m) and his Rolls (r) at some past index in 30

In 31, however, there are two worlds evoked:

(a)   The reference world of the present (don't be misled by the subjunctive verb forms) in which 'Max' has extension, but not the fact of Max's Rolls-Royce ownership (i.e. it is not true that Max owns a Rolls-Royce). This is represented by the circle in Fig. 2.5.
(b)   A nonfactual world, the ellipse in Fig. 2.5, in which Speaker imagines that Max exists and that he does own a Rolls.

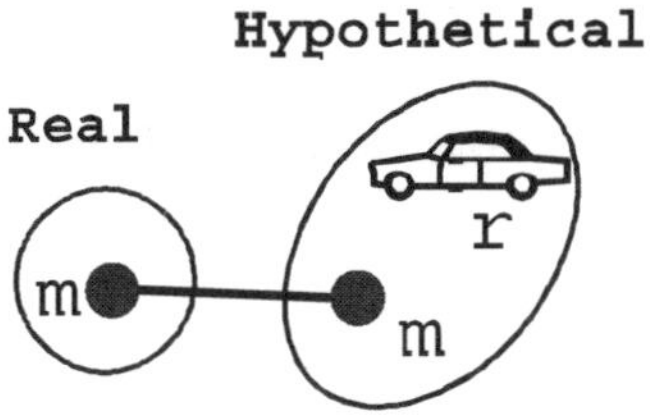

Hypothetical

Real

Figure 2.5 Speaker's model of the two worlds evoked in 31.

In fact, in 31, only the nonfactual (elliptical) world is actually spoken of; the factual world is implied. Because of the contrast between the two worlds, 31 is COUNTERFACTUAL, a special type of nonfactual. There are many difficulties with counterfactuals which we cannot discuss here.[8]

An example invoking a supposed but not necessarily counterfactual world is 32 or its equivalent, 33.

32 Should there be some eggs left, we'll eat them.
33 If there are any eggs left, we'll eat them.

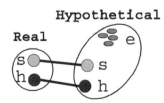

Hypothetical

Real

Figure 2.6 Speaker's model in 32–33. s = Speaker, h = Hearer, e = eggs. Is the (elliptical) hypothetical world containing eggs identical with the (circular) world spoken in?

Fig. 2.6 is only illustrative of 32–33 which do not pose the question in the caption (see Harder 1996:446f). But 32–33 do suppose that the world spoken in may possibly be identical to the hypothetical world. A semantically subjunctive verb does not always take a subjunctive form. Notice that in 33 the colloquial 'are' can be replaced by the subjunctive *should be*. In both 32 and 33 there is no extension for 'eggs' in the first clause, but there is extension for the coreferential 'them' in the second clause because you can't eat things that don't exist. Compare 34–35:

34 There are some eggs left, so we'll eat them.
35 *There are no eggs left, so we'll eat them.

36 There are no eggs left, so we'll buy $\begin{Bmatrix} \text{them} \\ \text{some} \end{Bmatrix}$ (and then eat them).

The explanation for the difference between 35 and 36 is straightforward: you can't eat eggs which aren't there; but you can buy eggs from elsewhere, then eat them. The interesting sentences are 32–33. The initial clause indicates that Speaker does not guarantee an extension for eggs, but is willing to suppose that there might be some eggs left; thus there is extension for 'eggs' in the supposed world (the ellipse of Fig. 2.6), and in that world they can be eaten.

OPAQUE or PROPOSITIONAL ATTITUDE verbs such as *look for, think, believe*, and *want* take NP objects or sentential complements that may themselves be nonextensional or which may contain NP constituents without extension.[9] For example, in 37(a) the italicized object NP presupposes extension, that in (b) does not. In 38 the extensionality of the object NP is ambiguous.

37 (a) I'm looking for *the person who drives the bus parked outside*.
     (b) I'm looking for *someone who can drive the bus parked outside*.
38 I'm looking for *someone who speaks Arabic*.

Where the NP lacks extension as in 37(b), *anyone* can substitute for 'someone'.

39 does not guarantee extension (i.e. truth) in the world and time Speaker inhabits for the proposition 'Harry has moved to Moscow'; but Speaker does attribute some credibility to the proposition.

39 I think Harry has moved to Moscow.

The status of the evidence for what is said is a matter of EVIDENTIALITY – so-called because the strength of Speaker's confidence in what s/he says is based upon the evidence supporting it.[10] The cooperative principle, in particular the maxim of quality, requires that Speaker admit any doubts s/he has about the preconditions on an utterance (§6.5).

The extension of a language expression e_{OL} is the entity, event, state, place, time, etc. denoted by e_{OL} that exists in a world (or set of worlds) spoken of or implied by what is said. There is a problem in deciding what constitutes existence. It is not only physical objects (e.g. you, this book) that exist, but also

(a)   events such as your reading of this book at this time,
(b)   your state of mind (happy, sad, excited, bored, confused, etc.),

(c)   the numbers 3 and Π,
(d)   the fact that $2 + 3 = 5$.

We saw that the truth of a proposition in a world w_i at time t_i is its extension at that index (D2.9). Historical people and events raise questions about extension: do Marilyn Monroe and her suicide exist today, or only in this world at a time now past? Obviously Marilyn Monroe doesn't exist the same way you do, as a living entity; but she exists as a dead entity, as a screen image, as a voice on a CD, and so forth. Fictional characters like Sherlock Holmes, and mythical objects like unicorns, have extension in some fictional or mythical worlds, but not here and now in this world. Do ideas and plans (the baby my sister is planning to have) have extension in this world, or in some imagined world? There are many philosophical problems with the notion of existence, and they spill over into a discussion of extension. We shall not be resolving them here.

Extensions that are tangible, such as that for *a dog*, are easily verified as such by extralinguistic means using sensory data, e.g. you can see, hear, feel, and smell a dog. There is circumstantial evidence for the abstract extensions of *justice, happiness, desire*. Things that have no extension, such as 'nobody' in *nobody is there*, are understandable (but not normally understood) by imagining a world in which somebody is there and denying the possibility of that world. A counterfactual (*if I were to own a Rolls-Royce* ...) can be explained by imagining a state of affairs in which it is factual. Yet it is only possible to describe understanding in this way because of the **intensions** of the words you are reading.

Extensionality in NPs is sometimes referred to as 'specificity' (cf. Partee 1972, Frawley 1992). For reasons that will be briefly examined, this is incorrect.

Definition 2.14   A SPECIFIC NP identifies a particular individual, set of individuals, or a particular part of a non-discrete mass.

Specificity interacts with extensionality and the definite – indefinite opposition (Chapter 13) – i.e. it is relevant to the choice between using a definite NP such as *the chocolate* and an indefinite such as *a chocolate*. Suppose Julie proffers Tom a box of chocolates with the words *Have a chocolate*: there is no question that the chocolates exist, but there is no specific chocolate that Tom is being offered – 'a chocolate' has extension but is nonspecific. Prior to Tom making his choice, there is no extension for something we can conveniently call *Tom's chocolate*. Of course, Tom might refuse the offer; in that case the NP *Tom's chocolate* persists in lacking extension and it is consequently inappropriate to use it. Being nonexistent, it is also inappropriate to refer to *a chocolate offered to Tom* because this identifies a specific chocolate. In order to talk about this non-entity we have to relate it to things that do exist, e.g. by saying *Tom was offered a chocolate, but refused to take one*. The word *one(s)* is the classic nonspecific pronoun (§2.7). Notice that whereas extensional indefinites may be either specific or nonspecific, indefinite NPs that lack extension are nonspecific – cf. 'a Rolls' in 31, 'any eggs' in 33, 'no eggs' in 36, 'someone who can drive the bus parked outside' in 37(b). Everything said about the singular countable NP *a chocolate* holds also for plurals and uncountables (Chapter 13). Suppose Julie had said *Take two* when offering Tom the box of chocolates; or had instead offered something named by a mass term, e.g. *Have some coffee*. Nonextensionals that are definite, e.g. *God does not exist*, are specific. To sum up:

(a)   Extensional indefinites may be either specific or nonspecific.
(b)   Nonextensional indefinites are all nonspecific.
(c)   Definites are specific whether they are extensional or nonextensional.

There are two classes of possible exceptions to (c). Definite NPs (nearly always pronouns) used of entities in nonfactual worlds when the antecedent reference to the entity is nonspecific may also be thought nonspecific; e.g.

40 If someone were to offer me *a Lamborghini*, I'd take *it*.

'[S]omeone' and 'a Lamborghini' are both indefinite nonspecific; 'me' and 'I' are definite specific. The sentence final 'it' is definite and arguably refers to the specific Lamborghini I am offered in some nonfactual world. But can we coherently conceive that the nonspecific Lamborghini of the *if* clause is specific in the second clause (apodosis)? The second kind of possible exceptions are definite NPs used attributively as in 24–25. From one point of view *the people who built Stonehenge* is specifically identifying certain people; from another point of view, Speaker is not specifically identifying anybody.

These difficulties aside, we see that identifying a particular individual, set of individuals, or part of a non-discrete mass – is a consequence of the interaction between extensionality and the definite–indefinite opposition which is examined in Chapter 13.[11]

This section has dealt with one of the most difficult areas of semantics: reference to things that either do not exist or whose existential status is unknown or uncertain. The discussion took us through comparisons between models, worlds, to opacity, evidentiality, and specificity.

Exercises

2.5.1 Does *Fred isn't a Mormon*: (a) indicate that 'Fred' has extension; (b) subsequently license the extensionality in the subject of *That Mormon tried to convert us*?

2.5.2 The idea of individuals performing differently in different worlds and/or times is necessary to understand such things as holding a belief that all politicians are liars, yet at the same time believing the man who tells you your tyre is flat, even though he turns out to be a politician and, in the political arena, is indeed a regular liar. We could represent the difference as follows: in M^{w_i,t_i} the man is believable; in M^{w_j,t_j} the man is not believable. Another example: the most likely interpretation of *In 1946 the President was a baby* is that the baby of 1946 grew up to become president; but the baby and the president exist in two distinct world–time pairs. Here are two true statements: *Bob Dylan wrote 'Blowin' in the wind'* and *Bob Dylan is Robert Zimmerman*. (a) Discuss the fact that the following is not true without qualification: *Robert Zimmerman wrote 'Blowin' in the wind'*. And (b) discuss the false conclusion in the following: If the Pope had been born a Protestant in Northern Ireland he'd be anti-Catholic. If he were anti-Catholic he'd hate the Pope. Therefore, if the Pope had been born a Protestant in Northern Ireland, he'd hate himself.

2.5.3 Which of (a) or (b) is presented as counterfactual? Explain what the meaning difference is.
(a) It rained today, so we didn't go to the beach.
(b) If it hadn't rained today, we would have gone to the beach.

2.5.4 In the real world that we inhabit the extension of *unicorn* is identical to the extension of *centaur*, namely null. Do these words have the same meaning? Give your reasons if you think the answer is no.

2.5.5 Discuss extension for the NPs and propositions of (a–d).
(a) Where did you leave my car?
(b) He has neither a pen nor a pencil.
(c) Grate me some cheese, will you?
(d) If he's written a book, I've never read it.

2.5.6 Explain what is peculiar about *Fred's bald, so he's gone for a haircut.*

2.5.7 How can *There might be some eggs left* be related to the extensionality of *There are some eggs left?*

2.5.8 Assuming some typical context for use in everyday English, discuss the extension of the italicized expressions in (a–h).
(a) My mother is knitting me *a sweater*.
(b) My cousin sent me *a postcard* from *Fiji*.
(c) *The accident* could have been prevented.
(d) *Bruce nearly crashed the car*.
(e) *Erica dropped the cup*.
(f) The vicar didn't realize that *Eric was Eric Clapton*.
(g) Roseanne dreamt that *she was Elle MacPherson*.
(h) *Nicole's dream* was that she could play tennis like Martina.

2.5.9 Disambiguate the extensionality of the object NP in *I'm looking for someone who speaks Arabic*.

2.5.10 Compare and comment on (a) and (b):
(a) There are some chocolates, $\left\{ \begin{array}{c} ??so \\ but \end{array} \right\}$ Harry can't have any.
(b) There aren't any chocolates, $\left\{ \begin{array}{c} so \\ ??but \end{array} \right\}$ Harry can't have any.

2.5.11 Are (a) and (b) equally ambiguous as to the extension of '... Versace jacket'? [In (b), suppose 'this' is indefinite, not demonstrative]
(a) Emma told me she wanted to buy a Versace jacket, but Harry dissuaded her.
(b) Emma told me she wanted to buy this Versace jacket, but Harry dissuaded her.

2.5.12 Suppose Julie offered Tom not a box of chocolates from which to choose one, but just held out a single chocolate for him saying *Have a chocolate*. On this occasion is the NP 'a chocolate' specific or nonspecific?

2.5.13 D2.14 reads 'A specific NP identifies a particular individual, set of individuals, or a particular part of a non-discrete mass.' Who does the identifying? What would happen if Speaker and Hearer make different identifications?

2.5.13 Look at the quote from Lewis Carroll's *Through the Looking-Glass* at the head of this section and comment on the King's use of 'Nobody'.

2.5.14 Suppose that the proposition that 'Nobody is there' is true, i.e. it has extension. How is this possible when the NP 'nobody' lacks extension?

2.6   Extensionality and generics

Definition 2.15 The common property of all generic expressions is that they are used to express law-like, or [g]nomic, statements. (Dahl 1975:99)

Some scholars link extension to TOKENS, and intension to TYPES (cf. Jackendoff 1983:94). You can think of a $10 bill or a £10 note as a token for the amount of $10 and £10 respectively, with the sum of money counting as type. My dog Zelda, as the extension of the NP *my dog Zelda*, is a token of dogginess – dogs being a type of entity. This relabelling does not help with the difficult questions about intension and extension, and it creates a new problem. If an individual dog is a token, then the genus of dogs is a type; hence it is often presumed that generic NPs lack extension. It is because generics express law-like statements that they denote types. The argument would be that only tokens of the genus can exist in any particular world w_i at time t_i; the genus or type itself does not. Whatever the philosophical justification for such a view, the fact is that speakers of English treat some generics as if they do have extension.

There are generic SENTENCES, e.g.

41 (a) Harriet blushes when she's embarrassed.

$$\text{(b) If you drink coffee at night it} \left\{\begin{array}{l} \text{may} \\ \text{will} \\ \text{can} \end{array}\right\} \text{keep you awake.}$$

    (c) As a rule, two magnets will either attract or repel each other.

There are three forms of generic NP in English. Two, the definite generic (italicized in 42) and the unmarked indefinite generic (43–44), typically have extension.

42 (a) *The kiwi* is a flightless bird. It inhabits New Zealand.
   (b) There is *the kiwi*. It is a flightless bird. It inhabits New Zealand.
   (c) Among flightless birds, there is *the kiwi* [and the ostrich].

43 (a) *Kiwis* are flightless birds that inhabit New Zealand.
   (b) There are *kiwis*, which are flightless birds that inhabit New Zealand.
   (c) Among flightless birds, there are *kiwis* [and emus].

44 (a) *Salt* is hygroscopic.
   (b) Among things that are hygroscopic, there is *salt* [and I don't know what else].

The fact that these two kinds of generic NPs can fall within the scope of a positive indicative existential in the (b) and (c) sentences proves that they have extension in $M^{w,t}$. Both of these generics can, of course, be used in nonextensional environments, e.g. *The dodo is extinct; Dodos are extinct; If weddell seals lived in the tropics, they'd have a lot less blubber.* However, a third kind of generic, the *a(n)*-generic, always lacks extension and is nonspecific; hence 45(b–c) cannot be interpreted as generic, and in them 'a dog' does have extension.

45 (a) *A dog* barks, *a cat* mews.
   (b) There is a dog, which barks.
   (c) ??Among things which bark, there is a dog.

Compare the relative unacceptability of 45(c) with the acceptability of the generic 45(d):

45 (d) Among things which bark, there is *the dog* [and the seal].

The *a(n)*-generic in 45(a) denotes the state of affairs indicated by the subjunctive in 46.

46 Normally, if $\left\{ \begin{array}{l} \text{something is a dog} \\ \text{there should be something which is a dog} \end{array} \right\}$ it will bark; ...

Some animal might replace 'something' in 46. If the generic is tautologous, e.g. *A bachelor is a man who has never married*, we get *necessarily* where 46 has 'normally':

47 Necessarily, if some man is a bachelor, he will be a man who has never married.

The facts presented above seem to be confirmed by the following generics which deny existence:

48 *The unicorn* does not exist in the real world.
49 There are no *unicorns* in the real world.
50 (a) ??A unicorn does not exist in the real world.
   (b) ?No unicorn exists in the real world.

Direct negation of the *a(n)*-generic is of doubtful acceptability; compare 50 with 51 in which the extensionality of a 'thing' is entertained before being dismissed if a unicorn is referred to:

51 (a) Such a thing as a unicorn does not exist in the real world.
    (b) No such thing as a unicorn exists in the real world.
    (c) There is no such thing as a unicorn in the real world.

In this section we have seen that generics express law-like statements; that in English, the definite generic and unmarked indefinite generic NP are both normally extensional while the *a(n)*-generic is nonextensional.[12]

Exercises

2.6.1 Comment on the extensionality of 'low-cut dress' and the anaphoric 'one' or 'it' or 'them' in the following:
    (a) I shan't wear a low-cut dress, because I look stupid in one.
    (b) I shan't wear a low-cut dress, because I'd look stupid in it.
    (c) I shan't wear a low-cut dress, because I look stupid in them.

2.6.2 In *Lions are dangerous* the intension of 'lions' is a genus; the extension is by implication the class of lions in the world and time spoken of as well as in all other worlds and times. Give a sense, intension, and extension for 'unicorns' in *Unicorns are mythical beasts*.

2.6.3 Some generics state contingent truths, others necessary truths: which of (a–b) is contingently true and which necessarily true? Is there any connection between (a–b) below and 46–47 of the main text?
    (a) Spiders are arachnids.
    (b) Spiders have eight legs.

2.6.4 Give a nongeneric context for *A dog barks, a cat mews*.

2.6.5 Why do you think it is acceptable to say *There is no dodo alive today in Mauritius*, but you cannot say **There is no dodo* (except as an elliptical response to e,g, *There's a dodo in that room*). You can also say *There are no longer any dodos in Mauritius* and *The dodo is no longer to be found in Mauritius*.

2.7 Some characteristic forms of anaphora: multiple references to something

Definition 2.16 ANAPHORA is the result of making successive references to the same thing or same kind of thing. Anaphors are semantically correlated with their governing expression (the first mention and/or the expression which c-commands the anaphor).

There are three kinds of anaphorical relation:

(a)   Coreferential identity.
(b)   Non-coreferential semantic identity.
(c)   Non-coreferential semantic overlap between instance and kind.

Pronouns are the most typical anaphors and (a), coreferential identity, is the most salient kind of anaphora. Typically, the first mention of something uses a semantically more complex form than its anaphoric second mention. Compare the two coreferential italicized (and co-indexed) NPs in 52.

52   *The bad-tempered old retired policeman who lives next door with his fourteen cats$_P$* had a heart attack yesterday. *He$_P$* got taken to hospital in an ambulance.

The ZERO ANAPHOR, indicated in 53 by $_{[\varnothing]}$, has no form at all.

53   *Max$_M$* came in and $_{[\varnothing_M]}$ sat down.

You understand from 53 that "Max sat down."

The form of the anaphor may be syntactically determined, as in 53, or partially syntactically determined in the case of the reflexive in 54:

54   *Max$_M$* congratulated *himself$_M$*.

54 reveals that there are also semantic constraints on anaphora: the referent 'Max' is male and this affects the gender of the pronoun. Syntactic constraints on anaphora are accounted by c-command (D2.13), and we shall say no more about them here.[13] However, note that the governing NP must c-command the pronoun in cases of CATAPHORA or BACKWARDS ANAPHORA, as in 55, where 'he' is coreferential to 'Eddy'.

55   When *he$_E$* did at last get home, *Eddy$_E$* fell asleep.

Cataphora also occurs in sentences like 56; placing the NP 'Eddy' at the end of the clause and leaving a pronoun in its original place within clause structure is called 'right-dislocation'.

56   Where did *he$_E$* go, *Eddy$_E$*?

There are also pragmatic and discourse conditions for choosing between different anaphoric forms.[14] These include the use of EXOPHORIC PRONOUNS to refer to something or somebody in the situation of utterance; e.g. when someone says of a passing punk:

57 Wow, did he look weird!

If the cooperative maxims are properly observed, the semantics of the exophoric pronoun 'he', "the male one", are assigned some easily identifiable referent in the situation of utterance. Clarity and style are motivations for repeating 'Bill' in 58:

58 John and Bill went fishing. Bill fell off the rocks and was washed out to sea.

Out of context, the interpretation of

59 The vet smelled the dog's breath when she bit her

is based on the pragmatic likelihood that the dog bit the vet; but this is not necessarily the case. Nonetheless, if Speaker is correctly observing the cooperative maxims, s/he will make the intended meaning explicit if it is the abnormal one of the vet biting the dog. On either the probable or the improbable interpretation, the coreferential pronoun requires on semantic grounds that the vet be female.

Anaphora typically results from making successive references to the same entity. As a rule, any two successive references to an entity involve some kind of change to it on the second and subsequent reference; for instance, in 60 (a text that may turn you vegetarian).

60 Catch $[$a chicken$_1$ $]$. Kill $[$it$_2$ $]$. Pluck $[$it$_3$ $]$. Draw $[$it$_4$ $]$. Cut $[$it$_5$ $]$ up. Marinade $[$it$_6$ $]$. Roast $[$it$_7$ $]$. When you've eaten $[$it$_8$ $]$, put $[$the bones$_9$ $]$ in the compost.

All nine subscripted NPs refer to the creature first identified in 'a chicken$_1$', which refers to a live chicken. By $_2$ it is dead, by $_3$ featherless, by $_5$ dismembered, by $_7$ roasted, and by $_8$ eaten. $_9$ refers to the chicken's bones after the flesh has been stripped from them. Thus $_7$, for instance, refers not to the chicken in $_1$, but to the caught, killed, plucked, drawn, cut up, and marinaded pieces of chicken. The successive states of the chicken can be presented as temporally sequenced changes in the world spoken of – $M^{w,t}_{1-9}$. It is exactly such information increment that goes to BUILDING UP A FILE ON A REFERENT (cf. Heim 1983). This process is at the root of world creation, and is the means by which knowledge about the real world is developed and through which story worlds are created. It is crucial to normal understanding in natural language.

The semantics of the different object pronouns in 61 identifies non-coreference in (a), self-congratulation in (b), and reciprocal congratulation in (c).

61 (a) Max and Jo congratulated them.
     (b) Max and Jo congratulated themselves.
     (c) Max and Jo congratulated each other.

As well as people and things, there are anaphors for places and times:

62 Ed is going to *Spain* and Jo's going *there* too.
63 Eva came to Britain in *1939*, but I didn't know her *then*.

An anaphor may identify a referent indirectly, by referring to the location within the utterance of some earlier reference to it.

64 Sue stared at *the pumpkin$_P$* and the squash, then declared she preferred *the former$_P$*.
65 At the checkout, Jo rummaged through her purse and pulled out *a kleenex$_K$*, a 20 cent piece, and *ten dollar note$_S$*, then absent-mindedly handed the cashier *the first of these$_K$* instead of *the third$_S$*.

All the foregoing anaphors are coreferential and typically they have extension in $M^{w,t}$. In 66, 'someone' and 'they' are coreferential but NONEXTENSIONAL because it is not known whether the referent exists.

66 If there's *someone who knows the answer$_?$*, will *they$_?$* please raise *their$_?$* hand?

In addition to being an example of GENDER-NEUTRAL anaphora, 'they' and 'their' in 66 are permissible because the request applies to a hypothetical world in which there may or may not be a person who knows the answer. Similar in some respects is the example of sentential anaphora in 67:

67 I'm not going to *wear a kilt$_W$* because *it$_W$* wouldn't suit me.

The subjunctive clause 'it wouldn't suit me' instructs Hearer to imagine a world in which Speaker wears a kilt. In that hypothetical world, the kilt does not suit Speaker; for that reason, Speaker refuses to wear a kilt in the world spoken **in**.
    Many anaphors do not indicate identity of reference but non-coreferential semantic identity. The classic nominal anaphor with this function is *one(s)*:

68 Ed ordered *a lite beer$_E$*, and I had *one$_l$*, too.
69 White *cars$_W$* stay cooler than black *ones$_B$*, because they reflect the heat.

In 68 'one' stands for *a lite beer*; in 69 'ones' stands for *cars*. In 69, 'they' is coreferential with 'White cars'.
    The same functions in a wide range of contexts as anaphoric on a semantically identical NP or sentence.

70 (a) Ed ordered *a rogan josh*, then Jo ordered *the same*.
    (b) Harry thought *that Susan ought to have got the job*, and I thought *the same*.

Another example of a pronoun used for semantic rather than referential identity is 'it' in 71, sometimes called a pronoun of laziness (Geach 1968:128) or 'sloppy identity' (a term due to Ross 1967).

71 If a lizard loses *its tail*, *it* grows again.

Here 'it' refers to the lizard's tail, but if the tail grows again we could say *the lizard has a new tail*, emphasizing its nonidentity with the old tail. Recall the traditional declaration on the death of a British monarch: *The King/Queen is dead, long live the Queen/King*, where the continuity of office is declaimed. Another (cf. Karttunen 1969) is 72:

72 The man who puts *his pay-cheque* in the bank is wiser than the man who takes *it* to the casino.

This compares the behaviour of two kinds of men ('the man' is a definite generic): "the wise man" and "the foolish man". The wise man's pay-cheque is not identical with the foolish man's pay-cheque, and what 'it' in 72 indicates is semantic identity with the co-textual NP 'his pay-cheque', except that the possessive no longer pertains to the wise man but to the foolish man. Rather similar in some ways is:

73 Every farmer who owns *a donkey* beats *it*.

There is a huge literature on such 'donkey anaphora' and we cannot do it justice in a line or two.[15] However, note that in 73 'it' does not refer to "the donkey that every farmer owns", because there is no guarantee that every farmer does own a donkey. To check the truth of 73 you have to check every farmer to see whether s/he owns a donkey, and then check the subset of donkey-owning farmers to see whether they all beat their donkeys. So 'it' here refers to a member of the set of donkeys owned by a subset of farmers – not necessarily all farmers (on sets and subsets see Chapter 7).

Anaphors for predicates and VPs standardly indicate semantic non-coreferential identity. For instance, there is the zero anaphor for the predicate in 74, sometimes called a 'gap':

74 Harry$_H$ *kissed* his$_H$ wife and Bill$_B$ $_{[\varnothing]}$ his$_B$.

The zero anaphor is understood as "kissed". Here 'his$_B$' is elliptical for *his wife*, meaning "Bill's wife" and once again we have semantic but not referential identity.

So do and *do (so) too* are VP anaphors:

75 Harry *kissed* his father and *so did* his wife.
76 Jo got *dressed* and Max *did so too*.

The anaphor is semantically correlated with its governing expression. Sometimes a pronoun refers not to the particular individual but to the genus of which the referent of the governing NP is a member:

77 *A poodle* bit me yesterday; *they*'re horrible dogs.

Similar are 78–80.

78 Don't give me *alcohol*, I can't take *the stuff*.
79 Bring *Harry*, I love *the man*!

80 Don't bring *that spider* near me, I loathe *those things*.

Each of 78–80 uses for the anaphor an abstract category term which names the kind of thing that the governing NP consists of: alcohol is a kind of stuff (the category for non-discrete phenomena typically named in mass terms); Harry is a man (the adult male kind of human being); spiders are things (the category for discrete phenomena).

The converse picks out an instance of the kind.

81 Tony's got *several cars*. I like *the Porsche* best.

Semantic implication gives rise to the anaphor in 82, relying on the fact that *guitarist* means "player of the guitar".

82 Ed became *a guitarist* because he thought *it* was a beautiful instrument.

There are category terms used as anaphors for adjectives and adverbs in the following ways:

83 I was looking for a *purple* wombat, but couldn't find $\left\{ \begin{array}{l} \textit{such a wombat.} \\ \text{one } \textit{that colour.} \end{array} \right\}$

84 Emma *weighs 90 kilos*, but George is not $\left\{ \begin{array}{l} \textit{that} \\ \textit{so} \end{array} \right\}$ *heavy.*

85 Max drives *dangerously*. Yeah, I really don't like $\left\{ \begin{array}{l} \textit{the way} \\ \textit{how} \end{array} \right\}$ he drives.

ANAPHORIC PREDICATE NPs ascribe semantic properties to the referent, much as a predicate does (Chapter 7).

86 Ed is a fink, I hate *the bastard*.
87 Tom's sent me flowers, *the sweetie*.
88 Don't bring Harry, I hate *con-men*.

It necessarily follows from 86 that Speaker thinks Ed **is a bastard** (predicate in bold), from 87 that Tom **is a sweetie**, and from 88 that Harry **is a con-man**.

In this section we have reviewed anaphora with the intention of demonstrating its great variety. Most anaphors have coreferential identity with their governing expression; many anaphors are semantically but not coreferentially identical to their governing expression; a few anaphors show other kinds of semantic overlap with their governing expression. The typical anaphor is a pronoun. There is only a small set of pronominal anaphors in a language and they have very little semantic content: e.g. none for the zero anaphor; "the male one" for *him*. This allows each anaphor to be used for a wide range of reference. It also has the consequence that anaphors place especially heavy demands on context to fix their reference. Nevertheless, anaphors exist to make language more efficient than it would be without them.

Exercises

2.7.1 It was said of 60, *Catch $_[$a chicken$_1]$. Kill $_[$it$_2]$. Pluck $_[$it$_3]$. Draw $_[$ it$_4]$. Cut $_[$it$_5]$ up. Marinade $_[$ it$_6]$. Roast $_[$it$_7]$. When you've eaten $_[$it$_8]$, put $_[$the bones$_9]$ in the compost* that a file is built up on successive states of the chicken, that links the nine references to it. Is there also a file built up on the actor, and what will be in it?

2.7.2 There are anaphors for sentences. How would you interpret the italicized pronoun of (a)?
  (a) Emily was having an affair with Bill, but Ivy didn't know *it/that*.

2.7.3 Why can't we say instead of 78: *Bring Harry, I love the thing* – after all, Harry is a thing? Note that instead of 79 we can say *Don't bring that spider near me, I loathe those creatures*.

2.7.4 Discuss the pairs of italicized constituents in the following.
  (a) Tom asked *Ed $_[\emptyset]$* to come.
  (b) Where is *it, Lamu*?
  (c) *No schoolkid with an attitude* wears *their* baseball-cap peak to the front.
  (d) Harriet never *wears red*, because *it* doesn't go with her hair.
  (e) Sheila has lots of *boyfriends*, but Ed is the only *one* with charm.
  (f) Sheila has lots of *boyfriends*, but *Ed* is the only one with charm.
  (g) Harry paid *fifty bucks* for his, but mine was *cheaper*.

2.8 Summary

The purpose of this chapter has been to explore and develop the notion 'world and time spoken of' ($M^{w,t}$), introduced in Chapter 1, and to develop methods for relating language to the things that language is used to talk about. This involved the difficult task of defining and differentiating the terms *sense, denotation, reference, intension*, and *extension* – which are labels for different aspects of what is loosely called *meaning*. It is important for language users to establish the existential status of what is spoken about, and we examined ways in which this is accomplished. This led us to a preliminary semantics of negatives, subjunctives, opacity, nonspecifics, and generics. A review of multiple reference took us to a discussion of anaphora. All the concepts developed in Chapter 2 are used in later chapters.

The next three chapters review aspects of lexicological semantics. Chapter 3 looks at the structure of a lexicon; distinguishes a lexicon from an encyclopedia; and proposes that the lexicon forms part of an encyclopedia.

● Key words and phrases whose meaning you should know, or know better, after reading this chapter are:

abstract category terms
ambiguity
anaphora (D2.16)
anaphoric predicate NPs
attributive reference
Bedeutung (Frege)
building and updating a file on a referent
cataphora (backwards anaphora)
c-command (D2.13)
contingent truth
coreferentiality
counterfactual
denotation (D2.6)
donkey anaphora
"e_M" (an expression in the metalanguage) (D2.11)
e_{OL} (an expression in the object language)
evidentiality
existence
exophora
extension (D2.7)
extension at an index
gender-neutral anaphora
generics (D2.15)
homography
homonymy (D2.2)
homophony
index

intension (D2.10)
model (M)
$M^{w,t}$, the world and time spoken of
negation
nonextension
opacity
opaque verbs (contexts)
polysemy (D2.1)
possible world
propositional attitude verbs
reciprocal pronoun
reference (D2.5)
reflexive pronoun
semantic identity
sense (D2.3)
sentence meaning
Sinn (Frege)
sloppy identity
speaker meaning
specificity (D2.14)
subjunctive
(linguistic) tautology (D2.12)
tokens
truth at an index (D2.9)
truth condition (D2.8)
types
utterance meaning (D2.4)
world–time pairing, <w,t>
zero anaphor

● Principle 2.1 stated that the terms 'denotation', 'extension', 'intension', 'reference', and 'sense' must be defined by the semanticist such that any particular use of the term is theory-bound. Ideally this principle should be applied to all terms used.
● Ambiguity arises when any language form can be assigned more than one meaning.
● A lexicon (= dictionary) gives the sense or senses of a listeme.
● The sense of a language expression, e_{OL}, is a description of its informational content in terms of some other language expression "e_M" (A2.1).
● Discovering the optimum form for "e_M" is one task for semantics.
● Sentence meaning, i.e. the sense of a sentence, is an abstract property of the language (A2.2).
● When Speaker makes utterance U, Speaker uses the intensions of language expressions to refer to the things that U and its constituents denote.

● Utterance meaning is what Hearer (or an outside observer with relevant contextual knowledge comparable to that of Hearer) takes a particular utterance to mean in the context in which it has been uttered.

● Speaker meaning is what the Speaker intends the utterance to mean in the conditions under which it was uttered.

● Semantics as the topic of this book includes pragmatics (the study of utterance or speaker meaning). But semantics is sometimes contrasted with pragmatics, in which case it is restricted to the study of sense and sense relations.

● Reference is what Speaker does, what s/he talks about.

● $M^{w,t}$ is the Speaker's or Hearer's model of the world w and time t spoken of. The pair <w,t> is an index.

● Denotation is a relation between language expressions and the content of worlds spoken of and/or implied by what is said.

● There are two kinds of denotation: extension and intension.

● Extension is one kind of denotation. Things that exist in a world are said to have extension in world w_i at time t_i. However, the notion of existence is problematical, so the determination of extension is also problematical. A language expression e_{OL} is said to have extension if it denotes something that exists in M^{w_i, t_i}. When e_{OL} has extension it (or a paraphrase of it) can usually fall under the scope of a positive, indicative existential *There is/are*, etc.

● A proposition has extension at an index if it is true at that index (D2.9)

● The intension of e_{OL} is the set of properties a denotatum of e_{OL} must perforce have for e_{OL} to be used appropriately in the language.

● Intension and sense have a common ancestor in Frege's notion *Sinn*.

● A metalanguage expression "e_M" describes the intension of expression e_{OL} in the object language.

● Intensions are the content of concepts (A2.4). They are not tied to any particular world or time (A2.5).

● Sameness of extension does not imply sameness of meaning. For instance, the word *I* is typically used to denote Speaker; so too is Speaker's proper name, and a whole variety of descriptions – e.g. *you sweetie, that mean bastard, the guy next door*. All of these can have the same extension, but they do not have the same intension because they do not have the same extension in every possible world and time.

● Two language expressions differ in intension when it is possible for them to differ in extension (A2.6).

● It is important for Speaker to make manifest to each participant in language interaction the degree of confidence s/he has in the existential status of phenomena within $M^{w,t}$ (A2.7). The world spoken of is a possible world: it can be the real world, or an imagined, desired, or supposed world.

● Negation is constrained by the fact that Speaker does not deny the existence of X, unless X's existence is normally taken for granted, and/or there has been some earlier assertion of X's existence (2.8).

● We saw that c-command identifies (a) the scope of a negative, and (b) the domain for pronominalization and other kinds of anaphor.

● A language expression e_{OL}, which has intension in some possible world w_i at time t_i but has no extension in M^{w_j,t_j} (a particular world w_j at time t_j), is interpreted in model M via its intension.

● When e_{OL} falls within the scope of negation, it is nonextensional, i.e. does not exist within the M^{w_i,t_i} (except perhaps when utterance meaning is detached from sentence meaning, e.g. in cases of irony like *Oh, I'm too slow to catch you, am I?*).

● Subjunctives imply no extension in (at least) one world, but extension in some accessible hypothetical world(s).

● Opaque or propositional attitude verbs are typically ambiguous as to the extension of their complements.

● Whereas extensional indefinite NPs may be either specific or nonspecific, nonextensional indefinite NPs are nonspecific. Definite NPs are normally specific.

● Although some scholars regard generic NPs as nonextensional, the grammatical evidence is that the definite generic and unmarked indefinite generic NPs are both normally extensional (though they may occur in nonextensional environments). On the other hand, the *a(n)*-generic is nonextensional.

● Three kinds of anaphorical relation were identified: coreferential identity, non-coreferential semantic identity, and non-coreferential semantic overlap between instance and kind.

● The relationship between governing expression and anaphor was described, and certain syntactic, semantic, pragmatic, and discourse conditions on anaphora were exemplified.

● Pronouns are the most typical anaphors.

● There is a comparatively small set of pronominal anaphors in a language and they have very little semantic content. This allows each anaphor to be used for a wide range of reference.

● Typical coreferential anaphora results from making successive references to the same entity. As a rule, any two successive references to an entity involve some kind of change to it on the second reference. To keep track of such developments we figuratively build and update a file on the referent.

2.9 Notes on further reading

[1] Lyons 1977 is well worth reading on the topics covered in this chapter. His perspective is slightly different from the one presented here.

[2] On various approaches to lexical ambiguity resolution, see Small, Cottrell, and Tanenhaus (eds) 1988.

[3] On different interpretations by different hearers, see Dummett 1991:85, Chomsky 1995:48, Marconi 1997:120.

[4] On interpreting nonliteral language, see Searle 1975b, Bach and Harnish 1979, Allan 1994b, Lakoff and Johnson 1980, Taylor 1986, Lakoff 1987, Johnson 1987, Kittay 1987, Noppen and Hols 1990, Sweetser 1990.

[5] On Frege, see Dummett 1981. On intensional logic and/or model theoretic semantics, see Carnap 1956, Montague 1974, Lewis 1970, Cresswell 1973, Dowty, Wall, and Peters 1981, E. Bach 1987, Benthem 1988, Chierchia and McConnell-Ginet 1990, Cann 1993.

[6] On abstract entities, see Plato's *Meno*, Katz 1981, Katz and Postal 1991.

[7] On speaking of nothing, see Donnellan 1974, Parsons 1980, Hirst 1991.

[8] On counterfactuals, see Lewis 1973, Traugott et al. (eds) 1986, Bybee, Perkins, and Pagliuca 1994, Veltman 1994, Bybee and Fleischman (eds) 1995b, Athanasiadou and Dirven (eds) 1997.

[9] On the character of opaque and propositional attitude verbs, see Quine 1956, 1961, Cresswell 1985, Chierchia 1989.

[10] On evidentiality, see Chafe and Nichols (eds) 1986.

[11] The view of specificity presented here is quite similar to that in Fodor and Sag 1982; however, they use the term 'referential' where this book uses 'extensional'. The accounts of specificity by Enç 1991 and Diesing 1992 are unsatisfactory because their arguments hinge in large part on judgments of grammaticality that are simply wrong for dialects of English such as I speak.

[12] On generics, see Carlson and Pelletier (eds) 1995. Most authors invoke a generic operator of one kind or another (e.g. Krifka (ed.) 1988, Diesing 1992); but none of the world's languages offers any morphological support for such an operator. Genericness is inferred.

[13] On the syntax of anaphora see Reinhart 1976, 1983, Chomsky 1981, 1986, Aoun 1985, May 1985, Dalrymple 1993, Pollard and Sag 1994 Ch.6.

[14] On discourse constraints on anaphora, see Halliday and Hasan 1976, Givón (ed.) 1983, Fox 1987, Ariel 1990.

[15] On 'donkey anaphora', see Geach 1968:128ff, Kamp 1981, Heim 1990, Reinhart 1986, Gamut 1991, Seuren 1994, Heim and Kratzer 1998 Ch.11.

3 The lexicon and the encyclopedia

Semantics without an adequate treatment of the lexicon is no semantics at all.

(Bonomi 1987:69 quoted in Marconi 1997:161)

3.1 Where we are heading

Definition 3.1 was forecast in Chapter 1:

Definition 3.1 The LEXICON is a bin for storing listemes (cf. D1.4).

This chapter and the next are on lexicology.

Definition 3.2 LEXICOLOGY studies listemes.

This chapter reviews the structure of lexicon entries and the relationship between the lexicon and the encyclopedia. Chapter 4 discusses what constitutes a listeme. §3.2 of this chapter identifies the three main components of a lexicon entry: formal, morphosyntactic, and semantic specifications. §3.3 examines the relationship between the three components and modes of accessing the lexicon. §3.4 distinguishes the lexicon from the encyclopedia and suggests there is more than one lexicon and more than one encyclopedia. §3.5 makes a detailed study of Kripke's idea that names are 'rigid designators'. §3.6 discusses the semantics of proper names and their place in the lexicon. Finally, §3.7 argues that the lexicon is part of the encyclopedia. §3.8 summarizes the chapter.

3.2 The main components of a lexicon entry

Definition 3.3 LEXICOGRAPHY is the construction of dictionaries and models of the mental lexicon.[1]

The way that a lexicon is organized depends on what it is designed to do.

(a)   The traditional desk-top dictionary is organized into alphabetically ordered entries in order to maximize look-up efficiency for the literate user.

(b)   *Kitab al-Ayn*, the Arabic dictionary of Al Khalil Ben Ahmad, has a phonetically based listing, beginning with velars and ending with bilabials (Kniffka 1994).

(c)   A grammar that requires random lexical entry according to morphological class needs to access a lexicon through the morpho-syntactic category of the lexicon entry.

(d)   Hearer accesses the mental lexicon from the phonological or graphological form of the entry.

(e)   Speaker accesses the mental lexicon through the meaning.

(f)   Someone producing an alliteration (e.g. *around the rugged rocks the ragged rascal ran*) needs to access the onsets to phonological forms.

(g)   Someone looking for a rhyme needs to be able to access entries via the endings of the phonological form.

(h)   The meaning of one word can remind you of another with a similar or contrary meaning; this suggests that meanings in the lexicon must be organized into a network of relations similar to those in a thesaurus. Miller and Johnson-Laird 1976 speculated that some basic concepts such as motion and possession give rise to semantic fields (A8.7). Concepts such as cause or instrument will connect many different semantic fields.

Summing up, a lexicon needs to be accessible from three directions:

FORM — phonological and graphological, by onset and rhyme; related forms must be accessible from each other.

MORPHO-SYNTACTIC CATEGORY — items from the same category are accessible to each other.

MEANING — an item's intrinsic meaning and also its location within a semantic field should be identified, thus making items with related meanings mutually accessible.

None of these three is intrinsically prior to the others; any precedence results from the particular needs of a user (or grammatical theory) accessing the lexicon on a particular occasion.

3.2.1 Formal specifications

FORMAL SPECIFICATIONS include graphological specification such as alternative spellings, hyphenation location, use of upper case (e.g. in abbreviations like *USA*, the initial capital letter of a proper name, *Fiji*). The phonological specification will include information on alternative pronunciations, syllable structure, the relative pitch and/or tone of the various syllables. For semantic (though not other) purposes the only prosodic information required from the phonological specification of an English listeme is the normal location of primary stress – if any – on the item as uttered in isolation.[2] If a token of the item is uttered with primary stress on a different syllable from the norm, it is either a speech error, or the primary stressed syllable is being focused upon, e.g. *I said* **PER***ception not* **CON***ception*, which focuses on the distinction between the two words.

3.2.2 Morphosyntactic specifications

MORPHOSYNTACTIC SPECIFICATIONS include morphological and syntactic properties such as the inherent morphosyntactic (lexical) category of the item. Traditionally, the nouns *helicopter* and *move*, and the semantically related verbs *helicopter* and *move*, are all different listemes. Semantically-related homonyms (D2.2) are different listemes when they are in different lexical classes (e.g. the two listemes *gay* N, *gay* Adj). On the other hand, despite their different syntactic properties and concomitant meaning differences, the transitive verb *move* and the intransitive verb *move* traditionally share the same polysemous dictionary entry (D2.1) under different subheadings. The *COBUILD English Dictionary* lists all forms of a listeme; e.g. for *clear* they have *clearer, clearest, clears, clearing, cleared* (which are not divided between the Adj and the V listemes as one might expect). It would be traditional to identify both the Adj *clear* and the V *clear* as regular. This is comparable to identifying the declension and gender of, say, Latin nouns:

> first declension feminine *puella, puellae* "girl";
> third declension feminine *nox, noctis* "night";
> third declension masculine *rūmor, rūmōris* "rumor";
> third declension neuter *sīdus, sīderis* "star".

And the conjugation of verbs: e.g. French *parler* "speak" is first conjugation, *sentir* "feel" is third. It is necessary to list IRREGULARITIES in inflexion, e.g. the past tense of English 'strong' verbs such as *drink* (*drank*) or *think* (*thought*). Also located among the morphosyntactic specifications are constraints on range: e.g. *-ize* is suffixed to nouns (*atomize*) and adjectives (*legalize*) (Chapter 4); an object NP can interrupt the V⌢vPrt of phrasal verb *run down* (*run NP down* "denigrate NP"), but not *put up with NP* (*put *NP up with* "endure NP").

3.2.3 Semantic specifications

SEMANTIC SPECIFICATIONS are discussed from Chapter 7 on. A point to take up here is the meaning of the lexical category names *noun, verb*, and *adjective*, and of morphological categories such as *feminine* (gender). Used in the morphosyntactic specifications, such category terms are part of the metalanguage, not the object language. But they also appear in the lexicon as expressions in the object language. In principle, we should not confuse metalanguage with object language; on the other hand, it wastes a resource not to exploit the situation. Suppose that the sense "typically names a person, place, thing or abstract entity" has an address in the lexicon (I'll explain such addresses in §3.3). Next, suppose that in the lexicon of English, one form at this address is *noun*. Further suppose that in the lexicon of French, one form at this address is *nom*; and in the lexicon of Greek, it is όνομα. It seems appropriate to take a further step and say that in the lexicon of the metalanguage there is a form N (or even *noun*) at this same address. This move simply reflects the well known and widely accepted fact that there are translation (near) equivalences between object language and metalanguage, just as there are between different natural languages. The suggested link between an entry in the lexicon of one language and an entry in the lexicon of another language appears more radical than it is, given the proposal to be discussed in §3.4 that there are many lexicons for any one language: one must assume there is an overlap between the different lexicons of a given natural language, with some items shared.

3.2.4 Other specifications?

Bauer 1983:196 proposed a category of 'stylistic specifications' to distinguish between *piss, piddle*, and *micturate*, i.e. to reflect the kind of metalinguistic information found in traditional desk-top dictionary comments like 'colloquial', 'slang', 'derogatory', 'medicine', 'zoology', etc. Such metalinguistic information is more appropriate to the encyclopedia entry. I shall argue later in this chapter that an encyclopedia is directly connected with every lexicon entry. The encyclopedia will also supply etymological (historical) information and an account of the connotations (§3.5) of listemes.

Bauer also suggested a signalling of 'related lexemes' such as that *edible* is related to *eat, knowledgeable* to *knowledge*, and *destruction* to *destroy*. The relationship between *edible* and *eat* is etymological. Etymology certainly is lexical, but etymological facts are encyclopedic information not essential to the proper use of the listemes. The semantic relationship between *edible* and *eat* will be identified through the semantic specification. Indeed, the semantic specification of *edible* might specifically differentiate its meaning from *eatable* (cf. Lehrer 1990:210 'Once when an acquaintance was served a very thick submarine sandwich, she described it as *uneatable*. In this context *inedible* would not have been appropriate'). The *COBUILD English Dictionary* lists 'antonyms' of listemes (strictly speaking they are contraries (D6.5)); the contrary of *good* is *bad*, that of *light* is *dark*. It makes subentries for derived words; e.g. under the listeme *clear* is the Adv *clearly*. Contraries and antonyms are linked to a listeme via its semantic field (A8.7). Derived words are either generated from the listeme by morphological rules, or else they are distinct listemes (Chapter 4).

It is tempting to propose extending the function of the category of 'related lexemes' to all the cross-referencing required in the hypothetical lexicon. For instance, metalanguage terms used in semantic specifications are often semantically identical with object language listemes; e.g. Pustejovsky 1995:101 specifies *book* as a "physical object" that "holds" "information" created by someone that "write[s]" it and whose function is to be "read". Certainly, there is a relation between *book, write*, and *read* that needs to be accounted for either in the semantic specification or the associated encyclopedia entry. For their part, morphological and syntactic relations should presumably be dealt with in theories of morphology and theories of syntax, or within the various subcategories of morphosyntactic specification. For instance, one might wish to retrieve all listemes beginning with /d/ or rhyming with *cord* and, although this task will use the lexicon, there is no compelling reason to cross-reference e.g. *cord, board, fraud, hoard, sword, sward* in the lexicon just because they rhyme; it is more efficient to search all entries for those whose first segment is /d/ or whose final segments are /ɔɔd/. Similarly, the best way to compile a list of all nouns in the lexicon is not to cross-reference every noun with every other noun, but to search the morphosyntactic specification of every entry. Finally, as part of the semantic specification of an item, it will be located within its semantic field, related to superordinate items, contraries, antonyms, and the like (Chapter 8). In any case, many of these relations are not primarily lexical, but arise from the relationships characteristic of the denotatum of a listeme: e.g. because a cat is perceived to be a kind of animal, the listeme *animal* is superordinate to the listeme *cat*. Any two listemes may be connected through their formal, morphosyntactic, and/or semantic specifications in the lexicon, and the stylistic or etymological properties identified in the encyclopedia. It seems that most of the information one might consider putting into a 'related lexemes' category probably ought to be located elsewhere.

3.2.5 The necessary specifications

I conclude that only formal, morphosyntactic, and semantic specifications are needed in a lexicon entry, although not every entry will exhibit all three. The zero-morph has no form, but a variety of syntactic functions and semantic effects. According to Jackendoff 1995 expressions like *ouch, wow, yippee* have formal and semantic specification, but no morphosyntactic entry. Jackendoff may be mistaken because traditionally they are interjections – it depends on one's theory of syntax. Expressions like *tra-la-la* and *e-i-e-i-o* have neither morphosyntactic specification nor semantic content (we can say what they are used for but not what they mean). And there is arguably no semantic specification for the English infinitive marker *to*, nor for some names (§3.7 below).

Exercises

3.2.1 From what aspect do you access the lexicon when performing the following tasks?
  (a) What word means "a vehicle you sit astride and propel by pedalling"?
  (b) What is a homonym of *tail*?
  (c) How many verbs can you list with a past tense form like that of *ride*?

3.2.2 Where is the normal primary stress location in the following English listemes, uttered in isolation: *perception, conception, affirm, affirmation, -ize* (as in *legalize*), *-ity* (as in *topicality*).

3.2.3 What kind of context would justify the use of (a) and how would you interpret it?
  (a) phoTOgraphic = /fə'tɒgrəfɪk/

3.2.4 Would you ascribe meaning to *yippee, tra-la-la,* and *e-i-e-i-o*?

3.3   The networked components in a lexicon entry

Let's adopt Lyons's suggestion (1977:516) that each lexicon entry be assigned an index (a random number) that serves as its address for access through any of the three modes we have identified. The index can be represented as a connector between the three kinds of specifications for the typical lexicon entry. In Fig. 3.1, F = formal specifications, M = morphosyntactic specifications, S = semantic specifications.

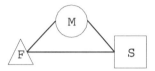

Figure 3.1 Indexed access to the lexicon presented as a network

One effect of this proposal is that every difference in meaning, and every difference in morphology or syntax, and every difference in form is assigned a numerical index. Assuming extensive cross-referencing, the end result is more effective coverage of the material in a hypothetical lexicon than is found in traditional desk-top dictionaries. Another advantage is that a given sense of a word in one language could be linked with the appropriate form in the lexicon of another language, giving rise to multilingual lexicons.

This proposal is very similar to one in Jackendoff 1995, 1997. Jackendoff's lexical licensing theory 'licence[s] the correspondence of certain (near-) terminal symbols of syntactic structure with phonological and conceptual structures'. For present purposes, Jackendoff's 'conceptual structures' correspond to our 'semantic specifications' (they are examined in detail in Chapter 12). Jackendoff proposes that a lexicon entry has the three parts in Fig. 3.2, where they are tagged with our specification types. The subscripts act in a similar way to numerical indices, but with one significant difference. The post-minimalist grammatical theory Jackendoff presupposes has independently generated phonological, syntactic, and semantic structures that are linked by correspondence rules indicated by $\longleftrightarrow$ in Fig. 3.3. Listemes establish part of the linking between components, so that the lexicon is part of the correspondence rule component.

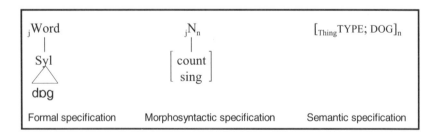

Figure 3.2 Jackendoff-style lexicon entry for *dog*

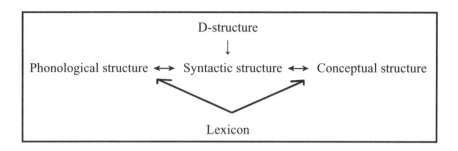

Figure 3.3 Jackendoff's post-minimalist grammar

In Jackendoff's theory,[1] the morphosyntactic specification is the linchpin that is co-indexed $_j$ with the formal specification to the left-hand, and $_n$ to the semantic specifications on the right. Jackendoff's method of indexing solves a problem that arises from our equal treatment of the three main components in a lexicon entry. If you ask someone the meaning of the word *fly* (which is many ways ambiguous) two possible answers are "travel though the air" (V) and "cloth cover for an opening" (N). Similarly, the word *dog* means "canine animal" (N) and "follow dog-like" (V). The word *canine* means "a member of the dog family" (N) and "pertaining to the dog family" (Adj). The difference between such pairs as these is indicated by the combination of formal and morphosyntactic specification – which corresponds to Jackendoff's subscript $_j$ in Fig. 3.2. This distinguishing factor is exactly the reason that a traditional desk-top dictionary identifies the morphosyntactic category immediately after identifying the form of a listeme. Note that *tra-la-la* is no recognized part of speech; it is onomatopoeic like *cockadoodledoo* (Chapter 4), and so there is nothing much to say about it semantically.

If we look at the nonsense words in 1, we see how much morphosyntax contributes to meaning.

1   The toves gimbled in the wabe.

'[T]oves' is clearly a plural noun and therefore denotes more than one entity. '[G]imbled' is the past tense of a verb and so denotes some act or state of the toves. '[W]abe' is a noun; and because it falls within the scope (D2.13) of the preposition 'in', 'wabe' identifies a place or time. Thus does the morphosyntactic specification of these words give us some meaning to work on – as suggested by Jackendoff's subscript $_n$ in Fig. 3.2. In addition, the form enables us to make a distinction between the nouns 'tove' and 'wabe'.

For Speaker, the main function of the lexicon is to find a form to express the intended meaning; but not just a form, also its morphosyntactic category, which is often at least partly determined by the content. For instance, reference to a thing will usually require

---

1. Note that Jackendoff has no place for LF (logical form) in Fig. 3.3. In Jackendoff 1997 he argues against LF. I take no position on the matter here, and will not attempt to resolve the matter in this book.

using a noun; reference to an event, a verb (Jackendoff would use a subscript $_v$). Except when parroting a phrase (which is abnormal language use) it is impossible when speaking a language to use a form without assigning it morphosyntactic specification. It is impossible to assign a morphosyntactic specification to a meaning without also assigning it a form (the appropriate form for a zero morph is, of course, null). The speaker of 2 may not be able to retrieve the form *retaliate*, but the intended meaning is conveyed using the forms of other lexemes.

2   What's the word that means 'get back at'?

The point is that Speaker goes from semantic specifications to a combination of formal and morphosyntactic specification, and not just one or the other of these. In terms of Fig. 3.2, this implies going from $_n$ on the semantic specification to the morphosyntactic specification $_jN_n$ which links to the formal specification through the $_j$ subscript.
  For Hearer the main function of the lexicon is to attach meaning to forms that normally occur within syntactic structures, so it is a matter of finding a semantic specification for something that is both formally and morphosyntactically specified. In terms of Fig. 3.2, this goes from $_j$ to $_n$.
  The upshot of this discussion is a revision of Fig. 3.1 to Fig. 3.4 in which Jackendoff-type indices (subscripts) correspond to connection points for bidirectional lines in a network (which shows that their sequence with respect to F, M, and S is a convention without substance – i.e. $_fF = F_f$, $_fM_s = M_{f,s}$, etc.).

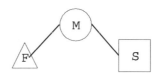

Figure 3.4 Networked components of an entry in the hypothetical lexicon

The network presented in Fig. 3.4 significantly oversimplifies. Suppose there are the components in Table 3.1. The formal and semantic addresses are randomly selected numbers, tagged with $_f$ and $_s$ respectively. In the semantic specifications, the metalanguage terms **dog'** and **follow_like_a_dog'**, etc. are symbolically differentiated from their object language counterparts by the final prime (') and being printed in **bold** type, yet otherwise share their form and core meaning. This is the notational device I use for much of the vocabulary in the metalanguage.

F	M	S
$f8899dog$	$f8899 N_{s0017}$	$\textbf{dog}'_{s0017}$
	$f8899 V_{s3214}$	$\textbf{follow\_like\_a\_dog}'_{s3214}$ (or $\textbf{follow\_like\_a\_}{}_s\textbf{0017}'_{s3214}$)
$f7656canine$	$f7656 N_{s7439}$	$\textbf{conical\_pointed\_tooth}'_{s7439}$
	$f7656 Adj_{s1227}$	$\textbf{pertaining\_to\_a\_dog}'_{s1227}$ (or $\textbf{pertaining\_to\_a\_}{}_s\textbf{0017}'_{s1227}$)

Table 3.1 Partial entries for dog and canine

The examples in Table 3.1 ignore the fact that the semantic specifications must somehow reflect the facts that a dog is an animal, a living thing, a physical object. They ignore the need to identify the kind of countable and uncountable environments in which a noun can conventionally occur (Chapter 13).[3] They ignore the thematic structure, valency, or frame of a verb (Chapter 11), and the gradability of an Adj (Chapter 8).[4] In Fig. 3.5, which represents a part of this network of relations, there are yet other meanings for *dog* and *canine* and only the graphological form is given for *canine*. The question of how the graphological and phonological forms should be correlated is also not accounted for. We shall return to lexicon entries when we discuss idioms in Chapter 4 and proper names later in this chapter.

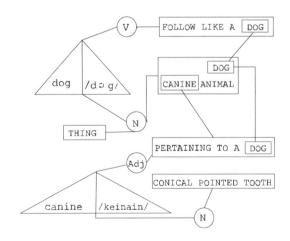

Figure 3.5 Part of the network for the lexicon entries for
dog (N and V) and canine (N and Adj)

The form of a lexicon entry is a co-indexed tripartite network in which the indices correspond to bidirectional connectors between the components of a lexicon entry as shown in Fig. 3.4. Such connectors model cognitive pathways that presumably have a neurological basis and could be empirically disconfirmed, e.g. by studies of aphasics. Even if the connectors prove to have no biological basis, the network can be utilized in retrieving data electronically from an on-line lexicon. There is, however, nothing to be gained by rewriting desk-top dictionaries in terms of networks if they are going to be consulted in the same way human beings have consulted them in the past. Each of the three kinds of specification in the lexicon has a number of subcategories. There are several aspects of phonological classification as well as graphological representation among the formal specifications; several aspects of morphology and syntax among the morphosyntactic specifications; and so forth. Boguraev and Briscoe 1989:5 add encyclopedic knowledge to this list. The next section argues for division of labour between lexicon and encyclopedia.

Exercises

3.3.1 What does the revised version of indexing the components in the hypothetical lexicon do to the idea of linking multilingual lexicons?

3.3.2 The four place numbers used for illustrative purposes in the indexical subscripts would be inadequate in an exhaustive model of the English lexicon. Why is this so?

3.4   The lexicon gives the meanings of listemes, the encyclopedia gives information about their denotata

The other kids at school nicknamed him Ix, which in the language of Betelgeuse Five translates as "boy who is not able satisfactorily to explain what a Hrung is, nor why it should collapse on Betelgeuse Seven."

(Douglas Adams Hitchhiker's Guide to the Galaxy 1992:44)

The lexicon is a bin for storing the meanings of those language expressions whose meaning is not determinable from the meanings (if any) of its constituents (Definition 3.1).

Definition 3.4 The ENCYCLOPEDIA functions as a structured data-base containing exhaustive information on many (perhaps all) branches of knowledge.

Important for linguistic semantics is:

> *Research question 3.1* How much information is it necessary to
> include in a complete semantic representation in the lexicon?

In school, comprehension of a text is usually tested by having a student either summarize the text or answer questions on it, or both. Attempts in the field of artificial intelligence to program a machine to interpret a text so as to answer questions on it or to provide a summary for it reveal that the project requires input from what Schank and Abelson 1977 call 'scripts', Lakoff 1987 'idealized cognitive models', Minsky 1977 and Barsalou 1992, Fillmore 1975, 1982a, Fillmore and Atkins 1992 'frames' (Chapters 8–10). These are by no means identical, but they all call extensively upon encyclopedic knowledge. The normal practice before the 1980s was to favour parsimonious dictionary knowledge against elaborated encyclopedic knowledge, but things have changed. Haiman 1980b:331 claimed 'Dictionaries *are* encyclopedias' which is certainly true of some existing dictionaries – *The New Grove Dictionary of Jazz* is more encyclopedia than lexicon. Jackendoff 1983:139f suggested that information in the lexical entry 'shades toward "encyclopedia" rather than "dictionary" information, with no sharp line drawn between the two types'. Wierzbicka developed semantic descriptions very similar to those in an encyclopedia (compare her proposed entry for *tiger* (Wierzbicka 1985:164) with the entry quoted from the *Encyclopaedia Britannica* (Wierzbicka 1985:194). Langacker (1987:154) says that the information in a lexicon IS encyclopedic:

> The distinction between semantics and pragmatics (or between linguistics and extralinguistic
> knowledge) is largely artifactual, and the only viable conception of linguistic semantics is
> one that avoids false dichotomies and is consequently **encyclopedic** in nature. [*Sic*]

Leech (1981:84) offers the contrary view:

> [T]he oddity of propositions like 'The dog had eighty legs' is something that zoology has
> to explain rather than conceptual semantics.

Leech is surely correct, but there has to be a cognitive path from the listeme to directly access encyclopedic information about dogs (or whatever) because of Hearer's ability to 'shadow' a text very rapidly – that is, to begin understanding it and making appropriate inferences milliseconds after Speaker has presented it (cf. Marslen-Wilson 1985, 1989b).

Assumption 3.1 The lexicon entry is one access point into the isomorphic set of
encyclopedia entries, all of which are activated by recognition of the listeme.

If the encyclopedia is a database, then the lexicon forms an integral component of the encyclopedia. It would seem incontrovertible that encyclopedic data was called upon when extending a proper name like *Kleenex* to denote facial tissues in general, *Hoover* to denote vacuum cleaners and vacuum cleaning, and to explain the formation of the verb *bowdlerize* from the proper name *Bowdler*. It is equally obvious that encyclopedic data is called upon in statements like 3–5.

3   Caspar Cazzo is no Pavarotti!
4   Nellie Norman is another Janis Joplin!
5   Harry's boss is a bloody little Hitler!

3 implies that Caspar is not a great singer. We infer this because Pavarotti's salient characteristic is that he is a great singer. 4 implies that Nellie is an accomplished (and probably white) blues singer and/or perhaps that she has severe problems with her self-image. Such comparisons draw on biodata that cannot be expected to come out of a lexicon; it must be drawn from the encyclopedia entry for the person who is the standard for comparison (secundum comparationis). Because of the encyclopedic entry for the name *Hitler* (given in 6), 5 is abusive.

6   **Hitler** *proper name* for **Adolf Hitler**, primarily responsible for World War II and castigated for being a fascist dictator who was ultimately responsible for the liquidation of six million Jews, and countless Slavs, gypsies, homosexuals, and others whom he regarded as socially undesirable. Comparisons with Hitler imply a ruthless dictatorial manner, someone willing to murder millions of the people he disapproves of.

A more carefully composed encyclopedic entry for *Hitler* would contain more genuine historical fact. Yet the prejudices of language users are just as relevant to a proper account of language understanding as the true facts.

> *Ideological problem 3.1* Will the lexicon and encyclopedia institutionalize the mainstream stereotype? If not, how will the prejudices of different groups within the community be represented?

> *Research question 3.2* Should the lexicon contain every word in the language and the encyclopedia contain exhaustive information on all branches of knowledge, or should they be modular, rather like a collection of human minds?

For instance, a medic's lexicon is full of medical jargon and a medic's encyclopedia contains medical knowledge unknown to the average patient; a botanist knows more about plants than I do and has the lexicon to talk about that knowledge; and so forth through the community for different interest groups. No one is sure what constitutes the common core of a lexicon nor of an encyclopedia. Even if they can be identified, they will have to be connected to specialist modules with jargon dictionaries and specialist encyclopedias. And a modular system would need an archiving device to facilitate information incrementation and update both lexicon and encyclopedia. There are two reasons for favouring multiple lexicons and encyclopedias:

(a)   It would model individual human capacities.
(b)   It would divide data and processing into manageable chunks

As already shown in 6, the encyclopedia will contain entries for people under their proper names. In reality, individuals in a community will have different mental encyclopedias, i.e. partially different information (cf. Katz 1977b). For example, suppose Speaker$_k$ says:

7   I know four Annas.

There is no requirement that Hearer knows, or even knows of, any of the Annas referred to. It does, however, call for lexical knowledge about the name *Anna*, because it implicates Speaker$_k$'s assumption that Hearer will understand "Speaker$_k$ knows four female human beings each of whom is called *Anna*." On the other hand, when Speaker$_k$ utters 8, it is normally expected that Hearer will understand not merely that Speaker$_k$ had a letter from some female human being named *Anna* but will, in addition, identify further facts about the person spoken of from the assumed common ground.

8   I had a letter from Anna yesterday.

Being able to identify the referent means being able to access information about her, and information about name-bearers is entered into a mental encyclopedia. In uttering 8 Speaker$_k$ normally assumes that s/he and Hearer have partially coincidental encyclopedia entries for the intended referent. Speaker$_k$ can have different expectations of different addressees. For instance, if Speaker$_k$ utters 8 to Hearer$_b$ at time t_x, the latter assumes the referent is Anna$_s$ for whom they share an encyclopedia entry with a considerable amount of additional information about the referent, some of which is mutual. If 8 is addressed to Hearer$_j$ at time t_y, the latter assumes the referent is Anna$_b$. On the other hand, Speaker$_k$ should not utter 8 to Hearer$_a$ at time t_z without some contextual clarification, because they each know that they each have encyclopedia entries for both Anna$_c$ and Anna$_w$, so a potential referential ambiguity must be resolved. We conclude that the name *Anna* will evoke one or more encyclopedia entries, depending on the number stored.

Information about people is stored in the encyclopedia and one means of access will be via a person's proper name. (The whole encyclopedia entry can be accessed through part of the information in it, enabling the name and further information about the referent to be retrieved.) 9 sketches the encyclopedia entry for *Aristotle*.

9   [1]**Aristotle** *proper name* of an ancient Greek philosopher, born in Stagira in C4 BCE.
        Author of *The Categories, On Interpretation, On Poetry*, ... Pupil of Plato and
        teacher of Alexander the Great ...
    [2]**Aristotle** *proper name* of **Aristotle Onassis**, C20 CE Greek shipping magnate ...
    [3]**Aristotle** *proper name* of **Ari Papadopoulos**, friend whose phone number is 018 111
        ...

The information here is clearly not of the kind that anyone should expect to find in a lexicon because it is not lexicographical information about a name in the language. Instead, it is encyclopedic information about particular name-bearers. Similarly for information about things, whether natural kinds such as gold and dogs, or unnatural kinds such as polyester and computers. Information about the ways in which cats differ from dogs will be culled from encyclopedia entries. The semantic difference between *cat* and *dog* as lexicon entries is minimal.

Exercises

3.4.1 Why are there specialist dictionaries and specialist encyclopedias?

3.4.2 Write a brief comparison of dictionary and encyclopedia entries for one of *tiger, water*, or *compass*.

3.4.3 Why do (a) and (b) have very different interpretations?
   (a) Caspar Cazzo is no Pavarotti!   (b) Caspar Cazzo is no Bill Gates!

3.4.4 What are the conditions that make the standard for comparison appropriate (try putting your own name there, for instance, or *hero* or *woman*)?

3.4.5 Discuss differences between an individual's encyclopedia and a published one such as the *Encyclopaedia Britannica*.

5 Names as rigid designators

Hitler, Elizabeth Taylor, Alfred the Great, the Virgin Mary, God, Santa Claus, Brooklyn, the Bronx, Mexico City, the City of London, Ayers Rock, I-40, the Pacific Ocean, the Mayflower, the Bodleian, WordPerfect, Tampax, Picasso's 'Les Demoiselles d'Avignon', the *OED*, Pink Floyd, the Grateful Dead, the Hopi, the Mafia, Zabar's, Factory-2-U, Oxford University Press [the publishers], General Motors, the Himalayas.

The typical proper name refers to an individual (a 'particular') but also named are: collections (whose members share some common property); real and imaginary people; pets; newly discovered and cultivated biological specimens; places and topological features, buildings, institutions, businesses, radio stations, pop groups, orchestras, acting companies; events like wars and epidemics; computer files, books, newspapers, films, TV shows; manufactured products of all kinds. *The Ford Motor Company* is a proper name, but *a Ford* (sc. a make of car) is not. Why is it, then, that the noun 'Ford' in the latter is standardly written with an upper case *F* in positions other than sentence initial? Algeo reminds us:

Most but not all proper nouns are capitalized in English, and a great many things that certainly are not proper nouns are regularly capitalized. Present-day English has some words like *Chevrolet* that are usually capitalized, some like *Roman* that are often capitalized, some like *devil* that are occasionally capitalized, and some like *first base* that are rarely capitalized. (Algeo 1973:17)

In the rest of this section we discuss some additional characteristics of proper names in the course of reviewing Kripke's 1972 account of names as 'rigid designators'.

Frege believed that a proper name has sense(s):

The sense of a proper name is grasped by everybody who is sufficiently familiar with the language or totality of designations to which it belongs. Footnote: In the case of an actual proper name such as 'Aristotle' opinions as to the sense may differ. It might, for instance, be taken to be the following: the pupil of Plato and teacher of Alexander the Great. Anybody who does this will attach another sense to the sentence 'Aristotle was born in Stagira' than will a man who takes as the sense of the name: the teacher of Alexander the Great who was born in Stagira. So long as the reference remains the same, such variations of sense may be tolerated, although they are to be avoided in the theoretical structure of a demonstrative science and ought not to occur in a perfect language. (Frege 1966:57 [1892])

This is the CHECKLIST or CLUSTER theory of proper names that gives a 'bundle of qualities', at least one of which is supposedly necessary in order to correctly identify the referent.[5] The sense of a listeme is a description of the attributes of the typical denotatum, not a description of the attributes of a PARTICULAR referent. So, Frege has not given the sense of the name *Aristotle* (Kripke 1972:272, 277); instead, he gives part of an encyclopedia entry for one bearer of the name *Aristotle*. Consequently, Frege's quoted remarks are open to the following objection:

If 'Aristotle' meant *the man who taught Alexander the Great*, then saying 'Aristotle was a teacher of Alexander the Great' would be a mere tautology. But surely it isn't; it expresses the fact that Aristotle taught Alexander the Great, something we could discover to be false. So, *being the teacher of Alexander the Great* cannot be part of the sense of the name. (Kripke 1972:258)

Kripke's solution is that the name *Aristotle* referring to the Stagirite, the philosopher, the teacher of Alexander the Great, is a RIGID DESIGNATOR.

Definition 3.5 'Let's call something a *rigid designator* if in any possible world it designates the same object' (Kripke 1972:269).

This is a refinement on Mill 1881 and a grammatical tradition that extends back at least as far as the Alexandrian grammarian Dionysos of Thrace *c*.100 BCE. Non-rigid designators would be such definite descriptions as *the teacher of Alexander the Great* and *the author of 'On Interpretation'*. These are rigid in some possible worlds but not every possible world. In a counterfactual world, Aristotle might not have been the teacher of Alexander the Great, but he'd still have been Aristotle; he might not have written 'On Interpretation', but he would still have been Aristotle. The name remains the same even in counterfactual worlds – that is why Kripke calls it a rigid designator. Therefore, we can make counterfactual statements like *If Aristotle had not been born, scholarly life would have been so much the poorer* – in which the word 'Aristotle' refers to Aristotle and rigidly designates.

It is not essential that the name-bearer be real for the name to rigidly designate. Historians believe that Homer may never have existed in fact; and even if he did, that he was just one contributor to the *Iliad* and the *Odyssey*. The historical facts make no difference whatsoever to Homer's expositors or other language users. The proper name *Homer* rigidly designates just as well when it is a convenient fiction as it would if it were historically validated as the true name of the real and sole author of the *Iliad* and *Odyssey*. If it turns out that someone else is authenticated as the author of the *Iliad* and the *Odyssey*, Homer will be redesignated in the encyclopedia 'formerly the supposed author of the *Iliad* and the *Odyssey*', but the name *Homer* will remain a rigid designator.

Although Kripke never refers to anything like an 'encyclopedic entry for the name', he does talk about evidence for fixing the reference of the rigid designator, and the evidence is composed from exactly the kind of information that goes into the encyclopedia entry.

Assumption 3.2 Definitions are one means of fixing reference.

Reference can be fixed in more than one way. The measurement name *metre* is a rigid designator; the length was fixed in 1875 as the length between marks on a platinum iridium bar at normal atmospheric pressure at 0°C. A *metre* is also defined as 1,553,164.13 wave lengths of red cadmium light, and as 1.093614 of a yard. For the average person, it is a length identified by whatever ruler or tape-measure is to hand. All these are some of the many ways of fixing the reference of *metre*. Similarly, the reference of the rigid designator *Aristotle* can be fixed by means such as identifying him as the pupil of Plato, the teacher of Alexander the Great, the philosopher born in Stagira, etc. Plato could have fixed the reference of *Aristotle* for, say Eudoxus, by OSTENSION: i.e. by pointing out Aristotle and telling Eudoxus the equivalent of *That's Aristotle*. Not everyone will fix reference in the same way, but the rigid designator holds for everyone for whom it designates the same referent; cf. Kripke 1972:331. This is so even when a $person_i$'s encyclopedic information is minimal, such that the reference of, say, *Aristotle* is merely "a historical personage". If $person_i$ has only this information about *Plato*, too, all that keeps Aristotle distinct from Plato is the form of the name.

A rigid designator is translatable. The form of the name is determined by the particular (variety of) language being used, and its reference is fixed by the norms and conventions of that language. For example, many proper names change across languages:

> London = Londres, Cuk Şon = Tucson, Uluru = Ayers Rock, Kirinyaga = Mount
> Kenya, Athēnai = Athens, Αριστοτέλης = Aristotle

London is a rigid designator when speaking English but not when speaking French, where the same referent is called *Londres*.

Londres and *London* are alternative names for the same referent. Such alternative names abound within a given language where most people have more than one version of a proper name. In some societies a person will have a public name and a secret name, the latter known to a very few privileged people (see Chapter 5). Many people have nicknames or familiar names in addition to their official name. *Michael* alternates with *Mike* in different, though overlapping, sets of contexts. A jazz buff will know that *Bird* refers to the same person as *Charley Parker*. Stage names are rigid designators also; and the name *Bob Dylan* identifies the same person as bears the name *Robert Zimmerman*, and *Marilyn Monroe* the same person as bore the name *Norma Jean Baker*. The designators are rigid, but used in different contexts.

10 Bob Dylan wrote 'Blowin' in the wind'.
11 Robert Zimmerman wrote 'Blowin' in the wind'.

11 is misleading because Robert Zimmerman's name does not appear on the credits – Bob Dylan's does. To make 11 felicitous, it needs qualifying: *Robert Zimmerman wrote 'Blowin' in the wind' under his stage name of Bob Dylan*. It is a necessary fact that Bob Dylan = Bob Dylan, and that Robert Zimmerman = Robert Zimmerman; but it could be false that Bob Dylan = Robert Zimmerman. Only someone aware of the contingent equivalence can infer 10 from 11 and vice versa.

> *Assumption 3.3* Referents are 'baptized' with rigid designators that are subsequently passed down through the community (Kripke 1972:302, 309).

The baptism 'initiates a proper name using practice' (Evans 1982). Lehrer 1992a reports experimental confirmation of what intuition suggests:

> *Assumption 3.4* There are semantic constraints on naming: it is not the case that 'anything goes'.

Judgments about the appropriateness of names are judgments of semantic and pragmatic acceptability arising from the connotations of the names.

> *Definition 3.6* The CONNOTATIONS of a language expression are semantic effects that arise from encyclopedic knowledge about its denotation and also from experiences, beliefs, and prejudices about the contexts in which the expression is typically used.

(See Chapter 5 for more discussion.) Connotations vary between contexts and speech communities independently of sense and denotation. For example, *Mike* and *Michael* can have the same reference but different connotations. Just as *John* is an unsuitable name for your new-born daughter, so is *Springtime in Paris* an inappropriate name for a 1200cc Harley-Davidson motorbike or an auto-repair shop. *Wheels and Deals* might be a good name for a used car mart, but not for a new strain of corn, nor for a maternity boutique. People are well aware of these facts, and marketing folk exploit such knowledge to the full. Consequently, when Lehrer ran a questionnaire on the suitability of a set of names for a variety of denotata (this was an exercise in EMPIRICAL SEMANTICS), she found a high degree of inter-subject agreement on the matter.

Lehrer 1992a reports on the names for models of American cars. The name of the make, e.g. *Ford*, or model, e.g. *Mustang*, is a proper name. The name of a particular car, as in *I drive a Mustang*, is not a proper name. The connotations of proper names for car models must be able to attract buyers from a significant section of the general public, so there are naming patterns for car models. As one would expect, many model names have associations with power and/or importance (Monarch, Le Baron, Ambassador, Jaguar, Laser), luxury (Malibu, Monte Carlo), speed (Mustang, Falcon, Corsair, Dart, Grand Prix, Le Mans, Volare), macho (Challenger, Matador, Maverick, Fury), and travel (Safari, Ranger). It is notable that car models are not named after trees, human body-parts, or mundane things like articles of clothing and items of household furniture; for a start, none of these things move. And if there are models with names like *Cyclone*, a word with connotations of speed and force, it is unlikely one would find a car model named *Rain* or *Overcast*. *Firebird, Thunderbird, Falcon,* and *Hawk*, even *Skylark*, are found; but the names of nondescript unexciting birds such as sparrow, crow, pigeon, chicken, goose, turkey are not used. Table 3.2 compares the connotations of *hawk* with those of *pigeon* to suggest why one is an appropriate model name, and the other is not.

Name:	*Hawk*	*Pigeon*
Attributes:	A hawk is a high-flying bird of prey. It soars and swoops and has an efficient aerodynamic appearance.	A pigeon is a compact-bodied, short-legged bird that waddles when it walks. It has ungainly take-off and flappy flight. It is friendly but mundane.
Comment:	These are attributes appropriate to a reasonably prestigious car, with a macho image.	If any car were to be called a *Pigeon*, it would surely have to be a runabout.
Used by:	Humber, Studebaker.	No one.

Table 3.2 What's in a name?

In principle a new car model could be called anything at all; in practice it cannot. The connotations of names affect their appropriateness. Similar constraints hold for all potential baptisms. Lehrer's review of the proper names of car models, rock bands, beauty salons, streets, and university buildings shows that baptisms are mostly systematic, and each genre develops its own naming themes and styles based on connotation. At the same time, all proper names are constrained by the nature of their denotation because, by Definitions 2.9–10 it is reflected in their senses.

Names can be descriptive, picking up on a salient characteristic perceived in, wanted for, or (sometimes ironically) imputed to the referent. Examples are the topographical names Green River, Black Mountain, Shiprock; Ghanaian day names such as Akua (woman born on Wednesday), Kofi (man born on Friday); the Puritan christian name If-Christ-Had-Not-Died-For-You-You-Had-Been-Damned; the characteristics Shakespeare imputed to

Doll Tearsheet, Pistol, Justice Shallow; the implications of nicknames like Shorty and Four-eyes, adopted names like Sid Vicious and Yahoo Serious, or family names like Baker and Smith. All these names were motivated as descriptions, yet once the referent is baptized (in Kripke's sense) the name becomes a rigid designator of that referent.

A rigid designator persists, but the characteristics of the referent may change over time. A baby baptized *PN* can, and often does, bear the name *PN* at all stages in his or her life (even when various bodily organs have been removed and replaced by organs transplanted from other people). And, of course, the name continues to rigidly designate after death. The membership of a pop group or orchestra may change from time to time without affecting the name of the ensemble. Cities grow or they fall into ruin, all the while retaining their proper name. This kind of chronological mutation in the characteristics of the denotatum is equally applicable to common names, and it is irrelevant to semantic theory.

> *Assumption 3.5* Once a proper name exists in the language, there is presumed to be a HISTORICAL CHAIN stretching back through users of the name to the original baptism (Kripke 1972:302).

This notion of the historical chain is a variation on a long established view that a history of conventional usage characterizes the vocabulary in the language and allows successive generations to communicate easily. The motivation for Kripke's historical chain conjecture is that the proper name persists in time denoting just the name-bearer, whereas common names denote a class of entities each of which is distributed in time. Note, however, that the class or kind persists, and Kripke 1972:328 does propose that kind terms are rigid designators.

> This conclusion [that names are rigid designators] holds for various species names, whether they are count nouns such as 'cat', 'tiger', 'chunk of gold', or mass terms such as 'gold', 'water', 'iron pyrites'. It also applies to certain terms for natural phenomena, such as 'heat', 'light', 'sound', 'lightning', and, presumably, suitably elaborated, to corresponding adjectives – 'hot', 'loud', 'red'.
>
> (Kripke 1972:327)

Compare

> The man called John = the man thinking of whom we say "John"
> a cat = an animal thinking of which one would say "cat"   (Wierzbicka 1972:22)

The *SOED* entry for *cat* describes it as 'A carnivorous quadruped' and in the context of zoology 'A member of the genus *Felis* or *Panthera*'. Both senses are followed by lists of species, i.e. encyclopedic information. *Gold* is also given a largely encyclopedic entry in the *SOED*: 'The most precious metal; characterized by its yellow colour, non-liability to rust, high specific gravity, and great malleability and ductility. Chemical symbol Au.' Clearly these are guides to fixing the appropriate denotation – which is a good practical aim for a dictionary.

Assumption 3.6 The semantic specification of natural kind terms locates them in a natural taxonomy, but is otherwise similar to the semantic specification of a proper name.

Defining the cat as a "carnivorous quadruped" merely describes what cats are, it does not give a semantic description of the word *cat*. Consider Putnam's 1962 notion that cats may turn out to be alien automata that we humans (and our dogs) have been hoodwinked into believing are animals: in this circumstance, is *cat* truly a rigid designator? Kripke says 'Cats are in fact animals!' the alien automata would be automata 'in a cat-like form' (1972:321). Though Putnam disagrees, Kripke seems to be right. The unnatural history of such cats is surely part of the encyclopedia entry. Putnam and Kripke are discussing an outlandish possibility; there is in fact a good deal of renaming in the various branches of biology when research leads to life-forms being relocated in new tribes, or families, or superfamilies, and so forth; or else a new variety or subspecies is recognized. This is straightforwardly indicated in reference books:

12 *Stribolanthes* species (syn. *Goldfussia*)', 'syn.' = "synonymous with", '*Tibouchina* species
(formerly *Lasiandra*)   (Moore et al. 1980:220, 221)

Australian chats Family Epthianuridae [The molecular biology work of Sibley & Ahlquist indicates the chats *are* true honeyeaters and they include them in the prior Family Meliphagidae. We separate them in this classification for the present.]
(Simpson and Day 1993:347 [*sic*])

The encyclopedia will record the changes, and the lexicon will record some of them, too, e.g. the entry for *Lasiandra* should be cross-referenced with *Tibouchina* and, perhaps in future, *Epthianuridae* with *Meliphagidae*. Because animacy is both semantically and syntactically relevant in the English language, it will need to be indicated in the lexicon; so, given the Putnam/Kripke scenario, if cats turn out to be automata yet continue to display all the characteristics of animates (e.g. they are born, breathe, nurture themselves, die), then at least some automata can be grammatically classified along with animates! Proper names may also be changed over time. Constantinople became Istanbul; St Petersburg became Leningrad and then, once again, St Petersburg. People change names for a variety of reasons. In some communities women get a new name on being married. Transsexuals change their name as they change sex. None of this presents a problem: each name is the rigid designator of an entity over a certain period of time.

It is far from obvious why Kripke did not include the names for non-natural kinds as rigid designators – not that he explicitly excludes them. The process of naming a new human being, a new town, a newly discovered mineral, and a new invention seem broadly similar. The way that the names are transmitted through a historical link is exactly parallel. If there are philosophical problems with non-natural kinds, the linguistic facts seem to force a comparison with natural kind terms.[6]

Assumption 3.7 Rigid designators name referents, they do not classify them.

At the beginning of §3.5 I said that *a Ford*, denoting a car marque, is not a proper name despite the fact that it derives from a proper name and looks like one. However, it denotes an non-natural kind and is, therefore, a rigid designator. So too is *a Toyota*; compare 13 with 14.

13 (a) There are three Toyotas in my garage.
   (b) In my garage there are three cars of the same kind/make: they are Toyotas.
   (c) In my garage there are three cars with the same name: *Toyota*.

14 (a) There are three Susans in my class.
   (b) *In my class there are three girls of the same kind/make: they are Susans.
   (c) In my class there are three girls with the same name: *Susan*.

13(a) means the same as 13(b), which is explicitly classificatory. The most probable interpretation of 13(c) is also 13(b). It could, however, mean that each car was baptized with the same proper name, *Toyota*, in which case it is feasible that one car could be a Ford, another a BMW, and a third a Hyundai (it has been known for someone to name their cat *Dog*). Note that in these unlikely circumstances, 13(c) has a different meaning from 13(a–b). 14(a) means the same as 14(c) but not the (would-be) classificatory 14(b). There is a class of objects with certain common characteristics that identify them as Toyotas, and a subset of these characteristics is not shared with other cars. Although all Susans are (probably) females, there are many females who are not Susans. There is no defining characteristic of all things called *Susan* that will systematically distinguish them from all things called *Anna* except that they bear different names. The form of the proper name marks the difference, and not its semantic (or morphosyntactic) specification. It follows that something can unproblematically bear both names without being a hybrid; furthermore, *Susan Anna* is a rigid designator distinct from *Anna Susan*.

This section adopted Kripke's thesis that within a community of speakers K a particular referent R or a class of denotata D is baptized with a name N, and afterwards is known within K as N. Many Rs and Ds are baptized with more than one N, each of which is a rigid designator; the form of N may also change over time, or if borrowed into another language. There are usually contextual constraints on which N is applicable in $M^{w,t}$ (the world and time spoken of). Baptisms of the same natural kind are likely to be different among different language communities, which is why the thing called *dog* is also called *chien, Hund, pies, ájá, kare, mbwa*, and many other names besides. The historical chain explains as well as anything does how the listeme N becomes conventionalized within a community. There are constraints on the baptismal name: life would be tough for a boy named *Sue*; it was even tough for the American who had his name changed to *One Zero Six Nine* – he had to go to four courts in two states before he found a sympathetic judge; and (Adrienne Lehrer tells me) even then he was required to spell the numbers and not use numerals. Some names are initially descriptive, but after the baptism they become rigid designators. The reference is fixed for a rigid designator by ostension (pointing out and naming), definition, or description which constitute part of the encyclopedic information about the referent (ostension is included for an "encyclopedia" that represents visual or auditory images – as our mental encyclopedias surely do).

Exercises

3.5.1 In a counterfactual world Aristotle's parents might have named him *Eudoxus* instead of Aristotle. If Aristotle hadn't been called Aristotle, would that undermine Kripke's claim that the name *Aristotle* is a rigid designator?

3.5.2 In Chapter 2 we discussed the meaning of *God does not exist*. Is 'God' a rigid designator? Explain your answer.

3.5.3 If *Cicero hailed the news of Caesar's murder* means the same as *Tully hailed the news of Caesar's murder*,
    (a) What does this tell you about Cicero and Tully?
    (b) Try to explain why it is that *Sam believes that Cicero hailed the news of Caesar's murder* does not mean the same as *Sam believes that Tully hailed the news of Caesar's murder*?

3.5.4 Discuss the likelihood that car models will be named after farmyard animals such as pig, cow, and goat.

3.5.5 Check people's responses to *Norma Jean Baker starred in 'Gentleman Prefer Blondes'*.

3.5.6 Ask five people to give five names and five unlikely names for a new baby girl, and also five names and five unlikely names for a new baby boy. Discuss the outcome.

3.5.7 Do either (a) or (b):
    (a) Collect names for beauty salons = hair boutiques = hairdressers and names for lawyers or financial advisors. How and why do the two differ?
    (b) Do the names of rock bands, past and present, give any clues to the characteristics of the band, such as whether they are all male, all female, what kind of music they play?

3.6 Proper names in the lexicon

> [I]t may be conventional to name only girls "Martha", but if I name my son "Martha" I may mislead, but I do not lie.
>
> (Searle 1958)

Many people share the same family name, more share the same given name, some share their entire proper name with others; the *Elizabeth Taylor* listed in the 1989 Tucson AZ phone directory was not the frequently husbanded British-born movie-star. What do language users do about this state of affairs? Well, take *London, Ontario* versus *London, England*, or *Boulder, Utah* versus *Boulder, Colorado*. The strategy used in the proper identification of incomplete names is to add further information to the proper name, thus turning it into a more complete and explicit name with perhaps some non-rigid descriptive material to fix the reference. Paradoxically, although the incomplete proper name is a rigid designator, the more complete proper name – e.g. *Aristotle, the ancient Greek philosopher* – may not be. In practice, what saves proper names as rigid designators is that they are typically used in a context in which they can felicitously function as incomplete names.

> **Assumption 3.8** If many proper names are shared by different name-bearers, there must be a stock of proper names. This stock must surely be located either partially or wholly in the lexicon.

The sense of a proper name *PN* is given in 15 and exemplified in 16. Note the direct link between formal and semantic specifications.[7]

15   PN_f —— $_fN_s$ —— $_s$"bearer of the name $_fPN$"
     |_____|

16   **Aristotle** /'ærɪstɒtl/$_{f500}$ —— $_{f500}N_{s600}$ —— $_{s600}$"bearer of the name $_{f500}$*Aristotle*"

16 makes no reference to any particular individual such as the 4th century BCE philosopher from Stagira, or a shipping magnate who married the widow of an assassinated US president, or my friend Ari Papadopoulos, or any of thousands more bearers of the name. Furthermore, this formula looks extremely plausible because it yokes together the proper name with the name-bearer, and that is exactly what we want to do. The point of identifying senses of language expressions is to represent them in a lexicon and to display their semantic structure and the semantic relations they enter into. It is the semantic specification that identifies the noun as a proper name. Somewhere it must be recorded that where *PN* is used as a rigid designator it will not merely be a noun, but a noun phrase.

      16 is inadequate. For instance, we know that the statements in 17 are anomalous whereas those in 18–21 are not.

17   *John washed herself.
     *Mary washed himself.

> *Definition 3.7* A phrase or sentence is ANOMALOUS if it cannot denote in any possible world or time because it contains a contradiction (D6.6), as in the NP *a round square*, or because its meaning is indeterminable, as in the sentence *This verb is in the indicative tense* (D6.11, D8.4).

18   John washed himself.
19   Mary washed herself.
20   Robin washed himself.
21   Robin washed herself.

The gender of the pronoun is normally determined by attributes of the referent. The anomaly of 17 derives directly from semantic incompatibility (Chapter 8) of the proper name and its clause-mate reflexive pronoun, and indirectly from the fact that the typical denotatum of *John* is male and the name is therefore of masculine gender, whereas *Mary* typically denotes a female and is feminine. *Robin* may denote either a male or a female, and so is semantically compatible with a pronoun of either gender. There are quite general gender constraints on names. **Richard is lactating* is anomalous. *Mary's just had a baby* normally means she has given birth, whereas *John's just had a baby* means that his female partner has given birth. The most significant characteristic of a personal proper name is that it identifies the gender of the name-bearer.

> Based on a comparison of sixty societies, Alford (1988:66–8) finds that the sex of an individual is the most common item of information conveyed by first names. This is certainly the case for the United States, where names typically convey gender. Androgynous names are relatively uncommon even at present: In New York State not one of the leading 100 boys' names overlaps with the leading 100 girls' names.
>
> (Lieberson and Mikelson 1995:933)

Thus gender expectations need to be indicated in the lexicon entry.

22   **John** /jɒn/$_{f100}$ —— $_{f100}$N$_{s200}$ —— $_{s200}$"bearer of the name $_{f100}$*John*, normally a male"

23   **Mary** /'meərɪ/$_{f110}$ —— $_{f110}$N$_{s210}$ —— $_{s210}$"bearer of the name $_{f110}$*Mary*, normally a female"

24   **Robin** /'rɒbɪn/$_{f120}$ —— $_{f120}$N$_{s220}$ —— $_{s220}$"bearer of the name $_{f120}$*Robin*, either male or female"

The gender of *Robin*'s referent on a particular occasion can be determined from further information about the bearer, which either emerges from the context or can be attached as part of a more complete name.

From a lexicological viewpoint, alternative spellings and pronunciations of names should be included. For example, the lexicon might contain something like the following entries. The position of the subscripts relative to what they index is of no consequence. In 25–27, 'V' (from Latin *vel*) symbolizes "or"; cf. Chapter 6.

25    $_{f150}$**Robin** V $_{f151}$**Robyn** /'rɒbɪn/ —— $_{f150-1}$N$_{s250-1}$ —— "bearer of the name $_{f150}$*Robin*, either male or female"$_{s250}$ V "bearer of the name $_{f151}$*Robyn*, normally female"$_{s251}$

26    $_{f160}$**Graeme** V $_{f161}$**Graham** /'greiəm/ —— $_{f160-1}$N$_{s260}$ —— "bearer of the name $_{f160}$*Graeme* V $_{f161}$*Graham*, normally a male"$_{s260}$

27    $_{f170}$**Colin** /'kɒlɪn/ V $_{f171}$/'koulɪn/ —— $_{f170-1}$N$_{s270}$ —— "bearer of the name $_{f170-1}$*Colin*, normally male"$_{s270}$

Alternative names such as *Mike* and *Michael* should also be linked. This is a generally applicable rule of English, and different from a completely contingent circumstance asserted in *Daddy is the bearer of the name Fred*, which identifies alternative descriptions of a particular individual not a class of individuals. However, we need to accommodate the facts that there is a stylistic difference between *Mike* and *Michael* or *William* and *Bill*, and that some name-bearers accept only one of these names and reject the other. So I propose that the entries will look something like 28, where the ellipse contains encyclopedic information.[8]

28    $_{f130}$**Bill** /bɪl/ —— $_{f130}N_{s230}$ —— "the bearer of the name $_{f130}$*Bill*, normally a male"$_{s230}$

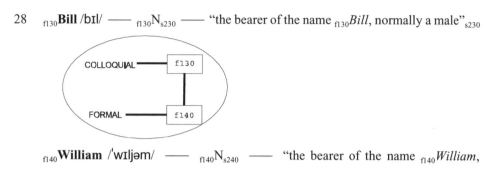

$_{f140}$**William** /ˈwɪljəm/ —— $_{f140}N_{s240}$ —— "the bearer of the name $_{f140}$*William*, normally a male"$_{s240}$

We have established that there is a stock of proper names in the lexicon for people to draw upon when baptizing name-bearers-to-be – even if many names are novel creations. And we have seen what the lexicon entries for proper names must include.[9]

Exercises

3.6.1 (a) Are the two referents for *Elizabeth Taylor* identified successfully in the first paragraph of this section?
   (b) In what way are they distinguished?
   (c) Is there one rigid designator here, or two?

3.6.2 How do books of names, e.g. for new-borns, differ from any other specialist lexicon?

3.6.3 Do you think that the lexicon should recognize that *Dobbin* is typically the name for a horse, *Rover* a dog, and *Spot* the name for an animal, often a dog?

3.7 The lexicon is part of the encyclopedia

Lexicon entries supply one means of the access to encyclopedia entries; consequently, the lexicon is very closely correlated with the encyclopedia. The most important thing the lexicon does is identify the senses of an item within it; and the sense of an item is a description of salient characteristics of the typical denotatum of that item (Definitions 2.9–10). Information about denotata is stored in their encyclopedia entries. It is this information from which the senses of isomorphic listemes are abstracted. Such abstraction from particulars is evident in the ontogenetic development of listemes by children. Eve

Clark 1973 reports a child's extension of *bird* to any moving creature (sparrows, cows, dogs, cats), *moon* to any round object, *bow-wow* to things that are bright, reflective and round (?based on the dog's eyes) such as a fur piece with glass eyes, pearl buttons, cuff links, a bath thermometer. The same process operates when adults encounter a new name or a new use for a name. The idealized model of the encyclopedia and lexicon requires a heuristic updating facility of this kind. Suppose that Z has only ever encountered female bearers of the name *Beryl*, so that the semantic specification in Z's lexicon entry is "bearer of the name *Beryl*, normally a female". If Z comes across the name *Beryl* used of a man, not only is Z's encyclopedia expanded, but also Z's mental lexicon entry will be updated to "bearer of the name *Beryl*, normally a female, but attested for a male".

Given names are included in the lexicon. There seems no good reason to exclude from the English lexicon such common family names as *Smith* and *Jones* with an entry such as "bearer of the name *Smith*, normally a family name". To do this recognizes that some names typically occur as family names and are retained in memory as such. A question arises whether or not foreign family names like *Sanchez, Papadopoulos*, and *Pavarotti* have any entry in an English lexicon. Native speakers of English readily recognize some names as Scottish, or Welsh, or Cornish, or Jewish; and immigrants to an English-speaking country who wish to assimilate sometimes Anglicize their names: e.g. *Piekarsky* becomes *Parkes, Klein* becomes *Clyne*. So it seems that even family names have lexical properties. *Papadopoulos* should be tagged as originally a Greek name, and *Pavarotti* Italian.

Although the family name offers a clue to the bearer's ancestry, it gives no guarantee of it being a fact. This reflects a general truth about proper names which distinguishes them from common names.

Assumption 3.9 The common name *a cat* necessarily names something animal, but the proper name *Martha* only most probably names a female.

Unusual names like *If-Christ-Had-Not-Died-For-You-You-Had-Been-Damned* or *Yahoo Serious* would presumably have empty lexicon entries leading directly to encyclopedic entries. A name such as *If-Christ-Had-Not-Died-For-You-You-Had-Been-Damned*, or *Boy-who-is-not-able-satisfactorily-to-explain-what-a-Hrung-is,-nor-why-it-should-collapse-on-Betelgeuse-Seven*, and a topographical name beginning *Mount* or *River*, is interpreted via the lexicon just like any other polyword listeme (Chapter 4). Once the component meanings are assembled and an interpretation determined for the name, a matching encyclopedia entry is sought and, if none already exists, a new entry is created. Where Hearer encounters a new proper name, a lexicon entry is established on the basis of its formal and syntactic characteristics, and any sense that is assigned to the lexicon entry derives from encyclopedic information about the name-bearer.

A3.10 derives from D3.1 and D3.4.

Assumption 3.10 A lexicon contains information about listemes, whereas an encyclopedia contains information about what listemes are used to refer to (cf. Katz 1977d).

The meanings of 'content words' – nouns, verbs, adjectives, adverbs – are influenced by the things that they denote and the circumstances in which the words are used. That is, semantic information in a large part of the lexicon is distilled from encyclopedic information about the salient characteristics of typical denotata.[10] We have already suggested that some lexicon entries for names contain no semantic information but function merely as access points to the encyclopedia (A3.1).

Assumption 3.11 *The encyclopedia is a general knowledge base of which lexical knowledge is a proper part – lexical information is just one kind of encyclopedic information.*

The combined lexicon-encyclopedia entry would no longer be the tripartite network of formal, morphosyntactic, and semantic specifications, co-indexed via the morphosyntactic specification ⟨F⟩—(M)—[S]. Instead it is quadripartite, where the additional member is the encyclopedic specification E in Fig. 3.6 (E symbolizes encyclopedic information other than that contained in F, M, and S).[11]

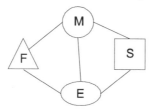

Figure 3.6 Components of the lexicon within the encyclopedia

An example is 29, where encyclopedic information is marked by index $_e$.

29    $_{f500,_fe500}$ **Aristotle** /ˈærɪstɒtl/

$_{f500}$N$_{s600}$

$_{s600}$ "bearer of the name $_{f500}$*Aristotle*, normally a male"$_{s}$e701–3

$_{f}$e500 Derived from Greek Ἀριστοτέλης

$_{s}$e701 — Ancient Greek philosopher, born in Stagira in C4 BCE. Author of *The Categories, On Interpretation, On Poetry* ... Pupil of Plato and teacher of Alexander the Great ... etc.

$_{s}$e702 — **Onassis**, C20 CE Greek shipping magnate ... etc.

$_{s}$e703 — **Papadopoulos**, friend whose phone number is 018 111 ... etc.

A fragment of the corresponding network is presented in Fig. 3.7.

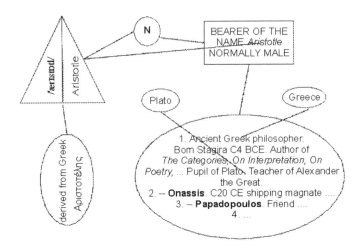

Figure 3.7 Networked fragment of the combined
lexicon-encyclopedia entry for Aristotle

For simplicity's sake much cross referencing has been omitted. There is no encyclopedic information on N included, none on (Ancient Greek) philosophers, poetry, Stagira, Plato, etc. Further complexity would result from there being more than one encyclopedia or if THE encyclopedia is divided into cross-referenced modules.

3.8 Summary

The purpose of this chapter has been to review the structure of lexicon entries and the relationship between the lexicon and the encyclopedia.[12] The evidence strongly suggests that a lexicon is the part of an encyclopedia which stores information about the formal, morphosyntactic, and semantic specifications of listemes. Some scholars believe that ALL information about listemes should be considered part of the lexicon; but I have argued for a division of labour between lexicon and encyclopedia. Etymological and stylistic information, for instance, are encyclopedic data that are not strictly a part of the lexicon even though they must be closely networked with it. Similarly, encyclopedic data on the denotata of listemes must be closely networked with the lexicon entries. Di Sciullo and Williams (1987:3) wrote: 'The lexicon is like a prison – it contains only the lawless, and the only thing that its inmates have in common is lawlessness.' We have seen that this view of the lexicon is erroneous.

The next chapter, Chapter 4, pursues the lexicological theme by seeking to answer the question: what counts as a listeme?

● Key words and phrases:

alternative name

anomaly (D3.7)

(Kripke) baptism

checklist or cluster theory of proper names

conjugation

connotation (D3.6)

declension

denotatum (PL denotata) (D2.6)

empirical semantics

encyclopedia (D3.5)

etymology

fixing reference

formal specifications

gender

historical chain

hypothetical lexicon

(numerical) indexing

inflexional irregularity

kind term

lexicography (D3.3)

lexicology (D3.2)

lexicon (D3.1)

lexicon entry

listeme

mental lexicon

morphosyntactic specifications

name

name-bearer

natural kind (term)

networking

ostension

polyword listeme

proper name

rigid designator (D3.5)

semantic specifications

semantic field

unnatural kind (term)

● Research question 3.2 asked whether there should be just one lexicon, and we answered that there should be many connected specialist lexicons.

● A lexicon entry has just three major connected components: formal specification is connected to morphosyntactic specification, and the morphosyntactic specification is connected to semantic specification in the following manner: F_f —— $_fM_s$ —— $_sS$. The indices function like bidirectional connectors in a network, (Fig. 3.4). We subsequently proposed that all these components are connected to encyclopedia entries; cf. Fig. 3.6.

● We suggested that there be many connected encyclopedias reflecting specialist knowledge modules and also different prejudices and points of view.

● The lexicon differs from the encyclopedia by identifying the meanings of listemes rather than giving information about their denotata; by identifying the formal and morphosyntactic specifications of listemes, rather than giving information on their history and relationships with other listemes.

● The lexicon will contain lexicographical information about a name in the language, and the encyclopedia information about name bearers.

● The lexicon entry is one access point to the encyclopedia entry (A3.1).

● Kripke 1972 demonstrates that a proper name is a rigid designator because in every possible world and time it has the same referent. His theory is in opposition to the checklist or cluster theory of proper names, which claims that the meaning of a proper name is given by at least one of a cluster of attributes of the name-bearer.

● Although Kripke never refers to an encyclopedic entry for the name he does talk about evidence for fixing the reference of the rigid designator, and the evidence is composed from exactly the kind of information that goes into the encyclopedia entry.

● Definitions are one way of fixing reference (A3.2).

● Referents are 'baptized' with rigid designators that are subsequently passed down through the community (A3.3). Once a rigid designator exists in the language, there is presumed to be a historical chain stretching back through users of the name to the original baptism (A3.5). This is a version of the belief that meaning and form are correlated by convention.

● We saw that there are constraints on naming (A3.4). These involve attributes of the typical denotatum and also connotation.

● Kripke argues that natural kind terms are rigid designators. They differ from proper names in that their semantic specifications locate them within a natural taxonomy (A3.6). We extended the notion of rigid designator to non-natural kind terms, too.

● Rigid designators name referents, they do not classify them (A3.7).

● Rebaptism occurs, and names change over time and across languages. The same referent may have more than one rigid designator. A name may begin as a description, but once it becomes idiomatic it is a rigid designator.

● Proper names are located in the lexicon (A3.8).

● A phrase or sentence is anomalous if it cannot denote in any possible world and time.

● We concluded that a lexicon is a part of an encyclopedia and that entries in the combined lexicon and encyclopedia form a quadripartite network of formal,

morphosyntactic, semantic, and (other) encyclopedic specifications, 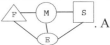. A

lexicon entry will be minimal because most of the so-called semantic information will be encyclopedic – this answers Research Question 1.

● In any human community there are people with widely different areas of specialized knowledge and the vocabulary to go with it. This can be modelled by a bank of encyclopedias, each containing a lexicon, and all accessible to one another.

3.9 Notes on further reading

[1] On lexicography, see Boguraev and Briscoe (eds) 1989, Mel'cuk et al. 1984, 1984–91.

[2] On primary stress in English, see Pike 1945, Halliday 1970, Brown et al. 1980, Ladefoged 1982, Allan 1986.

[3] On countability, see Allan 1980.

[4] On the gradability of adjectives, see Lehrer and Lehrer 1982, Rusiecki 1985, Cruse 1986, Allan 1987b.

[5] On the checklist theory of proper names, see Frege 1892, Russell 1905, Searle 1958, Strawson 1959.

[6] On philosophical problems with non-natural kinds, see Schwartz 1980, Pulman 1983 Ch. 7.

[7] On the semantics of proper names, see Russell 1918:221, Kneale 1962:630, Loar 1976, 1980, Katz 1977b, 1990, K. Bach 1987:135f, Fodor 1987:85f.

[8] Conditions for using alternate names are more complicated than 28 suggests. For a fascinating and very thorough discussion of the different conditions for using alternate Russian personal names such as *Katerina, Katen'ka, Katjuša, Kat'ka, Katjuxa, Katja, Katënok,* and *Katënyš,* see Wierzbicka 1990a, 1992b.

[9] For other views on names, see Lieberson and Bell 1992, McCulloch 1989, Pulman 1983 Ch. 6, Recanati 1993, Schwartz (ed.) 1977.

[10] On the derivation of intension and sense from typical denotata, see Ch.10, Jackendoff 1983, 1990, Wierzbicka 1985, Allan 1986 §2.9, Lakoff 1987.

[11] Marconi 1997:67–76 has tantalizing hints from neuropsychological research for dislocation of the connectors between one component and another of the networked lexicon-encyclopedia.

[12] For other views on the lexicon, see Boguraev and Briscoe (eds) 1989, Haiman 1980b, Hüllen and Schulze (eds) 1988, Jackendoff 1975, 1995, 1997, Lyons 1977 Ch.13; Mel'cuk 1992.

4 Morphology and listemes

[S]entences and phrases describe, while lexemes – some of which are produced by word-formation – name.

(Bauer 1983:142)

4.1 Where we are heading

This chapter takes up two assumptions arising from the definition of semantics (D1.1).

Assumption 4.1 It is a necessary condition on semantic theory to semantically specify every language expression in the object language.

Assumption 4.2 One goal for semantic theory is to account for semantic relationships between language expressions.

The goals expressed in A4.1–2 cannot be achieved without identifying the set of listemes in the object language, and the relationships between them. This chapter continues the lexicological theme of Chapter 3 by discussing what counts as a listeme and the part played by the lexicon in identifying the relationships between them.

Good traditional dictionaries list not only words, but also morphemes.

Definition 4.1 A MORPHEME is the smallest unit of syntactic analysis with semantic specification.

Listemes include all morphological roots, inflexional and derivational morphemes, all non-derived and most derived lexemes, onomatopoeic and phonesthetic items, polyword idioms, and probably stems as well. All these terms are explained in this chapter, which focuses on their semantic properties. §4.2 introduces some relevant terminology and discusses the place of inflected and derived words with respect to the lexicon. §4.3 differentiates polyword listemes (compounds, phrasal verbs, idioms) from phrases. §4.4 examines listemes created by sound symbolism (onomatopoeia, phonesthesia, etc.). §4.5 summarizes the chapter.

4.2 Meaning and morphology

> Since its foundation 32 years ago, one of the group's core and inviolable rules had always been non-interference in each other's affairs – for there was much to non-interfere with.[1]

> [T]he big hitters Munich Re, Gerling Re and St Paul Re have called for premium rate increases in the January renewal period.[2]

The meaning of the English word *rabbits* is transparently composed from the meaning of the noun *rabbit* and the plural morpheme PL indicated by the final '-s'. The plural morpheme in English is instantiated by a variety of ALLOMORPHS, e.g. the bold italic parts of 1.

1   cat*s*, bush*es*, th*ese*, ox*en*, m*ice*, dat*a*, cherub*im*, two sheep (ZERO MORPH)

Whereas the MORPH is a form (and sometimes described as an ETIC category), the morpheme is EMIC, i.e. an abstract theoretical construct. (The term *listeme* is exceptional in that it applies to the form as much as to a theoretical construct.) To introduce some more morphological jargon, consider the structure of the plural noun *undesirables* "people who are undesirable".

2   $[_N undesirable \frown -s_N]$
       STEM -SUFFIX   (This suffix makes the noun stem plural)

3   $[_{Adj} undesirable_{Adj}] \, [_N \varnothing_N]$
       STEM $\frown$ZERO AFFIX   (The zero affix turns the adjective stem into a noun)

4   $[_{Adj} un- \frown desirable_{Adj}]$
  PREFIX-   STEM   (This prefix makes the adjective stem negative)

5   $[_V desire_V] \frown [_{Adj} -able_{Adj}]$
  ROOT & STEM   -SUFFIX   (This suffix turns the root verb into an adjective)

An AFFIX attaches to a STEM, and the most deeply embedded stem is the ROOT. Affixes that precede the stem are PREFIXES, those which follow the stem are SUFFIXES. The only INFIX in English is where an expletive is infixed into the stem, e.g. the bold part of *kanga**bloody**roo*; in this example, the stem is the root, *kangaroo*.

---

1. Note the neologism *non-interfere*. Peter Hartcher 'Send in the troops but make it ASEAN [Association of South East Asian Nations]' *Australian Financial Review* Tuesday September 14, 1999, p.8.

2. Note the use of the prefix *Re* as an independent word (meaning "reinsurance"). Bernard O'Riordan 'Reinventing reinsurance after the worst year on record' *Australian Financial Review* Wednesday September 15, 1999, p.16.

At each level in the structure of *undesirables* (2–5), it is the right-most part of the word that determines the syntactic category. This is known as the 'right-hand head rule' (Williams 1981:248). At 5, the base level, the suffix *-able* on the verb *desire* creates an adjective. In 4, *undesirable* remains an adjective because the stem *desirable* is to the right and it is an adjective. In 3, the zero affix is conventionally suffixed to the right in morphological analysis because (in this case) it converts the adjective *undesirable* into a noun. In 2, the plural suffix shows that the noun is plural. *Undesirables* is, for syntactic and semantic purposes, a plural noun; this confirms that 'affixes more relevant to syntax appear outside affixes less relevant to syntax' (Di Sciullo and Williams 1987:70).

Assumption 4.3 All lexical roots are listemes.
Assumption 4.4 All affixes are listemes.

The term *word* ambiguously denotes a language expression with both form and meaning. We will adopt Bloomfield's 1926 definition of it as 'a minimum free form' which accords with Sapir's 1921:33f abduction that words have psychological reality in isolation.

Definition 4.2 A FREE form is one that can stand alone in some syntactic structure in the object language. Otherwise the form is BOUND.

Words may consist of:

(a)   a single free morpheme, *rabbit*;
(b)   a combination of free and bound morphemes, *cat-s, re-call*;
(c)   a combination of free morphemes, *chair-person*;
(d)   a combination of bound morphemes, *abb-ess*.

A LEXEME is usually referred to by its UNMARKED or CITATION FORM. For instance, in desk-top dictionaries and books on language, *give* is normally used to represent the lexeme **give′**. The lexeme is found in a number of different words; cf. 6 – where bound morphemes are glossed to the right.

6   *give*   **give′**
    gives   **give′.3.S.SUBJECT**   [3= "third person", s="singular"]
    gave   **give′.P**   [P= "past tense", D11.11]
    giving   **give′.p**   [p= "present participle"]
    given   **give′.Pp**   [Pp= "past participle"]
    to give   **give′.INFINITIVE**

Assumption 4.5 The minimal lexeme is a free morpheme.
Assumption 4.6 Every nonderived lexeme is a listeme.

Bound morphemes fall into two major categories: inflexional and derivational.[1] The differences between them are summarized in Table 4.1. The points identified in the different cells are taken up for discussion below the table.

INFLEXION	DERIVATION
(I1) Adds to the meaning of a lexeme by producing related forms of the same stem lexeme.	(D1) Produces new (derived) lexemes.
(I2) Paradigms typically have no gaps.	(D2) Processes typically apply inconsistently to lexemes from the same class.
(I3) The combination of stem and inflexion is typically semantically transparent.	(D3) The combination of stem and derivational morpheme is often semantically opaque.

Table 4.1 Contrasting inflexional with derivational morphology

(I1) Inflexions typically add the meaning of a secondary grammatical category to that of the basic lexeme: e.g. aspect, tense, mood, person, voice to a verb lexeme, as in 6 (and Chapter 11); number, gender, case to a noun lexeme; cf. 1, 2. Except for uncommon instances where grammatical and natural gender coincide as in Latin *fēmina* "woman", the gender of a noun is predetermined on grounds that are obscure to the ordinary language user.[2] Number and case are to some extent context dependent: number is usually determined by the state of affairs in which the referent of a noun plays a part (Chapter 13); case is typically determined by the role the noun's referent plays in the state of affairs spoken of (Chapter 11).

(I2) The advantage of inflexions to the language user is that the morphs can be learned as paradigms. Irregularities are readily dealt with by means of a small set of exception rules. There is a tendency to regularize inflexions: e.g. regular English plural *syllabuses* prevails over Latin-based *syllabi*.

(I3) is evident in 1, 2, and 6. Meanings of inflected words can be computed from the combination of the semantic specifications of the stem lexeme and the semantic specifications of the inflexions. Methods for computing the meanings of morphosyntactically combined words are discussed in Chapters 7, 11–13. Therefore,

Assumption 4.7 Inflected words (e.g. *rabbits, gave*) are not listemes.

(A lexicographer might nonetheless choose to list them, as in *The COBUILD English Dictionary*.) The root lexeme and any inflexions are listemes (A4.3–4). Depending on its derivational status, the stem lexeme usually is a listeme.

(D1) A derivational morpheme changes the morphosyntactic specification of the stem (cf. 3, 5) and/or produces a new (derived) lexeme from the stem lexeme (cf. 3, 4, 5).

(D2) Derivational processes are often irregular, typically applying inconsistently to lexemes from the same class. Most derivational morphemes apply to only a small subset of members of the class of the stem word. For instance, *-en* attaches to some adjectives to turn them into CAUSATIVE verbs "make (more) Adj" or INCHOATIVE verbs "become (more) Adj".

7   blacken, redden, sadden, widen, fatten
8   *greenen, *bluen, *happien, *narrowen, *thinnen

Conversely, the verbs *narrow* and *thin* have no counterpart verbs #*wide* and #*fat*:

9   (a)   The road narrowed.   (b)   *The road wided.
10 (a)   Harry thinned the paint.   (b)   *Harry fatted the pig.

Note that: (a) all Adj that take *-en* are monosyllables; (b) *-en* does not attach to a stem ending in a sonorant – thus adjectives *long* and *strong* switch to their nominal form as the *-en* stem: **lengthen, strengthen**.

A few of the 150 or so derivational affixes in English are PRODUCTIVE – i.e. they apply freely and transparently to new items. One of these is the EFFECTOR NOMINALIZER *-er/-or*, which is suffixed to citation forms of V lexemes to produce the meaning "one who Vs" (*worker, baker, creator, sailor*) or "instrument that Vs" (*cooker, fastener, vacuum-cleaner*). The result is commonly called an 'agentive noun', but most are not agentive as defined in Chapter 11 – though they are effectors. A few effector nominals, e.g. *porter, author, doctor*, have no extant verbs. The missing verbs are called LEXICAL GAPS (D8.9). Occasionally the gap is filled by a BACK-FORMATION, e.g. the verb *edit* was backformed from *editor*, and *lech (on)* from *lecher*. The development of a verb **auth* is probably blocked by the existing verb *write*, and a verb **port* by the existing *carry, handle*, and *take*.

Definition 4.3. The BLOCKING PRINCIPLE: If a listeme already exists to express a meaning, do not construct another one without good reason for doing so.[3]

Definition 4.3 embodies the requirement that new coinings are semantically and pragmatically motivated, and do not arise from applying morphological rules just for the hell of it. It raises the question: what constitutes 'a good reason'? To which there is no certain answer. Apparent counterexamples to the blocking principle are the doublets in 11.

11 appropriacy = appropriateness   falseness = falsity   linguistician = linguist
    candidacy = candidature   flippancy = flippantness   normality = normalcy
    complacence = complacency   lech = lecher   suitableness = suitability

And there are dozens of terms current for copulation and the body parts associated with it. They result from stylistic and politeness considerations, euphemism, and the desire to speak vividly (Allan and Burridge 1991). We must conclude that the blocking principle is a constraint, not a prohibition.

(D3) Seeking to predict the meaning of a derived lexeme from the meanings of its derivational components, we will often be led astray. The derived lexeme, once constructed, attains independence from its derivational origins by being recognized as a word in its own right. Thereafter, its meaning may change with use, and eventually even obscure its original, once predictable, meaning. In many derived lexemes the semantic content of the stem plus the derivational morpheme is only consistently transparent in recent coinings. Contrast the well-established, widely used *cooperate* with the newer, less common *co-occur*:

12 *co-occur*   **together_with′–occur′**   "occur with"

  co-operate   **together_with′–operate′**   "work with"   ⇒   "work together with, be helpful"

In 12 'A⇒B' indicates SEMANTIC SHIFT from source A to target B. Thus, the more frequent a derived form is, the more likely it is to become autonomous. Very striking are the various semantic effects of the causative *-ize* suffix (this morph is shorthand for **cause_to_become (like)′**; an allograph is *-ise*).

13 *legalize*   "cause to become legal"   = "make legal"

  atomize   "cause to become like atoms, reduce to atoms"   = "make like atoms"

  fraternize   "create friendly relations with"   ?⇐ "cause to become like a brother"

  revolutionize "bring about a revolution"   ?⇐ "cause to become like a revolution"

  computerize "convert for use by a computer" *⇐ "cause to become like a computer"

  womanize   "promiscuously seek relations with women"   *⇐ "cause to become like a woman"

On many occasions the meaning contributed by the *-ize* suffix to the meaning of the stem is predictable, e.g. *legalize, atomize*. In *fraternize*, the meaning has probably shifted from ('?⇐') "being like a brother to" to its present meaning. Similarly with *revolutionize*. The current meanings of *computerize* and *womanize* are not predictable from ('*⇐') their components, although they are obviously semantically related to them. This is a situation that pervades derivational morphology and has the consequence that lexemes composed from derivational morphemes such as *-ize* need to be entered into the lexicon as listemes. Even a lexeme such as *legalize*, whose meaning is transparent from its components, should be included in the lexicon because it is a widely attested lexeme. Rarely used derived lexemes whose meaning is transparent could be omitted from the lexicon for reasons of economy. Unfortunately, the grounds for deciding which lexemes are rare enough to be excluded from the lexicon will always be arbitrary.

It is not uncommon for there to be multiple derivational morphemes within a derived lexeme; e.g. the derivation of *legalization* (N_4) from *law* (N_1) (the order of suffixing is governed by stratal law in morphology).[4]

14 $_{[N}$**law'**$_]$ $= N_1$ *law*   "law"

$N_1 \frown _{[Adj}$**al'**$_]$ $\Rightarrow Adj_2$ *legal*   "according to law"

$Adj_2 \frown _{[V}$**ize'**$_]$ $\Rightarrow V_3$ *legalize*   "cause to become according to law" = "make legal"

$V_3 \frown _{[N}$**ation'**$_]$ $\Rightarrow N_4$ *legalization* "the action of being caused to become according to law" = "action of legalizing"

There is also *legal-ity* "the state of being legal"; *legal-ist* "someone concerned with legality"; *legal-ist-ic* "being concerned about legality", whence the adverb *legal-ist-ic-ally*. Cf. *nation, national, nationalization, nationality, nationalist, nationalistic, nationalistically*. Etymologically, *nation* is a nominalization from the past participle *nat-* of a Romance root verb *nascor* "be born", a fact only indirectly relevant to contemporary English because the semantic relations between all the aforementioned *nat-* words and others such as *natal, native, nativity* will all be cross-referenced in the lexicon-encyclopedia.

There are many controversial issues in morphology about the meaningful contribution of morphemes to lexemes. Consider the words in 15.

15 *north* – *south*
    east – *west*

Should we recognize a bound longtitudinal morph *-th* and a latitudinal morph *-st*? Perhaps, but they are restricted to just these words, and the residues are also bound to these words. In *nor-nor-east* and in *souwester*, the *nor-* and *sou-* respectively seem to result from elision of a final *-th* rather than being independent morphemes. And *ea-* and *we-* certainly occur nowhere else with the appropriate senses. It is best to conclude that there is no payoff in making such an analysis.

With ZERO-DERIVATION (or CONVERSION) a morpheme with no associated morph attaches to an existing lexeme, causing it to shift its lexical class and therefore change its meaning and become another lexeme. The derived lexeme adopts the syntactic distribution, syntactic function and regular inflexional morphology of the new lexical class. For example, from the noun *waitress* comes the zero-derived verb *waitress* with a full regular verb morphology.

16 $_{[N}$**waitress'**$_{N]} \frown _{[V}\emptyset_{V]} \Rightarrow _{[V}$**waitress'**$_{V]}$

By definition, a zero morph cannot be located in a traditional desk-top dictionary, but it can have a numerical index in the hypothetical lexicon (§3.3) even though there is no form.

V⇒N and N⇒V zero-derivation is very productive in English. There is usually a close semantic relationship between the source and the derived lexeme with just the semantics of the lexical class making the difference; cf. 17–22.

17 The noun *age* names a characteristic state from birth or inception to a later reference
time; it gave rise to the denominal verb *age* which means "causing or achieving
age, becoming aged".

18 The noun *balloon* names something characteristically elastic and inflatable; the zero-
derived verb denotes the act of swelling up like a balloon, i.e. becoming inflated.

19 The noun *sandwich* denotes an object in which food is squeezed thinly between two
outer layers of bread, the denominal verb denotes the act of squeezing or being
squeezed between two things.

20 The verb *catch* gave rise to a noun denoting variously an act of catching (e.g. in a ball
game), the thing caught (e.g. when fishing), or a device for catching (e.g. a door
catch).

21 The verb *reject* gave rise to the deverbal noun denoting something rejected.

22 The verb *sneak* gave rise not to what was sneaked, but whatever does the sneaking.

However, particularly with older coinings, the semantic distance between source and
derivation can be considerable. Compare the noun *wolf* and the verb *wolf (food)*; or *doctor*
– which is a nonderogatory noun but a derogatory verb. Both the verbs *wolf* and *doctor*
result from behaviour once associated with the typical referent.

23 The verb *dog* "follow like a dog" is recorded 350 years earlier (1519) than the verb
wolf, so despite the fact that all members of the family Canidae wolf their food, and
this is despised, the act was inconsistent with the meaning of the existing verb *dog*.
Furthermore, the most despised dog was the wild and supposedly savage wolf; hence
the verb *wolf* "eat in the manner of a hungry, savage, wolf".

24 For centuries, doctors were despised because of the ineffectiveness of their curative
powers; this prejudice is retained in the verb – which, incidentally, does not fill the
lexical gap *doc(t)* "do what a doctor does".

A few deadjectival verbs, such as *savage, shy* mean "act in a Adj manner". Most,
however, are causative with the sense "cause to become Adj" e.g. *blind, clear, dirty, idle,
slim, sour, tame*. A partial exception is *total* "cause to become totally wrecked/destroyed".
Deadjectival nouns fall into several kinds.

(a)   Colour adjectives like *red* give rise to colour names.
(b)   *The*-generic expressions for classes of human beings having suppleted Adj^N forms
to denote individuals: *the Dutch (a Dutch girl/man/person* not **a Dutch), the English, the
French, the Welsh* – all these nationality names end with a palatal sibilant, unlike some
other examples: *the poor, the unemployed, the workshy*.
(c)   Deadjectival nouns denoting human beings: *a black, an Argentinian, a newly-wed,
a regular, an undesirable*, etc.
(d)   In predictable contexts *a canine* means either "a tooth" or "a dog"; *a strawberry and
two choc-chips* refers to "flavours of ice-cream"; *a short-black* to "coffee".

(e)   Cyclical recurrent events: *a daily, my monthly, an annual, the biennial*. Note that the last two end in *-al*: many other derived adjectives in *-al* function as zero-derived nouns, e.g. *a musical, an oral, a practical, a professional, a sessional*.

The evidence suggests

Assumption 4.8 Most, if not all, derived lexemes are listemes.

Exceptions to A4.8 are derived lexemes that are both semantically transparent – such as recent coinings – and/or rare, e.g. *holier-than-thou-like, unwashability*. There are also those few derivational affixes, like the effector nominalizer *-er/-or* and the abstract nominalizer *-ness*, which do have semantically predictable effects.

In *be giving* and *have given*, the participles are inflexional. The gerund *Giving* [*is what Christmas is all about*] and Adj [*Tiny's*] *given* [*name is Tim*] are zero-derived from them. In 25, the complement 'was broken' is ambiguous between Adj and **Pp** (past participle). The difference is that **be'**⌒Adj is STATIVE and means "The window was already broken" whereas **be'**⌒**Pp** is nonstative and means "The window got broken".

25 The window *was broken* $\Big\{$
    be' + Adj   "was already broken"
    be' + **Pp**   "got broken"

Compare 25 with 26–27 in which the Adj is stative and the V nonstative. In 27 the symbol '∦' means "is synonymous with, means the same as".

Definition 4.4 (preliminary) A is SYNONYMOUS with B, symbolically A ∦ B, only if when A is true, then B is true, and vice versa. (It follows that if A is false, then B is false, and vice versa.)

26 The window is open.
27 The window is opened ∦ The window got opened.

A stative interpretation for the V 'opened' in 27 is blocked by the semantically equivalent Adj *open*.

Language users not only know the meanings of lexemes, but also the meanings and functions of derivational morphemes – including the zero affix. This is what enables speakers to coin new words using derivational morphemes and hearers to interpret novel derivations. The fact that all derivational morphemes are listemes is properly included in A4.4. Obviously, derivational morphemes semantically relate many, perhaps all, of the lexemes in which they are found (cf. A4.2).

Assumption 4.9 All lexical stems not listemes on other grounds should be entered in the lexicon, because they provide a potential basis for neologisms.

For instance, the stem *-duce* "lead" found in the nouns *duke* and *dux* and in the verbs *abduce, adduce, conduce, deduce, educe, induce, introduce, produce, reduce, seduce, traduce, transduce*. If you were to encounter *perduce as a novel term you could interpret it in terms of *per-* "through" and *-duce* "lead" (cf. *perchance, persuade*). The lexeme **rejuvenate**' consists of a verb prefix *re-* "(do) again", a root *juven* "young" (cf. *juvenile*) and the suffix *-ate* "make" (cf. *create, facilitate, separate*). Each of these will appear in the lexicon; but so perhaps should **juvenate**' which is a potential stem for **dejuvenate* – a verb that could be used to describe the effect of HIV-AIDS or progeria (a disease in which symptoms of old age appear in a young child).

In AGGLUTINATIVE LANGUAGES a complex stem will serve as the basis for yet more complex words to a much greater extent than is the case in English. For instance, Turkish *ceplerimizdekilerdenmiş* analyses into

28 *cep*   "pocket"
   -ler   PL
   -imiz   1.PL.POSSESSSIVE
   -de   LOCATIVE "in"
   -ki   RELATIVIZER
   -ler   PL
   -den   ABLATIVE "from"
   -miş   DUBITATIVE

"[it] is/was supposedly or reportedly from (among) those that are/were in our pockets"

(Hankamer 1989:396)

Curiously, the order of morphemes in English is, except for PL, the reverse of their sequence in the Turkish word. In Turkish many affixes can reapply as in the example of *göz-lük-çü-lük-çü-lük* "the occupation of being a lobbyist for the oculist profession" based upon *göz* "eye", *-lük* "thing for", and *-çü* "person for". Some recursion is possible in English, e.g. *re-re-V* (**re**-remarry, **re**-retype, **re**-reread) and *un-un-V* (**un**-undo, **un**-uninvite) but it is more often an aspect of verbal play than serious and regular usage.[5] Instead of being a productive characteristic of English morphology as it is in Turkish, the language resists it, causing English speakers to feel uncomfortable about the repetition. For instance, adjectives that end in *-ly* do not happily take the adverbial suffix *-ly*, cf. *sillily, friendlily, worldlily*. Something else which sounds odd is attaching the effector nominalizer *-er* to a verb ending in *-er* such as *tinker, scamper, pamper* to generate *tinkerer, scamperer, pamperer*. On the other hand, we sometimes hear *putter upperer* "someone who puts up with things, puts up people" with excessive recursion. English does not welcome recursions of derivational affixes as agglutinative languages do. Hankamer has calculated that, in Turkish, a full listing of all words, including derived words (as proposed in Jackendoff 1975), would result in at least 200 billion entries – which he claims is more than a human brain could tolerate if it is to do other things than search for words. The solution would be to list all roots, inflexional and derivational morphemes, and some morphologically complex forms (though Hankamer does not identify which). What seems clear is that there is no certainty which complex stems should be included in a lexicon. The earlier suggestion for English is that all common derived words such as *legalize* should be listed but rare ones with transparent semantics need not be listed. On these criteria, certainly *gözlükçülükçülük* and almost certainly *ceplerimizdekilerdenmiş* would NOT be listed in the Turkish lexicon.

In this section I have established that the inventory of listemes includes: all lexical roots; all inflexional and derivational affixes; all non-derived lexemes; most, if not all, derived lexemes (but not inflected words); and, somewhat controversially, all lexical stems not otherwise satisfying the criteria for being a listeme. Additionally, I defined the blocking principle, gave a working definition of synonymy, and suggested that the criteria on a listeme may differ between languages.

Exercises

4.2.1 The difference between etic and emic is primarily a difference between concrete, physically manifest forms (etic) and abstract theoretical constructs (emic) which looks in the present instance "PLURAL" very much like meaning. But it is sometimes said that an utterance is the etic counterpart of emic sentence; and, of course, the English phoneme /p/ has the etic allophones [p], [pʼ], [pʰ]. (a) Does it still look as if etic categories are form and emic categories meaning? (b) Is there a correlation between emic and intensional, etic and extensional?

4.2.2 If the emic to etic correlation for *cat(s)* is as follows

     Emic   **cat′**.PL   **cat′**.S

     Etic   *cat⌢-s*   *cat*

What is the distribution of morphemes to morphs in *sheep* [PL] and *sheep* [S]?

4.2.3 Discuss the following as effector nominals: *truck-driver, butcher, butler, cleaner, cooker, lawn-mower, lawyer, mixer, toaster.*

4.2.4 Why do you think we have, in English, *drum***mer** but *percussion***ist**, and *fidd***ler** but *violin***ist**?

4.2.5 *Cherry* and *pea* were sort of back-formations. Look up their histories.

4.2.6 Identify the root and intervening stems of the verb [*to*] *waitress.*

4.2.7 Is the prefix *in-* of *invincible* the same prefix as that in: (a) *impossible*; (b) *ingressive*; (c) *illicit*; (d) *ill-conceived*; (e) *inevitable*?

4.2.8 Does the order of affixation have semantic consequences? Compare *reundoable* with *unredoable.*

4.2.9 Consider *abbot, abbess* and *abbey*. Etymologically, *abbot* derives from Latin *abbatem* (accusative of *abbas*), *abbess* from *abbatissa*, and *abbey* from *abbadia*. But does it make sense to say that for modern English the bound morph(eme) *abb-* has a specific meaning, as does *-ess*; perhaps *-ot* can be linked to the final syllable of *bigot, patriot, pilot* (except these are not now restricted to males), and *-bey* to the *-by* in place names ("inhabited place")?

4.2.10 How would you analyse into morphemes: (a) *admissible*; (b) *readable*; (c) *possible*; (d) *invincible*?

4.2.11 It is common for the meaning of novel zero-derivations to be predictable, as in the following parody.

> General Alexander Haig has contexted the Polish watchpot somewhat nuancely. How, though, if the situation decontrols can he stoppage it mountingly conflagrating? Haig, in Congressional hearings before his confirmatory, paradoxed his auditioners by abnormalling his responds so that verbs were nouned, nouns verbed, and adjectives adverbised. He techniqued a new way to vocabulary his thoughts so as to informationally uncertain anybody listening about what he had actually implicationed. (London *Guardian* February 3, 1981)

Explain how you figure out the meanings of the verbs 'contexted', 'abnormalling', 'vocabulary', the nouns 'confirmatory', 'responds', the adverb 'mountingly' and the Adv⌢V 'informationally uncertain'.

4.2.12 Describe the relationship between the homonymous nouns and verbs: *lamb, bicycle, button, chair, neck, group, stack, heap, loop.*

4.2.13 Compare the denominal verbs in **salt** *the potatoes*, **dust** *the crops*, and **dust** *the furniture*.

4.2.14 Do you think it is just accidental that the verb *father* is ambiguous in a way that the verb *mother* is not, and that there are no conventional verbs *sister, brother*?

4.2.15 How come you can *bicycle to work* and perhaps *bus to work* but not *car to work, train to work* "travel to work by train"? Discuss.

4.2.16 (a) The suffix *[N]-ology* means "the study of [N]". What is [N], and does the gloss enable you to make correct predictions about the meanings of derived lexemes such as *anthropology, ornithology, psychology,* and *phonology*?
(b) The prefix *tele-* from ancient Greek τηλε meaning "from afar" occurs in many English words, including the familiar *telephone* (stem from the Greek word meaning "sound") and *television*. Are the meanings of *telephone* and *television* truly predictable from the meanings of their component morphemes?

4.2.17 Bauer 1983:93 claims that '**a two-carred man* or **a black-shoed lady* are not possible.' Do you agree, or can you imagine a context in which one or both of these are perfectly satisfactory?

4.3   Polyword listemes: compounds, phrasal verbs, and idioms

A dictionary is a frozen pantomime.

(Bolinger 1965:567)

Phrases are polyword expressions (i.e. they consist of more than one word) that differ from listemes in that their meanings are consistently computable from their components (by processes yet to be described). We have established that almost all lexemes are listemes; in this section two criteria are described that distinguish polyword lexemes from phrases.

> *Criterion 1* A LEXEME IS A MEMBER OF A PARTICULAR LEXICAL CLASS (N, V, Adj, Adv, etc.) with the morphosyntactic specifications, distribution, functions, and class meaning typical of that lexical class. Phrases are not members of a lexical class.

It follows from Criterion 1 that lexemes often permit affixation and phrases do not.[3] In 29 the suffix -*like* scopes over the noun 'bird' and not the whole NP 'a green bird creature'. Whatever 'it' in 29 refers to is one of the class of creatures that is green and like a bird; it is not a creature-like thing in a green-like colour.

29 It's a green birdlike creature.

A non-event does not mean "not an event" – which negates the whole NP – but an "event not worthy of the name" because *non-* negates the head noun.

> *Criterion 2* LEXEMES ARE ISLANDS.
>   C2a: They prohibit lexical insertion within their boundaries.
>   C2b: They prohibit internal disjuncture (pause) when pronounced normally.
>   C2c: They prohibit extraction of any of their parts by syntactic processes.

The only exception to C2a is that an intensifying expletive can be inserted if (a) the vowel preceding the expletive is tensed and (b) a stressed syllable follows the expletive.[6]

30

		Expletive insert	Other insert
LEXEME	absolutely	abso*bloomin*lutely	*abso*ever*solutely
LEXEME	fantastic	fan*fucking*tastic	*fan*ever*sotastic
LEXEME	kangaroo	kanga*bloody*roo	*kanga*hopping*roo
PHRASE	a new house	a new *bloody* house	a new *brick* house

---

3. Because possessive -'s/s' can be suffixed to the last constituent in a NP it is a CLITIC not an inflexion; e.g. *the man with the torn overcoat's [companion], the man who left's [wife]*.

To illustrate C2b, *understandably* in 31 cannot normally contain disjuncture (pause) indicated by a slash '/'. By contrast the phrase *understandably shy* in 32 will, in an appropriate context, permit disjuncture between the lexemes.

31 *u/nderstandably, *under/standably, *understand/ably, *understandab/ly
32 understandably / shy

Thus the (a) example in 33–35 is a lexeme, (b) is a phrase.

33 (a) a blackbird   "a species of bird"
     (b) a black / bird   "a bird which is black (not some other colour)"

34 (a) a metal container   "a container for metal"
     (b) a metal / container   "a container made of metal (not some other material)"

35 (a) the man in the street   "the ordinary person"
     (b) the man / in the street   "the man who is in the street"

Disjuncture typically marks the boundary of a sense-group.[7] Consequently, the inadmissibility of disjuncture within lexemes is evidence of their semantic islandhood in contrast to phrases.
     To illustrate C2b, compare 36–38.

36 There is a $_{[N}$bird$_{N]}$ over there.
37 There is a $_{[N}$blackbird$_{N]}$ over there.
38 There is a $_{[Adj}$black$_{Adj]}$ $_{[N}$bird$_{N]}$ over there.

We can isolate the adjective 'black' from the phrase in 38 but not the component 'black-' from the compound in 37. Thus 39 is synonymous with 38, but not 37.

39 There is a bird over there which is black.

> *Definition 4.5 (preliminary).* If A is THE CONTRARY OF B it cannot be the case that both A and B are concurrently true in $M^{w,t}$.

Black and *brown* are contraries: a bird which is predominantly black cannot at the same time be predominantly brown. So, 40(a–b) are anomalous.

40 (a) *There is a brown black bird over there.
     (b) *There is a black bird over there which is brown.

In fact there are subspecies of blackbirds with brown females, thus 41 is coherent (A ⫴ B symbolizes "A is synonymous with B", D4.4).

41 There is a brown blackbird over there ⫴ There is a blackbird over there which is
                                                                                      brown

The compound *blackbird* is a lexeme. Its parts cannot be isolated for grammatical purposes in the same way that parts of phrases can be. The semantic-syntactic islandhood of the lexeme prohibits *black-* or *-bird* being cleft from it. 42(a–b) necessarily mean "Ed saw a black bird", and not "Ed saw a blackbird".

42 (a) It was black, that bird Ed saw.
   (b) It was a bird, that black thing Ed saw.

Compounds satisfy all criteria for lexemes, phrasal verbs most of them, and idioms some of them.

4.3.1 Compounds are listemes

> a oh-what-a-wicked-world-this-is-and-how-I-wish-I-could-do-something-to-make-it-better-and-nobler expression
>
> (Jerome K. Jerome, quoted in Bauer 1983:164)

Definition 4.6 Compounds are members of a particular lexical class (Criterion 1) that are composed from two or more free forms.

43 is a sample of noun compounds.

43 *chimney sweep* "one who sweeps chimneys", *play-goer* "one who goes to plays", *heavy-smoker* "one who smokes heavily", *looker-on* "one who looks on", *stay-at-home* "one who stays at home", *cheapskate* "someone who does things on the cheap, ungenerously", *night owl* [fig.] "one who stays up late at night, like an owl", *left-wing* [fig.] "people holding socialist views", *skyscraper* [fig.] "a building so tall it seems to scrape the sky", *hand-me-down* "something handed down" *girlfriend* "a friend who is a girl/woman", *bakehouse* "a place where baking is done", *bus-stop* "a place where the bus stops", *drive-in* "a place one drives into for service", *light bulb* "glass bulb containing a filament that lights up when an electrical current is passed through it", *air pump* "a pump supplying compressed air", *airgun* "a gun using compressed air" (extended to "guns using a spring"), *fighter-bomber* "a plane that is both a fighter and a bomber", *blackbird* "a species of bird in which the male is characteristically black", *eating-apple* "an apple for eating", *junk food* "appetising food with little nutritional value", *soda pop* = *soft drink* "nonalcoholic, sugary, water-based beverage", *snail mail* "regular mail as contrasted with electronic mail", *teaching profession* "the profession of teachers", *cockfight* "fight between roosters", *small talk* "talk about insignificant matters", *hairdo* "the outcome of having one's hair done", *crew cut* "hair cut very short", *Piss Christ* is the name of a photograph by Andres Serrano of a crucifix in urine, *Parkinson's Disease* "a disease discovered by P", *Kinsey Report* "the report written by K", *Valentine's Day* "day commemorating St. Valentine", *Australia Day* "day commemorating the white invasion (first settlement) of Australia", *River Thames*.

Long as this list is, it does not exhaust the different types of noun compounds.[8] In addition, there are

(a)   compound verbs, e.g. *aircondition, mass-produce, two-time;*
(b)   compound adjectives, e.g. *cut and dried, easygoing, uncalled for;*
(c)   compound adverbs, e.g. *down-under, far-off.*

Not only are there conventional compounds like those exemplified so far; there are nonce compounds like Jerome K. Jerome's Adj *oh-what-a-wicked-world-this-is-and-how-I-wish-I-could-do-something-to-make-it-better-and-nobler* quoted above.

In noun compounds, a plural suffix will usually attach to the head noun constituent of the compound if there is one; otherwise it will be suffixed to the end of the compound.

44 blackbird*s*, housewive*s*, court*s* martial, looker*s*-on, son*s*-in-law, drive-in*s*, stay-at-home*s*

When the final constituent of a noun compound is a noun other than the head constituent, the suffix is sometimes attached there, cf. *son-in-laws*. The whole compound may fall within the scope of a derivational affix, whereas the same affix attached to a homonymous phrase only scopes over the lexeme to which it is affixed. In 45 the suffix *-like* scopes over the noun *bird*; but in 46 the same suffix scopes over the noun *blackbird*.

45 It's a black *bird*-like creature.
46 It's a *blackbird*-like species.

The scope of the suffix *-like* is the stem word, whether compound or not. Notice the illegitimacy of *??It's a black bird-like species*. Birds do not constitute a species, they are a biological class, *Aves*. In 45, whatever 'it' refers to is one of the class of creatures like a bird. In 46, 'it' refers to a species like a blackbird. The scope of a prefix may, similarly, be the whole compound; it cannot be a phrase. A *non-blackbird* is something that is not a blackbird. A *non-black bird* is a bird that isn't black. The scope of the prefix *non-* is the stem word, be it compound or non-compound.

Compounds are islands. With respect to C2a (Criterion 2a), the compound *man-in-the-street* cannot be expanded into *man who is in the street* like the homonymous phrase can. *Blackmetalbird* might be "bird made of black metal" or "metal bird which is black" – both of which are phrasal paraphrases – but it cannot be "metal blackbird". Intensifying expletives can be inserted: *blackfuckingbird, man-in-the-bloody-street*. C2b as it applies to the compounds *blackbird, metal container,* and *man in the street* was demonstrated in (a) sentences of 33–35.[9] C2c was seen to apply in the discussion of 36–42.

On all possible criteria, compounds are lexemes.

No one has developed a theory that can be guaranteed to predict the meaning of a randomly selected compound lexeme from its component words. Like many other derived lexemes, the meaning of a compound is only occasionally predictable from the meanings of its components. Often, long usage obscures an earlier transparency, e.g. the Old English compounds *hlafweard* "loaf-warden" and *hlæfdiȝe* "loaf-kneader" have been reduced (and upgraded) to the opaque *lord* and *lady* respectively. Surprisingly, Downing found no difference in the complexity or ingenuity of the interpretations people offered for conventional compounds like *bullet hole* and novel ones like *pea-princess*. Interpretations given for *bullet hole* were not restricted to the typical sense "hole made by a bullet"; but included such things as "a hole in which to hide bullets", "part of a bullet-forming apparatus" (Downing 1977:820).

> *Assumption 4.10* When asked to interpret a compound out of context, people put their imagination to work. The same is true for the interpretation of any language expression.

Implausible compounds such as *fork-spoon* and *hog-pork* were judged acceptable when a person could think of something for the compound to denote (Chapter 10); e.g. a piece of cutlery that is a fork at one end and a spoon at the other could be called *a fork-spoon*. 'When soy-pork is a common dish, hog-pork will describe the genuine article' (Downing 1977:833). However, a negative relationship has to be morphologically signalled: *a cousin-chair* cannot be "a chair reserved for noncousins" (Downing 1977:824).

> *Assumption 4.11* Compounds from the categories N, Adj, V, Adv name rather than describe.

> If two meaning elements are, by their content, highly relevant to one another, then it is predicted that they may have lexical or inflectional expression [i.e. occur as a listeme], but if they are irrelevant to one another, then their combination will be restricted to syntactic expression. [...] In English we have a lexical item *walk* which means "to go on foot by taking steps". If we add the meaning "through water", we can express both meanings together in the verb *wade*. These two semantic notions may be expressed together in a single lexical item because whether one has one's feet on dry land or in water is quite relevant to the act of walking. In contrast, whether the sky is sunny or cloudy is not usually relevant to the act of walking, so the hypothesis predicts that languages will not have a separate lexical items for "walk on a sunny day" vs "walk on a cloudy day". The latter two combinations would be more likely to have syntactic expression.   (Bybee 1985:13)

> *Assumption 4.12* Something named is either stable and enduring, or else recurrent.

E.g. *a cow-tree* was described as 'a tree under which cows LIKE to stand or TEND to gather' (Downing 1977:834, *sic*). On the other hand, compounds often serve as ad-hoc names for entities or categories deemed nameworthy. Bauer 1983:164 cites some other novel compounds: *a don't-tell-me-what-to-do-look, stick-to-it-iveness, with-itness,* and *get-at-able*. The existence of such unusual compounds suggests

> *Assumption 4.13* The number of possible compounding relationships is unbounded.

This is only possible because both Speaker and Hearer presume the cooperative principle to be in operation. Hence,

Assumption 4.14 One strategy Hearer will use to interpret a compound is pattern-matching with existing compounds. Because of the boundless variety of relationships that exist between the constituents in compounds, the results of pattern recognition will be checked in the light of the compound's constituent meanings, and the context in which the compound is used.

For instance, Downing (1977:818) cites the use and correct interpretation of *apple-juice seat* recognizable from context as the only seat at which there was a glass of apple-juice.

Conventional compounds are listemes. Novel compounds, like any newly-coined derived lexemes, will not be entered in the lexicon as wholes, and so their meanings will need to be determined from the meanings of their constituent lexemes and the context. In fact, they will be subject to the same interpretative process as inflected words, phrases, and larger structures.

Exercises

4.3.1.1 How far can you generalize on the compound *redhead*?

4.3.1.2 The following words are BLENDS (cf. Lehrer 1996). Suggest how each one is derived, and offer comments on the possible meaning: (a) *smog*; (b) *brunch*; (c) *workaholic*; (d) *wargasm*; (e) *shopathon*; (f) *shampagne*. A novel kind of blend is (g) *ambisextrous*.

4.3.1.3 Does hyphenation in the graphological form define a compound?

4.3.1.4 How would you explain the following data?
my hand-*me*-down, *your* hand-*me*-down, *his* hand-*me*-down, *your* hand-**you*-down, *his* hand-**him*-down, she is a *stay-at-home*, she is a **stays-at-home*.

4.3.1.5 Many women are quite happy to be *Madam Chairman* and many speakers of English do not believe this phrase is a blatant contradiction. Explain. (This is a linguistic question and not primarily about sexual politics.)

4.3.1.6 Suggest derivations for and give meanings of (a)–(e); also, where possible, make comparisons with more familiar compounds. (a) *book-novel*; (b) *ground-flower*; (c) *time-hour*; (d) *banana-fork*; (e) *rain sock*.

4.3.1.7 Using the techniques demonstrated here, show whether or not the following are compounds: (a) black and white film, (b) black hole, (c) chain gang, (d) goal post, (e) open heart surgery, (f) best seller, (g) high rise building, (h) bank cheque (cashier's check), (i) telephone answering machine, (j) Beam me up, Scotty.

4.3.2   Phrasal verbs are compounds, but some are discontinuous

Phrasal verbs are compound verbs[10] consisting of a verb followed by a particle or two, e.g. *cut **up**, egg **on**, give **in**, look **after**, type **up**, make do **with**, cut **down on**, put **up with**, wake **up to***. They satisfy Criterion 1 in having normal verbal affixes. But some phrasal verbs create difficulties for Criterion 2 because they are DISCONTINUOUS in that object NPs can be placed between the verb and the particle, and sometimes have to be.

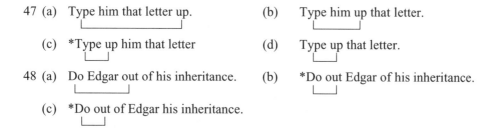

47 (a)   Type him that letter up.   (b)   Type him up that letter.

   (c)   *Type up him that letter   (d)   Type up that letter.

48 (a)   Do Edgar out of his inheritance.   (b)   *Do out Edgar of his inheritance.

   (c)   *Do out of Edgar his inheritance.

Discontinuity is mostly restricted to the placing of object noun phrases between the verb constituent and the particle constituent, cf. 47–48. The passive *by*-phrase cannot interrupt (49), nor can most adverbials (50).

49 *The onions were chopped by Max up.
50 (a)   *Max chopped quickly the onions up.
   (b)   *Ed made the story on impulse up.
   (c)   *Max chopped last night up the onions.

However, in speech, manner adverbs in -*ly* are often found between the object NP and the particle. The result is unstylish, and is avoided in the written medium.

51 (a)   Max chopped the body carefully up into little pieces.
   (b)   Ed looked the property cursorily over.
   (c)   They took the body quickly away.
   (d)   June played the men skilfully off against one another.

So the discontinuity which sets many phrasal verbs apart from other lexemes is severely restricted.
     When the parts of a phrasal verb are contiguous, they satisfy C2b – compare 53 with disjuncture between 'look' and 'up', against 54, without it.

52 Look, / up the tree! / Can you see the kookaburra?
53 ??Look / up the tree / in *Native Trees of Australia*.
54 Look up the tree / in *Native Trees of Australia*.

52 uses an adverbial prepositional phrase that directs Hearer where to look. 54 means "find the name of the tree by looking in *Native Trees of Australia*". Discontinuous instances of

phrasal verbs do not comply with C2b when a nonrestrictive relative clause appositive to
the object NP is interposed:

55 He cut the tree, / which had fallen across the road, / up into firewood.

56–57 show that C2c applies. The Adv 'up' in 56 can be cleft (56(b)), but vPrt 'up' in
57 cannot.

56 (a)   Ed climbed $_{[Adv}$up the mountain$_{Adv]}$.
   (b)   It was $_{[Adv}$up the mountain$_{Adv]}$ that Ed climbed.

57 (a)   Tom $_{[V}$chopped $_{[vPrt}$up$_{vPrt]}$ $_{V]}$ the onions.
   (b)   *It was $_{[vPrt}$up$_{vPrt]}$ the onions that Tom chopped.

Despite the name *phrasal verb* and the restricted discontinuity, phrasal verbs share most
of the characteristics of conventional compounds and, like them, are listemes. At least one
particle, *up*, has a meaning in many phrasal verbs that it does not have elsewhere: it is
completive. Compare the meaning of *cut* with *cut up*; *eat* with *eat up*; *close* with *close up*;
finish with *finish up*. In its completive sense (which will appear in the lexicon) *up* is
productively compounded with verbs to coin new phrasal verbs.

Exercises

4.3.2.1 With compound verbs, where do the verb inflexions apply?

4.3.2.2 Show that *close down* is a phrasal verb lexeme but *walk up* is not (despite the fact
it gives rise to the compound adjective/noun *walk-up*).

4.3.3   Idioms are phrasal or clausal listemes

> [W]e would be surprised to find a language which had an idiom of the form *divulge the
> information* with the meaning "spill the soup", as in *The waiter divulged the information all
> over my new suit*.
>
>   (Nunberg, Sag, and Wasow 1994:530)

Definition 4.7 An idiom is a polyword listeme that looks like a phrase or
clause and the meaning is figurative and not predictable from the literal
meanings of its constituents.

Sentential idioms are often proverbial: *It is the early bird that gets the worm. Time is
money. Birds of a feather flock together*. Idioms usually use a concrete vehicle, e.g. *spill
the beans*, to denote an abstract target – "reveal a secret". Idioms are typically used for

stylistic effect to mark an attitude or evaluation; therefore, they are often vivid, hyperbolic, or flippant.

Many idiomatic compounds readily satisfy both criteria on lexemes: e.g. the nouns *hot-dog* "frankfurter in a bun", *red herring* "diversion from the point", *man-in-the-street* "(ordinary) person". Others satisfy Criterion 1. In *rain cats and dogs* and *fight tooth and nail* the verbs 'rain' and 'fight' have their usual meaning; but the conjoined NPs have the semantic function of a manner adverb. In the case of *cats and dogs*, the interpretation cannot be derived from the components of the NP. *Fight tooth and nail* is, however, a HYPERBOLE (overstatement) and a figurative semantic extension of $_{[V}fight_{V]}\widehat{}_{[Adv}with\ tooth$ *and nail*$_{Adv]}$. The conjoined NPs have in common the semantic specification **in_a_hard_ manner**$'_{s_i}$ (the subscript identifies the semantic index) coreferenced with the morphosyntactic specification Man.Adv$_{s_i}$. There are at least three formal specifications to co-index with the latter:

(a) A context free form $_{f_j}hard$ (the subscript identifies the formal index).
(b) The context sensitive forms
    $_{f_k}cats\_and\_dogs$ when the adverb scopes over a verb meaning **rain**$'$
    $_{f_l}tooth\_and\_nail$ when the adverb scopes over a verb meaning **fight**$'$.

Nothing is lost by appealing to rules which check the co-text of an item, because context-sensitive rules will be needed for other purposes: e.g. *indicative* modifies *mood* and not *tense*; *past* modifies *tense* but not *mood*; *benign* meaning "non-cancerous" is applicable to *tumour* and nothing else (McCawley 1968b).

The idiom *by and large* superficially consists of Prep^Conj^Adj, yet it is a sentential adverb (cf. *mostly* and *more or less*) that quantifies states. In 58 it indicates the degree to which 'he is successful'.

58 $_{[Adv}$By and large$_{Adv]}$ he is successful.

It derives from a nautical expression meaning "to sail slightly off the line of the wind" hence the derived meaning "close to, but not completely". It was originally a conjunction of adjectives used as a compound adverb, compare 59.

59 He was sailing $_{[Adv}$by and large$_{Adv]}$.
   He was doing it $_{[Adv}$nice and slow$_{Adv]}$.

The syntactic specification must recognize this idiom as a degree adverb with an unusual substructure.

Weinreich 1980 Ch. 6 proposed that idioms are generated by the usual rules of syntax, and that non-terminal nodes such as VP and NP are inspected by a device searching for idioms. Jackendoff 1995, 1997 has shown that his lexical licensing theory dispenses with the need for such an idiom-matching device. Jackendoff's analysis of the idiom *kick the bucket* is the basis for 60. The subscript letters correspond to Chapter 3's numerical addresses. The postsubscript $_e$ in the semantic specification identifies the position of the person who dies (the 'EXTERNAL argument').

60 $_a$/kɪk/ $_b$/ðə/ $_c$/bʌkət/ —— $[_{VP}\ _a[V]\ [_{NP}\ _b[Det]\ _c[N]\ ]\ ]_h$ —— $[DIE\ ([\ ]_e)]_h$

In terms of a Chapter 3 network, the (partial) lexicon–encyclopedia entry is shown in Fig. 4.1.

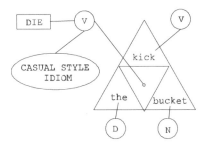

Figure 4.1 The lexicon+encyclopedia entry for
kick the bucket, presented as a network

Once again we see that the separation of the three categories of specification is advantageous because it enables us to readily incorporate idioms into the lexicon, and relate them to other components of the grammar.

There are problem idioms, though. *The straw that breaks the camel's back* is a complex NP that can be interpreted in terms of *the last/final straw*. Although the breaking of a vertebrate's back is a recognized metaphor for disaster (Chapter 9), the reference to a camel is opaque. (There are similar proverbs in other languages. This one is first recorded in Dickens's *Dombey and Son* and is apparently based on the now archaic *It is the last feather that breaks the horse's back*.) The idiom functions as a NP, which is not a lexical category. However, proper names such as *John*, *the Himalayas*, and *the Shah of Persia* also function as NPs, and some are polyword idioms. Their morphosyntactic category is Proper Name. Pronouns like *they* and *who* also function as NPs; their morphosyntactic category is Pronoun. In this vein, the lexicon should recognize Nominal Idiom as the syntactic category of *the straw that breaks the camel's back*, and Verbal Idiom as the category of *kick the bucket*.

Idioms containing a verb all have normal affixation on the verb – just like phrasal verbs. None of the other components in these idioms vary their affixes, though.

61 (a1) shot the breeze   (a2)   shooting the breeze*(s)

   (b1) kicks the bucket   (b2)   kicked the bucket*(s)

   (c1) It'll rain cats and dogs   (c2)   It rained *(a cat and a dog)

   (d1) blew the lid off   (d2)   blows *(some) lid*(s) off

   (e1) the straw that is breaking the   (e2)   ?? a straw that will break a
         camel's back   camel's back

Because idioms are lexemes, they can sometimes be modified in a similar way to other lexemes in their class; cf.

62 (a) a cold *hot-dog*
   (b) the ordinary *man-in-the-street*
   (c) Jed *kicked the bucket* after a long illness.
   (d) We had a smoke and *shot the breeze* for an hour.
   (e) It was *the last straw*, the one *that broke the camel's back*.

But compare 63 with 64.

63 (a) It rained }
       They fought } very hard.

(b)   It rained }
       They fought } harder.

64 (a) *It rained very cats and dogs.   (b)   ??It rained more cats and dogs. [?OK
                                                   if jocular]
   *They fought very tooth and nail.   *They fought more tooth and nail.

64 can be explained as a violation of Criterion 2 on the islandhood of lexemes – but only
if *rain* and *fight* – which have their usual meanings – constitute part of the listeme. Since
we earlier preferred a lexicon with redundancies (such as listing all stems) against a very
parsimonious one, it is consistent to list *rain cats and dogs* and *fight tooth and nail* in their
entirety.

   Many idioms are discontinuous in that they have open slots, e.g. *take NP to the
cleaners, pull NP's leg*. These challenge Criterion 2 on lexemes, just as phrasal verbs do.
However, contiguous idioms are islands that prohibit lexical insertion and disjuncture
within their boundaries (C2a–b). 65–66 cannot be interpreted as idioms.

65 ??They shot the light breeze.
66 She kicked the empty bucket.

Predictably, the idiom is maintained when a intensifying expletive is inserted: *She kicked
the fucking bucket* can mean "she died". Nevertheless, internal modification of the idiom
is only possible if the figure is maintained, intensified, or made more pertinent to the case
in hand – compare 67 and 68.

67 take full advantage of
68 take unfair advantage of

This observation is a truism, because it seems to be impossible to legislate the boundaries
of permissible modifications to idioms. Yet, 69 can only be taken literally. 70 can be
idiomatic if Tom has only one leg. 71 might go through as an idiom if it can be recognized
from the context that the joke played upon Tom tormented rather than teased him.

69 Tom had his left leg pulled.
70 Tom had his one remaining leg pulled.
71 Tom's leg was stretched to breaking point.

Idioms are syntactic islands, subject to very few syntactic processes such as change from active to passive (or vice versa in the case of passive idioms like *the die is cast, be/get caught short, be made for each other*). Although idioms such as *shoot the breeze* "chat" and *kick the bucket* can be questioned (72), they cannot be passivized (73), individual constituents cannot be cleft from them (74), and coordinate omission of a constituent is impossible (75). In 74–75 A ⫤ B symbolizes "A is not synonymous with B".

72 Did Harry finally kick the bucket, then?
73 *The breeze was shot by the boys.
74 It was the bucket that Ed kicked ⫤ Ed died
75 The cow kicked the milkmaid and the bucket ⫤ The cow kicked the milkmaid
    and died

Discontinuous idioms of the type *take NP to the cleaners, pull NP's leg* will submit to passivization (76), or being cleft apart (77), or permit coordinate omission (gapping, 78), all of which sets them apart from other lexemes.

76 Tom's hair was pulled a little, and his leg a great deal.
77 It was Tom's leg, not his neck, that was pulled.
    [Meaning "Tom thought he was going to be hanged,
    but it turned out to be a practical joke on him"]
78 (a) Jim held his horses and Martha her breath.
    (b) Martha held her breath, and Jim his horses.

Although the weight of evidence requires that polyword idioms be listed in the lexicon, they fit the two criteria on lexemes little better than square pegs fit round holes.

We turn briefly to other semantic aspects of idioms. There are often clusters of idioms with similar or related meanings. Those in 79 all mean "reveal a secret".

79 (a) spill the beans
    (b) let the cat out of the bag
    (c) $\left\{\begin{matrix} \text{take} \\ \text{blow} \end{matrix}\right\}$ the lid off
    (d) blow the whistle on

But there are different contexts in which they are likely to be used: (a) might be appropriate to use in situations where a person is revealing some personal information about someone else, while (b–d) might be used to talk of revealing secrets about governmental corruption. 80 implies that Harry is upset and perhaps embarrassed as much as angry. 81 suggests he is spoiling for a fight. 82 implies that he was unable to contain his anger.[11]

80 Harry got hot and bothered about being passed over for promotion.
81 Harry was bristling with anger at being passed over for promotion.
82 Harry blew his stack at being passed over for promotion.

Gibbs 1990 reports experimental confirmation of acceptable and unacceptable sequences among the idioms; e.g. 83 is fine, but the sequence of events reported in 84 is incoherent.

83 John's bad manners rubbed Sally up the wrong way, and started to get on her nerves,
    but she didn't blow her top.
84 ?*John's bad manners made Sally blow her top, and started to rub her up the wrong
    way so that he got on her nerves.

There are no meaning differences among the options in 85–87.

85 blow the $\left\{ \begin{array}{l} \text{whistle} \\ \text{gaff} \end{array} \right\}$ on

86 this is not getting the baby its $\left\{ \begin{array}{l} \text{dress} \\ \text{bottle} \\ \text{bonnet} \end{array} \right\}$

87 build $\left\{ \begin{array}{l} \text{castles} \\ \text{palaces} \end{array} \right\}$ in the $\left\{ \begin{array}{l} \text{air} \\ \text{clouds} \\ \text{heavens} \\ \text{sky} \end{array} \right\}$

Such idioms are figurative expressions that encourage spontaneous variations which are interpreted by relating them to a standard form of the idiom. In this way, idioms leak out of the lexicon.

All idioms are figurative and there is experimental evidence for simultaneous processing of both literal and figurative meaning of idioms (Gibbs 1990:427f). He further suggests that children find it easier to learn decomposable idioms like *button your lips* "keep quiet" where there are useful clues available from the meanings of its parts, than nondecomposable idioms like *kick the bucket* and *shoot the breeze* whose components reveal nothing about their idiomatic meaning. Obviously a lexicon cannot be expected to hold all the figurative expressions in a language, since novel ones are often produced: this is one of the more creative aspects of normal language use. *Bread and butter* has a literal meaning "bread and butter", and also a figurative meaning "source of income"; but it is uncertain whether the latter should be entered into the lexicon as an idiom. It is similarly doubtful that all the figurative uses of, say, *strong* should be listed separately in a lexicon:

88 (a) strong candidate
    (b) strong beer
    (c) this magazine's strong stuff
    (d) he's strong on Sanskrit phonology

Whereas we have been able to refer to criteria for deciding which compound and phrasal verb lexemes should be listed in the dictionary, these criteria apply only loosely to idiomatic polyword expressions. Most will certainly be listed in the lexicon. The meanings of a few, like those of other figurative expressions, will have to be determined from the meanings of their constituents and common ground.

Exercises

4.3.3.1 The etymology of *rain cats and dogs* is obscure; the most plausible suggestion is that *cats and dogs* is a reinterpretation of Greek *catadupa* "cataract, waterfall". If correct, this would be a case of FOLK ETYMOLOGY. (a) One kind of folk etymology is re-analysis of the nouns that are today *apron, adder, orange* (and, if you are Australian, *ocker*), *nickname,* and *pea.* (b) Another example is *I could of done it.* (c) A third kind is exemplified by the distress call *Mayday,* the score *love* in tennis, the phrase *check mate* in chess, and the compound (Australian) noun *chaise-lounge.* For all (a,b,c), find the original forms and explain what probably happened.

4.3.3.2 Create a partial lexicon-encyclopedia network for *shoot the breeze* (cf. Fig. 4.1).

4.3.3.3 Expressions like *as old as Methuselah, as old as the hills,* and *as dry as a bone* are similes that have become clichés. What distinguishes a cliché from an idiom?

4.3.4   Polyword listemes: conclusions

In §4.3, on the basis that all nonderived lexemes and most derived lexemes are listemes, we have established two criteria for lexemes against which to test compounds, phrasal verbs, and polyword idioms. Except for a handful of novel examples, the meanings of compounds, phrasal verbs, and idioms cannot be correctly determined from the meanings of their component words – they therefore need to be listed in the lexicon. To what extent are they like the majority of lexemes? Compounds have all the attributes of a typical member of one or another morphosyntactic class and they exhibit semantic, syntactic, and prosodic islandhood – just like any other lexemes. Many phrasal verbs and some superficially phrasal or clausal idioms can be discontinuous. This can lead to difficulties in morphosyntactic assignment and it looks like violation of the islandhood constraints on lexemes. Nonetheless, those constraints invariably apply to contiguous phrasal verbs and contiguous idioms; and there are strong constraints on the grammatical processes than do apply to their discontinuous counterparts. All in all, phrasal verbs, phrasal and clausal idioms are more like lexemes than like phrases, and there can be no doubt that they are listemes.

4.4   Sound symbolism

> I caught this morning morning's minion, king-
> > dom of daylight's dauphin, dapple-dawn-drawn Falcon, in his
> > > riding
> > Of the rolling underneath him steady air, and striding
> High there, how he hung upon the rein of a wimpling wing

In his ecstasy! then off, off forth on swing,
  As a skate's heel sweeps smooth on a bow-bend: the hurl and
    gliding
Rebuffed the big wind. My heart in hiding
Stirred for a bird, – the achieve of, the mastery of the thing!
  (Hopkins 'The Windhover' ll.1–10, 1877)

Human beings often seek to explain things that confront them in terms of causal relations. Over the ages, many scholars have believed there is a causal relation between word forms and their original meanings. The study of word history is called ETYMOLOGY meaning "the study of true form" because it was supposed that the original denotation of a word somehow gave rise to its original form "naturally", such that the form–meaning correlation was transparently obvious and did not need to be learned. This hypothesis became known as the NATURALIST HYPOTHESIS. Opposing naturalism is CONVENTIONALISM, which claims that the relationship between meaning and form is entirely arbitrary but at the same time conventional because it needs to be learned from the language community and cannot be directly perceived from the denotatum. The classic discussion of these opposing hypotheses (a.k.a. the *physis–nomos* controversy) is to be found in Plato's dialogue *Cratylus* c.385 BCE. A problem for conventionalism is to explain how the original correlation between meaning and form became conventionalized, a question we explored in Chapter 3. The naturalist explanation for the spread of words through a community is that people perceive the natural connection between a word and its meaning. But how does a naturalist explain that a canine animal is called *dog* in English, *chien* in French, *Hund* in German, *pies* in Polish, *ájá* in Yoruba, *kare* in Hausa, *mbwa* in Swahili, etc.? In *Cratylus*, Plato's mouthpiece Socrates says that different communities find different forms suitable – just as different craftsmen fashion a particular kind of tool or utensil in different ways. Let's allow that suitability is a matter of cultural taste, but the question remains how does the naturalist believe that the form of a word is naturally related to its denotatum?

   The answer lies with SOUND SYMBOLISM. For instance, in *Cratylus*, Socrates suggests that the phone [r] represents motion, [s] and other fricatives 'imitate what is windy', [l] expresses smoothness, etc. Plato's degree of confidence in this foundation is indicated by having Socrates say: 'I think my notions about the primary words are quite outrageous and ridiculous, though I have no objection to imparting them to you if you like, and I hope that if you can think of anything better, you will tell me' (426b). These phones certainly do not consistently have the properties Socrates claims for them throughout the whole vocabulary of any language anywhere. Consider *smooth*: it has fricatives at both ends, but it does not denote nor connote windiness. *Lollop, laugh, hall*, and *toll* all contain [l], but none has a sense of smoothness. The [r] in *rust, rot*, and *round* imparts no sense of motion to them. Indeed, when arguing against naturalism in 434e–435c of the *Cratylus,* Socrates himself cites counterexamples like these to force the conclusion that the form–meaning correlation in a word must be conventional and arbitrary – since it does not matter what the form of a word is, he says, if its meaning is 'sanctioned by custom and convention'.

   Some sound symbolism is what Rhodes 1994 calls 'wild', when people try to directly mimic sounds e.g. saying *The duck went* /kwæʔkwæʔ/ rather than conventionalizing it to the semi-wild /kwækwæk/ or the fully 'tame' *The duck quacked*. The vowel æ is laryngealized, which is not normal in the phonology of English. Other wild forms (from cartoons and graffiti) also show abnormal phonology, e.g. *phzz, hmm, pting, bwang, fwee(t/p), shtoing, ZZZzzzz, Aaaauuugh* (cf. Oswalt 1994). However, the vast majority of sound symbolism is language-specific and conventional, not wild. It is one form of ICONICITY in language (Chapter 9).[12] In sound symbolism, the form of the language expression mimics some aspect of the denotatum; for that reason it is sometimes referred to as 'mimesis' (Bolinger 1992).

Definition 4.8 ONOMATOPOEIC words mimic sounds.

Onomatopoeic words differ from language to language and obey the phonological conventions of the language in which they occur: English *cockadoodledoo*, French *cocorico*, German *kikeriki*, Japanese *kokekokkoo* are translation equivalents. In a kind of metonymy (Chapter 5), other onomatopoeic words name the denotatum by mimicking the sound that it makes, e.g. English *cuckoo*, Hausa *babur* or *butubutu* "motorbike", Hunanese *niao* "cat", Tzeltal *lohp* "gulp, large swallow of liquid". The meanings of onomatopoeic words in an unknown language cannot be accurately predicted from the form. However, once the meaning is known, the form–meaning correlation is often recognizable. Check the examples just given, and the Tzeltal and English pairs in Table 4.2.

	Tzeltal (Mayan; cf. Berlin 1968)		**English**
"squirts of liquid"	b'ihš	piss
"sound emitted from blows on metal object"	ćan	chang, clang
"blows, cuts with machete"	ćehp	chip
"sound emitted from vibrating object (e.g. bells) due to blows"	ćin	ching, ting
"drops of liquid on a hot object"	ćuh	hiss
"cries of ducks"	c'ihp	cheep
"sound from blows on metal"	kan	clang
"action, sound, of drawing bow across strings of a violin, etc."	kić	screech
"items crushed in fist"	mohč	mash
"cries of geese, frogs"	pehp	peep
"sounds of horn, trumpet"	pihp	beep

Figure 4.2 Onomatopoeia compared in two unrelated languages

In many languages 'stops are used for abrupt sounds and acts, and continuants for continuing sounds and acts, fricatives are used for quick audible motion of an object through the air, nasals are used for ringing, reverberating sounds' (Hinton, Nichols, and Ohala 1994a:9f).[13] Stop phonemes word initially or word finally tend to mark abruptness, the voiced ones being correlated with louder or larger noises than voiceless ones. Compare the pairs in 89.

89 peep–beep, ping–bang, ting–ding, phut–thud, w(h)ack–w(h)oosh

Final nasals and fricatives tend to mark continuing sounds, cf. *boom, dong, bang, splash, w(h)oosh*, etc. The names for iterated acts and events are usually multisyllabic, cf. *ding-dong, ring-ring, wiggle-waggle*; Japanese *katya-katya* "hard objects such as keys hit each other and make a variety of noises", *gyoro-gyoro* "to look around inquisitively and indeterminately with eyes bulging out", *pyoko-pyoko* "something light flip-flops" (Hamano 1994). Lengthening is used as an iconic marker of duration, intensity, or expansiveness: e.g. the English adjectives *long* and *bad* may be extended to double or triple their normal length to indicate something very very long or very very bad. Childs 1994 contrasts Gbaya (North Volta-Congo) *dir* "a rumble like thunder" with the lengthened *dirrr* "a long rolling rumble like thunder or like an earthquake"; *feεε* "a long breath of air" contrast *feε* "a breath of air", Vai (Western Mande) *cɔ́ɔ́ɔ́* 'descriptive of liquid pouring in a steady stream'. High pitch, rapid delivery, and increased amplitude is characteristically used for enthusiasm, perhaps because it is a natural effect of excitement. These variations of the norm are iconic because the form of expression presents a sound picture of the meaning. Although such principles of imitative word formations apply across languages, the particular morphological forms that result from them are language-specific. Despite it being obvious from the inspection of onomatopoeic words that sound symbolism motivates the form – meaning correlation for them, the meaning is NOT predictable from the form.

> *Assumption 4.15* Onomatopoeic words are listemes that have to be learned like any others.

Phonesthesia is the kind of sound symbolism that Socrates in *Cratylus* (426d–427b) suggests as the basis for the naturalist hypothesis.

> *Definition 4.9* PHONESTHEMES are phoneme clusters that recur in words from one or two lexical classes, and which have a common element of meaning.

All languages have phonesthetic networks which differ from language to language. Consider the following examples from English. Some are word onsets, others are stressed rhymes (word endings).

90 /kl-/   clack, clam, clamp, clang, clank, clap, clash, clasp, clatter, click, clip, clobber, [slang] clock, clop, clout, club

The verbs in 90 have a common semantic element of "sharp contact".

91 /kl-/   clag, clamber, clamp, clasp, claw, clay, clench, climb, clinch, cling, clod, clog, clot, cloy, clutch

The nouns and verbs in 91 all pertain to "clinging".

92 /gl-/   glacé, glade, glamour, glance, glare, glass, glaze, gleam, glimmer, glimpse, glint, glisten, glister, glitter, gloaming, gloom, gloss, glow, glower

The nouns or verbs in 92 involve something "eye-catching" because of the emission, reflection, or passage of light.

93 /gr-/   greet [dialect for "wail"], grim, grime, grin [archaic sense "bare the teeth in threat"], gripe, grisly, grizzle, groan, [colloquial] gross, grotty, grouchy, grouse, growl, grudge, gruesome, gruff, grumble, grumpy, grunge, grunt

The verbs and adjectives in 93 are deprecatory words.

94 /fl-/   flack, flag, flail, flame, flap, flare, flash, flay, flee, flick, flicker, flinch, fling, flip, flirt, flit, flood, flop, flounce, flounder, flourish, flow, fluent, flurry, flush, fluster, flutter, flux, fly

The words in 94 are mostly verbs, and all suggest "a sudden or violent movement".

95 /-æš/   clash, crash, dash, flash, gash, gnash, lash, mash, slash, smash, thrash, trash

All of these rhymes in 95 occur in verbs signifying "violent impact". The set extends to some words in /-ɒš/: *quash, squash, cosh, slosh.*

96 /-ʌmp/   bump, chump, clump, crump. dump, flump (down), frump, hump, jump, lump, plump, pump, rump, slump, stump, sump, thump.

    /-ʌm/   bum, [M]drum, dumb, glum, gum, [M]hum, numb, plum, slum, [M]strum, [M]thrum, thumb, tum

    /-ʌmbl/   bumble, fumble, grumble, humble, mumble, rumble, stumble, tumble

All the words in 96 have a semantic component of "dull, heavy, untidy action"; those in [M]-*um* pertain to music making.

97 /-ætə/   batter, chatter, clatter, natter, patter, scatter, shatter, smatter(ing), spatter, splatter, tatter(ed), yatter

    /-ɪtə/   flitter, fritter, glitter, jitter, litter, skitter, titter, twitter, witter

    /-ʌtə/   clutter, flutter, scutter, sputter, splutter, stutter

97 are all verbs signifying a "formless collection of iterated things, actions, events." In addition, *-itter* words suggest "bittiness", and *-utter* words suggest "untidyness, ungainliness, imperfection". Similar are: *bicker, dicker, flicker, snicker; potter, totter; dodder; shudder; stagger, swagger; snigger.*

    In English, phonesthemes are either

(a)   An initial consonant cluster, e.g. *gl-* and *fl-*.

(b)   Rhymes commencing with a stressed syllable, e.g. *-ASH, -UMBle, -ATter, -ITter, -UTter,* that recur in words from just one or two lexical classes.

Phonesthetic words may be either monosyllabic or disyllabic, and the second syllable of disyllabic phonesthetic words is either a consonant or an unstressed vowel. Ignoring syllable boundaries, the general structure of phonesthetic words in English is 98:

98   CvC(V)   C = one or more consonants
                                           v = vowel with primary stress
                                          (V) = optional unstressed vowel

      C-   -vC(V)

Either the onset C- or the rhyme -vC(V), or both, may be phonesthemes. It is notable that:

(a)   Phonesthemes form incomplete syllables.
(b)   No phonestheme may contain a morpheme boundary within it.

It seems probable that phonesthesia was first motivated by onomatopoeia: imitate a dog growling and you make a [gr] sound. But a phonestheme can function equally well from a purely arbitrary symbolic basis – e.g. the *gl-* phonestheme of 92 must have developed in the pattern of some prototype word. Whatever the original basis for the development of a phonestheme, the words instantiating it provide a pattern for new additions; and one member of a phonesthetic set can be responsible for the development of a subset centred on its peculiar semantics.

    Linguists disagree about the morphological status of phonesthemes. Some (e.g. Bolinger 1950:130 and Marchand 1969:403) believe they are morphemes, others (e.g. Matthews 1974:15f) don't. Phonesthemes obviously contribute to the structure of words, and comply with Hockett's definition of a morpheme as 'the smallest individually meaningful element in the utterances of a language' (1958:123). However, they fall into all the most troublesome areas of morphological analysis:

(a)   Phonesthemes have a vaguer and more subjective meaning than do most morphemes.
(b)   Their phoneme sequences occur in many words with no hint of the relevant meaning. For example there is a large number of words beginning with /gr-/ that have no identifiable characteristic in common, e.g. *grace, grade, graft, grail, grain, grammar, grand, grant, grape, graph, grass, grateful, grave, gravitate, graze, grease, great, greed, green, greet, grey, grieve, grill, groin, groom, groove, group, grow.* Others do: *grab, grapple, grasp, grip, grit (one's teeth), grope* are all verbs that include as part of their sense "take a firm hold". *Grate, grind, grub* are verbs meaning "to create or gather little bits"; the noun *grit* seems to fit here, too. So we have uncovered at least three homophonous /gr-/ phonesthemes, as well as a large set of exceptions to all three classes.
(c)   Phonesthemes consist of incomplete syllables, and combine with word remnants that have no independent status as morphemes; some of the remnants are *b-, ch-, d-, h-, j-, l-, r-; -ack, -ag, -ail, -ame, -ick, -ip, -op, -ux.*

> *Assumption 4.16* Because phonesthemes contribute to the structure and meaning of vocabulary items in a similar manner to bound morphemes, they too must be listemes.

The difference between phonesthesia and SYNESTHESIA is that phonesthemes are language-specific whereas synesthesia is a cross-language phenomenon.

Definition 4.10 'Synesthetic sound symbolism is the process whereby certain vowels, consonants, and suprasegmentals are chosen to consistently represent visual, tactile, or proprioceptive properties of objects, such as size or shape. For example, segments such as palatal consonants and high vowels are frequently used for diminutive forms and other words representing small objects. Expressive intonation patterns are also used synesthetically, as in the case of deep voice and vowel lengthening in speaking of large objects.' (Hinton, Nichols, and Ohala 1994b:4)

Synesthesia is best explained by Ohala 1994:326: 'sound symbolism is a manifestation of a much larger ethological phenomenon that is also seen in the vocal communication and certain facial expressions of other species.' In nonhumans, the sounds made by a confident aggressor (or one which wants to appear so) are typically harsh and have a low F_0 (= fundamental frequency). Submissive or non-threatening individuals utter cries with a high F_0. F_0 is correlated with the size of the larynx (syrinx in birds) and hence with body mass. It follows that among humans and animals, high F_0 correlates with smallness, deference, appeasement; low F_0 correlates with assertiveness, authority, confidence, and aggression. In a cross-language survey, Ultan 1978 found almost 90 per cent of the languages he sampled had diminutives marked by high front vowels. High tones and high frequency consonants are also associated with high frequency sounds, small size, sharpness, and rapid movement; low tones and low frequency consonants are associated with low frequency sounds, large size, softness, and heavy, slow movements.[14] Thus in English, a high front vowel is used to mark narrowness or smallness, and a low frequency open vowel the opposite – particularly in nonce terms and verbal play; cf. Table 4.3.

/ɪ/, /iː/	/aɪ/,/æ/,/ʌ/, /ɒ/,/ou/
incy-wincy, itsy-bitsy, teeny-weeny	*ginormous*
slim	*fat*
chip [of wood]	*chunk, chop*
stick	*trunk, bole* [of a tree]
piddle	*puddle*
trickle	*flood*

Table 4.3 The semantics of vowels

However, in no language is this a consistent trait through the vocabulary, e.g. *little* may contrast with *large*, but *big* and *small* are out of line. And contrary to most universalist claims, Diffloth 1994 finds that in the Mon-Khmer language Bahnar

99 high vowels   /i/, /u/   correlate with "enormous" or "big"
    high-mid vowels   /e/, /o/   correlate with "big"
    low-mid vowels   /ɛ/, /ɔ/   correlate with "small"

He explains

> In the articulation of high vowels, the tongue occupies a much larger volume in the mouth
> than it does for low vowels. [...] In this perspective, two different languages may easily use
> the same phonetic variable (vowel height) to convey the same range of sensations (size), and
> come up with exactly opposite solutions, both being equally iconic. [...] Iconicity can be
> both physiologically motivated and culturally relative at the same time.   (p. 113)

This is an important consideration for cognitive semantics (Chapter 9).

In many African, Australian, and Asian languages there are IDEOPHONES (or
EXPRESSIVES, Japanese *gion-gitaigo*). They form a large part of the vocabulary, as much
as 25 per cent in Nupe (Benue-Congo, Childs 1994).

> *Definition 4.11* An ideophone is 'A vivid representation of an idea in sound.
> A word, often onomatopoeic, which describes a predicate, qualicative or
> adverb in respect to manner, colour, smell, action, state, or intensity. The
> ideophone is in Bantu a special part of speech, resembling to a certain extent
> in function an adverb.' (Doke 1935:118)[15]

This holds for other languages, too. As with imitative sound symbolism, in many languages
ideophones display aberrant phonological features, e.g. in Hausa most segments are CV,
but ideophones are typically CVC (Childs 1994). In Yir-Yoront (Australian) ideophones
are 'based on the phonetic inventory found in ordinary words plus and minus a few sounds,
and with expanded phonotactic possibilities' (Alpher 1994:162). Ideophones are often set
apart by a preceding pause and accompanied by a paralinguistic gesture. They tend to be
used in informal styles and serve individual expressiveness. Some examples:

100   Bahnar (Mon-Khmer, Diffloth 1994)
       /blɔɔŋ-blɔɔŋ/   "numerous reflections caused by rays of light on a small object"
       /blɔɔŋ-blɛɛɛw/   "numerous reflections caused by a single ray of light on a small
                        shiny object"
       /təbriil/   "pair of big spherical objects"
       /təbrɛɛl/   "pair of small spherical objects"
       /jəhuuh/   "something large, gaping, and awe-inspiring"
       /jəhooh/   "something large and gaping"
       /jəhɔɔh/   "something small and gaping"

101   Yir-Yoront (Australian, Alpher 1994)
       chichichi   "of a dog running"
       churr   "of spearing a man"
       fffft   "of blowing a fire"
       lhop   "of being swallowed by the Rainbow Serpent"
       pill   "of shooting star's flight"
       pillii   "of woman's sexual arousal"
       thak   "of a sudden strike"

The similarity of ideophones to adverbials can be illustrated from Yir-Yoront:

> *Chor* (of splitting or ripping open) is recorded with several different verbs: *Chor yeng 'y* "chor! I cut [*yeng*] it [the belly] open," *Ngerr chor yiyawrrnh 'l* "the belly [*ngerr*] split open, chor!" *Ngul chor, anhth yawrronl ungh, thaw maq marrpiy* "then [*ngul*] chor! where [he] opens [*yawrronl*] it [*ungnh*] up, [he] tore [*marrpiy*] the mouth [*thaw*] at the bottom [*maq*]." *Chor* occurs verblessly (see below) in *Purrthurr 'y yapa, chor, chor ...lalpuym* "I put it down [*purrthurr*] in the leaves [*yapa*], cut it up, and [tied it up] in a bundle [*lalpuym*]."
>
> (Alpher 1994:167)

Alpher says that the use of the ideophone *chor* in place of a verb leaves the appropriate action to be inferred.

In this section we have reviewed semantic aspects of sound symbolism: onomatopoeia, phonesthesia, synesthesia, and ideophones. Every language has some listemes based on sound symbolism. All tame and semi-wild onomatopoeic words are listemes, but not wild ones. Phonesthemes and ideophones are listemes. Synesthesia will be noted as encyclopedic information – an attribute of listemes sharing some phonetic attribute.

Exercises

4.4.1 Try to match the onomatopoeic words (1–8) from languages other than English with their meanings (a–h).

(a) thunder (crash)

(b) zigzag; every which way

(c) head over heels; tottering, stumbling

(d) thunder (boom)

(e) insistent rapping on the door

(f) pop-pop, sound of fried millet or a motorbike

(g) jouncing from side to side

(h) rope going taut

(1) hɔlithɛli

(2) kpuk-kpuk-kpuk

(3) qi

(4) ɔliali

(5) pô?-pô?

(6) t'um·   ([t'] is ejective)

(7) túlipāli

(8) t'o·x̱

4.4.2 What other voice qualities do you think might have a natural rather than an arbitrary basis? Hinton, Nichols, and Ohala (1994b) identify a category of corporeal sound symbolism. This includes involuntary sounds like sneezes (*Achoo!*), shrieks of pain (*Ouch! Aaaugh!*), coughs, the effects of diseases such as colds and emphysema, the effect of emotional stress such as excitement or fear. (a) Do these fit into the sound system of the language, do you think? (b) Do speakers make any deliberate use of any of them?

4.4.3 What differences do you see between onomatopoeia, phonesthesia, and ideophones?

4.4.4 Discuss which of the following can be abnormally lengthened to indicate "very very ...": *good, tall, short, little, small, tiny, gross.*

4.4.5 You might want to discuss the following. In many languages high pitch and reduced amplitude is a mark of deference; the high pitch very probably mimics the pitch of child's voice, and traditionally children are subservient to adults. It is also possibly a mimicking of a woman's rather than a man's voice because, until recently, in most societies women have been subservient to men. Ohala 1994 explains sexual dimorphism in humans as follows: until puberty, boys and girls have similar voice quality; at puberty, the male larynx grows to about 1½ times the size of the woman's, and concomitantly lowers to make the man's vocal tract 15-20 per cent longer than a woman's. Because this occurs at the same time facial hair develops on a male, for which the best explanation is so that the male can make a better aggressive display (cf. the facial hair on other male primates, a lion's mane, the antlers on a deer), Ohala hypothesizes that the deeper voice of the male was motivated to make him appear bigger for purpose of aggressive display.

4.5 Summary

The goal of semantic theory is to assign a semantic specification to every expression in the object language (A4.1) and to account for semantic relationships between language expressions (A4.2). Towards achieving that goal, this chapter identified which kinds of morphological items are listemes. We concluded that the English lexicon should include all roots (A4.3), all inflexional and derivational morphemes (A4.4), almost all lexemes including conventional compounds, phrasal verbs, and phrasal or clausal idioms – but excluding novel derivations, all tame and semi-wild onomatopoeic and phonesthetic items, and probably all morphological stems as well. In other languages there may be some differences: not all languages have inflexional morphology; the lexicon of an agglutinative language might not list all derived lexemes and stems; some languages will list ideophones, and so forth.

This chapter has identified morphological sources for listemes. In the next chapter, Chapter 5, we look at other sources for which the motivation is connotation (D3.6). Chapter 5 focuses on the power that words have and the semantic effects that arise therefrom. This includes a discussion of and explanation for jargon.

● Key words and phrases:

affix	citation form
allomorph	clausal listeme
back-formation	cliché
blend	clitic
blocking principle (D4.3)	compound (D4.6)
bound form (D4.2)	contrary (D4.5)

conventional compound
conventionalist hypothesis
derivational morphology
discontinuity
disjuncture (pause)
effector (agent) nominal
emic
end-clipping
etic
etymology
folk etymology
fore-clipping
free form (D4.2)
iconicity (mimesis)
ideophone (expressive) (D4.11)
idiom (D4.7)
infix
inflexional morphology
islandhood
lexical gap
listeme
lexeme
morph

morpheme (D4.1)
morphology
naturalist hypothesis
novel compound
onomatopoeia (D4.8)
(phrasal verb) particle
phonestheme (D4.9)
phrasal verb
polyword listeme
prefix
productive derivational process
reanalysis
root
semantic shift
semantic island
sound symbolism
stem
suffix
synesthesia (D4.10)
synonymy (D4.4)
syntactic island
zero-derivation (conversion)
zero morph

● Essential terms for discussing morphology were introduced: root, stem, affix, lexeme.
● Free form was defined (D4.2).
● The minimal lexeme is a free morpheme (A4.5) and every nonderived lexeme is a listeme (A4.6).
● Table 4.1 contrasted inflexional with derivational morphology.
● Inflexion adds the meaning of some secondary grammatical category to that of the basic lexeme, producing related forms of the same stem lexeme. The combination of stem plus inflexion is semantically transparent. Inflected words are therefore not listemes (A4.7).
● Derivation produces new lexemes. Derivational morphology is often irregular, inconsistent, unsystematic, and sometimes subject to individual variation. The combination of stem and derivational morpheme is often semantically opaque. The derived lexeme, once constructed, attains independence from its derivational origins by being recognized as a listeme in its own right. We concluded that all common derived lexemes should be listed, but not rare ones with transparent semantics. Unfortunately, the grounds for deciding which lexemes are rare enough to be excluded from the lexicon will always be arbitrary.
● The blocking principle was shown to be a constraint, not a prohibition.
● It is sometimes possible to isolate morphemes such as the *ea-* and *-st* of *east* for which there is no semantic or other grammatical payoff. They are not among the inventory of listemes.

• Zero-derivation (conversion) results when a morpheme with no associated morph attaches to an existing lexeme, changing its meaning and causing it to shift lexical class and become another lexeme.

• A derived lexeme attains independence from its derivational origins by being recognized as an island, an independent lexeme. Eventually, this obscures its originally predictable meaning. Thus nearly all derived lexemes are listemes (A4.8) excepting novel coinings.

• Given (A4.2), complex lexical stems should be entered in the lexicon because they are a source for neologisms (A4.9).

• Two criteria on a lexeme were identified. C1a: a lexeme is a member of a morphosyntactic class. C1b a lexeme therefore has attributes common to the class. C2 lexemes are islands that prohibit lexical insertion within their boundaries (C2a), internal disjuncture (C2b), and extraction of any of their parts by syntactic processes (C2c).

• When asked to interpret a language expression out of context, people put their imagination to work (A4.10).

• N, Adj, V, and Adv compounds name rather than describe (A4.11). Something named is either stable and enduring or else recurrent (A4.12).

• The number of possible compounding relationships is unbounded (A.4.13).

• A strategy for interpreting a language expression is pattern-matching with known expressions, if any, checking constituent meanings, if any, and using all available clues from the common ground. Cf. A4.14.

• Many phrasal verbs are a kind of discontinuous compound and, like compounds, are listemes.

• We found that idioms typically function much like one of the major categories N, Adj, V, Adv despite their internal composition. We likened Nominal Idioms to Proper Names in being NP rather than N. There is little doubt that most polyword idioms must be counted lexemes.

• Sound symbolism is not consistent throughout the whole vocabulary of any language anywhere, thus the correlation between the form and the meaning of a language expression is arbitrary, though conventional.

• Onomatopoeic words differ from language to language, and mostly obey the phonological conventions of the language in which they occur. A very small number of 'wild' sound imitations is to be found in a language. These typically contain violations of the phonological conventions of the language in which they occur. The variations from the norm are iconic because the form of expression presents a sound picture of the meaning.

• Onomatopoeic words are listemes (A4.14).

• There are three kinds of 'secondary onomatopoeia' (Ullmann 1962:84) or 'conventional sound symbolism' (Hinton, Nichols, and Ohala 1994b): phonesthesia, synesthesia, and ideophones (expressives).

• Phonesthetic words in English may be either monosyllabic or disyllabic, and the second syllable of disyllabic phonesthetic words is either a consonant or an unstressed vowel.

• Because phonesthemes contribute to the structure and meaning of vocabulary items, they are listemes (A4.15).

• Although the particular forms of synesthesia are language-specific, it is a cross-language phenomenon that has characteristics in common with animal communication. In particular, high-frequency segments are associated with smallness, appeasement, deference; and low-frequency segments with their opposites. These are attributes to be mentioned in an encyclopedia rather than a lexicon.

• Although English has no ideophones, their typical functions in other languages were described. Ideophones are listemes.

4.6   Notes on further reading

[1] The difference between inflexional and derivational morphology was first recognized by Varro around 45 BCE as 'declinatio naturalis' and 'declinatio voluntaria':

> *voluntaria declinatio refertur ad consuetudinem, naturalis ad rationem*
> "voluntary affixation is a matter of usage, and natural affixation is a function of a logical
> system"   (Varro *De Lingua Latina* 10:15)

[2] On the semantics of gender, see Zubin and Köpcke 1986, Aikhenvald 2000.

[3] On blocking, see Aronoff 1976:43f, Scalise 1986:158–63, Di Sciullo and Williams 1987:10–14, Lehrer 1990, 1992b.

[4] On stratal law, see Mohanan 1986, Carstairs-McCarthy 1992, Katamba 1993.

[5] On recursive affixes, see Keyser and Roeper 1992, Lehrer 1995.

[6] On expletive infixes, see Bauer 1993, Macmillan 1980, McCarthy 1982.

[7] On the use of disjuncture to mark sense group boundaries, see Bolinger and Gerstman 1957, Jones 1960:274, Allan 1986.

[8] Attempts to classify the kinds of relationship that exist between the component words of a compound serve to demonstrate their boundless variety. See Marchand 1969, Adams 1973, Levi 1978, Selkirk 1982, Bauer 1983, 1992, Scalise 1986, Jensen 1990, Carstairs-McCarthy 1992, Katamba 1993.

[9] Many compounds are normally stressed on their first constituent word, e.g. BLACK*bird*; AIR*condition; Aus*TRA*lia Day*, whereas the homonymous phrase is normally stressed elsewhere. But not all compounds are front-stressed, cf. *head*MAS*ter* and *string* QUAR*tet;* and phrases can be front stressed in order to emphasize the stressed word. On stress in compounds, see Bauer 1983, Allan 1986.

[10] On phrasal verbs, see Kruisinga 1932, Bolinger 1971.

[11] There are many metaphors, mostly idiomatic, on the theme of anger – see Lakoff 1987:380–409.

[12] On iconicity in language, see Haiman (ed.) 1985.

[13] On common cross-language interpretations of articulatory types, see Rhodes 1994, Oswalt 1994.

[14] On synesthesia, see Hinton, Nichols, and Ohala 1994b, Morton 1994, Ohala 1994.

[15] Compare Doke's definition of ideophones with those in Alpher 1994, Hamano 1994, Matisoff 1994, Diffloth 1994.

5 The power of words: connotation and jargon

Who ever stubbed his toe in the dark and cried out, 'Oh, faeces!'?

(Adams 1985:45)

5.1 Where we are heading

In Chapter 4 we touched on morphological processes through which new words are created from existing resources. This chapter looks at other sources for new vocabulary. It begins by examining the power of connotation in motivating (a) the choice between near synonyms and (b) the development of new language expressions, so as to avoid injury, or to indicate in-group solidarity, politeness, deference, 'political correctness', insult or aggression. Over time, we can trace the rise and fall in what Leech 1981 has called the AFFECTIVE MEANING of listemes. §5.2 introduces euphemism and dysphemism as alternative effects of connotation. §5.3 describes the connotations of different forms of address and naming. §5.4 discusses the power of knowing someone's name and explains why the names of gods and dangerous animals are tabooed. §5.5 attributes the power of 'dirty words' to strong naturalist beliefs in the community that transfer to the listeme the distaste that its denotatum evokes. We see why homonyms of taboo terms drop out of use. §5.6 is on terms that upgrade, downgrade, and deliberately deceive. Euphemism and dysphemism, as effects of connotation, give rise to language change through the loss of some senses of terms, and the cycling of terms from one style to another; §5.7 looks at a dozen ways in which this leads to the development of new vocabulary. We shall also see that a new sense for a listeme may have multiple sources. §5.8 defines and examines jargon; explains why it is necessary; and shows how it is abused. You may think you don't use jargon, but like everyone else, you willingly do. §5.9 summarizes the chapter.

5.2 Connotation, euphemism, and dysphemism

In Chapter 3 we encountered connotation in the naming of cars, businesses, and bands, among other things.

> *Definition 3.6* The connotations of a word or longer expression are semantic effects that arise from encyclopedic knowledge about its denotation and also from experiences, beliefs, and prejudices about the contexts in which the expression is typically used.

Consequently, connotations vary independently of sense and denotation; and they vary between speech communities. Take the different connotations of 1 and 2:

1   Tom's dog killed Jane's rabbit.
2   Tom's doggie killed Jane's bunny.

As Gazdar 1979:3 points out (without, incidentally, mentioning connotation), in 2 Speaker 'is either a child, someone posing as a child, someone who thinks that they are addressing a child, or someone posing as someone who thinks that they are addressing a child'. A dog can be referred to by any of the nouns in 3.

3   dog, dish-licker, bow-wow, cur, mutt, mongrel, whelp, hound

Dish-licker smacks of dog-racing jargon (§5.8); and *bow-wow* either racing slang or baby-talk (cf. *gee-gee*). *Cur* is pejorative along with *mutt, mongrel,* and *whelp*, which have additional senses, as does *hound*, except that it connotes a noble animal. *Dog*, however, connotes nothing in particular, being the unmarked lexeme among the others. Because of the blocking principle (D4.3), it is rare to find words which are synonymous (D4.4) enough that they can substitute for one another in every context; each takes on associations from the various contexts in which it is used.

The effects of connotation can be either euphemism or its opposite, dysphemism.[1]

> *Definition 5.1* A dysphemism is a word or phrase with connotations that are offensive either about the denotatum or to the audience, or both.

'Dirty words' are dysphemistic in contexts where they are tabooed.

> *Definition 5.2* That which is taboo is forbidden. Taboo(ed) words are those considered offensive, shocking, or indecent when used in certain contexts. There are strict conditions on their use and penalties for violating these conditions.

A tabooed term, a strong dysphemism, is often replaced by a more positively viewed euphemistic word or phrase whose original meaning has been semantically extended to create a new sense for it. For instance, instead of saying *My father died* someone may say *My father passed*. Euphemism is talking about something distasteful in a nice way.

> *Definition 5.3* A euphemism is a word or phrase used as an alternative to a dispreferred expression. It avoids possible loss of face: either Speaker's own positive face (D1.29) or, through giving offence, the negative face (D1.30) of Hearer or some third party.

Connotation, euphemism, and dysphemism are richly illustrated in what follows.

Exercises

5.2.1 The use of the noun *man* or *mankind* for "*Homo sapiens*, human beings" and the use
of the generic masculine pronouns *he, him*, etc. for both males and females (as in 'the
reader should always keep the distinction at the back of his mind,' Allwood et al.
1977:22) is condemned for being sexist. Does the condemnation arise because of the
connotations of such usage?

5.2.2 Comment on connotations that attach to the nouns in either (a) or (b).
(a) *babe, bimbo, bird, bitch, broad, chick, dog, girl, honey, lady, madam, sheila, tart,
woman* (all of which could potentially be used of the same person, say, in her late
twenties, and if she were to travel between USA, Britain, and Australia). You might
want to think up a comparable list applicable to her male companion.
(b) *bathroom, bog, can, head, jakes, john, lavatory, littlest room, loo, shithouse, toilet,
washroom* on the assumption that all refer to the same place.

5.3   Connotations in naming and addressing and their effects on vocabulary

[*Falstaff, Shallow, Pistol, et al. outside Westminster Abbey on the Coronation of Henry V.*]

FALSTAFF: Stand here by me, Master Robert Shallow; I will make the king do you
                       grace: I will leer upon him as a' comes by; and do but mark the
                       countenance that he will give me.

                       [...]

[*Enter the King and his train, the Lord Chief Justice among them*]

FALSTAFF: God save thy Grace, King Hal! my royal Hal!
PISTOL: The heavens thee guard and keep, most royal imp of fame!
FALSTAFF: God save thee, my sweet boy!
KING HENRY V: My Lord Chief Justice, speak to that vain man.
LORD CHIEF J.:   Have you your wits? know you what 'tis you speak?
FALSTAFF: My king! my Jove! I speak to thee, my heart!
KING HENRY V: I know thee not, old man: fall to thy prayers; ...

                                              (Shakespeare *Henry IV, Pt 2* V.v.3–48)

As you see from the Shakespeare quotation above, the connotations of names and terms
of address have serious social consequences.[2] Context – both situation of utterance and
world and time spoken of, but particularly the former – is important. The style of naming
and addressing depends on two considerations:

(a)   The role Speaker perceives Hearer and/or the person or thing named to have
(adopted) relative to Speaker in the situation of utterance.

(b)   Speaker's attitude towards Hearer-or-Named at the time of utterance.

Personal relations are a function of power and social distance.

> *Definition 5.4* Power is a function of the perceived ability of one or the other interlocutor to control or affect the other.

> *Definition 5.5* Social distance is a function of the relative familiarity, social standing, and group affiliation of interlocutors – differences in age, gender, ethnicity, class, religion, ideology, etc.

A parent has power over their young child but the social distance is minimal. A police officer who books a speeding doctor has superior power, but the situation would be reversed if the police officer was undergoing a medical examination: in both scenarios, particularly the former, the social distance is likely to be large.

When the person or thing addressed or named (henceforth HEARER-OR-NAMED) is more powerful than Speaker, and/or there is a great social distance between them, the normal polite behaviour is for Speaker to be DEFERENTIAL and to use a STYLE whose degree of formality is less personal than, or equal to, 'consultative' on the scale in 4.

4 $\begin{bmatrix} \text{MOST-PERSONAL STYLE} \quad \text{LEAST-PERSONAL STYLE} \\ \text{intimate} - \text{casual} - \text{consultative} - \text{formal} - \text{frozen} \end{bmatrix}$

These five points of reference are intended to exhaust all possible manners of addressing and naming; however, it is not possible to recognize firm boundaries between adjacent pairs; cf. Joos 1961:11. Where Speaker is inferior to Hearer-or-Named, s/he will use unreciprocated (or conventionally unreciprocable) deferential forms such as *Your/Her Majesty, Your/His Highness, Your Lordship, Mr President, Madam Chairman*, etc. all of which are 'frozen' or 'formal' style. These titles do not include names, but identify roles or social positions; thus, to some extent, they impersonalize. So do terms like *Sir, Madam, this lady, the gentleman*, etc. which are used in 'frozen', 'formal', and 'consultative' styles. Children addressing adults sometimes use the titles *Mr* or *Mrs* alone, which is reminiscent of 'consultative' style. Even within that style, it would be dysphemistic from an adult Speaker. In rather stilted English, Hearer can be addressed in the third person, as *the astute reader* will doubtless be aware; one used to occasionally encounter similar forms in the more expensive shops, e.g.

5   If Madam so desires she could have our tailor alter the waistband just a touch.

This impersonalizing manner of naming and addressing is comparable with the regular use in some languages of third person address forms to Hearer. The deferential Polish question in 6 contrasts with the familiar version in 7 – which roughly corresponds to the 'intimate' or 'casual' styles of English.

6   *Co   mama   robi?*
    what   mother   3.s.do   "What are you doing mother?"

7 *Co   robisz,   mama?*
   what 2.S.do,   mum   "Wotcha doin', mum?"

In the canonical speech situation (D1.2) where Speaker and Hearer are in face to face conversation, there is a greater psycho-social distance, and often a greater physical distance, between Speaker and a third person than between Speaker and Hearer. This difference in relative distance is captured in the terms 'first', 'second', and 'third persons'.

> **Assumption 5.1** Because third person is intrinsically more distant from Speaker than second person, its use to Hearer exaggerates the social distance between Speaker and Hearer.

Such exaggeration is a widely-used strategy for indicating deference.

Another way for Speaker to indicate deference is to address or name not the individual Hearer-or-Named but to include Hearer-or-Named among a number of people. This becomes conventionalized so that in French, for example, Speaker uses the second person plural as a deferential mode for addressing a singular Hearer in 8, the 'intimate' or perhaps 'casual' form in 9.

8 *Vous êtes très gentille, madame.*
   2.PL   are   very kind   madam   "You are very kind, madam."

9 *T'es   très gentille, maman.*
   2.S.are very kind   mummy   "You're very kind, mummy."

The deferential address form in German uses the third person plural form *sie* orthographically marked by an initial capital, *Sie*, plus the 3rd person plural verb form. Spoken Tamil shows respect by using a third person plural form when naming a third person singular. Where the vehicle for respect is a plural instead of the singular form for a single Hearer-or-Named, the convention has it that Speaker acts on the normal presumption that any individual is representative of a group, and derives social standing accordingly. Because there is safety in numbers, Hearer-or-Named is less vulnerable as a member of the group than if s/he were alone: any threat to Hearer-or-Named threatens the whole group. This strategy exaggerates the relative power of Hearer-or-Named by pretending to greater respect for Hearer-or-Named than if Hearer-or-Named were a lone individual. It is less impersonalizing than the use of third person in place of second person. The strategies discussed can be ranked on the PERSONALIZING SCALE in 10.

10 ⎡ MOST PERSONALIZED   LEAST PERSONALIZED ⎤
   ⎣ 2.S   —   2.PL   —   3.S   —   3.PL ⎦

No language employs more than three of these (e.g. 18th century German), and most employ only one or two. So, rather than conflating the two strategies for marking deference on one personalizing scale correlating with relative status, it is more appropriate to recognize two distinct communicative strategies motivated by the components of social status: namely, social distance and power (Haiman 1980a:530).

Definition 5.6 The distance strategy is used when deference to Hearer is marked by exaggerating the social distance between Speaker and Hearer, e.g. by using third person to Hearer.

Definition 5.7 The power strategy is used when deference to Hearer-or-Named is marked by exaggerating his or her power relative to Speaker, e.g. by using plural number of a single referent.

The conventions of a particular language severely constrain the choices available to an individual speaker. In every language, Speaker may register a change in attitude towards Hearer-or-Named by changing the style of naming or addressing from that which s/he has been using in prior discourse, or which s/he normally uses.

Returning to the use of naming and addressing with the 'consultative' style in English: Speaker will use 'consultative' style to address or name using *title ⁀surname* for the task, e.g. *Mr Smith*, (a) where Speaker is superior in status to, but of friendly disposition towards, Hearer-or-Named or (b) where Speaker and Hearer-or-Named are of similar social status but there is considerable social distance between them. If Speaker is superior in status to Hearer-or-Named, s/he can choose either to maintain the status difference or choose to be less formal and show solidarity by using IN-GROUP MARKERS that demonstrate a concern to enhance Hearer-or-Named's positive face (D1.29) by seeking to make Hearer-or-Named feel good about themselves. Where Speaker and Hearer-or-Named are of similar social status and there is little social distance between them, the informal in-group language found in 'casual' and 'intimate' styles is the regular mark of solidarity. These styles are marked by contractions, ellipsis, diminutives, colloquialisms, and perhaps slang and swearing (cf. Brown and Levinson 1987). Among adults, address forms in 'casual' style include given name or nickname, perhaps with the surname; also American *bud(dy)*, Australian and southern British *mate*, northern British (Geordie and Cumbrian) *marra*, southern British *old boy* (possibly archaic), and *brother* or *sister* in various American, Australian, and British sociolects. These forms of address are also used in 'intimate' style, and in addition to the address forms just mentioned we find such terms as *auntie, babe, baby, daddy, darling, dear, duckie, ducks, fella(s), gorgeous, grandad, guys, handsome, honey, hunk, love (luv), lover, mac, momma, sexy, sis, sugar, sweetheart*, and a whole lot more.

In many English-speaking families it remains dysphemistic to address or name consanguineal (blood) kin of an ascending (older) generation by their given names. Instead we use kin titles such as *Dad, Nan, Grandpa*, etc. for lineal kin; and for lateral kin, a kin title like *Auntie*, or *kin_title ⁀given_name*, e.g. *Aunt Jemima*. If lineal kin of the second and higher ascending generations need to be distinguished from a collateral with the same title, *kin_title ⁀surname* is the usual form used, e.g. *Grandma Robinson* versus *Grandma Carter*. The social taboo against omitting the kin title is weakest with kin from the first ascending (i.e. parents') generation who are about the same age as Speaker, particularly collateral kin and step-kin; it is strongest with kin of the second and higher ascending generations. These are, of course, asymmetric conventions: given name only is the norm when Hearer-or-Named is close kin of a descending generation; though more distant affinal kin (i.e. kin by marriage) from a descending generation may warrant *title ⁀surname*. Amongst the religious groups of Old Order Amish and Old Order Mennonites in Pennsylvania, USA and Ontario,

Canada, everyone gives and receives first names only, regardless of relative familiarity, status, age, and sex. Furthermore, first names are derived only from the Old Testament and there is a limited number of family names; in the small Mennonite town of St Jacobs in Waterloo County, Ontario, there were at one time 27 David Martins registered at the local post office! So, most people have a distinguishing nickname (often gently mocking) that can be used to refer to some absent person.

Many Austronesians and Papuans traditionally taboo names for some kinsfolk, especially affines and, to a lesser extent, cross-consanguineal kin – in particular, siblings of the other sex, cross-cousins, and 'clan brothers and sisters'; cf. Simons 1982:177–9. In many societies, e.g. among the Zia, a non-Austronesian people who live in Morobe Province in south-eastern Papua New Guinea, personal names are not used among spouses, siblings, and often not to descending generations. Instead they use kin titles and the translation equivalents of terms like *person, man, woman, boy, girl*. Other societies use public names, nicknames, clan names, and kin descriptions like *mother of X*. Because relationships with in-laws are notoriously difficult in all societies, the so-called 'mother-in-law' languages (cf. Dixon 1971) and all similar taboos on naming and addressing kinsfolk are perhaps grounded in the desire to maintain social harmony.

A lot of vocabulary items maintain and encourage a community attitude that downgrades women. Since the 1960s feminists have sought to change public language to make it less dysphemistic towards women, and they have since been joined by other reformers resisting what is perceived to be DISCRIMINATORY LANGUAGE against a variety of disadvantaged groups. Many such reformers hold a belief that revising habits of language use will change community attitudes, and to that end there have been a large number of guidelines for nondiscriminatory, especially non-sexist, language usage in private and public institutions.[3] Speakers and writers are advised to choose the neutral alternative from such lists as 11 (a 'locution' is a "form of expression" D1.9).

11 **Dysphemistic locution**   **Neutral locution**

    man(kind)   human beings, humanity, people

    chairman   chairperson, chair

    policeman   police officer

    foreman   supervisor

    salesman   salesperson

    actress   actor

    (air) stewardess   flight attendant

Obviously, the -*man* locutions are appropriate when referring to a male person, and the neutral locution is primarily intended to name the office (job) itself so as to acknowledge that a woman may hold such an office. The is a view that terms suffixed -*ess*, and others such as *lady/woman doctor*, should be acceptable to a female referent. The objection is that these are marked terms, and that women referred to using such terms are less highly valued than their male counterparts. Consequently, the neutral alternatives are preferred for a female referent. Neutral terms are understandably preferred in contexts when there is to be no specific mention of gender; so why not on all occasions?

Gender differentiation between third person singular pronouns in English leads to the use of the doublets 'her/him', 'him or her', 's/he', 'he or she', 'hers/his', etc. in intensional contexts. Because the third person plural – *they, them, their(s)* – is not gender differentiated, it is recommended for use wherever possible.

12 If *anyone* needs to know about semantics, *they* should read this book from cover to cover.

Many prescriptivists (including feminists; cf. Frank and Treichler 1989:181) object to sentences like 12 – which is sadly pedantic in view of the fact that such usage has been common practice for many centuries, especially in colloquial speech; cf. Smith 1985:50–3. Whatever one's views on the use of plural pronouns for singular referents in intensional contexts, it is stylistically preferable to write 13 rather than 14, because the plural version does less violence to the cooperative maxim of manner (D1.26).

13 As *readers* can judge for *themselves.*
14 As *the reader* can judge for *him or herself.*

Sexist language displays just one type of -IST dysphemism, others include racist, ageist, speciesist, and classist putdowns. All of these have the same dysphemistic pivot: they fail to demonstrate respect for some personal characteristic which is important to Hearer-or-Named's self-image.

> *Definition 5.8* An -IST dysphemism fails to demonstrate respect for some personal characteristic important to Hearer-or-Named's self-image; therefore, whether deliberate or unpremeditated, it causes a face affront (D1.30) to members of an out-group.

For instance, racist dysphemisms occur when Speaker refers to or implicates Hearer-or-Named's race, ethnicity, or nationality in such terms as to cause a face affront to Hearer-or-Named. Among the racist dysphemisms of English, are: *mick* for Irish person, *frog* for a French person, *kraut* and *hun* for a German, *chink* for a Chinese, *jap* or *nip* for a Japanese, *slant(ie)* for any East Asian, etc. Some racist terms are not intrinsically dysphemistic, and in certain contexts can be used without prejudice. *Blacks* is not necessarily any more dysphemistic than *whites*; and in Australia, *boong* and *gin* are not invariably dysphemistic, no more so in fact than are *lebo* "Lebanese", *wog* "Caucasian Australian who is not Anglo-Celtic" and *skip(py)* "(young?) Anglo-Celtic Australian" (perhaps from a television series "Skippy the bush kangaroo"). Most, if not all, of these 'racist' terms can be used without irony between people of the group identified by it. For example, Folb 1980:248 glosses *nigger* as follows:

> **nigger** Form of address and identification among blacks (can connote affection, playful derision, genuine anger, or mere identification of another black person; often used emphatically in conversation).

Similarly, Greek Australians, for example, often refer to themselves as *wogs*, though it is perceived as derogatory when used by Anglos. Something comparable holds true for most -IST terms:

Assumption 5.2   -IST dysphemisms are disarmed by being used as in-group
solidarity markers by the targeted group.

Nonetheless, the encyclopedia entries for the racist terms exemplified above will need to
mark the degree to which they are dysphemistic: e.g. *black* should probably NOT be marked
as dysphemistic, but rather as neutral; on the other hand, *nigger* should be marked as
typically dysphemistic except when used between, e.g., members of the African diaspora.

In all the cases reviewed in this section, the connotations of some existing word often
lead to its replacement by another word or phrase, usually with some revision of its earlier
meaning, e.g. *server* in place of *waitress* and *waiter*. Sometimes, however, an entirely new
listeme is created, e.g. *salesman* ⇒ *salesperson*. Although these novelties are usually
euphemistic and have positive connotations, a few (such as the -IST terms) are primarily
dysphemistic and have negative connotations.

Exercises

5.3.1 Explain King Henry V's reaction in the quotation from Shakespeare's *King Henry
IV Pt 2* at the head of this section.

5.3.2 Try to assign the following to one (at most two) of the five styles:
   (a) How are you today, Harry?
   (b) G'day, Harry!
   (c) Sweetie, turn the light out.
   (d) Doctor, I have a very sore throat.
   (e) If your worship pleases.
   (f) Do you have Calabrese salami?
   (g) Hello Mrs Johnson, terrible weather, isn't it?
   (h) Professor Chomsky is not only responsible for a revolution in linguistics, ...

5.3.3 How do you think the so-called royal *we* fits into the picture of address terms?
   (Supposedly, Queen Victoria used the first person plural instead of the first person
   singular.)

5.3.4 Not all *-ist* suffixes are dysphemistic, cf. *botanist, linguist, typist, violinist*. Also,
   there are many -IST dysphemisms not mentioned here. Discuss.

5.3.5 Survey community reactions to the roughly synonymous NPs: (a) the aged; (b) old
   people; (c) old folks; (d) senior citizens; (e) the chronologically gifted.

5.4   Empowerment and danger in knowing the name: how this affects vocabulary

> Good name in man and woman, dear my lord,
> Is the immediate jewel of their souls.
> Who steals my purse steals trash; 'tis something, nothing;
> 'Twas mine, 'tis his, and has been slave to thousands;
> But he that filches from me my good name
> Robs me of that which not enriches him,
> And makes me poor indeed.
>
> (Shakespeare *Othello* III.iii.155)

Personal names are taboo among some peoples on all the inhabited continents, and on many of the islands between them. 'The name of a person, in Kwaio [Austronesian] culture, is associated with the essence (*to ʔofungana*) of that person' (Keesing and Fifiʔi 1969:159). For many peoples, a person's name (like their mind, spirit, soul, shadow, and reflection) is perceived to be an inseparable part of the body, and this is often reflected in the grammar of their language. To utter a tabooed name is to assault the owner of the name. And just as malevolent magic can be wrought with one's body and bodily effluvia, nail parings, or hair clippings, it can be practised by someone in possession of one's true name. Consequently, many 'true' names are kept secret from outsiders. In ancient Egyptian mythology, Isis gained power over the sun god Ra because she persuaded him to divulge his name. The discovery of a villain's name can destroy his power – as in the case of Rumpelstiltskin. In many Australian and Austronesian societies, as well as elsewhere, names of the dead are (or were until recently) taboo – lest uttering the name call the dead from their resting-place.

What applies to the names and naming of ordinary folk applies *a fortiori* to rulers and to gods, because any threat to their power endangers the entire society they dominate. Perhaps as an antidote to downgrading a ruler, naming or addressing them often involves extreme euphemism, not to mention pomp and circumstance.[4] Now that we have constitutional monarchs and democratically elected presidents, the terror which our rulers once inspired has been replaced by a notional respect (terror has become the mark of guerrillas and the petty dictator). Yet the language used to rulers has remained much the same, even if it is no longer so very different from the respectful deference extended to other persons of superior power to Speaker. At the March 1989 coronation of Prince Mangkubumi in Yogyakarta, Indonesia, the new Sultan was given the following title: *Ngarso dalem kanjeng ratu inkang sinuhan sri sultan hamengku buwono adipati ingalogo ngabdurahman sayidin panoto gomo kalifatullah kaping X* "His Exalted Majesty, whose Honour Shines Bright, Sultan of all the world, Commander in Chief, Servant of God, Protector of Religion, Assistant to God, the tenth." This mode of naming and addressing exaggerates the importance of Hearer-or-Named by magnifying their perceived or alleged higher social status.

Taboos on the names of gods seek to avoid metaphysical malevolence by counteracting possible blasphemies (even, perhaps, profanities) that arouse their terrible wrath. Thus in the Holy Communion service of the Anglican Church, the minister says 'Thou shalt not take the Name of the Lord thy God in vain: for the Lord will not hold him guiltless, that taketh his Name in vain' (*The Book of Common Prayer* 1662). To avoid blasphemy, the word *God* is avoided in euphemistic expletives such as the archaic *'Od's life!, Zounds!, by gad!* and the more contemporary 15:

15 Gosh!   Gorblimey!   Goodness (knows)!   (Oh) Lord!
    Golly!   Gordonbennet!   (Good) gracious!   Lawdy!
    Cor!   Gordon'ighlanders!   For goodness' sake!   La!

These examples demonstrate the generation of new vocabulary by various kinds of REMODELLING, including clippings and substitutions of phonetically similar words. *Jesus* is end-clipped to *Jeeze!* and *Gee!* (which is also the initial of *God*); *Gee whiz!* is a remodelling of either *jeeze* or *jesus*. More adventurous remodellings are in 16:

16 By jingo!   Jeepers creepers!   Jimminy cricket!   Crikey!
    Christmas!   Cripes!   Crust!   Crumbs!

One of the best disguised remodellings is *For crying out loud!* which is a euphemism for *For Christ's sake*. The Devil's name is avoided in *Old Nick, Old Harry, Old Bendy, Old Bogey*, etc. *What the dickens...* replaces "What the devil..." And so forth.

Note that the denotation of *Gee!, Jeepers!* and *Jesus!* is identical. From a purely rational viewpoint, if one of them is blasphemous, then all of them are. What is different is that the first two have connotations that are markedly different from the last. Connotation is seen to be a vocabulary generator.

Even in today's English, the power of names is not lost; we continue to use phrases like those in 17.

17 make a name for oneself   have a good name
    bring one's name into disrepute   clearing one's name

Names come to be linked with name-bearers, and a few proper names enter the general lexicon. There is direct reference to an original celebrated or infamous name-bearer as in the case of *He's a little Hitler*; and also use of proper names as general vocabulary items like the verbs *lynch, boycott,* and *hoover* and the common nouns *kleenex* and *biro* (Chapter 3).

Many peoples have taboos against mentioning the names of dangerous animals. The motivation can be gleaned from the Ukrainian proverb *Pro vovka pomovka a vovk u khatu* "One speaks of the wolf and it runs into the house" and the Korean *holangito ceymal hamyen ontayteni* "Speak of the tiger and it comes" – both are reminiscent of the English proverb *Speak of the devil and he comes running*. This attitude reflects a fear that animals can understand human language, and if a dangerous creature hears its proper name, it will respond to the call. Consequently, it is often named euphemistically. In most Slavic languages, for instance, the bear is called something like 'the honey eater'; and the English word *bear* derives from "[the] brown one" – compare *Bruno the bear* in which 'bruno' is Italian for "brown". Among the Zia of Papua New Guinea, fishermen avoid talking about, and try even to avoid thinking about, dangerous creatures like sharks, rays, and saltwater crocodiles for fear of inviting attack. If such creatures are seen they are referred to using the class name *woo* "fish" instead of *bawang* "shark" or *beoto* "ray"; and the crocodile will not be called *ugama* but *emo meko* "bad man" instead. In many communities a hunter will not name the game that he is hunting, even if he sees it. Sometimes hunters and fishermen will not address their fellows by name lest their quarry hear them and take revenge. In all such cases a term is tabooed because it has frightful or frightening connotations; as a result, the vocabulary of the language is increased either through SEMANTIC EXTENSION of some existing word or phrase, or by coining a new one.

Exercises

5.4.1 Almost every society has strong taboos against the mention of death. (a) Why do think this is so? (b) In what ways is this taboo manifest in English?

5.4.2 Discuss the following: 'People always grow up like their names. It took me thirty years to work off the effects of being called Eric. If I wanted a girl to grow up beautiful I'd call her Elizabeth. ...' (Letters of Eric Blair, a.k.a. George Orwell).

5.5   Why dirt clings: the power of naturalist beliefs

The ordinary reaction to a display of filth and vulgarity should be a neutral one or else disgust; but the reaction to certain words connected with excrement and sex is neither of these, but a titillating thrill of scandalized perturbation.

(Read [1935] 1977:9)

The words listed under the heading 'Dysphemistic locutions' in 11 (*foreman, actress*, etc.) are dispreferred by many and taboo to a few. It is not the denotation but the connotations of these vocabulary items which are controversial. Identifying the connotations of a term is to identify the community attitude towards it. Many words suffer PEJORIZATION, i.e. downgrading, through society's perception of a word's tainted denotatum contaminating the word itself. Throughout the ages countryfolk have been held in low esteem by townies. Latin *urbanus* "townsman" gives rise to *urbane* "sophisticated, elegant, refined" versus *rusticus* "rustic" with connotations of "clownish, awkward, boorish". *Boorish* means "ill-mannered, loutish, uncouth" and derives from the noun *boor* (Old English (*ʒe*)*búr* 'dweller, husbandman, farmer, countryman'; cf. Dutch *boer* "farmer") whose original meaning lives on in *neighbour* ("near-dweller"). English *churl* once meant "countryman of the lowest rank", and *churlish* already meant "ill-tempered, rude, ungracious" by the early Middle English period. The pejorization of these words, and also in many terms denoting women seems to have been extraordinarily rapid, a century at most, if we are to believe the *OED*.[5]

   Pejorization is most clearly seen with regular taboo terms – especially 'dirty words'. There is no *a priori* basis for distinction between the euphemism and the taboo term. It is mysterious why the euphemisms *pass (away), misappropriate, We'll have to let you go,* and *I'm going to the loo* have fewer unpleasant connotations than their taboo (dispreferred) counterparts *die, steal, You're fired,* and *I'm going for a piss*. The difference presumably derives from a persistent belief, A5.3.

> *Assumption 5.3* The form of an expression somehow communicates the essential nature of whatever it denotes.

In Frazer's words: 'the link between a name and the person or thing denominated by it is not a mere arbitrary and ideal association, but a real and substantial bond which unites the two' (1911:318). This is the naturalist hypothesis that there is a causal relation between words and their original meanings (§4.4). Today, controversies over the earlier forms of words are generally left to experts trained in historical and comparative linguistics; but even so, there is a strong body of public opinion that the proper meaning of a word is its original meaning. This is sometimes revealed in school textbooks and frequently in letters to newspaper editors asserting that the new meanings for words are 'misuses'. It is the view expressed in the following remarks about the English word *nice*.

> **nice** This word is very much overworked and misused. Its real meaning is *precise, exact, and delicately, fine;* e.g.
> A nice difference in meaning.
> A nice ear for music.
> The word is now often used to mean *agreeable, delightful, pleasant,* etc. – because it
> is easier to say *nice* than to think of a more suitable word.   (Wright 1978:91)

You should ask yourself what Wright means by saying 'it is easier to say *nice* than think of' some other word: 'easier' implies greater communicative efficiency, which is laudable not reprehensible. Wright's remarks about *nice* are simply incorrect. Today, the 'real meaning' of *nice* includes "agreeable", "delightful", "pleasant" just as much as (and arguably more than) it includes "precise", "exact", and "delicately fine", which were its 17th–18th century meanings and are now archaic. English *nice* derives from Latin *nescius* "ignorant", and we can trace a path through its earlier senses to its present meaning:

18 *nice* from Latin *nescius*   "ignorant"
          14th–16th C   "ignorant", "stupid", "foolish", "foppish"
          16th–18th C   "foppish", "fastidious", "precise"
          18th–19th C   "precise", "balanced", "agreeable"
          20th C   "agreeable", "pleasant", "pleasing"

To speak of one or more of the earlier meanings being the 'real' meaning of *nice* is absurd. It suggests that the current meaning is in some way degenerate. The degeneracy of contemporary language is, in fact, a recurrent theme in the naturalist tradition, because the naturalist hypothesis leads to a belief that the original word bore the proper form and proper meaning, therefore any subsequent change is a degeneration from the perfectly natural original form; a decline that should be halted or preferably reversed. However, we should ask for evidence that the original (form of the) language was a better instrument of communication than the language of today, or, indeed, of another time in recorded history. The answer is, of course, that there is no such evidence.

The connotations of taboo terms are contaminated by the taboo topics which they denote; but by definition euphemisms are not – or not yet – contaminated.

Assumption 5.4 Euphemisms often degenerate into taboo terms through contamination by the taboo topic.

For example, in 45 BCE Cicero observed that Latin *penis* "tail" had earlier been a euphemism for *mentula* "penis": 'But nowadays,' he wrote, '*penis* is among the obscenities' (*Epistulae ad Familiares* IX,xxii). As a 'learned term' borrowed from Latin (see §5.7), it is not among the obscenities of present-day English. English *undertaker* once meant "odd-job man" (someone who undertakes to do things), which was used as a euphemism for the person taking care of funerals; like most ambiguous taboo terms, the meaning of *undertaker* narrowed to the taboo sense alone, and is now being replaced by the euphemism *funeral director*. What often happens with euphemisms like this is that they start off with a modifying word, 'funeral' in *funeral undertaker*, then the modifier is dropped as the phrase ceases to be euphemistic. Other examples are *deranged* derived from *mentally deranged* ("mentally disordered"), and *asylum* from *lunatic asylum* ("place of refuge for lunatics"). *Toilet* (from French *toile* "cloth") is fading as a euphemism and may well disappear, as did *necessary house* (Grose 1811); it has almost been superseded by *bathroom* or *restroom* in American and *loo* in spoken British and Australian. All these examples support the view that taboo terms such as those for body parts connected with sexual reproduction and defecation, along with those for the correlative effluvia, are classified as such because of a belief, be it ever so vague, that their form reflects the essential nature of the taboo topics they denote. This is exactly why the terms themselves are often said to be unpleasant or ugly-sounding, why they are miscalled 'dirty words.' It is the result of the powerful hold that naturalist beliefs have upon the community.

There are two reasons why language abandons homonyms of taboo terms. One is the relative salience of taboo terms, the 'titillating thrill of scandalized perturbation' as Read 1977:9 describes it. Osgood, Suci, and Tannenbaum 1957 discovered a general tendency for any derogatory or unfavourable denotation or connotation within a language expression to dominate the interpretation of its immediate context. MacWhinney et al. 1982:315 found that 'sentences with profane and sexually suggestive language elicited responses quite different from those [without ...] Sentences with off-color language possess a memorability that is quite independent of their role in conversation.'[1] The other reason for abandoning the homonyms of taboo terms is that a speaker won't risk appearing to use a taboo term

---

1. The reason for this could be that obscene vocabulary is stored or accessed differently in the brain from other vocabulary; the evidence for this comes from people manifesting 'Gilles de la Tourette's syndrome, which is characterized by unusual tics progressing to involuntary outbursts of foul language (coprolalia)' (Valenstein and Heilman 1979:431). These people may lose all other language ability, which would only be possible if the means of storage and/or access were separate from that of obscene vocabulary; though why there should be such separation is a mystery.

when none was intended. For example, there are some (mostly older) English speakers who, if they catch themselves using the adjective *gay* in its pre-1960s sense will, with mild embarrassment, explicitly draw attention to this intended meaning. Their late 19th century forebears, fearful of seeming impropriety, avoided the terms *leg* and *breast* even when speaking of a cooked fowl, referring instead to its *dark* (or *red*) *meat* and *white meat*. The British still use *cock* to mean "rooster"; but, because of the taboo homonym meaning "penis", this sense of *cock* started to die out in American in the early 19th century; it is nowadays very rare in Australian. There has also been an effect on words containing *cock*: e.g. former Mayor Ed *Koch* of New York City gives his surname a spelling-pronunciation /koč/; the family of Louisa May *Alcott* (author of *Little Women*) changed their name from *Alcox*; and although there were other factors at work too, the use of *haystack* in place of *haycock*, and the use of *weather-vane* as an alternative to *weather-cock*, were undoubtedly influenced by taboo avoidance. Although *cockroach* is often foreclipped to *roach* in American, *cockpit* and *cocktail* show no sign of being avoided. The reason may lie in the fact that in these words *cock-* is not the head of the noun (recall the right-hand head rule of Chapter 4).

Where there is little likelihood of being misunderstood, the homonyms of a taboo term are likely to persist in the language. This is the case, for instance, with *queen* "regina" which is under no threat from the homonym meaning "gay male" simply because one denotatum is necessarily female, the other is necessarily male. The converse holds for the end-clipped American epithet *mother* "motherfucker". Similarly we experience no constraint in saying *It's queer* but we generally avoid saying *He's queer* if we mean "He's peculiar" preferring *He's eccentric* or *He's a bit odd*. *Bull* meaning "bullshit" is dissimilated from *bull* "male, typically bovine, animal" because it heads an uncountable NP instead of a countable one.

A word or longer expression with bad connotations (however unjustifiable) will suffer pejorization; hence the proverb *Give a dog a bad name*. Polysemous words with taboo senses are downgraded by SEMANTIC NARROWING to the taboo senses alone.[6] Words with a taboo homonym tend to be downgraded out of use.

Exercises

5.5.1 If the naturalist hypothesis were correct, would you know the meaning of Maasai *kiteng* or *abol* and Tzeltal *čan* or *c'ihp*, without the need for a dictionary?

5.5.2 There is a wealth of evidence that where a language expression is ambiguous between a dysphemistic sense and a non-dysphemistic sense its meaning will often narrow to the dysphemistic sense alone.
(a) Look up the history of the meaning of *villain*.
(b) Check the history of English *hussy*, French *fille*, and German *Dirne*.
(c) Check the history of the English noun *accident*.
(d) Why did *coney* (rhymes with *honey*) get replaced by *rabbit* in the late 19th century?
(e) What is the most salient sense for you of the adjective *gay*? Would your grandparents say the same?

5.5.3 The words *meat, girl, disease,* and *ejaculation* have all been subject to semantic narrowing (not necessarily in consequence of taboo). Explain.

5.6   Upgrades, downgrades, and deceptions

> Bribes, graft and expenses-paid vacations are never talked about [in the US House of Representatives] on Capitol Hill. Honorariums, campaign contributions and per diem travel reimbursements are.   (*Time Australia* April 17, 1989:36)

There is a whole batch of euphemisms for avoiding the mildly distasteful, upgrading what is favoured and downgrading what isn't. Some euphemisms are downright deceptive. With reference to the quote above, the terms *honorarium, campaign contributions,* and *per diem travel reimbursements* are used as alternatives to the dispreferred expressions *bribes, graft,* and *expenses-paid vacations* – because they have positive instead of negative connotations. Take the example of a widow who prefers to say she has *paying guests* rather than *lodgers* because, to her mind, *paying guest* has fewer negative connotations than does *lodger.* An author who reads in a publisher's letter *After careful consideration we have regretfully concluded that your manuscript falls outside the scope of our current publishing program* interprets it to mean "We don't want to publish your lousy manuscript." *We'll have to let you go* replaces "You're fired", even when *dehiring* is merited. People arrested but not yet charged are *helping the police with their enquiries.* If a soldier is hit by *incontinent ordinance* (a kind of friendly fire) s/he may suffer a *ballistically-induced aperture in the subcutaneous environment* or worse. If you jump out of a 10th-storey window, you won't just go splat when you hit the ground, you'll suffer *sudden deceleration trauma.* The final remark on the hospital chart of a case of *negative patient care outcome* was 'Patient failed to fulfill his wellness potential' (Lutz 1989:66); it is not reported whether this resulted from *therapeutic misadventure.* On a lighter note, whereas simple dieting would involve you in *negative expenditure,* you might be willing to pay for *nutritional avoidance therapy.* A *sanitation engineer* sounds more exalted than a *garbage collector*; a *vermin control officer* has replaced the *ratcatcher.* The *night watchman* has become a *night entry supervisor.* A *preloved* object sounds more attractive than a *second-hand* or *used* one does; they can be found in an *opportunity shop,* which specializes in *reutilization marketing.* One is, at best, *comfortably off* oneself; other people are *wealthy* or even *filthy rich.*

Many times a euphemism is linked with Speaker's point of view, dysphemism with some other view – it is an *us* versus *them* situation. For instance, consider the import of the parenthetical remark in the following:

> I cross the swinging footbridge over Salt Creek pestered all the way by a couple of yellow cowflies (cattlemen call them deerflies).   (Abbey 1968:40)

Abbey's point is that by calling these blood-sucking pests *deerflies,* cattlemen seek to avoid all responsibility for their numbers by associating them with feral beasts rather than their own multitudinous charges. Similarly, Speaker's military heroes *disengage from the enemy* or make a *tactical withdrawal*; the enemy *retreats.* Speaker's troops cause *collateral damage*; the enemy commits *terrorist acts against civilians*. We get *invited in*; they are *aggressors*. Employees *take industrial action* which their employers call a *strike*. Company officials *misappropriate* goods; burglars *steal* them.

Dysphemisms are used in talking about Speaker's opponents, things Speaker wishes to show disapproval of, and things Speaker wishes to (be seen to) downgrade. A dysphemism, then, is used for precisely the opposite reason that a euphemism is used. Dysphemistic terms of insult include:

(a)   Comparisons of people with animals that are conventionally ascribed certain behaviours, e.g. calling someone a *bitch, chicken, dog, galah, louse, mule, rat, snake*, etc.
(b)   Epithets derived from tabooed bodily organs (e.g. *asshole, prick*), bodily effluvia (e.g. *shit*), and sexual behaviours (e.g. *fucker, poofter, wanker, whore*).
(c)   Ascriptions of mental 'defect', such as *idiot, airhead, moron, maniac*; or physical 'defect', e.g. *baldy, four-eyes, spastic, weakling*.
(d)   Sexist, racist, ageist, and other -IST dysphemisms.
(e)   Finally there are terms of insult or disrespect, some of which invoke slurs on the target's character, such as *bag, battle-axe, biddy, codger, crank, crone, fogy, fuddy-duddy, fuss-budget, galoot, geezer, grump, hag*.

Many euphemisms are deceptive. Companies *restructure* and *downsize*, they don't *lay off* employees, let alone *sack* them.

> Fifteen employees at Clifford of Vermont, Inc. weren't laid off. "This was not a cut back nor a lay-off. It was a career-change opportunity," said John McNulty, president. *Valley News* (Conn.), 3 May 1990.   (*Quarterly Review of Doublespeak* 17/1, 1990:1)

McNulty was just *eliminating redundancies in the human resources area* by *releasing* these employees. *Life insurance* is, ironically, "insurance for when you are dead". A barrister's *refresher* is "the fee for the second and each subsequent day of a hearing". *Adult videos* are pornographic. And a *starter home* or a *cosy cottage suitable for renovation* is so much more enticing than a *small dilapidated dwelling*. Calling vinyl *vegetarian leather* may be kind of a joke; not so the Third Reich's *final solution* nor *ethnic cleansing* in the Balkans during the mid-1990s. Hopefully, the *strange fruit* that *decorated the cottonwoods* in the American south will never be seen again.

Exercises

5.6.1 See if you can identify the kind of work done by people filling the following job descriptions:
   (a) moving domestic engineer; (b) an intimate apparel field support manager; (c) urban transportation specialist; (d) member of the vertical transportation corps; (e) automative internist; (f) price integrity coordinator.

5.6.2 During the Cold War (*c.*1945–90), reference would be made by members of the Western alliance to *the so-called democracies of the Eastern bloc*. Comment on the force of 'so-called' and 'bloc'.

5.6.3   Divide the following military terms between *us* and *them*.

the leader is resolute	the leader is ruthless
press briefings, reporting guidelines	propaganda, censorship
Abu Nidal is a freedom fighter	Abu Nidal is a terrorist
kill, destroy	take out, neutralize, eliminate
cower in foxholes	dig in
first or pre-emptive strike	sneak or unprovoked attack
hordes	boys
brave, loyal dare-devils	mad, fanatical cannon-fodder

5.6.4 Comment on comparisons of personal behaviour like

    (a)   Bertrand Russell's celebrated conjugation *I am firm, you are stubborn, he is pigheaded.*

    (b)   I'm generous, but she's spendthrift.

    (c)   I'm careful, but he's mean.

5.7 Sources for euphemisms and dysphemisms: revising the vocabulary of a language

Assumption 5.5 Euphemism and dysphemism motivate language change by promoting new expressions, or new meanings for old expressions, and causing some existing vocabulary to be abandoned.

(a)   One source of new terms is REMODELLING. This has given rise to *gee* by end-clipping either *Jesus* or *God* (§5.4). In the jargon of nursing it has led to the folk-etymological (Chapter 4) substitution of *carative* from *curative* because nurses *care* for patients whereas doctors *cure* them.

(b)   PHONETIC SIMILARITY creates a new sense for *sugar* or *shoot* as euphemistic dysphemisms in place of dysphemistic *shit*. To express anger, frustration, or anguish, the remodelled forms *Shoot!, Sugar!, Shivers!, Shucks!* are euphemistic, but the act of uttering them is no less dysphemistic than is the act of uttering *Shit!* Cf. *darn* and *dang* from *damn*, and much else besides.

(c)   There are also ACRONYMS like *snafu* for "situation normal, all fucked (euphemistically, 'fouled') up".

(d)   ABBREVIATIONS like *S.O.B.* for "son-of-a-bitch". Unlike acronyms, abbreviations are written and pronounced as strings of letters rather than as words in their own right, i.e. /es ou bii/ ≠ /sɒb/ (or /sab/); contrast /snɑfu/.

(e)   Another source is VERBAL PLAY. Rhyming slang adds a sense to *cobblers* "rubbish, nonsense", *Brahms* "drunk", and gives the noun *jimmy-riddle* "urinate" (the reader can supply the relevant rhymes).[2] Alliteration and quasi-reduplication are at work in *pull the pope, crank the shank, jerkin' the gherkin* and many other expressions for "masturbate"; also *over-shoulder boulder-holders* ("bra", *bra* being from end-clipped *brassiere*).

(f)   Where euphemism or dysphemism use CIRCUMLOCUTION, e.g. *categorial inaccuracy* or *terminological inexactitude* for "lie", there is only an addition to the lexical stock when the circumlocution becomes a listeme (as a compound or idiom). We often get a polyword paraphrase of a short expression that is a kind of semantic analysis: e.g. *pet* becomes *companion animal*; *rape* becomes *criminal sexual assault* or (as the newspapers used to call it) *a serious offence against a woman*. Many language expressions castigated as jargon (§5.8) are paraphrases of this kind.

(g)   HYPERBOLES (overstatements) are found in euphemisms like *flight to glory* meaning "death".

(h)   There are euphemistic UNDERSTATEMENTS like *sleep* for "die". Many general-for-specific euphemisms are also understatements, e.g. *thing* for whatever, allowing US President Richard Nixon's neologistic references to *prething* and *postthing* where 'thing' referred to the 1972 Watergate break-in which brought him down. Other examples are *nether regions* for "genitals", and *go to bed with*. The legal term *person* for "penis" uses a similar strategy.

(i)   Using *person* for "penis" is true METONYMY – whole-for-part. Classic metonyms, neither dysphemistic nor euphemistic, would be *Next semester we are studying **Shakespeare*** referring to a work (or some works) of Shakespeare. *My aunt has a poodle, **they**'re horrible dogs*.

(j)   When Grose 1811 uses *the monosyllable* as a euphemism for *cunt*, the phrase simply acts as a SUBSTITUTE; cf. the use of *bottom* for "arse/ass", *smalls, frillies* or *jocks* for "underwear"; *break a leg* instead of "Good luck" in the theatre.

(k)   SYNECDOCHES are part-for-whole figures, e.g. *have someone by the short and curlies / by the balls* meaning to have them at your mercy; and *I've got a cough* may ignore the stuffed up nose, post-nasal drip, and running eyes. Classic synecdoches are e.g. *the Crown* for the executive government in Great Britain; *a fleet of ten **sail*** for ten ships; *the girl on the roan **has a good seat*** meaning she rides well. In truth, *metonymy* is often used for both what is here called 'metonymy' and also 'synecdoche'. Etymologically *metonymy* means "one name exchanged for another" and *synecdoche* "to take with something else": thus they were almost synonymous.

(l)   BORROWING from other languages is another source for euphemisms. The use of Latin-derived synonyms provides Standard English with additional vocabulary for bodily effluvia, sex, and the associated acts and bodily organs. The use of *perspire* instead of *sweat*, *expectorate* instead of *spit*, *defecate* and *faeces* instead of *shit*, *copulate* instead of *fuck*, and so forth, is accepted practice when using Standard English. The Latin vocabulary

---

2. For the reader who can't: cobblers awls = balls; Brahms and Liszt = pissed; jimmy-riddle = piddle

was borrowed for the purpose because Latin was for many centuries a language known to the formally educated (who were mostly male) and largely unintelligible to the young and innocent, and to many women (who weren't supposed to hear, and certainly not speak, of such things). Latin is not the only foreign language source for English euphemisms. There is also French: *po* for "chamber pot" from French *pot* [po], *lingerie* for "women's underclothing", and *brassiere* (which is not, of course, the French noun for one). In America, particularly in proximity to New York, Yiddish is a source for euphemistic terms, e.g. *schlong* "penis" from Yiddish *schlang* "snake, penis"; *tush(y)* "bottom" from Yiddish *tokhes/tukhes*, itself a euphemism derived from Hebrew *takhath* "under".

Many euphemisms and dysphemisms are figurative, e.g. *the cavalry's come* for "I've got my period," representing the onset of catamenia as the arrival of the redcoated cavalry; and *go to the happy hunting grounds* for "die"; *two cans short of a six-pack* for "stupid" – a picturesque variant of *not all there*. These are motivated by the desire to speak vividly, a trait that is not uncommon in ordinary everyday language use even if it is more highly developed in rhetoric and poetry.

A much less obvious figure is *pussy* "vulva and/or vagina", which has become established through a network of interacting associations.

(a)   **puss** (pɒs), *n.*[1] Also 6–7 **pus**, **pusse**. [A word common to several Teutonic langs., usually as a call-name for the cat (rarely becoming as in Eng. a synonym of 'cat'): cf. Du. *poes*, LG. *puus*, *puus-katte*, *puus-man*, Sw. dial. *pus*, *katte-pus*, Norw. *puse*, *puus*; also, Lith. *puž*, *puiž*, Ir. and Gael. *pus*. Etymology unknown: perh. originally merely a call to attract a cat.]   (*OED*)

The salience of pubic hair on the human body leads to the names of several furry animals – *beaver, bunny, pussy, ferret, rat* – becoming slang terms for the genitalia of women and men.

(b)   There is a link between rabbits (conies, cunnies [see ex. 5.5.2(d)]), hares, and cats. Grose 1811 notes that *ma(u)lkin* or *mawkin* is a "cat or awkward woman" and in Scotland "a hare". The *OED* gives "hare" as one sense for *puss* (17th–19th centuries). Partridge 1970:1351 lists "rabbit" as one meaning for *pussy* in Australian.

(c)   There is a long tradition of likening women to cats (men to dogs, ferrets, rats, cocks). As an endearment, a woman is likened to a *puss* and a kitten – *kitty*.

(d)   The *OED* lists *pusse* and *pus* used disparagingly of a woman from the early 17th century. From the 16th century, *Kit* was a typical pseudonym for a prostitute and became a term for female genitalia, giving rise to the euphemism *kit has lost her key* for "menstruate".

(e)   A *kitty*, like a *purse*, serves as a source or store of money. There are many figures which treat genitalia – but especially female genitalia – as a source or store of wealth. Cf. *(family) treasure, treasury, crown jewels, jewel, money, moneybox*.

(f)   *Purse* has long been used (cf. Irving 1979 for a recent instance) as one of the hundreds of euphemisms for female genitalia, partly for the reason mentioned in (e) and partly because of the visual resemblance between a slit-top coin purse and the vulva (and also lips, cf. *purse the lips* and, in this context, there is possible influence from Irish *pus* "lips, mouth"; cf. modern English slang *puss* for "face"). The earliest recorded form of *pussy* in the sense under discussion was in fact *puss*, and this is a spelling pronunciation for *purse* in some English dialects. Compare the more or less synonymous doublets in Table 5.1, in which those on the left are colloquial with a short lax vowel, the standard counterpart on the right has a long tense vowel.[3]

Colloquial: short lax vowel	Standard: long tense vowel
ass	arse
bass	barse
bubby	baby
buss	burse "purse"
bust	burst
crick	creek
critter	creature
cuss	curse
gal	girl
hoss	horse
hussy	housewife /hu•swi•f/
mot	mort "young woman"
sassy	saucy
tit	teat
whids	words
wud	world

Table 5.1 Synonymous doublets: colloquial–standard

It is certain that *puss–purse* is one of these doublets.[7]

Fig. 5.1 shows motivations (a–f) falling together to inform and confirm the meaning of *puss* and its endearment variant, *pussy*.

Three semantic processes have just been demonstrated:

(i)   METAPHORICAL EXTENSION of *puss –purse* to the human female sex organ. In Chapters 9–10 we shall review other examples of metaphorical extension.

---

3. Some forms dubbed colloquial, e.g. *crick*, are standard for certain English dialects. Other "colloquial" forms, e.g. *cuss*, have entered the standard language with a meaning that overlaps the "standard" counterpart but are no longer synonymous with it.

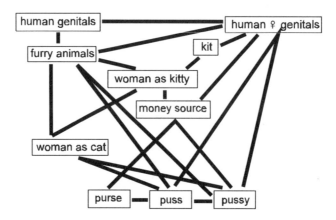

Figure 5.1 A semantic network: the pussy net of (diachronic) semantic relations

(ii)   There was the kind of LEXICAL CONFUSION found in folk etymology of *puss –purse* with *puss* "cat" on the basis of semantic networks that associate women with cats, and furry animals with genitalia (Fig.5.1).

(iii)   This has led to the SEMANTIC TRANSFER of modern *pussy* to these networks and a severance of its historical relation to *purse*.

Euphemism and dysphemism give rise to language change through the loss of some senses of terms, and the cycling of terms from higher to lower styles, perhaps with concomitant replacement by a synonym in the higher style. The substitution of one term for another creates a synonym that is not subject to the blocking principle. A euphemism can be borrowed from another language, but more often arises by semantic extension of an existing lexeme. The semantic extension is usually figurative; but is possibly an example of either metonymy or synecdoche, or an instance of remodelling. Remodelling can also give rise to novel listemes. Last, there are circumlocutions, which affect the lexical stock of the language only when they become compounds or idioms. Metaphorical extension and lexical confusion contribute new meanings to old forms. A new listeme may have multiple sources.

Exercises

5.7.1 What have the following listemes got in common? *Booboo, byebye, choo-choo, dada, geegee, hush-hush, mama, night-night, tata, wee-wee.*

5.7.2 The following are called ABLAUT-COMBINATIONS; they are mostly of the form $C_a \widehat{\ } I \widehat{\ } C_b \text{-} C_a \widehat{\ } æ \widehat{\ } C_b$, a few have /ɒ/ instead of /æ/: *dilly-dally, fiddle-faddle, mishmash, riffraff, ding-dong, flip-flop.* These are cases of quasi-reduplication (cf. Thun 1963). Can you think of any comparable words with a slightly different pattern?

5.7.3 The current meaning of the English noun *bead* was transferred from its former meaning "prayer". Explain.

5.7.4 We have seen that euphemisms are borrowed from other languages. There are two other motivations for borrowing: (a) Language L_a will borrow from L_b the name for something unfamiliar to speakers of L_a; (b) Language L_a will borrow from L_b because L_b has more prestige (in some semantic field) than L_a. Can you think of any borrowings of these kinds?

5.7.5 Discuss language aspects of one or more of the following taboos: (a) HIV and AIDS; (b) menstruation; (c) bodily effluvia; (d) death.

5.8 Jargon is the language peculiar to a trade, profession, or other group (and it is something that everyone uses)

The word *jargon* probably derives from the same source as *gargle* and (probably) *gag*, namely Indo-European **garg-* meaning "throat", and it originally referred to any noise made in the throat. In Middle English it was generally used to describe the chattering of birds, or human speech that sounded as meaningless as the chattering of birds (*OED* 1,3). It came to be

> applied contemptuously to any mode of speech abounding in unfamiliar terms, or peculiar to a particular set of persons, as the language of scholars or philosophers, the terminology of a science or art, or the cant of a class, sect, trade, or profession. (*OED* 6)

This has now become the primary sense, as witness the *Macquarie Dictionary* entry for **jargon**:

> **1**. the language peculiar to a trade, profession or other group: *medical jargon*. **2**. speech abounding in uncommon or unfamiliar words. **3**. (*derog.*) any talk or writing which one does not understand. **4**. unintelligible or meaningless talk or writing; gibberish. **5**. debased, outlandish or barbarous language.

Sense 1 from the *Macquarie Dictionary* is the basis for

Definition 5.9 JARGON is the language peculiar to a trade, profession, or other group.

We will see why it is that senses 2–5 are consistent with D5.9.

Assumption 5.6 Members of a trade, profession, or other group who use a particular jargon are IN-GROUPERS with respect that jargon. People not within the group are OUT-GROUPERS.

D5.9 employs the term *jargon* to include what some scholars call 'specialist' or 'technical' language, 'restricted' language (Firth 1968:98), 'sublanguage' (Kittredge and Lehrberger (eds) 1982), and others 'register' (e.g. Zwicky and Zwicky 1982, Wardhaugh 1986). For instance, Hirschman and Sager (1982:27) define 'sublanguage' as

> the particular language used in a body of texts dealing with a circumscribed subject area (often reports or articles on a technical speciality or science subfield), in which the authors of the documents share a common vocabulary and common habits of word usage.

One notable difference between *jargon* and synonymous terms is that only *jargon* is used pejoratively. Jargons involve more than just lexical differences; they often differ from one another grammatically and sometimes phonologically or typographically. Consider the following examples:

19 MARGINSON — Robyn and David welcome with love on 23rd May, Catherine May Emma (8lbs 11ozs.). A sister for Ryan and Lachlan. All are well and wish to thank the Doncaster Police for the escort in as well as all at Frances Perry House, especially Pat Foster, Jenny Chamberlain, Jane Harper and Dr Max Cole.

> (*The Age*, Melbourne, Thursday, 25th May 1989:19)

20 Syntagmatic relations are characteristically based on the co-occurrence of elements in the speech chain, while paradigmatic oppositions only obtain within the total system, all elements of each network of relations but one being absent from the actual string of phonemes or words through which *langue* manifests itself in *parole*.

> (Atkinson, Kilby, and Rocca 1988:106)

21 STOLE
    Materials: Quantity of handspun wool (the finer the wool the lighter the stole); wooden peg needles approx. 2cm (5/8ths) dowel.
    Cast on 63 sts: Knit 6 rows plain knitting.
    7th row: K4, wl. fwd. K2 tog to the last 3 sts. K3.
    Repeat row 7 until work measures 2 metres or length desired. Knit 6 rows plain knitting, cast off.   (*Weekly Times Farmers' Handbook* (6th edn) Melbourne 1978:239)

22 Note that the reduced cost on transmission inventory in plant 1 at the end of period 2 (*INTRP1T2*) is 1,831.82. The dual price on labor in plant 1, period 2 is 20.1313. It takes 90 hours of labor to assemble a single transmission in plant 1. Carrying a single transmission in inventory at the end of period 2, in plant 1, might thus be interpreted as being equivalent to "throwing away" 90 hours of labor supply. But $90(20.1313) = 1,811.82 < 1,831.82$. How do you explain this discrepancy of $20?   (Eppen and Gould 1979:339)

23

> *Sue and Graeme Cannon*
> *together with*
> *Anne and Bob Ervin*
> *extend a warm invitation to*
>
> ## Natalie and friend
>
> *to share with us the joyous occasion of the wedding of*
> *Vikki and Ken*
> *in the gardens of Nathania Springs, Olinda-Monbulk Road, Monbulk*
> *at 4.45pm on Sunday 10th May 1992*
> *Following the ceremony, a celebration will be held*
> *in their honour at the adjoining reception centre.*
>
> R.S.V.P.
> 1st May, 1992

24 EXPLANATORY NOTE

Regulation 3 of the Local Government (Allowances) Regulations 1974 ('the 1974 regulations') (S.I. 1974/447) made provision prescribing the amounts of attendance and financial loss allowance to members of local authorities. Regulation 3 of the Local Government (Allowances) (Amendment) Regulations 1981 ('the 1981 regulations') (S.I. 1981/180) substituted a new regulation for regulation 3 of the 1974 regulations. Regulation 3 of the Local Government (Allowances) (Amendment) Regulations 1982 ('the 1982 regulations') (S.I. 1982/125) further amends regulation 3 of the 1974 regulations, with effect from 8 March 1982, by increasing the maximum rates of attendance and financial loss allowances. [Etc.]   (Cutts and Maher 1984:57)

25 A fast-medium right arm inswing bowler needs two or three slips, a deep third man, a gully, a deepish mid-off, a man at deep fine leg and another at wide mid-on.

If you are unhappy about calling all of 19–25 'jargon' it is probably because you are thinking of jargon in the same way as Bryson, in the following:

At a conference of sociologists in America in 1977, love was defined as 'the cognitive-affective state characterized by intrusive and obsessive fantasizing concerning the reciprocity of amorant feelings by the object of the amorance'. That is jargon – the practice of never calling a spade a spade when you might instead call it a manual earth-restructuring implement.   (Bryson 1984:85)

A close examination of jargon shows that although some of it is vacuous pretentiousness (see Lutz 1989), and therefore dysphemistic, its proper use is both necessary and unobjectionable. Our purpose here is to explain what jargon is and how jargon comes to be both dysphemistic on the one hand and unobjectionable or even euphemistic on the other.

A jargon is identified by one or more of the following criteria.

(i) LEXICAL MARKERS:

(a)   Vocabulary specialized for use in some particular DOMAIN (the subject-matter of a jargon). The lexical relations among specialized vocabulary will reflect the accepted taxonomies within the domain (e.g. forms, varieties, species, genera, families, orders, classes in biology).

(b)   Idioms and abbreviations, e.g. in telecommunications, *DNA* "does not answer", *MBC* "major business customer", *HC&F* "heat coil and fuse", *LIBFA* "line bearer fault analysis"; in linguistics, *Noun Phrase* and NP; in logic, *if and only if* and *iff*; in biology, ♂ and ♀.

(ii) SYNTACTIC MARKERS such as imperatives in recipes and knitting patterns, large numbers of impersonal passives in reports of scientific experiments (e.g. *It was observed that* ...), full noun phrases in place of pronouns in legal documents (this will be discussed shortly).

(iii) PRESENTATIONAL MARKERS:

(a)   Prosodic (voice quality, amplitude, rhythm, etc.) and paralinguistic and/or kinesic (gaze, gesture, etc.) characteristics within a spoken medium, typographical conventions within a written medium; e.g. a hushed tone and minimal kinesic display is more frequently expected in funeralese than in football commentary or anecdote; in mathematics, {a,b}, <a,b>, and (a,b) will normally have different and conventionally prescribed interpretations; in linguistics, language expressions that are mentioned rather than used are usually italicized.

(b)   Format in which a text is presented: compare 19–25 in this respect. Format is particularly evident in the written medium.

Jargons are often characterized solely in terms of their vocabularies; cf. Wardhaugh 1986:48, Nash 1993, and the *Macquarie Dictionary* sense 2. There are two reasons for this. First, novel words or words used in new ways are more noticeable to most people than are syntactic or phonological novelties. Second, because the specialized vocabulary names those things which are special to the domain in which the jargon is used. However, if you reflect on the language and form of 19–25 in the light of what has just been said about the syntactic, prosodic, etc. aspects of jargon, you will quickly perceive that there is much more to jargon than just vocabulary.

Jargon has two functions:

Assumption 5.7 The primary function of jargon is to serve as a technical or specialist language.

Assumption 5.8 The secondary function of jargon is to promote in-group solidarity, and to exclude as out-groupers those people who do not use the jargon.

To the initiated, jargon is efficient, economical, and even crucial in that it can capture distinctions not made in the ordinary language. A linguist would claim that ordinary nonspecialist language cannot adequately capture all the precision that linguisticalese (the jargon of linguistics) can. Outside the discipline of linguistics there already exists an extensive non-technical vocabulary used by the lay public when talking about language; but unfortunately, the terminology is too imprecise to be of use in the discipline of linguistics. Linguists are therefore faced with having to narrow and redefine everyday terms like *sentence, word, syllable* and *grammar*, as well as add a number of new terms to overcome the imprecisions and to distinguish things that nonlinguists ignore and therefore ordinary language lacks terms for. For example, linguists find the term *word* insufficiently precise for all their purposes and so occasionally need to distinguish between *grammatical, orthographic*, and *phonological words* as well as introducing new terms like *lex, lexeme, morph* and *morpheme* to capture additional distinctions. To achieve its purpose, 20 has to use jargon because one mark of a linguist is control of linguisticalese, e.g.: 'syntagmatic relations', 'co-occurrence of elements', 'speech chain', 'paradigmatic oppositions', 'system', 'string of phonemes', '*langue*', '*parole*'. The text can only be paraphrased for a nonspecialist by extensive and discombobulating circumlocution involving a partial account of Saussure's (1974) linguistic theory. If this were quantum mechanics and not linguistics, no one would question the right to furnish the discipline with a technical vocabulary all of its own. But to the non-linguist such practice often seems unnecessarily pedantic. The technical language is perceived as intellectual hocus-pocus and all the more dysphemistic precisely because it deals with familiar subject-matter.

There are many distinguishing aspects of legal vocabulary. One is the preponderance of borrowings from Latin and French; e.g. *de novo* "from the beginning, anew"; *ex aequo et bono* "on the basis of what is fair and good"; *mens rea* "guilty mind"; *chose in action* "incorporeal personal property right enforceable in court of law"; *voir dire* "to say truly". Another is the common practice of stringing together two, sometimes three, synonyms as 'doublets' or 'triplets': *act and deed; goods and chattels; in my stead and place; cease and desist; remise, release, and forever discharge; rest, residue and remainder*. These derive from an early literary practice of conjoining one noun of Germanic origin with a synonym of Romance origin, as in the case of *false and untrue; will and testament*. But the most befuddling aspect of legalese to out-groupers is probably its grammatical structure. Long and extremely complex sentences can render a piece of legalese very difficult for the general reader to comprehend. Section 1 of Form S6/147 (Guarantee for Existing or New Advance) issued by the Australia and New Zealand Banking Group Limited consists of one sentence about 1270 words long. The average length of a sentence in a legal document is 55 words, which is twice the number for scientific English and eight times the number found in dramatic texts (Danat 1980:479). In 26 below, the subject 'a term of sale' is separated from its predicate 'is void' by a complex of embedded material containing as many as 11 propositions expressed in 88 words. Section (2) includes a string of negatives 'not', 'exclude', 'restrict', 'unless', 'inconsistent' and this significantly complicates the comprehensibility of the passage.

26 (1) A term of a sale (including a term that is not set out in the sale but is incorporated in the sale by another term of sale) that purports to exclude, restrict or modify or purports to have the effect of excluding, restricting or modifying –

(a) the application in relation to that sale of all or any of the provisions of this Part [of the act];

(b) the exercise of a right conferred by such a provision; or

(c) any liability of the seller for breach of a condition or warranty implied by such a provision –

is void.

(2) A term of a sale shall not be taken to exclude, restrict or modify the application of this Part unless the term does so expressly or is inconsistent with that provision.

(Sales Act, State of Victoria, Australia)

It would be dysphemistic for a lawyer not to use jargon when creating a legal document: that is exactly what legalese is for. However, the combination of esoteric vocabulary, grammatical complexities like abnormally long sentences, large numbers of passives, nominalizations, multiple embeddings, intrusive phrases, and multiple negatives, as well as the unconventional presentation and maintenance of topics, typically leads the out-grouper to perceive a legal document as having a discourse structure that is hard to follow. So when the public are presented with documents written in legalese, they will often feel offended by the perception that the writer has violated the cooperative maxim of manner (D1.26) by requiring them to expend unreasonable effort in order to understand what the document means. As a result they may feel incapable of understanding the implications of what is said without help from a lawyer. At worst they see legalese as a kind of secret language that maintains the exclusivity of the legal profession and keeps all the rest of us in the dark (Benson 1985:530ff). This accounts for the many social and political movements currently pushing for clear and simple English, particularly in laws, legal documents like contracts, and government documents of all kinds. Similar movements seem to have sprung up throughout Europe; for example, Cutts and Maher's *Gobbledygook* 1984, quoted above, is the work of a British society for plain English. There are also plain English movements in America and Australia (cf. publications by the Law Reform Commission of Victoria on 'Plain English and the Law'). In Sweden there is currently a strong push for comprehensible Swedish officialese in place of *krångelsvenska* "muddled Swedish", and in Norway there are courses on 'Plain Norwegian for Bureaucrats'. Parallels exist in Germany and France (Danat 1980:451f).

For in-groupers jargon is 'a kind of masonic glue between different members of the same profession' (Hudson 1978:1). Yet it binds not only professionals, but members of any group who use a particular jargon. The way to show in-group membership is to use the appropriate jargon. This is why in the medical and legal professions, for which there is a long and difficult apprenticeship, there is a consequent feeling amongst in-groupers that they belong to an exclusive club. Prestige is awarded to those who command the jargon, which can be used as a form of display. For instance, patients have certain expectations of their physicians, and most of them would probably prefer the jargon expression *patellar tendon reflex* to everyday *knee-jerk*, *dysmenorrhoea* to *period pains*, and whereas *pityriasis rosea* sounds like an expert diagnosis, *rash* does not; indeed, after the latter diagnosis a patient might well wonder why s/he has bothered to pay for a medical opinion at all! Full command of medical jargon is viewed as part of the competence of a medical expert. From another point of view, there are people who might prefer to say, euphemistically, they have *spirochaetal* or *luetic disease* than *syphilis*, just as people may prefer to say *Excuse me a moment* or *I have to go to the loo* instead of *I have to urinate / have a piss*. Not only medicalese and legalese, but also street jargon, druggie jargon, criminalese, and the like, have many terms with synonyms in other jargons; these serve as in-group recognition devices and (purportedly) disguise meanings from out-groupers. Consider examples from several regions: *work* for "work as a prostitute", *a trick* or *a john* for "a prostitute's client"; *tea* or *grass* for "marijuana", *shit* for "cannabis resin", *speed* for "amphetamines", *horse* or *brown sugar* for "heroin", *snow* for "cocaine", *the works* or *a fit* for a mainliner's "hypodermic syringe and spoon"; *a grass* for "a police informer"; *doing porridge* or *at college* for "being in prison"; etc.

The hamburger industry's use of the term *autocondimentation* as opposed to *precondimentation* is an economical way of distinguishing a client's right to sauce his or her own hamburger; but it is certainly not necessary to use *autocondimentation* in order to get the meaning across. So why use it? The answer is, of course, that it confers on the hamburger industry a certain dignity. The dignity comes from the Graeco-Latinate lexicon used, because it is reminiscent of such prestigious jargons as legalese and medicalese. Jargons like bureaucratese (the language of government and corporate offices; cf. Exercise 6.4.4) have two motivations. One, shared with criminal jargon, is the exclusion of out-groupers. The other, and more prevalent, is shared with the hamburger industry. The matters with which bureaucrats deal are mostly mundane and can be fully described and discussed in sixth-grade English such as one finds in the tabloid press. In order to augment their self-image, therefore, bureaucrats create synonyms for existing vocabulary using a Graeco-Latinate lexicon, seeking to obfuscate the mundane (and often trivial) and endow it with gravity; hence lexical substitutions such as

[*Emendation to the traffic plan for a London borough*] Line 5. Delete 'Bottlenecks', insert 'Localised Capacity Deficiencies'.   (Quoted in Cutts and Maher 1984:45)

In American English the general term for bureaucratese is *gobbledygook*, whereas in British and Australian English the sense of this word has generalized to mean "(any type of) incomprehensible language". The word was coined by the pseudonymous Maury Maverick 'thinking of the old bearded turkey gobbler back in Texas, who was always gobbledy-gobbling and strutting with ludicrous pomposity. At the end of this gobble there was a sort of gook' (Partridge 1952:16). In other words, *gobbledygook* is the mouthing of a turkey, which is the American term used for someone who in Australian is *a dork, dill*, or *dag* and in British *a wally* or *prat*.

Because it is founded on a common interest the most remarkable characteristic of a jargon is often its specialized vocabulary and idiom. While jargons facilitate communication among in-groupers on the one hand, on the other they erect communication barriers to keep out-groupers out. It is, of course, out-groupers who find jargon 'abounding in uncommon or unfamiliar words', and therefore 'unintelligible or meaningless talk or writing; gibberish' (*Macquarie Dictionary*). If the out-grouper is sufficiently rancorous s/he might also conclude the jargon is 'debased, outlandish or barbarous'.

We have seen that jargon is a variety of language used among people who have a common work-related or recreational interest. Its principal function is to serve as an in-group language that is an essential tool in precise and economical communication using devices not found in other varieties of the language. For some jargons such as legalese or linguisticalese, the relevant community of speakers (in-group) is fairly well-defined. For others, such as stock-market reports, and games such as bridge, football, cricket, there is barely an in-group at all except among professionals. For language dealing with death (outside of the funeralese of the bereavement industry), birth notices, and recipes, there is even less of an in-group – though there is a special vocabulary and there are conventional patterns of expression for all of these. The facts are clear: where in-groupers are associated with a particular trade or profession, they constitute a well-defined group; they are somewhat less well-defined by a common recreational interest; and the most ill-defined in-group are those defined merely by a temporary interest in the topic of the jargon – such as those members of the public who publish birth notices.

Assumption 5.9 Every text (discourse), including social chit-chat, is jargon of one kind or another.

Assumption 5.10 Everybody uses at least one jargon. Almost everybody controls several, often many, jargons.

A5.9 is the basis for A5.10. It is often the case that an expert in one domain (an in-grouper with respect to its jargon) needs to explain something within the domain to a novice outside the domain (an out-grouper) with minimal use of jargon. An example would be where a lawyer needs to explain some point of law to a client; or a doctor needs to explain a medical condition to a patient. Any jargon is in constant contact with others.

Some, and perhaps all, kinds of slang are jargons; or perhaps slang amounts to one style within a jargon.

Assumption 5.11 There are styles within a jargon.

Within legalese, for instance, four of the five basic styles of English identified in 4 can occur in different settings. 'Frozen' style typically occurs in written documents like wills, but can also be spoken in the case of jury instructions or in a witness's pledge to *tell the truth, the whole truth, and nothing but the truth*. Written 'formal' style is found in statutes and briefs, and can be spoken in the court room in the arguments of counsel and the examination of witnesses. 'Consultative' style is spoken in lawyer–client interaction and lay witness testimonies. 'Casual' style usually occurs only during in-group interaction: for example, in conversations between lawyers. In the casual style one might expect elements of slang such as *beak* for magistrate.[8]

Assumption 5.12 Jargons are not discrete from one another, all of them borrow from language that is common to other jargons.

The boundaries of a jargon are difficult if not impossible to draw, which makes any particular jargon difficult to define precisely.

This section defined jargon and attempted to rehabilitate its reputation by describing its motivations and functions, and indicating its universal use. Choice of a particular jargon involves the choice of a form of language with consequent connotations that affect the meaning of what is said. That is within the purview of semantic theory.

Exercises

5.8.1 Some things you could do:
  (a) Take any four of the different examples of jargon in examples 19–25 and identify
      for each one exactly what you find to be characteristic of the jargon it represents.
      Compare them, where you think it is enlightening to do so.
  (b) The term *jargon* is normally used to refer only to **vocabulary** and not to all aspects
      of a specialized language. Say whether or not you think it would be preferable to
      use a term such as *sublanguage* for what we have been calling 'jargon', and restrict
      the term *jargon* to meaning "the vocabulary of a sublanguage".
  (c) Investigate and compare the jargons of some of the following domains: a sport or
      recreation (cricket, netball, dressage, etc.); cooking recipes; wine appreciation; road
      reports on cars; stock market reports; animal husbandry *or* bird-watching.
  (d) Take a recipe and translate it into bureaucratese.

5.9 Summary

The purpose of this chapter was to examine the power of connotation in directing Speaker's
choice of words and inspiring the creation of new vocabulary. This led to an examination
of jargon and what motivates it.

Chapter 5 ends the lexicological part of the book begun in Chapter 3. The next two
chapters introduce formal tools for doing semantics – tools that derive from logic and
mathematics. We shall be using these tools from time to time in the remainder of the book.
Chapter 6 introduces propositional calculus, then closely examines conversational
implicature and presupposition, all within the context of establishing semantic relations
between sentences.

● Key words and phrases:

abbreviation	(social) distance strategy (D5.6)
ablaut-combination	domain (of a jargon)
acronym	(dysphemistic) downgrade
affective meaning	dysphemism (D5.1)
borrowing	euphemism (D5.3)
bureaucratese (AmE. gobbledegook)	formal style (4)
casual style (4)	frozen style (4)
circumlocution	Hearer-or-Named
connotation (D3.6)	hyperbole
consultative style (4)	in-group (with respect to jargon) (A5.6)
deceptive euphemisms	in-group marker
deference	intimate style (4)
discriminatory language	-IST dysphemism (D5.8)

jargon (D5.9)
legalese
lexical confusion
linguisticalese
metaphorical extension
metonymy (usually whole for part)
out-group (with respect to jargon) (A5.6)
pejorization
personalizing scale (10)
phonetic similarity
(relative) power) (D5.4)
power strategy (D5.6)
presentational marker of jargon
register
remodelling
semantic extension

semantic narrowing
semantic network (Fig.5.1)
semantic relations
semantic transfer
social distance (D5.5)
solidarity
sublanguage
substitute expression
synecdoche (usually part for whole)
synonymous doublets
syntactic marker of jargon
taboo term (D5.2)
tabooed topic
understatement
(euphemistic) upgrade
verbal play

• Because of the blocking principle, it is rare, if not impossible, to find words which can substitute for one another in every context. This is because their connotations differ.

• The connotations of names and terms of address have serious social consequences. The style of naming and addressing used depends on: (a) the role Speaker perceives Hearer-or-Named to have (adopted) relative to Speaker in the situation of utterance; (b) Speaker's attitude towards Hearer-or-Named at the time of utterance.

• Joos 1961 identified five styles for English, intimate — casual — consultative — formal — frozen; ranging from most personal to least personal.

• In some languages there is a personalizing scale in pronouns of address. Cross-linguistically, there are two distinct systems motivated by the components of social status: (a) Deference to Hearer can be marked by exaggerating the social distance between Speaker and Hearer (A5.1, D5.6). (b) Deference to Hearer-or-Named can be marked by exaggerating his or her power relative to Speaker (D5.7 and 10)

• In every language, Speaker may register a change in attitude towards Hearer-or-Named by changing the style of naming or addressing from that which s/he has been using in prior discourse, or which s/he normally uses.

• -IST dysphemisms are found in sexist, racist, and ageist putdowns. -IST terms are disarmed by being used as in-group solidarity markers among members of the targeted group (A5.2).

• The bad connotations of a discriminatory expression may lead to its replacement by another word or phrase, usually with some revision of that word's earlier meaning; sometimes, however, an entirely new listeme is created (11).

• Personal names are taboo among some peoples the world over. Names for dangerous animals and animals being hunted are also frequently taboo. In all such cases a term is tabooed because it has frightful or frightening connotations. As a result, the vocabulary of the language is extended either through semantic extension of some existing word or phrase, or by coining a new one.

• The names of cross-kin (of opposite sex to ego) are often tabooed. These taboos are perhaps grounded in the desire to maintain social harmony.

- What applies to the names and naming of ordinary folk applies more strongly to rulers and to gods, because any threat to their power endangers the entire society they dominate.
- A word or longer expression with bad connotations (however unjustifiable) will suffer pejorization, i.e. downgrading, through society's perception of a word's tainted denotatum contaminating the word itself (A5.3).
- Words denoting women are pejorized in many languages.
- The degeneracy of contemporary language is a recurrent theme in the naturalist tradition, because the naturalist hypothesis leads to a belief that the original word bore the proper form and proper meaning, therefore any subsequent change is a degeneration from the perfectly natural original form, a decline that should be halted or preferably reversed.
- Words for body parts connected with sexual reproduction and defecation, along with those for the associated effluvia, are 'dirty' words because of a belief that their form reflects the essential nature of the taboo topics they denote. Therefore, euphemisms often degenerate into taboo terms through contamination by the taboo topic (A5.4).
- Polysemous words with taboo senses are downgraded by semantic narrowing to the taboo senses alone. Words with a taboo homonym tend to be downgraded out of use.
- There are two reasons why language abandons homonyms of taboo terms. One is their relative salience; the other is that a speaker won't risk appearing to use a taboo term when none was intended. Where there is little likelihood of being misunderstood, the homonyms of a taboo term are likely to persist in the language.
- There is a whole bunch of euphemisms for avoiding the mildly distasteful, upgrading what is favoured and downgrading what isn't. Many times a euphemism is linked with Speaker's point of view, dysphemism with some other view – it is an *us* versus *them* situation. Dysphemisms are used in talking about Speaker's opponents, things Speaker wishes to show disapproval of, and things Speaker wishes to (be seen to) downgrade. A dysphemism, then, is used for precisely the opposite reason that a euphemism is used.
- Five kinds of dysphemistic terms of insult were identified.
- Euphemism and dysphemism motivate language change by promoting new expressions, or new meanings for old expressions, and causing some existing vocabulary to be abandoned. 12 ways of creating new listemes or meanings were identified and described: created by: remodelling, phonetic similarity, acronyms, abbreviations, verbal play, circumlocution, hyperbole, understatement, metonymy, substitution, synecdoche, borrowing. A new listeme or new meaning for an existing listeme may come about through the convergence of semantic processes such as metaphorical extension, lexical confusion, and semantic transfer.
- A jargon is identified by one or more of the following criteria: (a) specialized vocabulary; (b) specialized idioms and abbreviations; (c) certain syntactic norms; (d) its own prosodic, typographical, and kinesic norms; (e) a specialized text format.
- Jargon has two functions. The primary function is to serve as a technical or specialist language (A5.7). The secondary function is to promote in-group solidarity, and to exclude as out-groupers those people who do not use the jargon (A5.8).
- Jargons like bureaucratese (the language of government and corporate offices) have two motivations. The first, the exclusion of out-groupers, is shared with criminal jargon; the second, and more prevalent, is to confer upon the in-groupers a sense of dignity. Prestigious jargons such as legalese and medicalese use a Graeco-Latinate vocabulary; the matters with which bureaucrats deal are mostly mundane and can be fully described and

discussed without a specialized vocabulary. In order to augment their self-image, therefore, bureaucrats create synonyms for existing vocabulary using a Graeco-Latinate lexicon, seeking to obfuscate the trivial and the mundane and endow it with unwarranted gravity. This gets jargon a bad name.

• All language, including social chit-chat, is jargon of one kind or another (A5.9). Everybody uses at least one jargon (A5.10).

• There are styles within a jargon (A5.11).

• Jargons are not discrete from one another; all of them borrow from language that is common to other jargons (A5.12).

5.10 Notes on further reading

[1] On euphemism and dysphemism, see Bolinger 1980, Allan and Burridge 1991.

[2] On the connotations of names and terms of address, see Brown and Ford 1961, Brown and Gilman 1960, 1989, Ervin-Tripp 1969, Ervin-Tripp et al. 1984, Wierzbicka 1992c.

[3] On guidelines for nondiscriminatory language, see Frank and Treichler 1989, Pauwels 1991, Miller and Swift 1995.

[4] For pomposity in naming rulers, see Swift [1735] 1958:24 on the titles of the Emperor of Lilliput.

[5] On the pejorization of terms denoting women, see Allan and Burridge 1991, Miller and Swift 1991, Ng and Burridge 1993.

[6] On types of semantic change, see Stern 1965.

[7] On the historical data in the account of *pussy*, check Grose 1811, *OED*, Partridge 1970, Shipley 1977, Allan and Burridge 1991.

[8] On legal style, see Danat 1980:470–2.

6 Semantic relations between sentences

6.1 Where we are heading

This chapter introduces or redefines some fundamental concepts used in establishing relations between sentences and presents the most basic formal tools for analysing the meanings of sentences in truth-conditional semantics. Because they have been tried and tested over many centuries, these tools are invaluable in semantic analysis.

A sentence consists of one or more propositions. A proposition is essentially the meaning of a declarative clause (D1.8). §6.2 introduces propositional logic as a means of calculating the truth values of connected propositions. Except insofar as a proposition is assigned a value of either T (true) or F (false), its content is ignored. Thus no consideration is given to the pragmatic relevance of a sequence of propositions. Partly for this reason, some linguistics students find propositional logic challenging; but it is well worth the effort of mastering what is in this chapter, because many of the concepts are used extensively in later chapters. §6.3 redefines entailment and synonymy more formally than before. Entailment is compared with conventional implicature, a relation applicable to non-propositional sentence constituents. It is included here to show, on the one hand, its similarity to entailment, and on the other, its dissimilarity with the pragmatic relation of conversational implicature, first introduced in Chapter 1. In §6.4, conversational implicature is defined as an inference that arises from expectations about the way language is usually used. Unlike entailments and conventional implicatures, conversational implicatures are probabilities over a type of utterance that may not be valid for a particular token of the type and, indeed, may be explicitly cancelled without contradiction. §6.5 discusses presupposition (*Bill is smart, he's stopped smoking* presupposes Bill exists and that he used to smoke). The common definition for semantic presupposition is rejected in favour of a definition that says a presupposition is a proposition whose truth Speaker takes for granted in making the utterance. This corresponds to a conversational implicature arising from the precondition on an illocution (D1.10). This accounts for that fact that, like conversational implicatures, presuppositions can be cancelled without self-contradiction. §6.6 summarizes the chapter.

6.2   Propositional calculus: a brief sketch

The propositional calculus establishes the truth conditions between propositions (symbolized p, q, r) joined by LOGICAL CONNECTIVES. Because the function of these connectives is to define a truth value, they are also known as TRUTH FUNCTORS.

CONNECTIVE	TRUTH FUNCTION (MEANING)	NAME
$\wedge$ "and"		conjunction
$\vee$ "and/or"		inclusive disjunction
$\underline{\vee}$ "or else, only one of"		exclusive disjunction
$\rightarrow$ $p \rightarrow q$ "if p then q"		semantic implication (conditional)
$\longleftrightarrow$ $p \longleftrightarrow q$ "p if and only if (=iff) q"		semantic equivalence (biconditional)

Table 6.1 The truth functors (connectives)

The truth value of a connected pair of propositions is based jointly on (a) and (b):

(a)   The truth function (meaning) of the connective.
(b)   The truth value of each proposition in the construction.

   For our purposes, the facts concerning connected propositions are best seen in a truth table. In Truth Table 6.2 the negative operator is used: $\neg p$ means "not-p, it is not the case that p". The symbol 'T' stands for "true" and 'F' for "false".

1	2	3	4	5	6	7	8	9
p	q	$\neg p$	$\neg q$	$p \wedge q$	$p \vee q$	$p \underline{\vee} q$	$p \rightarrow q$	$p \longleftrightarrow q$
T	**T**	$\neg$T=**F**	$\neg$T=**F**	T$\wedge$T=**T**	T$\vee$T=**T**	T$\underline{\vee}$T=**F**	T$\rightarrow$T=**T**	T$\longleftrightarrow$T=**T**
T	**F**	$\neg$T=**F**	$\neg$F=**T**	T$\wedge$F=**F**	T$\vee$F=**T**	T$\underline{\vee}$F=**T**	T$\rightarrow$F=**F**	T$\longleftrightarrow$F=**F**
F	**T**	$\neg$F=**T**	$\neg$T=**F**	F$\wedge$T=**F**	F$\vee$T=**T**	F$\underline{\vee}$T=**T**	F$\rightarrow$T=**T**	F$\longleftrightarrow$T=**F**
F	**F**	$\neg$F=**T**	$\neg$F=**T**	F$\wedge$F=**F**	F$\vee$F=**F**	F$\underline{\vee}$F=**F**	F$\rightarrow$F=**T**	F$\longleftrightarrow$F=**T**

Truth Table 6.2

The rows of Ts and Fs are known as VALUATIONS. In Truth Table 6.2, the value for each cell is explicitly computed. This is not usually done; normally only the result that follows '=' in Truth Table 6.2 would be listed as the valuation. For the valuations in columns 5–9, the value to the left of the truth functor comes from column 1 and the value to the immediate right comes from column 2.

Definition 6.1 In traditional systems of logic, truth is bivalent, i.e. there are only two values possible: any proposition p is either true or else it is false.

This state of affairs is captured in the 'law of the excluded middle' and the 'law of non-contradiction'. It follows that $\neg p$ is true if, and only if, p is false.

Let's compare the meanings of the truth functors in Truth Table 6.2 with the meanings of the closest English connectives: '$\wedge$' with *and*, $\vee$ and $\underline{\vee}$ with *or*, $\rightarrow$ with *if...then*, and $\leftrightarrow$ with *if, and only if.*

Truth conditionally $p \wedge q$ is synonymous with $q \wedge p$. This is obvious in 1 (the truth conditions on '$\leftrightarrow$' are given in column 9 of Truth Table 6.2).

1   Paul is 40 and Emma is 20 $\leftrightarrow$ Emma is 20 and Paul is 40.

But 2 do not mean the same as 3, because natural English *and* often has the meaning "and then" and sometimes "if *p* then *q* will be the consequence":

2   (a)   Max got onto his horse and rode off into the sunset.
    (b)   Emma married Paul and got pregnant.
    (c)   The thief broke the circuit and an alarm bell went off.
    (d)   Lean out that window any further, and you'll fall.

3   (a)   Max rode off into the sunset and got on his horse.
    (b)   Emma got pregnant and married Paul.
    (c)   An alarm bell went off and the thief broke the circuit.
    (d)   ?*You'll fall, and lean out that window (any) further.

Truth conditionally, *and* is identical with logical '$\wedge$'. Take 2(b) and 3(b): if either of them is true then each of the constituent propositions 'Emma married Paul' and 'Emma got pregnant' must necessarily be true. The difference in meaning between 2(b) and 3(b), and each of the other pairs, will be accounted for by the pragmatic relation of conversational implicature.

In the discussion above, each of *p* and *q* was replaced by several clauses of English: e.g. *p* by 'Paul is 40' (1), 'Max got on his horse' (2a), 'Emma married Paul' (2b); *q* by 'Emma is 20' (1), '[Max] rode off into the sunset' (2a), etc. We shall refer to *p* and *q* as propositional VARIABLES. The clauses that replaced them are CONSTANTS.

Assumption 6.1 A variable is rather like a third person pronoun in that it can be used to refer to many different things. Any particular one of these can be given a name, which is a constant.[1]

---

1. Warning: If this footnote confuses you, ignore it altogether. If you like conundrums read on. If *p* and *q* (or x and y) are variables, then it is possible that *p* = *q* (and x = y). It is, however, normally assumed that the different labels *p* and *q* are distinct unless there is a statement to the contrary. In other words, the labels are treated like names, i.e. constants. Coherent discourse would otherwise be very very difficult!

Again because of conversational implicature (see §6.4 and Exercise 6.4.3), most natural English disjuncts, signalled by *or*, are EXCLUSIVE, $p\underline{\lor}q$.

4   Max is either in his office or he has gone home for the day.

The disjunction is true if only one of the two conjuncts is true. It is false if both are false or if both are true.

5   Ron is either 70 or 71 $\longleftrightarrow$ It is not the case that Ron is both 70 and 71, nor that he is neither 70 nor 71.

INCLUSIVE disjunct $p\lor q$ is only false if both p is false and also q is false; otherwise it is true. In natural English, Speaker often indicates inclusive disjunction by the combination *and/or*, 6. Exclusive disjunction can be made explicit by *or else*, 7.

6   Max is in his office *and/or* eating lunch.
7   Max is in his office *or else* he has left for the day.

We shall make much use of semantic implication, $p\rightarrow q$ ("if p then q"), also known as the CONDITIONAL. $p\rightarrow q$ is true for all conditions except when p is true and q is false – as can be seen in Truth Table 6.2.

8   Harry killed Bill $\rightarrow$ Bill is dead.

There is, however, a problem arising from a belief among classical logicians that anything at all can follow from a false statement. According to the Truth Table, 8 is true whenever Bill is dead – even if Harry didn't kill him. It is also true when both propositions are false. There are various ways out of this problem: we shall appeal to the maxims of the cooperative principle, in particular the maxim of relation (D1.25).
There is an ironic idiomatic use of the conditional:

9   (a) If p then I'm a Dutchman.
    (b) If snow is black then I'm a Dutchman.

9 is used (a) when Speaker believes 'p' to be false, and (b) Speaker is known NOT to be a Dutchman.
The formula known as MODUS PONENS is exemplified in 10.

10 $p\rightarrow q$ If Max is in the pub, then he's drinking   (a1)
      $\land p$ Max is in the pub   (a2)
    _____   _____

      $\rightarrow q$ Max is drinking   (c) by modus ponens

Computation of $(((p\rightarrow q)\land p)\rightarrow q)$ proceeds from left to right as shown in Truth Table 6.3. Every valuation can be represented like the fourth row, though this is not the usual way to do it. In row 4 column 4 'T∧F', 'T' is the value of $p→q$ from column 3 and 'F' is the value of p from column 1.

p	q	$p→q$	$(p→q) ∧p$	$((p→q) ∧p) →q$
T	**T**	T	T	**T**
T	**F**	F	F	**T**
F	**T**	F→T=**T**	T∧F=**F**	F→T=**T**
F	**F**	T	F	**T**

Truth Table 6.3

The bracketing in formulae such as $(((p→q) ∧p) →q)$ indicates structure comparable with that in an unlabelled tree structure:

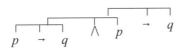

Brackets are omitted wherever possible; e.g. $¬p$ is preferred to $¬(p)$. But brackets are needed to distinguish, e.g. $¬(p∧q)$ from $¬p∧q$ (see Exercise 6.2.6).

The converse of modus ponens is MODUS TOLLENS, $(((p→q) ∧¬q) →¬p)$: from $p→q$ infer that if $¬q$ then $¬p$ either.

11 $p→q$ If that's a cat, then it's an animal   (a1)
    $∧¬q$ It's not an animal   (a2)
    _____   _____

    $→¬p$ It's not a cat   (c) by modus tollens

The Latin terms *modus ponens* and *modus tollens* are widely used.

We shall make extensive use of semantic equivalence, $p↔q$, read "p if, and only if (or *iff*) q". In other words, p and q have the same truth value. The double arrow symbol indicates that semantic equivalence is mutual semantic implication, i.e. $p↔q$ only if $p→q$ and at the same time $q→p$. For this reason it is also called the BICONDITIONAL. Remember that 'semantic equivalence' in propositional logic means "have the same truth value".

12 (a1)   Joe is a bachelor → Joe is a man who has never married
    (a2)   Joe is a man who has never married → Joe is a bachelor
    _____

    (c)   Joe is a bachelor ↔ Joe is a man who has never married

Generalizing:

13 (a1) $p \to q$
   (a2) $q \to p$
   _____
   (c) $p \leftrightarrow q$

The Stoics of Ancient Greece were responsible for establishing 14.

14 $\neg \neg p \leftrightarrow p$

The logical validity of *two negatives amount to a positive* is easy to show on a truth table: we use $\neg$-introduction twice (columns 2 and 3) to change the value in the previous column; and then we introduce $\leftrightarrow$ in column 4.

p	$\neg p$	$\neg \neg p$	$p \leftrightarrow \neg \neg p$
T	F	T	**T**
F	T	F	**T**

Truth Table 6.4

The first and third columns have identical truth values. Although $p \leftrightarrow \neg \neg p$ is logically valid, it needs to be carefully applied in the analysis of natural language. For instance 15 means the same as 16, not 17.

15 She can't not visit her mother on Christmas Day.
16 She really ought to visit her mother on Christmas Day.
17 She can visit her mother on Christmas Day.

And whereas in logic any p can be freely substituted by $\neg \neg p$ (and by $\neg \neg \neg \neg p$, etc.), no such thing is possible in normal language use. For instance, I would introduce my wife to someone using 18 but not 19.

18 This is my wife, Wendy.
19 It is not the case that this is not my wife, Wendy.

The logical form of 19 is perfectly correct; but, although well-formed grammatically, this monstrosity is unacceptable in ordinary language use because it violates the cooperative maxim of manner (D1.26). Every language expression that Speaker chooses to employ contributes to utterance meaning; consequently, double negations like that in 19 are normally reserved for the correction of denials by others, or, occasionally, for humour.

Propositional logic is limited to assigning a truth value to sentences consisting of propositions connected by truth functors. A 'meaningful' sentence is one that is true; false sentences are, by definition, 'meaningless'. This is obviously inadequate for natural language semantics because the constituents of false propositions are not meaningless, cf. *My brother is an only child* (false because it contains a contradiction). We examine the

internal structure of propositions in Chapter 7. Furthermore, there is a distinction between
the truth of a statement and its credibility, and what matters in ordinary language use is
credibility (see the answer to Exercise 6.2.12).

Exercises

6.2.1   Explain why the inference from $p{\wedge}q{=}T$ to $p{=}T$ is valid; but the converse, the
inference from $p{=}T$ to $p{\wedge}q{=}T$, is invalid.

6.2.2   If $p{=}T$, why is $p{\vee}q$ a valid inference but not $p\underline{\vee}q$?

6.2.3   Suppose $p{\wedge}q{=}T$. Are (a) and/or (b) true?   (a) $p{\vee}q$ (b) $p\underline{\vee}q$

6.2.4   Show that the number of conjoined propositions can exceed two without changing
the conditions on conjunction we have identified for the conjunction of just $p{\wedge}q$.

6.2.5   Suppose you have an exclusive disjunction of four propositions $(m\underline{\vee}n\underline{\vee}p\underline{\vee}q)$.
How many would have to be false for the whole disjunction to be false, i.e. $(m\underline{\vee}n\underline{\vee}p\underline{\vee}q){=}F$?

6.2.6 Why are the brackets needed to distinguish $\neg(p{\wedge}q)$ from $\neg p{\wedge}q$?

6.2.7   If $p{\wedge}q{=}F$, is $\neg(p{\wedge}q)$ valid?

6.2.8   Confirm modus tollens by completing the following truth table.

p	q	$p{\to}q$	$(p{\to}q){\wedge}\neg q$	$((p{\to}q){\wedge}\neg q){\to}\neg p$
T	T	T	F	T
T	F	F	F	T
F	T	F	T	T
F	F	T	T	

6.2.9   Complete the truth table below to demonstrate the biconditionality of $p{\to}q$.

p	q	$p{\to}q$	$q{\to}p$	$(p{\to}q){\wedge}(q{\to}p)$	$p{\leftrightarrow}q$	$((p{\to}q){\wedge}(q{\to}p)){\leftrightarrow}(p{\leftrightarrow}q)$
T	T					
T	F					
F	T					
F	F					

6.2.10 Using the following truth table, show whether $(p\underline{\vee}q) \to \neg(p\wedge q)$ is true.

p	q	$p\underline{\vee}q$	$\neg(p\wedge q)$	$(p\underline{\vee}q) \to \neg(p\wedge q)$
T	T			
T	F			
F	T			
F	F			

(handwritten margin note: ? $(p\underline{\vee}q) \Leftrightarrow (\neg p \Leftrightarrow q)$)

6.2.11 Using truth tables, show the truth of (a) and (b).
   (a) $p\underline{\vee}q \longleftrightarrow \neg(p \longleftrightarrow q)$ (b) $\neg(p \longleftrightarrow q) \to \neg(p\wedge q)$

6.2.12 It was said above that credibility matters more than absolute truth in ordinary language use. How can this be? *(handwritten: Co-operation principle)*

6.2.13 The following are disjuncts that could turn out to be inclusive. Explain.
   (a) It is either 3.50 or the clock has stopped. *(handwritten: $p\underline{\vee}q$ (it could be both))*
   (b) Max is either in his room or he is having lunch. *(handwritten: $p\underline{\vee}q$ (eating in room))*
   (c) Is Ed tall or short? *(handwritten: $p\underline{\vee}q$ (subjective, p.o.v))*
   (d) Either the speaker was dull or I was too tired to appreciate that talk! *(handwritten: $p\underline{\vee}q$ (could be both or neither))*

6.3   Entailments and conventional implicatures

Entailment was informally defined in Chapter 4. We update both it and the definition of synonymy in terms of conditional and biconditional semantic implication.

> *Definition 6.2* If A and B are sentences of the object language and their respective semantic descriptions are respectively *a* and *b*, then A ENTAILS B, A‖B, iff $a \to b$ in all possible worlds.

(handwritten: Sophia is a tabby ‖ Sophia is a cat)

> *Definition 6.3* If A and B are sentences of the object language and their respective semantic descriptions are respectively *a* and *b*, then A IS SYNONYMOUS WITH B, A‖‖B, iff $a \longleftrightarrow b$ in all possible worlds.

(handwritten: a wife is a married woman ‖‖ a married woman is a wife)

An example of entailment is 20.

20 The cat is on the mat ‖ An animal is on the mat
   (handwritten: P   q)

If it were false that an animal were on the mat, then it would necessarily be false that *The cat is on the mat*. Thus 21 is incoherent because it contains a contradiction.

21 *The cat is on the mat, but there is no animal on the mat.

(handwritten: truth of p contingent on q)

By contrast, because of the entailment in 20, 22 IS coherent.

22 The cat is on the mat, but there is no other animal on the mat.

There is a potential problem with the reference to possible worlds in our definitions. Suppose we take up Putnam's 1962 suggestion that in some possible world cats are Martian robots (Chapter 3). In such a world either (a) cats are not animals but robots; or else (b) cats are robotic animals, because cats are animals. By induction (Chapter 1), we choose (b) because human experience to date confirms Kripke's 1972 statement 'Cats are in fact animals!' The importance of human experience in establishing meanings is discussed in Chapter 9.

Grice 1975 identified conventional implicature as a non-truth-functional implication. There is no standard symbol meaning "conventionally implicates"; this book uses ▸ (solid arrowhead).

> *Definition 6.4* B is a CONVENTIONAL IMPLICATURE of A, A▸B, when in all possible worlds A implies B (but does not entail B) such that if B does not hold, then A does not hold, either.

The predicate 'does not hold' is used as the non-truth-functional counterpart to *is false*. Grice said very little about conventional implicature, and the only example he discussed in any detail is the use of 'therefore' in 23 (Grice 1975:44f).

23 He is an Englishman, therefore he is brave.

Because of its sense, Speaker's use of the connective 'therefore' indicates that "his being brave" is a consequence of "his being an Englishman". But being an Englishman does not entail being brave because *Every Englishman is brave* is false. More formally, where A ⊭ B "A does not entail B":

24 X is an Englishman ⊭ X is brave

It follows that *therefore* is not a truth functor, though its use does indicate consequence. This non-truth-functional meaning leads Grice to say that *therefore* conventionally implicates "consequence". This is what a linguist would mean by saying 'the sense of *therefore* is "consequently".' Lyons writes

> [A]ll sorts of meaning are encoded – i.e. in Grice's terms, made conventional – in the
> grammatical and lexical (and phonological) structure of particular languages.
>
> (Lyons 1995:276)

The notion of conventional implicature can be expanded to every kind of semantic implication consistent with its definition. For instance

25 four eggs ▸ at least two eggs.

Presumably an entailment would be a conventional implicature were it not truth-functional.[2] Indeed, the truth of 26 is entirely dependent on the conventional implicature (in other words the SENSE RELATION) in 25.

26 Four eggs are bad ‖ At least two eggs are bad

Perhaps the safest way to test conventional implicatures is to use them in connected propositions whose truth values can be evaluated.

Following Grice's initiative, the conventional implicatures of *but, too, either, also, even,* and *only* have been investigated.[1] In 27(a) the scope of 'Even' is the NP 'Harry'; its meaning is brought out in the entailed 27(b).

27 (a) Even Harry has dated Sally.
    (b) Many people have dated Sally, and of all the people who might have dated Sally (or anyone else), Harry is the least likely.

A denial of (b) cannot be conjoined with an assertion of (a) without contradiction. 28 is either contradictory or 'who' is coreferential with 'Harry'; 29 doesn't make any sense at all unless 'has dated her' is negated to *hasn't dated her*; and 30 is blatant contradictory nonsense (unless 'has dated' is construed as "has set up a date with").

28 Even Harry has dated Sally, who has never been on a date before.
29 *Harry is the most likely partner for Sally but even he has dated her.
30 *Even Harry has dated Sally, but they've never been on a date.

The conjunction *but* is truth-functionally equivalent to $\wedge$. It differs from *and* in that it conventionally implicates some sort of contrast, unexpectedness, or adversity. Contrast 31 with 32, which means much the same as either of 33–34.

31 Sally got pregnant and Harry was pleased.
32 Jodie got pregnant but Max was pleased.
33 Jodie got pregnant and, unexpectedly, Max was pleased.
34 Jodie got pregnant but, unexpectedly, Max was pleased.

Note that 31 and 32 have identical truth conditions: both are true when both propositions are true and false if one or both propositions is/are false. Although the conventional implicature of *but* can be strengthened, as it is in 34, it cannot be cancelled without incoherence – as shown in 35, which contrasts with 36.

35 *?Sally got pregnant but, not unexpectedly, Harry was pleased.
36 Sally got pregnant and, not unexpectedly, Harry was pleased.

---

2. Lyons 1995:126f (among others) uses 'entailment' for the non-truth-functional implications here called 'conventional implicature'. While this recognizes the similarity between entailment and conventional implicature, it creates problems for the truth based definition of entailment.

Though they differ truth-functionally, we have seen that entailment and conventional implicature are the same kind of relation: the entailed proposition ('B' in A‖B) and the conventional implicature ('B' in A▶B) cannot be falsified or cancelled (denied) without creating a contradiction or incoherence, cf. 21, 29, 30, 35. On the other hand, CONVERSATIONAL implicatures, which we discuss in the next section, are DEFEASIBLE, i.e. they can be cancelled without incoherence.

In Chapter 4 there was a preliminary definition of contraries. D6.5 refines that and contrasts with a definition for contradictories, D6.6. Some confusion arises because a sentence containing contraries is normally described as containing a contradiction; cf. *That black desk is brown* – colour names are contraries, so are *all* and *no* (Chapter 13). (X⊬Y means "X does not conventionally implicate Y".)

> **Definition 6.5** When ¬(A∧B) then A and B are CONTRARIES. Thus, A▶¬B and ¬B⊬A. When A and B are contraries, they are INCOMPATIBLE.

> **Definition 6.6** When ¬(A↔B), then A and B are CONTRADICTORIES. Thus, A↔¬B and A◀▶¬B. When A and B are contradictories, they are true ANTONYMS.

In bivalent logic *true* and *false* are contradictories and therefore antonymous; *all* is the contradictory of *not all*, and *no* is the contradictory and antonym of *a*.

Exercises

6.3.1 Identify relations of entailment between the following:
  (a) Someone trapped an animal.
  (b) John is in town.
  (c) Today is very hot.
  (d) My brother trapped a rat.
  (e) Today is Monday and it is very hot. p∧q
  (f) Harriet knows that John is in town.
  (g) Tomorrow is Tuesday.

6.3.2 What is the conventional implicature of *another* (the positive counterpart to 'no other [cat]' in 22)?

6.3.3 Why CONVENTIONAL implicature?

6.3.4 Show that (A↔¬B)↔(¬A↔B) but A↔¬B is not semantically equivalent to ¬B→A. (See D6.6 and D6.5 respectively).

6.4 Conversational implicature

The probabilistic character of conversational implicature is easier to demonstrate than define. If a stranger at the other end of a phone line has a high-pitched voice, you may infer that the speaker is a woman. The inference may be incorrect. Conversational implicatures are a similar kind of inference: they are based on stereotyped expectations of what would, more often than not, be the case.

> *Definition 6.7* In the formula A▷B, B is a CONVERSATIONAL IMPLICATURE of A, which is a part (or perhaps the whole) of Speaker's utterance U made in context C under conventional cooperative conditions. B is a pragmatic inference calculated from the meaning of U as being most probable given the common ground (D1.19), i.e. (i) the cooperative principle, (ii) the context C, and (iii) grammatical and encyclopedic knowledge. A conversational implicature is **defeasible** (can be cancelled) without contradicting the utterance which implicates it.

There is no standard symbol meaning "conversationally implicates"; this book uses ▷ (empty arrowhead). Conversational implicatures, first described by Grice 1975, are pragmatic counterparts to the semantic relations of entailment and conventional implicature. In all of A‖B, A▶B, and A▷B, 'B' is an inference from 'A'. In A‖B the inference is determined by truth-conditional logic. In A▶B and A▷B the inference is non-truth-conditional but semantically determined for A▶B and pragmatically determined for A▷B.

Chapter 1 discussed the following interchange:

37 [*The doorbell to Maggie and Frank's apartment rings*]

    MAGGIE [*voice off*]:   Did you hear the doorbell, dear? I'm in the bathroom.
        FRANK: I'll get it.

Many of the inferences drawn from it were conversational implicatures:

(a)   The generalized implicature attached to all spoken questions that Hearer is not deaf.
(b)   The particularized implicature that Maggie is presumably aware that Frank must have heard the doorbell himself.
(c)   Maggie's implicature that the caller needs to be attended to.
(d)   The implicature arising from the cooperative presumption that Maggie has some reason for saying that she is in the bathroom, and that it has particular relevance to fact that there is someone at the door – from which we conclude that she is unable to open the door herself.
(e)   The implicature that Frank's statement 'I'll get it' is a promise to answer the door more or less immediately.

Conversational implicatures are the principal device allowing Speaker to minimize the quantity of language expressed and, conversely, are the principal device Hearer must use to augment what is said in order to understand what is meant.

What sort of scenario would you imagine for 38?

38   STUDENT: Can I talk to you about my thesis proposal?
       PROFESSOR: Have you had lunch?

Under normal circumstances you will assume that the professor's rejoinder is a relevant response to the student's question (i.e. the maxim of relation is presumed) and that s/he is conversationally implicating that they could discuss the thesis proposal over lunch. There is a further implicature we readers draw from the relevance of the professor's rejoinder: that the conversation must have taken place not long before lunchtime (this would be common ground for the participants in 38).

Conversational implicatures arise from exploitation of the cooperative principle. They are therefore pragmatic. Whereas entailments and conventional implicatures are necessary inferences that Speaker cannot deny without self-contradiction, conversational implicatures are cancellable. Although implicatures are often discussed as though they arise only when FLOUTING the cooperative maxims, in any consistent account of implicature they must also arise from OBSERVING the maxims. This is obvious from an interchange like 39.

39   QUESTION: You did some time at Yale, didn't you?
       ABBEY: Two weeks. I went to Yale in the fall of '54.

                                   (Hepworth and McNamee 1989:125)

There is a generalized conversational implicature that a questioner seeks a relevant answer. We the readers, like the questioner, make the assumption that Abbey is responding truthfully: we could legitimately say *In 39 we have Abbey's word for it that he went to Yale for two weeks in the fall of 1954.* It is conversational implicature that justifies the development of 'scripts' that structure dynamic event sequences such as what happens when someone goes to a restaurant.[2] In 40, (a) entails itself and conversationally implicates (b–i) – which constitute the restaurant script.

40 (a)   Sue went to a restaurant last night with her new boyfriend.
   (b)   Sue intended to eat at the restaurant with her new boyfriend.
   (c)   Sue entered the restaurant, probably with her boyfriend.
   (d)   Sue and her boyfriend sat down.
   (e)   They ordered food.
   (f)   The food was brought.
   (g)   They ate it.
   (h)   Either Sue or her boyfriend paid the bill.
   (i)   Then they left the restaurant.

None of the clauses in (b–i) describe events that necessarily occurred, but they are all likely given that (a) is true. Any that do not apply can be cancelled, as most are in 41.

41 Sue went to a restaurant last night with her new boyfriend, but as soon as they'd got inside the door they had a huge fight and left before even sitting down.

In calculating the meaning of an utterance such as 41, the entailments and conventional implicatures of its constituents take priority over conversational implicatures. 41 entails 42–46, each of which has implicatures (e.g. 46 conversationally implicates that they walked out of the restaurant).

42 Sue went to a restaurant last night with her new boyfriend.
43 Sue entered the restaurant with her boyfriend ('they'd got inside the door').
44 Sue and her boyfriend had a huge fight in the restaurant.
45 Sue and her boyfriend didn't even sit down.
46 Sue and her boyfriend left the restaurant ('and left').

❶ 42 conversationally implicates 40(b).
❷ 43 supersedes 40(c).
❸ 45 explicitly cancels 40(d).
❹ 46 supersedes 40(i).
❺ 45 and 46 together cancel 40(e–h).

Horn 1972 identified a category of scalar implicatures.[3]

Definition 6.8 Given any scale of the form $<e_1, e_2, e_3, ..., e_n>$, if Speaker asserts e_i then s/he potentially conversationally implicates that it is not the case that e_{i-1} holds nor e_{i-2} nor any e higher up the scale.

Some scales:

<all, most, many/much, some, a few/little, a(n)>
$<n\geq6, 5, 4, 3, 2, 1>$
<no, not all, few/little>
<excellent, good>
<hot, warm>
<cold, cool>
<love, like>
<always, often, sometimes>
<succeed in doing A, try to do A, want to do A>
<know that *p*, believe that *p*>
<necessarily/certainly *p*, probably *p*, possibly *p*>
<must, should, may>
<and, or>

If Speaker says *I have two children,* this implicates that s/he has no more than two children. In the case that, say, Ed asserts *I have two children* when in fact he has five, he utters a logical truth and yet can be accused of speaking "falsely" because he has failed to observe the conventions for the normal use of language and misled Hearer by ignoring the communicative significance of scalar implicatures.

Scalar implicatures are, of course, defeasible.

Scalar implicatures

47 Q: Did some of the students come to his talk?
A_1: Yes [some of them came], in fact all of them.
A_2: Yes, at least some, if not all.

In the answers A_1 and A_2 the truth of 'some' is admitted, but the implicature is cancelled (strictly speaking, suspended in A_2 pending possible cancellation) by the correction to 'all'. In the contrary state of affairs, it is necessary to deny the truth of Q's supposition, as we see from a comparison of the acceptable answer $48A_3$ with the unacceptable $48A_1$–A_2.

48 Q: Did all of the students come to his talk?
A_1: *Yes [all of them came], in fact some of them.
A_2: *Yes, at least all, if not some.
A_3: No [not all of them came], but some did.

Consider the semantic and implicative relations between the four sentences in 49.

49 (a) I have no money with me.
(b) I don't have much money with me.
(c) I have some money with me.
(d) I don't have much money with me, in fact none.

Let's assume (it will be demonstrated in Chapter 13) that *no⌒N* contradicts *some⌒N* and *none⌒of⌒N* is synonymous with *no⌒N*. The relations between 49(a–d) are given in the calculation table for 49. The table makes reference to logical transitivity:

> *Definition 6.9* The relation of LOGICAL TRANSITIVITY holds if, for all A, B, C, when $A \rightarrow B$ and $B \rightarrow C$, then $A \rightarrow C$.

It follows that if $A \Vdash B$ and $B \Vdash C$, then $A \Vdash C$.

(a)$\Vdash$(b)	If (a) is true, (b) must also be true.	1
(a)$\Vdash\neg$(c)	If (a) is true (c) cannot be true.	2
(a)$\dashv\Vdash$(d)	By inspection of the semantic content.	3
(d)$\Vdash$(b)	By 1 and 3 (transitivity). Also by inspection.	4
(d)$\Vdash\neg$(c)	By 3 and 2 (transitivity).	5
(b)$\triangleright$(c)	Scalar implicature.	6
(d)$\triangleright$(c)	By 4 and 6.	7
$\neg$[(d)$\triangleright$(c)]	By 5.	8
The implicature of the first clause in (d) is cancelled: 5 cancels the implicature in 7		9

Calculation table for 49

Scalar implicatures are one kind of quantity implicature (D1.23). Grice 1975:45 identified two:

(a)   Quantity1 enjoins Speaker, to make the strongest claim possible consistent with his or her perception of the facts.
(b)   Quantity2 enjoins Speaker to give no more and no less information than is required to make his/her message clear to Hearer.

Quantity1 results in negative upscale (conversational) implicature:

50 (a)   some ▷ not most   <most, some>

     (b)   three ▷ no more than three   <n≥4, 3>

     (c)   p or q ▷ not both p and q   <and, or>

     (d)   I ran over a dog ▷ The dog was not mine or yours   <definite,
                  yesterday   indefinite>

     (e)   Sally went out with ▷ The man was not her partner   <definite,
                 a man last night   indefinite>

     (f)   Kim had the ability ▷ Speaker doesn't know that   <do A, have an
                 to win that race   Kim did win that race   ability to do A>

Quantity2 implicatures are lexically and/or grammatically distinct from Quantity1 implicatures. Quantity2 implicatures can be thought of as common ground (including shared knowledge of language and its use) which Hearer uses to augment what is actually said. With Quantity2 implicature, because Speaker has not indicated otherwise, Hearer is expected to make the default interpretation, 51. There are many more Quantity2 than Quantity1 examples.

51 (a)   It's a bird ▷ It's capable of flight (if it's alive)

     (b)   Sally climbed and climbed ▷ Sally used her legs and feet and went
                                                                upwards

     (c)   Kim was able to win that race ▷ Kim won that race (cf.(50f))

     (d)   Emma got pregnant and ▷ Emma got pregnant and then later
                          married George   married George

     (e)   Sam and Jack bought a house ▷ They bought it together

     (f) If you mow the lawn, (then) I'll ▷ I'll give you $15 only if you mow the
                          give you $15   lawn

     (g)   Jack ate the cookies ▷ Jack ate all the cookies

     (h)   I don't believe we've met ▷ I believe we have not met

     (i)   Jack backed a horse ▷ It was a racehorse

(j)   Sam broke an arm ▷ Sam broke his own arm

(k)   The driver stopped the car ▷ by applying the footbrake

Quantity2 implicatures are what Jackendoff refers to as 'preference conditions'.[4] For example:

52 TERM   QUANTITY2 IMPLICATURE = PREFERENCE CONDITION

     bird   something which can fly [cf. 51(a)]

    climb   climb upward and use feet [cf. 51(b)]

      go   go forward

 X sees Y   X's gaze makes contact with Y and X has visual experience of Y

   walk   walk forward using legs and feet

Consider them in more detail, starting with 53.

53 I'm looking at a bird.

Especially when unaided by a natural context, 53 denotes a bipedal creature with beak and feathers that can fly. Even though some chicks are naked when they come out of the egg, and penguins and emus don't fly, these are all members of the category Bird. Jackendoff 1983:150 represents the condition that a typical bird can fly as 54.

$$54 \quad \begin{bmatrix} \text{TYPE} \\ \text{BIRD} \\ \text{P(CAN FLY)} \end{bmatrix}$$

Such conditions are common to reasoning in many areas of cognitive processing: scripts and frames, the perceived groupings of notes and chords in musical scores, and in visual perception.[5] In Fig. 6.1, for example, there is a preference condition that A continues behind B as indicated by the dotted line.

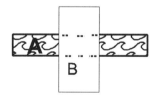

Figure 6.1 Bar B crosses bar A

Of course, the invited inference could be wrong: there may be a V-shaped contour in A that is masked by B; or A might end behind B and what appears to be a continuation to the right may be another rectangle. As common sense surely predicts, semantics is not autonomous from other aspects of cognition.

Preference conditions arise from reasonable expectations about the way the world is. In language, they are Quantity2 conversational implicatures. All conversational implicatures arise from the cooperative principle which identifies our normal expectations of the way people will behave when speaking to one another. Preference conditions are implicated whenever the common ground (including what S says) gives no indication to the contrary. Like all conversational implicatures, Quantity2 implicatures are open to cancellation. For instance, the Quantity2 implicature on *bird* is cancelled without contradiction in 55.

55 An emu is a bird that can't fly.

Take the verb *climb*.

56 X climbs → (X goes upward) ∨ (X moves in a vertical axis using legs and feet)
   X climbs ▷ (X goes upward) ∧ (X moves in a vertical axis using legs and feet)

Note that the semantic implication allows for only one of the two propositions *X goes upward* and *X moves in a vertical axis using legs and feet* to be true, but the default implicature draws the strongest inference possible (A1.9), i.e. that both propositions are true. Where A ≢ B "A is not synonymous with B":

57   Bill climbed the mountain ≢ { ⊢ Bill climbed up the mountain
                                  ⊬ Bill climbed the mountain on his knees.

58 Bill climbed down the mountain ≢ Bill climbed the mountain

59 (a) Bill climbed the valley.
   (b) Bill climbed down into the valley.
   (c) Bill climbed out of the valley.

Snakes, airplanes, and ambient temperature lack legs and feet they can use when climbing (presumably a metaphorical extension with these actors), hence:

60 (a) The snake climbed the tree.
   (b) ??The snake climbed down the tree.

61 (a) The airplane climbed to its cruising altitude.
   (b) ??The plane climbed down to land.

62 (a) The temperature climbed to 42.
   (b) ??The temperature climbed down to −10.

Jackendoff's 1985:288 lexicon entry for *climb* is 63.

63

$$\left[\begin{array}{l} \text{climb} \\ \text{+V,--N} \\ [\underline{\quad}(XP_j)] \\ \left[\begin{array}{l} \qquad\qquad\qquad \{j\} \\ \left[\text{GO}(i,\left[\begin{array}{l}\left\{\begin{array}{l}\text{TO TOP OF }[_{\text{Thing}}\,j] \\ \text{VIA }[_{\text{Place}}\text{ ON }[_{\text{Thing}}\,j]]\end{array}\right\}\end{array}\right]_{\text{Path}}\,\text{P(UPWARD)})\right] \\ {}_{\text{Event}}\quad \text{P}([_{\text{Manner}}\text{ CLAMBERING}])\end{array}\right]\end{array}\right]$$

In 63 'climb' is the formal specification. '+V,--N' is the morphosyntactic specification. '[___(XP_j)]' is the strict subcategorization indicating that *climb* may be either transitive or intransitive. XP is a variable for either NP or PP. The index i identifies the subject and theme location; j is the thing climbed – hence '$[_{\text{Thing}}\,j]$'. Climbing is an '$[_{\text{Event}}\,]$'. So, in Jackendoff's metalanguage:

64 Bill climbed $\longleftrightarrow$ CLIMB(BILL,$[_{\text{Path}}$])
65 Bill climbed that $\longleftrightarrow$ CLIMB(BILL,$[_{\text{Path}}$THAT$_j]$)
66 Bill climbed the mountain $\longleftrightarrow$ CLIMB(BILL,$[_{\text{Path}}$ TO TOP OF $[_{\text{Thing}}$ MOUNTAIN$_j]]$)
67 Bill climbed along the roof $\longleftrightarrow$ CLIMB(BILL,$[_{\text{Path}}$ VIA $[_{\text{Place}}$ ON $[_{\text{Thing}}$ ROOF$_j]]]$)

The two Quantity2 implicatures in 63 are P(UPWARD) and P(CLAMBERING) – the second one (from Fillmore 1978) being the counterpart to *moves in a vertical axis using legs and feet* in 56.

The verb *walk* potentially implicates "walk forward", any other direction must be made explicit. Similarly with *drive*.

68 She drove the car into the garage ▷ The car went forwards into the garage

Consequently there is no need for a verb *front* to be used as in 69, it is blocked by 68; but there is the need for a special verb *back* in 70.

69 *She fronted the car into the garage.
70 She backed the car into the garage.

Finally, consider the Quantity2 implicatures on *see*.

71 X sees Y $\longleftrightarrow$ X's gaze makes contact with Y $\lor$ X has visual experience of Y
   X sees Y ▷ X's gaze makes contact with Y $\land$ X has visual experience of Y

Hence:

72 Bill saw a movie.
73 Bill looked straight at me, but he didn't see me.
74 Bill saw a vision.

75 *Bill saw a vision, but he didn't notice it.

(Exercise 6.4.10 checks whether you understand the relevance of Quantity2 implicatures in 72–75.)
 Chapter 13 and Allan 2000 include some discussion of many of the other quantity implicatures of 50–51. To end discussion of them in this chapter, compare the lexically distinct 50(f) with 51(c).

50 (f) Kim had the ability to win that race ▷ Speaker doesn't know that Kim
                                                  did win that race   [Quantity1]
51 (c) Kim was able to win that race ▷ Kim won that race   [Quantity2]

The negative implicature of 50(f) is not valid for a non-past. Neither entailing sentence in 76–77 implicates that Kim will not win that race; but they do entail that s/he hasn't yet done so.

76 Kim has the ability to win this race ∥ Kim has not yet won this race
77 Kim will have the ability to win that race ∥ Kim has not yet won that race

The winner may play an active part in superseding competitors, e.g. when winning a race, or not, as in winning a lottery. When winning is the achievement of effort, there are the entailments in 78–79.

                        b   >   a
78 Kim won that race ∥ Kim was able to win that race [= 51(c)]
79 Kim was able to win that race ∥ Kim had the ability to win that race [= 50(f)]

It follows from 78–79 that

80 Kim didn't have the ability to win that race
      ∥ Kim wasn't able to win that race
      ∥ Kim didn't win that race

80 shows that despite their incompatible implicatures, 51(c) ∥ 50(f), a fact I will return to. If Kim won, then s/he proved her ability to win (whether honestly or corruptly). So if Speaker is speaking felicitously, the first conjunct of 81 must be uttered before Speaker is aware that Kim has won. In the present tense the difference between *have the ability to* and *be able to* is neutralized (a grammatical constraint on quantity implicature).

81 $_{[\Phi}$Kim $\left\{ \begin{array}{l} \text{has the ability} \\ \text{is able} \end{array} \right\}$ to win this race$_{\Phi]}$ and, in fact, $_{[\Psi}$she has won$_{\Psi]}$.

If sentence Φ^3 in 81 is felicitous at time t_1 then Ψ is only felicitous at a later time t_2. In *Kim had the ability to win*, Speaker entertains the possibility of Kim's having been capable

---

3. If you don't already know these upper-case Greek letters: 'Φ' is *phi* and 'Ψ' is *psi*.

of winning and the possibility would normally have been resolved by the facts of whether or not Kim won. To speak felicitously, Speaker should have chosen one of the sentences in 76, *Kim won that race* or *Kim was able to win that race* (=51(c)) if s/he knows that Kim won, hence the left-hand side of 50(f) implicates that Speaker doesn't know that Kim won – or in other words, implicitly admits the possibility that Kim did not win.

81Φ has the implicature *There are reasonable grounds for the belief that Kim has the ability/is able to win this race*. A reasonable ground would be Kim's performance in comparable races. The implicature arises from the maxim of quality (D1.24).

Looking back to 78–79, we can identify the following relations.

C > b > a

Kim won that race ⊩	Kim was able to win that race ⊩	Kim had the ability to win that race
outcome of ability	exercise of ability	potential ability

Pollyanna Principle

As a result of the pollyanna principle (positive evaluation is preferred wherever possible to adverse evaluation, Boucher and Osgood 1969), the exercise of ability is, by default, expected to lead to a successful outcome. Hence, the Quantity2 implicature in 51(c). Potential ability, however, has unknown outcome; hence the Quantity1 implicature in 50(f).

Kim was able to win that race ⊩ *Kim had the ability to win that race*, i.e. 51(c) ⊩ 50(f), despite their different implicatures. The reason is that implicature is partly a function of the choice of words in an utterance. Choosing the former indicates that the implicature of the latter does not apply. The same rule applies when *two* is used instead of *three*: *three* logically implies *two* and *two* implicates "no more than two", which is certainly not the implicature of *three* (Chapter 13). The rule applies just as well to *emu* and *bird*: the Quantity2 implicature "can fly", does not apply to *emu* despite the fact that *X is an emu* ⊩ *X is a bird*. It is, therefore, a regular effect of lexical choice that *Kim was able to win that race* does not implicate "Speaker does not know that Kim did win that race."

That's all for now on quantity implicatures; more is said about some of them elsewhere (Chapter 13). Together with the necessary semantic properties, quantity implicatures identify the typical attributes of the denotatum. They enable a rational explanation to be given for the application of a single lexeme such as *bird* to denotata with diverse characteristics such as birds that fly and others that don't. It is a lesson in capturing the flexibility of natural language in a principled manner.

Finally, here is a different kind of conversational implicature: 82 implicates that Speaker intended to say 83.

82 I've got my mires wuddled.
83 I've got my wires muddled.

The meaning of 'mires wuddled' is indeterminate at first. The cooperative principle leads us to invoke the communicative presumption (D1.27) and reasonableness condition (D1.28): in other words we presume that Speaker intended to communicate a coherent message. We therefore seek to resolve the indeterminacy by appealing to encyclopedic knowledge of language usage. This should lead us to recognize the spoonerism in 82:

" Spoonerism

Speaker has got the onsets to the words interchanged.[6] Thus 82▷83. In principle, the implicated 83 is defeasible because it may not be what Speaker intended to say in 82; e.g. a promoter of mud wrestling might have meant *I've got my mud fiddled*, a fireman *I've got my fires muddled*.

The conversational implicatures of an utterance U made in context C are pragmatic inferences that derive from stereotyped expectations about the use of the form of words in U in a context such as C. This section contrasted the defeasibility of implicatures with non-defeasible entailments and conventional implicatures. There are generalized implicatures, such as scalar implicatures, that match types of utterances with types of contexts; and there are particularized implicatures associated with some particular context. The implicature of any utterance or proposition within the utterance is calculated from the set of its implicatures minus any that have been superseded or cancelled by entailments of propositions in the immediate co-text. Finally, we compared Quantity1 implicatures which place negative restrictions on the interpretation of what is said with Quantity2 implicatures which augment what is said. There are lexical and/or grammatical constraints on which quantity implicature applies, but we only investigated them as they apply to *had the ability to* versus *was able to* (see Allan 2000 for more).

Exercises

6.4.1 Comment on the following interchanges.

(a)   MADGE: So what's happening between you and Harry?

      SUE QUICKLY LOOKS AT   Goodness! Is that the time? I must rush. Bye for
         HER WATCH: now.

(b)   JERRY: Wanna come to a movie tomorrow night?

     SHANA: I'm sorry, I have to wash my hair.

6.4.2 Explain how scalar implicature permits us to explain why it is that *or* is usually understood exclusively (i.e. as "or else" and not "and/or") in natural language. Use as a model sentence: *Sue is marking essays or watching Seinfeld*.

6.4.3 Explain the implicatures in (a)–(b).
(a) Gilbert wrote *The Mikado* ▷ Gilbert and no one else did so
(b) I think that *p* ▷ I don't KNOW that *p*

6.4.4 What cooperative maxim is exploited in the memorandum quoted below, and what is Lynn and Jay's resulting implicature?

Memorandum

To: *The Prime Minster*   *14 November*

From: *The Secretary of the Cabinet* [Sir Humphrey Appleby]

Certain informal discussions have taken place, involving a full and frank exchange of views, out of which there arose a series of proposals which on examination proved to indicate certain promising lines of enquiry which when pursued led to the realization that the alternative courses of action might in fact, in certain circumstances, be susceptible of discreet modification, in one way or another, leading to reappraisal of the original areas of difference and pointing the way to encouraging possibilities of significant compromise and co-operation which if bilaterally implemented with appropriate give and take on both sides could if the climate were right have a reasonable possibility at the end of the day of leading, rightly or wrongly, to a mutually satisfactory conclusion.

I [the Prime Minister] stared at the sheet of paper, mesmerised. Finally, I looked up at Humphrey. 'Could you summarise this please?' I asked.

He thought hard for a moment. 'We did a deal,' he replied.

(Lynn and Jay *The Complete Yes Prime Minister* 1989:402f)

6.4.5 Create a table showing the calculation of entailments and conversational implicatures for (a):

(a)   Some of the students came, in fact all of them.

6.4.6 In classical propositional logic if p is valid then so is $p \lor q$. However in natural language, when given one proposition you cannot freely introduce another proposition and disjoin it from the first. Why is that?

6.4.7 Show that one of $A \to B$, $\neg A \to \neg B$, or $\neg(A \underline{\lor} B)$ is logically implied by both $A \land B$ and $\neg A \land \neg B$.

6.4.8 Explain what each of the examples in 57–59 show. For example, 57 shows that Bill went upward and used his feet to do so.

6.4.9 Which implicatures hold for each of 72–75? (*Bill saw a movie. Bill looked straight at me, but he didn't see me. Bill saw a vision. *Bill saw a vision, but he didn't notice it.*)

6.5   Presuppositions and preconditions on illocutions

VINCENTIO: Come hither, you rogue. What, have you forgot me?
BIONDELLO: Forgot you! No, sir. I could not forget you, for I never saw you before in all
                my life.

(Shakespeare *Taming of the Shrew* V.i.49)

Everyone who knows a little of French history knows that 84 is false in the world we inhabit.

84 In 1990, France had a bald King.

France did not have a bald King in 1905 either, when Bertrand Russell claimed that 85 is false.

85 The present King of France is bald.

Both 84 and 85 entail that the King of France has extension at the relevant time.

84' There was in 1990 a King of France.
85' There is a King of France.

Both 84'–85' are false, hence, by modus tollens (11), 84–85 are false. 85' is also entailed by all of 86(a–e), thus they too are false (or similarly faulty if a truth valuation is not appropriate to 86(b–e)).

86 (a)   The present King of France is not bald.
    (b)   Where's the King of France gone?
    (c)   Is the King of France attending Di and Chuck's wedding?
    (d)   Shoot the King of France!
    (e)   That damned King of France!

Strawson 1950 said that a sentence like 85 does not entail but falsely PRESUPPOSES 85'.[4] The fact that both 85 and 86(a) presuppose 85' gives rise to the standard definition of presupposition, which uses the classical relation of entailment.

> *Definition 6.10* If A entails B and also ¬A entails B, then A SEMANTICALLY PRESUPPOSES B and ¬A SEMANTICALLY PRESUPPOSES B. Symbolically,
> $$(A \Vert B \lor \neg A \Vert B) \rightarrow (A \underline{\lor} \neg A) \gg B$$

In addition to definite NPs, there are about 30 other kinds of presupposition triggers.[7] Here are a couple. Factive predicates such as *know, realize, regret, be aware, be glad, be indifferent, be proud, be odd, be sad, be sorry* presuppose the truth of their complements.

---

4. In fact, Strawson 1950 used the term 'imply' and not 'presuppose' as he did later.

87 (a) Jo $\left\{ \begin{array}{c} \text{regrets} \\ \text{doesn't regret} \end{array} \right\}$ kissing Eric » Jo kissed Eric

   (b) Does(n't) Jo regret kissing Eric? » Jo kissed Eric

Verbs of judging presuppose their sentential complements:

88 (a) Sue $\left\{ \begin{array}{c} \text{accused} \\ \text{didn't accuse} \end{array} \right\}$ Ed of having an affair with Ann » Ed has been having an affair with Ann

   (b) Sam $\left\{ \begin{array}{c} \text{blamed} \\ \text{didn't blame} \end{array} \right\}$ Suzie for their being late » Sam and Suzie were late

   (c) Mike $\left\{ \begin{array}{c} \text{forgave} \\ \text{didn't forgive} \end{array} \right\}$ Jim for speaking out of turn » Jim spoke out of turn

Implicative verbs like *forget* (cf. the quote at the head of this section), *happen to, have the misfortune to, manage* presuppose the truth of their complements in declarative clauses, but not in interrogatives and imperatives. *Did Jack manage to speak to Harry* does not presuppose *Jack spoke to Harry* though it does presuppose *There is a question about whether or not Jack spoke to Harry*. Aspectual verbs like *begin, continue, stop, come to* and iteratives like *return, repeat, another time* have aspectual presuppositions.

89 (a) Harry $\left\{ \begin{array}{c} \text{started} \\ \text{didn't start} \end{array} \right\}$ to eat » Harry had not been eating before

   (b) Jerry $\left\{ \begin{array}{c} \text{stopped} \\ \text{didn't stop} \end{array} \right\}$ seeing Elaine » Jerry had been seeing Elaine

   (c) Harry $\left\{ \begin{array}{c} \text{repeated} \\ \text{didn't repeat} \end{array} \right\}$ the year » Harry had done the year before

   (d) Jack $\left\{ \begin{array}{c} \text{rang} \\ \text{didn't ring} \end{array} \right\}$ for a third time » Jack had already rung twice

Cleft and heavily stressed NPs have presuppositions such as in 90:

90 (a) It was(n't) Jack who called » Someone called

   (b) **JACK** $\left\{ \begin{array}{c} \text{went} \\ \text{didn't go} \end{array} \right\}$ » Someone went

You may have noticed a logical problem with D6.10:

(a)   A$\lor\neg$A is a logical tautology (not quite the same as a linguistic tautology D2.11). A logical tautology is a proposition that is necessarily true in every logically possible world; e.g. *Snow is white or else snow is not white. Grass is green or else grass is not green.* A tautology is truth-conditionally equivalent to every other tautology, e.g.

$(A\underline{\vee}\neg A) \hookrightarrow (B\underline{\vee}\neg B)$ or (*Snow is white or else snow is not white*) $\hookrightarrow$ (*Grass is green or else grass is not green*).

(b)   A tautology cannot (without contradiction) entail a non-tautology because $(p{\rightarrow}q)$=T whenever q=T, cf. column 8 of Truth Table 6.2. Therefore what is presupposed (B in D6.10) must be a tautology.

(c)   Given (a) and (b), every sentence presupposes all tautologies (cf. Katz 1973:258, Boër and Lycan 1976:6).

(d)   Although logically possible, from a cognitive point of view, (c) is absurd.

(a–d) violate the intuitive notion of presupposition. Despite the fact that D6.10 appears to account for many cases of presupposition, its consequences are unacceptable.[8]
     For a variety of technical reasons Gazdar 1979 and Levinson 1983 argue that semantic presupposition is simply not viable. One, already suggested in Strawson 1950, is that presupposition is essentially speaker-based in the sense that we interpret A»B as "A indicates that Speaker presupposes B". This is treats presupposition as PRAGMATIC. It is not always Speaker who does the presupposing; for instance with proprioceptive verbs of thinking and believing, or with verbs of saying:

91 Sam $\begin{cases} \text{says} \\ \text{believes} \\ \text{thinks} \\ \text{writes} \end{cases}$ that the King of France is coming to his party, which just
                                                                goes to prove the guy is nuts.

It is 'Sam' who presupposes there's a King of France; the 'which...' clause implicates that Speaker doesn't. Karttunen 1973 named verbs of this kind 'presuppositional PLUGS'.
     Presuppositions are pragmatic because they can be cancelled, unlike semantic/logical relations. For example, 92 cancels the presupposition of 85 and 93 the presupposition in 87.

92 The present King of France isn't bald, because there is no King of France at present.
93 Jo doesn't regret kissing Eric, because in fact she never kissed him in the first place.

These negations have the peculiar property of being refutations that are intuitively quotative – because it is appropriate to insert words to the effect of *as you claim* before the comma in 92–93. There may seem to be two types of negation:

(a)   an ordinary negative which does not negate the presupposition, e.g. *Jo doesn't regret kissing Eric*
(b)   PRESUPPOSITION NEGATION ('radical negation' in Seuren 1985, 'external negation' in Gamut 1991) which denies both the presupposition and the assertion (cf. 92–93).

In presupposition negation the presupposing clause has to be negated; retention of an affirmative creates incoherence:

94 *The present King of France is bald, because there is no King of France at present.
95 *Jo regrets kissing Eric, because in fact she never kissed him in the first place.

The difference between 92–93 and 94–95 arises from the fact that the *because* clauses in 94–95 entail the falsity of the presupposition in the first clause. This creates a self-contradiction similar to the phenomenon known as MOORE'S PARADOX (Moore 1952:542f); cf. 96 where 'this' = "linguistics is less rigorous than philosophy."

96 (a) *Linguistics is less rigorous than philosophy, but I don't believe this is true.
   (b) *Linguistics is less rigorous than philosophy and I don't know this for a fact!

97 (a) I don't believe that linguistics is less rigorous than philosophy.
   (b) I don't know for a fact that linguistics is less rigorous than philosophy.

In order to observe the cooperative maxim of quality (D1.24) and sincerely utter *Linguistics is less rigorous than philosophy*, Speaker must at least pretend to believe that the proposition is true. All 94–96 are contradictory because Speaker specifically denies this necessary precondition on felicitously uttering the sentence. In other words, Speaker can cancel an apparent presupposition but not deny a presupposition s/he implicitly holds to be true.

Imagine the stress, intonation, and tone of voice in which you would utter any of 98.

98 (a) The door wasn't green [as Harry claimed], it was blue.
   (b) George isn't tall and thin, he's short and fat; you're thinking of the wrong man!
   (c) There is no King of France, because France is a republic.

All of the sentences in 98 are explicitly contrastive and quotative. It is the quotative ('metalinguistic') characteristic of presupposition negation that distinguishes it from ordinary negation. This is not sufficient reason to identify a formal contrast between them. Furthermore, NO language has one morphological form for regular negation and a different form for presupposition negation.

Assumption 6.2 There is only one kind of negation.

The phrase *presupposition negation* is retained to describe the negating of presuppositions.[9]

The difference between 92 and 94 is proof enough that, when recognized, presupposition failure is marked by negation of the presupposing proposition as well as the presupposition. A purportedly true assertion such as 85, *The present King of France is bald*, contradicts an accompanying recognition of its presupposition failure; consistency requires it to be marked as not-true. Strawson 1950 suggested that statements with false presuppositions have no truth value. Quine 1960 dubbed this a 'truth-value gap' which gives rise to trivalent truth {T, F, #} where # = "neither true nor false". There are undoubtedly sentences whose truth value is difficult to determine; not only disputed sentences like 84–86 naming a nonexistent King of France, but also those like 82, *I've got my mires wuddled*, and word salads such as *This blue and on speak conferenced uply*. While none of 82, 84–86, and the word salad is true, they are not indisputably false either. Strawson and Quine are right to admit two kinds of not-true assertions:

Definition 6.11 Those sentences that are not-true are either false or INDETERMINABLE.

True and *false* are no longer contradictories, but contraries (D6.5). Indeterminable sentences are best dealt with as a pragmatic problem.

One kind of indeterminability arises from a failed precondition on the illocution. What is a precondition? It is an abbreviated label for what Austin 1962 called a 'preparatory condition'. Austin argued for four kinds of 'felicity' or 'happiness' conditions on an utterance (cf. Allan 1994a).

(a)   A FULFILMENT CONDITION is satisfied if Speaker's intended perlocutionary effect (A1.6) is achieved. That is, Speaker causes an effect in Hearer as a result of Hearer's understanding of Speaker's utterance. Chapter 1 put perlocutionary effect beyond the boundary of linguistic theory on the ground that it has only a contingent link with the language used; so we ignore the fulfilment condition.

(b)   An EXECUTIVE CONDITION is successful if the procedure invoked by the illocutionary act (D1.10) is 'executed by all participants correctly and completely' (Austin 1975:14). Austin exemplifies this with a misexecution: *I bet you the race won't be run today* said when more than one race was arranged for that day so that Hearer does not know which race is referred to. But such misexecutions should be dealt with under the cooperative maxim of quantity (D1.23). The only executive condition needed is for a class of speech acts known as 'declarations' (Allan 1994d) which bring about states of affairs such as marriage, job appointment and termination, legal verdicts and umpiring decisions. Speaker is sanctioned by a community or institution to perform the declarations under constraints specified in the preconditions (e.g. only certain persons may conduct a legal marriage ceremony and it may require a particular form of words to be uttered by the participants if the marriage is to be performed correctly).[10] An executive condition safeguards society's interests by seeking to ensure that the sanctions are respected.

(c)   A SINCERITY CONDITION has a similar function to the cooperative maxim of quality (D1.24). It has often been assumed that different kinds of illocutionary acts involve different kinds of sincerity conditions, but in fact they describe preconditions on a felicitous illocution as in the following bolded instances:

(i)   Assertions are sincere if **Speaker believes in the truth of the proposition asserted**.
(ii)   Requests are sincere if **Speaker believes Hearer has the capability and might be willing to carry out the act requested**.
(iii)   Declarations are sincere if **Speaker believes s/he has the proper authority to make the declaration**.[11]

Because sincerity reflects on whether or not Speaker upholds the preconditions, only one sincerity condition is necessary.

Definition 6.12 The GENERALIZED SINCERITY CONDITION: in making the utterance, Speaker knows or believes (or believes s/he knows) that all necessary clauses of the preconditions on its constituent illocutionary forces (D1.10) hold true.

This puts a burden on precise statement of the preconditions; but that seems exactly where it should lie, because:

(d)

Definition 6.13 PRECONDITIONS identify the particular circumstances appropriate to performing a given illocutionary act.

A precondition is what Austin called a 'preparatory condition'.

Preconditions identify what ought to be presupposed in a felicitous use of the illocution (= illocutionary force); cf. Karttunen and Peters 1979:10. For instance, the precondition on *France is a republic* is "Speaker has reason to believe that *France is a republic*." If Speaker had said *France is NOT a republic* we would condemn Speaker for being ignorant, deluded, insane, or maliciously attempting to mislead Hearer. This is exactly the normal response to sentences such as 84–86 that exhibit presupposition failure. In such cases, Austin would say 'the utterance is void' (1975:51).

Assumption 6.3 Hearer's normal response to presupposition failure is identical to the normal response to precondition failure for illocutions: Speaker is open to condemnation for being ignorant, deluded, insane, or maliciously attempting to mislead Hearer.

Take the precondition on thanking: "Hearer, or someone or something in Hearer's charge, has done some deed D with the apparent intention of benefiting Speaker (directly or indirectly)." If Speaker thanks Hearer for D when Hearer never did D, Hearer will either conclude that Speaker is deluded or is being sarcastic. Or, take the case of the tennis player in the US Open who claims his/her opponent's ball is *Out* when the umpire disagrees: the claim has no standing because the player is not a person sanctioned by the preconditions on this illocutionary act to declare the ball out of play. Again, by violating the precondition, Speaker risks condemnation.

Some inferences that have been described in the literature as presuppositions are more properly to be regarded as either entailments or conventional implicatures because they cannot be cancelled. They do, however (like all entailments and conventional implicatures), correspond to preconditions on Speaker's use of the illocution. Most propositions in temporal clauses are entailed (Levinson 1983:182 disagrees).

99   When Zeno was born isn't known ‖ Zeno was born
100 Harry cooked the fish while Sally made the chips
                    ‖ (Sally made the chips) ∧ (Harry cooked the fish)
101 Sam told me about the accident before John called
                    ‖ (John called) ∧ (Sam told me about the accident)

However, the semantics of the main clause may modify the entailment (cf. Heinämäki 1972, Gazdar 1979).

102 Jack died before he finished writing the book
                    ‖ (Jack died) ∧ (Jack was writing a book)

Here Jack's death terminates an ongoing activity before it reaches its proper conclusion, cf. *Jack hit the off-switch before the engine blew* and *The car broke down before they got to Wagga Wagga*. Many conventional implicatures of verbs have been called presuppositions, e.g. by Fillmore 1971, Lakoff 1971, Levinson 1983. In 103–6, impossible cancellations are given in square brackets (note that this applies to the senses and not to joking or sarcastic uses).

103 *credit NP with/for X* ▸ X is praiseworthy ∧ NP is responsible for X

> James *credited* his co-author with the invention that made them millions [*but he didn't believe his co-author had done anything praiseworthy].

104 *call NP a bitch* ▸ insult NP [denoting a female human, or a gay male human, or an inanimate object]

> Max called the young lady a bitch and she bridled at the insult [*but he wasn't insulting her].

105 *say NP looks terrific* ▸ compliment NP

> Fred told Zelda she looked terrific, and she complimented him in return [*but in fact he was insulting her].

106 *accuse NP of X* ▸ NP deliberately did reprehensible act X

> Sue accused Ed of having an affair with Sheila [*but neither Speaker nor Sue thought there was anything wrong with it].

The conversational implicature of 106 is that both Speaker and Sue believe X is reprehensible; it can be cancelled for one, but not both of them. *Blame NP for X* is similar.

This section has rejected the view that presupposition is a well-defined semantic or logical property. The weight of evidence is that presuppositions are the preconditions on illocutions, and presupposition failure arises through Speaker's failure to ensure the correct preconditions for what is said. Such failure causes Speaker to be judged ignorant, deluded, insane, or maliciously trying to mislead Hearer. Like conversational implicatures, presuppositions can be cancelled. If presuppositions arise from the preconditions on illocutions, then they are subject to the maxim of quality. For instance, someone who utters 85 implicates that s/he has reasonable grounds to believe that the proposition it contains is true and therefore implicates 85′. Similarly, the maxim of quality safeguards the implicature from 87 that *Jo kissed Eric*; and so forth for all the examples given.

> *Definition 6.14.* Presuppositions are those conversational implicatures that:
> (a) hold under negation, and
> (b) relate specifically to the preconditions on the speech act.

The hypothesis that presuppositions are a kind of conversational implicature explains why they share in the feature of defeasibility.

Exercises

6.5.1 Identify the presuppositions that distinguish the complement *Jay date Sally* in (a–e).
You may represent the complement sentence by simply D.

    (a)   Jay dreamed that he dated Sally.
    (b)   Jay tried to date Sally.
    (c)   Jay managed to date Sally.
    (d)   Jay congratulated himself on dating Sally.
    (e)   Jay stopped dating Sally.

6.5.2 The following sentences include some presuppositions within presuppositions, what
are they?
    (a) Mark was pleased that he'd bought the flowers.
    (b) Mark wasn't sorry that he'd managed to seduce Sharon.

6.5.3 Demonstrate the rule (cf. Seuren 1985:278): *If A ∦ B and B » C, then A » C*

6.5.4 What is entailed by *The car broke down before they got to Wagga Wagga*?

6.5.5 Identify the conventional implicatures for the verbs in (a–c).
    (a) praise NP for Ving
    (b) apologize to NP for Ving
    (c) thank NP for X

6.6   Summary

The purpose of this chapter was to iantroduce the most basic tools for analysing the
meanings of sentences in truth conditional semantics.[12] In the course of the book it is
shown that truth conditions alone are insufficient to account for meaning in a natural
language: the importance of implicature, and especially conversational implicature, makes
it imperative to introduce it as soon as practicable. The differences between semantic
implication, entailment, conventional implicature, and conversational implicature were
demonstrated. In the final section, semantic presupposition was dismissed in favour of
pragmatic presupposition defined as a kind of conversational implicature arising from the
preconditions on illocutions.

    Chapter 7 presents formal tools for investigating the semantic structure of the
constituents of a simple proposition. The chapter begins with predicate logic; then moves
on to the usefulness of sets and functions to linguistic semantics. There is consideration,
too, of other rigorous means for analysing the internal semantic composition of clauses and
sentences.

● Key words and phrases (TT = Truth Table):

bicondicional, ↔ (TT6.2)
bivalency, T⊻F (D6.1)
bracketing
calculating implicatures (49)
cancellation (defeasibility)
conditional, → (TT6.2)
conjunction, ∧ (TT6.2)
constant (A6.1)
contradictories (D6.6)
contraries (D6.5)
conventional implicature (sense
    relation), ▸ (D6.4)
conversational implicature, ▷ (D6.7)
cooperative principle
cooperative maxim
declarations
defeasibility (cancellation)
entailment, ‖- (D6.2)
exclusive disjunction, ⊻ (TT6.2)
executive condition
factive predicate
felicity condition
flouting a cooperative maxim
fulfilment condition
generalized implicature
illocutionary act (D1.10)
illocutionary force (illocution) (D1.10)
inclusive disjunction, ∨ (TT6.2)
indeterminability (D6.11)
inference
logical connective (truth functor)
maxim of quality (D1.24)
modus ponens (TT6.3)
modus tollens (11)
Moore's paradox (96)
negation (ordinary) (A6.2)
negative operator, ¬ (TT6.2)
non-truth-functionality

particularized implicature
perlocutionary effect (A1.6)
pragmatic presupposition (D6.14)
pragmatics
precondition (D6.13)
preparatory condition
presupposition (A»B)
presuppositional plugs (91)
presupposition negation
preference condition (Quantity2
    implicature)
propositional calculus (propositional
    logic)
Quantity1 (negative upscale)
    implicature (50)
Quantity2 (augmentative) implicature
    (51)
scalar implicature (D6.8)
script (40)
semantic implication (conditional, →)
    (TT6.2)
semantic equivalence (biconditional,
    ↔) (TT6.2)
semantic presupposition (D6.10)
(generalized) sincerity condition
    (D6.12)
speech act
synonymy, ‖‖ (D6.3)
(logical) transitivity (D6.9)
tautology
trivalence
truth conditions
truth functor (logical connective)
truth value
truth-value gap
valuation
variable (A6.1)

● A sentence may consist of one or more propositions. A proposition is essentially the meaning of a clause (D1.8).
● The propositional calculus is an algorithm for calculating the logical relationships between propositions connected by truth functors ∧, ∨, ⊻, →, ↔.
● The content of propositions is ignored in propositional logic, except insofar as they are assigned a truth value.

- Classical propositional logic is bivalent (D6.1), a proposition is either T or else F.
- The simplest means of demonstrating formal relations between propositions is a truth table. Truth Table 6.2 gives valuations for ¬ and all truth functors.
- p, q, and r are typical propositional variables. They can be replaced by particular propositions from a natural language which, by comparison, are constants. A variable is rather like a third person pronoun in that it can be used to refer to many different things; any particular one of these can be given a name, which is a constant (A6.1).
- $p \wedge q$ is true whenever both p and q are true and false otherwise (conjunction).
- $p \wedge \neg p$ "p and not-p" is a contradiction; it cannot be true.
- $p \vee q$ "p and/or q" is true whenever p and/or q is/are true (inclusive disjunction).
- $p \veebar q$ "either p or else q, but not both" is true whenever only one of p or q is true (exclusive disjunction).
- $p \rightarrow q$ "p semantically implies q" is true whenever p is false and/or q is true (conditional).
- $p \leftrightarrow q$ "p iff (if and only if) q" is true whenever p is true and q is also true or p is false and q is also false (biconditional).
- Modus ponens: $((p \rightarrow q) \wedge p) \rightarrow q$.
- Modus tollens: $((p \rightarrow q) \wedge \neg q) \rightarrow \neg p$.
- Entailment and synonymy were redefined in terms of semantic implication and semantic equivalence respectively (D6.2–3).
- Conventional implicature was defined as a non-truth-functional counterpart to entailment (D6.4). It is a sense relation, and a feature of lexical rather than propositional semantics.
- Conversational implicature was defined (D6.7) and its defeasibility, which sets it apart from entailment and conventional implicature, was exemplified. Of the three, only conversational implicature can be cancelled without contradicting the utterance which implicates it.
- Conversational implicature arises from expectations that people have about the way language is usually used; whereas the semantic relations of propositional logic, entailment, and conventional implicature are properties of the language itself.
- Although conversational implicatures are often discussed as though they arise only when flouting the cooperative maxims, in any consistent account of implicature they must also arise from observing the cooperative principle.
- The implicature of any utterance or proposition within an utterance is calculated from the set of its implicatures minus any that have been superseded or cancelled by entailments.
- Because conversational implicature is partly a function of lexical choice, it does not follow from the fact that A ⊩B ∧ B⊳C that A⊳C.
- The cooperative maxim of quantity (D1.23) has two distinct aspects. What has become known as Quantity1 (because it corresponds to the first of Grice's maxims in this category) has a negative upscale implicature. Quantity2, on the other hand, is that the default interpretation will augment what is said in some conventional and/or calculable way.
- There are lexical and/or grammatical clues as to which kind of quantity implicature applies in a particular utterance.
- If B is entailed by both A and ¬A, then B is a semantic presupposition of A and ¬A (D6.10). But this semantic definition has unwanted logical consequences.
- Presuppositions are defeasible, so they must be pragmatic.
- Presuppositions are denied through 'presupposition negation' which differs from regular negation only because a presupposition is negated along with the presupposing proposition.

However, no language has a distinct word or other morphological form for negating presuppositions. Languages have only one kind of negation (A6.2) – it is the scope that differs.

● Failure to deny the presupposing proposition when negating the presupposition leads to Moore's paradox.

● Presupposition failure renders a proposition indeterminable, i.e. neither true nor false (D6.11).

● Presuppositions were identified with the preconditions on illocutions (D6.13). The preconditions provide grounds for motivating Speaker to make the utterance and grounds from which Hearer will evaluate the illocutionary force expressed. They identify what ought to be presupposed in a felicitous use of the illocution and are therefore obligatory in the definition of illocutions (cf. Allan 1994d,e).

● Preconditions, under the name 'preparatory conditions', are one of four felicity conditions that Austin 1962 identified. The others are: (i) A fulfilment condition – important to nonlinguists concerned with perlocutionary effects of utterances. (ii) An executive condition to determine whether or not the speech act has been properly executed. (iii) A sincerity condition – which has a similar function to the cooperative maxim of quality. Just one sincerity condition is needed for all illocutions: it refers to the preconditions (D6.12).

● Violation of preconditions and presupposition failure – not surprisingly – the same effect: Speaker is condemned for being ignorant, deluded, insane, or maliciously attempting to mislead Hearer (A6.3).

● Preconditions are subject to the cooperative maxim of quality and therefore presupposition is a species of conversational implicature. This explains the defeasibility of presupposition.

6.7   Notes on further reading

[1] On conventional implicatures on non-logical connectives and adverbial particles, see Karttunen and Peters 1979. They take a different view from that presented here, essentially suggesting that conventional implicatures are semantic presuppositions (see also Chierchia and McConnell-Ginet 1990, Heim and Kratzer 1998). §6.5 of this chapter argues against semantic presupposition in favour of pragmatic presupposition. Perhaps the view presented in this book and the alternative presented by Karttunen and Peters et al. might be resolved if it turns out that, on the one hand, semantic presuppositions and conventional implicatures are substantially the same; and, on the other, pragmatic presuppositions and conversational implicatures are substantially the same (the latter view is taken in §6.5).

[2] On scripts, see Chapter 8 and Schank and Abelson 1977, Schank 1982, 1984, 1986.

[3] On scalar implicatures, see Horn 1989:232, Gazdar 1979:55–62, Levinson 1983:134.

[4] On preference conditions, see Jackendoff 1983 Chs 7–8, 1985, 1990:35ff.

[5] On scripts, see under [2]. On frames, see Chapter 8, Fillmore 1982, Fillmore and Atkins 1992, Barsalou 1992, Lehrer and Kittay (eds) 1992. On perceived groupings of notes and chords in musical scores, see Jackendoff 1983:131f, Lerdahl and Jackendoff 1982 Ch.3.

[6] On slips of the tongue, see Fromkin (ed.) 1980, Cutler (ed.) 1982.

[7] On presupposition triggers, see Karttunen 1973, Gazdar 1979:127, Levinson 1983:181.

[8] Not everyone agrees with this, by any means. For defenders of the view that semantic presupposition is viable, see especially Beaver 1997, 1999; also Gamut 1990, Heim and Kratzer 1998, McCawley 1993. Chierchia and McConnell-Ginet 1990 define semantic presupposition in terms of 'common ground at context c' (p. 290) – which, to my mind, is a pragmatic definition.

[9] On presupposition (radical, external. metalinguistic) negation, see Seuren 1985:238ff, Horn 1989.

[10] On declarations, see Searle 1979, Bach and Harnish 1979 (who call them 'conventional acts'), Allan 1986, 1994d.

[11] On different sincerity conditions for different speech acts, see Austin 1962, Searle 1969, Bach and Harnish 1979, Allan 1986.

[12] An excellent introduction to formal semantics, one which has stood the test of time, is Allwood, Andersson, and Dahl 1977. McCawley 1993 presents a linguist's approach to logic, and critically surveys a large number of formal theories. It is a useful reference work. Three other user-friendly introductions to formal semantics are Chierchia and McConnell-Ginet 1990, Gamut 1991, Cann 1993; all go very much further than this book. Hodges 1977 is an easy-to-read introduction to elementary logic.

7 Predicate logic, sets, and lambda: tools for semantic analysis

Essentially, semantics is concerned with the ways the truth values of sentences depend on the meanings of their parts and the ways the truth values of different sentences are related.

(Gamut 1991 I:92)

7.1 Where we are heading

In Chapter 6 we looked at truth-conditional relations between sentences and propositions. The purpose of this chapter is to identify some formal tools for the task of semantically specifying clauses and their constituents. These formal tools are borrowed from logic and mathematics, but this chapter concentrates on the concepts that are useful for linguistic semantics. §7.2 introduces predicate logic – the basis for analysing the structure of simple propositions. It is directly applicable to the semantic structure of clauses. §7.3 is on meaning postulates, used in the semantic specification of listemes. §7.4 discusses sets and tuples as aids in specifying the meanings of predicates. §7.5 shows why it is that the meaning of a predicate can be described as a function from entities to truth values, and it relates a formal notion of 'model' in model theoretic semantics to our informal notion of $M^{w,t}$ "model of the world and time spoken of" (Chapter 2). One function of semantic theory is to explicate how we interpret the meaning of a sentence such as *Someone is bald*. A step-by-step analysis is presented in §7.5. §7.6 describes the usefulness of the lambda or set operator in linguistic analysis. §7.7 summarizes the chapter.

7.2 L_P, the language of predicate logic

The simplest well-formed formula in L_P consists of a PREDICATE and a number of ARGUMENTS symbolized by TERMS.

Definition 7.1 A WELL-FORMED FORMULA (wff) is one that satisfies the rules of some logical system such as L_P.

The variables (A6.1) Φ, Ψ are used for formulae. Upper-case P, Q are variables for predicates. Lower-case x, y, z are variables for terms.

Px	is a **one place** predicate	(Pred₁)
Pxy	is a **two place** predicate	(Pred₂)
Pxyz	is a **three place** predicate	(Pred₃)

Definition 7.2 Where *n* is an integer, an *n* place predicate, Pred$_n$, is a predicate with arguments numbering *n*.

Conventionally the predicate symbol is to the left. The arguments are often enclosed within parentheses, e.g. Pxy can be rendered P(x)(y) or P(x,y). In the following examples '⟹' symbolizes "translates into", and minor language categories like tense and determiners are ignored. In 1 the intransitive verb *jog*, in 2 the complement adjective *be red*, and in 3 the complement NP *be a bachelor* are all Pred₁.

1 Max jogs **[in English]** ⟹ Jm **[in L$_P$]** [lit. "jog‸Max"]
2 The book is red ⟹ Rb [lit. "be_red‸the_book"]
3 Max is a bachelor ⟹ Bm [lit. "be_a_bachelor‸Max"]

Notice that the initial letters of the name for the predicate and the term are used as constants (A6.1) in the *L$_P$* translations. In 4–5 the transitive verbs *drink, admire*, and in 6 the relational complement *be wife to*, are Pred₂. Notice that the NP subject of a declarative clause is the leftmost argument.

4 (a) Max drank the beer
      (b) The beer was drunk by Max } ⟹ Dmb [lit. "drink‸Max‸the_beer"]

5 Archie admires himself ⟹ Aaa [lit. "admires‸Archie‸Archie"]

6 Mary is { Harry's wife / the wife of Harry } ⟹ Wmh [lit. "be_wife_to‸Mary‸Harry"]

The ditransitive verb in 7 is a Pred₃.

7 Archie gave Beatrice the camera ⟹ Gabc
      [lit. "give‸Archie‸Beatrice‸the_camera"]

Note the order of arguments in *L$_P$*; it is not variable as it is in English. *Archie gave the camera to Beatrice* is also Gabc and NOT Gacb.

Formulae in *L$_P$* can be negated, and all the familiar truth functors from propositional logic can be used between formulae. If Φ and Ψ are well-formed formulae (abbreviated wff) of *L$_P$*, then all of the following are also wff:

$$\neg\Phi; \quad \Phi\wedge\Psi; \quad \Phi\vee\Psi; \quad \Phi\underline{\vee}\Psi; \quad \Phi\rightarrow\Psi; \quad \Phi\leftarrow\Psi$$

The negation of 4 is 8.

8 (a) Max didn't drink the beer
    (b) The beer wasn't drunk by Max $\Big\}$ ⇒ ¬Dmb

¬Dmb can also be written ¬[Dmb] "It is not the case that [Max drank the beer]." Conjoined sentences have predictable translations, e.g.

9 Max drank the beer and fell ⇒ Dmb ∧ Fm

Note that the second of the identical arguments 'm' does not get omitted from L_p as it does in English; this is because L_p captures the meaning rather than the form of the second conjunct. In 10, the second conjunct 'F' is NOT a well-formed formula in L_p.

10 Dmb ∧ F   [Ill-formed]

Predicates such as *be the same height as, be near to* are symmetric predicates because the meaning of the sentence containing them is preserved when the order of their arguments is interchanged.

> *Definition 7.3* A two place predicate P is SYMMETRIC iff for any wff Pxy, Pxy⟷Pyx.

Sometimes there is a converse relation between predicates, 11–13.

11 X is husband to Y ⟷ Y is wife to X
12 X is the parent of Y ⟷ Y is the child of X
13 X buys Y from Z ⟷ Z sells Y to X

> *Definition 7.4* Two predicates P and Q are CONVERSE iff for any wff Pxy and Qyx, Pxy⟷Qyx

Predicate logic is made more expressive by the addition of two quantifiers: the universal quantifier ∀ "for all" and the existential quantifier ∃ "there is at least one". If Φ is a wff in L_p, the formulae ∀xΦ and ∃xΦ are also wff in L_p. In general terms

∀x[Px] means "every x is P, all x's P"
∃x[Px] means "some x Ps, there is at least one x that is P"

We symbolize *All bachelors are happy* and *Every bachelor is happy* as 14:

14 ∀x[Bx → Hx]   "for every x such that x is a bachelor, it is true that x is happy"

We say that the variable x is BOUND by the universal quantifier. Note that the universal identifies a rule applicable to bachelors. 14 can be true when there are no bachelors (cf. TT6.2), otherwise 15 follows from 14.

15   ∃x[Bx ∧ Hx]   "there is at least one x who is both a bachelor and happy"

In 15 the variable x is bound by the existential quantifier; so if 15 is true, then there is at least one bachelor in existence (in some relevant world and time).

The structure of 14 and 15 can be graphically represented in a tree diagram. The nodes are labelled for clarity: Φ is a formula, C is a connective (truth functor). In all other respects tree and formula are equivalent (i.e. alternative ways of saying the same thing).

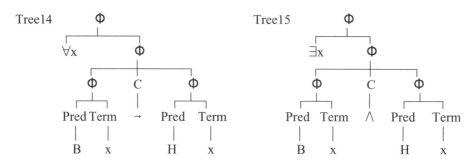

The quantifiers ∀ and ∃ often co-occur within the same expression; in which case their relative position determines their relative scope. A quantifier c-commands the variables in its scope (D2.12). Let Fxy mean "x is the father of y" or "x is y's father":

16   ∀y[∃x[Fxy]]   "for every y, it holds that there is an x such that x is the father of y" or *Everyone has a father.*

17   ∃x[∀y[Fxy]]   "there is an x such that it holds for every y that x is the father of y" or *Someone [e.g. God] is father to everyone.*

Notice that the variables x, y in 16–17 translate into pronouns 'someone', 'everyone'. Names and definite descriptions are typically constants. In the formulae of 16–17, the variable x is bound by the existential quantifier, and the variable y is bound by the universal quantifier. The scope difference is represented in different tree structures:

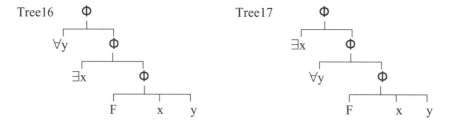

In Tree16 the universal quantifier c-commands the existential quantifier; vice versa in Tree17. In 16–17 we can reduce the symbolic clutter by omitting the outermost brackets and leaving the sequence of ∀ and ∃ to determine their relative scope. In fact, in 16–17, the brackets could be left out altogether; but there are formulae where brackets need to be incorporated to indicate quantifier scope. Compare 18 with 19.

18 ∃x[Pxy ∧ Qx]
19 ∃xPxy ∧ Qx

In 18 the scope of the existential quantifier is [Pxy ∧ Qx] in which both occurrences of x are bound. However in 19 the scope of the existential is just Pxy, so this occurrence of x is bound. Qx in 19 lies outside the scope of ∃x, so the x in Qx is said to be a FREE VARIABLE. Because any variable not bound by a quantifier is free, y in 18–19 is free – it is not within the scope of either ∃y or ∀y.

> *Assumption 7.1 Every variable is either bound by a quantifier (or* λ, *§7.6), or else it is free.*

Only formulae whose variables are bound count as coherent SENTENCES of L_p. Neither 18 nor19 is a sentence; they are PROPOSITIONAL FUNCTIONS. Supposing that P translates "patted" and Q translates "queer", 18 is the incomplete *Someone queer patted*. On the same assumption, an English translation of ∃x∃y[Pxy ∧ Qx], in which y is bound by ∃y, would yield the coherent sentence *Someone queer patted someone.*
    20–23 are examples of negation with the quantifiers.

20 Nobody likes Jo ⟹ ¬∃x[Px ∧ Lxj]   "there is no x such that x is a person and x
                                                            likes j"
21 Not everybody likes Jo ⟹ ¬∀x[Px → Lxj]   "not every x is a person such that x
                                                                    likes j"
22 Every woman dislikes Jo ⟹ ∀x[Wx → ¬Lxj] "for every x such that x is a woman,
                                                                    it is not the case that x likes j"
23 Not every woman dislikes Jo ⟹   ¬∀x[Wx → ¬Lxj]

Tree21

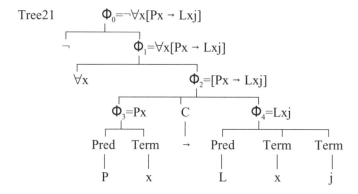

Tree22

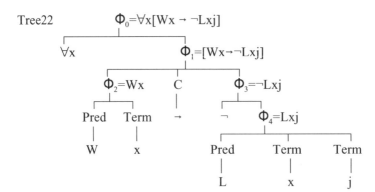

As you can see, in Tree21, ¬ c-commands ∀x, because the Φ_0 node immediately dominating ¬ is a branching node that also dominates ∀x and ¬ does not dominate ∀x. ∀x does not c-command ¬, because the Φ_1 node immediately dominating ∀x is sister to ¬. In Tree22, ¬ only c-commands Φ_4 and its constituents.

In this section we have seen how to translate simple clause predicates and their arguments from English into L_P, the metalanguage of predicate logic.[1] The best way to gain familiarity with the predicate calculus is to do the exercises below.

Exercises

7.2.1 Are (a–e) wff in L_P (assume that Φ and Ψ are wff)?
(a) $\Psi \longleftrightarrow \neg \Phi$;   (b) $\neg \Psi \wedge \Phi$;   (c) $\neg Pxy \wedge Qy$;   (d) $Pxyz \rightarrow Qzy$;   (e) $Px \rightarrow Q$

7.2.2 Translate (a–d) into L_P.
(a) Yasmin is tall and Sally is short. $Ty \wedge Ss$
(b) Harry didn't kiss Yasmin. $\neg Khy$
(c) Harry is Yasmin's father. Fhy
(d) If Jack sold Harry the car, then Harry is lucky. $Sjhc \rightarrow Lh$

7.2.3 Give an idiomatic English translation for (a) Rh   (b) Kbj   (c) Gefp
    Hank ran.   Bo kicked Jo.   Ellen gave Frank a pet.

7.2.4 (a) Let B symbolize *buy* and S *sell*; how would you translate their relationship into L_P? $Bijc$ $Sjic$
(b) Are *lend* and *borrow* symmetric predicates or converse predicates? Explain.
    $Lbhc$ $Bhlc$

7.2.5 Assuming that B is the predicate *be a bachelor* and H is the predicate *be happy*, why is the formula $\forall x[Bx \rightarrow Hx]$ true even if there are no bachelors?
    maybe

7.2.6 If ¬Lxy means "x dislikes y" and Jx means "x is a jerk" and Ry means "y is rich", translate into idiomatic English:
(a) $\exists x \forall y[(Jx \wedge Ry) \rightarrow \neg Lxy]$
(b) $\forall x \forall y[(Jx \wedge Ry) \rightarrow \neg Lxy]$

(c) $\exists x \forall y[(Jx \wedge Rx \wedge Ry) \rightarrow \neg Lxy]$
(d) $\forall y[Ry \rightarrow Jy]$

7.2.7 Show that
   (a) $\exists x[Px \wedge \neg Lxj] \longleftrightarrow \neg \forall x[Px \rightarrow Lxj]$
   (b) $\neg \exists x[Px \wedge Lxj] \longleftrightarrow \forall x[Px \rightarrow \neg Lxj]$

7.2.8 Construct a tree for $\exists x \forall y[(Jx \wedge Ry) \rightarrow \neg Lxy]$

7.3 Meaning postulates

The formal semantics of natural language cannot be expressed without recourse to the non-logical vocabulary of meaning postulates which identify the semantic properties of listemes (Carnap 1956:222–9).

> *Definition 7.5* A MEANING POSTULATE is the non-logical vocabulary (in this book, words of English) used in the semantic specification of a listeme.

	FORM	SEMANTIC SPECIFICATION		
24	*know*	(know that p)	$\rightarrow$	(p=T)
25	*believe*	(believe that p)	$\rightarrow$	possibly p
26	*alive*	(y is alive)	$\longleftrightarrow$	$\neg$(y is dead)
27	*dead*	(y is dead)	$\longleftrightarrow$	$\neg$(y is alive)
28	*kill*	(x kill y)	$\rightarrow$	(x cause (y become $\neg$(alive)))

Do meaning postulates really use the vocabulary of a natural language, as appears to be the case? The translation of the relevant part of 29 is 30.

29 Since the car crash, Max has been on a life-support system; he's neither dead nor alive.
30 $\neg$(Max is dead) $\wedge$ $\neg$(Max is alive)

But, given 26–27, 30 is contradictory. The same contradiction should be present in 29, yet 29 is an acceptable sentence of natural language. The apparent difference between the ordinary language of 29 and the logic of 26–27 and 30 is a matter of what is understood by the predicates 'is alive' and 'is dead'. In the real world the ethical and medical definitions of life and death are extremely controversial. The formal semanticist's solution is to stipulate meaning postulate 31, where parentheses are placed around arguments for the sake of clarity and **bold'** is a meaning postulate.

31 **be_dead'**(y) $\longleftrightarrow$ $\neg$(**be_alive'**(y))

This decision leaves 29 to be accounted for by conversational implicatures arising from the cooperative maxims of manner (D1.26) and quality (D1.24). 31 needs revising because a fire can be dead but not alive (see 32).

   A predicate decomposed by means of meaning postulates is used in formulae with the constituent order typical of L_P. The functions of square brackets and parentheses are the same. In 34, $\forall x,y[\Phi]$ is an alternative to $\forall x \forall y[\Phi]$. Also, the comma between the arguments in **kill′**(x,y) is for clarity; it can be omitted.

32 $\forall y[\mathbf{organism'}(y) \rightarrow (\mathbf{be\_alive'}(y) \longleftrightarrow \neg(\mathbf{be\_dead'}(y)))]$
33 $\forall y[\mathbf{organism'}(y) \rightarrow (\mathbf{be\_dead'}(y) \longleftrightarrow \neg(\mathbf{be\_alive'}(y)))]$
34 $\forall x,y[(\mathbf{kill'}(x,y) \rightarrow \mathbf{organism'}(y) \wedge \mathbf{cause'}(x,(\mathbf{become'}(\neg(\mathbf{alive'}(y)))))]$

32–34 are true for all admissible possible worlds, i.e. worlds that can be spoken of given the current state of English. In 32 **be_alive′**(y) is true and ¬(**be_dead**)(y)) is also true; each of these propositions is false in 33. Only one of 32 or 33 is needed because the other necessarily follows from it in the truth table for the biconditional (TT6.2). The asymmetrical relationship in 34 between **cause′**(x,(**become′**(¬(**alive′**(y))))) and **kill′**(x,y) contrasts with the symmetrical relationship of the formulae in 32 and 33. For sentences like 35, McCawley 1968c postulated a V⌢NP⌢NP structure reminiscent of Pxy in L_P, cf. Tree35. He postulated a rule called 'predicate raising' to combine the V nodes for lexicalization to *kill*, as in Tree35′.

35   x kills y

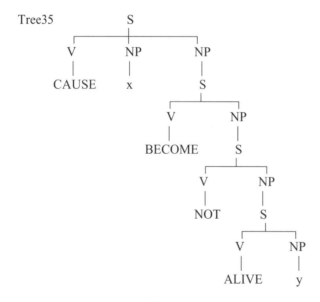

Tree35′

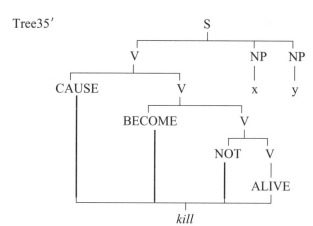

Predicate raising gives rise to all of 36, so constraints need to be specified that will block the unacceptable sequences (e–g) from surfacing.

36 (a) x kills y   ← x CAUSE BECOME NOT ALIVE y
   (b) x causes y to die   ← x causes y BECOME NOT ALIVE
   (c) x causes y to cease to be alive   ← x causes y BECOME NOT to be alive
   (d) ??x causes y to become dead   ← x causes y to become NOT ALIVE
   (e) ?*x causes y to become not alive
   (f) *x causes to become y not alive
   (g) *x causes to become not alive y

The hypothesis is faulty and it is not possible to identify all the necessary constraints. Imagine that Jim gets out of his car failing to put it in 'park' and pull on the handbrake; the car rolls away, gathering speed, and runs over two children, killing them. Whereas Jim could be sued for causing the death of the children through his negligence, he cannot properly be charged with killing them – the car did that. This shows that the true relationship between *kill* and *cause to die* is asymmetric, as in 34, Thus, although *kill* conventionally implicates (D6.4) *cause to die*, the form *kill* ought not to be mapped onto the semantic components CAUSE TO DIE. Similarly, *die* cannot simply be mapped onto BECOME NOT ALIVE (nor **cease_to_be_alive′** etc.) without reference to **die′**. Instead we postulate the logical relation in 37:

cause to die ≠ kill

37 $\forall y[\textbf{die}'(y) \leftrightarrow \textbf{cease\_to\_be\_alive}'(y)]$

Assumption 7.2 The meaning equivalences and implications of a form are NOT IDENTICAL WITH the composition of meaning for that form.

You can analyse bread into flour, yeast, sugar, and water plus a method for combining them. There is a value and purpose in doing this that is completely lacking in the hypothesis that the meaning of *die* is composed from BECOME NOT ALIVE. Confirmation for this observation may be had from 38. All (a–m) are logically equivalent, but it is absurd to suggest that (a) is a lexicalization of any of (b–m) because of the pragmatic differences.

38 (a) I have four children.
   (b) I have 1 child $\wedge$ 1 child $\wedge$ 1 child $\wedge$ 1 child.
   (c) I have two children and another two children.
   (d) I have one child $\wedge$ three children.
   (e) I have one less than five children.
   (f) I have sixteen less than twenty children.
   (g) I have one more than three children.
   (h) I have three more than one child.
   (i) I have four times one child.
   (j) I have two times two children.
   (k) I have two-squared children.
   (l) I have the square root of sixteen children.
   (m) I have the same number of children as there are 25s in 100.

Nonetheless, there is considerable evidence that some of these arithmetical processes are normal in the lexicalizing of number systems. For example, *fourteen* and *eighteen* are "four [+] ten" and "eight [+] ten" respectively (compare French *dix-huit* "ten [+] eight"). *Eight and twenty* sounds archaic, but it simply spells out the morphological components of *twenty-eight*. Compare also *forty* "four [×] ten" and *eighty* "eight [×] ten". French *quatre-vingts* "four [×] twenty" is the normal expression for 80, and 98 is *quatre-vingt-dix-huit*. The San Juan Southern Paiute *shuroxomaiy* "nine" is literally 'nearly complete hands', which is almost "one less than ten" (Bunte and Franklin 1988). Notice how the mathematics is biased towards human centredness, using hands and feet as bases for counting (Chapter 9).

    This section began with a discussion of meaning postulates.[2] The focus shifted to the idea of lexicalization over a structured complex of semantic components, which was developed under the sobriquet 'generative semantics'. The main thesis of generative semantics was that syntactic and semantic representations are labelled trees and a single system of rules relates the semantic representation to surface form through intermediate stages. The pros and cons of generative semantics were not discussed,[3] but it was shown that the meaning equivalences and implications of a form are not in themselves semantic specifications for the form. The semantic specifications for *kill* and *die* cannot do without **kill'**(x,y) and **die'**(y). The meaning is in the relationships identified in 32 and 34.

Exercises

7.3.1 Provide a colloquial English gloss for:
    $\forall$x,y[(**kill'**(x,y) $\rightarrow$ **organism'**(y) $\wedge$ **cause'**(x,(**become'**($\neg$(**alive'**(y))))))]
    Hunters kill prey.

7.3.2 Suggest meaning postulates (not necessarily exhaustive) for *bull, cow, calf, stallion, mare, foal, ram, ewe, lamb* that show the relationships between these listemes.

$\rightarrow$ meaning postulates ?

7.4   Sets and tuples

§7.4 considers some of the mathematical properties of sets, concentrating on the ones most useful to natural language semantics.

> *Definition 7.6* A SET is an unordered collection of MEMBERS (or ELEMENTS).

Members are conventionally separated by commas and listed between braces:

39   F = {your-eye, the-Vatican, b, a-night-with-Brigitte-Bardot, $\sqrt{2}$}
40   G = {a,b,c} = {b,a,c} = {c,a,b} = {c,b,a}

The-Vatican is a member of F (41(a)) but not of G (41(b)); and a is not a member of F, but it is a member of G (42). Symbolically:

41 (a) the-Vatican ∈ F   (b)   the-Vatican ∉ G
42 (a) a ∉ F   (b) a ∈ G

Instead of listing the members, a set can be ABSTRACTLY DEFINED. Thus G would be:

43 {x:x is one of the first three letters of the English alphabet}

This reads (using English as a metalanguage) "the set of all x such that x is one of the first three letters of the English alphabet".

> *Definition 7.7* A is a SUBSET of B, A⊆B, iff every member of A is also a member of B. More formally: A⊆B ⟷ ∀x[x∈A → x∈B]

> *Assumption 7.3* Every set is a subset of itself.

For instance, {a,b,c}⊆G says "the set {a,b,c} is a subset of the set G" (40).

> *Definition 7.8* A set that consists of only one member, e.g. {b}, is a UNIT set.

Any set can be empty, thus

> *Assumption 7.4* One subset of every set is the NULL SET, ∅ = { }: therefore ∅⊆G.

The rest of the subsets of G in 40 are PROPER subsets because they are included within it along with other subsets.

44 {a}⊂G   {b}⊂G   {c}⊂G   {a,b}⊂G   {b,c}⊂G   {a,c}⊂G

> *Definition 7.9* A is a proper subset of B, A⊂B, iff every member of A is also a member of B but at least one member of B is not a member of A. More formally: A⊂B ⟷ [∀x[x∈A → x∈B] ∧ ∃y[y∈B ∧ y∉A]]

Definition 7.10 The COMPLEMENT set of A relative to B, A′, is equivalent to B−A ("B minus A"). $\forall x[x \in A' \leftrightarrow x \in B \wedge x \notin A]$[1]

Any set is the SUPERSET of its subsets, so G in 40 is the proper superset of, say $\{b\}$: $G \supset \{b\}$. Note the direction of ⊃ "superset of" is from greater to lesser, and ⊂ "subset of" from lesser to greater.

Definition 7.11 Any two sets are IDENTICAL iff they contain the same members. It follows that if B⊆A and also A⊆B, then A=B.

For example:

45 A={x:x is one of the first three letters of the English alphabet}
    G={a,b,c}
    ─────────────
    ∴ A=G

The relations 'subset of' and 'superset of' are logically transitive (D6.9). For instance, dogs are mammals and mammals are animals, therefore dogs are animals. More formally, given a set D={x:x is a dog}, a set M={x:x is a mammal}, and a set A={x:x is an animal}

46 $(D \subset M \subset A) \rightarrow (D \subset A)$

Dogs are a genus of mammal, and mammals are a class of animals. We say that *dog* is a HYPONYM of *mammal* and also a hyponym of *animal*. The semantic relation of hyponymy is identical in such cases to the relation 'proper subset of'. For the converse 'superset of' relation, e.g. A⊃D, we say that *animal* is a SUPERORDINATE of *dog*. (Other properties of hyponymy are discussed in Chapter 8, Table 8.4.)
    Look again at F and G.

F = {your-eye, the-Vatican, *b*, a-night-with-Brigitte-Bardot, $\sqrt{2}$};
G = {a,b,c}

They have one member, and hence one non-null set, in common. We say that F and G OVERLAP or INTERSECT, and their overlap is $\{b\}$; symbolically

47 $F \cap G = \{b\}$

─────────────

1. For the mathematical enthusiast: this is a relative complement; sometimes people talk about an 'absolute' complement. The 'absolute' complement of A is everything that is not a member of A, symbolically A′={x:x ∉ A}. Thus, if the set of all objects in the universe is U, then U = A∪A′ (see the definition of merge, D7.13) from which it follows that A′ = U−A. In other words, the absolute complement A′ is defined relative to U! Consequently, the so-called 'absolute' complement is usually treated as the complement relative to a universe of discourse.

Definition 7.12 Every member of A OVERLAP B is a member of A and also a member of B. More formally: $\forall x[x \in A \cap B \longleftrightarrow (x \in A \land x \in B)]$

Where H={x:x is a human being}, F={x:x is a female creature}, M={x:x is a male creature} then $(F \cap H)' = (M \cap H)$: the complement of the overlap of F and H is identical with the overlap of M and H.

Sets may be combined, and the MERGE or UNION of F and G is as follows:

48    $F \cup G$ = {*a, b,* your-eye, a-night-with-Brigitte-Bardot, $\sqrt{2}$, *c,* the-Vatican}

Definition 7.13 Any member of A MERGE B is a member of A and/or a member of B. More formally: $\forall x[x \in A \cup B \longleftrightarrow (x \in A \lor x \in B)]$

Notice in the definition of overlap the correlation between $\cap$ and $\land$, matched by the correlation of $\cup$ and $\lor$ in the definition of merge. If $A \subset B$ then $B = A \cup A'$ (where A' is the complement relative to B). If C={x:x is a cat}, D={x:x is a dog}, and P={x:x has a pink ribbon}

49    $b \in C \cap P$ = b is a cat with a pink ribbon
50    $b \in C \cup D$ = b is either a cat or a dog

You may have noticed the basis for

Definition 7.14 A predicate defines a set.

§7.5 elaborates on this function of a predicate.

In addition to unordered sets there are ORDERED TUPLES: pairs, triples, quadruples, ..., *n*-tuples. Sets and tuples are interesting to linguistic semantics because of the RELATIONS that hold between the members. First consider the relation determined by the symmetric predicate *the same height as* that holds between members of a set H={x,y:x is the same height as y}. 51 substitutes *Jack* for both x and y; 52 substitutes *Jack* for x and *Harry* for y; 53 substitutes *Harry* for x and *Jack* for y.

51 Jack is the same height as himself (=Jack).
52 Jack is the same height as Harry.
53 Harry is the same height as Jack.

51 is necessarily true, 52–53 are synonymous, so the relative sequence of constants substituted for x and y is of no semantic consequence. By contrast, the relation *is taller than* holds between an ordered pair (i.e. a two-tuple) if we are to retain truth-conditions: *x is taller than y* $\neq$ *y is taller than x*. The former is symbolized {<x,y>:x is taller than y} and the latter {<y,x>:y is taller than x}. It follows that 54 is a contradiction, and 55 and 56 are contraries (one entails negation of the other, but negating one does not entail the other because Nancy and Elle may be the same height).

54 *Nancy is taller than herself.

it's like Perl! (handwritten in left margin)

55 Nancy is taller than Elle.
56 Elle is taller than Nancy.

More generally, the ordered pair <a,b> is distinct from the pair <b,a>. The triples <x,y,z>, <z,y,x>, <y,x,z>, <x,z,y> are all distinct from one another. And whereas there is no redundancy in formula <a,a> which identifies a pair of like objects, there is a redundancy in the set {a,a} because it simply identifies the unit set {a} whose member is a; consequently {a,a} = {a}. By contrast <a,a> ≠ <a>.

This section examined the basic concepts and concomitant jargon of set theory that are fundamental to natural language semantics.[4] We saw that 'subset of' corresponds to the lexical relation 'hyponym of'; and 'superset of' to 'superordinate of' (but see Chapter 8 for a modification). In the next section we build on the fact that predication corresponds to set membership.

Exercises

7.4.1 An abstract definition of F={your-eye, the-Vatican, b, a-night-with-Brigitte-Bardot, √2} would be very problematic, even impossible. Why?
    No obvious pattern? (handwritten)

7.4.2 In the formula in (a), which letter is a constant and which a variable, and why?
    (a) $a \in$ {x:x is one of the first three letters of the English alphabet}
            x (handwritten)

7.4.3 What is the semantic difference between F⊂G and G⊆H?
            part (handwritten)   *all* (handwritten)

7.4.4 If G⊆H and G⊃H, then G=H. What is wrong with (a)?
    (a) *If G⊂H and G⊃H, then G=H
            NOT, could have F⊃I (handwritten)

7.4.5 (a)   If you don't own a dog, what is the set of dogs belonging to you? ∅ (handwritten)
      (b)   Suggest a set relationship between the set of daffodils (D) and the set of flowers (F).
                D⊂F (handwritten)

7.4.6 Given that H={1,3,5} list all the eight subsets of H, identifying which are proper subsets. *{1,5,3} {3,1,5} {3,5,1} {5,1,3} {5,3,1} {5} {3} {1}* (handwritten)

7.4.7 If D={x:x is a daughter} and F={x:x is female}
    (a) Is it true that D⊆F? *No* (handwritten)
    (b) Is it true that ∀x[Dx ⟷ Fx]? If not, what truth functor should you substitute for ⟷? *∀x[Dx⊂Fx]* (handwritten)

7.4.8 What is the overlap set that validates the statement "Any two sets whatsoever overlap"? ∅ (handwritten)

7.4.9 List the members of H∪I where H={x:x is one of the first three positive odd numbers} and I={x:x is one of the last three letters of the English alphabet}.
            {135xyz} (handwritten)

7.4.10 Where H={x:x is one of the first three positive odd numbers} and J={x:x is the square root of an odd number} what is H∩J? Is there any other relation you can identify between H and J?   *1, 3, 5*

7.4.11 Can you suggest a set relation of any kind between the set of daffodils (D) and the set of airplanes (A).

7.4.12 B is the set of natural numbers. A is the set of odd numbers. What is A′ with respect to B?

7.4.13 C={x:x is a human being}; D={x:x is a female creature}. E = C∩D.
  (a)   What is the abstract definition of E?
  (b)   What is the abstract definition of D′ with respect to C?

7.4.14 Sets are sometimes depicted by Venn diagrams – usually circles or ovals, but one of them here is rectangular. Members are crowded within the set boundaries. In the diagrams below set F is represented by a RECTANGLE and set G by a CIRCLE. b∈F and c∈G, see Fig. i.

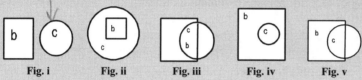

| Fig. i | Fig. ii | Fig. iii | Fig. iv | Fig. v |

Which Figure(s) represent(s):
  (a)   b ∈ F∩G
  (b)   c ∈ F∩G
  (c)   F⊂G
  (d)   F⊃G
  (e)   Identify F′ relative to G in Fig. i and Fig. iii.

7.4.15 How would you represent:
  (a)   Cats and everything with pink ribbons. *∀x y*
  (b)   John has a pink ribbon.
  (c)   female bovine animals *∀x[Fx &∨ Bx ∪ Ax]*

7.4.16 Do the digits in the written form of the number 120 form a triple? Explain your answer.

7.4.17 In (a–c), which is correct, 1 or 2?
  (a)   1 M={x,y:x is married to y}   2   M={<x,y>:x is married to y}
  (b)   1 M={x,y:x is near to y}   2   M={<x,y>:x is near to y}
  (c)   1 M={x,y:x is husband to y}   2   M={<x,y>:x is husband to y}

7.4.18 How would you explain a claim that the NPs in *the hunter killed the buffalo* form an ordered pair?

7.5   Functions and models

> So what *is* MT [model theoretic] semantics? It is *a theory of the semantic effects of composition.*
>
> (Marconi 1997:107, his italics)

Functions are a kind of relation. Symmetric predicates (D7.3) exhibit a SYMMETRIC RELATION aRb↪bRa (*a is near b* ↪ *b is near a*). Converse predicates (D7.4) exhibit a CONVERSE RELATION aRb↪bSa (*a is husband of b* ↪ *b is wife of a*). D6.9 defined the TRANSITIVE RELATION (aRb ∧ bRc) → aRc ((*a is taller than b ∧ b is taller than c*) → (*a is taller than c*)). There are also the REFLEXIVE RELATION aRa (*Joe shaves [Joe]*) and an EQUIVALENCE RELATION like *be the same height as* where the two arguments form a cohort or equivalence class of things that are the same height. A relation can be one-to-one (person to fingerprints), one-to-many (natural parent to children), many-to-many (library books to readers), many-to-one (siblings to a natural parent).

> *Definition 7.15* A FUNCTION is a special type of relation which takes as input a set of objects called its DOMAIN and 'maps' every member of the domain to one member of a set of outputs called its RANGE.

Speed is a function of distance over time: i.e. the function $\frac{d}{t}$ takes distances and times and maps them into speeds, its range. The function "sex" takes living organisms for its domain and maps them into the set {male, female}, its range. Within truth-conditional semantics a VALUATION FUNCTION takes sentences as its domain and assigns a value in the range {true, false}. The valuation function can be thought of as a machine that takes for its domain the set of sentences in a language. It inputs a sentence and outputs a value from the range {1,0} where, by convention, 1 means "true", 0 means "false" (empty set); cf. Fig. 7.1. This valuation function is bivalent; a different function would map sentences to {true, false, indeterminate}.

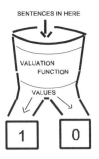

Figure 7.1 The valuation function

Suppose that the domain of the function from sentences to truth values is just the set {*Blood is red, Grass is green, Snow is black*} and nothing else. Further suppose that the machine is programmed to reflect the state of affairs in the real world. If the range is the set {1,0}, then:

> *Blood is red* ↘ 1
>
> *Grass is green* ↗
>
> *Snow is black* → 0

The function from sentences to truth values can be associated with the application of a clause predicate to denotations of NPs in the clause; e.g. the predicate *is red* is true of blood, hence the sentence *blood is red* is true.

Think of members of the domain as entities within the world and time spoken of. Suppose the world spoken of contains only Harold, Jack, and Frank of whom the latter two are bald. We refer to this state of affairs as a MODEL, and we'll call it M_1; cf. Fig. 7.2. There is a domain, A, consisting of the set {Harold, Jack, Frank}. For the sake of formality, we'll say A={h,j,f}. Within the domain is another set B={x:x is bald} = {j,f}.

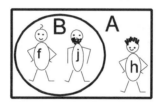

Figure 7.2 Model M_1

Suppose we want to answer question *Who is bald in M_1?* or, equivalently, *In M_1, what is the extension of 'being bald'?* $[\![\alpha]\!]$ symbolizes the denotation of α.

Assumption 7.5 $[\![bald']\!]^{M_1}$ symbolizes "the denotation of *being bald* in M_1".

$[\![bald']\!]^{M_1}$ is an interpretation function that takes h, j, and f as inputs. It outputs {1,0} in accordance with conditions in M_1. More generally,

Definition 7.16 Function $[\![bald']\!]^{M_1}$ applies to a member x of the domain A in model M_1 and assigns a value from the range {1,0}. The value is 1 when it is true that x is bald in M_1 and 0 otherwise.

57 FUNCTION   MEMBER OF DOMAIN   → VALUE IN THE RANGE {1,0}

$[\![bald']\!]^{M_1}$ =   j ↘
                                                      f ↗ 1
                                                      h → 0

$[\textbf{bald}']^{M_1}$ is also a CHARACTERISTIC FUNCTION because it defines a set B whose characteristic is the baldness of members of the domain A. 57 captures the facts that justify 58–60.

58 $[\textbf{bald}']^{M_1}=\{j,f\}$ [Identifies the extension of *being bald* in M_1]
59 In M_1, $\textbf{bald}'(x)=1 \longleftrightarrow x\in\{j,f\}$ [x is the name of someone bald in M_1]
60 In M_1, $\textbf{bald}'(x)=0 \longleftrightarrow \neg[\textbf{bald}'(x)]=1 \longleftrightarrow x=h, \therefore \{h\}=B'$ relative to A

60 demonstrates that negation corresponds to set complement: the set of people who are NOT bald is B' relative to A.
    Suppose we wanted to evaluate the truth in M_1 of 61.

61 Someone is not bald $\Rightarrow$ $\exists x[\neg[\textbf{bald}'(x)]]$

The interpretation function in 57 names who or what satisfies the predicate – i.e. it answers a *wh-* question. A VARIABLE ASSIGNMENT FUNCTION can be used to answer the question *Is there something that satisfies the predicate?*

> *Definition 7.17* Variable assignment function, g, has the set of all variables in the language as its domain and its range is D, the domain of all entities in a model M.

> *Assumption 7.6* The denotation of term t in M is symbolized $[t]^{M,g}$ meaning "the interpretation of term t in model M under assignment g".

The assignment function takes in turn every variable in the formula as input and outputs a denotation – just one – from among the members of domain D, in a wholly mechanical fashion. The method is to replace the variable, e.g. x, with a symbol for a member of the domain, e.g. by $h\in A$. For any formula Φ, this is symbolized $V^{M,g[d/x]}(\Phi)$ "valuation V based on model M under assignment g which replaces a variable x in the formula Φ by d which is a member of the domain D". The substitution of d for x is symbolized [d/x]. Consider how this applies to the valuation of 61 in M_1.

62 $V^{M_1}[\exists x[\neg[\textbf{bald}'(x)]]]=1$ iff, for some g, $V^{M_1,g}[\exists x[\neg[\textbf{bald}'(x)]]]=1$

This says that 61 is true iff it is true on some assignment g for at least one member of domain A in M_1 (i.e. if there is someone in A who is not bald). So,

63 $V^{M_1,g}[\exists x[\neg[\textbf{bald}'(x)]]]=1$
        iff, for at least one member d of domain A, $V^{M_1,g[d/x]}[\exists x[\neg[\textbf{bald}'(x)]]]=1$

What this says is that the truth of 61, $\exists x[\neg[\textbf{bald}'(x)]]$, can be evaluated by systematically substituting for the variable in $\neg[\textbf{bald}'(x)]$ a member of the domain A, i.e. $d\in\{j,f,h\}$. So,

64 $V^{M_1,g[d/x]}[\exists x[\neg[\textbf{bald}'(x)]]]=1$ iff, for some $d\in A$, $\neg[\textbf{bald}'(d)]=1$

We mechanically check each member of A in turn:

65 Let $[\![x]\!]^{M_1,g}=j$ (i.e. let j be assigned to x)

    $g = x{\to}j$

    $V^{M_1}[\neg[\mathbf{bald}'(j)]]=0$ ∴ 61 is not validated on this assignment.

66 Let $[\![x]\!]^{M_1,g'}=f$ (i.e. let f be assigned to x)

    $g = x{\to}f$

    $V^{M_1}[\neg[\mathbf{bald}'(f)]]=0$ ∴ 61 is not validated on this assignment.

67 Let $[\![x]\!]^{M_1,g''}=h$ (i.e. let h be assigned to x)

    $g = x{\to}h$

    $V^{M_1}[\neg[\mathbf{bald}'(h)]]=1$ ∴ 61 **is** validated on this assignment.

67 demonstrates that 61 is true in M_1. One function of a semantic theory is to make explicit how we interpret language expressions. The processes shown in 57–67 make explicit what we intuitively perform in microseconds.

Formula Φ is true in a model M on assignment g iff $[\![\Phi]\!]^{M,g} = 1$. Let's glimpse how to go beyond L_P to bring in worlds and times. Consider two cases:

(i) In the counterfactual 68 Max doesn't own a Rolls in the reference world, but in an imagined world he does (Chapter 2, 31).

68 If Max owned a Rolls, he'd be a lucky man.

In a model theoretic account we evaluate Φ = *Max owns a Rolls* within a single model, M_i, but with respect to different worlds, w' and w'': $[\![\Phi]\!]^{M_i,w',g}=0$ and $[\![\Phi]\!]^{M_i,w'',g}=1$.

(ii) A proposition such as Ψ = *Jack is bald* may be true at one time and false at an earlier time. Thus its validity is determined in a model with respect to time, t. Where $t' {<} t''$ ($<$ symbolizes "precedes"): $[\![\Psi]\!]^{M_2,w',t',g'}=0$ but $[\![\Psi]\!]^{M_2,w',t'',g'}=1$. Generalizing:

> *Definition 7.18* A formula Φ is TRUE IN A MODEL M with respect to a world w and a time t iff, for any assignment g, $[\![\Phi]\!]^{M,w,t,g}=1$

The expansion of L_P to include worlds and times leads to intensional logic – which we shall not investigate here.[5]

In this section we saw that a function is a relation that maps members from the set that forms its domain to a single value – a member from the set that constitutes its range. Particularly significant in semantics is the valuation function from sentences to truth values. The predicate within a proposition serves as a characteristic function to map the denotation of its arguments to truth values, thus defining a set within the domain of which the predicate holds true. Model theory was introduced. A model M consists of a domain D, which is a non-null set of entities and states of affairs. For purposes of exposition, the models were restricted to a very small number of states of affairs, but principles of semantic interpretation are applicable to much larger domains: the class of models for a language is defined on the need to assign a denotation to every sentence (and sentence component) of the language.

Exercises

7.5.1 Where W={Jo, Sue, Ann}, L={x:x is left-handed}, W∩L = {Jo}, T={0,1}: assign values from the range T mapped to the domain W by the function *is left-handed*.

7.5.2 A={h,j,f}; B={j,f}; B={x:x is bald}.
Which is INcorrect among (a–c)? (a) B⊂A;   (b) B⊆A;   (c) B⊃A

7.5.3 There is a law of extensional substitutivity known as Leibniz's Law. It is given in two parts (i) and (ii) below. How would you gloss each of these?
  (i)   (a=b) → (Φ↔[b/a]Φ)
  (ii)   ∀x[Ax↔Bx] → (Φ↔[B/A]Φ)

7.5.4 Show that in model M_1, ∀x[**bald′**(x)]=0.

7.5.5 Let **loathe′** be a $Pred_2$ such that **loathe′**(x,y) means "x loathes y" and this is distinct from **loathe′**(y,x). Consider an expansion of M_1 to M_2 which is exactly like M_1 but in addition Jack loathes Harry and Frank loathes Jack, i.e. in M_2, **loathe′**(j,h)=1 and **loathe′**(f,j)=1, **loathe′**(h,j)=0, **loathe′**(h,f)=0, **loathe′**(h,h)=0, **loathe′**(j,f)=0, **loathe′**(j,j)=0, **loathe′**(f,h)=0, **loathe′**(f,f)=0. Because, e.g. **loathe′**(h,j)=0 and **loathe′**(j,h)=1, it is clear that we must take account of the fact that the arguments of the $Pred_2$ **loathe′** form an ordered pair. Generalizing, the interpretation function [[**loathe′**]]^{M_2} applies to pairs of entities in domain A to assign a value from the range {1,0}; the value is 1 when the first member of the pair loathes the second, and 0 otherwise.
  (a)   In the formula [[**loathe′**]]^{M_2}={<j,h>, <f,j>} what is {<j,h>, <f,j>}?
  (b)   What is meant by: in M_2, **loathe′**(x,y)=1 ↔ <x,y>∈{<j,h>, <f,j>}?

7.5.6 Given M_2 as defined in 7.5.5, validate (a)
  (a) $V^{M_2,g}$[∃x∃y[**loathe′**(x,y)]]=1
Here's how to begin.
  V^{M_2}[∃x∃y[**loathe′**(x,y)]]=1 iff, for some assignment g and {d,d′}⊆A, [**loathe′**(d,d′)]=1. Let the output of an assignment function g be as follows:
    g =x → h   i.e. [[x]]^{M_2,g}= Harry
       y → j   i.e. [[y]]^{M_2,g}= Jack
  V^{M_2}[**loathe′**](h,j)=0 ∴ (a) is not validated
Next take assignment g which is a minimally different assignment of values to variables in M_2; thus, assume g(x)=g[h/x] as above, but g(y)=g[f/y].

7.6   The lambda operator, λ

The existential and universal quantifiers ∃, ∀ bind individual variables that, if they have any denotation at all, denote entities. The LAMBDA OPERATOR, λ, also known as the abstraction or set operator, was introduced into mathematical logic by Church 1941 to operate on sets rather than individuals. In consequence, λ can bind predicates or sets of entities having the property specified by the subformula within λ's scope. λ is not an operator within standard first-order predicate calculus; it is a corner stone of model theoretic semantics using type theory (Church 1940). This book does not use the formalism of type theory, but this section will refer to certain functional types that are definable in type theory. As we shall see, use of the λ-operator increases the explanatory value of the metalanguage for semantic analysis because it allows us to extend the metalanguage beyond L_P in a way that more closely resembles natural language syntax.

The open formula in 69 is a propositional function that contains a free variable, x; cf. 18-19 above.

69   **bald′**(x)

We can construct from 69 the λ-expression in 70, in which λx binds the variable x within its scope (as defined by the brackets).

70   λx[**bald′**(x)]

70 is not, however, a sentence. The lambda expression λx[**bald′**(x)] can be read "the set of x's such that x is bald" or "the property of being an x such that x is bald" or "the property x has of being bald". In other words λx[**bald′**(x)] is equivalent to the abstract set {x:**bald′**(x)}. So, 70 is an expression of the same type as the predicate **bald′**, or more generally,

> *Definition 7.19* λxΦ, in which x is a free variable within formula Φ, is of the same functional type as Pred$_1$, and therefore it is not a sentence but THE NAME OF A FUNCTION – a function (λ) from entities (x) to truth values (Φ) (provided certain conditions are met).

To become a sentence, the function must be applied to an argument. Let's see how.

Suppose we translate 71 from English into the L_P of 72:

71   Jack is tall and bald   ⇒
72   Tj∧Bj

(For convenience we'll resume using capital letters as predicate names, so 'B' in 72 symbolizes 'is bald'.) 72 is accurate in representing the fact that Jack is a member of the set of tall things and also a member of the set of bald things. But 72 does not explicitly represent the fact that Jack is a member of the overlap set: the set of things which are both tall and bald. This property of 72 can be captured by using the λ-expression in 73.

73 $\lambda x[Tx \wedge Bx]$ "the property of being tall and bald" or "the set of individuals that are
                                      both tall and bald"

73 is not a sentence, and it is not yet a translation of 71. It is a function looking for an argument to become a sentence in order to yield a truth value. This requirement can be met by applying 73 to a constant j, as in 74. 74 translates 75.

74 $\lambda x[Tx \wedge Bx](j)$
75 $j \in \{x : Tx \wedge Bx\}$

74 is a sentence that yields a truth value. We convert 74 into a standard formula of L_P, namely 72, by replacing the variable, x, with the constant, j.

> **Definition 7.20** For every occurrence of the variable bound by λ, LAMBDA CONVERSION substitutes the term given in the parentheses immediately following the scope of lambda. The latter is then deleted, along with the λ-operator, its bound variable, and any extraneous brackets (in 76, deletion is marked $\lambda x[\ ](j)$).

76 $\lambda x[Tx \wedge Bx](j)$ $\left\{ \genfrac{}{}{0pt}{}{\rightarrow}{[j/x]} \right\}$ $\lambda x[\ Tj \wedge Bj\ ](j)$ $\rightarrow$ $Tj \wedge Bj$

In 76 '[j/x]' symbolizes "substitute constant j for variable x". To get from 71 to 72 by way of 73–74 adds an important snippet of information to the semantic analysis; it is not just a Duke of York gambit (The Grand Old Duke of York, / He had 10,000 men; / He marched them up to the top of the hill, / Then he marched them down again).

Additional evidence for the explanatory value of λ-expressions is to be had from a discussion of active–passive pairs. Because they are truth-functionally synonymous, active–passive pairs, such as 77, have the same translation in L_P, cf. 4 and 8.

77 (a)   Frank admires Harry $\left. \right\}$ $\Rightarrow$ Afh
     (b)   Harry is admired by Frank

The surface structure difference between the English sentences (which has discourse consequences we can't begin to go into) is lost in the direct translation into L_P. Using the λ-operator in the translation rectifies the situation. In this case, because **admire'** is of type Pred$_2$, two variables are separately bound by two λ-operators. Glosses for the subformulae we shall use are

78 $\lambda y[\lambda x[Axy]]$ "the property of x admiring y"
79 $\lambda x[\lambda y[Axy]]$ "the property of y being admired by x"

Conversion proceeds from wider scope to narrower scope, i.e. from left to right. The leftmost λ-bound variable is associated with the leftmost constant.

77(a)′ λyλx[Axy](h) (f) $\left\{ \begin{array}{c} \rightarrow \\ [h/y] \end{array} \right\}$ λx[Axh](f) $\left\{ \begin{array}{c} \rightarrow \\ [f/x] \end{array} \right\}$ Afh

77(b)′ λxλy[Axy](f)(h) $\left\{ \begin{array}{c} \rightarrow \\ [f/x] \end{array} \right\}$ λy[Afy](h) $\left\{ \begin{array}{c} \rightarrow \\ [h/y] \end{array} \right\}$ Afh

The different paths to Afh are explicit. Notice how the surface subject is the last term to be converted (innermost λ-bound variable, outermost constant following the scope of lambda). Glosses for the medial subformulae, both the same type as Pred$_1$, are:

77(a)″ λx[Axh]   "the property of Harry's being admired by something (=x)" or
                  "the set of individuals that Harry is admired by"

Thus λx[Axh] = {x:x admires Harry}, which is a Pred$_1$ type expression as distinct from the sentence type: λx[Axh](f) = f∈{x:x admires Harry}

77(b)″ λy[Afy]   "the property of Frank's admiring something (=y)" or "the set of individuals that Frank admires / that are admired by Frank"

The Pred$_1$ type expression is λy[Afy] = {y:y is admired by Frank}, and the sentence type expression is λy[Afy](h) = h∈{y:y is admired by Frank}. Notice how the Pred$_2$ **admire′** is decomposed into a pair of Pred$_1$ type expressions; this is characteristic of type theory. The decomposition can be seen in Tree77(a)′.

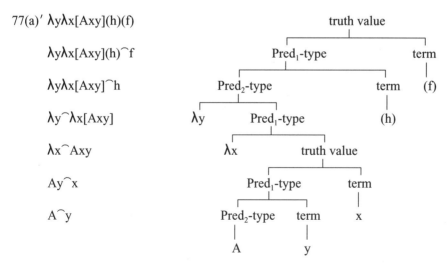

77(a)′ λyλx[Axy](h)(f)

        λyλx[Axy](h)^f

        λyλx[Axy]^h

        λy^λx[Axy]

        λx^Axy

        Ay^x

        A^y

The λ-operator can occur with the universal and the existential quantifiers. For instance, 80 translates as 81 (ignoring complications) and 81 converts to 82.

80   Tom ate a sausage Angeline cooked   ⇒
81   ∃x[λy[Sy∧Cay](x) ∧ Etx]
82   ∃x[Sx∧Cax∧Etx]

Glosses for subformulae are:

83   Pred₁ type: λy[Sy∧Cay]   "the property of being an Angeline-cooked-sausage" or
                               "the set of individuals that are Angeline-cooked-
                               sausages"
84   Sentence type: λy[Sy∧Cay](x)   "x has the property of being an Angeline-cooked-
                               sausage" or "x∈{y:y is an Angeline-cooked-
                               sausage}"

The existential quantifier binds x, so ∃x[Sx∧Cax∧Etx] translates "there is at least one x
which has the property of being an Angeline-cooked-sausage and Tom ate it." Again the
λ-operator spells out the semantic composition of the English sentence in a manner closer
to the surface structure of English than is possible in the standard L_P metalanguage.
    λ can bind predicate variables as well as term variables.

Definition 7.21 λPΦ is function (λ) from predicates (P) to truth values (Φ)
(provided certain conditions are met).

For example the sentence λP[∃x[Px]](B) has the structure 85.

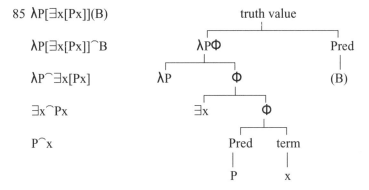

85 λP[∃x[Px]](B)   truth value

    λP[∃x[Px]]^B   λPΦ   Pred

    λP^∃x[Px]   λP   Φ   (B)

    ∃x^Px   ∃x   Φ

    P^x   Pred   term

                            P   x

λP[∃x[Px]] means "P is a property true of at least one individual" or "P is a set of sets that
include at least one individual." Applied to predicate B, 85 is converted to ∃xBx. *Jack is
bald* could derive from either 86 or 87. There is the subtle difference in emphasis indicated.

86 λPλx[Px](B)(j) = "Jack is a member of the set of things which are bald"

Tree86 λP[λx[Px]](B)(j)

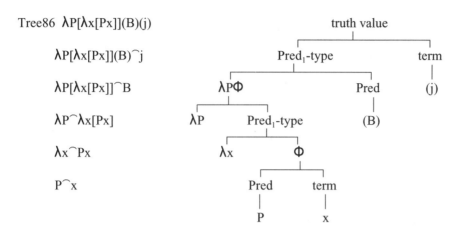

87 λxλP[Px](j)(B) = "Being bald is one of the set of properties predicable of Jack"

Tree87 λx[λP[Px]](j)(B)

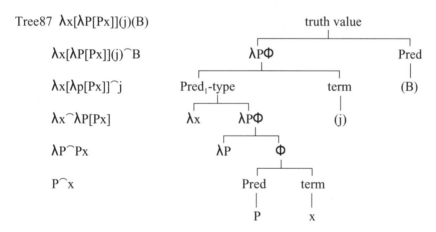

The λ-operator offers a means of representing the semantics of natural language expressions in a manner that more closely resembles natural language structure than does direct translation into L_P. This book uses it mostly to identify membership of overlapping sets.[6]

Exercises

7.6.1 Which of (a) and (b) is (i) well-formed and (ii) will yield a truth value?
   (a) λx[Px]   (b) λx[Py]

7.6.2 Using a λ-expression and λ-conversion translate the following and add glosses:
   (a) Sally runs and jumps.   λx [Rx ∧ Jx](s)
   (b) Ed is a tall man.   λx [Tx ∧ Mx] (e)

(c) Stuart jogs but is fat.

7.6.3 Gloss all the following. Assume j=Jo, and that j, B, and S are constant throughout this exercise.
    (a) S={x:x is short}, B={x:x is brunette}   (b) j ∈ S∩B
    (c) λx[Sx ∧ Bx](j)   (d) λx[Sx ∧ Bx]

7.6.4 Using a λ-expression and then λ-conversion, translate *Jo hated a tie that Ed wore.*

7.6.5 Translate the following active–passive pair using a λ-expression and then λ-conversion:
    (a) Helen reviewed the book.
    (b) The book was reviewed by Helen.

7.6.6 Consider the following sentences in which k=Karen and m=Mona:
    (a) λyλx[**think'**(x,**be_clever'**(y))](k)(k)
    (b) λyλx[**think'**(x,**be_clever'**(y))](k)(m)
    (c) λyλx[**think'**(x,**be_clever'**(y))](m)(k)
    (d) λyλx[**think'**(x,**be_clever'**(y))](m)(m)
    (e) *Karen thinks she's clever and Mona does too.*
    Which of the following conjuncts of (a–d) gives an acceptable reading for the ambiguous (e)? Spell out the meanings for the others.
    1. (a) ∧ (b)   2. (a) ∧ (c)   3. (a) ∧ (d)   4. (b) ∧ (c)   5. (b) ∧ (d)   6. (c) ∧ (d)

7.6.7 Where might you use the λ-operator to differentiate between (a) and (b)?
    (a) Someone drinks and someone smokes.
    (b) Harry drinks and smokes.

7.6.8 Do the λ-conversions on the expression λPλQ∀x[Px→Qx](B)(H).

7.7   Summary

The purpose of this chapter has been to assemble tools for analysing the semantic structure of clauses and clause constituents by reviewing the basic concepts of predicate logic, meaning postulates, set theory, relations, functions, and the λ-operator. Subsequent chapters in this book make extensive use of concepts from predicate logic, set theory, and lambda calculus in the semantic specifications of listemes.

The next chapter, Chapter 8, begins to make use of such tools. Chapters 8–10 review cognitive and functional approaches to semantics; that is, approaches that take account of human awareness and experience and the purposes which human language serves. Chapter 8 examines semantic frames, semantic fields, and lexical analysis in terms of semantic components or primitives. It appraises semantic primitives, what a semantic description is meant to achieve, and who or what a semantic specification is designed for.

● Key words and phrases:

argument

bound variable (A7.1)

c-command

characteristic function

complement set (D7.10)

connective (truth functor)

constant (name) (A6.1)

converse predicates (D7.4)

converse relation

denotation: $[\![t]\!]$ of a term t, $[\![P]\!]^M$ of predicate P in model M (cf. D7.16)

domain (D7.15)

entity (e)

equivalence relation

existential quantifier, $\exists$

formula, Φ, Ψ, ...

free variable (A7.1)

function (D7.15)

generative semantics

hyponym of

identity of sets (D7.11)

intensional logic

interpretation function

lambda (abstraction or set) operator, λ

$\lambda x\Phi$ function from entities to truth values (D7.19)

$\lambda P\Phi$ function from $Pred_1$ to truth values (D7.21)

lambda conversion (D7.20)

Leibniz's Law (Law of Substitutivity)

L_P predicate calculus

meaning postulate (D7.5)

member of a set, $\in$

merge (set union), $\cup$ (D7.13)

model, M

model theoretic semantics

null set, $\varnothing$ (A7.4)

overlap (set intersection), $\cap$ (D7.12)

predicate, P, Q, ... (D7.14)

predicate logic (calculus)

$Pred_n$ (n-place predicate) (D7.2)

proper subset, $\subset$ (D7.9)

propositional function

quantifier binding (A7.1)

range (D7.15)

reflexive relation

scope (D2.12)

set (D7.6)

subset, $\subseteq$ (D7.7)

substitution of [d/x] in Φ

superordinate of

superset

symmetric predicate (D7.3)

symmetric relation

term (variable or constant)

(logical) transitivity

transitive relation

truth value (t)

truth in a model (D7.18)

tuple

type categorial language

unit set (D7.8)

universal quantifier, $\forall$

valuation function

variable (A6.1)

variable assignment function, g (D7.17)

well-formed formula (wff) (D7.1)

● A simple proposition consists of $Pred_n$ and n arguments (D7.2).
● A constant has a fixed value (denotation) (A6.1). Constant symbols for individuals are conventionally taken from the beginning of the alphabet or the initial letter of a name. Constant symbols for predicates conventionally use the initial letter of the name of the predicate.
● A variable (A6.1) has no fixed value, though there may be certain contextual conditions that limit the possibilities. Φ and Ψ are variables for formulae; p and q are variables for propositions; P and Q are variables for predicates; x, y, z are variables for individuals.
● If Φ and Ψ are well-formed formulae, their negations and the formulae that result from their being connected by truth functors are also well-formed.

- If $Qx\Psi$ is a subformula of Φ, and Q is a quantifier such as $\forall$ or $\exists$, or an operator such as $\neg$ or λ, then Ψ is in the scope of Q.
- A bound variable x is one within the scope of $\forall x$, $\exists x$, or λx, otherwise it is free.
- A sentence of L_p was distinguished from a propositional function.
- Meaning postulates can be employed in defining a set, e.g: $G=\{x:\mathbf{man}'(x) \wedge \exists y((\mathbf{love}'(x,y) \wedge \neg(\mathbf{love}'(y,x))) \rightarrow \mathbf{sad}'(x))\}$ "G is the set of men who, if they love someone or something and are not loved in return, are sad"; $F=\{<x,y>:\mathbf{man}'(x) \wedge \mathbf{love}'(x,y) \wedge \neg(\mathbf{love}'(y,x))\}$ "F is a pair such that one, x, who is a man, loves something y, but is not loved in return"
- The relation 'subset of' was linked to the lexical relation 'hyponym of'; 'superset of' to 'superordinate of'. (Hyponymy is further discussed in Chapter 8.)
- We distinguished sets whose members are unordered from tuples whose members are ordered with respect to one another.
- The predicate within a proposition serves as a function to map its arguments to truth values, and in so doing maps the proposition or sentence to truth values. Particularly significant in semantics is the valuation function from sentences to truth values.
- A predicate is a characteristic function because it characterizes a set relative to its domain.
- A model M consists of a domain D, which is a non-null set of entities and states of affairs. A model is comparable with our notion of $M^{w,t}$ "model of the world and time spoken of".
- We looked at two formalizations for the interpretation of formulae. An interpretation function which names who or what satisfies a predicate for some domain within a model. An assignment function g which mechanically assigns each member of the domain to each argument of a predicate enabling a proposition to be evaluated for truth on that assignment. These functions explicitly model the way in which language is applied to the world and time spoken of.
- Leibniz's Law, a.k.a the Law of Substitutivity or of Identity. If a has the same extension as b, b can substitute for a in any formula without changing the truth value (but not necessarily without changing intensional meaning).
- The λ-operator is a set abstraction operator. For instance given $F=\{<x,y>:\mathbf{man}'(x) \wedge \mathbf{love}'(x,y) \wedge \neg(\mathbf{love}'(y,x))\}$, F is a pair such that one, x, who is a man, loves something y, but is not loved in return. The same set F can be defined using the λ-operator: $\lambda x\lambda y[\mathbf{man}'(x) \wedge \mathbf{love}'(x,y) \wedge \neg(\mathbf{love}'(y,x))]$. The principal use for it in this book will be to capture properties of set overlap such as were illustrated in 73–76.
- In model theoretic semantics, the λ-operator is generally used within type categorial languages. In such a language the two primitive types are t "truth value" and e "entity"; all other types are composed from these. We did not examine type languages because we shall be making no further use of them. We shall use lambdas as a convenient extension to predicate calculus.
- Lambda expressions convert into the formulae of L_p.
- Formal semantics treats language as an abstract entity; it can be thought of as a rational model of cognitive behaviour, though by no means a chart of cognitive behaviour.

7.8   Notes on further reading

[1] On predicate logic, see Allwood et al. 1977, Cann 1993, Gamut 1991, Hodges 1977, McCawley 1993.

[2] On meaning postulates, see Carnap 1956, Chierchia and McConnell-Ginet 1990, Lyons 1977, 1995.

[3] On generative semantics, see Gruber 1965, 1967, Lakoff 1965, McCawley 1968a,b,c, Newmeyer 1980, Allan 1986, Harris 1993.

[4] On set theory, see Allwood et al. 1977, McCawley 1993 for a linguistic orientation, Devlin 1993, Vaught 1995 for maths-oriented introductions.

[5] On intensional logic, see Carnap 1956, Kripke 1963, Montague 1974, Lewis 1970, Cresswell 1973, Bradley and Swartz 1979, Benthem 1988, Chierchia and McConnell-Ginet 1990, Gamut 1991, Cann 1993, McCawley 1993.

[6] There is, of course, much more to lambda calculus than is presented here and there are complications we have not considered; see Church 1941, 1956, Partee, Meulen, and Wall 1990.

A few short words on type theory. There are two primitive types, e "entity" and t "truth value". If α is an expression of type <a,b> and β an expression of type a, then the functional application of α to β will yield an expression of type b. $\lambda x \Phi$ is of Pred$_1$ type <e,t> – a function from entities to truth values. $\lambda P \Phi$ is of type ≪e,t>,t> – a function from a function from entities to truth values to truth values. A Pred$_2$ is of type <e,<e,t≫ – a function from entities to a function from entities to truth values. A manner adverb is normally of type ≪e,t>,<e,t≫ – a function from a function from entities to truth values to a function from entities to truth values (roughly a predicate upon a predicate). ¬ is of type <t,t> – a function from truth values to truth values, and the logical connectives are <t,<t,t≫. On type theory for linguists, see Lewis 1970, Allwood et al. 1977, Montague 1974, Dowty, Wall and Peters 1981, Partee, Meulen, and Wall 1990, Gamut 1991, Heim and Kratzer 1998.

Scripts - event sequences

Frames - structural relations
between items & concept

?. Fields - relations between
names & concepts

8 Frames, fields, and semantic components

Principle of Discrete and Exhaustive Analysis. Meanings can be analysed in a fully determinate way; that is, any complex meaning can be decomposed into a combination of discrete other meanings, without circularity and without residue.

(Goddard 1994:8)

8.1 Where we are heading

The purpose of this chapter is to explain the significance of semantic frames, semantic fields, and componential analysis within lexical semantics. It will be evident that

> **Assumption 8.1** Semantic properties and relations are constrained and informed by the categories and relations that we humans perceive in nature, and/or have experience of in the world around us, and/or conceive of in abstract fields such as knowledge and moral or ethical behaviour.

The meanings of language expressions reflect speakers' perceptions of their denotata; as a result, we cannot account for senses and sense relations without recourse to intensions and through them to extensions in some world, real or imagined. These findings will be strongly confirmed in the chapters that follow.

We begin with scripts in §8.2 so as to get a proper perspective on the semantic frames and fields discussed later in the chapter. Scripts are structured representations of event sequences, whereas frames identify the structural relations of listemes and the concepts they name. Semantic fields are constructed from the semantic relations among names for concepts. §8.3 describes semantic frames and their place in constraining the combining of listemes: how can we account for the (apparent) anomaly of *Colorless green ideas sleep furiously* (Chomsky 1957:15)? Some constraints are imposed by the rules of syntax. 'Selection restrictions' have been proposed as semantic constraints on the co-occurrence of listemes; but identifying selection restrictions proves impracticable, if not impossible. The goal can be achieved by using the semantic frame for every listeme to create well-formedness conditions on its collocation (co-occurrence) with other listemes. §8.4 looks at semantic fields and the semantic relations that exist between items within a field. §8.5 is on componential analysis, which seeks to identify the meaning components in listemes. The principal means of accomplishing this is has been through the structuralist method of contrastive distributional analysis. §8.6 appraises the search for those quintessential semantic components called 'semantic primitives', focusing on the work of Anna Wierzbicka and colleagues. Their 'natural semantic metalanguage' is critically examined. Despite the breadth of data they have investigated, the set of primitives postulated is far too limited to be convincing. §8.7 summarizes the chapter.

8.2   Scripts

> *Definition 8.1* 'A script is a structure that describes appropriate sequences of events in a particular context. A script is made up of slots and requirements about what can fill those slots. The structure is an interconnected whole, and what is in one slot affects what can be in another. Scripts handle stylized everyday situations. They are not subject to much change, nor do they provide the apparatus for handling totally novel situations. Thus, a script is a predetermined, stereotyped sequence of actions that defines a well-known situation. Scripts allow for new references to objects within them just as if these objects had been previously mentioned; objects within a script may take 'the' without explicit introduction because the script itself has already implicitly introduced them [i.e. they are common ground].' (Schank and Abelson 1977:41)

When we think about how the meaning of such verb phrases as *eating out* or *going to a restaurant* relates to other parts of the vocabulary, we surely think in terms of scripts such as the one below, adapted from Schank and Abelson 1977:43f (the original restaurant script was implemented by a computer program).

The   Restaurant   Script

Roles: Customer, Server, Cook, Cashier (optional)
Props: menu, food, tables, chairs, cutlery, etc., bill, money
Entry conditions: Customer is hungry. Customer has money
Results: Customer has less money. Customer is not hungry. Customer is pleased
             (optional).

Scene 1: Entering

I1 Customer goes into restaurant
I2 Customer looks for a table
I3 Customer decides where to sit
I4 Customer goes to a table

Scene 2: Ordering   *M1–M6 will be omitted if menu is to hand*

M1   Customer signals to Server
M2   Server goes to Customer   *M2–M3 may be skipped*
M3   Customer says "need menu" to Server
M4   Server gets menu
M5   Server goes to Customer
M6   Server gives menu to Customer

R1   Customer takes menu
R2   Customer reads menu
R3   Customer chooses food
R4   Customer signals Server
R5   Server goes to Customer
R6   Customer tells Server "want food"
R7   Server goes to Cook
R8   Server gives order to Cook
R9   Cook tells Server "no food" OR ELSE GO TO R13   *R9 is a dispreferred*
                                                         alternative to R13
R10 Server goes to Customer
R11 Server tells Customer "no food"
R12 RETURN TO STEP M4 OR R2, OR ELSE GO TO X1
R13 Cook prepares food (food preparation script)

Scene 3: Eating

E1   Cook gives food to Server
E2   Server gives food to Customer
E3   Customer eats food
E4   RETURN TO STEP M1 OR ELSE GO TO P1

Scene 4: Paying

P1   Customer signals Server
P2   Server goes to Customer
P3   Customer asks Server for bill
P4   Server writes bill
P5   Server gives Customer bill
P6   Customer gives Server money OR ELSE Customer pays Cashier
P7   Customer leaves tip   *P7 is optional*

Scene 5: Exiting

X1   Customer leaves restaurant

The vocabulary used in the script evoked by *going to a restaurant* indicates its semantic associations. Listing the terms in alphabetical order is unhelpful.

bill, cashier, chairs, cook, customer, drink (omitted from Schank and Abelson's script), *eating, entering, exiting, food, hunger, menu, order, ordering, paying, selecting, server (waiter, waitress), signalling, tables, taking/writing the order, tipping*

The script is much more valuable because it shows how the semantic associations are organized in respect of one another. Some are logically necessary. You cannot exit from a place before being in it. In order to be in it, you have to enter. Other parts of the script are simply conventional and can vary: in some establishments (not all) you pay before getting food; in some (not all) the cooking precedes the ordering.

The motivation for scripts is

Assumption 8.2 Beyond earliest childhood, VERY LITTLE WE ENCOUNTER IS TOTALLY NEW IN ALL ITS ASPECTS. Most of what we hear and read can be interpreted wholly or partially in relation to structured knowledge arranged into modules of information.

Speaker presupposes (D6.14) this common ground when constructing a text so that e.g. understanding *Went to a restaurant last night* is to invoke the restaurant script as a set of conversational implicatures (Chapter 6, 40). A script contains information that Speaker does not need to repeat to Hearer unless Hearer is, for instance, a small child predicated to have no notion what *going to a restaurant* means. Scripts enable what is said to underspecify meaning on the assumption that, when interpreting utterances, Hearer will expand the explicit text by systematically adding what is implicit in it.

Some additional facts.

Assumption 8.3 Scripts contain structured information about dynamic event sequences. Regular components of a script are predictable and DEVIATIONS FROM A SCRIPT ARE POTENTIALLY NEWSWORTHY.

Assumption 8.4 There is a very large number of scripts. Many overlap and there must be networking among scripts.

For instance, entering a restaurant has much in common with entering any other business premises and is distinct from entering a private home. Schank 1982, 1986 proposes a sort of hierarchy: at the top, very generally applicable, script-like memory organizational packets have more specific scripts (like the one above) and finer-grained scenes within them. There is much research to be done, but it is certain that communication and language understanding make use of scripts, and that the vocabulary used in describing the scripts constitutes a semantic field of words whose interrelationships are defined in terms of the frames and event sequences in the script.[1]

Exercises

8.2.1 What sort of script is invoked in the following?

One morning Tom found his Jaguar wouldn't start. He phoned Ed and asked him to come and look at it. Ed didn't really want to, but he came anyway. He saw that the plugs were worn, and advised Tom to fit some new ones. Tom did so. After that the car worked perfectly.   *fixing a car*

8.2.2 Write a script for telephoning to make an appointment to see a doctor, dentist, or lawyer.

8.2.3 Suppose that Bill is a plumber. Would you infer something different from (a) and (b)? Give reasons.   *script*

(a) Bill went to the restaurant.   (b) The plumber went to the restaurant

to eat   *to fix something*

8.3   Frames and selection restrictions

[A] word's meaning can be understood only with reference to a structured background of experience, beliefs, or practices, constituting a kind of conceptual prerequisite for understanding the meaning. Speakers can be said to know the meaning of the word only by first understanding the background frames that motivate the concept that the word encodes. Within such an approach, words or word senses are not related to each other directly, word to word, but only by way of their links to common background frames and indications of the manner in which their meanings highlight particular elements of such frames.

(Fillmore and Atkins 1992:76f)

There is a distinction between the restaurant script – consisting of a dynamic structure of event sequences – and a restaurant frame identifying the function of a restaurant and what kind of thing it is.

Definition 8.2 FRAMES identify the characteristic features, attributes, and functions of a denotatum, and its characteristic interactions with things necessarily or typically associated with it.

A restaurant is a public eating-place. Its attributes are: (1) business premises where, in exchange for payment, food is served to be eaten on the premises. Consequently, (2) a restaurant has a kitchen for food preparation, and tables and chairs to accommodate customers during their meal. A frame is built from encyclopedic knowledge. The frame for *people* registers the fact that, being living creatures, people have the attributes of age and sex. The attribute sex has the values male and female. It can be represented formally by a function **be_sexed'** applied to the domain D={x:x is a person} to yield a value from the set {male, female}. The function **be_aged'** applies to the same domain to yield a value from a much larger set. Frames interconnect in complicated ways. For instance, the social status and the appearance of a person are usually partly dependent upon their age and sex, but not necessarily so. Such knowledge is called upon in the proper use of language. Part of the frame for *bird* is

1   $\forall x \begin{bmatrix} \mathbf{bird}'(x) \rightarrow \lambda y[\mathbf{feathered}'(y) \wedge \mathbf{biped}'(y) \wedge \mathbf{beaked}'(y)] \\ \mathbf{bird}'(x) \rhd \mathbf{can\_fly}'(x) \end{bmatrix}(x)$

The functions **feathered'**, **biped'**, and **beaked'** applied to a domain yield a value from the range {true, false}; applied to D={x: **bird'**(x)} they have the value true. The function **can_fly'** applied to D={x: **penguin'**(x)} yields the value false. Birds are sexed, and a (normal) female bird has the attribute 'can lay eggs' with the value true. Barsalou 1992:28 describes attributes as slots in the frame that are to be filled with the appropriate values.

Attributes for events include participants, location, and time of occurrence, e.g. the verb *buy* has slots for the attributes buyer, seller, merchandise, payment: these give rise to the THEMATIC STRUCTURE (valencies, case frames) of the verb (Chapters 11–12). An act of buying occurs in a certain place at a certain time – a world–time pair with values relevant to evaluation of truth. Fillmore and Atkins 1992 make a detailed discussion of the various semantic frames for the verb *risk*. Simplified and abbreviated, the attributes within the frame for *risk* are:

(a)   An actor.
(b)   Something valued that may be lost by the actor doing act A.
(c)   A hoped-for gain that motivates act A.

Fillmore and Atkins assign attributes a syntactic classification. In an active clause the actor is typically the subject [NP$_{SU}$]; the thing at risk is typically the first (direct) object [NP$_{O1}$]; the hoped-for gain is expressed in a [prepositional phrase$_{PP}$]. Examples are:

2   [He $_{SU}$] risked [his life $_{O1}$] [for her $_{PP}$].
3   [She $_{SU}$] risked [her reputation $_{O1}$] [for the chance to become rich $_{PP}$].
4   [A speculator $_{SU}$] risks [money $_{O1}$] [in the hope of making more $_{PP}$].

The thing done or the purpose is often named in a nonfinite [clause$_{S}$]:

5   She risked her life [swimming to get help $_{S}$].
6   He risked his reputation [to get rich $_{S}$].
7   He risked the family fortune [by investing in junk bonds $_{S}$].
8   We risked surfacing the submarine [to race to a new attack position $_{S}$].

A well structured and more comprehensive approach to what are here referred to as semantic frames is to be found in Pustejovsky's 1995 'lexical semantic structures'. His 'generative lexicon' entries potentially have four components.

ARGUMENT STRUCTURE specifies the number and type of logical arguments and how they are realized syntactically (Chapters 11–12 have more on this topic).

EVENT STRUCTURE defines the event type as state, process, or transition. For instance, the event structure of the verb *open* involves a process wherein x carries out the act of opening y, creating a state where y is open (Chapter 12 has more on this topic).

QUALIA STRUCTURE (*qualia* is the plural of Latin neuter noun *quale* "the quality (nature) of a thing") identifies the characteristics of the denotatum. There are four types:

CONSTITUTIVE: material constitution, weight, parts and components.

FORMAL: orientation, magnitude, shape, dimension, colour, position.

TELIC: purpose and function or goal.

AGENTIVE: creator, artifact, natural kind, causal chain.

LEXICAL INHERITANCE STRUCTURE, e.g. Fig.8.1, identifies relations within what Pustejovsky calls the lexicon, but which is encyclopedic information in terms of Chapter 3 of this book.

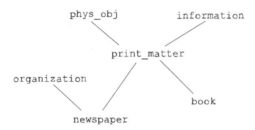

Figure 8.1 From Pustejovsky 1995:95

Fig.8.1 demonstrates that *book* and *newspaper* have in common that they are print matter, and that *newspaper* can refer to both the readable product and the organization that produces it. Pustejovsky's (1995:101) entry for *book* is 9.

$$
9 \quad
\begin{bmatrix}
\textbf{book} \\
\text{ARGSTR} =
\begin{bmatrix}
\text{ARG1} = \textbf{x:information} \\
\text{ARG2} = \textbf{y:phys\_obj}
\end{bmatrix} \\
\text{QUALIA} =
\begin{bmatrix}
\textbf{information.phys\_obj\_lcp} \\
\text{FORMAL} = \textbf{hold(y,x)} \\
\text{TELIC} = \textbf{read(e,w,x.y)} \\
\text{AGENT} = \textbf{write(e}'\textbf{,v,x.y)}
\end{bmatrix}
\end{bmatrix}
$$

In the qualia, **information.phys_obj_lcp** is a LEXICAL CONCEPTUAL PARADIGM (lcp) represented in a 'type cluster' that says *book* is a physical object that holds information, cf. ARG2 and ARG1 and **hold(y,x)** in the formal quale. The type cluster is:

information.phys_obj_lcp = {**information.phys_obj, phys_obj, information**}

All three members of the set are available for expression by *book*. In 9, the agent quale captures the fact that a book (**x.y**, i.e. **information.phys_obj_lcp**) is written by someone (**v**). The event of writing is **e**′. The telic quale captures the fact that a book (**x.y**) is for reading (**e**) by someone (**w**).

Although Pustejovsky's terminology is not used again in this book, his method is consistent with much that follows. But let's turn now to constraints on the permissible combinations for listemes.

Languages could not function as they do if they permitted just any old sequence of listemes.

> *Assumption 8.5* The primary function of language is to communicate meanings. This is done by combining the meaning encapsulated in listemes into the complex meanings of phrases, sentences, and longer texts. THERE CANNOT BE A LANGUAGE WITHOUT SYNTAX.

Combining listemes imposes a structural organization upon them conditioned by the rules of syntax. For this purpose up to five kinds of morphosyntactic specifications in lexicon entries have been proposed.

Morphosyntactic specification	Example
CATEGORY FEATURES	N, V, ...
STRICT SUBCATEGORIZATION FEATURES	[+ ___NP] for syntactically transitive verbs such as *kiss*
RULE FEATURES	Whether or not an object NP can occur between the V and vPrt of a phrasal verb (Chapter 4)
INHERENT FEATURES	[+ human, + female, ...] for *woman*; or [+ active, ...] for *go*
SELECTIONAL FEATURES	E.g. for a verb [+ [+ animate]___[+ abstract]] "has an animate subject NP and an abstract direct object NP"

The term 'features' is used simply as a matter of convenience, we are concerned only with the different kinds of co-occurrence constraints. Chapter 3 left no doubt about the need for category features.

> *Definition 8.3* STRICT SUBCATEGORIZATION identifies other syntactic categories that collocate with the listeme.

For instance, syntactically transitive verbs are defined by some notational variant of the strict subcategorization feature [+ ___NP] "takes a 1st object", e.g. *open* (as in *Fred opened the box*) has this feature, whereas the intransitive verb in *The door opened easily* has the feature [– ___NP]. The obvious correspondence suggests a single verb *open* with two different semantic frames; cf. Pustejovsky 1995:220ff. On comparable grounds, we could say that the strict subcategorizations for *risk* are:

$$10 \quad [+\underline{\quad}NP \, (\{ \begin{array}{l} \text{Prep P} \\ \text{Gerund} \\ \text{Infinitive} \end{array} \})]$$

Rule features (Lakoff 1970) will be ignored because have not been widely adopted, and have little direct semantic effect.

Our concern in the remainder of this section is with inherent and selectional features. Allegedly syntactic inherent features such as [+ human] or [+ active] are in fact semantic.[2] Because the selectional features of one listeme refer to the inherent features of collocated listemes, there are no grounds for syntactic selectional features. They were originally postulated to constrain a supposedly purely syntactic process of LEXICAL INSERTION into syntactic phrase markers. Today it is generally accepted that listemes are inserted into phrase markers under semantic conditions;[3] otherwise it would be impossible to generate meaningful sentences like 11–12.

11 Grace me no grace, nor uncle me no uncle.   (Shakespeare *Richard II* II.iii.87)
12 But me no buts.   ([= "don't prevaricate"] Scott *The Antiquary* Ch.XI)

Definition 8.4 SEMANTIC SELECTION RESTRICTIONS are postulated to block anomalies (D3.7).

Each reading [= sense] in the dictionary must contain a *selection restriction*, i.e. a formally expressed necessary and sufficient condition for that reading to combine with others.
                                        (Katz and Postal 1964:15)

In reality, an enormous range of features would be needed to express the full range of selection restrictions to be found in English [...].
(a) *That verb is in the indicative tense.
(b) *Bernstein's theorem is nondenumerable.
(c) *John diagonalized the differential manifold.
(d) *That electron is green.
(e) *I ate three phonemes for breakfast.
(f) *He pronounces diffuseness too loud.
(g) *My hair is bleeding.
(h) *That unicorn's left horn is black.   (McCawley 1968a:265)

There are clearly many more selectional restrictions than are referred to in most books and articles on linguistics. In McCawley's example (a), the grammatical terms 'indicative' and 'tense' have very restricted collocability: *indicative* with *mood*, and *tense* with perhaps a dozen attributives such as *past, future,* etc. What governs the co-occurrence of listemes is that the collocation has some possible denotation (be it substance, object, state, event, process, quality, metalinguistic statement, or whatever). Consider McCawley's (d–h). (d) is judged anomalous because electrons are theoretical constructs that cannot absorb or reflect light, and therefore cannot be predicated as green. But suppose an explanatory model of an atom were constructed in which an electron is represented by a green flash:

there would be no anomaly stating *That electron is green* with respect to such a model. Consider (e): phonemes are abstract entities, and one cannot eat abstract entities. Now imagine a situation in which a breakfast cereal is made in the shape of letters (*à la* alphabet soup); this cereal is fed to participants at a Linguistic Society conference and some wag eats a **p**, a **t**, and a **k**, and utters *I ate three phonemes for breakfast*. Such a statement is no more anomalous than Austin (1975:144) saying *France is hexagonal* – which no one has judged anomalous. Take (g): hair has no blood vessels, so it cannot bleed; but that wouldn't stop a child painting bleeding hair, or a computer game creating bleeding hair somewhere in cyberspace – both cases establishing conditions under which the utterance of (g) would not be anomalous. We could make similar stories for (f) and (h).

Sequences of listemes are ultimately judged in terms of their coherence and sensicalness, which are dependent upon what they denote.[4] Empirical evaluations of normal, unusual, and impossible sequences have to be matched in the grammar by well-formedness conditions, which are in part expressed by selection restrictions (i.e. the grammar must specify what constitutes a well-formed formula, cf. D7.2). We have seen that selection restrictions can only be determined by matching a sequence of listemes to the particular context it purports to denote.

Assumption 8.6 To describe the full set of well-formedness conditions for the occurrence of every listeme in a language would entail trying every conceivable combination of listemes in every conceivable context, and such a task is at best impracticable and at worst impossible. Moreover, speakers of a language learn the proper way to combine listemes without trying more than a few of the possible combinations.

Jackendoff 1972 proposed that lexical insertion be constrained by category features alone. This would disallow such infrequent but sensical sentences as 12 and novel zero-derivations like those in 13.

13 This, it was suppositioned, was a new linguistic harbingered by NATO during the time he [Alexander Haig] bellwethered it. But close observers have alternatived that idea. What Haig is doing, they concept, is to decouple the Russians from everything they are moded to.

(London *Guardian* February 3, 1991)

12 would be permitted if we accept Weinreich's 1966 suggestion that there be no constraints on lexical insertion to the major category nodes N, V, Adj, Adv. However, that would allow some true anomalies to be generated, e.g.

14 *The in anded some thes.
    *This blue and on speak conferenced uply.
    *Peter thated nine an equipment.

Noone can supply a context (even a metalinguistic one) in which any of 14 can convincingly make sense.

Identifying a complete set of selection restrictions appears to be impracticable, and perhaps impossible. It is not acceptable to postulate a theoretical device such as selection restrictions when there is no method for identifying them. A more useful course of action is to systematically describe semantic frames for every listeme, for instance, along the lines of Pustejovsky's 'lexical semantic structures'.

In this section we have seen that semantic frames have an encyclopedic basis. They contain metaphorical slots to capture the attributes of denotata. Values for these attributes are assigned to slots in the frame. They are spelled out in the various kinds of specifications identified for a lexicon entry in Chapter 3. Although different researchers probably understand the term *frame* differently, the consensus would be that it is the structure for information about a listeme that identifies its form and meaning and constrains its collocation with other listemes. The frame creates co-occurrence conditions on listemes that replace the traditional but impracticable 'selection restrictions'.[5]

Exercises

8.3.1 Imagine a *car* frame. What would you guess to be the attributes of a car? What criteria do you use to establish the attributes of a car?

8.3.2 Do you think that frames can be invoked to explain the anomaly of (a–c)?
(a) The lamb miaowed.   (b) The lion chirruped.   (c) The cat bleated.

8.3.3 What would be the semantic frame and strict subcategorization feature of the verb *wound*?

8.3.4 How do the semantic frames of *award, bequeath, donate,* and *give* differ from one another?

8.3.5 Chomsky 1957 created a sentence that was supposed to be syntactically acceptable but semantically anomalous, it was *Colourless green ideas sleep furiously.* Can you think of any context that will make this sensical?

8.3.6 In trying to establish the semantic frame of every listeme, will the same difficulties be met with as are encountered in trying to identify selection restrictions?

8.4   Semantic fields and relations within them

The idea of semantic fields derives from the fact that a conceptual field such as colour (Table 8.3), kinship, or cooking terms (Fig. 8.3) is covered by a number of listemes in a language, each denoting a part of the field. Different languages, and at different times in history any one language, may divide the field differently among listemes.

Assumption 8.7 The SEMANTIC FIELD of a listeme is determined from the conceptual field in which its denotatum occurs. A semantic field is structured in such a way as to mirror the structure of the conceptual field.

Each listeme in the field was said by Saussure 1974 to have a 'valeur'; this is NOT identical with the 'value' of an attribute (§8.3).

Definition 8.5 The DIFFERENTIAL VALUE (Saussure's 'valeur') of any listeme is that part of the conceptual field that it denotes in contrast with the part denoted by other listemes in the same semantic field.

The notion of semantic fields goes back at least to Humboldt 1836 and possibly to Herder 1772.[6] Semantic fields are primarily useful in establishing meaning relations among the listemes of a language.

Assumption 8.8 A strong structuralist motivation for the study of semantic fields is to identify the differential value of a given listeme in its semantic field.

For instance, all languages have BASIC COLOUR TERMS (Berlin and Kay 1969).

Definition 8.6 A colour term is basic if all of (a–d) hold true.
(a) The term is monolexemic. English *blue* is basic; *navy blue* is not.
(b) The term is not a hyponym of any other colour term (Chapter 7) such that the colour named is not a kind of any other colour. *Red* is basic; *crimson*, which names a kind of red, is not.
(c) The term has wide applicability. *Blond* is not one.
(d) The term is not a semantic extension from something manifesting that colour. *Gold* and *charcoal* are not basic.

Some languages have only two basic colour terms: *warm-light* and *cool-dark*. From a purely abstract point of view, they can be analysed in terms of merges of sets[1] of the four primary hues (chromatics) **red′**, **yellow′**, **green′**, **blue′** and the achromatic poles of brightness **white′** and **black′**, Table 8.1.

warm-light = **white′** ∪ **red′** ∪ **yellow′**
cool-dark = **green′** ∪ **blue′** ∪ **black′**

Table 8.1 Two basic colour terms

---

1. Normally sets are defined on individuals that are countable. Colour is not. In Chapter 13, we shall incorporate sets within 'ensembles'. An ensemble is defined on parts and not individuals. That will nicely accommodate colour as an ensemble, not a set.

Some languages, e.g. Eskimo and !Kung, have five basic colour terms, Table 8.2. English
has 11, Table 8.3.

white'
red'
yellow'
grue = **green'** ∪ **blue'**
black'

Table 8.2 Five basic colours

white'
red'
yellow'
green'
blue'
black'
pink = **red'** ∩ **white'**
orange = **red'** ∩ **yellow'**
purple = **red'** ∩ **blue'**
brown = **red'** ∩ **black'**
grey = **black'** ∩ **white'**

Table 8.3 Eleven basic colours

With less than six basic colours there is a merge of sets and with more than six colours set
overlap. *Grue* is usually the last merge to survive. The earliest overlaps are between the
achromatics **black'** and **white'**. Later, chromatics overlap with **red'** (except for its
complementary, **green'**). There is some evidence that overlap with **blue'** may follow
(Allan 1986, I:119).[7] Tables 8.1–3 present an abstract analysis which, for reasons given
when we discuss cognitive semantics in Chapter 9 does not explain colour perception (cf.
MacLaury 1997). Colour naming is systematic, governed by a combination of
neurophysiological response to the sense data (Kay and McDaniel 1978) and choice of
what to focus on within the colour spectrum. Rosch 1973 showed that the Dani (Papuan,
Irian Jaya), who have two basic colour terms, can readily distinguish and refer to all the
colours that have distinct names in English – but their language doesn't make it so easy for
them as it is for English speakers. The way they do it is to compare the colour to something
in the environment e.g. *the colour of mud.* The presumption is that the Dani speech
community has not hitherto had any great need to make frequent reference to the same
number of colours as the English speech community. The conclusion to be drawn is that,
although the sensory data in the colour spectrum is the same for all human beings,
languages name parts of the field differently. Western Dani *laambu* divides the spectrum
in half. Its differential value is very different from English *yellow*, even though *laambu* is
a possible translation for English *yellow*. The value of *yellow* is only one-eleventh of the
colour spectrum: thus, *laambu* implies not-*mili* "not cool-dark", whereas *yellow* implies
"not-white, not-red, not-green, not-blue, not-black, not-brown, not-pink, not-purple, not-
orange, not-grey".

SEMANTIC SHIFT can result from the introduction of a new term into a field, because
the new term changes the differential values of the existing terms. For instance, in 13th

century English, *girl* denoted a child of either sex and only finally shifted to its present meaning around the 16th century. In the meantime, *knave* had shifted from meaning "boy" to its present meaning (13th century) and the word *boy* was introduced with the value of the former *knave*, causing *girl* to narrow to "female child, young woman".

Listemes in a semantic field are related in many ways (Lyons 1963, Lehrer 1974 are classic studies). For instance, in the field of colour, *red* is a HYPONYM of *colour*, and *vermilion* is a hyponym of *red* (Chapter 7).

15   $\lambda x[(\textbf{vermillion}'(x) \subset \textbf{red}'(x) \subset \textbf{coloured}'(x)) \rightarrow (\textbf{vermilion}'(x) \subset \textbf{coloured}'(x))]$

Typically a hyponym is "a kind of" its superordinate; e.g. red is a kind of colour. But this is not always the case. On the basis of psycholinguistic experiments, Chaffin 1992 identified five categories of supersets and four elements to hyponymy, as in Table 8.4.

Superset	Elements of hyponymy			
Type and *examples*	Physical similarity	Functional similarity	Same location	Countability
Taxonomic: *bird, tree, ball, cup*	+	–	–	+
Functional: *toy, weapon, pet, weed, vehicle*	–	+	–	+
Collective singular: *furniture, crockery, underwear*	–	+	+	+
Heterogeneous stuffs: *drugs, herbs, cereals*	–	+	–	–
Collective plural: *leftovers, groceries, contents*	–	–	+	+

Table 8.4 Four components of hyponymy (adapted from Chaffin 1992:280)

Subsets of 'collective plural' do not bear a 'kind of' relation to their superset. Birds bear a physical similarity to one another, whereas toys, items of crockery, different herbs, and grocery items can look very different from one another. There is a functional similarity between different weapons, different items of furniture, different kinds of drugs, but not between different birds or grocery items. Whether or not we quibble with Chaffin's conclusions, it is certain that there are different categories of hyponymy.

Definition 8.7 Hyponyms are NECESSARILY (logically) transitive only when they are in the same category.

Compare 16 with 17–18.

16 (a1)   A husky in a sled-team is a dog.   [Taxonomic]
   (a2)   A dog is a mammal.   [Taxonomic]
   _____

   (c) ⊢   A husky in a sled-team is a mammal.   [Taxonomic]

17 (a1)   A husky in a sled-team is a dog.   [Taxonomic]
   (a1)   A dog is a kind of pet.   [Functional]
   _____

   (c) ⊬   A husky in a sled-team is a kind of pet.

18 (a1)   A husky is a dog.   [Taxonomic]
   (a1)   A dog is a kind of pet.   [Functional]
   _____

   (c) ⊬   A husky is a kind of pet.

16(c) is valid, 17(c) and 18(c) are invalid: 17(c) is false and 18(c) is only possibly true.
   Obviously, in 15 the hyponyms are of the same category. The relations in 15 can also
be represented by ASYMMETRIC SEMANTIC IMPLICATIONS as in 19 (asymmetric because the
arrow cannot be reversed).

19   ∀x[**vermilion**′(x) → **red**′(x) → **coloured**′(x)]

Whereas *red* and *blue* are co-hyponyms of *colour*, *vermilion* and *blue* are not exactly co-
hyponyms in the way that *vermilion* and *crimson* and *scarlet* are co-hyponyms of *red*. We
need to attend to the level of semantic analysis, which can be represented by the tree in
Fig. 8.2.

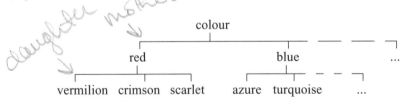

Figure 8.2 Some hyponyms of *colour*

In Fig. 8.2 mother nodes are superordinates and daughters are hyponyms, not constituents,
of mothers; sister nodes are co-hyponyms. Co-hyponyms are contraries and incompatible
with one another (D6.5).

20   ∀x[**scarlet**′(x) → ¬**crimson**′(x)]
21 (a)   The sheet is scarlet ‖ The sheet is not crimson
   (b)   The sheet is not crimson ‖̸ The sheet is scarlet

The incompatibility of colour names explains why *The flag is blue and white* ‖ *The flag
is part blue and part white*. A hyponym is incompatible with the co-hyponyms of its
superordinates, and with their hyponyms. For example, *crimson* is incompatible with

scarlet, and because *red* is incompatible with *blue*, its hyponym *crimson* is also incompatible with *blue* and with hyponyms of *blue* such as *azure*.

COMPARISON is made on a category scale having an upper and a lower end bounded by a pair of so-called GRADABLE ANTONYMS or RELATIVE PREDICATES, as in Table 8.5.[8]

DOWNSCALE POLE	CATEGORY SCALE "OF A CERTAIN …"	UPSCALE POLE
short	"height from base [relative to a human]"	*tall*
short	"length"	*long*
low	"height"	*high*
narrow	"cross dimension"	*wide*
shallow	"dimension from top surface down"	*deep*
young	"age"	*old*
light	"weight"	*heavy*
slow	"speed"	*fast*
cold	"temperature"	*hot*

Table 8.5 The gradable antonymy of relative predicates

Each of the scales is divisible in the manner demonstrated in the comparative scale in Table 8.6.

DOWNSCALE POLE	<	≤	≈	≥	>	UPSCALE POLE
short	shorter	as short	about the same height	as tall	taller	tall
cold	colder	as cold	about the same temp.	as hot	hotter	hot
early	earlier	as early	about the same time	as late	later	late

Table 8.6 Some comparative scales

Gradable 'antonyms' are in fact contraries and not true antonyms, cf. 22–23.

22   $\forall x[\textbf{tall}'(x) \rightarrow \neg[\textbf{short}'(x)]]$ e.g. Ed is tall ⊩ Ed is not short
23   $\forall x[\neg[\textbf{short}'(x)] \rightarrow \text{POSSIBLY}[\textbf{tall}'(x)]]$ e.g. Ed is not short ⊮ It is possible that
                                                                           Ed is tall

Relational scales involving more than two terms, e.g. the semantic incompatibles *hot, warm, cool, cold,* exhibit some interesting relationships that can be represented in a variety of different ways. In 25–26 >[PRED(x)] means "upscale of PRED"; in 27–28 <[PRED(x)] means "downscale of PRED". 24 means "something is temperate iff it is none of hot and/or warm and/or cool and/or cold". 25 means "something is hot iff it is upscale of (=more than) warm". In some contexts *tepid* is more appropriate than *temperate*; like other mid-points on relational scales, *tepid* and *temperate* are not gradable.

24    $\forall x[\textbf{temperate}'(x) \longleftrightarrow \neg[\textbf{hot}'(x) \lor \textbf{warm}'(x) \lor \textbf{cool}'(x) \lor \textbf{cold}'(x)]$
25          $\forall x[\textbf{hot}'(x) \longleftrightarrow >[\textbf{warm}'(x)]]$
26          $\forall x[\textbf{warm}'(x) \longleftrightarrow >[\textbf{temperate}'(x)]]$
          $\forall x[\textbf{warm}'(x) \;\triangleright\; \neg[\textbf{hot}'(x)]$
27          $\forall x[\textbf{cool}'(x) \longleftrightarrow <[\textbf{temperate}'(x)]]$
          $\forall x[\textbf{cool}'(x) \;\triangleright\; \neg[\textbf{cold}'(x)]$
28          $\forall x[\textbf{cold}'(x) \longleftrightarrow <[\textbf{cool}'(x)]]$

24–28 are illustrative not definitive and you can easily make alternative analyses.

Assumption 8.9 Choosing between alternative analyses should be determined by:
(a) The most accurate account of the data.
(b) The simplest account of the data given A8.9(a).
(c) Consistency with the semantic analysis of other language data in one's corpus.

In the semantic field of marital relations there are the converse predicates *be the husband of* and *be the wife of*:

29 $\forall x,y[\textbf{be\_the\_husband\_of}'(x,y) \longleftrightarrow \textbf{be\_the\_wife\_of}'(y,x)]$

In lexical semantics this relation is abbreviated by referring to the listeme *wife* as the converse of *husband*, and vice versa. Synonymy between *bachelor* and *man who has never married* is illustrated by 30.

30 $\forall x[\textbf{be\_a\_bachelor}'(x) \longleftrightarrow \lambda y[\textbf{be\_a\_man}'(y) \land \textbf{never\_married}'(y)](x)]$

Few scholars have undertaken extensive semantic analysis of a semantic field, but Backhouse 1994 is an extensive study of taste terms in Japanese, and Lehrer 1974 analyses cooking and sound terms. Lehrer identifies roughly the following structure within the semantic field for English cooking terms. (Lehrer does not use a tree structure. In this, as in Fig. 8.3, daughter nodes are hyponyms of mother nodes).

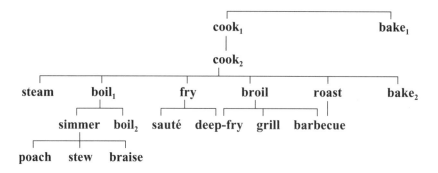

Figure 8.3 Part of the semantic field of cooking terms, after Lehrer 1974:71

Cook₁ (top tier) is a syntactically transitive verb with the attributes of a human agent preparing raw meat, fish, vegetables, etc. by cooking it/them in some way. *Bake₁* is also a transitive verb with a human agent who combines ingredients to produce bakery products such as cakes and bread (this may be North American dialect). *Cook₂* (second tier) is a causative process verb identifying something done to a type of food. The third tier is distinguished according to different cooking media. *Steam* is to cook in hot water vapour (Lehrer says that for some speakers *steam* is a kind of *boil₁*, which is not the case shown in Fig. 8.3). To *boil₁*, hot water or a water-based medium (not oil or fat) is used. To *fry*, hot oil or fat is used. To *broil* (*grill* in British English), fat or oil are often used and the cooking is done directly over or under the heat source. To *roast* overlaps both *broil* and *bake₂* because it is often done in the oven (but can be on a spit over open coals). A roast is basted in fat or oil. To *bake₂* uses an oven with an indirect heat source. The fourth and fifth tiers result from different manners of employing the cooking medium. *Simmer* and *boil₂* are differentiated by the intensity of the applied heat: *simmering* is done just below boiling point, and *boiling₂* above it. Different reasons for simmering are found in the fifth tier: *poaching* is slow simmering to maintain the shape of the food; *stewing* is long slow simmering to soften tough ingredients; *braising* involves first *browning* to seal in the juices, followed by slow cooking in a sealed container. There are two ways of frying in the fourth tier. To *sauté* involves quick frying with little oil or fat. To *deep-fry* (or *french-fry*) is both to fry "boil in oil or hot fat" and *broil* (but not *grill* in British English). The difference between *grill* and *barbecue* (or *charcoal*) is typically that heat is applied from an exposed heat source directly above in a grill and from below when barbecuing. The latter often has attributes of roasting over coals in the open air (or simulating this condition).

The field of cooking terms, unlike the field of colour terms, is not neatly circumscribed. It is more difficult to decide whether the whole field is covered by Lehrer's analysis, and what effect extensions or diminutions of the field will have. Since Lehrer wrote her book, microwave ovens have become ubiquitous. Microwaving best slots into the third tier, but one can *boil₁*, *roast*, and *poach* in a microwave: so the semantic field has been revised with the advent of this new form of cooking. Generalizing,

Assumption 8.10 When new objects and new ways of doing things come into existence there is a change in the conceptual field that usually leads to a change in the semantic field and the addition or semantic extension of listemes.

If, for convenience, we treat the verbs *stew, boil*, and *cook* as syntactically intransitive, then because stewing is a kind of simmering which is a kind of boiling₁ which is a kind of cooking:

31   $\forall x[\textbf{stew}'(x) \rightarrow \textbf{simmer}'(x) \rightarrow \textbf{boil}_1{}'(x) \rightarrow \textbf{cook}'(x)]$

Although some senses of the terms *finger, hand, arm,* and *body* are in the same semantic field, their relationship is quite different from that of the cooking terms above. They exhibit one kind of MERONYMY.

Definition 8.8 A is a MERONYM of B iff A is a part of B, such that A≤B.

32
$$\forall w,x,y,z \begin{bmatrix} \textbf{finger}'(x) \rightarrow \text{x is part of a hand} \\ \textbf{hand}'(y) \rightarrow \text{y is part of an *arm-hand} \\ \textbf{hand}'(y) \rightarrow \text{y is part of a body} \\ \textbf{arm}'(z) \rightarrow \text{z is part of an *arm-hand} \\ \textbf{arm}'(z) \rightarrow \text{z is part of a body} \\ \textbf{*arm-hand}'(w) \rightarrow \text{w is part of a body} \end{bmatrix}$$

There is no English term for the limb dubbed '*arm-hand'.

Definition 8.9 A LEXICAL GAP exists when there is no listeme in the language for a concept within a conceptual field in which adjacent concepts are named.

Arm-hand is a lexical gap in English. The hand and arm are distinct parts of the body. To *cut oneself* is to cut one's body, it could be on the hand, or arm, or elsewhere. To *cut one's hand* is not to cut one's arm, nor vice versa. Of course, because the fingers are attached to the hand and the hand is attached to the arm, to lose one's arm is to lose one's hand and fingers too. Note that in this case the meronymy is logically transitive: a finger is part of an *arm-hand and also part of a body. However, Chaffin 1992 shows that

Definition 8.10 Meronymy is necessarily transitive only when the same category of meronymy occurs in both premises.

The categories of meronymy are shown in the left-hand column of Table 8.7.

Meronymy Types and *examples*	Elements of meronymy			
	Separability	Spatio-temporal	Function	Homeomeronymy
Object : Component *cup : handle*	+	+	+	–
Event : Feature *rodeo : cowboy*	+	–	+	–
Collection : Member *forest : tree*	+	+	–	–
Mass : Portion *pie : slice*	+	+	–	+
Process : Phase *growing up : adolescence*	–	–	–	–
Area : Place *forest : glade*	–	+	–	+
Object : Stuff *lens : glass*	–	+	–	–

Table 8.7 Seven kinds of meronymy (adapted from Chaffin 1992:263)

A handle is separable from a cup, but a lens is not separable from the glass from which it is made. A cup and its handle are normally located together, whereas a cowboy is not normally located at the same time and place as a particular rodeo. Functional parts are restricted to a particular location and configuration. HOMEOMERONYMS are the same kind of thing as the whole (HETEROMERONYMS are not). We may quibble about the details, but the general picture seems correct. Compare the valid transitivity in 33 with the contrary in 34–35. 34(c) is incoherent and 35(c) is only possibly true.

33 (a1) The carburettor *is a component* of the engine.
    (a2) The engine *is a component of* the car.

    (c) ⊢   The carburettor *is a component of* the car.

34 (a1) Bart's head *is a component of* Bart.
    (a2) Bart *is a member of* my phonetics class.

    (c) ⊬   *?Bart's head *is a member of* my phonetics class.

35 (a1) The handle *is a component of* the tea-pot.
    (a2) The tea-pot *is made of* silver.

    (c) ⊬   The tea-pot handle *is made of* silver.

There is an important conclusion to draw from the discussion in this section. Scripts primarily identify the organization of event sequences, frames the structural relations of concepts, and fields the semantic relations between names for concepts. As was said in A8.1, so-called 'semantic relations' are constrained and informed by the relations that we humans perceive in nature, or have experience of in the world around us, or conceive of in abstract fields such as knowledge and moral or ethical behaviour. This is the principal tenet of cognitive linguistics discussed in Chapter 9. It will be continually confirmed that the meanings of listemes and more complex language expressions are related to one another in a way that reflects the language community's perception of relations among their denotata. This is known to be a problem for translators. Different language communities and subgroups within a community may divide up 'the same' sensory and purely conceptual data differently (e.g. doctors interpret symptoms differently from their patients; linguists see things in language that non-linguists don't). As a result, the meanings of the linguistic labels given to 'the same' denotata often overlap without being fully identical.

> *Assumption 8.11* Often, we cannot properly identify semantic relations between lexical items without making reference to their denotata. Perceptions and conceptions of these denotata may not be identical for different communities of speakers.

In other words, we often cannot deal with sense relations without recourse to intensions and through them to extensions in some world at some time or other (Chapter 2). Nor can we completely exclude the perceptions and conceptions of language users.

Exercises

8.4.1 The differential value of *rabbit* or *lamb* differs from that of *sheep* or *pig* because of the existence of the lexemes *mutton* and *pork*. Explain.

8.4.2 (a) What do the morphemes in *hyponym* contribute to its meaning? (b) What words other than *hyponym* can you think of with the prefix *hypo-*? (c) What is the difference in meaning between *hypo-* and *hyper-*?

8.4.3 Identify the kinds of semantic relations that hold between (pairs of) items in the following list: (a) *brother of,* (b) *child of,* (c) *female parent of,* (d) *male sibling of,* (e) *mother of,* (f) *parent of,* (g) *sibling of,* (h) *consanguineal kin.*

8.4.4 Translate (a) into colloquial English.
  (a) $\forall x[\textbf{be\_a\_bachelor}'(x) \leftrightarrow \lambda y[\textbf{be\_a\_man}'(y) \wedge \textbf{never\_married}'(y)](x)]$
  (b)   Give a couple of English sentences exemplifying (a) and show the entailment relations between them.

8.4.5 To *cut one's hand* usually implies a cut not of a finger, but elsewhere on the hand. Why should this be?

8.4.6 Can you make any sense of *He was born with hands but no arms*?

8.4.7 The is-part-of relation is manifest differently in *a minute is part of an hour, which is part of a day*, etc. Although a body can exist without an arm, an hour necessarily contains minutes; moreover a mutant body could have three arms, but an hour consists of exactly sixty minutes. Or does it?

8.4.8 *Kick* is related to *hoof* and *foot*. And *foot* is related to *ankle, leg, body* and *toe*, and to *boot, shoe, sock, stocking*. Is *kick* also related to *stocking*?

8.4.9 *Start, begin, commence, set out* are all related to *continue, keep on, go on*, and to *finish, end, terminate*. As soon as we begin to define the relationships between listemes, we also begin to define a semantic field. What else can you say about this one?

8.4.10 Why is there no anomaly in *Her lovely blue eyes were red from crying*? (How can her eyes be red if they are blue?)

8.4.11 The attributes of age and sex apply not only to people but to all creatures. What are some consequences of this for semantic inquiry?

8.4.12 To what extent is it the case that any word is partly understood in terms of its value? Consider ways in which one woman can make an insulting remark about another woman. First of all there is the semantic content of a word: to refer to her as a dog is to comment on her appearance, to call her a bitch is comment on her character. There is a choice of insults concerning character which appear to have degrees of disapprobation but are also constrained by matters of politeness style, etc. *something that rhymes with rich* is not so explicit as *bitch*; and there are much worse things to call someone. Discuss.

8.4.13 Try to analyse one of the following semantic fields:
  (a) Wind instruments (as musical instruments)
  (b) Tableware
  (c) Sea-food
  (d) Clothing

8.5 Componential analysis of listemes into their semantic components

Definition 8.11 COMPONENTIAL ANALYSIS expresses the sense of a listeme in terms of SEMANTIC COMPONENTS.

For instance, it was suggested in Chapter 7 that (x kill y) → (x cause (y become ¬(alive))) leading some people to say that CAUSE, BECOME, NOT, ALIVE are semantic components of *kill*.

Assumption 8.12 Every listeme is analysable into one or more semantic components.

Assumption 8.13 There is no consistent one-to-one correlation between semantic components and either the morphs or the morphemes of any language.

Assumption 8.14 Listemes that share semantic components are semantically related.

Assumption 8.15 Being components of sense, semantic components reflect the characteristics of typical denotata as identified in the intensions of listemes across possible worlds.

Assumption 8.16 There is a hierarchy of semantic components. Because semantic components reflect the characteristics of typical denotata, the hierarchy of components corresponds to perceived hierarchies among denotata (cf. White 1992). For instance, FELINE is a semantic component of *cat* and entails the semantic component ANIMAL which is also, therefore, a component of *cat*. This suggests a thesaurus-like structure for semantic components.

Together, A8.12 and A8.16 have the consequence that the set of semantic components for a language can be discovered by identifying all the relationships that can be conceived of among the denotata of listemes. In practice, this could be everything in all worlds, actual and non-actual. There have been a number of attempts to carry out such a task; among the most successful of them is Bishop John Wilkins's *An Essay Toward a Real Character and a Philosophical Language* 1668. Wilkins, like many of his contemporaries, accepted the Aristotelean tradition that although natural languages may differ from one another superficially, there is intertranslatability because human beings from different language communities have similar mental capabilities and share common experiences of the world around them which are encoded in natural language.

> Spoken words are the symbols of mental experience and written words are the symbols of spoken words. Just as all men do not have the same orthography, so all men do not have the same speech sounds; but the mental experiences, which these directly symbolize, are the same for all, as also are those things of which our experiences are images.
>
> (Aristotle *On Interpretation* 16a,3)

(This is compatible with a weak version of the Sapir–Whorf hypothesis D9.23). It was Wilkins's purpose to construct a universal or 'philosophical' language by categorizing all of human experience and labelling each category by a symbol (corresponding to a listeme) in his 'philosophical language'. Each such category is comparable to a semantic component. Wilkins described what he was doing in the following words.

> The second part shall contein [*sic*] that which is the great foundation of the thing here designed, namely a regular *enumeration* and *description* of all things and notions, to which marks or names ought to be assigned according to their respective natures, which may be styled the *Scientifical* Part, comprehending *Universal* Philosophy. It being the proper end

and design of the several branches of Philosophy to reduce all things and notions unto such
a frame, as may express their natural order, dependence, and relations.   (Wilkins 1668:1)

Wilkins invented a symbol for each 'thing and notion' in such a way as to represent its
place in the natural order and its relation to other 'things and notions'. These symbols
constitute the 'real character' of his title (Greek χαρακτήρ "distinctive mark"), and the
forms for writing his 'philosophical language'. Other parts of the *Essay* describe a
pronunciation system for the language; and, of course, there is a syntax for it, too. The final
part of the book consists of a dictionary which translates English words 'according to the
various equivocal senses of them' into the 'philosophical language'. The result is a
componential analysis. *Father*, for instance, is defined as "economical relation (= the first
and most natural kind of association of men into Families) of the consanguineous type, of
the species direct ascending, of the division male". Through the various components named
in this meaning definition, *father* can be semantically related to other words whose
meanings contain any of the same components. Since Wilkins's time no one has attempted
anything so comprehensive.

Within modern linguistics, the componential analysis of meaning was adapted from
distinctive feature analysis in morphosyntax which in turn had its roots in the methodology
of Prague School phonology.[9] It is a small step from the componential analysis of closed
morphosyntactic systems like noun and verb affixes to the componential analysis of closed
semantic fields like kinship systems. Anthropologists had for many years been comparing
widely differing kinship systems in culturally distinct societies by interpreting them in
terms of universal constituents that we can equate with semantic components, e.g. Kroeber
1909 postulated the following components of a kinship system. (Kin are described from
the perspective of EGO. In English, ego's female parent is her/his *mother*. Taking the
mother as ego: her male child is her *son*, her female child is her *daughter*.)

36   generation; relative age within a generation; consanguineal vs affinal; lineal vs
        collateral; sex of ego, kin, and linking kin; condition – living, or deceased – of kin.

Two of the earliest articles in componential analysis of meaning, Lounsbury 1956 and
Goodenough 1956, appeared consecutively in the same issue of the journal *Language*. Both
were analyses of kin terms. Lounsbury's paper begins with a comparison of the following
sets of English and Spanish kin terms, noting that there is in Spanish a regular superficial
marking for the sex of kin that has no compeer in English.

MALE		FEMALE	
uncle	ti-o	aunt	ti-a
son	hij-o	daughter	hij-a
grandfather	abuel-o	grandmother	abuel-a
brother	herman-o	sister	herman-a

English has no gender morphs corresponding to the Spanish suffixes -*o* and -*a*, but gender
is a significant component in the meaning of the English kin terms. Their covert gender

must be compatible with the sex of the person denoted; consequently, it is anomalous to call one's uncle *aunt*, or one's sister *brother*. When the terms *aunt* and *uncle* are extended to close friends of ego's parents, they are assigned on the basis of the sex of the referent. Children early become aware of the covert gender in English kin terms: Lamb 1965:37 quotes a six-year-old saying, 'Mommy, what are girl nephews called?' Although gender is covert in English kin terms, there are grammatical consequences. The personal pronoun anaphoric to *uncle* is *he/him*; the one for *aunt* is *she/her*. And whereas the sentence *My aunt is pregnant* is grammatical and could be true in our world, **My uncle is pregnant* is anomalous and can never be true in any world in which *uncle* has its present meaning.

Today it is no longer necessary to justify the study of semantic components using arguments about their syntactic effects. But in the 1950s, semantics was still regarded by many linguists as metaphysical and unfit for the kind of scientific enquiry into observable language structures that they believed linguistics should undertake. The early writers on componential analysis in morphosyntax and kinship systems were responsible for changing contemporary linguistic opinion on the status of semantic analysis by showing that it can be carried out using approved methods of structural analysis, such as those used to filter out the phonetic components of the Sanskrit stop phonemes. Just as we can compare and contrast Sanskrit phonemes /p/, /b^h/, and /g^h/ in terms of voicing, aspiration, and place of articulation, so we can compare and contrast *father, uncle*, and *aunt*. These three kin terms all have in common that they are FIRST ASCENDING GENERATION (many componentialists write the components in capitals). *Father* and *uncle* additionally have in common that both are MALE, whereas *aunt* is FEMALE. *Aunt* and *uncle* are both COLLATERAL, whereas *father* is LINEAL. Thus, via the semantic components we have identified, we can show the meaning relationships between *father, uncle,* and *aunt*.[10]

Hjelmslev 1961:70f, Lyons 1968:472, Lehrer 1974:46 suggest that the nine listemes *bull, calf, cow, ewe, foal, lamb, mare, ram, stallion* – which constitute a fragment of a semantic field – can be contrasted with one another in such a way as to reveal the semantic components in Table 8.8.

BOVINE	*bull*	*cow*	*calf*
EQUINE	*stallion*	*mare*	*foal*
OVINE	*ram*	*ewe*	*lamb*
	MALE	FEMALE	YOUNG
	ADULT		

Table 8.8 A componential table

Extrapolating from the table we can define the meaning of each listeme.

37   *bull* = BOVINE ∧ ADULT ∧ MALE
       stallion = EQUINE ∧ ADULT ∧ MALE
          ewe = OVINE ∧ ADULT ∧ FEMALE
          foal = EQUINE ∧ YOUNG

How can we be certain that the analysis is correct? The basis for claiming that BOVINE or MALE is a semantic component of *bull* cannot be a matter of language pure and simple. It is a relation speakers believe exists between the denotata of the terms *bull* and *male* and *bovine*. Doing semantic analysis of listemes, it is not enough to claim that 38 is linguistic evidence for the claim that MALE is a semantic component of *bull*, because 39 is equally good until a basis for the semantic (and therefore grammatical) anomaly has been established that is independent of what we are seeking to establish – namely the justification for the semantic components identified in Table 8.8.

38 A bull is male.
39 A bull is female.

THE ONLY LANGUAGE-INDEPENDENT DEVICE AVAILABLE IS AN APPEAL TO TRUTH CONDITIONS, and this takes us to the denotata of *bull* and *male*. In fact what we need to say is 40.

40 In every admissible possible world (and time) an entity which is a bull is male and in no such world is an entity which is a bull a female.

There is no point claiming that the semantic component MALE is a metalanguage symbol and at the same time not the English word *male*. Unless we are carrying out a pointless mental exercise, no matter what symbol we use for this component, the meaning for that symbol must be equivalent to the relevant sense of English *male*. Thus, on the assumption that semantic components reflect characteristics of typical denotata as revealed through their intensions across worlds and times, the justification for postulating the semantic components in Table 8.8 and 37 is a set of inferences such as those in 41.

41 For any entity x that is properly called a *bull*, it is the case that x is adult $\wedge$ x is male $\wedge$ x is bovine.

Let the relevant property of x be represented by **bull′**(x). From 41 we generate the meaning postulate 42, which is asterisked because it turns out to be false.

42 $*\forall x[\textbf{bull′}(x) \longrightarrow \lambda y[\textbf{male′}(y) \wedge \textbf{bovine′}(y) \wedge \textbf{adult′}(y)](x)]$

The equivalence between semantic components and semantic predicates is enshrined in a tradition stretching back to Aristotle (*Categories* 1b,13) and is recognized, for instance, by Bierwisch 1970:169. In fact, 41–42 are incorrect because two of the conjoined propositions, 42's **bovine′**(y) and **adult′**(y), are false.

Against **bovine′**(y) in 42. The noun *bull* is not restricted in application to bovines, it is also properly used of male elephants, male whales, male seals, male alligators, etc. The initial plausibility of 41–42 is due to the fact that it describes the prototypical ("most typical" A10.2) or stereotypical bull (D10.5). The world of the English speaker is such that *bull* is much more likely to denote a bovine than any other species of animal.

Assumption 8.17. PERIPHERAL USES *of bull are examples of* SEMANTIC EXTENSION *from bovines to certain other kinds of large animals. Consequently they require that the context make it abundantly clear that a bovine is* NOT *being referred to. This is often achieved by spelling it out in a construction such as bull elephant or bull whale which is of greater complexity than the simple noun bull used of bovines – a difference motivated by the principle of least effort.*

Definition 8.12 THE PRINCIPLE OF LEAST EFFORT (Zipf 1948): A less complex label tends to be used for things which are significant within the everyday life of a community – and so tend to be frequently referred to. A more complex label is used for less significant things.

Let's coin the term ***bozine** to fill a lexical gap (D8.9).

Definition 8.13 **Bozine* denotes the class of animals whose males are called 'bulls', females 'cows', and young 'calves'.

Against **adult'**(y) in 42. It is incorrect to say that *bull* is only predicable of adult animals since a new-born male calf is properly called a bull. Nonetheless, it is true that the sex of an animal is hardly significant until it is capable of reproduction – human languages are anthropocentric and therefore speciesist. Even for very young human beings the pronoun form can be *it* rather than *he* or *she*. It follows that a sex-differentiating term, like *bull*, is normally used of adult animals. When used of young animals the context must generally make Speaker's intention clear by using a phrase such as *bull calf* rather than the noun *bull* on its own. The choice of expression is entirely pragmatic, and we are attempting to establish the semantics of *bull*.

As Varro pointed out in *De Lingua Latina* IX, 56 (47 BCE), there are specific names for the male and the female of animals that are important to the community, but not for others. For instance, there are hens and cocks (roosters), and these terms are sometimes extended to other birds; e.g. in place of *female blackbird* we can say *hen blackbird*; instead of *male robin*, *cock robin*. The young of all birds can be called *chicks* – derived from *chickens*. There are not usually any special listemes for the young of reptiles. There are specific terms for distinctive forms of pre-adult creatures, e.g. *eggs, embryos, caterpillars, maggots, pupae* – but none of these is species-specific. Nor are there any specific nouns distinguishing male from female insects, arachnids, molluscs, or plants. This is not because of any conceptual difficulty: sex differentiation and growth stages are criterial attributes of all living things. But the principle of least effort (D8.12) decrees that in this area of nomenclature the number of lexical gaps far exceeds the number of listemes in use. The age and sex of a particular life form can always be referred to through circumlocution.

Although *bull* will more often refer to an adult than a young animal, this is not a significant characteristic of the expression *bull* itself, but – as already noted – a property of every expression which age or sex differentiates animals; cf. *lion, lioness, cub*. It is no part of a general semantic characterization of *bull* that it typically denotes adults. Rather, it is part of the general naming practice for complementary sets of male and female animals.

Typical bulls are ungulates and mammals and quadrupeds. These properties follow from the fact that bulls are bovine and are not significant properties in the semantic analysis of the word *bull*. For instance, a bull alligator is a reptile not a mammal; a bull whale is a cetacean not an ungulate. In consequence, though it is the norm that non-cetacean bulls are quadrupeds, a three-legged bull still counts as a bull, and the abnormality does not render the creature 'not a bull' only an 'abnormal bull'. By contrast, a so-called 'bull' that is not male does not count as a bull at all! Maleness is the defining attribute of 42. We must therefore correct 42 to 43.

43   $\forall x[\lambda y[\mathbf{bull'}(y) \wedge \mathbf{animal'}(y)](x) \longleftrightarrow \lambda z[\mathbf{male'}(z) \wedge \mathbf{*bozine'}(z)](x)]$

"For every x, x is a member of the overlap of bulls and animals if, and only if, x is a member of the overlap of males and *bozines."

The attributes of anything called *a bull*, provided it is an animal (this excludes a papal *bull* "edict"), are male and *bozine.

Are the relationships in a semantic field 'sense' relations – i.e. pure linguistic relations between listemes – or are they relations between the denotata of listemes? The discussion of scripts, frames, semantic fields, and the meaning of *bull* leads to the following:

Assumption 8.18 Relationships within a semantic field are not the relationships defined by nature or by human perceptions and conceptions of the world about them, but the relationships between the intensions of listemes which name things perceived and conceived of within the world about us (and within imaginary worlds, too).

Exercises

8.5.1 Attempt a componential analysis of *biscuit, bread, cake, roll, scone.*

8.5.2 In reality sex differentiation is more complicated than as presented here. Although there are natural occurrences of hermaphrodites among higher animals, they are abnormal; however, there are many species of living organisms which are normally hermaphrodites. There are also quite a number which undergo sex changes as part of their normal life-span. Thus the antonymy which we intuit for the listemes *male* $\underline{\vee}$ *female* is by no means so straightforward in its application; even though for most speakers the more complex combinations of sex alternations may never arise as a topic of conversation. What should the semanticist make of these complications?

8.5.3 Discuss the following quote from the text: 'sex differentiation and growth stages are criterial attributes of all living things. But in this area of nomenclature the number of lexical gaps far exceeds the number of listemes in use.'

8.6   Semantic primitives and the definition of listeme meanings

Natural Language Principle. Semantic primitives and their elementary syntax exist as a
minimal subset of ordinary natural language.

(Goddard 1994:10)

This section assumes that semantic components are, or are composed from, semantic
primitives, and investigates how many primitives are there.

In the mid-1960s Jerrold J Katz was largely responsible for establishing semantic theory
as one component of a transformational grammar. Katz's metalanguage was dubbed
'semantic markerese' by Lewis 1970, because so-called 'semantic markers' are the
principal kind of semantic component Katz uses. According to Katz 1967:129, 1972:38,
a semantic marker names a concept that any human being can conceive of; hence, semantic
markerese is applicable to all natural languages. However, Katz never properly justified,
evaluated, or even seriously discussed the vocabulary and syntax of semantic markerese.
We can only learn to interpret his metalanguage by abduction from his examples.
Unfortunately, there is little consistency among these examples, and semantic markerese
remains only a partially comprehensible language. Katz 1964b:744 compared the formal
constructs of his theory to chemical formulae; but unlike them it lacks both a conventional
vocabulary and a conventional syntax. It uses words and phrases from English combined
with one another in obscure ways, forcing one to conclude that Katz's metalanguage is a
degenerate form of English. Compare 44, the semantics for *chase* given in Katz 1967:169,
with 45, given in Bierwisch 1969:160.

44 (((Activity of X) (*Nature:* (Physical)) (Motion) (*Rate:* (Fast)) (*Character:* (Following
     Y)) (*Intention:* (Trying to catch ((Y) (Motion)))

45 [Physical] Activity $\wedge$ [Fast] Motion]X $\wedge$ [Following]XY $\wedge$ [Trying]X([Catch]XY) $\wedge$
     [Motion]Y

It is only in the vocabulary that there is any interesting similarity between the two; there
is a striking difference in structure. Bierwisch has used the standard and conventional
syntax of predicate logic, but the syntax of Katz's semantic marker is neither standard nor
conventional. The marker (Activity of X) classes *chase* with verbs such as *eat, speak, walk,*
and *remember* as against state verbs like *sleep* or *wait,* and process verbs like *grow,* or
freeze. The marker (*Rate:* (Fast)) distinguishes *chase* from *creep* and *walk.* (*Character:*
(Following Y)) distinguishes *chase* from *flee* or *wander.* The variables 'X' and 'Y' indicate
where the semantics of the actor and undergoer should be inserted, thus imposing a
structure onto the semantic interpretation. I'll say no more about semantic markerese.[11]

Like any language, a metalanguage for semantics consists of a set of symbols, a set of
axioms and rules for combining them into syntactically well-formed structures, and a set
of interpretations for these structures and for the individual symbols in isolation.

Definition 8.14 SEMANTIC PRIMITIVES are the primitive symbols and their
interpretations that constitute the vocabulary of the semantic metalanguage.

§8.4 referred to the search for primitive semantic components by Bishop Wilkins (1668). His contemporary, Antoine Arnauld, in *La logique, ou l'art de penser* 1662, recognized that the meanings of most words can be defined in terms of others, but that ultimately there are some undefinable semantically primitive words. In recent times, Weinreich (1980:50, 161, 300, 308f) identified a discovery procedure for a semantic metalanguage built upon natural language.

> *Assumption 8.19* (a) Stratify the language into a central core of semantic primitives whose members are definable only circularly and by ostensive definition such as "colour of the sky" in the entry for *blue.*
>
> (b) The next stratum out uses items whose definitions contain only core items without (further) circularity.
>
> (c) Each more peripheral stratum uses items from the preceding strata without
>
> circularity; as in the diagram 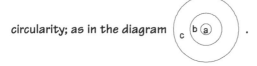 .

Since before 1972, Anna Wierzbicka has been carrying out this program in a cross-language context, searching for a universal set of semantic primitives expressed principally through the vocabulary of English. Goddard 1994:12 (Principle VI) claims that 'any simple proposition' expressed in NATURAL LANGUAGE METALANGUAGE (NSM) using any one natural language (e.g. English) will be expressible in NSM using any other language (e.g. Japanese). This embodies a claim that, like L_P (Chapter 7), NSM is linguistically and culturally unbiased and that there is a heuristic or algorithm for translation. In fact, there is none.

Wierzbicka's search for semantic primitives recalls the 'Swadesh-list' of basic vocabulary created to plot diachronic relationships between unwritten languages in Africa, the Americas, and elsewhere. The purpose of the Swadesh-list was to take a pair of languages and compare the 100–215 basic lexemes to see how many are cognates (see Swadesh 1955), hence one name for the program is 'lexico-statistics'. In making the comparisons, literal meanings are preferred to semantic extensions; e.g. the body-part sense of English *tongue* is preferred to the sense "language". Assuming that two languages being compared are in fact related, the time of divergence from a common mother language is estimated from the proportion of vocabulary common to both. The scale of vocabulary differentiation derives from studies of Indo-European languages for which there are historical records. The procedure is sometimes called 'glottochronology'.[12] Words in the Swadesh list are basic in the sense that they name things likely to be common to the experience of all human communities, hence they fall into categories such as personal pronouns, interrogatives, connectives (*and, if, because*), locatives and locations, position and movement, manipulations (*wash, hit, scratch*), time periods, numerals, quantifiers, size, natural objects and phenomena, plants, animals, persons, body parts and substances, bodily sensations and activities, colours, kin, and cultural objects and activities. The studies of semantic and lexical universals reported in Goddard and Wierzbicka (eds) 1994,

Wierzbicka 1996, Goddard 1998 are not concerned with diachronic relationships, but with the different differential values that listemes have both within and across languages.[13]

> [T]wo words (morphemes, etc.) can be identical in meaning despite belonging to different parts of speech or having different grammatical status; for example WANT can be either a verb or an adjective, FEEL can be a word in one language but a suffix in another, and so on. Naturally, two semantically identical words may have different patterns of allomorphy or allolexy in different languages; for example, SOMEONE may have just one lexical exponent in language A, but three or four in language B. Finally, semantically identical words may have very different ranges of use for cultural reasons, or because of different patterns of polysemy.   (Goddard 1994:23)

The number of semantic primitives identified by Wierzbicka grew from 14 in 1972 to nearly 20 in 1985, 37 in 1994, and 57 in 1998 (Wierzbicka 1996, Goddard 1998).

Substantives	I, YOU, SOMEONE/PERSON, SOMETHING/THING, PEOPLE
Determiners	THIS, THE SAME, OTHER/ELSE
Quantifiers	ONE, TWO, MANY/MUCH, ALL, SOME
Mental predicates	THINK (OF), FEEL, WANT, KNOW, SEE, HEAR
Speech	SAY, WORD
Actions/events	DO, HAPPEN, MOVE
Existence and life	THERE IS, LIVE, DIE
Evaluators	GOOD, BAD,
Descriptors	BIG, SMALL
Place	WHERE/PLACE, UNDER, ABOVE, FAR, NEAR, HERE, SIDE, INSIDE
Time	WHEN/TIME, AFTER, BEFORE, NOW, A LONG TIME, A SHORT TIME, FOR SOME TIME
Logical concepts	NOT, IF, CAN, BECAUSE, MAYBE, IF...WOULD
Intensifier/augmentor	VERY, MORE
Partonymy/taxonomy	PART OF, KIND OF
Similarity	LIKE

Table 8.9 Semantic primitives in NSM

In addition, 'allolexes' of these primitives are permitted, e.g. *me* for I, *who* and *what* for SOMEONE and SOMETHING, *thing* for SOMETHING, *could* for CAN, *for* for BECAUSE, *place* for WHERE. Exactly what constrains the proliferation of allolexes remains to be defined. Since 1972, WORLD has been dropped and IMAGINE has changed to IF. DISWANT has (mercifully) been replaced by NO for the following reason:

It is not black =
No, it is not black =
when I want to think: "I can think: 'it is black'", I think "no"   (Wierzbicka 1994:477)

Finally, BECOME has been replaced by HAPPEN on the following grounds:

X became Y =
(a) at some time, X was not Y
(b) after that something happened to X
(c) after that X was Y
(d) I say this after that time   (Goddard and Wierzbicka 1994:48)

Until around 1990, Wierzbicka's meaning descriptions used a lot of other items besides the primitives; cf. 1972:22,26,106. More recent semantic analyses stick closely to the primitives.

How do Wierzbicka's semantic analyses compare to those of scholars using other metalanguages? Compare her semantics for the verb *assert* with that of, say, Bach and Harnish 1979. The lines of each are numbered for comparative purposes

[1]   I say: X
[2]   I imagine some people would say this is not true
        I can say that this is true
[3]   I assume that people will have to think that it is true
[4]   I say this because I want to say what I know is true   (Wierzbicka 1987:321)

[1]   In uttering *e*, *S* asserts that *P* if *S* expresses
[2]   i. the belief that *P*, and
[3]   ii. the intention that *H* believe that *P*.   (Bach and Harnish 1979:42)

[1] is a description of asserting. [2] describes the preconditions under which Speaker can sincerely and appropriately make an assertion (D6.13). [3] describes the purpose of making an assertion, which is to have Hearer believe the asserted proposition. [4] is a sincerity condition not explicit in the Bach and Harnish quote, because it is presumed to hold under the cooperative maxim of quality (D1.24). The point of this comparison is to show that, after a quarter-century of dedicated scholarship by Wierzbicka and her colleagues NSM is an effective tool of semantic description that compares well with other semantic metalanguages.

Nevertheless, it is not possible to restrict viable semantic definitions to just the set of semantic primitives in Table 8.9. There is evidence in Wierzbicka 1972 that natural kind terms such as *tiger* are treated like semantic primitives: 'an animal thinking of which one would say *tiger*'. This would vastly expand the number of primitives postulated; but NSM practitioners offer no clear statements on the matter. The best that might be hoped for is a 'simplified' vocabulary of several hundred, perhaps several thousand words, such as is claimed for the *Longman Dictionary of Contemporary English*. The most recently identified Wierzbickan semantic primitives will constitute merely a small subset of this simplified vocabulary.

Wierzbicka has never defined the syntax of NSM. Goddard 1994 writes

> Semantic primitives have an elementary syntax whereby they combine to form 'simple propositions'. [...] Semantic primitives and their elementary syntax exist as a minimal subset of ordinary natural language.   (pp. 8,10)

It behoves the proponents of the theory to be more precise about the syntax and also to explain what differentiates a well-formed semantic definition or description from an ill-formed one.[14]

One of the most attractive features of NSM is that the ordinary reader can easily relate to the meaning definitions. Since about 1984, Wierzbicka's semantic definitions are presented like prose poems. They are deliberately 'naive'; consequently, some readers have remarked upon their childlike quality. Here is part of the semantic definition of *tiger*:

> [...] they are similar to cats in the way they look and in the way they move   *SIZE*
> but they are much bigger than cats
> being more like people in size than like cats
>
> they have black stripes on a yellowish body   *APPEARANCE*
> they have big sharp claws and big sharp teeth
>
> they attack other animals and people and kill and eat them   *BEHAVIOR*
> they can move quickly and without noise like cats [...]
>
>   (Wierzbicka 1985:164)

The expressions used in a semantic representation in NSM are supposed to match those that (a) children acquire early and (b) have counterparts in all languages (Goddard 1994:12). In her definitions, Wierzbicka is deliberately anthropocentric and subjective, referring to the natural world of sensory experience rather than intellectualized abstractions. She prefers to describe *red* as the colour of blood (1980:43, 1990b) or fire (1990b, 1992a) than as an electromagnetic wave focally around 695 nanometres in length.

> If we are trying to understand and to elucidate the intuitions of ordinary speakers, we cannot use in our definitions anything which is not independently attested to be accessible to that intuition. Translating colour terms into information about wavelength may tell us something about physiological and neurological processes but obviously it cannot tell us anything about the intuitive connections between different everyday concepts.   (Wierzbicka 1984:235)

I propose that *blue* involves more than one point of reference: not only the sky but also water – not water from the tap, but naturally occurring water, that is, the water of seas, lakes, rivers, and so on. Roughly:

> *X is blue*
> when one sees things like X
> one can think of the sky
> or of places (not made by people)
> where there is water   (Wierzbicka 1992b:222f)

This is a characteristic of cognitive semantics (Chapter 9).

Wierzbicka 1984:207 has commented that Labov's denotation conditions for *cup* 'need the help of a mathematician to understand' them and do not give the lexicographic meaning. However, 'the denotation conditions can be deduced from the meaning' (1984:209).

> The term *cup* is regularly used to denote round containers with a ratio of width to depth of $1 \pm r$ where $r \leq r_b$, and $r_b = \alpha_1 + \alpha_2 + \dots \alpha_v$ and α_i is a positive quantity when the feature *i* is present and 0 otherwise.
>
> feature 1 = with one handle
> 2 = made of opaque vitreous material
> 3 = used for consumption of food
> 4 = used for consumption of liquid food
> 5 = used for consumption of hot liquid food
> 6 = with a saucer
> 7 = tapering
> 8 = circular in cross-section
>
> *Cup* is used variably to denote such containers with ratios of width to depth of $1 \pm r$ where $r_b \leq r \leq r_t$ with a probability of $r_t - r/r_t - r_b$. The quantity $r \pm r_b$ expresses the distance from the modal value of width to height. (Labov 1973:366f, quoted Wierzbicka 1984)

Her own definition for *cup* (Wierzbicka 1984:222–4) is 831 words (two pages) long and extraordinarily detailed. It raises important questions about the playoff between the effectiveness of a definition and its accuracy.

> *Research question 8.1* What is the purpose of the semantic analysis?

> *Research question 8.2* Who or what is the semantic specification that results from the analysis designed for?

Wierzbicka's semantic definitions are not designed to be used by machines that simulate language understanding. She intends them to be easily accessible to a non-native speaker of the language. But every such reader will already know what a cup is, so a brief description would be sufficient. Many readers find Wierzbicka's two page definition of *cup* just as confusing as Labov's denotation conditions (Goddard 1998:233 successfully reduced it by 71 per cent). Consider the following 'dictionary representation' of *cup* given in Katz 1977b:49.

Physical Object
Inanimate
Vertical Orientation
Upwardly concave

Height about equal to top diameter
Top diameter greater than bottom diameter
Artifact
Made to serve as a container from which to drink liquid.

Katz's description is adequate, very much simpler than Labov's 'denotation conditions', and far more succinct than Wierzbicka's 'semantic definition' of 831 words. NSM practitioners would object that the terms Katz uses are more difficult than *cup* itself – but that is equally true for the semantics of *cup* in Wierzbicka 1984 and Goddard 1998.

> *Assumption 8.20* The purpose of semantic representations is to make useful revelations about the nature of human language and/or human cognition. They are not displays of the creator's ingenuity.

Wierzbicka has written: 'An adequate definition must show fully what the word in question means, not what it doesn't mean or how it differs in meaning from some other words which we happen to compare it with. [...A]n adequate definition of a word must constitute a faithful "portrait" of the concept encoded in it' (Wierzbicka 1984:227). This is inconsistent with her 1985 semantic definition of *tiger* quoted above, where she compared tigers with cats because we see tigers as a kind of cat. In different terms, all that Wierzbicka seems to be saying is that an adequate definition of what a listeme means will capture the intension of the listeme – which is exactly the view presented in this book. The prolixity of Wierzbicka's semantic definition for *cup* is unjustifiable: 'For dictionary purposes, the concept has only to be identified, not fully specified,' wrote Cruse 1990:396.

This section looked into the search for semantic primitives. The view of this book is that every listeme with semantic specification is a semantic primitive – that is exactly why it is a listeme. Different languages have different listemes, but a listeme in one language can be related to listemes in another language by means of entailment and/or conventional implicature and conversational implicature.

Exercises

8.6.1 Try writing semantic definitions using NSM for: (a) *X is red*.   (b) Either *sky* or *water*.

8.6.2 'For dictionary purposes, the concept has only to be identified, not fully specified' (Cruse 1990:396). What do you think?

8.7 Summary

The purpose of this chapter has been to explain the significance of semantic frames, semantic fields, and componential analysis within lexical semantics. In the chapters that follow we see how other linguists make use of semantic components. The goal for decompositional semantics is that 'any complex meaning can be decomposed into a combination of discrete other meanings, without circularity and without residue' (Goddard 1994, quoted at the head of this chapter). We shall see that there is a very long way to go before this goal is likely to be reached.

Throughout Chapter 8 it has been evident that semantic properties and relations are constrained and informed by the categories and relations that humans perceive and conceive of (A8.1). The meanings of language expressions reflect speakers' perceptions of their denotata. As a result, we cannot account for senses and sense relations without recourse to intensions and through them to extensions in some world and time. Chapter 9 takes up these matters by exploring the relation between word, percept, and thing spoken of, both language internally and across languages.

● Key words and phrases:

antonymy
asymmetric semantic implication
argument structure
attribute
basic colour term (D8.6)
bozine (filling a lexical gap) (D8.13)
category feature
category scale
cognitive semantics
collocation
comparative scale
componential analysis (D8.11)
componential table (Table 8.8)
contraries
conceptual field (A8.7)
converse predicates
co-occurrence condition (A8.6)
differential value (valeur) (D8.5)
event structure
frame (D8.2)
function
gradable antonyms (relative predicates)
heteromeronymy
homeomeronymy
hyponymy (15, Table 8.4)
incompatibility
inherent feature

kin term
kind-of relation (hyponymy)
lexical conceptual paradigm (lcp)
lexical inheritance structure
lexical insertion
lexical gap (D8.9)
meronymy (D8.8, Table 8.7)
natural semantic metalanguage (NSM)
part-of relation (meronymy)
peripheral use of a term
principle of least effort (D8.12)
prototype
quale/qualia
relational scale
script (D8.1)
selection restriction (D8.4)
selectional feature
semantic component (D8.11)
semantic extension (A8.17)
semantic field (A8.7)
semantic marker(ese)
semantic primitive (D8.14)
semantic shift
stereotype
strict subcategorization (D8.3)
synonymy
thematic structure (valency, case frame)

transitivity of hyponym (D8.7)   value of an attribute
transitivity of meronym (D8.10)

● Scripts are used in the construction and understanding of texts. Based on the assumption (A8.2) that little we encounter is entirely new, they specify structured information about dynamic event sequences, information that Speaker does not as a rule need to explicitly repeat to Hearer because the regular components of a script are predictable once the script is invoked. There is a very large number of scripts, and many overlap (A8.4).
● Scripts supply the grounds for determining what is worth reporting, because deviations from scripts are potentially newsworthy (A8.3).
● The frames for a listeme identifies the characteristic features, attributes, and functions of its denotatum, and the characteristic interactions of the denotatum with things necessarily or typically associated with it. The frame can be thought of as a number of slots into which the values of appropriate attributes are inserted, furnishing formal, morphosyntactic, and semantic specifications for the listeme.
● We communicate meanings by combining listemes into the larger, more complex, meaningful structures (A8.5). Semantic selection restrictions were postulated to provide the co-occurrence conditions regulating such text creation (D8.4). Identifying a full set of selection restrictions is at best impracticable and at worst impossible (A8.6).
● It is not acceptable to postulate a theoretical device such as selection restrictions when the means by which they are to be identified is left unspecified. A more useful course of action is to use the listeme's frame as a co-occurrence constraint. Pustejovsky's work on the lexical semantic structures of his generative lexicon suggest how the frames might be identified in a systematic manner for this purpose.
● The semantic field of a listeme e_1 is determined from the conceptual field in which its denotatum occurs (A8.7). Other parts of the conceptual field are labelled by other listemes e_2, e_3, ... e_n and all of these, together with e_1 are said to be in the same semantic field.
● Different languages – or, at different times in its history, any one language – may divide the conceptual field differently between lexemes. There is a corresponding difference (A8.8) in their differential value (D8.5).
● We saw how the semantic field of colour is divided differently in different languages (Tables 8.1–3).
● Hyponymy was reviewed. Chaffin 1992 identified seven categories of hyponym (Table 8.4).
● Co-hyponyms of some superordinate term are contraries and therefore incompatible with one another. Furthermore, a hyponym is incompatible with the co-hyponyms of its superordinates, and with their hyponyms.
● Gradable so-called 'antonyms' are incompatibles (contraries) ranged on a comparative scale (Tables 8.5–6).
● Three criteria for choosing among competing analyses of data fragments were given in A8.9: accuracy, simplicity, and consistency with major analyses.
● Semantics is affected by external events when new vocabulary has to be found for new discoveries.
● Meronymy (the part-of relation) was introduced (D8.8). Chaffin 1992 identified seven categories of meronym (Table 8.7).

• The assumptions underlying componential analysis are: every listeme is analysable into one or more semantic components; listemes that share semantic components are semantically related; there is a thesaurus-like taxonomy of semantic components that corresponds to hierarchies perceived and/or conceived of among denotata (A.12–16).

• Wilkins 1668 was an early attempt at componential analysis.

• In the 1950s and 1960s semantic components were identified through the established methods of contrastive and distributional analysis that had been so successful in phonology and morphology (cf. Harris 1951). However, this generally ignored the importance of knowledge about the denotata such as is captured in frames.

• The manner of naming is influenced by Zipf's 'principle of least effort' (D8.12).

• In trying to determine an accurate semantics for one of the lexemes *bull*, it was necessary to consider properties of the denotatum and use truth conditional semantics (43).

• Prototypical or stereotypical uses of *bull* were distinguished from peripheral uses. The latter often result from semantic extension and are assigned longer names (A8.17).

• Relationships within a semantic field are determined by relationships between the intensions of listemes which name things perceived and conceived of within the world about us (A8.18). Consider the following clash between semantics and reality. Suppose that Kim is a self-described *woman* but also one of the 'chicks with dicks', i.e. biological male, but with some physiological and all social characteristics of a woman. Semantically, $\forall x[\textbf{woman}'(x) \rightarrow \textbf{female}'(x)]$; but in these circumstances, *Kim is a woman* seems to be true, but *Kim is female* seems false.

• Semantic primitives are the basic vocabulary of the metalanguage (D8.14). Ideally, complex meanings should be decomposed into semantic primitives without circularity and without residue.

• Jerrold J Katz was important for carving a place for semantic theory within a modern linguistic paradigm. However, his semantic markerese is severely deficient as a metalanguage for semantics.

• Weinreich's recipe for a natural language metalanguage for semantics (A8.19) has been adopted and developed by Wierzbicka. NSM, Wierzbicka's 'natural semantic metalanguage', uses part of the vocabulary and syntax of a natural language. She says it is linguistically and culturally unbiased and therefore translatable into any other natural language. It has certainly been applied to languages from many different famillies.

• Wierzbicka's search for semantic primitives is distinct in kind from the Swadesh-list of up to 215 lexemes that are basic in the sense that they name things likely to be common to the experience of all human communities. The primitives of NSM are supposed to name basic concepts. The number has grown from 14 in the 1970s, 20 in the 1980s, and 57 in the late 1990s. If NSM is used to analyse more than a few fragments of any language, we may expect many more primitives to be needed.

• The syntax of NSM has yet to be properly described.

• NSM is deliberately informal, anthropocentric, and easy to read. But it is a good deal more wordy than its competitors, for instance Jackendoff's 'lexical conceptual structures' (studied in Chapter 12).

• We posed two very important research questions for a semantic theory: the purpose of the data analysis (RQ8.1) and the intended audience (RQ8.2). A partial answer to RQ8.1 was given in A8.20: to make useful revelations about the nature of human language and/or human cognition.

8.8   Notes on further reading

[1] On scripts, see Schank and Abelson 1977, Schank 1982, 1984, 1986.

[2] On the semantic basis for 'syntactic' inherent features, see Chomsky 1965 §2.3, Weinreich 1966, McCawley 1968a, 1968b, Jackendoff 1972.

[3] On lexical insertion into syntactic phrase markers, see Katz and Postal 1964, Chomsky 1965, Katz 1972, Allan 1986 I:295ff.

[4] Sequences of listemes are ultimately judged in terms of their coherence and ability to make sense in context, which are characteristics dependent upon what the sequences denote; cf. Fillmore 1971:274, Jackendoff 1972:379, Johnson-Laird 1981:115.

[5] On semantic frames, see Fillmore 1982a, Lehrer and Kittay (eds) 1992.

[6] The notion of semantic fields was initially developed among German scholars Herder 1772, Humboldt 1836, Trier 1931, Porzig 1950, Weisgerber 1950, Geckeler 1971. The most accessible discussions and exemplifications in English are Bendix 1966, Bierwisch 1967, Tyler 1969, Lehrer 1974, Lyons 1963, 1977, Lehrer and Kittay (eds) 1992, and Backhouse 1994. Peeters 1991 (and elsewhere) uses a term derived from André Martinet and refers to 'axiological fields'.

[7] On colour terms, see Chapter 9, Berlin and Kay 1969, Berlin and Berlin 1975, Kay and McDaniel 1978, Allan 1986, Wierzbicka 1992a, MacLaury 1997, Hardin and Maffi (eds) 1997.

[8] On the category scale, see Allan 1987b. On gradable antonymy, see Lehrer and Lehrer 1982, Lehrer 1985.

[9] On Prague school phonology and componential analysis, see Trubetzkoy 1939, Jakobson 1936, Harris 1948, Nida 1951, Allan 1986 I:166–8.

[10] On componential analysis, see Harris 1948, Nida 1951, 1975, Goodenough 1956, Lounsbury 1956, Hjelmslev 196,1 Lyons 1968, Lehrer 1974, 1992c.

[11] The definitive statement of semantic markerese is Katz 1972, see also Katz 1977a. For detailed critical evaluation of Katz's work, see (Janet) Fodor 1977, Allan 1986 Ch. 5.

[12] On glottochronology, see Embleton 1992 for a critique of the method.

[13] Goddard and Wierzbicka (eds) 1994 offers detailed accounts of the distribution of up to 37 semantic primitives across 14 languages; and there is additional material of a similar kind to be found in Wierzbicka 1991, 1992c, 1996, Goddard 1998. A set of 'primitifs sémantiques' for French is given in Peeters 1994:94.

[14] On the syntax of NSM, see Wierzbicka 1996:19–22, Goddard 1998, 329–36.

9 Cognitive semantics: backs, colours, and classifiers

[T]o study semantics of natural language *is* to study cognitive psychology.

(Jackendoff 1983:3)

9.1 Where we are heading

Meaning in natural language is an information structure that is mentally encoded by human beings.

(Jackendoff 1987a:122)

Unlike anybody's metalanguage, natural language is not a creation of conscious artifice, and in this respect it is like our minds and bodies. This chapter focuses on the influence of human perceptions and conceptions in determining semantic categories, properties, and relations. §9.2 emphasizes the human-centredness of language by making a close and detailed examination of the English listemes *back* to demonstrate the ways in which this body-part term has extended from humans to animals to inanimates, and jumped syntactic category from noun to adjective, verb, and adverb. People are well able to see similarities in the configuration of things that are in other respects distinct, and to exploit this perception in the semantics of their languages. §9.3 accounts for colour term use and understanding in terms of Vantage Theory (MacLaury 1997). In Chapter 8 we saw that the colour spectrum is carved up differently in different languages, but offered no explanation for the evolution of basic colour terms from two to eleven (Tables 8.1–3). §9.3 does. It also seeks to explain how it is that a speaker of the Mayan language Tzeltal, when asked to mark all the shades of colour that *k'an* "yellow" can refer to maps right over almost every shade that *čah* "red" refers to. It is because a Tzeltal speaker takes a certain point of view, or vantage, different from that of an English speaker. A vantage is the cognitive construction of what is perceived that leads a person to create categories of things that subsequently get named. In order for people to understand one another within a speech community there is a conventional way of seeing and talking about things: in other words, a conventionalization of vantage within the community. §9.4 examines the character and functions of different kinds of classifiers. Classifiers are found in many unrelated languages; they are markers attached to nouns, noun modifiers, anaphors, and/or predicates in order to indicate "I'm referring to such-and-such kind of thing" (just as English uses *he* or *she* to specify whether we are speaking about a male or a female). The similarities across languages lead to doubts about the Sapir–Whorf hypothesis that each language constrains the manner in which its speakers perceive the world. We also see why some groupings do not get named in a natural language. §9.5 summarizes the chapter.

A satisfactory theory of semantics is consistent with

> *Assumption 9.1* Language is a creation of human beings for the purpose of communicating with other human beings.

Implicit is the further assumption

> *Assumption 9.2* A semantic theory is a theory of one aspect of human cognitive ability.

Cognitive semantics is a branch of cognitive linguistics.[1]

> *Definition 9.1* COGNITIVE LINGUISTICS is the systematic study of language under assumption A8.1, that language is constrained and informed by the relations that human beings (a) perceive in nature – particularly in relation to themselves; (b) have experience of in the world they inhabit; (c) conceive of in abstract and metaphysical domains.

> *Definition 9.2* PERCEPTION is the categorizing of sensory data using both biologically and culturally determined criteria.

The main thrust of COGNITIVE SEMANTICS (including Jackendoff's CONCEPTUAL SEMANTICS) has been the influence of perception in determining linguistic categories, semantic fields, frames, and the like, that are assumed to be psychologically real.[2] There are cognitive foundations to functional linguistics.

> *Definition 9.3* FUNCTIONAL LINGUISTICS holds that grammatical structure is not 'autonomous' but can only be understood and explained with reference to its semantic and communicative functions (cf. Van Valin 1993a:2, Harder 1996).

The communicative function of a language expression arises directly from, and is informed by, Speaker's cognitive awareness of its intended effect upon Hearer.

Formalists tend to believe that functionalist and cognitivist accounts of semantic structure lack the rigour necessary for proper scientific inquiry. Cognitivists counter that formal semanticists prefer abstract semantic representations which are psychologically unreal. A charitable interpretation of the opposed positions suggests considerable overlap.

> *Assumption 9.3* (First premise) Formal representations are created by human minds and are interpretable by human minds. Therefore, they have cognitive reality. Moreover, formal models of meaning are models of human reason as it is expressed in language – which is an aspect of human cognition.
> (Second premise) The informal semantic metalanguages of the cognitivists – e.g. Jackendoff's conceptual semantics (Chapter 12) and Wierzbicka's NSM

(Chapter 8) – are creations of deliberate, consciously contrived artifice, just as much as any formal metalanguages are.
(Conclusion) Formalists, cognitivists, and functionalists all use contrived metalanguages that have cognitive reality.

9.2 The meanings of the English words *back*: the human-centredness of language[1]

NUMBERS

One—Yee'ur.
Two—Bul'chiba.
Three—Bulchiba-yeiyur.
Four—Bulchiba-bulchiba.
Five—Bulchiba-bulchiba-yeiyur.
Ten—Bulchiba bee'yun (two hands).
The Head denotes 10 as—Crown of head, eyes, ears, cheeks, nose, mouth, and chin.
The Body denotes 17 as—The back, shoulders, elbows, wrists, and fingers.
The Legs denotes 16 as—The hips, knees, ankles, and toes.
Head, hands, and feet, 30.   (*Australasian Anthropological Journal* 1, 1897:87)[2]

This section demonstrates that the human mind and body constrain our perception and cognition; they also provide a standard. We examine the senses of the words *back* and its relationship to *front, face,* and *behind*. The word *back* has been extended from humans to animals and inanimates and there are various associative (transferred) uses of the word. Finally, we see how a 'journey schema' explains extensions of the meaning of *back* from noun to verb and adverb. The analogical and metaphorical extensions of *back* are just one instance from a huge body of work that proves beyond any doubt that

> Assumption 9.4 LANGUAGE IS ANTHROPOCENTRIC. Humans necessarily describe the world of their experience with reference to the human body and its everyday experiences. All speech communities use the human body and its parts as a basis for describing and measuring other things in the world around them.[3]

Evidence:

---

1. A list of symbols peculiar to this section is found among the keywords section of the summary.

2. The language is Yorta Yorta. Today 1 = iyawa, iyung, 2 = bultjubul, 3 = bultjubul-iyung, 4 = bultjubul-bultjubul, 5 = bultjubul-bultjubul-iyung, 10 = bultjubul biyin "see two hands" or wuta djirtj "all fingers" (Bowe, Peeler, and Atkinson 1997).

(a)   Traditional counting systems are mostly based on the numbers 4 (fingers on one hand), 5, 10, or 20, because of the structure of our hands and feet. See the quote at the head of this section, and the San Juan Southern Paiute (Uto-Aztecan):

ma-nuxi-y	*shu - roxo - mai - y*	*toxo - mai - y*	
hand-?-NOM	nearly-complete-hand-NOM	complete-hand-NOM	
"five"	"nine"	"ten"	(Bunte and Franklin 1988)

(b)   Traditional units of measurement are also determined by the human body, e.g. English *inch, hand, foot, yard, fathom, mile.*

(c)   Most people are right-handed, and in many cultures the right hand is regarded more positively than the left hand – used in many cultures to handle the impure. Latin *sinisteritas* "left-hand" is the source for *sinister*. English *cackhanded* and *gauche* derive from "left-handed".

(d)   Assigning gender terms to animals is often determined by whether or not the sex of the animal is of significance to a sizeable proportion of the language community (Chapter 8).

These, and much more, demonstrate the human-centredness of language and, indirectly, of the human cognition that language reflects.

In what follows we need to take note of some additional facts.

Definition 9.4 The CANONICAL HUMAN BEARING is the upright bipedal human being confronting the world by looking, and walking, forward.

Definition 9.5 In the CANONICAL HUMAN ENCOUNTER two people confront one another face-to-face (H.Clark 1973:35).

The human body is a standard for relative locations as well as measurement. A direct effect of recognizing a body part within the configuration of the whole body, is to recognize it as a LOCATION as well as a proper part. The noun *back* correctly names a proper part of or location on the human body provided that D9.6–8 hold true. (S_H abbreviates "spine of a human").

Definition 9.6(S_H) PROTOTYPICAL ("most typical") NOTION BACK. The part or location named *the back* is located across the shoulders and lengthways co-extensive with the spine.

The *Oxford English Dictionary*, among others, categorizes D9.6(S_H) as the prototypical sense of *back*; probably because the spine is seen as necessary for keeping humans upright and bipedal, which marks us off as a species from other animals (D9.4). Nonetheless, this sense of back is the one transferred to creatures most like human beings, i.e. vertebrate animals. The structural function of the spine, and the facts that it curves forward and is used for burden bearing, all turn up in semantic extensions of *back*.

D9.7(I'_H) is the sense of *back* most widely extended from humans to other entities. (I'_H abbreviates "opposite to the interactive-side of a human"; the prime notation indicates "opposite to".)

> *Definition 9.7(I'_H)* The INTRINSIC CORE BACK. The part or location named *the back* is on the opposite side of the body from the 'interactive-side' of a human being. This is the side where the mouth, breasts, belly and external genitals are located and from which the limbs extend. The 'interactive-side' is named for being the side of principal interaction and access to a person.

'Interactive-side' is placed within quotes to mark it as a technical term for a proper part of and/or location on a body or thing and not merely a description. A creature's mouth, teats and breasts (if any), genitals, and limbs all interact with the physical environment, and often with other animals of the same species in social, sexual, or nurturant behaviours. The collection of body parts identified as components of the 'interactive-side' are those body parts principally involved in food ingestion, sexual reproduction, neonate nurturing, and various kinds of social interaction. These functions are the very stuff of life – which explains the salience of the 'interactive-side', and by implication the human front. It is the front of a person that includes the face and makes him/her most readily recognizable. It is one's front that bears the most important sensory organs (eyes, ears, hands, nose, mouth) and which, consequently, is the plane that normally interacts with other people and with inanimate objects. The components of the 'interactive-side' are the principal means and locations of interaction with and access to a creature. These properties are figuratively transferred to identify a front, and hence the back, of animate and many inanimate objects. *Back* is defined in terms of the front of the body, rather than vice versa, just because the front is the more salient and significant body location.

The primary model for the notion "back" is the human being in upright stance and walking with the front of the body proceeding forward (D9.4). Consistent with D9.7(I'_H), a human normally walks in the direction s/he faces, and not sideways or backward, because of the way our bodies have evolved: forward is the direction over which a human has optimal perceptual regard (D9.4). In short, it is normal for the front to be the leading edge. In D9.8(L'_H), L'_H abbreviates "opposite to the leading edge of a human".

> *Definition 9.8(L'_H)* The PERIPHERAL BACK. The part or location named *the back* is on the opposite side from the leading edge when a person, H_1, is walking normally (i.e. forward). The leading edge is named *the front* and this confronts viewer H_2, another person, facing H_1.

The notion of a leading edge transfers to animals determining their front (end) but not their backs. An animal's back is opposite the 'interactive-side', which for vertebrates is where the spine is (see below). The spread to inanimate mobile objects, however, does define their backs: think of the front and back of a bike, car, train, or plane.

So, there is a central notion "back", and a peripheral one; cf. A8.17 on peripheral uses of *bull*. A similar distinction is to be found with other body-part terms in other languages; e.g. a single term for "eye" (central) and "face" (peripheral), or one for "face" (central) and "front" (peripheral).[4] Due to the principle of least effort (D8.12), it is typical of a semantic extension and a peripheral notion that terms instantiating "peripheral back" all require augmentation of the basic lexeme *back*, e.g. *the back of the body*, *the back of the head*, *backside* ("buttocks" or "behind"), *back(s) of the legs*, and even *back(s) of the arms*. In all these examples, the component *back* is a PROPER part noun derived from the body-part noun – i.e. *back of the leg* is a meronym (D8.8) of *leg*.

A consequence of the intrinsic back, D9.7(I'_H), is D9.9(C'_H) where C'_H means "side of a human opposite the side which confronts the viewer".

> *Definition 9.9(C'_H)* DEFAULT BACK. The part or location named *the back* is on the opposite side of a person H_1's body from *the front*, which is the side that confronts H_2, another human viewer, facing H_1.

This gives the default condition for identifying the back of something in the event that it has no intrinsic back. It arises because most languages reflect the fact that the human viewer's visual field defines what objects face him/her. The English verb *face* derives from the isomorphic body-part noun and is figuratively extended from a prototype in which two people are face to face in the canonical encounter (D9.5).

The components of the meaning of *back* as applied to the human body have been extended to other animate creatures and to inanimate objects. To begin with, humans have spines in common with other vertebrate animals, so $S_H \Rightarrow S_A$ (where $\Rightarrow$ symbolizes "copies to, extends to", and S_A="spine of a non-human animate").

> *Definition 9.6(S_A)* A VERTEBRATE'S CORE BACK. The part or location named *the back* of a vertebrate animal is located across the shoulders and lengthways co-extensive with the spine.

Also D9.6(S_H) $\Rightarrow$ D9.6(S_N), where S_N="spine of an inanimate", perhaps (but not necessarily) with input from D9.6(S_A). D9.6(S_H) does not productively transfer to inanimates, presumably because of its limited appropriateness. However, there is a figurative extension arising from the fact that breaking the spinal column of a human or vertebrate animal renders the victim helpless.

> *Definition 9.6(S_N)* The part or location named *the back* of an inanimate object is a crucial sustaining structure that, if broken, is disastrous to the object.

Cf. *the back/spine of a book*, *the back of a wave*, *break the back of a ship*, *break the back of the task*.

D9.7(I'_H) is a very productive source for semantic transfer. $I'_H \Rightarrow I'_A$ ("opposite to the interactive side of a non-human animate").

> *Definition 9.7(I'_A)* A CREATURE'S INTRINSIC CORE BACK. *The back* names the proper part or location of any animate creature's body that is the opposite side of the body from the 'interactive-side', i.e. that side of an animate creature's body which contains the mouth(parts), teats and breasts (if any), belly (if appropriate), and external genitals, and from which the limbs (if any)

extend. This is the side of principal interaction with and access to the creature.

This readily accommodates invertebrates, including those without head or hindquarters. For example, the back of a jellyfish floating in the ocean is universally recognized as being opposite its 'interactive-side' – it faces the sky. Certainly it is normal for the back of an animal to be roughly horizontal and face skyward; but "the part of an animal roughly horizontal and facing skyward" is not sufficient as a definition for its back, and it is easily falsified by jellyfish stranded on its back upon the sand. The 'interactive-side' of an oyster, clam, or mussel is the side which opens to interact with its environment; so, the back of these bivalves is where the hinge is.

Also, D9.7(I'_H) ⇨ D9.7(I'_N).

Definition 9.7(I'_N) The back names the proper part or location of a STATIC CONCRETE INANIMATE OBJECT that is on the opposite side to an intrinsic front if, and only if, the front is the 'interactive-side', designed to be the side of principal interaction with and access to the object and, consequently, the side which normally confronts the human viewer facing the object.

Humans and animals have intrinsic fronts and backs as body-parts. Many manufactured goods and artifacts – computers, cupboards, fridges, houses – also have intrinsic fronts and backs as proper parts. The front of such objects is the side which under normal circumstances confronts the human user. Their fronts are also defined by analogy with the human 'interactive-side' as the side having the principal locations and means of normal interaction with and access to the object.

(a)   Someone using a computer looks at the VDU and, from time to time, the keyboard – which are both to the front of a computer, as are the floppy disk and CD ports (usually). S/he also interacts with all these.

(b)   The user looks at and into the front of a cupboard or fridge and interacts with them in order to put things in and get things out.

(c)   On walking from the street to enter the house, the human viewer faces the house front; so, the front of a house conventionally faces the street it is on. Once upon a time, houses would have only one door (many huts, shanties, hogans, and wickiups still do); consequently, the front was the side from which one would enter. For many houses, the front is still the side from which entry is most often made. The entrance is therefore perceived as the side which confronts the person entering, and at the same time it is the place of common access and interaction with the house – the counterpart to the 'interactive-side' of humans and animals.

D9.8(L'_H) "opposite to the leading edge of a human" is extended to animates and thence inanimates.

Definition 9.8($L'_{A/N}$) The part or location named *the back* or *back/tail end* or *rear* of AN OBJECT CAPABLE OF MOBILITY is on the opposite side or end from the leading edge when the object is in motion. The part of the object named *the front*, which confronts the human viewer facing it, ranges between the leading edge through to halfway back; therefore the part, location, or end opposite the leading edge (from about halfway along) is the peripheral back.

The front of a cow or a snake or a tarantula is determined from where its head is, because that is the part of the animal that leads when the animal is travelling normally. Significantly, it is also the part which confronts the human viewer facing it (D9.9(C$'_H$)). This criterial fact makes it irrelevant that the front legs of many spiders precede the head when the arachnid walks; and it accommodates crabs who move crabwise, and crayfish who walk backwards. With respect to the side opposite the leading edge, a significant difference between nonhuman animates (D9.8(L$'_A$)) and inanimates (D9.8(L$'_N$)), is that for inanimates it is properly labelled *the back*, but not for animates. Appropriate names for the part or location defined by D9.8(L$'_A$) are *back/tail end, rear, rump, hind quarters*, etc. The contrast between *back (end)* and *front* is what justifies the expression *back legs* for *legs AT the back* – not legs that extend out from an animal's back. The different locations of an animal's back and its butt makes it unlikely that animals provided the original model for defining the fronts and backs of objects capable of mobility. However, it is likely that L$'_A$ was extended from animals to vehicles (L$'_N$): compare *the back wheels of a car* with *the back legs of an ox*. But there is no overriding zoomorphic analogy that licenses **the car's back* meaning "the car's roof" by analogy with *the ox's back* – English is anthropomorphic and not zoomorphic.[5]

D9.9(C$'_H$), where C$'_H$ refers to the side of a human opposite the side which confronts the viewer, does not transfer to nonhuman animates, all of which have intrinsic fronts and backs defined by any or all of D9.6(S$_A$), D9.7(I$'_A$), D9.8(L$'_A$). However, it does extend to inanimates, i.e. D9.9(C$'_H$) ⇨ D9.9(C$'_N$).

Definition 9.9(C$'_N$) The part or location named *the back* of anything is the side opposite (or behind) its front. If a static concrete inanimate object is assigned no intrinsic front, the part or location of the object facing the human viewer is contingently named *the front*, and the part or location on the opposite side or end of the contingent front is named *the back*.

For example, the front and back of a vase, a wine glass, a tree. Among speakers of English, trees do not have intrinsic fronts and backs, but Heine 1989 observes that among the Chamus (a dialect of Maa, Eastern Nilotic) they do. The front of the tree is determined by analogy with the 'interactive-side': if a tree leans, the front is the side to which its trunk inclines; so its back is on the other side. The source for this figurative extension is that humans normally lean to the front, e.g. when bending over or walking. But of course, not all trees lean over, and the Chamus identify the front of a vertical tree as the side where the biggest branch or largest number of branches are located because this looks something like the extended limbs of the upright human. So, ascribing a front and back to a tree in the Chamus dialect of Maa is based on its likeness to a human being.

Because the 'interactive-side' of a human being contains the face and the front, people who are face to face normally have their respective fronts oriented towards one another. The characteristics of the canonical encounter between humans are transferred to the encounter between a human being and a nonhuman object; with the result that the viewer faces the front of the object, and it confronts him/her. In most languages, including

English, the vast majority of inanimate objects are assigned fronts, and consequently backs, on the basis of which side confronts the human viewer.

Although the physical configuration and neurosphysiological apparatus of human beings give us all a common starting-point for the way we experience the world, our perceptions of it are differentiated by individual cultures.

Assumption 9.5 The way in which speakers perceive the world and, as a result of their perceptions CONCEIVE of it, informs their linguistic categorization.[6]

(Compare A1.1.) The one alternative to imagining that the object which the human viewer faces, faces the human viewer in return, is to imagine it facing in the same direction such that the human viewer faces the object's back. This alternative is selected in Hausa (Chadic), Swahili (Bantu), and Maasai (Eastern Nilotic). Whether the human viewer is facing the front or the back of such an object, the same set of conditions is in operation:

Assumption 9.6 A front and back are ascribed to a static inanimate object depending which side of it the human viewer is facing.

It is a matter of cultural convention whether the viewer is facing the front of the object, or its back. In English, the human viewer faces the front of the object, consequently, the contingent back of an object is out of sight.

There are several kinds of ASSOCIATIVE *back*. All four senses applicable to humans, D9.6(S_H), D9.7(I'_H), D9.8(L'_H), and D9.9(C'_H), combine to give rise to D9.10($Æ_H$).

Definition 9.10($Æ_H$) The part or location named *back* or *rear* of a crowd of human beings facing in a particular direction is that part of or location in the crowd from about halfway through the crowd in the direction that the backs of its individual members are facing.

Cf. *the back of the audience, the back of the line/queue*. A further derivation from this is the noun *back* as in a football team, since it is someone who defends the back of the field. D9.10($Æ_H$) extends to inanimates: D9.10($Æ_N$).

Definition 9.10($Æ_N$)   PLACES in which a group of people have an institutionalized orientation to face in a certain direction have fronts and backs ascribed by meaning transfer from the location of associated human backs. The part or location named *back* is that part of the space normally occupied by the back or rear of the group that occupies it.

By association with the proper parts of the group of people for whom it exists, a theatre or classroom has a front and back derived by meaning transfer (Chapter 5). The front and the back of the stage in a theatre are associated with the actors facing the audience; thus the front of the stage is closest to the front of the audience that is facing it – which is analogous to the classic interactive configuration for individual human beings recognized in D9.9(C'_H).

The obvious similarity between the back of human crowd and the back of a herd of animals provides the condition for D9.10($Æ_H$) $\Rightarrow$ D9.10($Æ_A$). Since herds are wont to move, D9.10($Æ_A$) is also partly motivated by D9.8(L'_A).

> *Definition 9.10($Æ_A$)* The part or location named *back* or *rear* of a collection (herd, flock, caravan) of animals facing in a particular direction is that part of or location in the collection from about halfway through the collection in the direction the back-ends (rears) of its individual members are facing.

The spine and/or peripheral back of a human, D9.6(S_H) $\lor$ D9.8(L'_H), give rise to

> *Definition 9.10($Æ_N$)* A part or location of an inanimate object is named *the back* when it clothes, supports, or otherwise has the function of being in close contact with the human back to the effect that it is shaped or configured to accommodate the human back.

The back of my shirt, a chairback are principally associated with D9.6(S_H) but *the back of my trousers/skirt/shoes* are associated with the peripheral back, identified through D9.8(L'_H).

The denominal adjective (Chapter 4) *back* may also be counted associative. It is restricted to attributive position – *DET back N*, e.g. *a back door*. The corresponding predicative construction is explicitly locative – *DET N at/in the back [of* $_{NP[}α_1]$, e.g. *a door at the back of the house.*

> *Definition 9.11 $Back_{Adj}$*. An object β which is a part or location of an animate or inanimate object α is named *DET back* $_{N[}β_1$ if, and only if, it is either part of or else closely associated with the back of α, and there is at least one similar β to the front of α. It is *DET* $_{N[}β_1$ *at/in the back of* $_{NP[}α_1$ and *behind* some comparable β.

The front and the back of the mouth are instances of D9.7(I'_N) and from this we get *a back tooth, a back vowel*, etc. *A back door* would also derive via D9.7(I'_N) in some instances, and D9.10($Æ_N$) in others. A combination of all subcategories of the sense "opposite the leading edge", namely D9.8($L'_{H/A/N}$), give rise to adjectival *back* in expressions such as *backside, back end, back legs, back wheels* or *back seat* [of a car]. Associative human and inanimate backs, D9.10($Æ_{H/N}$), combine produce to *back marker*. The idiomatic *a back number* derives from the journey schema discussed below.

To this point we have seen that human back is the model for many other kinds of backs. D9.6(S_H) extends to the intrinsic backs of vertebrate animals and a few inanimates. D9.7(I'_H) extends to the intrinsic backs of animals of all kinds, and to those of many artifacts that are likely to remain in situ for long periods of time. D9.8(L'_H) has been extended to define the intrinsic back end of animals and the back (end) of inanimate objects capable of motion (vehicles). The default case, D9.9(C'_H), is extended to define the contingent back of static inanimate objects that have no intrinsic back. There are various kinds of associative *back*, based on a proper part relation, being located at or in (or otherwise in close association with) a back or back end of one kind or another; e.g. the back of a crowd of humans or herd of animals, the back of an institution holding an audience; something shaped to accommodate the human back. The network of semantic relations is illustrated in Fig. 9.1.

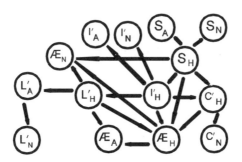

Figure 9.1 The radial semantic network of the noun *back*

Consider next the semantic relations for today's predicative and adverbial uses of *back*. These all derive from the JOURNEY SCHEMA, which is an elaboration of the one presupposed in D9.8(L$'_H$) "opposite to the leading edge of a human".

Assumption 9.7 B 🐾 🐾 P 🐾 D   A person H$_1$ moving forward

through place P going towards place D (destination) from place B (base) journeys through both space and time. Let P stand also for the time at which H$_1$ is at P, B for the (earlier) time at which H$_1$ was at B; then B ≺ P ≤ D. (≺ "precedes"; ≤ "precedes or is simultaneous with" – allowing that P is identical with D)

Taken together with D9.8(L$'_H$) this entails that H$_1$'s back is toward B. Although the schema is based on the human model, it readily allows for H$_1$ to be substituted by anything that moves or is moved from B through P to D. Hence:

Definition 9.12 JOURNEYING. Anything (person or thing) that moves itself or is moved forward through place P going towards place D from place B journeys through both space and time. Let P stand also for the time at which the person or thing is at P, B for the (earlier) time at which the person or thing was at B; then B ≺ P ≤ D. The back of the person or thing is towards B, the front is towards D.

In the journey schema, the human back is literally turned upon a place one leaves; hence the figure *turn one's back on*, and the wishful *I'll be glad to see the back of X*. D9.12 gives rise to the spatial and temporal locative predicates *back*.

Definition 9.13 Back_{Stative.Adv}. Relative to P, B together with the people and things at B are *back there* (e.g. *a mile back*) and *back then* (e.g. *an hour back*).

Many things that extend in time and/or space, such as life-spans, discussions, dramas, narratives, are treated metaphorically as journeys starting at B and ending at D, e.g. *back at the start, a few pages back, a back number*. Similarly for any durative or iterative event.

Definition 9.14 Back_{Dynamic.Adv}. Anything that moved itself or was moved from place B and has reached place P can be said to be *going* [*moving, travelling*, etc.] *back* or *moved* [*put*, etc.] *back* to B only if that person or thing is returning/returned to B.

Through *back_{Relational.Loc}*, D9.12 gives rise to the notion *behind*.[7]

Definition 9.15 Back_{Relational.Loc}. Anything (person or thing) that moves itself or is moved forward through place P going towards place D from place B journeys through both space and time. All points in space and time between P and B, and also B itself, are *behind* the person or thing journeying.

If β is coming from B and moving forward through P₁ going towards P₂ and D at the same time α on the same journey is going through P₂, then *β is behind α* (conversely, *α is in front of β*). Furthermore, if β started out from B at the same time as α, then *β has fallen behind α*. There are figurative expressions that play on the temporal aspect of journeying such as *fall behind* in one's work. Learning impairment is described using the same basis in expressions such as *β is behind the others, β is slow, β has been kept back a year, β is held back by his disability, β is backward*. A *backwater* is a backward place. The 'back' in *stand back* or *hold/keep back*, literally "not move forward, prevent from moving forward, hinder", derives from the same source.

D9.12 provides the basis for the motional verb *back*.

Definition 9.16 Back_{Motional.V}. Anything that moved itself or was moved from place B and has reached place P can be said to *back away/off* from P, or *back (up)* from P to B only if that person or thing *goes* [*runs*, etc.] *backwards* with its back as the leading edge when moving from P.

Back is defined in relation to the front, which in humans is the 'interactive-side'. *In front of* is also defined in relation to the front, as are its converses *behind* and *at the back of* or *in back of*. The dependence of *back* on the front is not restricted to the noun; the motional verb *back* is also a marked term. As we saw in Chapter 6, its converses are not *front* or *forward*, but the basic verbs *go* and *move*, whose Quantity2 implicatures are "go/move forward". Hence a synonym for *back_{Motional.V}* is the marked *go/move back(ward)*. Vehicles *back (up)* "move in reverse", such that their back end is the leading edge. People and animals *back off, back away* and *back down*, which in the their literal uses mean "retreat backwards", again making the back a leading edge. *Backwards* means "in the direction the back points". The 'back' in *backslang* and in *He's written it backwards* appear to be abstractions from the notion of the back end functioning as a leading edge. The real world allows us to go back in space but not time; we can only go back in time in an imagined world, or when using the expression figuratively to recount past history. $Back_{Motional.V}$ is also metaphorically extended to moving in the opposite direction from a position once held in discussion or argument.

The expression *back (someone) (up)* meaning "give support to" arises directly from D9.12 and D9.15, and is probably boosted by the fact that, traditionally, humans and certain domestic animals carry heavy loads on their backs. Leader α goes forward with his/ her supporters (β and everyone) following; if β follows, β *is at* α*'s back*.

> *Definition 9.17* $Back_{Support.V}$. β backs α if β is supporting α in some endeavour and also β is typically located behind α in a formal parade.

Here *back* is a non-motional act. Together with D9.6(S_H), D9.17 has given rise to *back* in the sense of "create a back for" as in *back the curtains*. The *backing group* for a singer is named for their supporting function, but is doubtless strengthened by the fact that they typically stand behind the virtuoso (D9.13, D9.15). Bleaching (fading) of the concrete locational implication gives rise to *back up*, where there is no requirement that β is physically placed behind α. Many a dictator has *military backup* to maintain power. A notion of support in the sense almost of "insurance, subsidiary" is abstracted in the expression *back-up file* (in computing) and perhaps *backchannel* in engineering. And then there are people who commit money in support of someone or something – *financial backers*; the effector nominal (Chapter 4) is very rarely used for other kinds of supporters. A related notion of committing money in support of something is to *back it* by making a wager.

That completes this very detailed survey of the meanings of the English words *back*. There are two reasons for not using the formal apparatus of Chapters 6–7 in the definitions: (1) it would have taken too much space to set up; (2) it would distract from the purpose of this chapter – which is to focus on the perceptual and cognitive motivations for meanings. We have seen that semantic extensions of English *back* are human-centred. This is just one piece of evidence for a powerful image of 'the body in the mind' (Johnson 1987) and of its effects upon language. The senses of *back* developed from the name for a human body-part, using as a foundation the model of the prototypical upright human being engaged in typical human activities such as walking or interacting with fellow human beings and other things in the environment. Essentially, "back" is where the action and interaction isn't – because it is the intrinsic part, location, or direction directly opposite where the action and interaction goes on. Figure 9.2 summarizes the semantic-syntactic network of *back*.

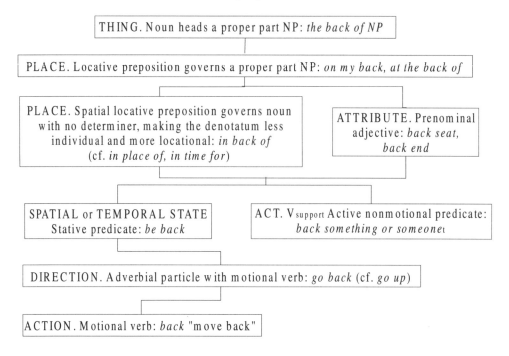

THING. Noun heads a proper part NP: *the back of NP*

PLACE. Locative preposition governs a proper part NP: *on my back, at the back of*

PLACE. Spatial locative preposition governs noun with no determiner, making the denotatum less individual and more locational: *in back of* (cf. *in place of, in time for*)

ATTRIBUTE. Prenominal adjective: *back seat, back end*

SPATIAL or TEMPORAL STATE Stative predicate: *be back*

ACT. V_support Active nonmotional predicate: *back something or someone*ι

DIRECTION. Adverbial particle with motional verb: *go back* (cf. *go up*)

ACTION. Motional verb: *back* "move back"

Figure 9.2 The semantic-syntactic network of the words *back*

Exercises

9.2.1 What is the relationship between these measurements and body-parts: *inch, hand, foot, yard, fathom, mile*?

9.2.2 (a) Why do you think *the back of the hand* and *the back of the arm* are on opposite sides of the same limb?
       (b) Where is the back of a book in relation to its front?

9.2.3 By which criteria do we assign backs to the following?
       (a) a frisbee   (b) a curtain   (c) a sea-urchin   (d) a leaf   (e) a picture-postcard

9.2.4 Imagine a house with a garden/yard in front of it and another garden/yard behind it. Where is the back of each of these gardens/yards? Why?

9.2.5 Why turn to speak to someone behind you? Why is it more important to turn your head towards an interlocutor than your legs?

9.2.6 (a) Why is it rude to turn your back on someone?   (b) When is it not rude to do so?

9.2.7 Compare (a–c).   (a) back someone up   (b) back up to someone   (c) front up to someone

9.3   Colours and Vantage Theory

		R				YR				Y				GY				G				BG				B				BP				P				RP		
0	A	1	2	3	4	5	6	7	8	9	0	1	2	3	4	5	6	7	8	9	0	1	2	3	4	5	6	7	8	9	0	1	2	3	4	5	6	7	8	9	0	9.5
0	B	2	2	2	2	2	2	2	2	4	6	6	6	6	2	2	2	2	2	2	2	2	2	2	2	2	2	2	2	2	2	2	2	2	2	2	2	9.0
0	C	6	6	6	6	6	6	6	8	14	16	16	14	12	12	12	4	10	8	8	6	6	6	6	4	4	4	4	4	4	6	6	4	4	4	4	6	6	6	6	6	6	8.0
0	D	8	8	10	10	10	14	14	14	12	12	22	12	12	6	10	10	10	8	8	8	8	6	6	6	6	6	8	8	8	6	6	6	6	8	8	10	10	8	8	7.0
0	E	12	12	12	14	16	12	12	12	10	10	10	10	10	8	12	12	10	10	10	10	8	8	8	8	8	8	8	8	10	10	10	8	8	8	8	10	10	10	10	12	12	6.0
0	F	14	14	14	16	14	12	10	10	8	8	8	8	8	10	10	12	12	10	10	10	10	8	8	8	8	8	8	10	12	12	10	10	10	10	10	12	12	12	14	14	5.0
0	G	14	14	14	14	10	8	8	6	6	6	6	6	6	12	8	8	10	10	10	10	8	8	8	6	6	8	8	10	10	12	12	10	10	10	10	12	12	12	12	14	4.0
0	H	10	10	12	10	8	6	6	6	4	4	4	4	4	10	6	6	8	8	10	8	6	6	6	6	6	6	6	8	10	10	12	10	10	10	10	10	10	10	10	3.0
0	I	8	8	8	6	4	4	4	2	2	2	2	2	2	4	4	4	6	6	6	4	4	4	4	4	4	6	6	6	8	10	8	8	8	6	6	8	8	8	8	2.0
0	K	2.5	5	7.5	10		5		10		5		10		5		10		5		10		5		10		5		10		5		10		5		10		5		10	0.5

Key: R=red, Y=yellow, G=green, B=blue, P=purple

Figure 9.3 Black and white chart of the 330 Chip Munsell colour array used in the World Color Survey. Boxed numbers indicate degree of saturation from 0–16. Left column of unsaturated achromatics from white (top) through eight greys to black. Cf. Maclaury 1997:11

In Chapter 8 basic colour terms were described in terms of set theory: *warm-light* = **white'∪red'∪yellow'**, *cool-dark* = **green'∪blue'∪black'**, *pink* = **red'∩white'**, *orange* = **red'∩yellow'**. This accurately describes the relationships of the colours named; but it does not explain what people do with colour terms. For example, in experiments on colour FOCUS, subjects are asked to identify the best example for a given colour term (e.g. in Fig 9.3, English *red* is around G1, *yellow* C10, *green* F17, etc.). With composite colours such as *grue* (**green'∪blue'**), subjects may locate the focus in green, or in blue, or in both – it is largely dependent on which language they speak, though there is also some individual variation. Set theory has no explanation to offer, but MacLaury 1997 offers a cognitive solution in terms of Vantage Theory.

Definition 9.18 VANTAGE THEORY is a theory of categorization in terms of point of view (vantage). Vantage Theory holds that categorization reflects human needs and motives. It explains how people construct categories by analogy to the way they form points of view in space-time, how categories are organized, how they divide, and the relations between them.

Vantage Theory (but not set theory) also offers an explanation for the evolution of colour terms from composites (merges) to overlaps. For English speakers, the colour orange is an overlap **red'∩yellow'** that cannot properly be named by either *red* or *yellow* because colour TERMS do not overlap (there is an explanation for the discrepancy at the end of this section). *Orange* ≠ *red∩yellow* because *orange, red,* and *yellow* are contraries.

Vantage Theory explains the cognitive dynamics of colour naming and mapping. In the World Color Survey (of which MacLaury's research is a counterpart) the researcher takes 330 Munsell colour chips and asks a language consultant to do three things.[8]

(a)   In a randomly ordered array, to name the colour of each chip.
(b)   In an ordered array (Fig. 9.3), to identify the focus for each colour term. And
(c)   Place a rice grain on every chip a name can apply to; then to repeat the process on the remaining chips until it is impossible to do any more. The result is a ranked sequence of mappings.

Despite the fact that all human beings (and other primates; cf. Maffi and Hardin 1997:358f) with normal sight experience the same sensory colour data, Berlin and Kay (1969) established that languages reveal an evolutionary sequence from two to eleven basic colour terms with only minor cross-language variations (Tables 8.1–3). MacLaury 1997:104 explains the evolution in terms of gradual change that 'consists of rearranging cognitive relations among pre-existing terms and pre-existing categories'. This is to be expected in a closed semantic field such as colour and is much like Saussure's notion of differential value (D8.5). For MacLaury: 'Cognition consists of the ways in which people modify their perceptions by means of selective emphasis [on similarity and/or difference]' (1997:93). The selective emphasis is the adoption of a vantage.

Colour-category evolution seems to be induced by increased societal complexity in which novelty and difference come to be more highly valued than similarity. Nevertheless, discrimination is physiologically constrained. There is a physiological basis for the fact that the starting-point for colour naming is the contrast between bright and dark, not between different hues. Attention to brightness precedes attention to hue because brightness is perceived before hue in real time: neural channels conveying luminance respond faster than those conveying hue sensations (Peralta 1980, MacLaury 1997:44, 470f). The photoreceptors in the eye are rods and cones. There are three types of cones: short, medium, and long. Discrimination between blue and green depends mainly on change in excitation of short cones. Short cones are sparse, slow, and peripherally distributed in the retina; they are therefore at a disadvantage in relaying information to the visual cortex. Colour discrimination that depends on long and medium cone outputs, such as that between red and yellow, yellow and green, or red and blue is more acute. So, warm hues come to be dissimilated before the cool hues (MacLaury 1997:92).

A colour category never consists of equal emphasis on brightness and hue, but all or greater attention to only one of these. People using only two basic colour terms do respond to the sensation of hue but nevertheless ATTEND TO the similarities between the components of **white′**∪**red′**∪**yellow′** or **green′**∪**blue′**∪**black′** more than their differences.

Assumption 9.8 EMPHASIS ON SIMILARITY will favour composite colours because attention to similarity contracts cognitive distance between stimuli. EMPHASIS ON DIFFERENCE (distinctiveness) protracts cognitive distance between stimuli so that it favours individual hues and the lexical partitioning of categories.

According to MacLaury, a colour category is fashioned by analogy to physical experience as though it were one or more points of view on a spatial terrain, referred to as 'space-motion coordinates'. Reminiscent of gestalt theory (Chapter 10) is the claim that a category is the sum of its coordinates, plus their arrangement into one or more vantages by selective emphasis. 'The maker of the category, in effect, names the ways he constructs it rather than the set of its components as detached from himself' (1997:153). The categorizer's perspectives can be illustrated by an ornithologist 'zooming in' to see a mallard among the ducks on a lake, or alternatively 'zooming out' to see the assembled mallards, widgeon, and pintails as ducks. On both views there is a pair of coordinates which we can loosely differentiate as 'species' and 'genus'. What MacLaury refers to as the 'fixed coordinate' (the one fixed upon by the viewer as the ground for reference) is the one zoomed to. The other he calls a 'mobile coordinate'. A vantage is a point of view constructed in reference to coordinates. For instance, in the warm category (**red′∪yellow′**), when the two colour mappings are somewhat different, there is a single vantage: **red′** (R) dominates at the primary level of concentration – level 1 in Fig. 9.4. Attention is on similarity, S in Fig. 9.4, as the mobile coordinate. At level 2 concentration, attention to the mobile coordinate Y (**yellow′**) notes its similarity to R. At level 3 there is attention to D, the difference of fixed coordinate Y from R.

CONCENTRATION		COORDINATES		BEHAVIOUR
Zoom_in		**Fixed**	**Mobile**	**Focus and range**
↓	Level 1	R	S	Red focus, breadth of range
↓			✓	
↓	Level 2	S	Y	Warm range
↓			✓	
	Level 3	Y	D	Margin of range
	Synopsis:	Y is more similar to R than Y is different		

Key: R=red, S=similarity, Y=yellow D=difference.
Figure 9.4 Red focus in the warm composite category; cf. MacLaury 1997:145

Assumption 9.9 A person concentrates on only ONE RELATION AT A TIME between fixed and mobile coordinates.

A mobile coordinate is treated as fixed by assuming that it is background information, and a new mobile coordinate is related to it. Every fixed coordinate is thereby contextualized. Concentration on similarity or difference is relevant to the acceptance or cancellation of quantity implicatures such as that a bird is something that can fly (Chapter 6, Chapter 8,1). If the bird in question is a parrot, then it is similar to the typical bird because it can fly. If the bird is an emu, it is different from the typical bird because it cannot fly and the Quantity2 implicature on *bird* must be cancelled.

Definition 9.19 When two colour terms are COEXTENSIVE, there is about equal emphasis on their similarity and difference. They typically overlap by >50% when mapped. The mapping of each covers the focus of the other.

Usually, one of the coextensive terms will dominate. In Fig. 9.5, *k'an* "yellow" is mapped over a greater area than *ćah* "red" by a speaker of Tzeltal, whose second mapping of *ćah* is shown as grey not black. The crosses mark foci. *K'an* dominates; *ćah* is recessive.

> *Definition 9.20* The DOMINANT term is used in naming more individual chips
> and selecting more of the array during mapping. It is more centrally focused
> than the RECESSIVE term; and the mapping steps are larger.

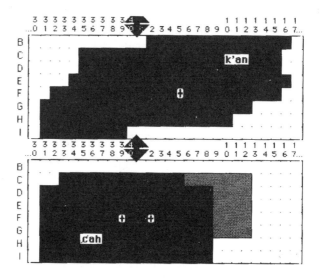

Figure 9.5 Mapping of *k'an* and *ćah* by a Tzeltal woman,
aged 85, from MacLaury 1997:132

The colour categorization in Fig. 9.5 is modelled in Fig. 9.6. *K'an* is dominant and *ćah* is similar to *k'an*, hence *k'an→S→ćah* in the fixed column of the dominant vantage. *Ćah* is only distinctive as a fixed coordinate at the third level of concentration; cf. Fig. 9.4. In short, *ćah* is more similar to *k'an* than different. The recessive range focuses on the distinctiveness of *ćah* at level 1. *K'an* is recognized as distinct from *ćah* at level 2 but similar to *k'an* at level 3. So the fixed coordinate of the recessive vantage has *ćah→D→k'an* as more attention is paid to difference: *k'an* is more different from *ćah* than it is similar. Fig. 9.6 (p. 305) shows that a person keeps in mind several levels of coordinates while concentrating on no more than two coordinates at a time.

> *Assumption 9.10* A dominant vantage has broad central focus, even distribution
> in mapping, and frequent naming. The viewer zooms in from naive attention to
> similarity to analysis. A recessive vantage is always cognizant of the dominant
> vantage. It has narrow marginal focus, skewed mapping, sparse naming. The
> viewer zooms in from analysis to synthesis and, probably, to abstract
> formulation.

Vantages		Dominant		Recessive	
Zoom_in		Fixed	Mobile	Fixed	Mobile
↓	Level 1	k'an	S	ćah	D
↓		✓		✓	
↓	Level 2	S	ćah	D	k'an
↓		✓		✓	
	Level 3	ćah	D	k'an	S

Figure 9.6 Vantages in the mappings in Fig. 9.5.

People who make a single colour focus are maximally subjective, unaware of any other vantage. People with two foci are aware of more than one vantage and able to categorize from a reflective standpoint. People with three foci – such as linguists – must view the language from the external viewpoint of another language.

Speakers of the same language, even within the same generation and from a small community, may differ in the number of basic colour terms they manifest (MacLaury 1997:452). Furthermore, with cool composite colours there is much evidence of variation in foci and individuals cancelling a focus in one hue and locating it in another. 'In some cool categories, the naming range of a single term may be skewed toward one hue and its mapping skewed toward the other. The focus may land anywhere' (p. 455). This raises a serious question about how people can (apparently) succeed in communicating when talking about colour (and much else besides). MacLaury's answer is that a particular colour term denotes the dominant or recessive range – a cognitive structure – rather than wavelengths of light reflected by a particular set of chips in the colour map. The catch is that the cognitive structure itself – assuming it is a refined version of structures represented in Fig. 9.4 and Fig. 9.6 – makes reference to colour, i.e. to reflected wavelengths of light. In short, Speaker has a mind's-eye view of the typical denotatum (or range of denotata).

> *Assumption 9.11* Given common ground (knowing the language and context of utterance), understanding what Speaker says is partly by means of Hearer analysing what was actually said and comparing this with what s/he supposes could be said.

This is a heuristic process of analysis by synthesis, not so different from coming to terms with the phonological system of an unfamiliar speaker, particularly one with a marked regional accent that has to be accommodated on the fly.

This section has given a Vantage Theory account of the use and development of colour terms. There is much more to say about colour perception and the semantics of colour terms.[9] The point to draw from this short essay is that the meanings of colour terms are based upon the vantage or viewpoint of selective emphasis adopted by the human being responding to the sensory data that present themselves to her or him. However, the individual's perception can only be communicated to others by adapting their private perceptions to the conventional perceptions publically current in their speech community.

Although Vantage Theory explains the use and development of colour terms, it tells nothing about the semantic specification of a term such as English *green*. Unlike lampposts, lettuces, and democracy, colour is perceptible ONLY through vision. The sound waves of music are tangible to the profoundly deaf, but a congenitally blind person cannot experience colour at all. They will be told about it, of course, and have transferred experiences such as that *red* is characteristic of something very hot, *green* is the texture of vegetation. What a person blind from birth understands by a colour term such as *green* is conceptual and analogical, not experiential. Sighted human beings experience colour as light waves reflected from things: *red* is the colour of fresh blood (seen in daylight), *green* is the colour of live vegetation (seen in daylight). Wierzbicka 1992b and Goddard 1998:128ff restrict the semantics of colour listemes to such *colour-of* descriptions, but this is only half the story. If you tell a blind person *A banana is yellow* they will know this colour-of relation without ever knowing what *yellow* means, because they can't know what yellow is. There is neuropsychological evidence for what Davidoff 1997 calls an 'internal colour space' separate from 'object-colour knowledge'. The 'internal colour space' contains the colour yellow, the colour of the banana is part of one's 'object-colour knowledge'. I therefore suggest that colours be defined in terms of the inclusive disjunct in D9.21.

Definition 9.21 For every x that is labelled *green*:
[colour x reflects light in the range 470–580 nanometres, and focally around 512 nm] ∨
[colour-of there is some y such that, if y is a living leaf then, in daylight, the wavelengths of light reflected from x (i.e. the colour of x) is approximately identical with the wavelengths of light reflected from y]

The disjunction in D9.21 suggests one explanation for the fact that **orange′= red′∩yellow′** (verified by wavelengths and colour charts) but the terms *orange, red,* and *yellow* are contraries. The proposition **orange′= red′∩yellow′** is true for the internal colour space: orange is reflected light in the range 590–610 nanometres: both yellow and red stretch their periphery through this range. However, as object-colour knowledge, each of orange, red, and yellow is distinctive: the citrus fruit orange is not the colour of blood, nor the colour of a banana.

Exercises

9.3.1 Looking at Figs 9.5–6, how might you add to the formula: ∃x[**colour_chip′**(x) ∧ (**ȼah′**(x) ...)]?

9.3.2 In Chapter 8 the two basic colour terms of Dani, *laambu* and *mili* were discussed. In the Figure below (MacLaury 1997:50), the foci of these colours are located squarely in red and blue respectively. Discuss this.

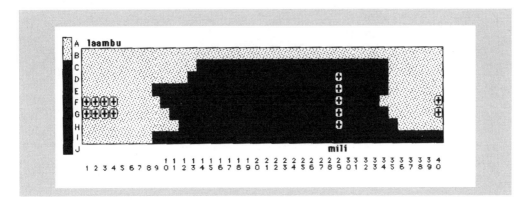

9.4 The semantics of classifiers

In many unrelated and geographically separated languages from Africa, the Americas, Asia, Australia, and Oceania, there are certain syntactic environments that require a 'classifier' to be used.

Definition 9.22 A CLASSIFIER is a morpheme or lexeme denoting perceived or imputed characteristics of the denotatum of the associated noun, thereby classifying the referent according to one or more of eight categories – which often overlap.[10]

material make-up	e.g. human(-like), animate, female, tree(-like)
function	e.g. piercing, cutting, or writing instruments; for eating, drinking
shape	e.g. long (saliently one-dimensional), flat, round
consistency	e.g. rigid, flexible, mass
size	including diminutives and augmentives
location	for inherently locative entities such as towns
arrangement	e.g. a row of, a coil of, a heap of
quanta	e.g. head of cattle, packet of cigarettes

Table 9.1 The eight categories of classification in the world's languages

There are several kinds of classifier; among the commonest are the so-called NUMERAL CLASSIFIERS. For example, Thai (Tai) uses classifiers in expressions of quantity (1–4), demonstrative and anaphoric expressions (5–7); classifiers are in bold type. (Tones: à = low, á = high, ǎ = rising, a = neutral.)

1 *bùri•*   *sɔ̌•ŋ*   **muan**
   cigarette two   rolled-up.thing
   "two cigarettes"

2   *bùri•   sɔ̌•ŋ   sɔ•ŋ*
    cigarette two   pack(et)
    "two pack(et)s of cigarettes"

3   *bùri•   sɔ̌•ŋ   lŏ•*
    cigarette two   dozen
    "two dozen cigarettes"

4   *mǎ•   sì•   tua*
    dog   four   body
    "four dogs"

5   *mǎ•   tua   nán*
    dog   body   that
    "that dog"

6   *tua nán*
    "that" [animal, coat, trousers, table]

7   *sì• tua*
    "four (of them)" [animals, coats, pairs of trousers, tables]

The usefulness of classifiers has been well illustrated by Becker, who presents the data in Table 9.2.

"river"	"one"	CL	TRANSLATION
miyiʔ	tə	yaʔ	"river one place" (e.g. destination for picnic)
miyiʔ	tə	tan	"river one line" (e.g. on a map)
miyiʔ	tə	hmwa	"river one section" (e.g. fishing area)
miyiʔ	tə	'sin	"river one distant arc" (e.g. path to sea)
miyiʔ	tə	θwɛ	"river one connexion" (e.g. tying two villages)
miyiʔ	tə	'pa	"river one sacred object" (e.g. in myth)
miyiʔ	tə	khu'	"river one conceptual unit" (e.g. in a discussion of rivers in general)
miyiʔ	tə	miyiʔ	"river one river" (default)

Table 9.2 Exploitation of Burmese classifiers, after Becker 1975:113

RELATIONAL classifiers occur in possessive constructions. Examples 8–10 are from Kosraean (Micronesian, Lichtenberk 1983:156).

8 *sikutuhr* **okuh**-*k*
   scooter   vehicle-my
   "my scooter"

9 *mos*   **suhnuh**-*k*
   breadfruit plant-my
   "my breadfruit tree"

10 *lohm* **sih**-*k*
   house land-my
   "my house"

Classifiers occur in the PREDICATES of some languages, e.g. Dogrib (Athapaskan, Davidson, Elford, and Hoijer 1963):

11 *let'e*   *niyeh*-**tši**
   bread I.pick.up-PERF.flat.flexible.entity
   "I pick up a slice of bread"

12 *let'e*   *niyeh*- **ʔa**
   bread I.pick.up-PERF.round.entity
   "I pick up a loaf of bread"

Also in Caddo (Caddoan), 13–14, and Cayuga (N. Iroquoian), 15, (Mithun 1986):

13 *Kapì:* **kan**-*čâ:ni'ah*
   coffee liquid-buy.**P**
   "He bought (liquid) coffee"

14 *Kapì:* **dân:**-*čâ:ni'ah*
   coffee powder-buy.**P**
   "He bought (ground) coffee"

15 *Kéi* *niwak*-**wiy**-*áę'*
   four so.I-children-have
   "I have four children"

The commonest classifiers are NOUN CLASSES (Aikhenvald 2000). These include GENDERS in Indo-European languages (Corbett 1991) and are characterized by being bound morphemes and the fact that every noun falls into a noun class. (This distinguishes them from NOUN CLASSIFIERS which are usually free morphemes and a noun may occur with none or with more than one.) And in some languages, notably Bantu languages, noun classes are marked by CONCORDIAL CLASSIFIERS, e.g. the Swahili *vi*- (class 8) which is the plural classifer for artifacts (mostly):

16 *Vi-su*   *vi-dogo* *vi-wili* *hi-vi*   *amba-vy-o* *nili-vi-nunua* *ni* *vi-kali*   *sana*

   vi-knife *vi*-small *vi*-two this-*vi* which-*vi*   1.S.**P**-*vi*-buy be *vi*-sharp very

   "These two small knives which I bought are very sharp"

In Luganda the noun stem -*ganda* is classifed by the prefix *mu*- to refer to one person, *ba*- to refer to more than one person (hence, in English, we speak of the Baganda), the prefix *bu*- marks reference to the country of the Baganda, and *ki-ganda* denotes the culture of the Baganda.

   Other kinds of classifiers are DEICTIC CLASSIFIERS which typically identify the spatial location and or visibility of a referent and LOCATIVE CLASSIFIERS which are have been found only in some South American languages and which identify the nature of a particular location (what Allan 1977 called 'locative classifiers' would now be called 'deictic classifiers').

   It seems likely that the original criterion for noun classification was material, extended from identical entities (such as trees) to similar entities (such as things made of wood, or tall things), weakening the material connection and strengthening those of shape, consistency, and size implicit in the most typical members of the class. Gandour et al. 1985 found that Thai aphasics lost configurational classifiers more frequently than material classifiers, suggesting that the latter are more basic. In confirmation, shape categories are often given labels based on material names such as 'stick-like', 'rope-like', 'fabric-like', 'plank-like', 'stone-like', 'bush-like', 'seed-like'.

> The Caddo classifier for small round objects, *ič'ah-*, is also the noun stem for 'eye'. The Mundurukú classifier for circular or spherical objects, a^2, is the noun for 'head'. That for long, rigid, cylindrical objects, ba^4, is the noun for 'arm'. That for long, flexible cylindrical objects is bu^2. the noun for 'finger'.   (Mithun 1986:390)

If we focus on the prototype rather than on the category as a whole, a 'fabric-like' classifier, for instance, can be judged a material classifier ranging over fabric and other flat flexible entities of real or imputed similarity to it. But it seems preferable to treat such a classifier as identifying things with a saliently two-dimensional shape and a flexible consistency. There is strong evidence of the semantic basis for classification from the fact that native speakers of the language have the ability to readily classify new objects and this is generally consistent among speakers. This ability has been witnessed for such diverse languages as Burmese (Sino-Tibetan, Burling 1965:249), Dyirbal (Australian, Dixon 1968:199f), Fula (Niger-Congo, Arnott 1967:54f), and Navajo (Athapaskan, Ervin and Landar 1963:51). In the simplest case, a noun is classified on the basis of some physical or metaphysical characteristic shared by its referents. Furthermore, when children are learning the language they tend to make mistakes that reveal they have focused on some characteristic that just happens not to be the conventional determinant for classification; cf. Carpenter 1991. Instead of using *muan* for classifying cigarettes, Gandour et al. (1984) report the use of *thɛŋ* "one-dimensional rigid entity" and *lɔɔ̀d* "tubular entity". There are many instances of such perception based misclassifications.

   The eight categories of classification – material make-up, function, shape, consistency, size, location, arrangement, quanta – range over all the predictable bases for classification except colour – which is surprising because in experimental situations people from many cultural backgrounds will group objects according to colour. There are three reasons for not using colour as a systematic category of classification. First, colour varies with the ambient lighting, and in the dark is unreliable as an identifying characteristic. Second, a shapeless blotch of colour does not systematically identify anything; line drawings or black and white photos do identify things. Last, colour is perceived through only one mode – sight – whereas all other categories of classification are perceivable through more than one. Thus there are no classifiers solely reliant on the faculties of smell, taste, or hearing either.

The fact that all languages use only up to the same eight categories of classification is not surprising if one takes the view that human perceptions are generally similar and that they stimulate a cognitive classification of the world which is reflected in the meanings of language expressions. But it is a view at variance with a strong interpretation of the SAPIR–WHORF HYPOTHESIS expressed in the following quotations:

> The fact of the matter is that the 'real world' is to a large extent unconsciously built up on the language habits of the group. No two languages are ever sufficiently similar to be considered as representing the same social reality. The worlds in which different societies live are distinct worlds, not merely the same worlds with different labels attached.
>
> (Sapir 1956:69)

> The "linguistic relativity principle" [...] means, in informal terms, that users of markedly different grammars are pointed by the grammars toward different types of observations and different evaluations of externally similar acts of observation, and hence are not equivalent as observers but must arrive at somewhat different views of the world.   (Whorf 1956:221)

The review of colour terms in §9.3 suggests that people name colours according to the conventions of their language. But, at the same time, all human beings see all the hues in the Munsell array depicted in Fig. 9.3. A strong version of the Sapir–Whorf hypothesis is therefore untenable.

Definition 9.23 A WEAK VERSION OF THE SAPIR–WHORF HYPOTHESIS is that a language directs its speakers towards certain aspects of perceived phenomena – but, because perception is independent of language, other aspects of phenomena can be commented upon, if desired, by circumlocution, or by the novel use of a language expression.[11]

Speaker may use an unusual classification (ranking on a scale between dead metaphor and innovation) to get some particular point across; e.g. tall people can be classified by the "long" classifier instead of the "people" classifier in some Bantu languages, in Japanese, and in the Mayan language Yucatec.

Assumption 9.12 The basis for classification is the characteristic perceived or believed to be salient in the referent.

Cognitive linguistics holds that language categories are not randomly created in a completely arbitrary fashion, but reflect human perceptions and conceptions about the things humans use language to refer to. Although the form of a root listeme is constrained by the phonological system of the language, the form is arbitrary with respect to what the listeme denotes (despite the evidence of sound symbolism in §4.4). In contrast,

> **Assumption 9.13** The scope of a listeme's denotation is motivated, and essentially determined, by human perception.

Examples of possible listemes are:

(a)   English *put up with*.
(b)   The Maasai verb *abol* "to hold a cow/bull by the mouth".
(c)   The Chinook word *ania'lot* meaning "I give him to her" (Boas 1911).

Impossible in any language would be a verb **mimp* meaning "marry a woman allergic to": there can be no sentence *I mimped cats* with the meaning "I married a woman allergic to cats" (cf. McCawley 1971).

> **Assumption 9.14** The partial noun phrase *a woman allergic to*, consisting of a head NP and part of its restrictive relative clause, is AN INCOMPLETE NOTION – which is not the case with any normal NP.

In many languages there is a verb with the meaning "marry a woman, take a wife" (e.g. Maasai *ayam*). In theory, there could be a language which has a verb meaning "marry a woman who is rich" because this is a complete notion. If **zamp* were to mean "marry a woman allergic to cats", then *I zamped* would be acceptable, and *I zamped cats* would be a tautology (D2.12) similar to *I bought it for money*.

The fact that the scope of a lexeme's denotation is motivated explains why there is no possibility of a naturally occurring noun *voogs* denoting the membership of the set

{your-eye, the-Vatican, *b*, a-night-with-Brigitte-Bardot, $\sqrt{2}$}

No such motley collection, lacking any common physical or functional or even metaphysical attribute, would be named by a root listeme in any language. Category names such as *bird* serve to differentiate a class of entities with one or more common or closely related attributes (a family resemblance or semantic chain) from some other class of entities such as bats. However, categories like rugs and carpets, or cups and mugs, or shrubs, bushes, and small trees seem to merge gradually one into another rather than starkly abut one another; so that, although the prototypical exemplars of each category are clearly different, the boundary between e.g. a small carpet and a large rug is fuzzy. Prototype semantics (Chapter 10) was developed to investigate these matters.

> **Assumption 9.15** Co-classification is rational and motivated.

The title *Women, Fire, and Dangerous Things* (Lakoff 1987) is a description of the *balan* classifier in the Australian language Dyirbal. There are four noun classifers in Dyirbal; cf. Dixon 1972, 1982:[3]

I.	*Bayi*:	bats, some birds, boomerangs, most fishes, hunting spears, most insects, kangaroos, men, the moon, possums, rainbows, most snakes, storms ...
II.	*Balan*:	bandicoots, most birds, crickets, dogs, echidna, fighting implements (shields, spears, etc.) and the fighting ground, anything to do with fire, fireflies, some fishes, the hairy mary grub, platypuses, scorpions, some snakes, stars, the sun, some trees, anything to do with water, women ...
III.	*Balam*:	cake, cigarettes, all edible fruit and the plants that bear them, ferns, honey, tubers, wine.
IV.	*Bala*:	bees, parts of the body, grass, language and noises, meat, mud, some spears, stones, most trees, yamsticks, the wind ...

Lakoff suggests that class IV is a default, and the other three classes are built around prototypical members as follows:

I.	*Bayi*:	human males
II.	*Balan*:	human females
III.	*Balam*:	edible plants
IV.	*Bala*:	everything else

(Lakoff 1987:99)

Animals are mostly in class I. But most birds are in class II because they embody the spirits of dead human females; birds that are mythical males go into class I. Crickets are mythically 'old ladies', so they go in class II. Storms and the rainbow are mythical men, and therefore in class I. The moon is husband to the sun, so the moon is in class I and the sun in class II. Stars, lightning, and fire are in class II, presumably through association with the sun. Stinging and biting creatures (e.g. the hairy mary grub, scorpion, stonefish, platypus, and echidna) and plants (e.g. stinging nettle vine) that cause pain similar to a burn are in class II, presumably chained to fire. Fighting implements are in class II, perhaps because they are chained to the natural things that sting and bite. Because edible fish are in class I, so is fishing gear; boomerangs are in class I because they are used by class I men in hunting the animals in class I. Fruit trees are in class III, but their wood is in class IV, as are non-edible trees and plants. Somewhat unexpectedly, water is in class II, for which Lakoff offers not even a tentative hypothesis. Water is the antithesis of fire, and not the kind of dangerous thing that bites or stings. Is it that flooding can be almost as devastating as wildfire? Is it because it is life-giving like a mother's milk? Or associated with the

---

3. Dixon would not call these classifiers, but noun class markers. Dixon 1986 claims that classifiers are always lexemes, whereas noun class markers define a 'a closed grammatical system, on a par with number and case and tense' (p.106). The evidence doesn't support this claim. But in any case, it is a question for morphologists and is not relevant to the semantics of noun classification that we are pursuing in this chapter.

'breaking of the waters' (amniotic fluid) as a woman gives birth? Speculations along such lines need to be confirmed by myth before we can accept them. We need to be mindful of misinterpreting. For instance, Lakoff suggests that the platypus and echidna are in class II because they are 'unusual' animals. They may be unusual for an American, but there is no reason to suppose that the Dyirbal think that way. It is more likely the monotremes are in class II because of their poisonous spurs. Lakoff also suggests that the hawk is in class I because it is unusual as a bird; but a more positive reason is that the hawk is a (respected) hunter and therefore in class I along with men.

The importance of Lakoff's analysis is that it shows the rational basis for what at first sight seems a fairly random classification of unlike phenomena into the available noun classes of Dyirbal. Although the classification of objects cannot be accurately predicted, some of the constraints on classification can be identified. Once the core distinctions have become established according to the three prototypes and the default (human male vs human female vs edible plants vs other) the three prototypes begin to attract additional members to the class. It is notable that class III failed to do this, and in young people's Dyirbal its members have been subsumed to class IV (Lakoff 1987:98, Schmidt 1985), which justifies Lakoff's claim that the basic contrast is between the robust classes I and II. The salience of the distinction between human males and females has linguistic effects in almost every language. Class I either extends to animates in general, or it attracts things associated with men's business such as hunting and fishing – unless there are beliefs or myths to counter the attraction. Class II encompasses mythical as well as actual females, including female animals. Why it encompasses water is mysterious; but Lakoff's account of the semantic extension chain is a convincing explanation for the inclusion of dangerous things. Another possibility, revealed in a quote from a 33-year-old Dyirbal man (Lakoff 1987:101), is that many of the things in class II, including women, are a potential hazard for the male human prototype for class I. What is absolutely clear is that there is no single property that is uncontrovertibly common to all members of class II.

In this section we have seen that in many languages there are certain syntactic environments that require a classifier to be used. The eight categories of classification found across languages were described. Numeral classifier, predicate classifier, and concordial classifier systems were illustrated. Because the basis for classification is the characteristic perceived or believed to be salient in the referent we can find a rational basis for what may superfically seem a fairly random classification of unlike phenomena by one classifier.

Exercises

9.4.1 Echoing a gun-lobby maxim, we might say *Language doesn't classify the world, people do*. But just as guns are a tool that constrain and facilitate the way in which people kill, so language constrains and facilitates the way in which people think about what they experience. Discuss.

9.4.2 Here is a list of classified items for just three of 13 classifiers in a language. Identify a possible basis for classification for each classifier.

(I) pencil, pen, hunting knife, folding (or pocket) knife, crowbar, wood rasp, metal file, one and two-handled wood saws, length of iron pipe, cigar, cigarette, match, fork, spoon, rake, shovel, hoe, pickaxe, axe, hatchet, car key, rifle, shotgun, metal or wooden ruler, carpenter's T-square, carpenter's level, metal bolt, nail, screw, wire brad, baseball bat, flashlight, flashlight battery, hammer, wrench, piece of firewood, cradleboard, clothespin/peg, arrow shaft, bow, fence post, blade of grass, log.

(II) pail, washbasin, drinking glass, coffee cup, frying pan, kerosene can, tin can (all sizes), shoe, boot, spool of thread, spool of wire, cake of soap, loaf of bread, box of detergent soap, box of matches, pack of cigarettes/cigars/chewing tobacco, car/truck tyre, chair, table, light bulb, kerosene lantern, brick, book, egg, apple, peach, pear, potato, acorn, walnut, peanut, coins, cigarette lighter, beer/wine bottle, milk container, burden basket, flat basket, wallet, Dutch oven, coffee pot, revolver, pocket watch, shoebox, saddle, cooking tin, kernel of corn, grain of salt, oil/gasoline drum, bale of hay, pebble.

(III) piece of paper, paper money, blanket, horse blanket, saddle pad, pillow case, sleeping bag, buckskin, trousers, T-shirt, shirt, tortilla, paper sack, burlap (feed) sack, sock, towel, piece of canvas, brassiere, woman's slip, woman's dress, diaper/nappy, sweater, pillow.

9.4.3 Comment on a view that the prototype for Dyirbal class I is male and the prototype for class II is female while, at the same time, the prototype male is human, as is the prototype female.

9.4.4 One of the characters in the sitcom "Mad about you" raised a laugh by telling how she'd arranged all the books on the shelves according to their colour. What uses can you imagine for grouping things by colour alone?

9.4.5 Discuss the following:

It is fundamental to understanding what [Whorf] said about linguistic relativity to appreciate that although he thought each language embodies a distinctive world view, this overall conceptual orientation towards experience is generated at least in part by the way speakers of a language habitually and unconsciously 'segregate different *essentials* out of *the same situation*'

(Lee 1996:90. Lee's italics in the quote from Whorf 1956:162)

9.5   Summary

But mortal men imagine that gods are begotten, and that they have human dress and speech and shape. (Fr.14)

If oxen or horses or lions had hands to draw with and to make works of art as men do, then horses would draw the forms of gods like horses, oxen like oxen, and they would make their gods' bodies similar to the bodily shape that they themselves each had. (Fr.15)

The Ethiopians say their gods are snub-nosed and black-skinned, the Thracians that they are blue eyed and red-headed. (Fr.16)

(Xenophanes of Colophon C6th BCE (Hussey 1972:13))

The purpose of this chapter was to examine the influence of human perceptions and experience in determining semantic categories, properties, and relations. It began with a systematic analysis of the meanings of the words *back* which clearly showed how what is known about the physical characteristics of the human body serves as a cognitive model for extensions of meaning to animate and inanimate objects, attributes of place, time, direction, and to actions. Our canonical stance and motion, the manner in which human activity and perceptions are determined by our anatomy and physiology, all have a bearing on the semantic properties of the words *back*, and many other vocabulary items in English and in all other languages.

According to MacLaury 1997, the way humans name and discriminate colours depends on the way they categorize what they see. Colour (and other) categories are constructed in terms of selected perceptions, i.e. vantages: reciprocal and mutable emphases on similarity and difference. One coordinate is a fixed point of reference, the other is attended to in relation to this – typically in terms of its similarity or difference. Each vantage is open to independent lexical or morphological identification. Vantage Theory (1) explains how a category is formed, extended, shaped, and bounded; (2) specifies the viewer's relation to the category; and (3) accommodates a means for the viewer to change the size and composition of the category. But Vantage Theory does not give the semantic specification for elemental colour terms such as English *red, blue, green*. To do that we reverted to a formula introduced in Chapter 2,11 which defined colour in terms of a disjunct of electromagnetic wavelength and the colour-of relation.

Classifiers function like a cataloguing system, identifying which grouping an entity belongs to. This reduces the processing load on language production and understanding. A cross-language review of classifiers revealed constraints on the ways in which humans classify. There are only eight categories of classification across languages even though the basis for classification is the characteristic perceived or believed to be salient in the referent. Co-classification was shown to be rational and motivated (A9.15). What may superficially seem a fairly random classification of unlike phenomena under one label may, on investigation, reveal a rational basis.

The term 'typical denotatum' has been used from time to time in this book. Chapter 10 seeks to elucidate this term by investigating and comparing prototype semantics with stereotype semantics. It forges a formal link between cognition and intension and formulates a procedure for identifying reference.

● Key words and phrases:

Æ$_{H/A/N}$ "associative (human, or animate, or inanimate)" (D9.10)

I'$_H$ "opposite to the interactive-side (human)" (D9.7)

L'$_H$ "opposite to the leading edge (human)" (D9.8)

S$_H$ "spine (human)" (D9.6)

analysis by synthesis (A9.11)

anthropocentricity of language (A9.4)

(associative) chains of (semantic) similarity

associative senses of *back* (D9.10)

back — where the spine is (D9.6)

back — opposite the 'interactive side' (D9.7)

back — opposite the leading edge (D9.8)

back — opposite the side that confronts the viewer (D9.9)

basic colour term (D8.6)

body-part

the body in the mind

canonical human bearing (D9.4)

canonical (human) encounter (D9.5)

categories of classification (Table 9.1)

categorization

classifier (D9.22)

coextension (D9.19)

cognitive linguistics (D9.1)

cognitive semantics

colour discrimination

colour mapping

colour naming

colour term

(in)complete notion (A9.14)

composite category

concentration level (Fig. 9.4)

conceptual structure

concordial classifier

cone (photoreceptor)

coordinate (fixed, mobile)

core sense

deictic classifier

(perceived) difference (A9.8)

dominant vantage (D9.20, A9.10)

evolution of basic colour terms

fixed (upon) coordinate

focus (best exemplar of a colour term)

functionalist linguistics (D9.3)

green (D9.21)

human-centredness (anthropocentricity)

journeying (D9.12)

journey schema (A9.7)

least effort (principle of) (D8.12)

locative classifier

mapping (of colour terms)

metaphorical extension

metonymic extension

mobile coordinate

noun class

noun classifier

numeral classifier (1–7)

overlap

perception (D9.2)

peripheral sense

predicate classifier (11–15)

proper part

quantity implicature

recessive vantage (A9.10)

relational classifier (8–10)

Sapir–Whorf hypothesis (D9.23)

selective attention (vantage)

semantic extension

semantic network (Figs 9.1–2)

semantic structure

semantic-syntactic network (Fig. 9.2)

(perceived) similarity (A9.8)

typical denotatum

vantage (selective attention)

Vantage Theory (D9.18)

zooming

● The structure of meaning reflects the fact that language is a creation of human beings for the purpose of communicating with other human beings (A9.1). This makes semantics the study of one aspect of human cognitive ability (A9.2).

- Formalists, cognitivists, and functionalists all use contrived metalanguages that have cognitive reality (A9.3).
- Cognitive linguists believe that language is informed by what human beings perceive in nature (particularly in relation to themselves (A9.4), or have experience of in the world they inhabit, or conceive of in abstract and metaphysical domains (D9.1).
- The ways in which speakers perceive and conceive of the world inform their linguistic categorization (A9.5).
- *Back* is defined in terms of the front of the body, rather than vice versa, just because the front is the more salient and significant body location.
- Three basic senses of (human) *back* are: "co-extensive with the spine" (D9.6), which identifies the core back; "opposite the 'interactive-side'" – opposite those body-parts principally involved in food ingestion, sexual reproduction, neonate nurturing, and various kinds of social and physical interaction (D9.7); "the part or location that is on the opposite side from the leading edge when a person, H_1, is walking normally" (D9.8) – arising from the canonical human bearing (D9.4). The leading edge confronts viewer H_2, another person, facing H_1 – whose back is on the opposite side of their body (D9.9).
- *Back* was extended from humans to animals and inanimates.
- There are also several associative uses of the term *back* (D9.10–11).
- The journey schema (A9.7, D9.12) explains verbal and adverbial extensions of the meaning of *back* (D9.13–17).
- Vantage Theory (D9.18) is a theory of categorization that accounts for the facts of colour naming, mapping the extension of a colour term, and the evolution of basic colour terms.
- Vantage Theory plots the interaction of cognition with perception, hypothesizing that the simplest cognition consists of selective attention to perception. There is reciprocal weighted emphasis on similarity and difference that can differ among individuals within a community and does differ across languages. Frequent 'unmarked' choices are referred to as the dominant range, and marked choices the recessive range.
- A dominant vantage has broad central focus, even distribution in mapping, and frequent naming. The viewer zooms in from naive attention to similarity to analysis. A recessive vantage has narrow marginal focus, skewed mapping, sparse naming. The viewer zooms in from analysis to synthesis to abstract formulation. (A9.10)
- A colour category is fashioned by analogy to physical experience as though it were one or more points of view on a spatial terrain, referred to as fixed and mobile coordinates. A person concentrates on only one relation at a time between fixed and mobile coordinates. (A9.9)
- The fixed upon coordinate is the one zoomed to at a particular level of concentration. There may be a number of levels of concentration, but only the top one is salient; others are in the back of the mind.
- Studies of colour term usage confirm a common trait in language understanding: Hearer analyses the locution and and compares it with what s/he supposes could be said (A9.11).
- In many languages certain syntactic environments require the use of a morpheme or lexeme denoting perceived or imputed characteristics of the denotatum of the associated noun, thereby classifying the referent according to one or more of eight categories (Table 9.1). There are no classifiers solely reliant on the faculties of sight, smell, taste, or hearing.
- The basis for classification is the characteristic perceived or believed to be salient in the referent (A9.12).

● Numeral classifiers are used in expressions of quantity, and often in demonstrative and anaphoric expressions, too. Relational classifiers typically classify a possession, occasionally the possessor. Some languages have extensive concordial systems in which class membership is marked on nouns, determiners, and predicates. A few languages include noun classifiers within their predicates; yet others have other kinds of classifiers.

● The original criterion for noun classification was material. It extended from identical entities (such as trees) to similar entities (such as things made of wood, or tall things), weakening the material connection and strengthening the importance of similarities in shape, consistency, and size implicit in the prototypical members of the class.

● Cross-language comparison of classification systems shows that a weak version of the Sapir–Whorf hypothesis is tenable: namely, that a language directs its speakers to attend to some aspects of phenomena and not others; but it will not prevent them from seeing what any other human being can see (D9.23).

● The scope of a listeme's denotation is motivated by human perception (A9.13).

● Root listemes name complete notions. An incomplete notion such as the partial noun phrase *a woman allergic to* will never constitute a listeme in any natural language (A9.14).

● Co-classification is rational and motivated (A9.15).

9.6   Notes on further reading

[1] On cognitive linguistics, see Fauconnier 1985, Haiman (ed.) 1985, Herskovits 1986, Lakoff and Thompson 1975, Langacker 1987, 1991, Pinker 1989, Talmy 1978.

[2] On cognitive semantics, see Backhouse 1994, Brugman 1983a, Fillmore 1975 onwards, Jackendoff 1983 onwards, Lakoff 1987, Lakoff and Johnson 1980, Lehrer 1983 onwards, Sweetser 1990, Fauconnier and Sweetser (eds) 1996, Tsohatzidis (ed.) 1990, Vandeloise 1990, Wierzbicka *passim*.

[3] On semantic extensions of body part terms in languages from many families across the world, see Basso 1967, Hill 1975, 1982, Fillmore 1982, Brugman 1983, Heine 1989, MacLaury 1989, Heine, Claudi, and Hünnemeyer 1991, Vandeloise 1991, De León 1992, Levinson 1992, Svorou 1994, Allan 1995a. On the body in the mind, see Johnson 1987.

[4] On core and peripheral body-parts, see Anderson 1978:358, Brown and Witkowski 1983:75, MacLaury 1989:121.

[5] In some languages, e.g. the Eastern Nilotic language Maasai (Heine 1989), the Uto-Aztecan language Tohono O'odham (= Papago in Svorou 1994), and the Mixtecan languages Chalcatongo Mixtec (Brugman 1983) and Trique (Hollenbach 1990) the name for an animal's back is used for "roof of", "cover of", "on"; the word for its buttocks or anus is used for "in back of". Nevertheless, the human model is prior to the animal model.

[6] On ways human perception and conception influences linguistic categorization, see Allan 1977, 1986; Brugman 1983b (discussion of her example 43); H. Clark 1973; Johnson 1987; Langacker 1987; Lakoff 1987; Svorou 1994.

[7] The journey schema underlies what is sometimes called the 'landmark' model in e.g. the West Caucasian language Abkhaz, Navajo (Athapaskan), Tigre (North Ethiopic), where terms for "trail", "track", "trace", "footprint" are used when English uses *back* (Svorou 1994:80); cf. English *back there, back then*.

[8] For alternative representations of colours, see Hardin and Maffi (eds) 1997.

[9] On Vantage Theory, see MacLaury 1986, 1987, 1991, 1995, 1997. Recently, Vantage Theory has been extended to the semantics of colour in many other languages, the category of person in 16th century Aztec, literacy choices for Yaquis in Arizona, various kinds of semantic extension in Zapotec, English, and Spanish, terms of address in Japanese, etc.

[10] On classifiers, see Allan 1977, Craig (ed.) 1986, 1994, Aikhenvald 2000. On relational classifiers, see Lichtenberk 1983, Carlson and Payne 1989.

[11] On the Sapir–Whorf hypothesis, see Sapir 1956, Whorf 1956, Lucy 1992, Lee 1996, Gumperz and Levinson (eds) 1996, Pütz and Verspoor (eds) 2000.

10 Using the typical denotatum to identify the intended referent

Psychological research (e.g. Keil 1986, Neisser 1987b) has emphasized that adult and even very young speakers are quite aware that superficial, perceptual criteria are insufficient for guising the application of many words.

(Marconi 1997:140)

10.1 Where we are heading

Chapter 2 defined intension as follows:

> *Definition 2.10 (preliminary)* The INTENSION of expression e_{OL} in the object language is the characteristic property or set of properties that a typical denotatum must perforce have for e_{OL} to be used in a conventional manner within the (object) language.

D2.10 relies on a common sense interpretation of 'typical denotatum'. This chapter elucidates the idea by discussing possible interpretations and matters arising from them. One possibility is that a typical denotatum is a 'prototypical denotatum'. §10.2 discusses and evaluates prototype semantics which says that a bird which flies (e.g. a crow) is closer to the prototypical ("most typical") denotatum of *bird* than one which doesn't (e.g. a penguin).

> *Definition 10.1* In prototype semantics, a PROTOTYPE is the most typical exemplar of a category.

Prototype semantics was a strike against checklists of necessary and sufficient conditions within semantic specifications before those specifications included the defeasible conditions indicated by quantity implicatures (Chapter 6). §10.3 considers the possibility that a typical denotatum (e.g. for *politician*) is the stereotype (politician), which is compared with the notion of a Gestalt. §10.4 discusses typicality and argues that the typical denotatum is more stereotype than best exemplar. The definition of intension D2.10 (repeated above) is revised in the light of the discussion in §§10.2–3. §10.5 describes a procedure whereby Speaker chooses an appropriate label for a referent and Hearer interprets the language expression so as to correctly identify Speaker's intended referent. §10.6 summarizes the chapter.

10.2 Prototype semantics

The Prototype idea is roughly this. Instead of the meaning of a linguistic form being
represented in terms of a *checklist* of conditions that have to be satisfied in order for the
form to be appropriately or truthfully used, it is held that the understanding of meaning
requires, at least for a great many cases, an appeal to an exemplar or prototype – this
prototype being possibly something which is innately available to the human mind, possibly
something which, instead of being analysed needs to be presented or demonstrated or
manipulated.

(Fillmore 1975:123)

There is a division among cognitive semanticists between those who make the
decomposition assumption (A10.1), and those who do not.

Assumption 10.1 The meaning of a lexeme or more complex expression e_{OL} in
(object) language L_{OL} can be EXHAUSTIVELY DECOMPOSED into a finite set of
semantic or conceptual primitives that are together necessary and sufficient to
determine the sense and denotation of every instance of e_{OL} in L_{OL}.

Necessary conditions can be identified for most if not all listemes, but these conditions are
often insufficient to distinguish a given listeme from others in the same semantic field.
Among those who believe in necessary and sufficient conditions on decomposition are
proponents of NSM (Wierzbicka and her colleagues, §8.6), semantic markerese (Katz
1966:70–73), and formal semantics.[1] Among those who don't are Lakoff (since 1972),
Fillmore (since 1975), and Jackendoff (since 1983). For simplicity's sake, the following
discussion is restricted to lexemes, though the principle applies to any object language
expression e_{OL}.

Discussing the componential analysis of *bull* in Chapter 8 we saw that the semantic
components ADULT $\wedge$ MALE $\wedge$ BOVINE often attributed to it are appropriate to the most
typical denotatum for *bull* – e.g. when interpreting 1 out of a 'normal' context.

1   Look at that bull!

An important finding was that the range of possible referents for the word *bull* is not restricted to adults or bovines.

Assumption 10.2 The PROTOTYPE HYPOTHESIS is that some denotata are better exemplars of the meaning of a lexeme than others, therefore members of the category denoted by the lexeme are graded with respect to one another.

Definition 10.2 PROTOTYPE SEMANTICS holds that some senses of a listeme are more salient than others.[2]

In addition to using our intuition and/or diagnostics like those described in Chapter 8 for 1, how do we discover prototypes?

Coleman and Kay 1981 investigated the semantics of the verb *lie* "speak falsely". They found that notions of prototype and gradience are relevant to describing something as a lie. They argued that for the worst kind of lie

Definition 10.3 Speaker LIES if Speaker asserts that Φ and conditions (a–c) hold:
(a) Φ is false.
(b) Speaker believes that Φ is false.
(c) In uttering Φ, Speaker intends to deceive Hearer.

Coleman and Kay then presented very short stories in which conditions D10.3(a–c) were varied such that all hold, two hold, one holds, or none hold. They found that

subjects fairly easily and reliably assign the word *lie* to reported speech acts in a more-or-less, rather than all-or-none, fashion; and ... subjects agree fairly generally on the relative weights of the semantic prototype of *lie*.   (Coleman and Kay 1981:43)

The general rule is that the more prototype elements a story contains, the higher it scores on the lie scale.   (p. 33)

D10.3(b) was the condition given most weight, and D10.3(a) the least; see Table 10.1 (p. 326). Sweetser 1987:62f writes

A lie is simply a false statement – but cultural models of information, discourse, and power supply a rich context that makes the use of *lie* much more complex than this simple definition indicates.

Lying is, therefore, deemed to occur when the cooperative maxim of quality (D1.24) is violated. The prototypical lie occurs when Speaker knowingly utters a deliberate falsehood (or otherwise intentionally speaks insincerely). The next most important element is Speaker's perceived intent to deceive Hearer. The least important element is whether Φ is actually false.

	D10.3(a)	D10.3(b)	D10.3(c)
Worst lie	Yes	Yes	Yes
	Yes	Yes	No
	No	Yes	Yes
	No	Yes	No
	Yes	No	Yes
	Yes	No	No
	No	No	Yes
Not a lie	No	No	No

Table 10.1 The evaluation of a lie

Assumption 10.3 The significant aspect of lying is what it reveals of Speaker's credibility and intentions towards others – its social interactive effects.

It follows that when an untruth is told to save or enhance Hearer's face, or to play down Speaker's achievements, the resulting 'social lie', 'white lie', 'understatement' or 'exaggeration' is acceptable social behaviour and not denigrated as a 'real' reprehensible lie.

Battig and Montague 1969 asked students to list as many Vegetables, or Fruits, or Diseases, or Toys, etc. as they could in 30 seconds (as in Exercise 10.1.1 above). They hypothesized that the most salient members in each category would be (a) frequently listed and (b) high on the list. They found, for instance, that a carrot is the prototype for Vegetable, i.e. the best exemplar of the category because frequently listed near the top. (Where did it figure on your list?) In folk belief, a tomato belongs to two categories: Vegetables and Fruit (some people say that it is a Vegetable in folk belief and technically a Fruit). On the Battig and Montague scale, a tomato ranked 6th as a Vegetable and 15th as a Fruit. Using their figures for salience and frequency, we can compute the tomato's degree of membership of the category Vegetable as 68 per cent and of the category Fruit as only 14 per cent. Lakoff 1972/1975 interprets such rankings in terms of FUZZY SETS of objects with a continuum of grades of category membership between 0.0 and 1.0.[3] If we assume that a category like Vegetable is a fuzzy set, then (on Battig and Montague's finding) a carrot is the best instance with a value 1.0, a tomato has the value 0.68 (and 0.14 membership in the fuzzy set Fruit), an onion 0.14, and a pickle only 0.006. Any entity assigned a value greater than 0.0 is a member of the category, i.e. the pickle is a Vegetable no less than the carrot. What the value of a fuzzy set member indicates is how good or bad an exemplar of the category a certain population of speakers perceives that entity to be.

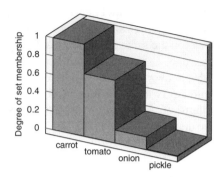

Figure 10.1 Four members of the fuzzy set Vegetable

Just how important to semantics is this? One's interpretation of the noun *tomato* does not – even on reflection – lead to the thought that we are dealing with something nearly five times more of a vegetable than a fruit! What is more important to natural language semantics is that the tomato's ambiguous status is reflected in the semantic frame of *tomato*.

(a)   A tomato is vegetable-like because it is eaten, often with other vegetables, as part of an hors d'oeuvre or main course. It is not eaten, alone or with other fruits, for dessert.
(b)   A tomato is fruit-like because it grows as a fruit well above the ground and not on or below it. Also, it is often eaten raw and the extracted juice is drunk like fruit juices.
(c)   Flowers are cultivated for ornamentation, but tomatoes are cultivated for food.

> **Assumption 10.4** Our practice of eating tomatoes as if they are vegetables rather than as if they are fruit is what explains the relative ranking in each category (as revealed in the Battig and Montague figures).

Rosch 1973 replicated the Battig and Montague 1969 finding that the best exemplar of the category Vegetable is a carrot; but she also found that the common cold is a very poor exemplar of Disease – which conflicted with the Battig and Montague finding. The discrepancy between the two findings could be explained by A10.4(a) (where ➤ means "is a better exemplar than") and/or A10.4(b).

> **Assumption 10.5** (a) Rosch listed six exemplars of each category and asked people to rank them. The resulting ranking for Disease was:
>
> cancer ➤ measles ➤ malaria ➤ muscular dystrophy ➤ rheumatism ➤ cold
>
> Obviously, a cold is the mildest of the diseases under consideration.
> (b) The number of people suffering from colds at the time of the experiment would affect its salience in the subjects experimented upon.

A10.4(a–b) reveal a weakness in experimental evidence for prototypes: establishing the prototype depends upon the experiences and beliefs of the population investigated. The claimed prototypicality ranking might be valid for the community surveyed, but not for all speakers of the language, or even the same speakers on a different occasion.

What explains the Armstrong, Gleitman, and Gleitman discovery that *3* is a better exemplar of the category Odd Number than is *15*? Given our decimal system, the numbers *0, 1, 2, 3, 4, 5, 6, 7, 8, 9* hold a privileged position, making single-digit numbers 'more prototypical' than double digits; cf. Armstrong at al. 1983:276. Because of the structure of human hands and feet, the numbers *4, 5, 10* and *20* are privileged in being the common bases for counting systems throughout the world.

Experiments to identify prototypes may indeed identify salient exemplars of a category, but there is no reason to assume that these are necessarily what we think of, or are subconsciously aware of, when a category is named. Indeed, Rosch herself warns against it: 'Prototypes do not constitute a theory of representation of categories' (1978:40).

> **Assumption 10.6** The intension of the linguistic expression naming a category is NOT identical with the prototype of that category.

If semantic structure reflects conceptual structure, we have yet to discover exactly what the latter is.

When a class of linguistics students is asked to write down as many Fish as they can think of in 30 seconds, it is common for cetaceans, cephalopods, and crustaceans to be listed. This is not due to ignorance of standard biological taxa, but to the greater influence on ordinary language users of the semantic fields of Aquatic Creatures and Sea-food. It suggests that a prototype for categories named by superordinate terms with many hyponyms, e.g. *fish, vegetable, furniture*, do not have such clear and convincing prototypes as BASIC LEVEL CATEGORIES like Bull. Instead there are 'family resemblances' between category members (Wittgenstein 1953:I,66–71). There are, for instance, root vegetables like carrot, turnip, and potato; green vegetables like cabbage and spinach, broccoli and cauliflower; there are pumpkin, squash, peas and beans; lettuce and celery; capsicum and tomato; etc. It is probable that noun classifier systems (Chapter 9) in which denotata are associated through similarities of substance, configuration, shape, or function develop on such a basis. Lakoff 1987 Ch. 2 gathers together ethnobiological evidence for the salience of the GENUS as the basic level for categorization and naming by human beings. He locates it within the rank scale in Table 10.2. The different levels give rise to hyponymy relations between lexemes naming members. Categories such as Vegetable are 'life form' categories such that the noun *vegetable* denotes a 'life form' category. Terms like *root vegetable* and *green vegetable* denote an 'intermediate' level, whereas *carrot* and *tomato* name 'genus' categories.

danger w/ prototypes (margin annotation)

UNIQUE BEGINNER	(plant, animal)
LIFE FORM	(tree, bush, bird, fish)
INTERMEDIATE	(leaf-bearing tree, needle-bearing tree)
GENUS	(oak, maple)
SPECIES	(sugar maple, white oak)
VARIETY	(cutleaf staghorn sumac)

Table 10.2 Levels of categorization from Lakoff 1987:33

Definition 10.4 A BASIC LEVEL CATEGORY is one at which:
(a) There is a perceived homogeneity of shape, and a single mental image (Gestalt, §10.3).
(b) There is the fastest identification of category members.
(c) It is the highest level at which there are similar motor actions for interacting with category members (compare *stroke a **cat*** with *stroke an **animal***).
(d) It is the level at which terms are used in neutral contexts (compare *There's a **dog*** on the porch vs *There's an **animal*** on the porch vs *There's a **wire-haired terrier*** on the porch).
(e) It is the first level to enter a language as a new listeme, the first to be named by a child acquiring their first language.
(f)   It is the level with the most commonly used label for category members, the lowest level with non-compound lexemes.

Cf. Rosch et al. 1976. The genus level is the lowest ranked category to be named using single nouns because the principle of least effort (D8.12) is in operation. The genus is more salient within the community and is more often referred to than the more specific 'species' and 'varieties' which, consequently, are named by compounds.

   An alternative approach to discovering the prototype is to present subjects with a variety of (pictures of) objects and ask the name for them. For example, people were asked to label items such as those in Fig. 10.2 as either cup, mug, bowl, glass, goblet, or vase, perhaps on the basis of the figure alone, or where it was to be imagined that someone was drinking coffee from the container, or it was full of mashed potatoes, or had soup in it, or was on a shelf with cut flowers in it. In the experiments reported by Labov 1978 the decisions were made on the following bases:

(a)   The shape and configuration of the container – proportion of height to width, whether or not the container is tapered, whether or not it has a handle.
(b)   The material from which the container is made.
(c)   The purpose to which the container is put.

Most people add that the potential accompaniment of a saucer is criterial in distinguishing a cup from a mug. Experiments like Labov's directly link language with denotata, whereas the Battig and Montague or Rosch experiments more directly reveal conceptual or cognitive structures.

Figure 10.2 Pictures of containers, Labov 1978

One kind of family resemblance is the CHAIN OF SIMILARITY. In Fig. 10.2 you can perceive certain chains of similarity. For instance, in the top row, object 3 is a better exemplar of a cup than 2, which is a better exemplar than 1; in the left column, 5 ➤ 6 ➤ 7 ➤ 8 ➤ 9. The Japanese classifier *hon* is normally used of saliently one-dimensional (long thin) objects such as sticks, canes, pencils, rolled-up scrolls, candles, ropes, wire, hair. However, the class is extended by chaining to various kinds of context, ping-pong rallies, movies, letters, telephone calls, and radio programs – among other things (Lakoff 1987:104). The chain goes:

From **sticks** to **martial arts contests** that use sticks or swords. From these to **judo contests**, and **contests between Zen master and student** to outdo each other with Zen koans such as *What is the sound of one hand clapping?*
From **ropes** and **the contest chain** to the trajectory of the ball in a ball-game: **hits** and sometimes **pitches** in baseball, **shots** in basketball, **serves** in volleyball, **rallies** in ping-pong.
From **ropes** to **rolls of tape or film**, and thence to **movies**.
From **scrolls** to **books and letters**. From **letters and wires** to **telephone calls**. From books, telephone calls, and movies to **radio and TV programs**.

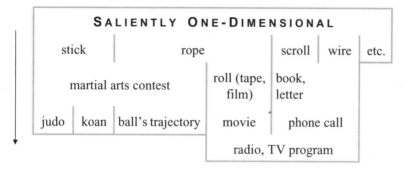

Figure 10.3   The associative semantic chains of Japanese *hon*

Semantic extension proceeds stepwise along a chain in which the first and last links are semantically quite distant (e.g. scrolls and radio programs).

Take the example of *mother*.

2   The **prototypical mother** is the woman who produces the ovum, conceives, gestates, gives birth, and then nurtures ego.

Radiating from this are more peripheral attributes of *mother*.

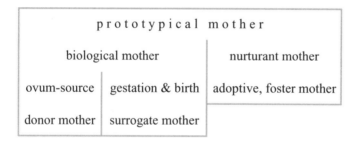

Figure 10.4   The associative semantic chains of *mother*

3   The **natural or biological mother** is the woman who produces the ovum, conceives, gestates, and gives birth to ego.
4   The **genetic or donor mother** supplies the ovum that becomes ego to a **surrogate mother** in whose womb the genetic mother's ovum is implanted and in whose body the foetus develops till ego is born.
5   The **nurturant mother** may be an adoptive mother, a foster mother, the genetic mother, or the surrogate mother.

In addition there is the **stepmother** "ego's father's current wife"; and **mother-in-law** "ego's spouse's mother" – who may in principle be any one of the foregoing categories of mother. (Polygamous societies offer additional complexities.) The metaphor in *necessity* *is the mother of invention* hinges on the prototypical or natural mother. The status of a mother is recognized in the convention of referring to *mother nodes* in a tree structure. The status of the nurturant mother is invoked in *house-mother*, and *spiritual mother* and *mother superior* in a religious context. By contrast, descriptions like *single mother* and *working mother* connote challenges to the individual's capacity as a nurturant mother.

Another kind of family resemblance is the radial structure. In terms of Langacker 1987, 1990, the core sense of *over* can be represented by the IMAGE SCHEMA of a TRAJECTOR, T, being located above a LANDMARK L, cf. Fig. 10.5. Either of T and L may be any shape, and may extend beyond the boundaries of the other.

Figure 10.5 T *over* L

The various meanings, listed in Table 10.3, seem to radiate out from two basic meaning components: "T is above L", and the dynamic counterpart to this: "T goes above (and across) L". Given that *ufa* means "up", *over* once meant "more up" '*Over* was thus in origin an old comparative of the element *ufa, ove,* in *ab-ove*' (*OED*). So modern *over* maintains links with its origins.

THE DIFFERENT *OVERS*	ENTAILMENT OF EACH SENSE OF *OVER*
T is [1]**over'** L	T is directly above L (*The painting is over the fireplace. A power line stretches over the yard*) ⇨ T has power over L (*oversee the operation, a standover*)
T is [2]**over'** L	T covers L → T wholly or partially conceals L unless T is transparent (*a sheet over the chair, litter all over the campground, a board over the broken window, it clouded over*)
L is [3]**over'** NP/Adv$_{Place}$	L is across from T (*Max lives over the river*)
T Vs [4]**over'** L	T is above L and takes a path across L from one side to the other (*jump or climb over the gate, drive over the bridge*)
T is [5]**over'** L⎫ L is [5]**over'** ⎭	T has crossed L and is on the other side (*the show's over, get over an obsession*)

T ^{6}**over'**-V L	T Vs beyond L (*there's over 10 miles ahead of us, it'll take over an hour*). L = the capacity of T to V properly, appropriately, or normally (*overestimate, overflow, overlook the fine detail*)
T goes ^{7}**over'**	T=L ∧ T is up somewhere, or upright, and goes to being no longer up or upright, being wholly or partly affected by gravity (*drop over the wall/cliff, Ed pushed Jo over, Sherry rolled over, PTO*)
Agent V$_{sudden.contact}$ T ^{8}**over'** L	Agent moves T above and across L to bring T into sharp contact with L (*hit over the head, Ed broke the stick over his knee*)

Table 10.3 The senses of *over*

Sense 1 (^{1}**over'**) gives rise to 2, 8, and perhaps to 7. 1, and perhaps 3, give rise to 4 (it is alternatively possible that 3 derives from 4). 4 gives rise to 5. 5 gives rise to 6. Thus, sense 1 is a radial category, and 1 ⇒ 4 ⇒ 5 ⇒ 6 form a chain. See Fig. 10.6.

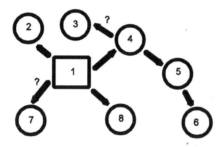

Figure 10.6 Connections between the various senses of *over*[4]

Semantic chains can be explained once they exist, but cannot be predicted. For instance, the cognates English *ride* and German *reiten* were both used to denote the act of riding on horseback – prototypically sitting astride a horse and using it for transportation. In German there is an extension to *auf einem Balken reiten* "sit astride a beam"; English *ride a beam* sounds unusual and pointedly metaphorical. However, in English we do *ride a bike*, sitting astride this means of transport. German uses the verb *fahren* for bike-riding (*radfahren*) and also for travelling in vehicles such as coaches, cars, and trains that English speakers *ride in*. This comparison of English and German (cf. Lyons 1977:263) suggests that whereas German extended the "legs astride" attribute of *reiten* and ignored the transportation attribute, English focused on the latter attribute.

Exercises

10.2.1 (a–e) contain falsehoods that don't count as reprehensible lies. Explain why.
  (a) My boss is a real pig.
  (b) It's so hot out there you could fry an egg on the sidewalk!
  (c) I had a great time at your party on Saturday. [Speaker was in fact bored.]
  (d) HE: What have you got me for my birthday then?
        SHE: Nothing. [She has in fact bought a present.]
  (e) Your girlfriend bought you that lovely tie? Ditch her. ['lovely'?]

10.2.2 A tomato is said to be 68% vegetable and 14% fruit. Why don't these percentages
  add up to 100%?

10.2.3 Kay and McDaniel 1978 argue that the boundaries of colour categories are defined
  by the foci of adjacent colours. The area between the boundary foci is a fuzzy set,
  where the colour focus has the value 1, e.g. a yellow green with a wavelength of 520
  nm is 0.67 green and 0.33 yellow (and 0 red, 0 blue). Overlaps like pink and orange
  (**red'∩yellow'**) have a focus at 0.5, which is a problem. Kay and McDaniel simply
  double every overlap membership number to counteract it. Is this justifiable?

10.2.4 (With apologies to Pulman 1983:113), rank the following verbs on a scale from 1,
  best exemplar to 7, worst exemplar:
  (i)   Category = Kill. Verbs to rank: (a) *assassinate*; (b) *commit suicide*; (c)
          execute; (d) *massacre*; (e) *murder*; (f) *sacrifice*.
  (ii)   Category = Speak. Verbs to rank: (a) *drone*; (b) *mumble*; (c) *recite*; (d) *shout*;
          (e) *stutter*; (f) *whisper*.
  (iii) Category = Walk. Verbs to rank: (a) *limp*; (b) *march*; (c) *pace*; (d) *saunter*;
          (e) *stride*; (f) *stumble*

10.2.5 Rank the following in terms of the category levels quoted from Lakoff: (a) *African
  elephant*, (b) *animal*, (c) *elephant*, (d) *mammal*, (e) *pachyderm*.

10.2.6 Tversky 1990:336 writes 'It's innocent to offer you a ride home in my "car" but not
  to offer you a ride in my "Ferrari" or my "vehicle".' What is she talking about here?

10.2.7 Does *father* exhibit similar prototype characteristics to *mother*?

10.2.8 Explain the positive connotations of (a) by comparison with the negative
  connotations of (b) in terms of the 'good is up' metaphor from Lakoff and Johnson
  1980.
  (a) (i) having high hopes   (b) (i) feeling low (*or* feeling down)
        (ii) she's on the up and up   (ii) she's a snake in the grass

10.2.9 If Jake is taller than Slim and stands up against Slim, is it true that *Jake stands over
  Slim*? Would this be connected in any way with *a standover*?

10.2.10 Identify T (trajector) and L (landmark) in (a–d).
  (a) Sally poured water over the petunias.
  (b) A rope was thrown over the camel's back.
  (c) The boat sailed beneath the bridge.
  (d) Sam put the lamp on the table.

10.2.11 Explain why a tank can be *overfull* but there is something odd about describing a tank as *overempty*.

10.2.12 Test it on your friends, but objects 3–5 in Fig. 10.2 are usually agreed to be the most cuplike, 11 the most muglike. Opinion is divided on 10, although most agree it is more of a mug than a cup unless it forms a pair with a saucer. Objects 14–19 are very poor exemplars of cups or mugs.

10.3 Stereotypes and Gestalten

Prototype semantics selects a particular denotatum or a particular sense as the most typical exemplar for a lexeme. People have suggested that the prototypical bird is a robin, the prototypical vegetable is a carrot, and the prototypical disease either cancer or a cold. Putnam 1975 proposed a stereotype semantics ($[\![e]\!]$ is the denotation of e_{OL}, cf. Chapter 7).

> *Definition 10.5* STEREOTYPE SEMANTICS holds that the meaning of a language expression e_{OL} (typically a lexeme) is not a well-defined set of properties necessarily found in every denotatum for e_{OL}, it is rather A MINIMUM SET OF STEREOTYPICAL FACTS about the typical denotatum $[\![e]\!]$.

For example, the stereotypical bird flies, even though emus and penguins don't. The stereotypical politician is economical with the truth when his or her power or credibility is threatened. Putnam expressly allows for experts to have considerably more knowledge at their command than their fellows – which raises the interesting question:

> *Research Question 10.1* Do the words *elm* and *beech* have the same stereotype and meaning for a botanist as they do for an inner-city dweller who can't distinguish an elm from a beech?

Presumably not: Chapter 3 suggested that the expert has different encyclopedia entries from the layperson. However, if the botanist were to point out and name an elm, the inner-city dweller would know it is not a beech, even if s/he could still not recognize another elm thereafter. Putnam's notion of a stereotype incorporates connotation: a male chauvinist and a radical feminist will possibly have quite different stereotypes for *man* and *woman* – and yet have no difficulty picking the denotatum of one from the other. The close links proposed in Chapter 3 between lexical and encyclopedic information nicely accommodates Putnam's notion of a stereotype.

Very similar to the stereotype is the notion of a prototype as a GESTALT (Brown 1990, Lakoff 1987). The term 'Gestalt', coined by Wertheimer 1959, is borrowed from German because there is no convenient English translation (the phrase 'single mental image' used in D10.4 denotes a Gestalt). Classic examples of the use of Gestalten in perception are:

(a) Knowing the true configuration of a chair even though one can only ever see parts of it from a single viewpoint.
(b) Recognizing melody without being conscious of the individual notes from which it is constructed.
(c) Having a Gestalt of a particular word that enables you to "feel" that it is spelled correctly or incorrectly on a given occasion. A child learning to read is acquiring the Gestalten for words; people who are alexic presumably can't acquire them.

The intensions of some lexemes seem, intuitively, to constitute Gestalten. For instance, if you can conjure up a mental image in response to the lexeme *dog* some people would call it a Gestalt, others a prototype, yet others a stereotype. Whatever the definition of a Gestalt within psychology, it is ill-defined (if defined at all – though see Lee 1996) within semantics; nevertheless, it is more like a stereotype than a prototype.

Exercises

10.3.1 How would you differentiate the prototype from the stereotype in the cases of (a) *movie*; (b) *(to) take*?

10.3.2 Identify the attributes of the stereotypical dog, man, act of walking and compare these with the semantic specifications you would want to assign to the listemes *dog, man,* and *walk*.

10.4 Intension and the typical denotatum

Coleman and Kay 1981 include a long discussion of the difference between PROTOTYPICAL and TYPICAL characteristics, though by the latter they apparently mean "with stereotypical connotations". They discuss the following story which was not so well known then as it is now:

> A young man is involved in an automobile accident in which his father is killed. Seriously injured, the youth is rushed to hospital and a surgeon is called. Seeing the patient, the surgeon exclaims 'Oh my God! I can't possibly operate on my own son!'

The conundrum was founded on the fact that the (stereo)typical surgeon is male, but the surgeon in the story must be the boy's mother. Coleman and Kay write, 'But femaleness is by no means a property of TYPICAL surgeons' (*sic*, 1981:36). However, Coleman and Kay equate 'prototypical' properties with denotation and 'typical' properties with a connotation of *surgeon*: 'prototypical properties play a role in the meanings of words, while merely typical properties do not' (p. 37). This is illustrated by the fact that 'a female surgeon is no less a surgeon for being female, though female surgeons may be as rare as hens' teeth' (p. 36). This book does not use the terms 'prototypical' and 'typical' to distinguish denotation from connotation as Coleman and Kay do.

Cruse 1990 offers a different objection to the term 'typical'. He says that prototypicality seems to imply 'well-formedness'. A prototypical bird has two legs, two wings, one beak, etc.; injured birds and mutants don't fit the prototype. Nor, we may add, do they fit the stereotype. He then raises the following point:

> Anyone who is fond of collecting edible wild fungi, for instance, will know that well-formed specimens are in the minority: most are damaged, decayed or maggot-ridden, and the finding of an unblemished specimen is an occasion for rejoicing. One might hazard a guess that the typical mushroom is not well-formed.   (Cruse 1990:385)

Cruse's term 'typical' appears to be close in meaning to, if not synonymous with, the use of 'stereotypical' in D10.5. He implies that 'unblemished' mushrooms exist to motivate the prototype, even though the stereotypical mushroom is blemished. Whether or not Cruse has his data right, he has identified a real problem for prototype theory: what is the evidence for the well-formedness of a prototype? Consider the problem Plato identified in *Letter VII*: perfect geometric figures cannot exist except in the mind, so if a prototypical circle is well-formed, it cannot be based on experience. Yet cognitive semantics insists that prototypes and stereotypes ARE based in human experience; therefore either the foundations of cognitive semantics are misplaced, or Cruse must be mistaken in suggesting that prototypes are necessarily well-formed. Assume that cognitive linguistics is well founded and that Cruse is wrong with respect to the well-formedness criterion. He may be right in proposing another criterion of prototypes that he calls 'quality'.[5]

Definition 10.6 A prototype is as good an example as can be found for the purpose in hand.

D10.1 implies that the prototypical denotatum of a (object) language expression e_{OL} is the 'most typical exemplar of a category'. This has just been revised to as-good-an-exemplar-as-can-be-found among the class of things denoted by e_{OL}. This implies that the prototype is selected as superior to other denotata. A stereotype is not, hence we described it as a 'typical denotatum'. A problem that noone has resolved is how 'a (stereo-)typical denotatum of e_{OL}' is distinguishable from 'as-good-an-exemplar-as-can-be-found among the class of things denoted by e_{OL}'. One possibility is that the stereotype properly includes the prototype. For instance, whatever the stereotype of *vegetable* may be, it presumably properly includes the prototype carrot and the peripheral onion (Battig and Montague 1969, Armstrong et al. 1983). The stereotypical *vehicle* includes both the prototypical car and bus and the peripheral horse-drawn wagon. If this is correct, then it is obvious we should favour the stereotype in giving the semantics of listemes. The time has come to revise the definition of intension, D2.10 (quoted in §10.1).

Definition 10.7 (final) The intension of expression e_{OL} in the object language is all the attributes perceived in or conceived of the typical denotatum [e] of e_{OL} when e_{OL} is used in a conventional manner within the (object) language.

This definition of intension corresponds very closely to Lakoff's 'idealized cognitive model' (Lakoff 1987:68)

> An idealized cognitive model [i.e. intension] may fit one's understanding of the world either perfectly, very well, pretty well, somewhat well, pretty badly, badly, or not at all.
>
> (Lakoff 1987:70)

This is equally true for the intension of a language expression. The fit between intension and intended referent was what we saw tested in Labov's cup-or-mug experiments described in §10.2. Fitting the intension for *bachelor* "a man who has never married" to a potential referent is determined by what one knows of the person to whom this state is to be attributed: a nubile unmarried male is a good candidate; a male with a de facto but not de jure wife is probably not a bachelor; the Pope may legally be a bachelor, but he is not marriageable, so the attribute is inappropriate.

Exercise

10.4.1 How would you set about describing the intension of *cow*?

10.5 Identifying the referent

A child of 1-2½ years old will often over-extend word meanings, that is, they use words with too wide a denotational scope.[6] This behaviour reflects the fact that there are family resemblances between the denotata of many lexemes in the standard adult language. For instance, there are many different kinds of things labelled by *vegetable* or *furniture*, or even *dog*. Eve Clark 1973:79–81 lists many examples, among them: *bird* used to denote sparrows, cows, dogs, cats, any animal that was moving; and *mool* [⇐ *moon*] used to denote the full moon, cakes, round marks on a window, writing, round shapes in books, tooling on leather book covers, round postmarks, and the letter *o*. In the child's lexicon the semantic specifications for these two words are, apparently:

6 *bird* $\forall x[\textbf{bird}'(x) \longleftrightarrow \lambda y[\textbf{animal}'(y) \wedge \textbf{move}'(y)](x)]$
7 *mool* $\forall x[\textbf{mool}'(x) \longleftrightarrow \lambda y[\textbf{round}'(y) \wedge \textbf{small}'(y)](x)]$

In both these cases the child selected a salient attribute perceived in the original referent but limited exposure to language data led to ignorance of other attributes that restrict the scope of denotation of *bird* and *moon*.

Assumption 10.7 To know the conventional intension for a listeme e_{OL} is to know the attributes and preference conditions appropriate to a typical denotatum $[\![e]\!]$ for that listeme for speakers of the (object) language. The attributes are spelled out in the semantic specifications for e_{OL}.

Recognizing the attributes imputed to an intended referent is what enables Hearer to interpret *Look at that cow!* as referring on different occasions to a live animal, a photo of a cow, a sculpture of a cow, even abstractions such as those in Fig. 10.7 where only one of the items, (b), can reasonably be identified that way (and even then, not entirely felicitously).

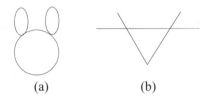

(a)   (b)

Figure 10.7 Which is the cow?

Consistent with the final definition of intension (and not altogether inconsistent with the definition of intension within intensional logic) are the predictable inferences when Speaker uses e_{OL}:

Definition 10.8 To LABEL AN INTENDED REFERENT $[\![r]\!]$ with an expression e_{OL} has the effect of ascribing to $[\![r]\!]$ the attributes of the typical denotatum $[\![e]\!]$ of e_{OL} as a function of e_{OL}'s intension.

This recognizes the necessity of including quantity implicatures within the semantic specifications of e_{OL}, so that the word *cow* ascribes the semantics in 8, the word *climb* the semantics in 9.

$$8 \ \forall x \left[\begin{array}{l} \textbf{cow}'(x) \longmapsto \lambda y[\textbf{female}'(y) \wedge \textbf{*bozine}'(y)](x) \\ \qquad\qquad \triangleright \ \lambda y[\textbf{bovine}'(y) \wedge \textbf{adult}'(y) \wedge \textbf{animal}'(y) \wedge \textbf{horned}'(y) \\ \qquad\qquad\qquad \wedge \textbf{uddered}'(y)](x) \end{array} \right]$$

$$9 \ \forall x \left[\begin{array}{l} \textbf{climb}'(x) \to \lambda y[\textbf{go\_upward}'(y) \vee \textbf{move\_in\_a\_vertical\_axis\_using\_feet}'(y)](x) \\ \qquad\qquad \triangleright \ \lambda y[\textbf{go\_upward}'(y) \wedge \textbf{move\_in\_a\_vertical\_axis\_using\_feet}'(y)](x) \end{array} \right]$$

From which follows:

Definition 10.9 RECOGNIZING THE INTENDED REFERENT. Assuming Speaker uses e_{OL} felicitously in referring to $[\![r]\!]$, the problem for Hearer when interpreting e_{OL} is to identify something in $M^{w,t}$ (the model of the world spoken of w_i at time t_i), whose attributes approximate to those of a typical denotatum [e] for e_{OL}.

There are, of course a host of problems that may be encountered when seeking to fix the reference, e.g. the figurative use of *cow* to refer to a person. We'd need several chapters to pursue the matter to a successful conclusion.[7]

Exercises

10.5.1 In D10.9, are [r] and [e] identical or only similar? Discuss both possibilities.

10.5.2 Suppose your intended reference consists of the pair of diagrams in Fig. 10.7. What is the [r] and [e] for this task?

10.5.3 Is an unmarried man with a de facto wife properly called a *bachelor*?

10.5.4 How is it possible for you to interpret *blue tomato*?

10.6 Summary

The purpose of this chapter was to discuss and evaluate prototype and stereotype semantics, and to define the links between labels, denotata, and reference. Chapter 2 said that Speaker uses intensions when referring. The purpose of this chapter was to define intension and explain how it is used in making reference. Because intension was defined in terms of typical denotata (D10.7) two relevant semantic theories were examined. The first was prototype semantics in which a prototype is the best exemplar for the purpose in hand (D10.6). Categories like Rugs and Carpets, or Cups and Mugs, seem to merge gradually one into another, although prototypical exemplars of each category are clearly different. Lakoff 1972/1975 proposed using fuzzy sets to index the exemplariness of a category member. The prototype was given the value 1.0, the worst example has a value close to 0.0. Although values of fuzzy set membership can be calculated from experiments such as the one described in Battig and Montague 1969, the achieved value is only valid for the tested population at the time of the experiment, not for all speakers of the language and not even for the same subjects on a different occasion. Rosch claimed that a robin is a good exemplar of the category Bird for North Americans. It would not be so good for Australians, for whom the emu, a big flightless bird, ranks much higher because the emu is a national icon (similarly with the kiwi for New Zealanders). Battig and Montague's figures demonstrated precisely how much more of a vegetable than a fruit a tomato is; but they don't reveal anything new about the meaning of the listemes *tomato* or *vegetable* or *fruit*. A tomato is both a fruit and a vegetable, but mostly it is used like a vegetable. Its characteristics are included in the internalized cognitive model of the tomato and contribute to the semantic frame of *tomato*. Prototype theory has no means of representing such facts. Even the poorest examples of a category remain within the category: the fact that an onion is a poor exemplar of a vegetable for a tested population does not change their perception that it is a vegetable. The prototype in no way defines the category: no one believes that a vegetable is a carrot! Furthermore, categories are independent of related categories with respect to prototypicality. For instance, a guppy is a good exemplar of the category Pet Fish, but it is not a good exemplar of either of the categories Pet and Fish.[8] All in all, prototype semantics has failed to deliver startling insights into semantics. Its greatest value was to make respectable the correlation of semantics with cognitive processes.

The stereotype is a mental image, mental construct, or Gestalt with the attributes of the typical denotatum. Putnam's stereotype even includes connotations, though these must be kept separate from the stereotype as the model for the intension of a lexeme. We concluded that the intension of a lexeme has all the attributes of the typical denotatum, and that the recognition of the referent of a language expression e_{OL} is a matter of identifying something in $M^{w,t}$ with characteristics that fit with the attributes of the typical denotatum of e – i.e. with its intension. The problem of compositionality remains to be solved. 10 is easily understood and a possible context for it can readily be imagined:

10 A blue tomato is not a tomato.

If we are to interpret *tomato* in terms of a typical denotatum, we have an incompatibility to be resolved with the colour *blue*. The fact is there are yellow tomatoes, black tomatoes, and striped tomatoes – but like flightless birds they are not typical. In principle there is probably no reason that blue tomatoes cannot be bred, however unlikely it is. Like a bearded woman, a blue tomato is contrary to expectation, but not contrary to reason, and the phrase *blue tomato* is not contradictory. There are millions of things that satisfy the description *not a tomato* and certainly no prototype or stereotype for them. As proposed in Chapter 2, we interpret *not a tomato* in terms of *tomato* on the basis of labelling described in §10.4.

This ends the general exegesis of linguistic semantics, approaches to it, and discussion of tools and methods to explain meaning in natural language. The remaining chapters in this book demonstrate the application of formal methods of semantic analysis to a corpus of data. The analyses confirm the cognitive and functional motivations for semantic composition. Chapters 11–12 look at aspects of clause semantics. Chapter 11 gives a partial semantics for the grammatical categories of mood, tense, and modality before turning to examine the semantics of thematic structure.

● Key words and phrases:

attributes of denotata
basic level category (D10.3)
category membership
checklist theories of meaning
cognitive linguistics (D9.1)
cognitive semantics
componential analysis
decomposition assumption (A10.1)

fuzzy set (membership values between 0.0 and 1.0) (Fig. 10.2)
genus (category level) (Table 10.2)
Gestalt(en)
idealized cognitive model
image schema
intension (D10.7, A10.7)
intermediate level category (Table 10.2)

● Chapter 9 identified the basis for noun classification as the characteristic perceived or believed to be salient in the referent. Human beings see the world through their mind's-eye, and categorize physical and metaphysical phenomena accordingly. These categorizations become conventionalized within language communities and are reflected in language. It is the linguistic consequences of such categorization that are studied in cognitive semantics.

● Traditionally, the meaning of a linguistic form is represented in terms of a checklist of necessary and sufficient conditions that have to be satisfied in order for the form to be appropriately or truthfully used (A10.1). Cognitivists like Wierzbicka believe this, too.

● Prototype theory holds that some denotata are better exemplars of the meaning of a listeme than others, therefore members of the category denoted by the listeme are graded with respect to one another (D10.1, A10.2). The grades can be measured as values between 0.0 and 1.0 when the members of the category are assigned to a fuzzy set (e.g. Fig. 10.1).

● Coleman and Kay 1981 argued that *lie* is a graded notion. It seems that lying is deemed to occur when the cooperative maxim of quality (D1.24) is violated (D10.3, Table 10.1). The prototypical lie is when Speaker knowingly and intentionally speaks insincerely (A10.3).

● In prototype experiments, categories that are salient (speedily accessed and frequent among subjects) are taken to be prototypical by psychologists. The resulting prototypicality ranking depends upon the experiences and beliefs of the population investigated: it is only valid for the community surveyed, not for all speakers of the language nor even for the same speakers on a different occasion (A10.5).

● The intension of the linguistic expression naming a category is NOT identical with the prototype of that category (A10.6).

● Levels of categorization (Table 10.2) have linguistic consequences; cf. D10.4.

● Family resemblances, associative chains, radial clusters, and semantic networks account for semantic extension and the development of semantic fields.

● Semantic extension may proceed stepwise along a chain in which two adjacent steps are very similar but the first and last links are semantically quite distant (Figs 10.3–4, 6).

● Many polysemous lexemes have a network of radial and chained semantic extensions (Figs 9.1–2, 10.3–4,6).

● An alternative to prototype semantics is stereotype semantics (D10.5).

● A prototype is the best exemplar, e.g. a robin is, for some people, the prototypical bird. A stereotypical bird is something with a beak and feathers that can fly.

● Are stereotypes the same for everyone in a speech community (RQ10.1)? It depends on the boundary of speech community. Does an expert and/or someone with a special interest exist in the same community as a disinterested lay person? If so the answer is *No*.

● Very similar to the stereotype is the notion of a meaning as a Gestalt – roughly, a single mental image or an idealized cognitive model.

● Coleman and Kay 1981 distinguished the typical denotatum from the prototypical denotatum by associating the former with connotation and the latter with denotation. Cruse 1990 says that the typical denotatum may be flawed, whereas the prototype is not. §10.4 concluded that 'typical denotatum' is best interpreted as "stereotypical denotatum", but rejected connotation as part of it.

● To know the conventional intension of a listeme is to know the attributes of its denotatum (A10.7).

● The basis for the referent recognition was described (D10.8–9).

● There are problems to be solved in the composition of meanings.

10.7 Notes on further reading

[1] The work of formal semanticists is reported in Chapter 7 and Dowty 1979, Dowty, Wall, and Peters 1981, Cann 1993, Chierchia and McConnell-Ginet 1990, Partee, Meulen, and Wall 1990, Gamut 1991, Kamp and Reyle 1993, Benthem and Meulen (eds) 1997.

[2] On prototype semantics, see Lakoff 1987, Tsohatzidis (ed.) 1990.

[3] On fuzzy sets, see Zadeh 1965, 1971, 1972, Kosko 1991, De Silva 1995, Klir and Yuan 1995.

[4] On the semantics of *over*, see Brugman 1983a, Lakoff 1987:416ff, Vandeloise 1990, Dewell 1994.

[5] Further discussion of Quality would take at least another chapter. For an entertaining account, see Robert M. Pirsig's *Zen and the Art of Motorcycle Maintenance* (1974).

[6] On the denotational scope of children's listemes, see E. Clark 1973, Anglin 1977.

[7] On problems fixing the reference, see Small, Cottrell, and Tanenhaus (eds) 1988, Kamp and Reyle 1993, Recanati 1993.

[8] On the weaknesses of prototype semantics, see Osherson and Smith 1981, Pulman 1983, Kamp and Partee 1995, Fodor and Lepore 1996.

11 Mood, tense, modality, and thematic roles

11.1 Where we are heading

Chapters 11 and 12 tackle major aspects of clause semantics: the semantics of clause-type or mood, tense, aspect, modality, predicate frames, and predicates themselves. §11.2 discusses the meaning and function of mood, which is read from the clause type (declarative, interrogative, etc.). There are only a handful of clause types, so the identification of mood is straightforward. It is shown that identifying the mood of the clause is the first step towards discovering the illocutionary point of an utterance (Speaker's message) – introduced in Chapter 1. §11.3 offers a simplified semantics for tense in terms of fuzzy sets of time points on a linear scale. It also touches on aspect in English. §11.4 addresses the semantics of English modal verbs *will, can, may, must*, etc. Watch out for ways in which your dialect differs from the ones described; it is an area of considerable variation. The section ends with a credibility metric for propositions. §11.5 looks ahead to Chapter 12 by defining a set of thematic roles. Roles like agent and patient are casually referred to in the linguistics literature as if they were well-defined uncontroversial concepts; but – as we see – their definition faces many uncertainties. §11.6 summarizes the chapter.

11.2 Mood as primary illocution

> [Protagoras, 490–420 BCE] was the first to classify utterances into four [moods], namely: optative-subjunctive mood [*euchōlē*], interrogative [*erōtēsis*], declarative [*apokrisis*], imperative [*entolē*].
>
> (Diogenes Laertius *Lives of Eminent Philosophers* 9:53f)

Assumption 11.1 The FORM of the utterance must be the starting point for Hearer's interpretation of its meaning (its illocutionary point). Thus, Hearer must recognize all (a–c):

(a) The locution, i.e. the sense (D2.3) of each clause.
(b) What Speaker intends the locution to refer to.
(c) The illocutions within the utterance.

Hearer hears the locution, recognizes its sense, looks to the context to figure out the apparent reference, and then seeks to infer Speaker's illocutionary intention (D1.12). The primary illocution is directly accessible from the locution. (The kind of inferences made were illustrated in §1.7 in the discussion of example 29; there is also a sample inference schema in Table 11.1 at the end of this section.)

> **Assumption 11.2** MOOD is the meaning of the clause-type. It is the initial clue to determining the illocutionary point of the utterance because mood indicates the primary illocutionary force of an utterance.

Suppose a herpetologist utters one of sentences 1–4 to his or her spouse. 1–4 have a common propositional content: "Hearer's not ever handling the cobra". The difference in meaning is indicated by the different clause-types and moods (S_n symbolizes "Speaker of n").

1   You never handle the cobra. S_1 **makes a statement** using the declarative

2   Do you never handle the cobra? S_2 **asks a question** using the interrogative

3   Never handle the cobra! S_3 **entreats** H_3 using the imperative

4   (a) Would that you never handle the cobra! ⎫ S_4 **expresses a wish** using the
     (b) If only you were never to handle the cobra ...⎭   subjunctive

Making a statement, asking a question, entreating, and expressing a wish are distinct illocutionary acts; i.e. Speaker is doing something different in each of 1–4. Because the same proposition is used, the difference must be a function of the different mood in each sentence.

Grammarians in the western classical tradition have recognized a degree of coincidence between clause-type and illocutionary force at least since the time of Apollonius Dyscolus (100 CE; cf. Householder 1981:12f) and probably since 300 BCE (cf. Diogenes Laertius 'Life of Zeno' VII, 65–8).[1] Palmer's 1986 monograph distinguishes the interrogative within the modality system, but Lyons 1977 argues against the identification of mood with clause-type because in the western classical tradition both the declarative and the interrogative are indicative in mood. However, there are not only interrogatives like 2 asking about the actual world, but also subjunctive interrogatives like 5 which ask questions about hypothetical worlds:

5   Would you never handle the cobra?

We return to the matter of the two interrogatives shortly.

Mood is the meaning of the clause-type; and 1–5 demonstrated that it indicates the illocutionary force. Fragments like declarative *John* in answer to *Who's that?*, interrogative *John?* [Is that you?], imperative *JOHN!* [Where the hell are you!], subjunctive *If only!* [that were so] are not a problem for this analysis because their clause-type is always recognizable.

Sadock and Zwicky 1985 surveyed 35 languages representing a wide range of language families and linguistic areas. They found that every language distinguishes

(a) a declarative to (among other things) make statements;
(b) an interrogative to ask things of people;
(c) an imperative to get people to do things.

These three moods are orthographically marked by '.', '?', and '!' respectively. Many languages have clause types with other functions – e.g. optative-subjunctive, expressive-exclamative, prohibitive, imprecative. English has not only the (optative-)subjunctive in 4 and 5, but also expressive(-exclamative) in mostly monolexical nonverb idioms of two kinds: those not necessarily addressed to anyone, 6, and those addressed to Hearer, 7. Note that some imprecations are listed.

6 (a) Goodness gracious!   (b) Shit!   (c) Wow!

7 (a) Thanks.   (b) Please.   (c) Sorry.   (d) Pardon.
   (e) Hi.   (f) Bye.   (g) Congratulations.   (h) Asshole!

Some of 7 have idiomatic counterparts with verbs:

8 (a) Thank you.   (b) How do you do?   (c) Screw you!

Imprecations of third persons appear to be expressives (9Y–10), but the clauses in 11 are imperative:

9   X: Suzie found Tom in her own bed with another woman!
    Y: Asshole!   ["Tom is an asshole"]

10   Fuck him!   [≠ "You copulate with him"]

11 (a) Apologize to him for me.   (b) Congratulate her.   (c) Thank him.

Often the expressives of 6–10 have similarly idiomatic counterparts in other languages.
    In the metalanguage, mood is represented as an operator on the propositional content of the clause.

> *Definition 11.1* The primary illocution of a DECLARATIVE clause:
>   <form> ⊢[Φ], or simply Φ (with a zero operator), an assertoric
>   clause (fragment) such as 1, 12.
>   <description> Speaker says that Φ.
>   <precondition> Speaker has reason to believe that Φ.
>   <illocutionary Speaker reflexively intends (D1.13) the utterance of the
>   intention> clause to be recognized as a reason for Hearer to believe
>   that Speaker has reason to believe that Φ.

Recognition of the form leads to its identification in the description. The precondition (D6.13) is part of one's knowledge about the proper grounds for uttering a declarative clause. The illocutionary intention of a declarative clause arises directly from Speaker's use of this mood, given the precondition. The primary illocution of the declarative clause is 'declarative' which is not to be confused with a 'declaration' (Chapter 6). The declarative performs an act of **saying**; a declaration performs acts of **declaring** legal verdicts and umpiring decisions, **effecting** states of affairs such as marriage, job appointment, etc.

12 (a) Jack is bald.   (b) Frank loathes Harry.   (c) [Q: Who called? A:] Jack.

> *Definition 11.2* The primary illocution of an INTERROGATIVE clause:
>
> <form> ?[Φ], e.g. 2, 13.
>
> <description> Speaker asks Hearer something (makes a **request**.)
>
> <precondition> Speaker has reason to believe that Hearer can or might be able to respond appropriately to what is asked in the clause.
>
> <illocutionary Speaker reflexively intends the utterance of the clause to be intention> taken as asking Hearer something.

13 (a) Will you mail this?   (b) What's the time?

Turning to imperative clauses: many are not at all imperious.

14 (a) Forgive me intruding.
   (b) Excuse me.
   (c) Let me help you with that.
   (d) Have a beer.
   (e) Take the first turning on your left and the third on the right.
   (f) Have a good day!

> *Definition 11.3* The primary illocution of an IMPERATIVE clause:
>
> <form> ![Φ], e.g. 3, 11, 14.
>
> <description> Speaker entreats Hearer to do A.
>
> <precondition> Speaker believes that Hearer can do A.
>
> <illocutionary Speaker reflexively intends Hearer to take the utterance of intention> the clause as a reason to do A.

Definition 11.4 The primary illocution of an EXPRESSIVE:

                <form> **X**[I], where 'I' is an expressive idiom, e.g. 6–10.

     <description> Speaker is reacting to Ω (read *omega*), i.e. something that has occurred, by uttering I.

    <precondition> Speaker believes it appropriate to express a reaction to Ω (showing some degree of feeling) by uttering I.

    <illocutionary Speaker (reflexively?) intends the utterance of the
       intention> expressive I to be taken as expressing a particular (sometimes perfunctory, sometimes strongly felt) attitude toward Ω.

Definition 11.5 The primary illocution of a SUBJUNCTIVE:

                <form> ¡[Φ], where '¡' is nonstandard, e.g. 4, 15.

     <description> Speaker imagines a world in which Φ.

    <precondition> Speaker has no reason to believe that it IS the case that Φ; indeed, Speaker may know it is NOT the case that Φ.

    <illocutionary Speaker reflexively intends the clause to be taken as a
       intention> reason for Hearer to believe that Speaker does not believe that Φ and Speaker reflexively intends Hearer to consider the implications of Φ in a world in which it IS the case that Φ.

15 (a) I wish *I were rich.*
   (b) I wish *I was rich.*
   (c) *Would that I were rich.*
   (d) *If Harry should call*, tell him I'll be back this evening.

The subjunctive environment is often the complement of a verb of wishing or wanting, invoking a hypothetical world (Chapter 2). In 15(a) the form *were* looks like a past tense, but is in fact the nonpast subjunctive – the tenses of all 15 are semantically nonpast.. However, in 15(b) the past tense FORM is used to mark the subjunctive. A past tense subjunctive would be *I wish(ed) I **had been** rich*. Note the use of modals *would* and *should* in (c) and (d). Conditional *if* marks a subjunctive clause when the proposition invokes a hypothetical world, so that *should* can be utilized in a paraphrase – e.g. (d) is a paraphrase of *If Harry calls* ....[2]

    English interrogative subjunctives are restricted to requests with only four backshifted modals; cf. 16. They are all notably tentative, which accounts for their use in polite contexts.

16 (a) Would you mail this for me?
   (b) Could you do me a favour?
   (c) Might he be there by now?
   (d) Should I write to him?

Definition 11.6 The primary illocution of an INTERROGATIVE SUBJUNCTIVE:

           <form> ?[ᵢ[Φ]], e.g. 5, 16.

  <description> Speaker asks Hearer about a hypothetical world in which Φ.

  <precondition> Speaker has reason to believe that Hearer can or might be able to respond appropriately to what is asked in the clause but wishes to appear tentative and not impositive.

  <illocutionary Speaker reflexively intends the utterance of the clause to
     intention> be taken as asking Hearer about Φ in some hypothetical world.

The form of the interrogative subjunctive suggests that the 'indicative' interrogative has an interrogative operator ranging over a declarative and it could be symbolized ?[⊢[Φ]]. However, since the declarative operator is effectively zero, this will reduce to ?[Φ], as in D11.2.

    The primary illocutions of the clause-types fall into four classes corresponding to Searle's 1975a notion 'direction of fit'.

(a)   Declaratives show a **words-to-world** fit: the words match the way the world was or is or will be.

(b)   Interrogatives and imperatives both show a **world-to-words** fit: things are to happen in the world to make it match the propositional content. They differ because Speaker expressly gives Hearer the option not to comply when using an interrogative; whereas with imperatives, Speaker expressly gives Hearer no option but to comply.

(c)   For expressives, direction of **fit is irrelevant**.

(d)   Subjunctives fit the **words to a hypothetical world**.

(e)   Interrogative subjunctives **seek to fit the actual world to a hypothetical world**: things are to happen in the actual world to make it match the words that describe the hypothetical world.

    The recognition of mood identifies the primary (or initial) illocution in the utterance, but not Speaker's illocutionary point. This has consequences for the interpretation of PERFORMATIVE CLAUSES.

Definition 11.7 A performative clause

(a) Has a main verb that names the illocutionary force of the clause, e.g. *admit, apologize, claim, deny, disagree, forbid, offer, promise, request, suppose, warn*.

(b) Is in present tense.

(c) Is in simple, occasionally progressive, aspect (e.g. *I promise Φ* or *I'm promising Φ*).

(d) Denotes the actualization of the illocutionary act, e.g. *I **admit** I was wrong* is performative, *I **might admit** I was wrong* is not, because no admission is made.

(e) Speaker must be agent for whoever takes responsibility for enforcing the illocutionary point, usually self.[3]

Gazdar 1981 assumes that performative clauses have only one illocutionary force: the main verb expresses the illocutionary point directly. But analysis of 17 makes this impossible: its primary illocution – like that of every performative clause – is (by D11.1) declarative (Cohen 1964, Lewis 1970, Bach and Harnish 1979).

17 I promise to go there tomorrow.

The primary illocution is: "S_{17} is saying that S_{17} promises to go there tomorrow." This is not the illocutionary point of 17, however. S_{17} is using this primary illocution as a vehicle for a further illocution to be read off the performative verb, namely: S_{17} reflexively intends the (primary) declarative to be a reason for H_{17} to believe that S_{17} undertakes and intends (i.e. S_{17} promises) to go there tomorrow. There is no further inference to draw, so this is the illocutionary point of 17. Speaker has no choice but to make a promise indirectly by means of a declarative; the grammar of English determines the matter.

What additional evidence is there that performatives are declaratives in primary illocution as well as form? First, there is the obvious similarity between 17 and 18.

18 I promised to go there tomorrow.

Unlike 17, which is in the present tense and has the illocutionary point of a promise, 18 is past tense (which violates D11.7(b)) and has the illocutionary point of a statement (or report) about a promise made in the past. The primary illocution of 18 is "S_{18} is saying that S_{18} promised to go there tomorrow." This is not the only parallel with 17, because H_{18} will interpret 18 (subconsciously, and not in so many words) as 19.

19 S_{18} reflexively intends the declarative to be a reason for H_{18} to believe that S_{18} did undertake and intend to go there tomorrow. There is no further inference to draw, so the illocutionary point of 18 is that S_{18} did undertake and intend to go there tomorrow.

Note that the undertaking in both 17 and 18 remains to be fulfilled. Although S_{18} is not actually making the promise in 18 as S_{17} is in 17, nevertheless, provided all normal cooperative conditions hold, S_{18} is as much obliged to fulfil the promise reported in 18 as S_{17} is in 17! The presumption that the primary illocution of explicit performatives is that of a declarative permits a commonsensical account of the similarity and difference between 17 and 18.

Second, there is a distinction between *saying Φ* and *saying that Φ*: the former reports locutions, the latter reports statements. Imperatives and interrogatives do not make statements, but declaratives do. Compare 20(a-d).

20 (a_i) Go!   (a_q) What's your name?
    (b_i) I said go.   (b_q) I said what's your name?
    (c_i) *I said that go.   (c_q) *I said that what's your name?
    (d_i) I said that you must go.   (d_q) I said that I want to know your name.

In order to be reported by *saying that*, the propositional content of imperatives and interrogatives needs to be recast as the declarative in 20(d); this is not the case with a performative because its primary illocution is already that of a declarative; cf. 21, where no (d) row is needed.

21 (a_d) The beer's cold.   (a_p) I promise to go there tomorrow.
    (b_d) I said the beer's cold.   (b_p) I said I promise to go there tomorrow.
    (c_i) I said that the beer's cold.   (c_p) I said that I promise to go there tomorrow.

Third, there is a set of adverbials which modify primary illocutionary acts, e.g. *honestly, for the last time, seriously, frankly, once and for all, in the first place, in conclusion*.[4] Consider 22:

22 *In the first place* I admit to being wrong; and *secondly* I promise it will never happen again.

22 means "The first thing I have to say is that I admit to being wrong; and the second thing I have to say is that I promise it will never happen again." It is clear that 'secondly' denotes a second act of **saying**, not a second act of **promising**; from which we may further deduce that 'In the first place' identifies a first act of saying, not a first act of admitting. Therefore, the evidence is strongly against the view that explicit performatives are primary illocutions, because primary illocutions are read off the mood which is in most instances readily identifiable from the clause-type.[5]

At the beginning of this section A11.1 refers to an inference schema for determining the meaning of an utterance: Hearer hears the locution, recognizes its sense, looks to the context to figure out the apparent reference, and then seeks to infer Speaker's illocutionary intention. We do not have the space to discuss the schema here.[6] Table 11.1 analyses stepwise an answer *It's 7.45* to a question *What's the time?* and as a contrast, Table 11.2 analyses *It's 7.45* in when Speaker and Hearer car-pool to work and need to leave by seven forty-five in order to arrive on time.

In uttering *It's 7.45* in answer to the question *What's the time?*, **Speaker intends Hearer to reason that:**	**B a s i s:**
1. Speaker utters U_1 in context of the question *What's the time?* [RECOGNITION OF THE UTTERANCE ACT]	Hearing Speaker utter U_1
2. U_1 consists of the locution *It's 7.45* in English. It means "Speaker says it is seven forty-five". [RECOGNITION OF THE LOCUTION]	1, cooperative principle, knowledge of English.
3. By 'it' Speaker means "the time". Speaker is using the locution to mean "Speaker says the time is seven forty-five". [RECOGNITION OF REFERENCE]	2, semantic theory, context.

4. Speaker reflexively intends U_1 to be taken as a reason for Hearer to believe that Speaker has reason to believe the time is seven forty-five. [RECOGNITION OF THE PRIMARY ILLOCUTIONARY INTENTION]	3, definitions of primary illocutionary acts.
5. Speaker is saying that there is reason to believe that the time is seven forty-five. [RECOGNITION OF THE PRIMARY ILLOCUTION]	4, definition of declaratives.
6. Speaker's reason for saying this is to answer the question *What's the time?* Speaker reflexively intends U_1 to be taken as a reason for Hearer to believe that (Speaker believes that) the current time is seven forty-five. [RECOGNITION OF THE SECONDARY ILLOCUTIONARY INTENTION]	5, cooperative principle, definitions of illocutionary acts.
7. Speaker is stating that the time is seven forty-five. [RECOGNITION OF THE SECONDARY ILLOCUTION]	6, definition of statements.
8. There is no reason to believe any further illocutionary intention can be inferred, therefore Speaker is stating that the time is seven forty-five. [CONCLUSION AS TO THE ILLOCUTIONARY POINT OF U_1]	3, 7, definitions of illocutionary acts, encyclopedic knowledge.

Table 11.1 Inference schema
for an utterance of *It's 7.45* as answer to *What's the time?*

In uttering *It's 7.45* when Speaker and Hearer need to leave by 7.45 in order to arrive on time, **Speaker intends Hearer to reason that:**	B a s i s:
1. Speaker utters U_2 in context of getting ready to leave for work at 7.45. [RECOGNITION OF THE UTTERANCE ACT]	Hearing Speaker utter U_2
STEPS 2–5 AS IN TABLE 11.1 – WITH U_2 SUBSTITUTED FOR U_1.	
6. Hearer knows that Speaker has not been asked to tell Hearer the time, therefore Speaker has some spontaneous motivation for drawing the current time to Hearer's attention; Hearer also knows that Speaker knows that they have both been getting ready to leave at 7.45 to car-pool to work. Hearer will therefore conclude that Speaker's motivation must be that because it is 7.45, it is time to leave for work. Hence, Speaker reflexively intends Hearer to recognize that "Speaker is asserting that the time is seven forty-five which is the time to leave for work." [RECOGNITION OF THE SECONDARY ILLOCUTIONARY INTENTION]	5, cooperative principle, definitions of illocutionary acts.

7. Speaker is asserting that the time is seven forty-five which is the time to leave for work. [RECOGNITION OF THE SECONDARY ILLOCUTION]	6, definition of assertives.
8. Hearer may reason that Speaker knows as well as Hearer does that if it is 7.45 it is time to leave for work; if Speaker and Hearer have not yet done so, then they must hurry themselves. Suppose that Hearer has grounds for believing that Speaker believes that Speaker is ready to leave for work but Speaker may not believe that Hearer is also ready (this would be made more probable if Speaker's tone of voice reveals that s/he is irritated). Given this belief, Hearer will conclude that Speaker reflexively intends U_2 to be taken as sufficient reason for Hearer to hurry up because Hearer is delaying their departure and so making them late. [RECOGNITION OF THE TERTIARY ILLOCUTIONARY INTENTION]	7, cooperative principle, context, encyclopedic knowledge, definitions of illocutionary acts.
9. Speaker is urging Hearer to hurry up because Hearer is delaying their departure and so making them late. [RECOGNITION OF THE TERTIARY ILLOCUTION]	8, definition of urgings.
10. If there is no reason to believe any further illocutionary intention can be inferred, Speaker is stating that the time is seven forty-five as a means of urging Hearer to hurry up because Hearer is delaying their departure and so making them late. [CONCLUSION AS TO THE ILLOCUTIONARY POINT OF U_2]	3, 9, definitions of illocutionary acts, encyclopedic know-ledge.

Table 11.2 Inference schema for a spontaneous utterance of *It's 7.45*

Exercises

11.2.1 What are the moods of (a–e) and which have truth values?
  (a) Congratulations!
  (b) You will do your homework!
  (c) If I were to apply, would they lend me $100,000?
  (d) I'm asking you what your name is.
  (e) Your name is ... ?

11.2.2 What is modified by the italicized adverbial (note its location) in each of (a–c)?
  (a) *Once and for all*, go to bed you wretched child.
  (b) *Frankly*, I don't believe you.
  (c) *Seriously*, do you have to return to Moscow tonight?

11.3 Tense

[Protogoras] was the first to distinguish the tenses of verbs.

(Diogenes Laertius *Lives* 9:52)

Every language has a set of listemes for time locations such as *yesterday, today, tomorrow*, and a boundless set of lexically complex expressions such as *last year, an hour ago, five minutes and forty-three seconds after Ivan arrived*. Not all languages have tense systems, but those that do represent events as ordered relative to one another in time, t.

Definition 11.8 TENSE consists of a small number of grammatical morphemes which systematically locate situations in time relative to a DEICTIC CENTRE t_d.

There are cycles of days, weeks, leap years, and seasons. For most peoples, each spring is new; but in some cultures (e.g. the Hopi of Arizona) the old spring returns: spring this year is the spring that was here before, not a different one (Whorf 1956:148, Lucy 1992:51ff, Malotki 1983). The semantics of tense takes no account of such a system. It also assumes that time travels from past to future, ignoring cultures such as Ancient Greek, Maori, and Trique that look back on the future (Chapter 9).[7]

In many languages different tenses mark distances from the deictic centre. In Kamba (Bantu, data from Angelina Nduku Kioko) there is no unspecific past tense form which corresponds directly with the English "he went"; instead there are:

23 *nǐwaenda*   "s/he went a few minutes ago"
    nǔendie   "s/he went earlier today"
    nǔnaendie   "s/he went a while ago [e.g. last week]"
    nǐwaendie   "s/he went ages ago"

(Orthographic *ǐ* is pronounced [e], *e* is [ɛ], *ǔ* is [o]). Similarly for the future:

24 *nǔkǔenda*   "s/he's going right now [in just a moment]"
    nǔkáenda   "s/he's going later today"
    nǔkàenda   "s/he's going in a year or two"

In Kamba the period from the deictic centre is partly determined by Speaker's point of view: thus the remote tense can be used for hyperbole, much like the English 25 can be used to indicate that Speaker feels s/he has been waiting long enough – even when s/he has in truth only been ready for a minute or two.

25 I've been ready for hours.

This section introduces just three semantic tenses: **P** "past", **N** "now, present", **F** "future". No attempt is made to give a comprehensive semantics for tense.[8] Past and present have in common that they are REALIS "real (actual, factual)" because they locate things that have happened or are happening. By comparison the future is IRREALIS "unreal (unactualized, nonfactual)"; this links it with subjunctive mood and modality.

Consequently, in English, the typical indicator for **F** is the modal auxiliary *will* and the future is discussed in §11.4. The two conceptual systems within tense are shown in Table 11.2.

past	nonpast	
P	**N**	**F**
realis		irrealis

Table 11.2 The time–tense–reality network

Definition 11.9 PRESENT TENSE means "the predication is located in time such that the situation is current at the time of utterance, t_0". **N** is a fuzzy set (Chapter 10) of instants of time such that $\mathbf{N}\Phi \supset t_{d=0}$.

The moment of utterance, t_0, is simultaneous with the deictic centre, t_d; this is abbreviated in the formula of D11.9 to $t_{d=0}$. The extent of the fuzzy set **N** is hugely variable: it can be just this very second in *He scores!* or a whole era in *Homo sapiens is a curious species.* The 'moment of utterance', $t_{d=0}$, is also a fuzzy set whose members include the instant when the utterance starts and the instant it finishes.

26   Thanks.
27   Stop thief!
28   *Peel*, *core*, and *slice* apples. *Cook* with water and sugar until soft. *Place* in greased pie dish, *cover* with combined topping ingredients.

26 expresses gratitude at the very moment of utterance: **X**[**N**[Thanks]]. 27 issues a demand for action at the moment of utterance: ![**N**[Thief, you stop]]. 28 issues a set of instructions for an apple dish that may be followed at any time which includes the moment of reading, i.e. they are habitually applicable: ![**N**[you peel the apples] ≺ [you core the apples] ≺ [you slice the apples] ≺ [you cook ...]]. The temporal sequence $\Phi \prec \Psi$ ("phi before psi") here is an implicature indicated by the sequence in which the propositions are presented. The difference between the punctual 27 and habitual 28 is also an implicature arising from context.

Punctual and habitual are aspectual properties.

Definition 11.10 ASPECT is the internal temporal contour of a situation; in other words, an aspect of the development of an event – initiation, ongoingness, termination, completeness, habitualness, iteration, punctualness, etc.

In this chapter, aspect is only mentioned in passing; but lexical aspect is examined in some detail in Chapter 12.[9]

Definition 11.11 PAST TENSE, **P**, means "the event or state of affairs spoken of has already taken place before the time of utterance and it is not current at the time of utterance." Symbolically, $\mathbf{P}\Phi < t_{d=0}$.

29   George Barton raised his glass of champagne. They drank. There was a pause – then one
       of the party slumped down in his chair, his face turning purple as he fought for breath.
                                                             (Agatha Christie *Sparkling Cyanide* 1945)

29 describes a sequence of events that occurred before the moment of utterance. It is notable that with punctual events such as the raising of glasses, the toast, the slumping down, there is a conversational implicature that they are completed and over with. This is represented by the completive aspectual operator FINISH in 30.

30   **P[They drink]** ▷ **P[FINISH[They drink]]]**

With duratives the implicature still holds, but it is more reasonably cancellable. For instance 31 has the implicature that Jim no longer lives in Edinburgh, but it can be cancelled as in 32, where ◊ "it is possible that" translates 'for all I know'.

31   Jim lived in Edinburgh ▷ **P[FINISH[Jim live in Edinburgh]]]**

32   ₍ₒ Jim lived in Edinburgh; and for all I know he still does ₒ₎
       Φ → **P[Jim live in Edinburgh]** ∧ ◊**N[Jim live in Edinburgh]**

The effect of cancelling the completive implicature of a punctual act is ludicrous:

33   George raised his glass of champagne; and for all I know he's still raising it.

       Two more cases:

34   Fred was singing [=Φ] when Tony came in [=Ψ] → **PΦ⊃PΨ**

35   ₍ₒ Mona began the ironing before George stopped eating ₒ₎
       Φ → **P[START[Mona do ironing]]** < **P[FINISH[George eat]]**
       Φ ▷ **P[START[George eat]]** < **P[START[Mona do ironing]]**

34 represents the time instants taken by Tony's entry as a proper subset of the time instants during which Fred was singing. 35 introduces the initiative aspectual operator START to complement FINISH.

As noted in §11.2,15, what Palmer 1990:44 calls the unreal or tentative meaning of the English past tense form is used in counterfactuals as a mark of the subjunctive mood (36); and also in some polite contexts (37). The subjunctive mood in 36 is best dealt with not in terms of time, but in terms of other worlds (Chapter 2).

36   If I *were* you, I wouldn't slam that door. → ¡**N[I am you** ∧ ¬**[I slam that door]]]**
37   I *wondered* if you and your wife would like to come to dinner with us on Saturday
       evening?

In 37 the nonpast *wonder* is also possible and there is no significant temporal difference between past and nonpast in this context. Even in the nonpast, the wondering occurs – or at least starts – before t_0. Rather more interesting is the backshifting seen in 39 ('regretted') when it is a paraphrase of 38.

38   Sue said that she regrets not meeting Sally →
                                        P[Sue say **N**[Sue regret not meeting Sally]]

39   Sue said that she regretted   } → { **P**[Sue say **N**[Sue regret not meeting Sally]]
            not meeting Sally   { **P**[Sue say **P**[Sue regret not meeting Sally]]

In 38 and one reading of 39, there is an entailment that Sue's regret holds at $t_{d=0}$, i.e. at the time of this report of it.

The PLUPERFECT is a relative tense denoting a time that precedes a past deictic centre for an event or state of affairs seen as narratively relevant at the deictic centre. In 40–41 the outer **P** is the deictic centre, i.e. $\mathbf{P}_d[\mathbf{P}\Phi \prec \Psi]]$ – hence the 'past in the past' sobriquet.

40   Ed had left when Max arrived → $\mathbf{P}_d[\mathbf{P}$[Ed leave] $\prec$ [Max arrive]]
41   Ted had been writing [$=\Phi$] when Max arrived [$=\Psi$] →
                                 $\mathbf{P}_d[\mathbf{P}$[START[Ted write]] $\prec$ [Max arrive]]

42 is ambiguous, as shown, between Sue saying (a) *I'd spent the money before I discovered I'd been sacked* and (b) *I spent the money before discovering I had been sacked.*

42   Sue said she had spent the money before discovering she was sacked

→ { **P**[Sue say $\mathbf{P}_d$[**P**[Sue spend the money] $\prec$ [Sue discover **P**[Sue sacked]]]]   (a)
    { **P**[Sue say **P**[Sue spend the money] $\prec$ $\mathbf{P}_d$[Sue discover **P**[Sue sacked]]]   (b)

The PRESENT PERFECT is like the past in locating an event that precedes the moment of utterance, but unlike the past it is used of an event or state of affairs located within a period of time whose endpoint is the moment of utterance.

43   John has been dead for six months → **N**[**P**[John be dead] $\wedge$ **N**$-$**P**=six months]
44   John has been dying for six months → **N**[**P**[START[John die]] $\wedge$ **N**$-$**P**=six months]

The difference between 45 and 46 lies with Speaker's presuppositions: in 45 Speaker presupposes Hearer has seen John and wants to know when it was; in contrast 46 is an open question about whether or not Hearer has seen John at all. Notice that 46 can only be felicitously asked while it is still morning, and morning is a period of time extended between **N** and **P**. The presumption in 47 is that John was seen at some time and it was necessarily in the past – that is what makes the use of the present perfect anomalous.

45   At what time did you see John this morning? → ?[i$\subseteq$**P**[you see John this morning]]
46   Have you seen John this morning? → ?[**N**[**P**[you see John this morning]]]

47 *At what time have you seen John this morning? →

$$\text{*?[i}\subseteq\mathbf{N}[\mathbf{P}[\text{you see John this morning}]]]$$

In English there are morphological grounds for a distinction between only two tenses because there is one bound morph for the past tense, and a zero morph for nonpast tense. In many languages the nonpast tense is used for both present and future.

> *Definition 11.12* FUTURE TENSE means "the event or state of affairs spoken of has not yet taken place at the time of utterance". Symbolically, $\mathbf{F}\Phi > t_{d=0}$.

To fly out is a punctual act, *to stay* somewhere is durative; hence the differences between 48 and 49.

48 We fly out today → $\mathbf{N}[\text{We fly out today}] \rhd \mathbf{F}[\text{START}[\text{We fly out today}]]$

49 $_{[\Phi}$ Sally's staying at the Sheraton $_{\Phi]}$

$\Phi \to \mathbf{N}[[\text{Sally stay at the Sheraton}] \wedge \neg[\text{FINISH}[\text{Sally stay at the Sheraton}]]]$

$\Phi \rhd \mathbf{N}[\text{START}[\text{Sally stay at the Sheraton}] \wedge \mathbf{F}[\text{FINISH}[\text{Sally stay at the Sheraton}]]]$

The implicature in 48 is that the flying out hasn't yet begun. In 49, the implicature is that the stay has begun, but not yet ended. There is further discussion of the future in §11.4.

The purpose of this section has been to review some basic facts about tense, summarized in Table 11.3, where t_d identifies the deictic centre and t_0 the moment of utterance. (An example of a future perfect is *Sally will have left by this time tomorrow*.)

past perfect

pluperfect	past	present perfect	present	future	future perfect
$\mathbf{P_d[P]}$	$\mathbf{P}$	$\mathbf{N_d[P]}$	$\mathbf{N}$	$\mathbf{F}$	$\mathbf{F_d[P]}$
$\mathbf{P_d} < t_0$	$\mathbf{P} < t_{d=0}$	$\mathbf{N_d} \supset t_0$	$\mathbf{N} \supset t_{d=0}$	$\mathbf{F} > t_{d=0}$	$\mathbf{F_d} > t_0$

Table 11.3 A summary of the semantics of English tenses

Although almost entirely exemplified from English, the method of analysis is applicable to the tense systems of other languages.

Exercises

11.3.1 We talk of the past being behind us, the future in front of us; we stride forward facing the unknown. There are languages (e.g. Trique, Maori, Ancient Greek, cf. Hollenbach 1990, Thornton 1987:70) where one faces the past. How can this be?

11.3.2 The difference between punctual and durative verbs is a difference of lexical aspect (Chapter 12). Briefly explain what you understand by the terms.

11.3.3 How would you represent the semantics of time in (a–d)? (For *She shot the dentist* it would be **P**[*she shoot the dentist*].)

(a) She saw a skin specialist.
(b) She's seen a skin specialist.
(c) She's been seeing a skin specialist.
(d) Fred cried when Toni came in.

11.4 Modals such as *will, can, may, must*

Although often spoken of as a tense marker, English *will* and its past tense form *would* are primarily modals. The ROOT (dynamic) meaning is "act on one's will, desire, want, hence insist on doing something".

50   Connie $\left\{ \begin{array}{c} \text{will} \\ \text{would} \end{array} \right\}$ telephone me at 11.30 at night.   →   **will′**$(x_A,[\textbf{do′}(x,[\text{PRED}(x...)])])$

The formula **will′**$(x_A,[\textbf{do′}(x,[\text{PRED}(x...)])])$ is generic. In 50, x_A is the clause actor 'Connie'; **do′** identifies the PRED 'telephone' as an active verb; 'me at 11.30 at night' gives substance to ... in the formula. The presence of the actor leads such modals to be called 'agent-oriented'.[10] '[W]ill' here is habitual, it is Connie's characteristic wilfulness in telephoning me. '[W]ould' means "it used (in the past) to be her habit". Neither of these in 50 is future, but even so there is an element of prediction, which characterizes the so-called EPISTEMIC (Greek ἐπιστήμη "knowledge") sense of *will*. Root meaning is stronger in the request in 51Q. The answer, 51A, is epistemic, PREDICTED[**do′**$(x_A,[\text{PRED}(x...)])$]; it shows that willingness to commit oneself to doing something does not imply a desire to do it.

51   Q: Will you take out the garbage?
       → ?[**N**[**will′**(you,[**do′**(you,[you take out the garbage])])]]

    A: Yes I will, though it's the last thing on earth I want to do.
       → **N**[PREDICTED[**F**[**do′**(I,[I take out the garbage])]]]

The main clause of 51A is not just a present prediction about Speaker's future behaviour but conversationally implicates a commitment to act in a certain way. Other examples of predictive *will* are 52–53, both of which are **N** rather than **F**, and can be replaced by the tensed versions without *will*, with consequential loss of the prediction.

52 Tell him it's Max, $\left\{ \begin{array}{l} \text{(a)   he'll know} \\ \text{(b)   he knows} \end{array} \right\}$ who I am.

     (a) → **N**[PREDICTED[he knows who I am]]
     (b) → **N**[he knows who I am]

53 It's ten o'clock; $\left\{\begin{array}{l}\text{Max'll be}\\\text{Max is}\end{array}\right\}$ in the canteen.

Because they are predictable situations, they are habitual states or reiterated events (and vice versa). For 53: if you check, Max will have been in the canteen at 10 o'clock. Statements like 'Max is in the canteen' in 53 pretend to be established fact, but they are de facto predictions in which Speaker has a good deal of confidence.

54 contains a past prediction.

54 She didn't think he was the sort of person that would cheat on her.
    → **P**[she think ¬[PREDICTED[he be the sort of person to cheat on her]]]

55 I think that their pool $\left\{\begin{array}{ll}\text{(a)} & \text{is}\\ \text{(b)} & \text{will be}\\ \text{(c)} & \text{would be}\end{array}\right\}$ about 10 metres long.

    (a) → **N**[their pool is about 10m long]
    (b) → **N**[PREDICTED[their pool is about 10m long]]
    (c) → ¡[**N**[their pool is about 10m long]]

55 is a guesstimate: (a) is least tentative, (c) most tentative – 'would' is not past tense, but subjunctive.

    A prediction need not be temporal, it can be of a remote place at the moment of utterance, cf. 56. 57 is the nonpredictive but virtually synonymous counterpart.

56 It's six o'clock now, here in Los Angeles, so it will be nine o'clock in New York
    → **N**[It is six o'clock in LA] ∧ **N**[PREDICTED[It is nine o'clock in NY]]

57 It's six o'clock now, here in Los Angeles, so it's nine o'clock in New York
    → **N**[It is six o'clock in LA] ∧ **N**[It is nine o'clock in NY]

In 56–57 the second clause is not an entailment of the first because the relationship is contingent upon time zones remaining defined as they are currently.

    Nonmodal futures (*it's raining tomorrow*) are used primarily for scheduled events, whereas predictions with a strong hypothetical implication generally use the modal future (*it'll rain tomorrow*).

58 I bet it *will* rain tomorrow, let's check the weather forecast. [CHECKS THE FORECAST IN A NEWSPAPER] Yep, it *'s raining* tomorrow.

    The so-called DEONTIC (Greek δεοντ- "binding") use of *will* states the requirement that Hearer do some future act, i.e. gives rise to commands.

59 **N**[REQUIRED[**F**[**do**′(you$_A$,[PRED(you ...)])]]] ← You will assemble here at
                                                0500 hours in battle order.

Here deontic *must, have to* and *are to* can substitute for 'will' and any subtle meaning difference arises from the root sense **will'**. In legalese, *shall* is still regularly used deontically in identifying legally binding conditions. 60 is from a property sale contract.

60 The rents and profits of the property hereby sold shall belong to the Vendor up to and
        including the date of possession and thereafter to the Purchaser and shall be dealt
        with as follows – ...

    Possibility is often expressed using the modal verbs *can, could, may* and *might*; but these verbs also have other meanings. The root meaning of *can* and *could* is linked to the Scots verb *ken*, the adjective *cunning* and north British dialect *canny*: "actor knows how, is mentally or physically able, to X".

61 Suzie can speak Swahili.
62 Can you swim?

Note the entailment relations in 63–64.

63 Suzie speaks Swahili ⊩ Suzie can speak Swahili
64 Do you swim? ⊩ Can you swim?

Hence the contradiction in 65, which contrasts with 66.

65 *Suzie speaks Swahili but she can't.
66 Suzie can speak Swahili but she doesn't.

66 is acceptable because the second clause cancels a Quantity2 implicature of the first clause (it is identified in 70(b)). The predicate in the scope of root *can* and its past counterpart *could* is regarded as some kind of enduring accomplishment; consequently, 67 is acceptable, but 68 is not. The reason is clarified by the (b) sentences.

67 (a) Harry had learned Spanish and could speak it well.
     (b) Harry had learned Spanish and in consequence of this accomplishment could
             speak it well thereafter.
68 (a) *Tom ran after the thief and could catch him.
     (b) *Tom ran after the thief and in consequence of this accomplishment could catch
             him (thereafter).

Habitual capability (*Hercule Poirot can catch thieves*) is indicated by *can* or *could* and a one-off ability by *be able to*, cf. 69.

69 Tom ran after the thief and was able to catch him.
     → ... **be'**(x,[**able'**(x,[PRED(x...)])])

Except as a case of irony, 69 does not justify *Tom catches thieves* on the pattern of *Suzie speaks Swahili* in 63. (However, *Suzie can speak Swahili* ‖ *Suzie is able to speak Swahili*.) The semantics for such sentences as 61–64 is given in 70.

70 (a) **do′**(x$_A$,[**can′**(x,[PRED(x...)])]) → **can′**(x,[PRED(x...)])
   (b) **can′**(x,[PRED(x...)]) ▷ **do′**(x$_A$,[PRED(x...)])

66, *Suzie can speak Swahili but she doesn't*, is semantically

66′ **can′**(Suzie,[speak (Suzie, Swahili)]) ∧ ¬[**do′**(Suzie,[speak (Suzie, Swahili)])]

The anomaly of **Suzie speaks Swahili but she doesn't* is explained by the fact that the left-hand side of 70(a) outranks and cancels the implicature on the right-hand side of 70(b).
    The root meaning of *may* is "actor has the power or right to do A"; cf. the noun *might*. Paradoxically, the auxiliary *might* has lost this sense today (see 82–83 for uses of *might*). Root *may* is constrained to the power to execute the speech acts known as declarations (p.208); it indicates that the actor is sanctioned to issue an authoritative.

71 The Minister may, at his or her discretion, grant a reprieve.
       do′(x$_A$,[**may′**(x,[PRED(x,y)])]) → **may′**(x,[PRED(x,y)])

A valid reprieve could only be successfully granted if the grantor has the power or right to do so.
    There are also deontic uses of *can, could, may,* and *might* which mean "actor is permitted to do A or prohibited from doing A". They derive from the right to exercise or not to exercise the root ability or power to act. The permitter or prohibitor is determined by implication (as distinct from being explicit in performatives like *The court permits you to stand down* and *I prohibit you from going out tonight*). 72 has the implicature "you are welcome to join us" as well as the entailment "you are allowed to come with us." Note that the permission applies to a future act.

72 Of course you $\left\{ \begin{array}{c} \text{can} \\ \text{may} \end{array} \right\}$ come to the party with us tomorrow.

    → N[PERMITTED[F[**do′**(you,[you come to the party with us tomorrow])]]]

73 You $\left\{ \begin{array}{c} \text{mayn't} \\ \text{can't} \end{array} \right\}$ come to the party with us.

    → N[¬PERMITTED[F[**do′**(you,[you come to the party with us])]]]

In 73, the scope of the negative defines the prohibition, which could just as well be expressed using *are not allowed to*. *Can(not)* is less formal than *may (not)*, compare

74 Wally can't go any place at this hour.   [Less formal]
75 Wally may not go any place at this hour.   [More formal]

For the semantics of possibility we concentrate on epistemic senses of *can, could, may*, and *might* "it is or was or will be possible that *p*" or $\Diamond\Phi$ (read "diamond phi"). This reflects the strength of Speaker's belief or knowledge that *p*. The epistemic sense derives historically from the root meanings. If actor has the ability to do A, then A is a possible act, but the converse does not necessarily hold, cf. *You could drive a car if you bothered to learn* (Hearer doesn't have the ability to drive even though it would be a possible act for her/him). Also in 62, *Can you swim?*, there is a possible world in which you know how to swim, but it may not be the real world. The shift in focus from the actor to the act gives rise to epistemic possibility, which resists paraphrase by "actor's ability to" or "have it in actor's power to" because these are irrelevant to the point being made, perhaps because there is no actor. 76, for instance, appeals to external circumstances (formula $\mathbf{do}'(\varnothing_A,\varnothing)$ means "someone does something").

76 I'll see $\begin{Bmatrix} \text{what can be done} \\ \text{whether something can be done} \end{Bmatrix}$ → N[PREDICTED[I see [?[$\Diamond$[$\mathbf{do}'(\varnothing_A,\varnothing)$]]]]]]

In 77 the subjunctive, indicated by the form 'could', is used to mark a tentative possibility. It evokes two hypothetical worlds, one of which is expected to match the real world.

77 John could be in his room or in the canteen
    → ¡[N$\Diamond$[[John is in his room] ⋁ [John is in the canteen]]]

Comparing *can* with *be able to*, 78 means "Will external circumstances allow Hearer to get 'here' quickly?"; 79 asks "Is it within Hearer's ability (power) to accomplish it?"

78 How quickly can you get here? ← ?[N$\Diamond$[$\mathbf{do}'$(you,[you get here quickly])]]
79 How quickly are you able to get here?
    ← ?[N[$\mathbf{be}'$(you,[$\mathbf{able}'$(you,[$\mathbf{do}'$(you,[you get here quickly])])])]]

There is no actor in 80; being generic it means something like "if you choose any dog at random, it probably has foul breath."

80 Dogs $\begin{Bmatrix} \text{may} \\ \text{can} \end{Bmatrix}$ have foul breath.

There are meaning differences between *can, could, may*, and *might*. 81–82 are rhetorical questions in which the expected has not yet happened. Both sentences have the precondition P[PREDICTED[N[they come]]]. 83 seeks information, and has the precondition N$\Diamond$[they come]. In 82–83 *might* is subjunctive and more tentative than *may*. Accents indicate pitch movement: ` fall,´ rise, ˇ fall-rise, ^ rise-fall. In 81–85 [*p*] = [they are coming].

81 $\begin{matrix} \text{(a)} \\ \text{(b)} \end{matrix} \begin{Bmatrix} \text{Càn} \\ \text{Còuld} \end{Bmatrix}$ they be cóming? → $\begin{cases} \text{(a)} & ?[N\Diamond[p]] \\ \text{(b)} & ?[¡[N\Diamond[p]]] \end{cases}$

82 $\begin{matrix} \text{(a)} \\ \text{(b)} \end{matrix} \begin{Bmatrix} \text{Mày} \\ \text{Mìght} \end{Bmatrix}$ they be cóming? → $\begin{cases} \text{(a)} & ?[N\Diamond\neg[p]] \\ \text{(b)} & ?[¡[N\Diamond\neg[p]]] \end{cases}$

83 (a) Mǎy ⎫ they be cǒming? → (a) ?[N◇[p]]
   (b) Mǐght ⎭   (b) ?[¡[N◇[p]]]

84–85 express a difference in Speaker's degree of confidence; note the difference in negative scope.

84 They cán't be còming!   →   N¬◇[p]

85 They ⎰ may ⎱ not be coming! → ⎰ N◇¬[p]
        ⎱ might ⎰   ⎱ ¡[N◇¬[p]]

Compare 86–87 which both question a current possibility.

86 You couldn't be mistaken?   → ?[¡[N¬◇[you be mistaken]]]
87 You couldn't have been mistaken? → ?[¡[N¬◇P[you be mistaken]]]

The perfect *have ⌒Pp* construction is the result of the NΦ[PΦ] configuration in the semantics of 87.

88 has a deontic use of *may*; it is a rhetorical exclamation, hence the inappropriacy of *might*.

88 Who says I ⎰ may ⎱ not paint my house purple! → N[¬PERMITTED[p]]
               ⎱ #might ⎰

The modal verbs that denote necessity are *must* (which can always be paraphrased by *have to*) and *need*. Deontic necessity speaks of obligations, requirements, and demands. The past tense of 90 is 91, note the suppleted modal. 92 is ambiguous.

89 You must leave now.   →   N[REQUIRED[p]]

90 Dogs ⎰ must ⎱ be on a leash. → N[REQUIRED[p]]
         ⎱ need to ⎰

91 Dogs had to be on a leash   →   P[REQUIRED[p]]

92 Dogs may not be on a leash.   ⎰ → N[REQUIRED[¬p]]
                                   ⎱ → N[PERMITTED[¬p]]

93 Dogs ⎰ need not ⎱ be on a leash. → N[¬REQUIRED[p]]
         ⎱ don't have to ⎰

94 is ambiguous between the deontic sense and an epistemic sense: "given what is known, the only possible conclusion is that *p*." This is about as close as natural language gets to logical necessity, so it is symbolized by box, □. It sits happiest with a stative or durative predicate.

94 The table must be six foot long. → $\left\{ \begin{array}{l} \text{REQUIRED[the table is 6' long]} \quad \text{(Deontic)} \\ \Box\text{[the table is 6' long]} \qquad\qquad \text{(Epistemic)} \end{array} \right.$

The common epistemic examples show more evidence of external forces. In some dialects, though perhaps not written standard English, invariant *needs* can substitute for *must* and can even occur before it.

95 After driving for eight hours you $\left\{ \begin{array}{c} \text{must} \\ \text{needs} \\ \text{needs must} \end{array} \right\}$ be tired. → **N**[...$\Box$[you are tired]]

96 The victim must have been shot weeks ago.
       → **N**[$\Box$[**P**[the victim be shot]] weeks ago]

$\Box\Phi$ here is NOT identical with $\Box\Phi$ in modal logic because the relevant propositions in 95–96 are not necessarily true in all possible worlds. However, $\Box\neg p$ standardly gives rise to *can't* but in some dialects *mustn't* and these are synonymous with $\neg\Diamond p$, cf. 84 and 97.[1]

97 The table $\left\{ \begin{array}{c} \text{can't} \\ \text{mustn't} \end{array} \right\}$ be 6 foot long

$\neg\Box\Phi$ is manifest by *not need to* or *not have to*:

98 You didn't $\left\{ \begin{array}{c} \text{need} \\ \text{have} \end{array} \right\}$ to have slapped me so hard!

The root meaning of *must* is that circumstances beyond actor's control necessitate something: **must'**(x_A,[**do'**(x,[PRED(x...)])]).

99 You must poke your nose into my business; you can't help yourself.

   To sum up this section. The root meaning of modals is close to their original meanings.

Definition 11.13 ROOT MODALS have the semantics

$\left\{ \begin{array}{l} \textbf{able'} \\ \textbf{can'} \\ \textbf{may'} \end{array} \right\}$(x,[PRED(x...)])

$\left\{ \begin{array}{l} \textbf{will'} \\ \textbf{must'} \end{array} \right\}$($x_A$,[**do'**(x,[PRED(x...)])])

Epistemic meanings arose by implicature from root meanings and express degrees of confidence in the facts.

---

1. In modal logic $\Box\Phi \leftrightarrow \neg\Diamond\neg\Phi$ and therefore $\Diamond\Phi \leftrightarrow \neg\Box\neg\Phi$

Definition 11.14 EPISTEMIC MODALS have one of the following three semantic operators:

PREDICTED[Φ] for epistemic *will, would*
◇Φ for epistemic *can, could, may, might*
□Φ for epistemic *must, needs, [not] need to, [not] have to*

There is an implicational scale < □Φ, PREDICTED[Φ], ◇Φ > such that the choice of a member to the right implicates none to the left apply, e.g. *It could rain tonight* ▷ ¬[*It will rain tonight*] ▷ ¬[*It must rain tonight*].

Deontic meanings denote permissions, prohibitions, obligations, requirements, demands, and the like which impose controls on participants in the situation.

Definition 11.15 DEONTIC MODALS have one of the following two semantic operators:

REQUIRED[Φ] for deontic *will, must, have to, need, may [not]*
PERMITTED[Φ] for deontic *can, may*

There is an implicational scale < REQUIRED[Φ], PERMITTED[Φ] >, cf. *You can bring your kids* ▷ ¬[*You must bring your kids*].

The modality system expresses different degrees of certainty.[11] People operate a credibility metric that is reflected in their languages. Ordinary language users judge a proposition true or false on the basis of its credibility. Therefore linguists (though perhaps not philosophers) need a credibility metric such as that in Table 11.4, in which complete confidence that a proposition is true rates 1, represented CRED=1, and complete confidence that a proposition is false rates CRED=0; indeterminability is midway between these two – CRED=0.5. Other values lie in between. Each level corresponds to a degree of commitment ranging between □*p* and □¬*p*.

1	Undoubtedly true	□*p*, I know that *p*
0.9	Most probably true	I am almost certain that *p*
0.8	Probably true	I believe that *p*
0.7	Possibly true	I think *p* is probable
0.6	Just possibly true	I think that perhaps *p*
0.5	Indeterminable	◇*p*
0.4	Just possibly false	It is not impossible that *p*
0.3	Possibly false	It is not necessarily impossible that *p*
0.2	Probably false	It is (very) unlikely that *p*
0.1	Most probably false	It is almost impossible that *p*
0	Undoubtedly false	□¬*p*, I know that ¬*p*

Table 11.4 The credibility metric for a proposition

In reality, one level of the metric overlaps an adjacent level so that the cross-over from one level to another is more often than not entirely subjective. Levels 0.1, 0.4, 0.6, 0.9 are as much an artifact of the decimal system as they are independently distinct levels. Nonetheless, there is no doubt that some variant of the credibility metric exists and is justified by the employment of the adverbials *probably* and *possibly* in everyday speech. This metric is used in some lexical entries (Allan 2000).

Exercises

11.4.1 Modal verbs split between realis and irrealis. Which category do the following fall into?
  (a) Although he's only three, Sean *can* swim.
  (b) I think I *might* go swimming.
  (c) She *must* get her application posted before noon today.
  (d) *Would* you come to the ball with me?

11.4.2 How would you describe the difference in meaning between (a) and (b)?
  (a) Can you help me lift this table?   (b) Will you help me lift this table?

11.4.3 Contrast the semantics of (a) and (b).
  (a) How long will it take?   (b) How long does it take?

11.4.4 What is the meaning of (a) and why is it consistent with the semantics given in 70 (p.361).
  (a) I know you CAN swim, but DO you?

11.4.5 Discuss *If it is possible for Harry to pass the exam, then he must have the ability to do so.*

11.4.6 What contribution does *can* make to the illocutionary point in each of (a–c)?
  (a) Come early and we can have a drink.
  (b) Can you pass the salt?
  (c) Jeez, that woman can talk!

11.4.7 What difference do you identify between (a) and (b)?
  (a) I can hear a dog barking.   (b) I am able to hear a dog barking.

11.4.8 Idiomatic expressions like (a–c) are ambiguous between epistemic ability and deontic meanings because their main function is to act as expressives. What is the implied meaning for each of them?
  (a) You can leave me off that list!
  (b) Fred can get stuffed!
  (c) You can say that again!

11.4.9 What is the semantics of the modal in *John can be out at any time of the day?*

11.4.10 There seem to be different implicatures in the most likely interpretations for (a) and (b). What are they?

    (a) I can't paint my house purple.   (b) I couldn't paint MÝ house purple!

11.4.11 Why do you think all the possibilities in (a) are OK, but (b) are dubious?

    (a) In her state of mind she could/may/might kill someone.
        It could/may/might be that prices will go down.
    (b) ??In her state of mind she can kill someone.
        ??It can be that prices will go down.

11.4.12 What is the difference between (a) and (b)?

    (a) You can go tomorrow.   (b) You could go tomorrow.

11.4.13 Compare the progressive aspect in (a) with the simple (aorist) aspect in (b).

    (a) Sue can't be singing, she had a throat operation last week.
    (b) Sue can't sing, though she thinks she can.

11.4.14 What is the meaning difference between (a) and (b).

    (a) You mustn't put words in my mouth.   (b) You needn't put words in my mouth.

11.4.15 Do you have any comment on (a) and (b)?

    (a) I must admit she looked stunning tonight.
    (b) ?I need to admit she looked stunning tonight.

11.4.16 In the light of 61–64, comment on *I don't ever waltz, but I can*.

11.5 Stepping-stones through the quagmire of thematic roles

Clause predicates denote actions, states, and events and their NP arguments denote participants in these actions, states, and events. The roles that participants play, such as effector, experiencer, theme, patient, are called 'thematic roles'.

> *Definition 11.16* The THEMATIC ROLE of an argument x of a predicate derives from the role that x plays in the action, event, or state denoted by that predicate.

The following quotes from Dowty 1991 deserve careful reading.

> From the semantic point of view, the most general notion of thematic role (type) is A SET OF ENTAILMENTS OF A GROUP OF PREDICATES WITH RESPECT TO ONE OF THE ARGUMENTS OF EACH. (Thus a thematic role type is a kind of second order property, a property of multiplace predicates indexed by their argument positions.)

[...] semantic distinctions like these entailments ultimately derive from distinctions in kinds of events found 'out there' in the real world: they are natural (physical) classifications of events, and/or those classifications that are significant to human life. There is no reason to believe that all such classes must have discrete boundaries.

[...] It is certainly not obvious that in ordinary reasoning and conversation people directly pay attention to or worry about whether something really was or was not a Theme or a Source or an Agent (in some sense of 'Theme', etc., exactly as defined by Jackendoff or some other linguist): but we do concern ourselves all the time, both in everyday life and in courts of law, and sometimes to a painstaking degree, with whether an act was really volitional or not, whether something really caused something or not, whether somebody was really aware of an event or state or not, or had a certain emotional reaction to it, whether something was moving or stationary, whether something changed in a certain way or not, whether an event was finished or not, and whether an act produced something as a result or not.   (Dowty 1991:552, 575)

There is no doubt that thematic roles are a significant part of the semantic frame of a predicate;[12] but there are problems determining the number, definitions, and boundaries of thematic roles – hence the title of this section. Significant to differentiating the different thematic roles for any particular language is A11.3.

> *Assumption 11.3* For any given role, there is a consistent set of entailments and/ or implicatures.

> *Definition 11.17* An EFFECTOR instigates the action or activity denoted by the verb.[13]

There are four different kinds of effector: agent, force, instrument, and means. Most, if not all, languages have some effectors that are agents.

> *Definition 11.18* (a) An AGENT wilfully instigates the action/activity of his, her, or its own volition.
> (b) An agent is sentient (capable of perceiving and cognizing) and therefore
> (c) causes an event to occur or causes a change of state in another participant, i.e. is the source for the action/activity.
> (d) An agent often moves in relation to another participant.
> (e) An agent typically exists independently of the event denoted by the predicate.

100 exemplifies the prototypical agent.

100 [Sue_agent] slapped Harry for insulting her.

Intuitively, agents play other roles as well (captured in Jackendoff's system of both action and thematic tiers, Chapter 12). For instance, in 100 Sue is the SOURCE of the slap. This violates the restriction first identified by Fillmore 1968:21 and enshrined in the theta-criterion of government binding theory (Chomsky 1981):

Definition 11.19 The Θ-CRITERION: no NP can fill more than one thematic role in a clause.

Assumption 11.4 Agent is always a pragmatic implication and not part of the semantic frame of any verb (cf. Holisky 1987, Van Valin and LaPolla 1997).

Forces and instruments differ from agents in not volitionally instigating the action/activity denoted by the verb and they are often not sentient. Forces share some properties with agents:

Definition 11.20 A FORCE is capable of independent motion and action, and can even 'use' an instrument.

101 $_[$The wind$_{force]}$ blew the door open.
102 $_[$The helicopter$_{force]}$ clipped the tree-tops with $_[$its rotor-blades$_{instrument]}$.

Definition 11.21 INSTRUMENTS are incapable of independent motion or action and must be controlled by some other effector.

103 $_[$Thea$_{agent]}$ cut the salami with $_[$a knife$_{instrument]}$.
    $_[$Thea$_{agent]}$ used $_[$a knife$_{instrument]}$ to cut the salami.

Definition 11.22 An abstract effector is MEANS.

104 (a)   Evita swept into power on $_[$the sympathy vote$_{means]}$.
    (b) $_[$The sympathy vote$_{means]}$ brought Evita into power.

105 (a)   Caesar was toppled by $_[$a conspiracy$_{means]}$.
    (b)   Governments increase revenue by $_[$raising taxes$_{means]}$.

In 104 the means may or may not be manipulated, in 105 there is no doubt that it is manipulated. When manipulated, the means is an abstract instrument; when it is not, it is an abstract force. These differences result from the entailments licensed by the semantics of the NPs, the predicates, and our knowledge of the world. The same assessment holds for all of the effector roles, creating further problems for the θ-criterion and Fillmore's 1968 constraint that no clause may contain more than one instance of a thematic role. Consider:

106 $_[$Joe$_{effector]}$ cut off his finger with $_[$his knife$_{effector]}$.

If both Joe and his knife are effectors, why is the former chosen for the clause subject in the unmarked clause? Because there is a dominance hierarchy among effectors (X ≺ Y means "X outranks (takes precedence over) Y").

Assumption 11.5 There is an EFFECTOR HIERARCHY:

$$\text{Agent} \prec \begin{cases} \text{force} \prec \text{instrument.} \\ \text{means} \end{cases}$$

This hierarchy correlates with other hierarchies such as that animates outrank inanimates and things capable of movement outrank things that are inherently incapable of movement. The subcategories of effector cannot save the θ-criterion: compare 106 with 107–8.

107 [Joe$_{effector}$] deliberately cut off his finger with [his knife$_{instrument}$].
108 [Joe$_{effector}$] accidentally cut off his finger with [his knife$_{instrument}$].

106 is ambiguous between between 107 and 108, with a preference for the latter because it is unusual for people to mutilate themselves. The manner adverbs in 107–8 simply clarify the intended meaning. There is no good reason to claim that in 106 Joe is anything other than an effector, i.e. no reason to claim that he is agent rather than force. However, being human, Joe outranks the knife as an effector. In 107 there is good reason to identify Joe as the agent, whereas in 108 it is more appropriate to regard him as a force. The distinction is clearly a consequence of the manner adverbs in the two sentences and not either the verb frame or the relationship between the verb and its argument.
    Turning to the knife, compare 109–11.

109 [The knife$_{effector}$] cut off Joe's finger.
110 ?The knife accidentally cut off Joe's finger.
111 ??The knife deliberately cut off Joe's finger.

109 is perfectly acceptable, and could apply either to a knife that fell off a shelf or to one that someone was using – although in the second case it would be usual to blame the knife-user not the knife. In our culture (at least) the manner adverbs in 110–11 cannot be literally attributed to the behaviour of the knife itself, and have to be interpreted as referring the behaviour of the knife-user. Because no knife-user is mentioned, the adverbs render the sentences very peculiar. Can we determine whether the knife in 109 is a force or an instrument? If it fell off a shelf it is a force, whereas if someone was using it, it is an instrument; however, out of context, 109 is ambiguous between these possibilities. As we shall see, the problem of deciding what sort of effector we have is typical of many thematic roles – as foreshadowed in the quotes from Dowty 1991 at the beginning of this section.

Definition 11.23   An EXPERIENCER is a sentient being which has an experience that is not volitionally or wilfully instigated.

Definition 11.24 A PERCEIVER is a subcategory of experiencer that undergoes a physical effect from some stimulus.

In 112 Harry is an agent as well as being a perceiver, but in 113 he is only a perceiver.

112 [Harry$_{agent}$] listened to the music.

113 [Harry$_{perceiver}$] heard the parrot screech.
114 [Sheila$_{perceiver}$] is feeling fluey.
   [The dog$_{perceiver}$] smelled the cooking bacon.

In 112 Harry volitionally and willfully does something, whereas this is not the entailment of 113–14.

> *Definition 11.25* A COGNIZER is a subcategory of experiencer that undergoes a mental effect.

115 [Jack$_{cognizer}$] knew the answer.
   [Emma$_{cognizer}$] wanted to buy the coat.
   [People$_{cognizers}$] believe that the Chief of Police is corrupt.

Perception surely involves cognitive awareness, so that perceivers are also cognizers.

Prepositions are a guide to the assignment of thematic roles in English, but many are multifunctional.

(a)   *By* is used with effectors in passive constructions, but *stand by **the window*** is LOCATIVE.
(b)   *With* is used with instruments, but *come with **me*** is COMITATIVE.
(c)   *To* is associated with experiencers in *known/appear to **NP*** but also GOAL in *go to **Paris***, RECIPIENT in *give it to **Jo***, and POSSESSOR in *belong to **NP***.

Random choices from a list of English prepositions – *after, around, at, before, beside, down, from, in, on, over, through, to, under, up* – suggest there must be many locative relations (cf. Landau and Jackendoff 1993). In addition to locations in space and time, there are ABSTRACT LOCATIVES such as recipient and possessor:[14]

116 The book was given to [Sue$_{recipient}$] by her father.
117 [Sue$_{possessor}$] has a new book.

The role of recipient often coalesces with that of beneficiary. BENEFICIARY (or, BENEFACTIVE) is exemplified in 118, where Ed is the beneficiary.

118 (a)   Sue bought a shirt for [Ed$_{beneficiary}$].
    (b)   Sue bought [Ed$_{beneficiary}$] a shirt.

In 119 there is both a recipient and a beneficiary and the latter is peripheral to the core clause and is denoted by a PP headed by *for* as in 118(a).

119 Sue gave [her mother$_{recipient}$] a shirt for [her father$_{beneficiary}$].

When there is no beneficiary marked, the recipient is understood to be beneficiary (or its contrary, MALEFICIARY, which is the same kind of thematic role but the act is bad for the referent instead of beneficial):

120 Sue gave $_{[}$her mother$_{recipient/beneficiary]}$ a shirt.
121 Sue gave $_{[}$her son$_{recipient/maleficiary]}$ a slap.

Returning to more typical locatives, many are complex; for instance, with dynamic verbs like *go*, PATH stretches from SOURCE to GOAL:

122 Harry went $_{[path}$ from $_{[}$London$_{source]}$ to $_{[}$Bangkok$_{goal] path]}$.

We need to distinguish locatives that form part of the semantic frame of a predicate from those that are peripheral. Although in normal discourse every state and event is located in space and time, reference to that spatio-temporal location is peripheral to what role and reference grammar calls the 'the core of the clause'. For instance, the italicized temporal and spatial adverbials in 123 are peripheral; the remainder, 'the Queen opened Parliament', is the core of the clause.

123 $_{[}$*Yesterday*$_{temporal]}$ *in* $_{[}$*London*$_{inessive]}$ $\left[\begin{array}{c} \text{the Queen opened Parliament} \\ \text{THE CORE OF THE CLAUSE} \end{array} \right]$

The verb *open* requires in its frame just two arguments: someone or something to do the opening, and something to be opened – neither of which is locative. The peripheral adverbials satisfy the requirements of a particular discourse context, and are not part of the meaning of *open*. The verb *go* also requires at least two arguments: someone or something to do the going and a path to go along, or a source to go from and also a goal to go to. The locative is an essential part of the verb frame – i.e. essential to understanding the proper meaning of *go*. The discourse context will decide which subcategory of locative is appropriate and whether it is to be made explicit or left to be inferred.

Typically, the various types of locative interact with a theme.

Definition 11.26 A THEME is causally affected by another participant only in terms of its location and not in terms of its character or configuration. A theme is also an entity whose location is referred to.

In 124–25 the theme is moved, but it is static in 126–27.

124 $_{[}$Harry$_{agent]}$ took $_{[}$the book$_{theme]}$ from $_{[}$the shelf$_{source]}$.
125 $_{[}$The book$_{theme]}$ was given to $_{[}$Sue$_{recipient]}$ by $_{[}$her father$_{agent]}$.
126 $_{[}$The mask$_{theme]}$ sits on top of $_{[}$the speaker-cabinet$_{locative]}$.
127 $_{[}$The rolling tumbleweed$_{force]}$ swept past $_{[}$the rock$_{theme]}$.

The abstract counterpart to a physical location is something possessed or owned.

128 $_{[}$Harry$_{locative]}$ kept $_{[}$the CD$_{theme]}$.
129 $_{[}$Wendy$_{possessor]}$ owns $_{[}$a BMW$_{theme]}$.
130 $_{[}$The BMW$_{theme]}$ belongs to $_{[}$Wendy$_{possessor]}$.

What experiencers experience is a theme:

131 Only [Sandy$_{cognizer}$] knows [the combination$_{theme}$].
[The combination$_{theme}$] is known only to [Sandy$_{cognizer}$]

132 [Wendy$_{perceiver}$] spied [a king parrot$_{theme}$].

Theme is the default thematic role with state and change of state predicates. The symmetric predicate ensures that 133 is synonymous with 134. The difference between them arises from discourse considerations such as topicality, familiarity, empathy, point of view, figure–ground hierarchy, etc.[15] 'Harry' and 'Fred' hold the same thematic role.

133 [Harry$_{theme}$] is as tall as [Fred$_{theme}$].
134 [Fred$_{theme}$] is as tall as [Harry$_{theme}$].

We see in 133–36 that stative symmetric predicates have two themes.

135 [Philadelphia$_{theme}$] is near [New York$_{theme}$].
136 [2+2$_{theme}$] equals [4$_{theme}$].

Active symmetric predicates like those in 137–38 have two effectors.

137 [Boris$_{agent}$] debated (with) [Anton$_{agent}$] at the Oxford Union.
138 [My computer program$_{force}$] played chess with [his$_{force}$].

The occurrence of 'with' in 137–38 suggests that the second agent is also comitative.
   Converse predicates are no problem. 139 express relative locations; 140 locate an entity with respect to something known.

139 (a) [The lamp$_{theme}$] is on [the table$_{locative}$].
     (b) [The table$_{theme}$] is under [the lamp$_{locative}$].

140 (a) [Sheila$_{theme}$] is [Bruce's mother$_{locative}$]
     (b) [Bruce$_{theme}$] is [Sheila's son$_{locative}$].

Assuming that Bruce is Sheila's son, 141(a) and (c) do not mean the same.

141 (a) [Sheila$_{possessor}$] has [a son$_{theme}$].
     (b) [Bruce$_{possessor}$] has [a mother$_{theme}$].
     (c) #Sheila has Bruce.

Definition 11.27 (a) A PATIENT's character or configuration is causally affected by another participant.
(b) It is often incremental. Sometimes the participant's condition changes perceptibly during the course of an event, cf. the patient of effective verbs like *build a house, knit a sweater* and destructive verbs like *tear up the paper into little pieces*: the house and sweater come into being incrementally; the paper gets torn up incrementally.

(c) A patient may come into existence or cease to exist as a result of the event denoted by the predicate.

(d) A patient undergoes a change of state.

(e) A patient either doesn't move or moves less than an effector.

142 exemplifies the prototypical patient:

142 $_{[}$Harry$_{effector]}$ broke $_{[}$the plate$_{patient]}$.

The original motivation for identifying thematic roles was to represent, within the semantic frames of verbs, the semantics of the surface cases and prepositional or postpositional phrases that the verb governs. This study of thematic roles has shown that even trying to define each role in terms of a common set of entailments or implicatures leaves many unresolved problems. There is probably a boundless number of thematic roles, so it is hardly surprising that no one has satisfactorily identified a full set of them for any language. Roles such as effector and locative have a number of subcategories (cf. Cruse 1973, Dowty 1991), and it is possible that ever finer distinctions can be drawn among them. §12.3.10 lists attributant, attribute, cognizer, consumed, consumer, creation, creator, desiror, effector, emitter, emoter, existant, experiencer, implement, indicator, judge, location, locus, mover, object of knowledge/belief, observer, patient, perceiver, performance, performer, possessed, possessor, sensation, speaker, stimulus, target of emotion/desire, theme, user. Goldberg 1995 has 'creator-theme, 'createe-way', 'hander', 'handee', 'handed', 'lurcher', and 'sneezer', among others. There are many occasions when a given NP seems to satisfy the conditions for more than one thematic role; sometimes two NPs (apparently) have the same thematic role. What today is called the θ-criterion (D11.19) is apparently untenable. For instance, there is no doubt that goals and sources can be agents with verbs like *give, buy, sell*. And symmetric predicates and resumptive pronouns in sentences like ***The door*** *has a wreath on* ***it*** show that more than one instance of a thematic role can occur in a simple sentence. The definition of thematic roles in grammar is unsatisfactory and there is no sign that the situation is about to improve. Better definition is possible if we admit just two macroroles 'actor' and 'undergoer' in the grammar. The macroroles are discussed in Chapter 12 in the context of role and reference grammar.

Exercises

11.5.1 Where possible, assign the italicized NPs in (a–d) and the zero anaphor in (a) one of the effector roles and briefly explain your decision.
  (a) *Sally* cut herself on *the broken glass* and *[ø]* yelled.
  (b) *The tornado* took the roof off the barn.
  (c) *The river* swept him away.
  (d) O J was prosecuted on *circumstantial evidence*.

11.5.2 Assign thematic roles to the italicized NPs in (a–k).

  (a) *Sandy* pretended to forget his name.
  (b) *The lamppost* was hit by *a truck*.
  (c) *Rex* just knew he was in trouble.
  (d) *Sally* gazed at Fabio.
  (e) *Jim* was bamboozled by *a con trick*.
  (f) *Ed* looked at *the bridge*.
  (g) *The loot* is under *the mattress*.
  (h) *The committee* meets at *10*.
  (i) Gim*me a chocolate*!
  (j) *Merv* has *a new car*.
  (k) *Everyone there* saw *the accident*.

11.5.3 In English, it is usual for there to be some clause structure in which an argument of the core of the clause does NOT fall under the scope of a preposition, e.g. the recipient in *George gave the bike to Harry* is under the scope of 'to' but this is not the case in *George gave Harry the bike*. The locative core argument of relocation verbs like *go* and *put* cannot lose their preposition. One test for whether an argument is core or not comes from asking questions like the ones below. (i) and (ii) are two model sentences; in answering questions (a–f), what is the smallest part of the clause that is acceptable? Why is (c) strange in this context?

(i) *Yesterday in London the Queen opened Parliament.*
(ii) *Sue went to Boston yesterday.*

  (a) What happened yesterday?
  (b) What happened in London?
  (c) ??What happened to Boston?
  (d) Where did she do it?
  (e) As briefly as possible, what did the Queen do?
  (f) As briefly as possible, what did Sue do?

11.5.4 The beneficiary and maleficiary are usually regarded as subsidiary roles; for instance in *Jed helped the old lady across the road* 'the old lady' is a beneficiary of the action, but the NP would usually be regarded as a theme; in *Jed battered the old lady to death* 'the old lady' is a maleficiary and Jed the malefactor, but 'Jed' has the thematic role of agent, and 'the old lady' that of patient. In *Harry sold Jim a mower* can you argue both that Harry is an agent and also a source for the mower? Is Jim not recipient, goal, and also beneficiary? What does this tell you about thematic roles?

11.6 Summary

Chapter 11 has focused on major aspects of clause semantics: mood, tense, modality, and thematic roles. Although grammatical aspect received short shrift, the only major omission has been any investigation of the passive. This is not fully justified by the fact that the passive is primarily motivated by pragmatic or discourse considerations.[16] Because mood indicates primary illocution, certain aspects of speech acts were briefly considered; but discussion was severely limited because speech acts are a quintessentially pragmatic category and this book seeks to stay – so far as is feasible – within semantics.

Chapter 12 builds on the discussion of thematic roles when describing the semantics of clause predicates. It begins with the semantic decomposition of predicates in terms of Jackendoff's lexical conceptual semantics; and then turns to the aspectually based categorization of predicates in Van Valin's role and reference grammar.

● Key words and phrases:

abstract locative (recipient, possessor, etc.)
actor
agent (D11.18)
aspect (D11.10)
backshifting
beneficiary
□, box, epistemic necessity operator
case (deep case)
clause-type (A11.2)
cognizer (D11.25)
comitative
converse predicate
core of the clause
counterfactual
credibility metric (Table 11.4)
cyclic time
declarative clause, Φ, $\vdash\Phi$ (D11.1)
deictic centre, t_d (D11.8)
deontic meaning (D11.15)
$\Diamond$, diamond, epistemic possibility operator
direction of fit
durative aspect
effector (D11.17)
effector hierarchy (A11.5)
epistemic modality (D11.14)
experiencer (D11.23)
expressive(-exclamative), $X[I]$ (D11.4)
FINISH, completive aspect operator

follows, $\succ$
force (D11.20)
future tense, $\mathbf{F}$ (D11.12)
goal
illocution(ary force)
illocutionary act
illocutionary point
imperative, $!\Phi$ (D11.3)
imprecative
inference schema for speech acts (Table 11.1)
instrument (D11.21)
interrogative, $?\Phi$ (D11.2)
interrogative subjunctive, $?[\text{¡}\Phi]$ (D11.6)
irrealis (Table 11.2)
locative
locution
macrorole
maleficiary
means (D11.22)
modal verb
moment of utterance, t_0
mood (A11.2)
outranks (takes precedence over), $\prec$
participant (thematic) role
past tense, $\mathbf{P}$ (D11.11)
path
patient (D11.27)
perceiver (D11.24)
performative clause (D11.7)

● The form of utterance is necessarily the starting-point for Hearer's interpretation of utterance meaning and consequently the illocutionary point of the utterance (A11.1, Table 11.1).

●The function of mood is to indicate primary illocution (A11.2).

● Six primary illocutions for English are indicated by mood (clause-type): declarative (D11.1), expressive (D11.4), imperative (D11.3), (declarative) interrogative (D11.2), interrogative subjunctive (D11.6), and subjunctive (D11.5). Most languages have about this number of primary illocutions ±1 or 2.

● The definitional components of a primary illocution are <form>, <description>, <precondition>, <illocutionary intention>. The last of these refers to Speaker's reflexive intention towards Hearer.

● The identification of primary illocution with mood renders explicit performatives (in which the illocutionary point is spelled out in the semantics of the verb, D11.7) 'indirect' illocutions. Every performative has the primary illocution of a declarative.

● *Saying Φ* reports locutions, roughly the form of words uttered. *Saying **that** Φ* reports statements.

● Table 11.1 demonstrated a schematic step-by-step inferential analysis of utterance meaning proceeding from the utterance act, through the locution, the act of referring, the primary illocution, and thence to the illocutionary point.

● Tense is a grammatical system that locates situations in time relative to a deictic centre (D11.8, Table 11.3).

● Grammatical aspect captures some aspect of the development of an event (D11.10).

● The realis–irrealis split (Table 11.2) interacts with both tense and modality. The subjunctive mood is an irrealis mood.

● The root meaning of modals is close to their original lexical meaning (D11.13).

● The epistemic meanings of modals, captured by the operators PREDICTED, ◇, and □, are derived by implicature from root meanings and express degrees of confidence in the facts.

● The deontic meanings of modals, captured by the operators PERMITTED and REQUIRED, denote permissions, prohibitions, obligations, requirements, demands, and the like which impose controls on participants in the situation.

● The argument of a predicate has a thematic role that derives from the role which the participant denoted by that argument plays in the action, event, or state denoted by the predicate.

● Thematic roles play both a syntactic and a semantic role, and the latter now dominates the discussion of thematic roles. The original motivation for identifying thematic roles was to indicate in the syntactic frame of a predicate which surface cases, prepositional, or postpositional phrases it governs.

● Thematic roles are referred to by many terms, e.g. 'valencies', '(deep) cases', and 'θ-/ theta roles'. Each such term is theory-dependent and the definition of a particular role in one theory is likely to be different in at least some respects from its definition in another theory, despite the same label (e.g. agent, patient) being used in both.

●There is a consistent set of entailments and/or implicatures for a thematic role (A11.3).

● Among the thematic roles identified were: effector (which includes agent (a pragmatic role A11.4), force, instrument, and perhaps means), experiencer (which includes cognizers and perceivers of various kinds), locative (which includes recipient, possessor and a host of spatial and temporal locations), theme (moved or static), and patient.

● There is a hierarchy among effectors (A11.5) and, we shall come to see, other roles.

● GB theory proposes a θ-criterion (Chomsky 1981, based on an earlier criterion in Fillmore's case grammar, 1968) that there is one thematic role per clause and no NP can hold more than one thematic role. The criterion has been shown to be incorrect; for instance, the arguments of a symmetric predicate hold identical thematic roles.

11.7 Notes on further reading

[1] On the long history of linking clause-type to illocutionary force, see also Sanctius 1585, Lancelot 1644, Lane 1700, Whitney 1888, Sadock 1974:16f.

[2] Not discussed here is the illocutionary contribution of embedded clauses (such as complements) to the illocutionary point of an utterance; see Allan 1986, 1994h.

[3] On performative clauses, see Austin 1962, 1963, Allan 1994c.

[4] On adverbials which modify primary illocutionary acts, see Allan 1986, Jackendoff 1972, Schreiber 1972, Sadock 1974.

[5] On mood, see Harnish 1994, Lyons 1977, Palmer 1986, Sadock and Zwicky 1985.

[6] On schemas for inferring the illocutionary point, see Searle 1975a, Bach and Harnish 1979, Allan 1986, 1994e.

[7] On looking back to the future, see Thornton 1987:70, Hollenbach 1990.

[8] On tense, see Comrie 1985, Declerck 1991, Huddleston 1995, Harder 1996 Part 3, Huddleston and Pullum 1997, Steedman 1997.

[9] On aspect, see Comrie 1976.

[10] On 'agent-oriented' modals, see Bybee 1985, Bybee et al. 1994, Bybee and Fleischman 1995a.

[11] On modals, see Lyons 1977, Coates 1983, Palmer 1986, Matthews 1991, Bybee, Perkins and Pagliuca 1994, Bybee and Fleischman (eds) 1995.

[12] Themantic roles are also referred to as 'valencies' in Tesnière 1959, '(deep) cases' in Fillmore 1968, 1977, J. Anderson 1971, Blake 1977; 'semantic roles' in Katz 1972, 1977a, Dillon 1977; 'θ-/theta roles' in Chomsky 1981, Marantz 1984, Wilkins 1988; 'role archetypes' by Langacker 1990; 'thematic roles' in Frawley 1992; and 'argument roles' in Goldberg 1995. The discussion of thematic roles in this chapter rests on Dowty 1991, Foley and Van Valin 1984 Ch. 2, Van Valin 1993a, Wilkins and Van Valin 1994, Van Valin and LaPolla 1997; in turn their work has been influenced, principally, by the insights of Gruber 1965, Fillmore 1968, 1977, S. Anderson 1971, Jackendoff 1972, 1976, 1987b, 1990.

[13] On effectors, see Foley and Van Valin 1984, Holisky 1987, Van Valin and LaPolla 1997.

[14] On locatives of possession and ownership, see Gruber 1965, Lyons 1967, 1977 Ch. 15, Anderson 1971, Jackendoff 1972, Allan 1998.

[15] On topicality, familiarity, empathy, point of view, figure–ground hierarchy, see Malkiel 1968, Kuno 1976, 1979, Kuno and Kaburaki 1977, Ertel 1977, Talmy 1978, Haiman 1985, Langacker 1987, Allan 1987a.

[16] On the passive, see Shibatani (ed.) 1988, Siewierska 1984.

12 The semantics of clause predicates

12.1 Where we are heading

This chapter builds on the discussion of thematic roles in Chapter 11 and continues the study of clause semantics and semantic frames by describing two approaches to the semantics of clause predicates. §12.2 reviews Jackendoff's lexical conceptual structure analysis of the meanings of verbs. Jackendoff decomposes verbs into a limited number of semantic primitives that function as predicates in what he calls 'function-argument structures'. §12.3 continues the study of the semantic frames and structures of predicates in §12.2 by examining their 'logical structures' in role and reference grammar (RRG). RRG decomposes verbs on the basis of their aspectual properties, i.e in terms of whether they denote activities, states, achievements, etc. Considerable attention is paid to the assignment of the macroroles actor and undergoer within the logical structures of verbs. §12.4 compares and evaluates the application of Jackendoff-style lexical conceptual semantics and RRG style logical structures to the same data. The section ends with commentary on the nature of semantic specifications in the metalanguage. §12.5 summarizes the chapter.

12.2 Jackendoff's 'lexical conceptual structures' for verbs[1]

Conceptual structure hypothesis
There is a *single* level of mental representation, *conceptual structure*, at which linguistic, sensory, and motor information are compatible.

(Jackendoff 1983:17)

This section uses Jackendoff's metalinguistic conventions when expounding his work. In particular, semantic primitives are written in UPPER CASE, and optional constituents are enclosed in < > or marked by dashed underlining.

Jackendoff adopts the view of his mentor Chomsky that the proper study for linguistics is what used to be called 'competence' (Chomsky 1965) and more recently 'I-language' (I = "internalized", Chomsky 1986). Conceptual semantics is intended to integrate with syntactic and phonological theories that have been intensely studied since the early 1960s. It is also an integral part of a general theory of the mind that Jackendoff has developed in

---

1. A list of symbols peculiar to this section is found among the keywords section of the summary.

several books (1983, 1987a, 1992a, 1997) in addition to what appears in *Semantic Structures* 1990. Relevant components of this theory of mental structure are presented in Fig. 12.1.

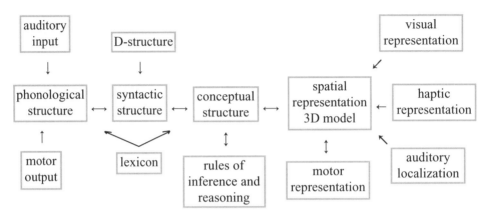

Figure 12.1 Mental representations, based on Jackendoff 1983, 1990, 1992a, 1997

According to Jackendoff, semantics is a part of conceptual structure in which linguistic, sensory, and motor information are compatible. This breadth of vision has a consequence that is unusual in semantic theories: Jackendoff believes that word meaning is a large, heterogeneous collection of typicality conditions with no sharp distinction between lexicon and encyclopedia.

> *Assumption 12.1* Knowing the meaning of a word that denotes a physical object includes knowing what such an object looks like. So, in addition to the traditional-style lexicon entry, conceptual structure must also contain a partial 3D (= three-dimensional) model structure based on visual perception (Jackendoff 1983:139, 1987a:201).

This is very likely true for a sighted person, but what about someone blind from birth?

> Any semantic distinction that makes a *syntactic* difference must be encoded in conceptual structure. Differences that appear only in 3D model structure can by hypothesis have no syntactic effects. For example, *run, jog,* and *lope* are syntactically parallel, as are *throw, toss,* and *lob.* Thus the members of each set can be identical in conceptual structure and differ only in the associated 3D model. [...] 3D model differences [... are] crucial in distinguishing word meanings.   (Jackendoff 1990:34)

Jackendoff implies that the actions denoted by *run, jog,* and *lope* look different but have a common semantic base represented by the primitive verb GO. (The claim is modified in Jackendoff 1996 in response to criticism from Taylor 1996, but not retracted.) A partial 3D model for such verbs represents the manner and stages of motion, but is unspecified so as to enable an individual to recognize different instances of running, jogging, etc. as the same kind of activity.[1]

> [V]isual distinctions of "manner of motion" (or at least a great many of them) are not the business of conceptual structure at all; conceptual structure has to encode primarily an appropriate argument structure, linked in the lexicon to a more detailed spatial structure encoding.
>
> (Jackendoff 1990:88)

It is the different manners of motion visible in each of *run, jog*, and *lope* on the one hand, and *throw, toss*, and *lob* on the other, that Jackendoff refers to as differences in 3D model structures. Along with visual differences are other sensory differences that would be perceived by the unsighted as well as the sighted person. No semanticist has discussed these, but if visual data is to be accounted for, so should other sensory data. All this information is encyclopedic rather than lexical (Chapter 3).

What are the linguistic clues to conceptual categories?

> Every content-bearing major phrasal constituent of a sentence (S, NP, AP, PP, etc.) corresponds to a conceptual constituent of some major conceptual category.
>
> (Jackendoff 1990:44)

S expresses STATE or EVENT. A NP can express almost any conceptual category. PP expresses PLACE, PATH, and PROPERTY. Jackendoff is principally interested in the semantic structure of verbs; with a secondary interest in 'function-argument structures in the spatial domain' – for 'function' read "predicate" (Chapter 7). He makes no attempt to semantically decompose nouns, treating them as semantic primitives. In his view, only kin terms and geometric figures admit of satisfactory semantic decomposition (1983:112f, 1987a:140). By contrast, he finds that verbs decompose into comparatively few classes.

Jackendoff's vocabulary of semantic primitives is very much larger than the set used by Wierzbicka and her co-workers (§8.6). The syntax of his lexical conceptual structure (LCS) is a configuration of functions ranging over arguments. For instance, 1 is a conceptual structure in which function F has two arguments [A] and [B].

1   [F([A],[B])]

Note that conceptual structures and primitives are bounded by square brackets, and the range of the function in parentheses. LCS makes no use of logical connectives.

2   [PLACE] → [$_{Place}$PLACE-FUNCTION([THING])]

Examples of Place-functions are AT, IN, ON, UNDER. (In the following, the LCS is to the left of ← and an italicized English phrase or clause containing the LCS is on its right.)

3   [$_{Place}$UNDER([$_{Thing}$TABLE])]   ← *under the table*

PATH is exemplified in 4, EVENT in 5, and STATE in 6. There are no representations for definiteness or tense.

4   (a) $[_{Path}TO([_{Thing}HOUSE])]$ ←   *to the house*

     (b) $[_{Path}FROM([_{Place}UNDER([_{Thing}TABLE])]$ ←   *from under the table*

5   (a) $[_{Event}GO([_{Thing}BILL], [_{Path}TO([_{Thing}BOSTON])])]$ ←   *Bill went to Boston*

     (b) $[_{Event}STAY ([_{Thing}BILL], [_{Place}IN([_{Thing}BOSTON])])]$ ←   *Bill stayed in Boston*

6   (a) $[_{State}BE([_{Thing}BILL], [_{Place}IN([_{Thing}BOSTON])])]$ ←   *Bill is in Boston*

     (b) $[_{State}ORIENT([_{Thing}SIGN], [_{Path}TO([_{Thing}PHOENIX])])]$ ←   *The sign points to Phoenix*

     (c) $\left[_{State}EXT([_{Thing}ROAD], \begin{bmatrix} FROM([TUCSON]) \\ _{Path}\ TO([NOGALES]) \end{bmatrix})\right]$ ←   *The road goes (extends) from Tucson to Nogales*

EXT in 6(c) means "extends". In 7, INCH symbolizes INCHOATIVE, i.e. becoming, turning into, growing Adj. (The conditions for postulating INCH are not always distinguishable from conditions on GO; see Jackendoff 1990:94.)

7   $[_{Event}INCH([_{State}BE([SKY], AT([_{Property}RED])])])]$ ←   *The sky turned red*

The reason that $[_{Property}$ RED] falls within the scope of the function AT can be deduced from the following conceptual structure for *The light changed from red to green*:

8   $\left[_{Event}GO([_{Thing}LIGHT], \begin{bmatrix} FROM([_{Property}RED]) \\ _{Path}\ TO([_{Property}GREEN]) \end{bmatrix})\right]$

If a property can be a source and a goal, presumably it is also a location. *The weathervane came to point north*; *The railroad finally reached Kansas City* are other examples.
    9 exemplifies CAUSE.

9   $[_{Event}CAUSE([_{Thing}BILL], [_{Event}GO([_{Thing}BEER],$
             $[_{Path}TO([_{Place}IN([_{Thing}MOUTH\ OF([_{Thing}BILL])])])])])]$ ←   *Bill drank the beer*

A preferred alternative to the double appearance of BILL in 9 is ARGUMENT BINDING, symbolized 'α' in the lexicon entry for *drink* in 10.

Assumption 12.2 Greek superscripts $^{α, β, γ}$ stipulate binding between argument positions.

10   $\begin{bmatrix} \text{drink} \\ \text{V} \\ \begin{bmatrix} CAUSE([_{Thing}\ ]^{α}_{A}, [_{Event}GO([_{Thing}LIQUID]_{<A>}, \\ _{Event}\qquad\qquad\qquad [_{Path}TO([_{Place}IN([_{Thing}MOUTH\ OF([_{Thing}α])])])])]) \end{bmatrix} \end{bmatrix}$

Subscript $_{<A>}$ marks an option: what is drunk must be liquid, but need not be mentioned (*Bill drinks*).

Assumption 12.3 All arguments are indexed by subscript $_A$. Thematic roles are assigned according to a thematic hierarchy by 'argument linking'.

Definition 12.1 ARGUMENT LINKING
(a) Order the A-marked constituents in the verb's LCS according to the thematic hierarchy Actor ≺ Patient/Beneficiary ≺ Theme ≺ Location, Source, or Goal. (X ≺ Y means "X takes precedence over Y".)
(b) Order the NP constituents in the syntactic structure according to the syntactic hierarchy Subject ≺ 1st (direct) object ≺ 2nd object.
(c) Optionally coindex APs, PPs, and S's freely into A-marked constituents in the LCS.
(d) Coindex the first through *n*th NPs with the remaining A-marked constituents in thematic order, choosing coindexations from among the possibilities in the network:

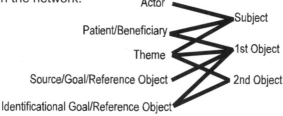

(Adapted from Jackendoff 1990:258, 261, 265f)

In 10, '$[_{Thing} \quad]^{\alpha}_A$' will be assigned what Jackendoff calls the 'actor' role (an effector, D11.17). '$[_{Thing} \quad]^{\alpha}_A$' is co-indexed with '$[_{Thing} \alpha]$' into whose mouth the liquid goes – namely 'Bill' in 9. The $_A$ in '$[_{Thing}LIQUID]_{<A>}$' indicates that it holds the role of theme. The theme NP is optional; syntactically intransitive *Bill drank* is nonetheless transitive in its semantic structure. The revised conceptual structure for *Bill drank the beer* is therefore 11.

11 $[_{Event}CAUSE([_{Thing}BILL]^{\alpha}_{A\text{-}actor}, [_{Event}GO([_{Thing\text{-}liquid}BEER]_{A\text{-}theme},$
$$[_{Path}TO([_{Place}IN([_{Thing}MOUTH \ OF([_{Thing}\alpha])])])])])]$$

The way that arguments get incorporated into the verb frame is by 'argument fusion'.

Definition 12.2 ARGUMENT FUSION. To form the conceptual structure of a syntactic phrase that has been linked with an LCS, fuse the conceptual structure of each indexed syntactic position to the coindexed conceptual constituent in the LCS (Jackendoff 1990:264).

Marking by $_A$ is motivated by the fact that there are many verbs like *break, open* and *slide* which can be intransitive and unaccusative, or transitive and causative; see Table 12.1

Middle voice

Intransitive and unaccusative	Transitive and causative
The window broke.	John broke the window.
The door opened.	Ed opened the door.
The box slid down the stairs.	Bill slid the box down the stairs.

Table 12.1 Verbs with transitive and intransitive alternates

Jackendoff proposes that the transitive and intransitive versions share a common lexicon entry in which the causative part is optional. For *slide*, he suggests the conceptual structure in 12, in which dashed underlining symbolizes optionality (presumably chosen because of the difficulty that would be met using < >).

12 $[_{\text{Path}}\text{CAUSE}([_{\text{Thing}}\ ],\ [_{\text{Event}}\text{GO}([_{\text{Thing}}\ ],\ [_{\text{Path}}\ ])]\ )]$

THING in the scope of GO is the subject of the intransitive clause, but the 1st object of the transitive clause. Jackendoff assumes that every clause needs an underlying subject, so one solution (known as the 'unaccusative hypothesis') is to index the lexical conceptual structure for the transitive as in 13 and stipulate a convention that, when the causative is not selected, $[_{\text{Thing}}\ ]_j$ is promoted to $[_{\text{Thing}}\ ]_i$ – note the changed subscript.

13 $[_{\text{Path}}\text{CAUSE}([_{\text{Thing}}\ ]_i,\ [_{\text{Event}}\text{GO}([_{\text{Thing}}\ ]_j,\ [_{\text{Path}}\ ]_k)]\ )]$

This is rejected. Jackendoff's preferred alternative is to index all arguments by $_\text{A}$, and leave the linking rules to determine the θ-role (thematic role, D11.16) of a particular argument according to D12.1. The lexicon entry for *slide* becomes 14 in which β is Theme and γ is Location.

14 $\begin{bmatrix} \text{slide} \\ \text{V} \\ [_{\text{Event}}\text{CAUSE}([_{\text{Thing}}\ ]^\alpha{}_\text{A},\ [_{\text{Event}}\text{GO}([_{\text{Thing}}\ ]^\beta{}_\text{A},\ [_{\text{Path}}\ ]^\gamma{}_\text{A})])] \end{bmatrix}$

Argument Binding by co-indexing with Greek letters resolves violations of the θ-criterion of government binding theory (D11.19). For example, there are sentences in which more than one NP holds a single θ-role, e.g. the italicized NPs in 15.

15 (a) *The box* has books in *it*.
　　(b) *Bill* carried four books with *him*.
　　(c) *The list* includes my name on *it*.

The arguments of verbs like *chase*, and the transaction verbs *buy* and *sell*, hold more than one θ-role, contrary to at least some statements of the θ-criterion. The problem disappears if Argument Binding is permitted. The lexicon entry for the verb *buy*, for example, is 16. 'AFF([α],[β])' means roughly "α affects β".

16
$$\left[\begin{array}{l} \text{buy} \\ \text{V} \\ \text{CAUSE}([\ ]^{\alpha}_{A}, \left[\begin{array}{l} \text{GO}_{\text{Poss}}([\text{Thing}\ ]^{\beta}_{A}, \left[\begin{array}{l}\text{FROM}[\ ]^{\gamma}_{<A>}\\ \text{TO}[\alpha]\end{array}\right]) \\ [\text{EXCH}[\text{GO}_{\text{Poss}}([\text{MONEY}], \left[\begin{array}{l}\text{FROM}[\alpha]\\ \text{TO}[\gamma]\end{array}\right])]] \\ {}_{\text{Event}}\ \text{AFF}([\alpha],[\beta]) \end{array}\right]) \end{array}\right]$$

The optional argument marking '$_{<A>}$' says that *buy* is optionally ditransitive when γ is explicitly mentioned (*Jo$_\alpha$ bought the bread$_\beta$ from Safeway$_\gamma$*). Otherwise, it is transitive (*Jo$_\alpha$ bought the bread$_\beta$*). In either case, '[$_{\text{Thing}}$]$^{\beta}_{A}$' is the 1st object. GO$_{\text{Poss}}$ indicates a change in the possession of β from γ to α; and there is a concomitant exchange of money from α to γ. Jackendoff defines a condition, D12.2, to uniquely link each syntactic argument with a conceptual argument, while allowing for (a) one NP to have more than one θ-role, and (b) one θ-role to be expressed by multiple NPs.

> *Definition 12.3* LINKING CONDITION (Neo θ-Criterion). Each index linking syntactic and conceptual structure in a lexical entry must appear only once in the entry's LCS. All other θ-roles that the co-indexed NP holds must be expressed by arguments bound to the indexed conceptual constituent (Jackendoff 1990:64).

AFF([α],[β]) in 16 represents the ACTION TIER in the LCS for *buy*. The action tier deals with actor-patient relations and co-exists with a THEMATIC TIER dealing with motion and location, often indicated by locative functions.

	Sue hit Fred		Pete threw the ball		Bill entered the room		Bill received	a letter
thematic tier	Th	G	S	Th	Th	G	G	Th
action tier	A	P	A	P	A			

Key: A=actor, G=goal, P=patient, S=source, Th=theme

Table 12.2 Jackendoff's action and thematic tiers

17 shows how the action tier is represented in conceptual structures.

17 [AFF([X],)]   X = Actor
   [AFF(,[Y])]   Y = Patient
   [AFF([ ],[Y])]   implicit actor
   [AFF([X],[ ])]   implicit patient

(There are unresolved inconsistencies among Jackendoff's superscripts for AFF, so they are omitted here.) In 16, 'AFF([α],[β])' indicates that α will be assigned the θ-role of actor and β has the θ-role of patient. On the thematic tier: for the exchange of possession, α is goal for the theme β, and γ is the source; for the exchange of money, money is the theme, α is the source and γ the goal. Two more examples.

18 $\begin{bmatrix} \text{CAUSE}([\text{HARRY}]^\alpha{}_A, \text{GO}_{\text{Poss}}([\text{BOOK}]^\beta{}_A, \begin{bmatrix} \text{FROM}\,([\alpha]) \\ \text{TO}([\text{SAM}]^\gamma) \end{bmatrix})) \\ \quad \text{AFF}([\alpha],[\beta]) \\ _{\text{Event}} \end{bmatrix}$

   ← *Harry gave the book to Sam*

Harry is actor and source; the book is patient and theme; Sam is goal.

19 $\begin{bmatrix} \text{GO}_{\text{Poss}}([_{\text{Thing}} \text{BOOK}]_A, [\text{TO}_{\text{Path}} ([_{\text{Thing}} \text{SAM}]_A)]) \\ _{\text{Event}} \text{AFF}([\ ],[\ ]) \end{bmatrix}$

   ← *Sam received a book* (unspecified actor)

Here the action tier is empty, and θ-roles are determined from the thematic tier.

16 and 18–19 have added a subscript to the primitive verb GO, namely GO$_{\text{Poss}}$ "possession". This is just one of many subscripts that can attach to GO, STAY, and BE that subcategorize these verbs and the associated locative functions such as AT, FROM, TO into a variety of semantic fields.

(a) POSSESSIVE:

20 (a) $[_{\text{Event}}\text{GO}_{\text{Poss}}([\text{WALLET}], [_{\text{Path}}\text{FROM}_{\text{Poss}}([\text{BILL}])])]$ ← *Bill lost the wallet*
  (b) $[_{\text{State}}\text{BE}_{\text{Poss}}([_{\text{Thing}}\text{RESTAURANT}], [_{\text{Place}}\text{AT}_{\text{Poss}}([_{\text{Thing}}\text{MAX}])])]$
    ← *Max owns the restaurant*

Compare French *Le restaurant est à Max* (literally, *the restaurant is at/to Max*, cf. Lyons 1967, 1977 Ch. 15).

(b) An IDENTIFICATIONAL field locates THINGs in a set denoting types or properties.

21 (a) $[_{\text{State}}\text{BE}_{\text{Ident}}([_{\text{Thing}}\text{ELISE}], [_{\text{Place}}\text{AT}_{\text{Ident}}([_{\text{Thing-type}}\text{PIANIST}])])]$ ← *Elise is a pianist*

  (b) $[_{\text{Event}}\text{GO}_{\text{Ident}}([_{\text{Thing}}\text{METAL}], \begin{bmatrix} \text{FROM}_{\text{Ident}}([\text{SOLID}]) \\ _{\text{Path}}\ \text{TO}_{\text{Ident}}([\text{LIQUID}]) \end{bmatrix})]$ ← *The metal melted*

(c) In the TEMPORAL field *The meeting is at four o'clock* uses BE$_{\text{Temp}}$ and AT$_{\text{Temp}}$. *We kept the meeting as originally scheduled* uses STAY$_{\text{Temp}}$. *The meeting was moved from four to six o'clock* uses GO$_{\text{Temp}}$ in 22, where *The* place prepositions are subcategorized $_{\text{Temp}}$.

22 $[_{Event}CAUSE(_{Thing}[\ ], [_{Event}GO_{Temp}([_{Event}MEETING], \begin{bmatrix} FROM_{Temp}([_{Time}FOUR]) \\ _{Path}\ \ TO_{Temp}([_{Time}SIX]) \end{bmatrix})])]$

(d)   The semantic field of CONTACT is indicated by subscript $_c$ in 23.

23 (a) $[_{State}BE_c([BILL], [_{Place}AT_c([PICTURE])])]$ ← *Bill touched the picture*
     (b) $[_{Event}INCH([_{State}BE_c([CAR], [_{Place}AT_c([TREE])])])]$ ← *The car hit the tree*

(e)   Other semantic fields identified include adherence, circumstance, and composition, e.g.

24 $[_{State}BE_{Comp}([TRIANGLE], [_{Place}AT_{Comp}([THREE\ LINES])])]$
     ← *The triangle consists of three lines*

The subscripting of a few primitive verbs with all these semantic field indicators greatly expands the range of the verbs, but it appears to be unconstrained, so that a new field indicator might be included whenever the analyst deems it useful.

Restrictive modification is very straightforward, e.g *big house* is a thing (*house*) with a property (*big*):

25 $\begin{bmatrix} HOUSE \\ _{Thing}\ [_{Property}\ BIG] \end{bmatrix}$

In *John went home quickly* there is AdvP modification of VP, yielding 26. *John went home at 6:00* has a PP modifier of VP and the temporal adverb is treated as a subcategory of place adverbs in 27.

26 $\begin{bmatrix} GO([_{Thing}JOHN], [_{Path}TO([_{Place}HOME])]) \\ _{Event}\qquad [_{Property/manner}QUICK] \end{bmatrix}$

27 $\begin{bmatrix} GO([_{Thing}JOHN], [_{Path}TO([_{Place}HOME])]) \\ _{Event}\qquad [_{Place}AT_{Temp}([_{Time}6:00])] \end{bmatrix}$

Definition 12.4 RESTRICTIVE MODIFIER RULE. If YP (the restrictive modifier) is the daughter of X″ in XP (X″ is one syntactic level above XP, e.g. mother to XP), and the conceptual structure of YP is $[C_y]$, then the conceptual structure of XP is of the form $\begin{bmatrix} ... \\ [C_y] \end{bmatrix}$ (Jackendoff 1990:56).

Where no head can be determined, as with $[_{PP}\ [_{PP}\ from\ the\ house]\ [_{PP}\ to\ the\ barn]]$, Jackendoff proposes

28 $\begin{bmatrix} FROM\ ([_{Thing}HOUSE]) \\ _{Path}\quad TO\ ([_{Thing}BARN]) \end{bmatrix}$

Every verb that involves PATH includes GO as part of its conceptual structure. Jackendoff introduces $[_{Event}MOVE([_{Thing} \;])]$ for, e.g. *The bear was dancing*. But if PATH is involved:

29 $[_{Event}GO([EMMA]^{\alpha}, [_{Path}TO([DOORWAY])]) [BY[MOVE([\alpha])]]]$
   ← *Emma danced to the doorway*

(See Jackendoff 1990:224 for details). BY is the function introducing the conceptual counterpart to an adverbial clause expressing "by means of". Other adverbial clause functions are FROM introducing causative clauses (e.g. *Harry sang **because he was happy*** or 30); FOR introduces purposive clauses (*Harry smiled **in order to ingratiate himself***), and WITH accompaniment clauses (31).

30 $\begin{bmatrix} [_{Event} \; INCH([_{State} \; BE_{Ident} \, ([_{Thing} \; JOHN]^{\alpha}, [AT_{Ident} \, ([_{Property} \; DEAD])])])] \\ [_{Cause} \; FROM \, ([_{Event} \; OVEREAT \, ([\alpha])])] \end{bmatrix}$

   ← *John died **from overeating***

31 $\begin{bmatrix} [_{Event} \; GO \, ([EMMA]^{\alpha} \, [_{Path}TO \, ([_{Place} \; IN \, ([_{Thing} \; ROOM])])])] \\ [_{Accompaniment} \; WITH \, ([_{Event} \; SMILE \, ([\alpha])])] \end{bmatrix}$

   ← *Emma came in **with a smile on her face***

To sum up this section. The syntax of Jackendoff's LCS is a 'function-argument' structure similar to that of predicate calculus. Although Jackendoff makes no use of logical connectives, some of his more complex formulae imply conjunction between the function-argument structures in a lexical conceptual structure. For instance AFF([ ]) is intuitively conjoined with the preceding function-argument structure. The set of primitive verbs so far identified is

32 BE, STAY, GO, ORIENT, EXT, CONF ("configured"), INCH, CAUSE, EXCH, AFF, REACT, MOVE

Many of these are subcategorized with the same subscripted categories as prepositions. In addition, $CS_{entrain}$ and CS_{launch} are found in the LCS for *drag* and *throw* respectively (1990:138). Several other verbs, CREATE, EAT, ENCOUNTER, FIND, OPEN, PREPARE, THINK also appear in Jackendoff's work, perhaps for notational convenience (e.g. EAT, PREPARE), or perhaps because they are primitive (e.g. THINK; cf. Wierzbicka 1996, Van Valin and Wilkins 1993). Although the vocabulary of functions seems to be restricted, the vocabulary of primitive arguments is unbounded.

Jackendoff uses superscripting and subscripting to expand the primitive vocabulary by subcategorization. There are inconsistencies in the superscripting of AFF, and CAUSE was reanalysed as in 33.

33 CS^{+} = CAUSE with successful outcome e.g. *Ed managed to leave.*
   CS^{-} = CAUSE with unsuccessful outcome e.g. *Ed failed to leave.*
   CS^{u} = CAUSE with unknown outcome e.g. *Ed tried to leave.*

The lexicon entry for *try* is

$$
34 \quad
\begin{bmatrix}
\text{try} \\
\text{V} \\
\begin{bmatrix}
\text{CS}^{\text{u}}([\alpha], [_{\text{Event}} \text{ AFF } ([\alpha],)]_{\text{A}}) \\
_{\text{Event}} \text{ AFF } ([\ ]^{\alpha}_{\text{A}},)
\end{bmatrix}
\end{bmatrix}
$$

The entries for *manage, fail,* and *try* simply differ in the superscripted feature on CS. Subscripting is more successful. For instance, the subscripts to the immediate right of a left-bracket, e.g. $[_{\text{Thing}} \ ]$ identify the conceptual kind. Other examples are:

35 $[_{\text{Thing-liquid}} \ ]$, $[_{\text{Place}} \ ]$, $[_{\text{Time}} \ ]$, $[_{\text{Path}} \ ]$, $[_{\text{Property}} \ ]$, $[_{\text{State}} \ ]$, $[_{\text{Event}} \ ]$, $[_{\text{Property/manner}} \ ]$.

Many predicates are subcategorized, also.

Most simple prepositions are treated as functions, but compound prepositions such as *into* are analysed into their component primitives: $[_{\text{Path}} \text{TO} ([_{\text{Place/Temp}} \text{IN}])]$. Prepositional subcategories include at least:

36 Possession, Identification, Temporality, Contact, Adherence, Circumstance, Composition.

This section sketches only a few aspects of Jackendoff's conceptual semantics, but it is sufficient to show that a semantic decomposition of verbs making extensive use of just a few primitives is a feasible project. Anyone acquainted with predicate calculus can construct a lexical conceptual structure in the style of Jackendoff despite the fact that a LCS does not employ standard logical formulae. Conceptual semantics is designed to integrate with a dominant syntactic theory in contemporary linguistics: A-marking links the semantic interpretation to a node in the syntactic phrase marker. Jackendoff 1992b, 1997, Culicover and Jackendoff 1994, suggest that argument binding in LCS (using Greek superscripts) does away with the need for the level of logical form (LF) in syntax. Intuitively, argument binding is a matter of semantics rather than syntax, e.g. the pronoun *she* appropriately refers to Mary for semantic not syntactic reasons. In German, *das Mädchen* "girl" is rendered neuter by its diminutive suffix *-chen* but is normally pronominalized in colloquial speech by the feminine *sie* and not the neuter *es*, though the matter is hotly debated and in the written language syntactic conformity is the norm. LF has not yet been abandoned in favour of conceptual structure; but Jackendoff's conceptual semantics is a real force within the development of grammatical theory.

Exercises

12.2.1 In (a–b) which are the functions and which the arguments?
  (a) $[_{\text{State}} \text{BE}([_{\text{Thing}} \text{BILL}], [_{\text{Place}} \text{IN}([_{\text{Thing}} \text{BOSTON}])])$
  (b) $[_{\text{Event}} \text{INCH}([_{\text{State}} \text{BE}([\text{SKY}], \text{AT}([_{\text{Property}} \text{RED}])])])]$

12.2.2 The idea of a 3D model would nicely offer one criterion for distinguishing kinds of animals from one another, e.g. cats from dogs. However, Jackendoff seems to imply that the model is purely visual. If this were true, blind people would be at a much greater disadvantage than appears to be the case – to use one of Jackendoff's examples, they wouldn't be able to distinguish running from jogging, which is simply not the case. How can we exploit Jackendoff's insight without such an unwelcome and unwarranted limitation?

12.2.3   Write conceptual structures for the following:
    (a)   to the floor
    (b)   onto the floor
    (c)   Harry pointed to the floor.
    (d)   Tom grew old.
    (e)   Harry went to London.
    (f)   The rug stretched from the study to the bathroom.
    (g)   Harry put the spoon in his mouth.
    (h)   The meeting is in the morning.
    (i)   The boss moved the meeting from four to six
    (j)   Harry sang because he was happy.   [Assume SING is a primitive].

12.2.4   Create Jackendoff-style lexicon entries for
    (a)   *eat*
    (b)   *sell*
    (c)   *fail* [e.g. fail to arrive]
    (d)   *open* [Assume the internal predicates are CAUSE(GO(TO(OPEN)))]

12.2.5   Given that the lexicon entry for the verb *butter* is

$$\left[\begin{array}{l} \text{butter} \\ [_V N] \\ [_{Event}\text{CAUSE}([_{Thing}\ ]^{\alpha}{}_A, [_{Event}\text{INCH}([_{State}\text{BE}([_{Thing}\text{BUTTER}], [_{Place}\text{ON}_{Dist}([_{Thing}\ ]^{\beta}{}_A)])])])] \end{array} \right]$$

In *Jo buttered the bread* where would the semantic content of the various listemes go during argument fusion? (The place function ON_{Dist} is distributive *on*, with the approximate meaning "all over".)

12.3   The logical structures of predicates in Role and Reference Grammar

12.3.1   Aspect-based verb classes

Vendler 1967 Ch. 4 identified the first four classes of verbs listed in Table 12.3 on the basis of the restrictions on their co-occurrence with adverbials and aspects, and certain of their conventional implicatures and entailments. Vendler's grammatical tests were further refined by Dowty 1979 in the context of Montague semantics, and later by Van Valin and co-workers in the context of RRG[2] – which was when causatives were included.

ACTIVITIES	*The water sparkled.*	The water does something
STATES	*The water is cool.*	The water is in a certain state of being
ACHIEVEMENTS	*The balloon burst.*	There is a sudden change of condition
ACCOMPLISHMENTS	*The water cooled.*	There is a gradual change of condition
CAUSATIVES	*Jo cooled the water.*	Jo caused something to happen

Table 12.3 Aspect-based verb classes

Van Valin claims, citing studies from eight language families, that the classification 'has proved to be of great cross-linguistic validity' (1993a:34). It underlies the 'logical', i.e. semantic, structures of verbs in Table 12.4.

Verb class	Logical structure
activity	$\textbf{do}'(x,[\text{PRED}(x \textit{ or } x,y)])$
state	$\text{PRED}(x \textit{ or } x,y)$
achievement	INGR PRED(x *or* x,y) *or* INGR $\textbf{do}'(x,[\text{PRED}(x \textit{ or } x,y)])$
accomplishment	BECOME PRED(x *or* x,y) *or* BECOME $\textbf{do}'(x,[\text{PRED}(x \textit{ or } x,y)])$
causative	Φ CAUSE Ψ

Table 12.4 The logical structures of verb classes in RRG

In Table 12.4 (x *or* x,y) indicates either one or two arguments; PRED is a variable to be replaced by the particular name of the predicate. A12.4 is a convention already used in Chapter 11.

Assumption 12.4 All activity verbs contain *do'*.

Assumption 12.5 All achievements contain the operator INGR (cf. *ingressive*) indicating instantaneous change of state or activity, e.g.
x shatters → INGR shattered'(x).

Assumption 12.6 All accomplishments contain BECOME indicating change of state or activity over some period of time, e.g. x melts → BECOME melted'(x).

12.3.2 Macroroles

MACROROLES, hereafter MRS, are defined on the logical structures of verbs. Dowty 1991 refers to something very similar as PROTO-ROLES.

Assumption 12.7 The maximum number of MRs is 2, the minimum is 0.

Definition 12.5 The two MRs are ACTOR and UNDERGOER. They roughly correspond to what is sometimes called 'logical subject' and 'logical object' respectively.
(a) If the MR is in the scope of **do'** or DO (§12.3.7), it is an actor.
(b) In an ACTIVE clause, the actor is (to use Langacker's 1987 terms) the trajector profiled in the clause and so becomes clause subject, while the undergoer is landmark and 1st object.
(c) In a PASSIVE clause the undergoer is trajector, and the actor is relegated to a peripheral PP.
(d) The prototypical actor is an agent, and the prototypical undergoer is a patient.

In the following examples, 'actor' is indicated by subscript $_{[}NP_{A]}$ and 'undergoer' by $_{[}NP_{U]}$.

37 (a) $_{[}Sue_{A]}$ slapped $_{[}Harry_{U]}$.
   (b) $_{[}Harry_{U]}$ was slapped by $_{[}Sue_{A]}$.

38 (a) $_{[}The\ truck_{A]}$ hit $_{[}the\ lamppost_{U]}$.
   (b) $_{[}The\ lamppost_{U]}$ was hit by $_{[}a\ truck_{A]}$.

39 (a) $_{[}Everyone\ there_{A]}$ saw $_{[}the\ accident_{U]}$.
   (b) $_{[}The\ accident_{U]}$ was seen by $_{[}everyone\ there_{A]}$.

40 (a) $_{[}Water_{A]}$ filled $_{[}the\ tank_{U]}$.
   (b) $_{[}The\ tank_{U]}$ was filled with water.

In 40(b) there is an implication that some unmentioned effector filled the tank, so 'water' is not an actor. 41 has 'psychological predicates'. 41(a) has an experiencer (D11.23) subject who is sentient and perceiving. 41 (b) has a stimulus subject who is the cause of emotional reaction or cognitive judgment in the undergoer (cf. Dowty 1991:579).

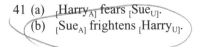

41 (a) $_{[}Harry_{A]}$ fears $_{[}Sue_{U]}$.
   (b) $_{[}Sue_{A]}$ frightens $_{[}Harry_{U]}$.

Assumption 12.8 The number of MRs a predicate has is less than or equal to the number of arguments in its logical structure.

It is often said that there is no proposition unless the predicate has at least one (understood if not explicit) argument. According to RRG, this aphorism does not hold for weather verbs like *rain* and *snow* because:

(a)   In many languages such verbs do not have overt arguments.
(b)   In English *It's snowing/raining*, 'It' is a syntactic argument, but semantically empty. 'It' appears to have no referent because we cannot say **the weather is snowing, *the sky is raining*.

Thus, Van Valin 1993a:46 claims that weather verbs like *rain* and *snow* have no arguments in their logical structure, and therefore no MR.

MRs are called 'MACROroles' because, as we have seen in 37–41, they each subsume a number of thematic roles; cf. Table 12.5.

a c t o r			u n d e r g o e r		
		← increasingly marked undergoer			
	increasingly marked actor →				
agent	experiencer		recipient	theme	patient
	cognizer	perceiver			
giver	thinker	hearer	given to	located	broken
runner	believer	feeler	sent to	moved	killed
killer	knower	taster			
speaker	presumer	smeller			
dancer					

Table 12.5   Some thematic roles and typical macroroles
(cf. Wilkins and Van Valin 1993)

Assumption 12.9 If a theme holds any MR, it is undergoer.

Stative symmetric predicates, e.g. *be like, be identical to, be related to, resemble, equal*, have two themes, but only one undergoer – the trajector subject. The trajector is determined on discourse considerations such as topicality, familiarity, empathy, point of view, figure–ground hierarchy, etc.

42   [Tom$_{U\text{-theme}}$] is as shortsighted as [Marge$_{theme}$].

With active symmetric predicates, the actor is the trajector.

43   [Boris$_{A\text{-effector}}$] debated (with) [Anton$_{effector}$] at the Oxford Union.

Assumption 12.10 Predicates with only one MR do not passivize (cf. 42–43).

Converse predicates (44) and reciprocals (45) have only one MR.

44 (a) $_{[}$The lamp$_{U\text{-theme}]}$ is on $_{[}$the table$_{locative]}$.

   (b) $_{[}$The table$_{U\text{-theme}]}$ is under $_{[}$the lamp$_{locative]}$.

45 (a) $_{[}$Sue and Tom$_{A]}$ made mad passionate love together.

   (b) $_{[}$Harry and Sally$_{A]}$ met by chance at the station.

Non-reciprocal counterparts to 45 can be passivized:

46 $_{[}$Sue$_{A\text{-agent}]}$ made mad passionate love with $_{[}$Tom$_{U\text{-patient}]}$.

$_{[}$Tom$_{U\text{-patient}]}$ was $\begin{Bmatrix} \text{made love to} \\ \text{fucked} \end{Bmatrix}$ by $_{[}$Sue$_{A\text{-agent}]}$.

47 $_{[}$Harry$_{U\text{-theme}]}$ was met by $_{[}$Sally$_{A\text{-agent}]}$ at $_{[}$the station$_{locative]}$

12.3.3 Activities

Definition 12.6 ACTIVITIES have the logical structure **do$'$**$(x_A,[\text{PRED}(x \text{ or } x,y)])$ and typically:

> occur with progressive aspect (when not future, *NP is Ving* → *NP has Ved for some time already*);
> occur with adverbs like *vigorously, actively*;
> occur with adverbs like *quickly, slowly*;
> occur in *V for an hour* → *V at all times in the hour.*

NON-VOLITIONAL VERBS OF MOTION like *roll* and *fall* have the semantics in 48.

48 **do$'$**$(x_A,[\textbf{roll}'(x)]) \wedge \textbf{do}'(x_A,[\textbf{fall}'(x)])$ ← *The ball$_x$ rolled and fell*

Because *roll* and *fall* are verbs of motion, their arguments are themes (D11.26); but the coreferential argument of **do$'$** has the thematic role of effector, in 48, force (D11.20). The thematic roles, however, are of less theoretical interest in RRG than the MRs, which have morphosyntactic consequences.

A NON-VOLITIONAL NON-MOTIONAL verb has the same structure:

49 **do$'$**$(x_A,[\textbf{squeak}'(x)])$ ← *The door$_x$ squeaks*

There is a semantic distinction between involuntary uncontrolled activity as in 50 and deliberate controlled activity like in 51.

50 $_{[}$Wendy$_{force]}$ cried when she heard that Bindi had had to be put down.

51 $_{[}$Sue$_{agent]}$, being a consummate actor, cried like someone who cared when the police
      told her her husband had been found dead in a ditch.

In RRG there is no semantic decomposition of verbs like *cry* that in any way links it with
the production of tears from the eyes and vocal noise of a certain kind. The agency in 51
is clearly based on the cancellable implicature of 'being a consummate actor, cried like
someone who cared'; for that reason the same logical structure, **do**$'(x_A,[$**cry**$'(x)])$, applies
in both 50 and 51.

    DYNAMIC COPULA COMPLEMENTS include Adj – *be brave/greedy*; *be rude/nice to NP*;
NP – *be a hero/clown/bastard*. They have the subject NP$_x$ doing something, represented
do$'(x_A,\varnothing)$, which is evaluated as being brave, or rude, or acting the clown.

52 $[$**do**$'(x_A,\varnothing) \rightarrow [$**greedy**$'(x)])]$

    PRED$_1$ ACTS (one place predicates, D7.1) include *smile, walk, talk, swim*; *vibrate, hum,
roll, roar*; *rain, thunder, snow* (which have no MR, according to RRG); *smoke, eat, drink*;
and aspectual verbs *keep, continue*.

53 **do**$'(x_A,[$**keep**$'(x,[$**vibrate**$'(x)])])$ $\leftarrow$ *The motor$_x$ keeps vibrating.*

PRED$_2$ ACTS (two-place predicates) include *drive a car, push a trolley*; *sit on/in, ride on/in,
write on/in*; *look for, listen for*; *listen to, watch, taste, feel, smell*; *pay attention to, keep
track of*.

54 **do**$'(x_A,[$**attend_to**$'(x,y_{theme})$ $\leftarrow$ *Harry$_x$ paid attention to her every word$_y$.*

    According to Van Valin 1990, 1993a, multiple argument activity verbs never have an
undergoer MR, and hence do not passivize:

55 (a) Harry is being a hero.
    (b) *A hero is being been Harry.
56 (a) Eddie drives a bus.
    (b) ?* A bus is driven by Eddie.

Counterexamples to the claim are explained by the fact that undergoers must have
extension in M^{w,t} (Van Valin and LaPolla 1997:149).

57 (a) $_[$The concert$_{U]}$ was listened to avidly by $_[$thousands of people$_{A]}$.
    (b) $_[$The food$_{U]}$ was tasted by $_[$all the kids$_{A]}$ one after the other.
58 (a) $_[$The book$_{U]}$ had been written in.
    (b) $_[$That bed$_{U]}$ was slept in by the deeply mourned Princess Di.

57(a–b) denote activities based on perception verbs which have two MRs:

57′ **do**$'(x_A,[$**hear**$'/$**taste**$'(x,y_U)])$

But 58 are not so easily explained away unless they are classed as active accomplishments (§12.3.8); otherwise, the claim that Pred$_2$ activity predicates have no undergoer is only true for some of them.

DEMONSTRATIONS like *x indicates y, x implies y, x proves y* are probably also Pred$_2$ acts (although Jackendoff 1990:139 suggests that they can be paraphrased along the lines of "x leads to y").

59 **do**$'$(x$_A$,[**imply**$'$(x,y$_{U\text{-theme}}$)]) ← $_[$*"Jo has one son"*$_{x]}$ *implies* $_[$*that she has no more than one son*$_{y]}$

12.3.4 States

Definition 12.7   STATES are primitive and have the logical structure
PRED(x *or* x,y). They typically
    do not occur with progressive aspect;
    do not occur with adverbs like *vigorously, actively*;
    do not occur with adverbs like *quickly, slowly*;
    occur in *V for an hour, spend an hour Ving*;
    occur in *V for an hour → V at all times in the hour*.

LOCATIONAL STATES include *be in/on/at, be located at, be found at, sit in/on, adhere to*; of paths etc. *extend, run, cross*.

60 (a) **be_on**$'$(x$_{locative}$,y$_{U\text{-theme}}$) ← *The book$_y$ is on the table$_x$*
    (b) **be_at**$'$(x$_{locative}$,y$_{U\text{-theme}}$) ← *Harry$_y$ is at the office$_x$*

The logical structure reverses the sequence of the surface NPs. This is acceptable because the semantic metalanguage supposedly applies to all languages and cannot therefore take surface word order into account. In RRG argument positions in the logical structure are mapped to their positions in syntactic representation via 'linking theory' which we shall not examine. Of more concern is that **be_on**$'$ and **be_at**$'$ look decomposable. The Jackendoff counterpart decomposes, e.g. [$_{State}$BE([$_{Thing}$ RAY, [$_{Place}$ AT([$_{Thing}$BRANDEIS])]. An alternative analysis for locatives and possessives is proposed in §12.4.

PERCEPTIONS AND COGNITIVE STATES include *see, hear, perceive; be proud of, be fond of; love, dislike, know, understand, believe, regret; dismay, please, surprise, be pleased about, be astonished at.*

61 **see**$'$(x$_{A\text{-experiencer}}$,y$_{U\text{-theme}}$) ← *Harry$_x$ saw a hairy-nosed wombat$_y$*

IDENTIFICATIONALS with a complement NP, e.g. 62, are usually analysed along the lines of 63 which, in effect, locates Bob among the class of lawyers.[3]

62 Bob$_x$ is a lawyer$_y$

63 **be**$'(x_{theme}, y_{locative})$

For instance, Jackendoff 1983:194 has

64 $[_{State}BE_{Ident}([_{Thing-token}ELISE], [_{Place} AT_{Ident}([_{Thing-type}PIANIST])])]$ ←   *Elise is a pianist*

Since Schwartz 1993, the RRG analysis has the attribute of being a lawyer$_y$ located at Bob$_x$. Note that 62–66 treat the copula as a Pred$_2$ (two-place predicate).

65 **be**$'(x_{U-locative}, y_{theme})$

The same analysis is given to attributive complements:

66 **be**$'(x_{U-locative}, y_{theme})$ ←   *Paolo$_x$ is happy$_y$*

66 is different from Foley and Van Valin 1984:47, where **tall**$'(x)$ and **sick**$'(x)$ are described as Pred$_1$s whose argument is a patient. In most formal semantic accounts, *happy* or *tall* would be treated as a predicate that denotes a set of entities of which the predicate holds true. Thus, in 66 Paolo would be a member of the set of tall entities. There is an obvious parallel with the usual (= other than RRG) analysis of 62. Furthermore, 65 presents a problem for RRG.

> **Assumption 12.11** When choosing between patient, theme, and locative for the MR of undergoer, patient ≺ theme ≺ locative.

65–66 (and by implication the RRG analysis of 62) violate A12.11. So what explains the current RRG analysis of these copular sentences?

   The Schwartz analysis, argued from data in French, Italian, Russian, and Dakota, has a certain similarity with the Montagovian notion of 'individual sublimation' (cf. Dowty, Wall, and Peters 1981:221ff, Cann 1993:173f). An individual is defined as the overlap of the set of all predications of it that give rise to true propositions, cf. Fig. 12.2.

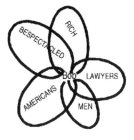

Figure 12.2 Individual sublimation

On reflection it will be seen that this is consistent with the traditional analysis in which Bob is located among lawyers. Chapter 3 recounted insuperable problems with this Fregean notion of a checklist of properties, at least with respect to proper names. What Schwartz does is turn the Montagovian definition of the individual on its head by (a) presupposing the individual and (b) locating the set of sets of properties at it. Schwartz's idea can be represented as 67, where b=Bob. 67 λ-converts (D7.20) to 68, which is the semantics for 62.

67 $\lambda P[P(b)]$(**lawyer′**)
68 **lawyer′**(b)

This process corresponds to the RRG rule of 'attributive/identificational predicate creation' (Van Valin 1990:234, Schwartz 1993:447). The rule incorporates the theme of Pred$_2$ into the predicate to create a Pred$_1$. Although details of the procedure and of the formal properties of the resulting predicate are not specified in the RRG literature, they presumably are:

Step 1.	**be′**$(x_{\text{U-locative}}, y_{\text{theme}})$	[Pred$_2$]
Step 2.	Apply attributive/identificational predicate creation	
Step 3.	[**be′**$+y_{\text{theme}}](x_{\text{U-locative}})$, e.g. **be_a_lawyer′**(b)	[Pred$_1$]

The effect is to arrive at a structure reminiscent of a translation of 62 and 66 into L_P (predicate logic), where such propositions are Pred$_1$. However, because RRG does not adopt the same compositional procedure for other Pred$_2$s, 'attributive/identificational predicate creation' must be treated with suspicion.

Can the traditional analysis of 63, in which the copular subject is theme and the copular complement is locative, be reconciled with the attributive/identificational predicate creation rule?

63 **be′**$(x_{\text{U-theme}}, y_{\text{locative}})$ ← *Bob$_x$ is a lawyer$_y$, Paolo$_x$ is happy$_y$*

To make this analysis work, the predicate would have to incorporate the locative at Step 3 in the attributive/identificational predicate creation rule, resulting in [**be′**$+y_{\text{locative}}](x_{\text{U-theme}})$. The evidence is against it. There is evidence for verb+theme and verb+patient compounds (D4.6) like 69, but none for verb+locative or verb+experiencer compounds such as 70.

69 (a) theme-head⌢V⌢-er ← *bookgiver* "someone who gives books"
   (b) patient-head⌢V⌢-er ← *platebreaker*

70 (a) locative-head⌢V⌢-er ≠ *Fredgiver* ≠ "someone who gives something to Fred"
   (b) experiencer-head⌢V⌢-er

A *Fredgiver* would NOT be "someone who gives something TO Fred" but "someone who gives Fred(s)" – in which 'Fred(s)' is a theme. This favours the RRG analysis. So does the fact that the verbs *buy* and *sell* incorporate the theme "money"; and ingestion verbs like *eat* and *drink* optionally incorporate their patients "food" and "drink" respectively (10). But there are implicit locative arguments for *remove* (source) and *travel* (path) that suggest incorporation, so the situation is far from clear (see Jolly 1993 and references cited there).

To sum up, the Schwartz analysis in 65 depends on the dubious attributive/identificational predicate creation rule to save A12.11. In §13.10 and Allan 1998 the traditional analysis of copula sentences (63) is favoured.

A12.11 faces challenges from other structures in which locatives become undergoers. The incorporation of theme works for a verb like *butter* in 71, which – if it is synonymous with 72 – has the logical structure in 73 (in which the '⊘' argument is understood as "something"; causatives like this are discussed shortly).

71   Harry$_x$ buttered the toast$_y$.
72   Harry$_x$ put butter$_z$ on the toast$_y$.
73   $[\textbf{do}'(x_A, \varnothing)]$ CAUSE [BECOME $\textbf{be\_on}'(y_{\text{locative}}, z_{\text{theme}})]$

Applying 73 to 72 gives the paraphrase "Harry did something that caused butter to come to be on the toast." 73 creates a problem for MR assignment, because in 71, 'the toast' is undoubtedly the undergoer and can be subject of a passive sentence 74.

74   The toast$_U$ was buttered.

Yet as we see from 73, 'the toast' is locative. Either A12.11 is too strong, or our intuitions with respect to the relations among 71–74 are wrong. The fact that locatives (including recipients) can function as undergoers even when there is an actor in the sentence may account for the acceptability in many dialects of sentences such as 57–58 and 75.

75   (a) $_{[}$This plant$_{U]}$ has been trodden on.
     (b) $_{[}$A painting$_{U]}$ is meant to be looked at.

We have not yet finished with copula sentences. Foley and Van Valin 1984 and Van Valin 1993a identify 76 as a (?resultant) 'condition'.

76   $\textbf{broken}'(x_{\text{U-patient}})$ ←   *The plate$_x$ is broken*

It is by no means clear how conditions differ from attributions that are analysed as Pred$_2$. Why is the primitive verb in 76 merely $\textbf{broken}'$ and not $\textbf{be\_broken}'$, like the states $\textbf{be\_on}'$, $\textbf{be\_at}'$ in 59? 76 is not analysed as $\textbf{be}'(x_{\text{U-locative}}, y_{\text{theme}})$ like 66, *Paolo$_x$ is happy$_y$*, was because:

(a)   x in 76 is a prototypical patient;
(b) $\textbf{broken}'$ derives from the verb *break*.

Obviously, semantic $\textbf{be}'$ is only partly similar to English *be* (cf. Van Valin and LaPolla 1997:103). So, is the analysis of 66 correct? If *Paolo is happy* is a habitual characteristic, then 65 does seem the correct analysis (in terms of RRG). If *Paolo is happy* is a temporary state that results from some event, 65 is NOT appropriate. (Spanish would use different verbs: the habitual characteristic would be expressed using *ser*, the temporary state using *estar*.) The temporary state of happiness is an achievement (§12.3.5) with the semantics in 77 (read "something happened that is causing Paolo to be happy").

77 [**happen**$'(\emptyset)$] CAUSE [BECOME **be**$'(x_U,y)$]

The difference between 66 and 76 cannot be explained away by claiming that NP complements of the copula are arguments, but adjectives and past participles are predicates. On that view, what is to be done with a copula like *feel* as in 78.

78 I feel $\begin{cases} \text{a fool.} \\ \text{so stupid.} \end{cases}$

In its current formulation the attributive/identificational-predicate-creation rule does not apply to 78 as it would to *I am a fool/so stupid*. The RRG analysis of these stative constructions containing copular complements (Adj, **Pp**, NP, and even PP) leaves many unanswered questions for which solutions are proposed in Allan 1998.

12.3.5 Achievements

Definition 12.8 ACHIEVEMENTS have the logical structure INGR PRED(x *or* x,y) or INGR **do**$'$(x,[PRED(x *or* x,y)]) in which the operator (second-order predicate) INGR indicates instantaneous (punctual) changes. Achievements typically:
> do not occur with progressive aspect;
> do not occur with adverbs like *vigorously, actively*;
> do not occur with adverbs like *quickly, slowly*;
> do not occur in *V for an hour, spend an hour Ving, take an hour to V* where these refer to duration of the event, and not to duration up to the event's inception.

PRED$_2$ LOCATIVES include *reach, leave, touch*; *arrive at, depart from, fall from*.

79 (a) INGR **be_on**$'(x_{locative},y_{U\text{-}theme})$ ← *The book$_y$ fell on the floor$_x$*
     (b) INGR **be_at**$'(x_{locative},y_{U\text{-}theme})$ ← *Harry$_y$ arrived at the office$_x$*

PUNCTUAL CHANGE OF STATE OR INVOLUNTARY ACTIVITY verbs such as Pred$_1$s *ignite, explode, collapse; awaken, fall asleep*; aspectuals *begin Ving/to V, cease Ving/to V, stop Ving* (INGR NOT).

80 (a) INGR **popped**$'(x_{U\text{-}patient})$ ← *The balloon$_x$ popped*
     (b) INGR **awake**$'(x_{U\text{-}theme})$ ← *Harry$_x$ awoke*
     (c) INGR NOT **do**$'(x_A,[$**breathe**$'(x)])$ ← *Jim$_x$ stopped breathing*

EXPERIENCE predicates: *spot, catch/lose sight of*.

81 INGR **see**$'(x_{A\text{-}experiencer},y_{U\text{-}theme})$ ← *Harry$_x$ spotted the hairy-nosed wombat$_y$*

12.3.6 Accomplishments

Definition 12.9 ACCOMPLISHMENTS have the logical structure
BECOME PRED(x *or* x,y) or BECOME **do'**(x,[PRED(x *or* x,y)]). BECOME is
an operator that indicates a gradual change. Accomplishments typically:
    occur with progressive aspect;
    do not occur with adverbs like *vigorously, actively*;
    occur with adverbs like *quickly, slowly*;
    occur in *V for an hour, spend an hour Ving, take an hour to V* where
    these refer to the duration of the event.

Differentiating BECOME from INGR is problematic because many verbs are punctual in
some contexts (82) and non-punctual in others (83). All such verbs are counted as non-
punctual accomplishments provided they satisfy the other criteria in D12.9. Those that are
punctual in all contexts are achievements (D12.8) if they satisfy the relevant criteria.

CRITERION	INGR	BECOME
Occurs with progressive	NO	YES
Occurs with adverbs like *quickly, slowly*	NO	YES
Occurs in *V for an hour, spend an hour Ving*	NO	YES

Table 12.6 Differentiating INGR from BECOME

82 (a) The stone broke the glass.
   (b) The embryo froze instantly when dipped in liquid nitrogen.

83 (a) The earth was breaking beneath them as the quake developed.
   (b) The pond gradually froze across the top.

GRADUAL CHANGE OF STATE verbs: $Pred_2$ – *turn into, become Adj.* $Pred_1$ – *melt, freeze,*
be born, die; darken, warm, sink, improve.

84 (a) BECOME **be'**$(x_{U\text{-locative}}, y_{theme})$ ← *Bob$_x$ became a lawyer$_y$; Sally$_x$ grew tall$_y$*
   (b) BECOME **dark'**$(x_{U\text{-patient}})$ ← *The sky$_x$ darkened*

POSSESSIVES: *get, lose, receive.*

85 BECOME **have'**(x_U, y) ← *Wendy$_x$ got a BMW$_y$*

EXPERIENCE verbs: *come to see, make out, come to realize.*

86 BECOME **do'**$(x_A, [\textbf{believe'}(x, y_U)])$ ← *Joe$_x$ gradually came to realize $_{[}$that*
                                        George was gay$_{y]}$

12.3.7 Causatives

Definition 12.10 CAUSATIVES occur when some proposition Φ, usually an activity, causes some proposition Ψ, usually an achievement or accomplishment, to come about. The logical structure is Φ CAUSE Ψ. Causatives typically:
    occur with progressive aspect;
    occur with adverbs like *vigorously, actively*;
    occur with adverbs like *quickly, slowly*;
    occur in *V for an hour, spend an hour Ving*;
    occur in *V for an hour → V at all times in the hour*;
    allow of a causative paraphrase containing the same number of NPs
    as sentence being paraphrased, e.g.
    Robin gives the book to Kim → "Robin causes Kim to come to have the book"
    Sandy runs ≠ "Sandy causes Sandy to run".

In examples 87-95 the actor MR is the argument furthest to the left in the logical structure; and the undergoer MR is the argument furthest to the right.
    EFFECTIVES: *make NP, create, build, erect; draw (a picture), knit (a sweater), dig (a hole)*.

87 $[\mathbf{do'}(x_A,[\mathbf{knit'}(x,y)])]$ CAUSE $[\mathbf{exist'}(y_U)]$ ← *Harriet$_x$ knitted a sweater$_y$*

AFFECTIVES/DESTRUCTIVES: *hide, (un)cover, crate, shell; kill, petrify, transmogrify, cook (the turkey), paint (a house), marry NP to NP; destroy, eat, melt (ice), erase, put NP down*. Temporary states might also belong here, as in 88 (rejected by Van Valin, personal communication). Also, compare 90 with 91 where the operator DO indicates that *murder* necessarily takes an agent, whereas *kill* in 90 does not.

88 $[\mathbf{happen'}(\varnothing)]$ CAUSE $[\text{BECOME } \mathbf{be'}(x_U,y)]$ ← *Paolo$_x$ is happy$_y$*
89 $[\mathbf{do'}(x_A,\varnothing)]$ CAUSE $[\text{BECOME } \mathbf{hidden'}(y_U)]$ ← *Harry$_x$ hid the loot$_y$*
90 $[\mathbf{do'}(x_A,\varnothing)]$ CAUSE $[\text{BECOME } \mathbf{dead'}(y_U)]$ ← *Jo$_x$ killed Sam$_y$*
91 $[\text{DO}(x_A,[\mathbf{do'}(x,\varnothing)])]$ CAUSE $[\text{BECOME } \mathbf{dead'}(y_U)]$ ← *Jo$_x$ murdered Sam$_y$*

In earlier versions of RRG, deliberate and unmediated agency was indicated by an operator DO.[4] Today, DO only appears in the few logical structures that necessarily take an agent. The argument of DO outranks all other arguments for the MR actor: $\text{DO}(x_{A\text{-agent}},[\mathbf{do'}(x,...)]...)$.

92 $[\mathbf{do'}(x_A,\varnothing)]$ CAUSE $[\text{BECOME NOT } \mathbf{exist'}(y_U)]$
    ← *The earthquake$_x$ destroyed the city$_y$*
93 $[\mathbf{do'}(\varnothing,\varnothing)]$ CAUSE $[\mathbf{do'}(x_A,[\text{BECOME } \mathbf{be\_at'}(y,x)]$ CAUSE $[\text{BECOME } \mathbf{broken'}(y_U)]$
    ← *The rock$_x$ broke the window$_y$*
94 $[[\mathbf{do'}(x_A,\varnothing)]$ CAUSE $[\mathbf{do'}(y,[\text{BECOME } \mathbf{be\_at'}(z,y)]]$ CAUSE
    $[\text{BECOME } \mathbf{broken'}(z_U)]$ ← *The boy$_x$ broke the window$_z$ with a rock$_y$.*

In 93, [**do**′(∅,∅)] recognizes an implied effector, higher ranked than 'rock' (cf. 94); but the MR for the clause must be a constituent of the surface clause.

95 [[**do**′(x$_A$,∅)] CAUSE [BECOME **be_at**′(y,z)]] CAUSE [**do**′(z,[**cut**′(z,y)])] CAUSE
      [BECOME **cut**′(y$_U$)] ← *Tom$_x$ is cutting the bread$_y$ with a knife$_z$*

92–95 shown that in the logical structure [[**do**′(x,[...])] CAUSE [**do**′(y,[...])] ..., the thematic role of force is indicated by the x argument, and that of instrument by the y argument.
      RELOCATIONS: *place/put NP into NP; drive/carry NP to NP; walk/push NP a block.*

96 (a)   [**do**′(x$_A$,∅)])] CAUSE [BECOME NOT **be_at**′(z,y$_U$)]
             ← *Mel$_x$ drained the water$_y$ from the pool$_z$*
      (b)   [**do**′(x$_A$,[**toss**′(x,y)])$_Φ$] CAUSE [$_Ψ$INGR **be_on**′(z,y$_U$)]
             ← *Joan$_x$ tossed the journal$_y$ on the desk$_z$*

12.3.8 Active accomplishments

ACTIVE ACCOMPLISHMENTS are a hybrid category represented by intransitive relocations such as *walk to, fly to, sit/lie (down) on/in, swim a mile* that do not meet the causative paraphrase criterion. Nonetheless, the relocation is a consequence of the activity (Φ<Ψ means "Φ precedes Ψ chronologically").

97 [**do**′(x$_A$,[**run**′(x)])$_Φ$] < [$_Ψ$BECOME **be_at**′(y$_{locative}$,x$_{theme}$)] ← *Bill$_x$ ran to the park$_y$*

12.3.9 Locating the macroroles

The MR of actor is chosen on the basis of the leftmost member of the hierarchy in Table 12.7. It correlates well with the thematic role hierarchy (A < B "A takes precedence over B").

Actor hierarchy	DO(x,... < do′(x,... < PRED(x,..
Thematic role hierarchy	agent < force < instrument < experiencer < locative

Table 12.7 Assigning actor

Some thematic roles that correspond to the argument x in Table 12.7 are:

DO(x,...   agent
do′(x,...   effector, mover, emitter, performer, consumer, creator, speaker, observer, user
PRED(x,y) location, perceiver, cognizer, desiror, judge, possessor, experiencer, emoter, indicator, theme

Assigning the MR of undergoer depends on the co-occurrence of an actor, as shown in Table 12.8.

Undergoer hierarchy +Actor	PRED(x) ≺ PRED(...,y) ≺ PRED(x,...
Thematic role hierarchy	patient ≺ theme ≺ locative ≺ experiencer
Undergoer hierarchy −Actor	PRED(x,... ≺ PRED(...,y) ≺ PRED(x)
Thematic role hierarchy	experiencer ≺ locative ≺ theme ≺ patient

Table 12.8   Assigning undergoer

Typical undergoers holding the specified argument in Table 12.8 are:

PRED(x,... location, perceiver, cognizer, attributant
PRED(...,y)   attribute, target of emotion/desire, stimulus, sensation, theme, object of knowledge/belief, possessed, performance, consumed, creation, implement, locus
PRED(x)   patient, existant

12.3.10 Predicates in RRG

§12.3 has examined aspectual classification of predicates and their logical structures, and considered the relation of thematic roles to macroroles. There are five categories of verbs:

❶   States indicated simply by PRED(x,..).
❷   Activities indicated by **do′**(x,...).
❸   Achievements indicated by the operator INGR.
❹   Accomplishments indicated by the operator BECOME.
❺   Causatives indicated by the operator CAUSE.

They differ from one another in that:

• Only causatives contain the CAUSE operator.
• Activities, achievements, and accomplishments are all dynamic; states are not.
• Accomplishments and achievements involve change of state or activity; activities do not.
• Achievements are inherently punctual; accomplishments are not.

In contrast to the uncertainty of assigning thematic roles, assigning MRs to a clause predicate is well defined. We have concentrated on this and said little about the functions of MRs in clause semantics, for which the interested reader should turn to recent works on RRG.

Exercises

12.3.1 What would you say is the thematic role of 'Jed' in *Francis made Jed carry the load*?

12.3.2 Classify the verbs in (a–e) according whether they are activities, states, achievements, accomplishments, or causatives.
(a) Sally is a virgin.
(b) Tom lost his wallet.
(c) Ed threw away his old love-letters.
(d) The frost killed the petunias.
(e) The wind is blowing noisily.

12.3.3 Write RRG-style semantic representations for the verbs in (a–j).
(a) The ice melted.
(b) The motor hummed.
(c) Sheila was astonished at Joe's promotion.
(d) The sky darkened.
(e) The sun melted the snowman.
(f) Mary shelled the peas.
(g) Eddie spotted his sister's umbrella.
(h) The meat was put in the fridge.
(i) Sally broke the window with her handbag.
(j) Harry skinned the rabbit.

12.3.4 Suggest a common logical structure for (a) and (b). How would the MR be chosen?

(a) Harry is Sue's husband.   (b) Sue is Harry's wife.

12.3.5 Why is (b) so much more unnatural than (a)? Can you suggest a common logical structure for (a) and (b). How would the MR be chosen?

(a) The lamp is on the table.   (b) The table is under the lamp.

12.4 Comparing two approaches to the lexical decomposition of clause predicates

Meaning is compositional and componential semantics seeks to identify the meaning components in listemes. §§12.2–3 reviewed two theories analysing the componential semantics of predicates. Although not dwelled upon, it is clear that the semantic frames of verbs and their logical or conceptual structure reflect speakers' perceptions of the denotata. The aspectual classification of verbs into activities, states, achievements, accomplishments, and causatives has led to some insightful componential analyses of predicates in RRG. This section discusses the respective RRG and Jackendoff analyses of *x turned red* (98), *x ran to y* (99), *x did y with/using z* (109).

98   (a)   x turned red$_y$

(RRG) BECOME **be'**($x_{\text{U-locative}}$,y_{theme})

(J)   [$_{\text{Event}}$INCH ([$_{\text{State}}$BE([X], AT([$_{\text{Property}}$RED])])])]

The presence of the operator BECOME marks 98(RRG) as an accomplishment predicate. Its counterpart in 98(J) is INCH. In RRG, operators (second-order predicates) are formally distinct from first-order predicates: as part of their Montague-via-Dowty heritage they are written in upper case instead of bold lower case + prime. No such regular distinction of semantic type is made in Jackendoff's metalanguage and none seems to be recognized. In Jackendoff's work, all semantic primitives are written in upper case, whatever their semantic type.

By convention, the form of 98(RRG) identifies it as an accomplishment because the operator BECOME scopes over a state predicate. In 98(J) the non-stativity of 98(a) is indicated by the subscript notation $_{\text{Event}}$. Consistent with this is the subscript notation of the domain of INCH as $_{\text{State}}$. Note that both theories analyse *be* as a Pred$_2$, but classify the roles differently – there are converse assignments of locative and theme (discussed in §12.3.4, 62–66). Otherwise, consistency in the representation of semantic type favours the RRG representation. Countering this is the fact that the RRG metalanguage is not a strict type-language in the sense of Chapter 7. Let's examine further examples.

99   (a)   x ran to y

(RRG) [**do'**(x_A,[**run'**(x)])]] < [[BECOME **be_at'**(y,x)]]

(J)

$$\left[\begin{array}{l} \text{GO}([_{\text{Thing}}x]^\alpha{}_A,[_{\text{Path}}\text{TO}([_{\text{Thing}}y])]) \\ \quad \text{AFF}([\alpha]) \end{array} \right]_{\text{Event}}$$

In RRG the primitive predicate is **run'** whereas in Jackendoff's conceptual structure it is simply GO, because in Jackendoff's view the difference between *run* and *go* is a matter for the encyclopedia and not the lexicon (§12.2). In 99(RRG), **do'** renders x an actor; in Jackendoff's metalanguage this is captured by the operator AFF. Whereas the relationship of **do'** to all other components of the semantic structure of the verb is indicated by a standard convention, the relationship between AFF and the components not within its immediate scope is not explicit. The nature of the relation between the thematic tier in the scope of GO and the action tier in the scope of AFF, generalized in 100, has not been explained.

100

$$\left[\begin{array}{l} \text{GO}(...) = \text{THEMATIC TIER} \\ \text{AFF}(...) = \text{ACTION TIER} \end{array} \right]_{\text{Event}}$$

From a logical point of view, these tiers can only be conjoined; this seems confirmed by the fact that *big house*, whose logical structure would be $\lambda x[\textbf{house}'(x) \wedge \textbf{big}'(x)]$, is also given a tiered structure:

101 $\begin{bmatrix} \text{HOUSE} \\ _{\text{Thing}} [_{\text{Property}} \text{ BIG}] \end{bmatrix}$

Applying this hypothesis to 99(a) we get an analysis which can best be paraphrased as 102 in which the order of conjuncts is logically irrelevant and so misrepresents the sequence of events reported in 99(a).

102 (x relocates to y) $\wedge$ (x does something)

The fault is not easy to correct in Jackendoff's conceptual structure framework. Jackendoff analyses the activity in 99(a) as $_{\text{Event}}$, the same category as 98(a). In RRG, the activity results in an accomplishment and it has a different semantic structure from the accomplishment in 98(a). Finally, whereas in Jackendoff the thematic tier is represented in terms of 103 in which GO and TO are primitive, these concepts are further decomposed in RRG to 104.

103 x GO TO y

104 BECOME **be_at**$'(y_{\text{locative}}, x_{\text{U-theme}})$ "it comes about that x is at y"

So, Jackendoff's GO is treated in RRG as the accomplishment of relocation; and Jackendoff's goal predicate TO is incorporated into this conceptualization. If the aim is maximal decomposition, then RRG does it, and Jackendoff does not – in this example. However, there are problems with RRG differentiating INGR from BECOME (achievements from accomplishments) when either of these is a subformula of a causative construction or an active accomplishment, e.g. in the logical structures for *cut with, toss, run to,* or *show* the criteria do not unambiguously apply. 104 is dynamic, not stative, hence we have a sense of "x coming to y or arriving at y or reaching y" and it is this property that BECOME marks in the logical structures of non-punctual predicates. Yet verbs like *arrive at* and *reach* are said to contain INGR **be_at**$'$. This surely cannot be correct. Although arrival can be punctual (Chapter 11), it is not necessarily so, e.g. in *The President is arriving at Kennedy Airport as I speak* the progressive indicates that arrival is ongoing. In reality the time of arrival is a fuzzy set: there is rarely a single instant of arrival, though there may be several time instants that can be claimed as possible contenders. Notably, the verb *arrive* is NOT used in a timed race to label the punctual events of breaking the tape, touching the end of the pool, etc. On further investigation, the difference between INGR and BECOME (Table 12.6) may prove to be illusory.

The systematic semantic relations established between, say, states, achievements or accomplishments, and causatives allow RRG to specify the semantic relatedness of *The water is cool, The water cooled,* and *Jim cooled the water*. Not yet captured in RRG is the systematic relation between something melting and its becoming liquid (as Jackendoff recognizes), and between someone crying and producing tears accompanied by a distinctive sound. In order to analyse *The ice melts* the expected RRG semantics would be 105.

105 BECOME **melted**$'(x_{\text{U-patient}})$

The translation into conceptual semantics is 106.

106 $[_{\text{Event}}\text{GO}_{\text{Ident}}([_{\text{Thing}}X], \begin{bmatrix} \text{FROM}_{\text{Ident}}([\text{SOLID}]) \\ _{\text{Path}}\ \text{TO}_{\text{Ident}}([\text{LIQUID}]) \end{bmatrix})]$

On this occasion, the conceptual semantics is more detailed – even if we substitute **liquid**$'$ for **melted**$'$ in the RRG analysis. Lexical decomposition in RRG has only been extensively discussed in respect of verbs of saying (Van Valin and LaPolla 1997:116-118) and the English verb *remember* and the corresponding verbs *irlpangke-* and *telare-* in the Australian language Mparntwe Arrernte (Van Valin and Wilkins 1993). Should we say that the logical structure of *melt* is BECOME **liquid**$'(x)$ and that of *cry* is **do**$'(x,[\textbf{cry}'(x)])$ or should we say instead that there are synonymies of the following kind:

107 *x melts* → [BECOME **melted**$'(x)$ ↤ BECOME **liquid**$'(x)$]
108 *x cries* → [**do**$'(x,[\textbf{cry}'(x)])$ ↤ **do**$'(x,[\textbf{go\_from}'(x\text{'s eyes,tears})])$]

In other words, there is not necessarily just one logical structure for a predicate.
   Now consider the different treatments of 109(a); this time glosses have been added.

109 (a)   x did V to y with/using z (e.g. *x opened the door with a key*)

   (RRG) $[[\textbf{do}'(x,\varnothing)] \text{CAUSE} [\textbf{do}'(y,[\text{BECOME } \textbf{be\_at}'(z,y)])] \text{CAUSE} [\text{BECOME PRED}(z)]]$
   "x's doing something that causes the relocation of y to z causes y to become V-ed"

   (J) $\begin{bmatrix} \text{CS}^+([_{\text{Thing}}x]^\alpha, [\text{INCH}([\text{BE}_{\text{Ident}}([y]^\beta, [V])])]) \\ \text{AFF}([\alpha],[\beta]) \\ [_{\text{Instr}} \text{ BY} \begin{bmatrix} \text{CS}^+([\alpha], [\text{AFF}([z]^\gamma, [\beta])]) \\ \text{AFF}([\alpha],[\gamma]) \end{bmatrix} \\ \text{Event} \end{bmatrix}$

   "x causes y to become V-ed and x does something by means of z doing something
   to y and x doing something to z" ↤
   "x does something and x causes y to become V-ed by means of x doing something
   to z and z doing something to y"

Note that the second gloss of 109(J) is more plausible because the sequence "Φ and Ψ" conversationally implicates that Φ is the cause of Ψ. Jackendoff marks the instrument with the predicate BY, which triggers the $_{\text{Instr}}$ label. On grounds of economy, therefore, the RRG analysis is to be preferred. Once again, the RRG analysis is more detailed than Jackendoff's because it accounts for the fact that the instrument z is relocated to y. However, there are two objections to this.

(a)   Not all instruments have the property of being relocated (e.g. *He looked at her with his one remaining eye*).
(b)   It is inconsistent to represent the fact of z being located at y without representing the concomitant fact that x is located at z (or vice versa).

And to be precise, it is probably not x but only some proper part of x that is located at z and only some proper part of z that is located at y! Imagine that Harry opened the door with a key: Harry will necessarily be grasping part of the key with some part of his anatomy, and only part of the key will act on the door – and not the whole door but only the lock on the door. We have gone beyond the semantics of 109(a) into the philosophy of action and causation.

> *Assumption 12.12 Decomposition needs to be constrained to the minimum necessary to make useful revelations about the nature of human language and/or human cognition (A8.20). A necessary condition on semantic theory is the compromise between recognizing all semantic distinctions that human beings can discern, and those that have lexical, morphological, and syntactic consequences within human languages.*

Semantic structures should ideally be applicable in all human languages. But it is important for the analyst to make the most detailed account possible of the semantic structure of a particular language and not merely to utter generalities applicable to all languages. There is no reason to suppose that there is much less variety in semantic structures across languages than there is in the cultures of the people who speak them.

Allan 1998 proposed that 110 and 111, usually taken to be synonymous, have quite divergent semantics – based respectively on 110′ and 111′. (Subscript $_{poss}$=possessor or holder[2], $_{loc}$=locative.)

110   Bill gave Fred the diary.
110′ $[\textbf{do}'(x_A,\varnothing)]$ CAUSE $[\text{BECOME } \textbf{have}'(y_{U\text{-poss}}, z_{theme})]$

111   Bill gave the diary to Fred.
111′ $[\textbf{do}'(x_A,\varnothing)]$ CAUSE $[\textbf{go}'(z_{U\text{-theme}}, [_{loc\text{-path}} \textbf{from}'(x_{loc\text{-source}}), [\textbf{to}'(y_{loc\text{-goal}})]_{loc\text{-path}}])]$

In 110′, the recipient/experiencer 'Fred' is the undergoer; in 111′ the relocation of undergoer 'the book' is indicated by **go**′ (subscripts are introduced to index the difference between the locatives: path, source, and goal). 111′ is consistent with 110′ in that the first argument of Ψ in the structure [Φ CAUSE Ψ] is profiled as landmark (1st object) in the main surface clause, and the dynamic relocation of the theme accounts for the occurrence of semantic **to**′ and lexical *to*. One justification for the introduction of **go**′ is the answer in 112:

---

2. The various verbs for **have**′ in Indo-European languages all derive from verbs meaning "hold" or "take"; cf. Meillet 1924.

112 [IN A DISCUSSION ABOUT WHO GOT WHAT PRESENTS OR BEQUESTS:]
     Q: Who got the book?
     A: The book went to Fred.

Precedents for 111' are examples like 113–14 in Jackendoff 1990.

113 $\left[\begin{array}{l} \text{CAUSE([HARRY]}^\alpha, \text{GO}_\text{Poss} ([\text{BOOK}], \left[\begin{array}{l} \text{FROM } ([\alpha]) \\ \text{TO([SAM]}^\beta) \end{array}\right]))) \\ \quad \text{AFF([}\alpha],[\beta]) \end{array}\right]_\text{Event}$

     ← *Harry gave the book to Sam*

114 $\left[\begin{array}{l} \text{GO}_\text{Poss}([\text{Thing} \text{ BOOK}], [\text{TO}_\text{Path} ([\text{Thing} \text{ SAM}]^\alpha)])] \\ \text{AFF([ ], [}\alpha]) \end{array}\right]_\text{Event}$

     ← *Sam received a book* (unspecified actor)

In 111' the complex locative argument of **go**' – $[_\text{loc-path} \textbf{from}'(x_\text{loc-source}),[\textbf{to}'(y_\text{loc-goal})]_\text{loc-path}]$
– is an abbreviation for 115, in which $\alpha < \beta$ symbolizes "α precedes β in time and space".

115 $[_\text{loc-path} [_\alpha \textbf{be}'(z_\text{theme},[\textbf{at}'(z_\text{theme},x_\text{loc-source})]_\text{loc})_\alpha]$
        $< [_\beta \text{BECOME } [\textbf{be}'(z_\text{theme},[\textbf{at}'(z_\text{theme},y_\text{loc-goal})]_\text{loc})]_\beta]_\text{loc-path}]$

Assumption 12.13 A possessor is a kind of locative.

Given A12.13, 111' expands to 116.

116 $[_\phi \textbf{do}'(x_A,\varnothing)_\phi]$ CAUSE $[_\psi [\textbf{go}'(z_\text{U-theme},[_\text{loc-path} [_\alpha \textbf{be}'(z_\text{theme},[\textbf{at}'(z_\text{theme},x_\text{loc-source})]_\text{loc})_\alpha]$
        $< [_\beta \text{BECOME } [\textbf{be}'(z_\text{theme},[\textbf{at}'(z_\text{theme},y_\text{loc-goal})]_\text{loc})]_\beta]_\text{loc-path}])]_\psi]$

A rough paraphrase would be "Bill did something that causes the diary located with him
to later come to be located with Fred." This makes the relationship between 110' and 116
(and by implication, 110' and 111') much more obvious. It is also obvious that 111' and
116 asymmetrically entail 110', cf. 117.

117 $[\textbf{do}'(x_A,\varnothing)]$ CAUSE $[\textbf{go}'(z_\text{U-theme},[_\text{loc-path} [\textbf{from}'(x_\text{loc-source}),[\textbf{to}'(y_\text{loc-goal})]_\text{loc-path}])]$
        $\rightarrow [\textbf{do}'(x_A,\varnothing)]$ CAUSE $[\text{BECOME } \textbf{have}'(y_\text{U-poss},z_\text{theme})]$

These analyses show that 111, in which the theme is undergoer (and 1st object), is
semantically prior to 110 in which the recipient/possessor is the undergoer. This view is
consistent with the fact that in most languages the preferred sequence is motivated by the
personal and/or animacy hierarchy in which the preferred sequence is **humans < other
animates < inanimates** (e.g. humans before diaries).[5] It favours the views expressed by
e.g. Dryer 1986, Goldberg 1995, and conflicts with the prevailing view in government
binding theory and RRG. To what extent this analysis generalizes to other ditransitives
awaits further research.

One objection to 111' is the fact that it fails to distinguish between *give* and *send*. This can be rectified by replacing the 'ø' of [**do**'$(x_A,ø)$] with a dissimilating specification of the semantics of *send*. Another objection is that 110' and 111' seem too different to be representations of the semantics of the same lexical verb *give*. This objection can be put aside because it is based upon a confusion between forms in the object language and forms in the semantic metalanguage. None of the semantic specifications offered in this book directly decompose lexemes of the object language (Chapter 8). They are structured as meaning postulates (D7.5); in effect they are translations into a metalanguage (Chapter 1). To speak of *give* being DECOMPOSED into 110' and 111' or 116 is fatally misleading because it would make the lexeme **give**' redundant: in semantic analysis it would be supplanted by 116. But lexemes are not redundant. As discussed in Chapter 8, componential analysis of an expression e_{OL} involves recognizing the conventional implicatures, entailments, and conversational implicatures of e_{OL}.

> *Assumption 12.14* Metalanguage structures such as those in Wierzbicka's natural semantic metalanguage, Jackendoff's lexical conceptual structures, the logical structures of role and reference grammar, and all others that have appeared in this and similar books are in fact just conventional implicatures, entailments, and conversational implicatures of e_{OL} translated into whoever's metalanguage.

The semantic representation **give**'(x,y,z) of the English listeme *give* has, among others, the implications shown in 118.

118 **give**'(x,y,z)
    → [**do**'$(x_A,ø)$] CAUSE [**go**'$(z_{U\text{-theme}},[_{\text{loc-path}}$ **from**'$(x_{\text{loc-source}}),[$**to**'$(y_{\text{loc-goal}})]_{\text{loc-path}}])]$

The upshot is that a listeme such as *give* is not in itself semantically decomposable, but it does have certain conventional implicatures, entailments, and conversational implicatures that, whether in metalanguage translation or within the object language itself, throw light upon its meaning.

12.5 Summary

The purpose of this chapter was to study the semantic frames and structures of clause predicates in Jackendoff's lexical conceptual semantics and Van Valin's role and reference grammar. Wierzbicka's Natural Semantic Metalanguage, discussed in §8.6, is purely lexicographical and makes no pretence to integrate with any theory of syntax. In contrast, the semantic theories reviewed in this chapter are integrated with a syntactic theory as part of a general theory of language structure. Role and reference grammar is constructed in the belief that 'grammatical structure can only be understood and explained with reference to its semantic and communicative functions' (Van Valin 1993a:2). Thus, syntax is not autonomous as it is for Jackendoff. Jackendoff offers a semantic theory that integrates with a dominant syntactic theory and so makes a contribution to grammatical theory in general. It has the additional advantage of employing conceptual structures of a type common to other kinds of cognitive processing. The rules for constructing semantic definitions in Wierzbicka's NSM are obscure. By contrast, the metalanguage employed in role and reference grammar and by Jackendoff in his conceptual semantics are, in both cases, a viable compromise between ordinary language use and a formal language such as predicate calculus or intensional logic (Chapter 7).[6] The vocabulary items used in the logical structures of RRG and in Jackendoff's lexical conceptual structures come from English otherwise we wouldn't understand them. There are certain specialized uses of **do'** and the operators DO and BECOME in RRG, and of GO in conceptual semantics. These are supplemented by such technical terms as INGR in RRG and INCH and CS in conceptual semantics. Nonetheless, it is obvious that knowing English is a prerequisite to understanding any of these semantic metalanguages. Perhaps Wierzbicka's NSM is easier to read than the other metalanguages we have been discussing, but it is harder to write, and a good deal more wordy, than RRG's 'logical structures' and Jackendoff's 'lexical conceptual structures'. It is a matter of opinion which metalanguage produces a 'better' lexical semantics. Finally, we picked up on comments made about semantic metalanguage in Chapters 1, 7, and 8 to emphasize that representations of semantic structures are simply translations into a metalanguage of the conventional implicatures, entailments, and conversational implicatures of object language expressions.

The next chapter, Chapter 13, shifts attention to the semantics of the noun phrase. It makes a detailed study of English quantifiers. Grammatical number, countability, and (in)definiteness are described so as to link meaning to morphological form. Chapter 13 ends with a detailed semantic analysis of a simple sentence which draws on much that has been discussed in the book to that point.

● Key words and phrases:

1st (direct) object
2nd object
3-D model (A12.1)
AFF "affected entity"
(argument) A-marking (A12.3)
accomplishment, BECOME (D12.9,
    Table 12.6)
achievement, INGR (D12.8, Table 12.6)
action tier, AFF([ ],[ ]) (Table 12.2)
active-accomplishment
active clause (D12.5)
activity (D12.6)
actor (17, D12.5)
agent (D12.5)
argument fusion (D12.2)
argument binding (A12.2)
argument linking (D12.1)
aspectual classifications of preds (Tables
    12.3–4)

attributive/identificational predicate
    creation
causative, CS, CAUSE (D12.10)
conceptual semantics
conceptual category
conceptual structure
conceptual constituent
CS$^+$ "CAUSE with successful outcome"
CS$^-$ "CAUSE with unsuccessful
    outcome"
CS^u "CAUSE with unknown outcome"
decomposition (A12.12)
DO (91)
do' (A12.4)
EXCH "exchange"
function–argument structure (1)
INCH "inchoative"
incorporation (69–70, 73)
individual sublimation (Fig. 12.2)

INGR "ingressive, or punctual inchoative"
I[nternalized]-language
landmark (D12.5)
LCS "lexical conceptual structure"
lexical conceptual structure, LCS
linking condition (D12.3)
logical structure
macrorole, MR (A12.7–8, D12.5)
metalanguage structures (A12.14)
passive clause (D12.5)
patient (D12.5)
personal/animacy hierarchy
possessor as locative (A12.13)
$Pred_{1-2}$
predicate (verb) frame
recipient as locative
restrictive modifier rule (D12.4)

role and reference grammar, RRG
state (D12.7)
semantic component
semantic primitive (33)
(Jackendoff's) subcategorization (35–36)
syntactic hierarchy (D12.1)
thematic tier (Table 12.2)
thematic role (Tables 12.5, 12.7–8)
(theta) θ-criterion (D11.19)
θ-/thematic hierarchy (D12.1, Tables 12.7–8)
θ-role
trajector (D12.5)
transitivity (Table 12.1)
undergoer (D12.5)
undergoer hierarchy (Table 12.8)
verb (predicate) frame
weather verb

● Jackendoff's conceptual semantics is an integral part of a general theory of the mind. Conceptual structure is the single level of mental representation, at which linguistic, sensory, and motor information are compatible. Conceptual semantics is a component of the description of I[nternalized]-language, intended to integrate with syntactic and phonological theories in the Chomskyan paradigm.

● In lexical conceptual structure (LCS) the noun lexeme is a semantic primitive; but verbs are decomposed into function–argument structures of the form F([A], ...) broadly similar to those in predicate logic (Chapter 7).

● To combine the semantic content from the separate lexicon entries of constituents in a phrase marker in an appropriate manner, Jackendoff A-marks arguments $[\ ]^{\alpha}_{A}$ (A12.3). The combinatorial process is called Argument Fusion (D12.2).

● Argument Linking (D12.1) attaches A-marked constituents in the LCS to appropriate nodes in the phrase marker consistent with the thematic and syntactic hierarchies.

● In argument $[\ ]^{\alpha}_{A}$ the α superscript is for Argument Binding (A12.2) which handles relations between θ-roles and arguments in the LCS.

● Jackendoff distinguishes between a thematic tier dealing with motion and location, and an action tier dealing with actor-patient relations (Table 12.2).

● Jackendoff restricts the vocabulary of functions, but the vocabulary of primitive arguments is unbounded. He uses subscripting and superscripting to expand the primitive vocabulary by subcategorization.

● The logical structure of predicates in role and reference grammar (RRG) was originally dependent on the work of David Dowty, in particular Dowty 1979, who, in turn, used the aspectual verb classification of Vendler 1967. In the most recent work, however, RRG has moved away from these origins.

● In RRG predicates are classified on a roughly aspectual basis into activities, states, achievements, accomplishments, and causatives (Tables 12.3–4). Their distinctive features are: only causatives contain the CAUSE operator; activities, achievements, and accomplishments are all dynamic; states are not; accomplishments and achievements involve change of state or activity; activities do not; achievements are inherently punctual, accomplishments are not. The distinction between achievements and accomplishments is often fuzzy.

● In RRG, thematic roles are of less theoretical significance than the two macroroles (MRs) of actor and undergoer (D12.5) which roughly correspond to what are loosely called 'logical subject' and 'logical object'. A clause may have from 0 to 2 MRs, but never more than there are surface arguments. There is some correlation between MR and thematic role, but MRs are defined on argument positions within the logical (i.e. semantic) structure of the clause predicate (Tables 12.7–8).

● A comparison of three structures in terms of LCS and RRG found that the RRG analysis fared slightly better.

● A12.12 recognized that semantic decomposition is a compromise between exquisite detail in analysis and identifying only semantic distinctions that have lexical, morphological, and syntactic consequences.

● There is reason to expect that detailed semantic analysis of particular languages is likely to be more fruitful than restricting attention to only those generalities that apply in all languages.

● Possessors (A12.13), recipients, and even experiencers are kinds of locative.

● Copular sentences typically profile a theme as trajector, and 'possessive' *have* sentences profile the possessor as trajector, and they have different semantic components even when they have the same truth conditions.

● Postulating two logical structures for the ditransitive *give* (a) disposes of the argument over whether *give*⌢NP_{theme}⌢*to*⌢$NP_{recipient}$ derives from *give*⌢$NP_{recipient}$⌢NP_{theme} or vice versa; (b) makes it unnecessary to postulate exceptions to the usual conditions for assigning the macrorole of undergoer in (at least some) ditransitives. However, it was shown that *give*⌢NP_{theme}⌢*to*⌢$NP_{recipient}$ semantically entails *give*⌢$NP_{recipient}$⌢NP_{theme}.

● Semantic decomposition is done in a metalanguage. The semantic decomposition demonstrated in semantic theories is metalanguage translation that represents and demonstrates the meaning of object language expressions but is not identical with it (A12.14). Symbolically, $e_{OL} \Rightarrow$ "e_M" but $e_{OL} \neq$ "e_M".

12.6 Notes on further reading

[1] Attempts to specify 2½D and partial 3D visual properties have been made by Marr 1982, Jackendoff 1987a, Landau and Jackendoff 1993, Levinson 1992.

[2] Major works on RRG are Foley and Van Valin 1984, Van Valin 1990, 1993a, Van Valin and LaPolla 1997. See also the readings listed at http://wings.buffalo.edu/linguistics/rrg/index.html.

[3] Gruber 1965, 1967, Anderson 1971, Jackendoff 1983, 1990 analyse the subject of the copula as theme and complement as locative.

[4] On the operator DO, see Ross 1972, Dowty 1979:118, Foley and Van Valin 1984:50.

[5] On the personal and/or animacy hierarchy, see Givón 1970, Hawkinson and Hyman 1974, Kuno 1976, 1979, Ertel 1977, Kuno and Kaburaki 1977, Morolong and Hyman 1977, Ransom 1977, Zubin 1979, Allan 1987a.

[6] On formal semantics and intensional logic, see Carnap 1956, Kripke 1963, Montague 1974, Lewis 1970, Cresswell 1973, Dowty, Wall and Peters 1981, Benthem 1988, Partee, Meulen, and Wall 1990, Gamut 1991, Cann 1993, McCawley 1993.

13 Quantifiers in English

A lathe is way too much tool for you.

(Paul's father to Paul in the sitcom 'Mad About You')

13.1 Where we are heading

This chapter is an intensive study of one of the most important aspects of noun phrase semantics. It identifies the tools and method to make a comprehensive, internally consistent description of number, countability, quantification, and (in)definiteness in English that links meaning to morphological form. §13.2 discusses the association between grammatical number and countability. It argues that countability is a property of NPs not nouns, but shows that nouns may show a preference for either uncountable or countable environments.

> **Assumption 13.1** Every English NP is either countable or it is uncountable.[1]

Various exploitations of number marking are examined. §13.3 establishes ensemble theory – a sort of combination of mereology with set theory – for the semantic definition of lexically related countables and uncountables from a common base. §13.4 introduces the notion of restricted quantification using generalized quantifiers formed on everyday quantifiers from the English lexicon. It provides the necessary paraphernalia for semantically specifying NPs containing 'determiners', i.e. articles and (other) quantifiers. §13.5 creates a semantics for the plural morpheme and the N_0 'bare' or citation form of a noun as a prelude to describing the semantic effects of quantifiers ranging over them and over other quantifiers too. §13.6 takes up the challenge that

> **Assumption 13.2** Every English NP is either definite or it is indefinite.

It argues that *the* is the prototypical definite and also a universal quantifier. It explains why *the* is said to mark identifiability and uniqueness of reference. §13.7 examines relationships among quantifiers as revealed by their entailment relations. §13.8 examines the relationships among quantifiers as a result of their scope. §13.9 describes the semantic foundations for associating an indefinite NP with its definite anaphoric successor. §13.10 uses insights from this and earlier chapters to make an exhaustive analysis of all the constituents of a simple classificatory sentence. §13.11 summarizes the chapter.

13.2 Countability in English NPs

The cat-fishes, of which there are about fifty distinct forms arranged in four families, constitute the largest group, with probably the greatest number of individuals per species. In some parts of the country where nets are little used and fishing is mainly done with traps and long lines, at least *three-quarters of the annual catch is of cat-fish.*

(Welman 1948:8, emphases added)

13.2.1 Countability and individuation

Definition 13.1 Countable denotata are denumerable by the quantifiers *a(n)*, *one, two* (and all natural numbers), *(a) few, several, many, each, every, both.*

Uncountables can be quantified by e.g. *much, little.* In English, the NUMBER system (to which quantifiers are linked) simply contrasts PLURAL "more than one" with SINGULAR "one". Many languages also have a dual, giving a three term system: "one", "two", "more than two". There is a trace of the duality in English *both, pair, couple,* and *brace (of partridge).* Some languages (e.g. Fijian) have yet more terms in their number system (Corbett and Mithun 1996).

Assumption 13.3 A noun is countable or uncountable only within the context of a particular NP (Weinreich 1966, Allan 1980, Bunt 1985).

All English NPs are either countable or uncountable. Typically, uncountable referents are perceived as an undifferentiated unity, whereas countables are perceived as discrete but similar entities; compare the two uses of *lamb* in 1.

1 It is because I like lambs that I don't like lamb.

In 1 the animals as individuals implicitly contrast with their meat – the edible stuff which they embody. An uncountable NP is used to refer to the meat when it is usual for the consumer to eat only part of the animal at a sitting. Much the same applies to NPs denoting other kinds of food: where more than one object is eaten at a sitting, a countable NP is used (Allan 1976). These Quantity2 implicatures are shown in 2–3.

2 For dinner we are having $\left\{ \begin{array}{l} \text{lamb.} \\ \text{rabbit.} \\ \text{chicken.} \\ \text{goat.} \end{array} \right\}$ ▷ Part of the animal at one sitting

3 For lunch we are having $\left\{ \begin{array}{l} \text{pilchards.} \\ \text{oysters.} \\ \text{an egg.} \\ \text{sandwiches.} \end{array} \right\}$ ▷ One or more at one sitting

13.2.2 Tests for countability

In English, grammatical number is registered in several ways. Prototypically by the absence or presence of plural inflexion on the NP head: *cats, oxen, mice, foci, data, cherubim*, etc. In 4 the noun *sheep* is uninflected, but recognizably plural because of NP-INTERNAL NUMBER REGISTRATION on the italicized demonstrative and NP-EXTERNAL number registration on the verb and the possessive pronoun in bold type.

4   *Those* sheep **are** wiggling **their** ears.

NP-internal number registration is normally CONCORDANT, cf. ✓*a chair* vs **a chairs*; ✓*these chairs* vs **these chair*.

Allan 1980 identified four syntactic tests for countability preferences in English nouns. Although each test identifies whether or not a NP is countable, head nouns vary in the number of countable environments they occur in: some are to be found in more types of countable NP than others revealing a scale of countability preference as in Table 13.1.

MOST COUNTABLE   LEAST COUNTABLE

car ≺ *oak* ≺ *cattle* ≺ *Himalayas / scissors* ≺ *mankind* ≺ *admiration* ≺ *equipment*

Table 13.1 Countability preferences among English nouns

Assumption 13.4 Tests 13.1–4 below show that a given occurrence of an English NP will be either countable or uncountable, but no noun listeme is intrinsically countable or uncountable. (This is why the interpretation of 'lambs' and 'lamb' in 1 is different; as are the two occurrences of the lexeme oak' in *Oaks are the source for oak*.) Nevertheless, the semantics of the noun interact with the semantics of countability.

TEST 13.1 If *a(n)* or *one* concatenates with a singular head noun, the NP is countable.

A car is a great blessing.	C
The council won't let him cut down *an oak* which is dead and dangerous.	C
*Every farmer has a sheep and *a cattle*.	U
⎰ *A Himalayas* without tourists would be a great thing.	⎱
⎱ ?Pass me *a scissor(s)* will you. [OK for some speakers, but not others]	⎰ ?C
Imagine *a mankind* with a preference for peace over war!	C
Hermione's is *an admiration* that Charles has long craved.	C
*We'll have to buy *a new equipment* to do this.	U

Scissors, and other pluralia tantum nouns such as *tweezers, pliers, pants*, are syntactically plural but semantically singular when they denote a single object. This is what leads some speakers to create singular forms such as *a scissor, a pant*. Because each of the NPs *the*

Himalayas, the Rockies, the Grampians denotes a range of mountains in which each individual mountain has its own name, the syntactic singular **a Himalaya* (etc.) is not used.

TEST 13.2 The NP is countable if a plural head noun is preceded by a fuzzy denumerator such as *(a) few, several, many, a dozen or so, about fifty*, and high rounded numbers.

Max owns *several cars*.	C
His garden contains *many oaks*	C
700,000 cattle died in the drought.	C
?How many Himalayas/scissors are there?	?C
*Few mankinds will be found distributed through the universe.	U
**George is vying for *several admirations* at the same time.	U
**We've bought *a dozen new equipments* this year.	U

TEST 13.3 If the NP takes external plural number registration, it is countable.

The cars *were* damaged by a falling wall	C
The oaks *are* in front of the house.	C
The cattle *are* in the truck.	C
The Himalayas/scissors *are* just there.	C
"Mankind *are* my favourite species," said Dr Who.	C
**Admiration(s) *are* what an academic craves.	U
**Equipment(s) *were* in short supply.	U

TEST 13.4 If *all* concatenates with a singular head noun and the NP has singular external concord, the NP is uncountable. (Below, asterisks indicate a preference for countable environments).

*All car is a mode of transport.	C
All oak is good timber for furniture making.	U
*All cattle is bovine.	C
{ **All Himalayas* is in Asia. { **All scissors* was removed from the kiddies' reach. }	C
All mankind was agog at the caped crusader's audacity.	U
All admiration does the ego good.	U
All equipment must be registered with the Dean's office.	U

The strongest evidence that a noun prefers a countable environment is where it succeeds in both Test 13.1 and Test 13.2. Nouns like *car* and *oak* are shown to be most countable, with *?Himalayas/scissors* dubious in this respect.

Many languages have morphological and/or syntagmatic marking of countables; but no language systematically marks uncountables while leaving countables unmarked. There is sometimes similar syntactic marking on uncountables and plurals, e.g. Sinhalese and noun class 6 in many Bantu languages.

Assumption 13.5 The principal motivation for countability is to identify the individual from the mass.

13.2.3 Number discord

In many English dialects, NP-EXTERNAL NUMBER DISCORD is possible where the NP head is a collective noun such as *admiralty, aristocracy, army, assembly, association, audience, board, class, clergy, committee, crowd, flock, government.*

5   The herd $\left\{ \begin{array}{c} \text{is} \\ \text{are} \end{array} \right\}$ getting restless and $\left\{ \begin{array}{c} \text{it is} \\ \text{they are} \end{array} \right\}$ beginning to move away.

Whereas singular NP-external registration (S.XR) indicates that the set as a whole is being referred to, the plural (PL.XR) indicates that the set members are being referred to. Thus 6 identifies the composition of the committee, while 7 identifies dissension among the membership of the committee.

6   The committee $\left\{ \begin{array}{c} \text{is} \\ \text{?*are} \end{array} \right\}$ composed of many notable scholars.

7   The committee $\left\{ \begin{array}{c} \text{?*is} \\ \text{are} \end{array} \right\}$ at odds with each other over the new plan.

NPs denoting institutions, e.g. *the company I work for, the BBC, the university* must be singular when the institution as a building, location, or single entity is referred to (8), but can have PL.XR when the people associated with it are referred to (9).

8   The library $\left\{ \begin{array}{c} \text{is} \\ \text{?*are} \end{array} \right\}$ located in the new civic centre.

9   The library $\left\{ \begin{array}{c} \text{charges} \\ \text{charge} \end{array} \right\}$ a heavy fine on overdue books.

When a plural NP is quantified by a numeral and also takes a predicate such as *be all, be enough, be sufficient, be too few, be too many,* number discord occurs when Speaker focuses on the quantity itself rather than the entities quantified.

10   Three crocodiles is too many to keep in your backyard; suppose they escape?
11   Two men isn't many, is it? Two isn't going to be enough.

The quantifiers in 10–11 cannot be replaced by any of the determiners *the, these, those* because these do not allow for focus on quantity.

Next, consider XR (external number registration) with five kinds of English classifier construction (D9.22).

UNIT COUNTERS   two *pieces* of equipment

FRACTIONALS   three *quarters* of the cake

VARIETALS   two *species* of wheat

MEASURES   two *pounds* of cabbage

ARRANGEMENTS   two *rows* of beans

Plural classifiers may take S.XR to focus upon the quantity, or PL.XR to focus upon plurality in the (italicized) classifier.

12 Four *pieces* of cake $\left\{ \begin{array}{l} \text{is} \\ \text{are} \end{array} \right\}$ enough for anyone but a glutton.

13 Three *quarters* of the cake $\left\{ \begin{array}{l} \text{was} \\ \text{were} \end{array} \right\}$ put on Ed's plate.

14 Two *pounds* of flour $\left\{ \begin{array}{l} \text{was} \\ \text{were} \end{array} \right\}$ what I needed.

Let's discuss 13. With S.XR 'was', *three quarters* forms a single semantic unit such that the two words cannot legitimately be separated by an adjective or even a pause; with PL.XR they can be, e.g. *three uneven quarters of the cake*. S.XR is appropriate where a single piece of cake amounting to (an undifferentiated unity of) three-fourths of the whole is put onto Ed's plate. PL.XR is appropriate where three separate quarters are all put onto Ed's plate.

A singular fractional, measure, arrangement, or collective classifier (e.g. *a* **bunch** *of bananas*) with a plural classified NP may have S.XR to focus on the classifier as a unit (italicized, 15, 17), or PL.XR to focus on the classified NP as individuals (bolded, 16–17).

15 One *half* of the diamonds *was* not enough for Sid.

16 A half of **the tomatoes were** bad.

17 A *row* of **trees** $\left\{ \begin{array}{l} \textit{stands} \\ \textbf{stand} \end{array} \right\}$ on the ridge.

13.2.4 Collectivizing

> *Definition 13.2* PRINCIPLE OF N_0 USAGE FOR ENGLISH. N_0, the form of the noun unmarked for number, is used when the denotation for N is perceived not to consist of a number of significant similar units.

The reference to 'similar units' is to account for use of N_0 in uncountable NPs headed by words like *furniture, equipment, crockery, silverware*. Where several pieces of furniture are similar in form and function, they are labelled using a countable NP such as *chairs, beds, tables*; similarly for *spoons, forks,* etc. Although what we call *furniture* or *silverware* consists of perceivably discrete objects, these are typically dissimilar in form and function (Wierzbicka 1988).

In certain contexts, 'collectivized nouns' (Allan 1976), such as the ones italicized in 18–19, are optionally inflected for plural:

18 These three *elephant* my great-grandfather shot in 1920 were good tuskers, such as you
       never see today.
19 Four silver *birch* stand sentinel over the driveway entrance.

Collectivizing of trees and other plants is much less common than collectivizing animals. Early uses of the collectivized form applied to animals hunted for food or trophies. Today, collectivizing occurs in contexts of zoology, ornithology, and conservation.

> **Assumption 13.6** In a plural NP headed by N_0, the absence of plural inflexion on the head noun marks COLLECTIVIZING. It signals hunting, conservation, or farming jargon because N_0 is characteristically used of referents that are NOT perceived to be significant as individuals. Early users of the collectivized form were not interested in the individual animals except as a source for food or trophies.

Contributing factors to the establishment of N_0 as the mark of collectivizing (see Chapters 5 and 9 on multiple sources for words) might have been the unmarked plural of *deer* – which once meant "wild animal, beast" – and the fact that meat nouns are N_0 (1–2 above).

Consider some MASS NOUNS such as *coffee, wheat, sugar, sand.* As the term *mass noun* suggests, the denotata are only significant *en masse.* In uncountable NPs such nouns denote a mass of perceivable natural units such as coffee beans or grains; grains, ears, spikelets, or stalks of wheat; granules of sugar; grains of sand. You might expect that mass nouns like these would share with collectives like *committee* or *herd* the option of taking either singular or plural external number registration; but no NP headed by a mass noun permits it.

20 The spilt sugar $\left\{ \begin{array}{l} \text{was} \\ \text{*were} \end{array} \right\}$ being carried away by ants.

> **Assumption 13.7** NATURAL UNITS which compose the denotata of mass nouns are conventionally perceived to be too insignificant as individuals to merit labelling individually.

Of course, language does permit us to label the components of the mass, but not by using a simple noun that uniquely labels them. Instead they are denoted by composed phrases such as *coffee bean, grain of sand,* which employ listemes like *bean, grain, coffee, sand* each with a broader meaning. As remarked several times, every language limits its vocabulary via the principle of least effort (D8.12): a less complex label tends to be used for things which are significant within the everyday life of a community (and so tend to be frequently referred to); a more complex label is used for less significant things. Where contextually identifiable ARTIFICIAL UNITS exist, so-called 'mass' nouns readily and very naturally occur in countable NPs:

21 Give me two $\left\{\begin{array}{l} \text{beers} \\ \text{coffees} \\ \text{sugars} \end{array}\right\}$, please.

Furthermore, although nouns such as *wine, wheat,* and *coffee* readily occur in the uncountable NPs of 22, they equally happily occur within the countable NPs of 23 to denote a variety, kind, or species.

22 (a) All wine is acidic.
   (b) All wheat is highly nutritious.
   (c) Coffee is grown at a lower altitude than tea.

23 (a) We have fifty wines on our list, madam.
   (b) Up in Nyeri, you need a wheat that likes a high altitude.
   (c) The Arabica and Robusta coffees provide most of the world trade in coffee.

Notice how the differentiation between singular and plural of mass terms is exploited for additional semantic effect. Such semantic exploitation of different grammatical forms is very common across languages.

§13.2 has shown that countability is a property of NPs not nouns, although nouns do show preference for occurrence in NPs of different countabilities. Semantic differences arise from the use of a noun in countable and uncountable NPs. This semantic difference is regularly exploited by language users. Likewise the variations in number marking on NPs found where there is number discord or collectivizing.

Exercises

13.2.1 Number in Fijian pronouns has four subcategories: singular, dual, paucal (approx. 3–12), plural, e.g.

   (a)   *E la'o mai*   3.SINGULAR go here   "He/She/It came"
   (b)   *Rau la'o mai*   3.DUAL   go here
   (c)   *Ratou la'o mai*   3.PAUCAL go here
   (d)   *Ra la'o mai*   3.PLURAL go here

Suggest enlightening translations for (b)–(d).

13.2.2 Comment on the countability of the italicized NPs in (a1–2) and (b1–2)
   (a1) Will you have *some more potato*?   (b1) We had *pie* for lunch.
   (a2) Will you have *some more potatoes*?   (b2) We had *pies* for lunch.

13.2.3 How would you interpret *We had lambs for dinner*?

13.2.4 What markers of NP-internal number registration can you think of?

13.2.5 Do three sheep constitute a flock or three people a crowd or a committee? It seems likely that the cardinality of the set denoted by a collective noun will necessarily be greater than three, and can be several thousand. How, then, would you explain the proverb *Two is company; three is a crowd*? (Note the number registration here; it is discussed immediately below.)

13.2.6 In the light of the discussion in §13.2.4, comment on the countability of the italicized NPs in (a–d).
  (a) *These cucumber* are doing well, it's good year for them.
  (b) *The machine gun* was assembled in the terrorist's car.
  (c) We saw *two giraffe* coming down to the water's edge to drink.
  (d) You should visit *the Teewah coloured sands*.

13.2.7 Comment on the fact that both singular and plural external number registration is possible with proper names like *the United States* and *the Himalayas*.

13.2.8 Explain the different semantic effects of singular and plural external number registration in (a-c).
  (a) Four pieces of cake is/are enough for anyone but a glutton.
  (b) Two pounds of flour was/were what I needed.
  (c) A row of trees stands/stand on the ridge.

13.3 Ensemble theory

> [T]here are parts of water, sugar, furniture too small to count as water, sugar, furniture.
> (Quine 1960:99)

We need a semantic representation for countable and uncountable NPs that captures the intuition in A13.8.

> **Assumption 13.8** Countables denote individual entities of a similar kind; uncountables denote an undifferentiated (comm)unity.

Contrast *knives and forks* with *cutlery*, or 24 with 25.

24 Harry bought some cream *cakes*.
25 Harry bought some cream *cake*.

Even more telling is 26 where the uncountable 'some cake' is followed by the countable 'which one' meaning "which [kind of] cake".

26 Do have some cake; which one would you like to try?

The pronoun *one(s)* indicates lexical/semantic identity and not coreference (Chapter 2, 68–69).

> *Assumption 13.9 Cake heading a countable NP is lexically and semantically identical with cake heading an uncountable NP. Similarly for other such nouns, e.g. oak, wine, potato.*

Set theory captures the semantics of countable NPs because a set takes individuals as members. Thus, the denotata of *some cakes* can readily be conceived as members of the set K={x:x is a cake}. Uncountables such as the NP *some cake* do not denote individuals; they

> refer to entities as having a part–whole structure without singling out any particular parts and without making any commitments concerning the existence of minimal parts.
>
> (Bunt 1985:46)

Exactly the contrary is presupposed for countable NPs.

We need a metalanguage that captures the properties of both countables and uncountables using something very like set theory but whose primitive notion is a part-of relation (meronym) for uncountables and a membership relation for countables. Recall that, in set theory, the relation A⊆B, "A is a subset of B", is defined by all members of A being also members of B, and not because A forms a part of B – even though it appears to be represented meronymically in a Venn diagram such as Fig. 13.1.

Figure 13.1 A⊂B

Linguistic semantics needs a metalanguage which uses the notion "part of" as primitive, but defines anything which is "the smallest part" as the member of a set. Ensemble theory, defined by Bunt (1976, 1979, 1985), is such a metalanguage.[2]

We will consider only essential characteristics of ensemble theory; details are presented in Bunt's works. Borrowing from conventions in mereology,[3] Bunt uses lower-case x, y, z as symbols for ensembles in order to differentiate them formally from the usual notation for sets. An individual is denoted by a unit set, and a set is just a special kind of ensemble (1985:57). Judging from 24–26, this very well reflects the way that languages express countability.

Definition 13.3 x⊆y "x is a subensemble of y".

Definition 13.4 IDENTITY: ∀x,y[x=y iff (x⊆y) ∧ (y⊆x)]

Definition 13.5 PROPER SUBENSEMBLE: $\forall x,y[x \subset y$ iff $(x \subseteq y) \wedge \neg(y \subseteq x)]$

Definition 13.6 TRANSITIVITY: $x \subseteq y \subseteq z \rightarrow x \subseteq z$

Definition 13.7 $x \cap y$ is the OVERLAP of ensembles x and y:
   $\forall a,x,y[a=x \cap y$ iff $(a \subseteq x \wedge a \subseteq y) \rightarrow \forall z[(z \subseteq x \wedge z \subseteq y) \rightarrow z \subseteq a]]$

Definition 13.8 $x \cup y$ is the MERGE of ensembles x and y:
   $\forall b,x,y[b=x \cup y$ iff $(x \subset b \vee y \subset b) \rightarrow \forall z[z \subset b \rightarrow (z \subset x \vee z \subset y)]]$

Definition 13.9 A non-null ensemble with no proper parts is ATOMIC. If x is atomic, then x has exactly one member (for '$\exists!z$' read "there is exactly one z"): $\exists!z[\forall x,y[x=\{z\} \wedge [x \subseteq y \longleftrightarrow z \in y]]$

Definition 13.10 A merge of atomic ensembles $x \cup y$ is a discrete ensemble or SET (1985:71).

Definition 13.11 ALL: $\bigcup x:x \subseteq u$ is the merge of all subensembles of u. The merge of all subensembles of u is uniquely equivalent to u. Thus,
   $\exists!u[\forall x,y[\bigcup x:x \subseteq u=u$ iff $(y \subseteq x \rightarrow y \subseteq u) \wedge x \cup y=u]]$

The formula in D13.11 translates "There is exactly one ensemble u such that for every ensemble x and every ensemble y, the merge of subensembles of u is identical with u only if, when y is a subensemble of x, then y is a subensemble of u and the merge of x with y is identical with u."

§7.4 defined a set abstractly using a formulation such as K={x:x is a cake} "K is the set of x's that are cakes." Ensembles are similarly defined; e.g. g=⌐x:x is gold⌐ "g is the ensemble of parts that are gold". More generally: f=⌐x:Px⌐, in which x is an ensemble and P names what kind of ensemble it is. (Every subensemble is an ensemble, just as every subset is a set.)

Exercises

13.3.1 Give a colloquial English gloss for (a–c).
   (a) $\forall x,y[x \subset y$ iff $(x \subseteq y) \wedge \neg(y \subseteq x)]$
   (b) $x \subseteq y \subseteq z \rightarrow x \subseteq z$
   (c) $\forall b,x,y[b=x \cup y$ iff $(x \subset b \wedge y \subset b) \rightarrow \forall z[z \subset b \rightarrow (z \subset x \vee z \subset y)]]$

13.3.2 Suppose that c={x} and c⊆b. Does it follow that x∈b or x⊆b?

13.3.3 The term 'parts' used in this chapter is borrowed from mathematical logic and refers to both "parts" and "pieces" or "bits". What is the difference between 'parts' as in *spare parts for a car* and 'pieces/bits' as in *pieces/bits of the car were littered all over the road*?

13.4 Preliminaries for a semantics of English quantifiers

Various standard relational symbols are used in this section: $\ll$ means "is very-much-less than",< "is less than", $\leq$ "is less than or equal to", = "equals, is identical with", $\approx$ "is approximately equivalent to, about the same number as", $\geq$ "is greater than or equal to", > "is greater than".

We shall treat familiar English quantifiers as 'generalized quantifiers'. A singular countable NP such as *a cat* is represented by the quantified subformula 27.[4]

27 [*a(n)* x: Cx]

The quantifier *a(n)* binds x and 27 is read "an x such that C of x". However, x is an ensemble and not an individual: it is *a(n)* that determines x is an atomic ensemble. In formulae such as 27, the predicate C denotes an ensemble $[\![c]\!]$. We define the ensemble $c = \lceil x{:}x$ is cat$\rceil$ using the uncountable predicate NP 'is cat' (undifferentiated catness) rather than the countable *is a cat*.

> **Definition 13.12** The noun lexeme is semantically unmarked for countability.

Note that any noun lexeme can occur in environments which are not countable; for instance, *travel by car, cat-obsessed, scissor-movement*.

27 sets a recurring pattern, [Qx: Fx], in the semantics of quantifiers. But it ignores the crucial fact that the quantifier *a(n)* defines a singular countable NP.

> **Definition 13.13** The quantifier Q in the subformula [Qx: Fx] determines a MEASURE FUNCTION which takes the (sub)ensemble x as its domain and outputs a quantity, $|x|$.

We need to capture the fact that 27 tells us that x is a set such that the number of x's is at least one, i.e. $|x| \geq 1$.[1] Line (ii) in 28 does this. (Below I will explain why we say 'the number of x's is at least one' rather than *the number of x's is exactly one* such that $|x|=1$.) The sentence *a cat is sick* is represented by the formula in line (i) of 28, where $C = \lceil x{:}x$ is cat$\rceil$ and $S = \lceil x{:}x$ is sick$\rceil$.[5]

28 [*a(n)* x: Cx](Sx)   (i)
    [*a(n)* x: Cx] ▸ $|x| \geq 1 \wedge x \subseteq c$ (ii)
    $x \subseteq s$ (iii)
    [*a(n)* x: Cx](Sx) $\rightarrow$ $|x| \geq 1 \wedge x \subseteq c \cap s$ (iv)
    [*a(n)* x: Cx](Sx) $\longleftrightarrow$ $|c \cap s| \geq 1$ (v)

Let's take this line by line. Line (i) is read "an x such that C of x, and S of (that) x (which is C)". The subformula [*a(n)* x: Cx], is not a proposition but a RESTRICTED QUANTIFIER

---

1. In this chapter, 0 and 1 have the numerical values "zero" and "one".

(Hailperin 1957): quantification is restricted to x's which are C, and only those x's satisfying this condition are predicated by S. Because [a(n) x: Cx] is not a proposition the conventional implicature (D6.4) appears in line (ii). On the left-hand side, 'x' is quantified by *a(n)* and this conventionally implicates '$|x| \geq 1$' on the right-hand side.

> *Definition 13.14* When the measure function on ensemble x yields a number greater than or equal to 1 ($|x| \geq 1$), x is a set and any ensemble of which x is part is a set. Consequently, the NP IS COUNTABLE.

Obviously *a(n)* is being treated as synonymous with *one*, which is preferred to *a(n)* when the focus is on the quantity (see §13.6, A13.12). Note the existential presupposition in line (ii); of course, like any presupposition it may turn out to be false. Line (ii) of 28, [a(n) x: Cx] ▸ $|x| \geq 1 \wedge x \subseteq c$, depicted in Fig. 13.2, needs to be interpreted as purportedly true within $M^{w,t}$ (the model of the world and time spoken of).

Figure 13.2 Rough sketch of 28(ii)

The x⊆s in line (iii) follows from our interpretation of Sx in line (i); x remains bound by [a(n) x: Cx]. In line (iv), [a(n) x: Cx](Sx) → $|x| \geq 1 \wedge x \subseteq c \cap s$, the last conjunct x⊆c∩s "x is a subensemble of the overlap of c and s" follows from lines (ii–iii), (x⊆c) ∧ (x⊆s); it is depicted in Fig. 13.3. Truth functors appear in lines (iv) and (v) because the formula to their left is a proposition.

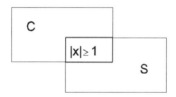

Figure 13.3 Rough sketch of 28(iv)

Line (v), [a(n) x: Cx](Sx) ⟶ $|c \cap s| \geq 1$, follows from line (iv) and means "*a cat is sick* is true if and only if the number of sick cats ≥ 1". $|c \cap s|$ symbolizes the measure function on the overlap ensemble of cat and sick entities; its value is >1 if x⊂c∩s "x is proper subset of c∩s" but exactly 1 if x is an improper subset of c∩s, i.e. x=c∩s. For example, *A cat is sick* is true if (but not only if) *three cats are sick*:

29   Three cats are sick. ⊩ A cat is sick.

In normal language use, quantifiers form a class of scalar implicatures (D6.8). Relevant scales for present purposes are:

<all, most, many/much, some, a few/little, a(n)>
<n≥6, 5, 4, 3, 2, 1>
<no, not all, few/little>.

Use of an item conversationally implicates that no item to its left is applicable. If Speaker asserts *a cat is sick* s/he conversationally implicates that only one cat is sick and that it is not the case that few or some or many or most or all cats are sick. The standard conversational implicature of quantified NPs is just as important to their semantic specification as the truth condition. Consequently, 28 needs an additional line, (vi).

28 $[a(n) \text{ x: Cx}](Sx) \longmapsto |c \cap s| \geq 1$ (v)

$[a(n) \text{ x: Cx}](Sx) \triangleright |c \cap s| = 1$ (vi)

Based on the assumption that $x \subseteq c \cap s \longmapsto (x = c \cap s \veebar x \subset c \cap s)$ in line (iv) of 28, the implicature adopts the strongest, most specific interpretation in the disjunct, namely that $x \subseteq c \cap s \triangleright x = c \cap s$.

Scalar implicatures relate to the quantity scale in Fig. 13.4. *Some* is omitted because it is compatible with any quantifier to the right of *all* and to the left of *no*.

$$\text{all} > \text{most} > \left\{ \begin{array}{l} \text{many} \\ \text{much} \end{array} \right\} > \left\{ \begin{array}{c} \text{several} \geq \text{a few} \\ \text{a little} \end{array} \right\} > \left\{ \begin{array}{l} \text{few} \\ \text{little} \end{array} \right\} > \left\{ \begin{array}{l} \text{a(n) / one} \\ \text{?a (tiny) bit of} \end{array} \right\} > \text{no}$$

Figure 13.4 The quantity scale.

(Possible alternatives to *a (tiny) bit of* are *very little* and *almost no*.) Any quantifier **conventionally** implicates all quantifiers downscale to its right except for *no* (X ⊬ Y = "X does not conventionally implicate Y").

all N ▸ many N ▸ one N ⊬ no N.

In addition to the implicational scales and the quantity scale in Fig. 13.4, there is the comparative scale in Table 13.2 (cf. Table 8.5 and Allan 1987b).

DOWNSCALE POLE	<	≤	≈	≥	>	UPSCALE POLE
few	fewer	as few	about the same number	as many	more	many
little	less	as little	about the same quantity	as much	more	much

Table 13.2 A comparative scale of quantifiers

As pointed out by Lakoff 1972, Rusiecki 1985, a person's height is implicitly compared against a fuzzy norm. The same is true for the polar quantifiers *few, little, many, much.*

30 *Sam is tall* → Sam's height > typical height expected for such men
31 *Ed is short* → Ed's height < typical height expected for such men

> *Definition 13.15* The REFERENCE ENSEMBLE (SET) is the (usually fuzzy) standard for a comparison or quantification.

The number of people Speaker refers to when using *few* in 32 will depend on the size of the class enrolment (≪ means "very-much-less than").

32 Few students turned up to my class today. ⊣⊢
       The number of students who turned up to my class today ≪ the number enrolled.

Few out of an enrolment of 100 would be appropriate where nineteen attended, whereas this number would be *many students* out of a class of twenty-five. In 32, the reference set, the number of students enrolled, is well defined; but this is not always the case.

33 Many people are living in poverty. ⊣⊢ The number of people living in
       poverty > the number of people we should expect to live in poverty.

33 can be true when less than 1 per cent of the population is living in poverty, just because the reference set is not the population as a whole.
       Questions about quantity use *How much/many?* from the high or upper end of the scale. This is quite usual – all the italicized adjectives in 34 are from the upper end of the scale (Table 8.5, Allan 1987b).

34 (a) How *tall* are you?
     (b) How *wide* is it?
     (c) How *good* is she?
     (d) How *beautiful* is it?

An explanation for this may be the pollyanna principle: the universal human tendency to use evaluatively positive words more frequently and diversely than evaluatively negative words (Boucher and Osgood 1969). Whereas 35 is an open question about the number of party-goers, 36 has the implicature "Speaker presupposes that not many people attended."

35 How many people went to Harry's farewell party?
36 How few people went to Harry's farewell party?

An explanation for the fact that *A few people went* is more positive in its evaluation than *Few people went* (similarly for *a little* versus *little*) will be given in §13.7.

This section identified a category of generalized quantifiers, symbolized Q, which includes articles (see §13.6) and denumerators. In the formula $[Qx:Fx](Gx)$, Q binds x within the restricted quantifier $[Qx:Fx]$, and the restricted quantifier in turn binds the x within (Gx). Predicates F and G denote ensembles f and g respectively, of which x is a part. Q determines a measure function $|x|$ on ensemble x. $x \subseteq f$ such that Q determines $|f|$, the quantity of ensemble f, in this context. The semantic facts about quantification need to be supplemented with standard conversational implicatures. We also saw that there is a quantity scale, and a comparative scale of quantifiers. Finally we identified a reference ensemble for comparative quantification.

Exercises

13.4.1 Would it be true to say of $[a(n)$ x: Cx$](Sx)$ that $a(n)$ binds x and the predicates C and S denote ensembles $[\![c]\!]$ and $[\![s]\!]$ respectively of which x is a part? If you agree, how would you represent that x is a part of c and s?

13.4.2 In the formula $[a(n)$ x: Cx$](Sx)$, is C in the domain of S? In other words, is S a second-order predicate?

13.4.3 Give a semantics, based on $[a(n)$ x: Cx$](Sx)$, for *One man is tall*.

13.4.4 If the scalar implicatures <*all, most, many/much, some, a few/little, a(n)*> and <*no, not all, few/little*> are right then (a) and (b) should be acceptable. What is your judgment?
  (a) Many of the apples in that box are rotten, in fact all of them.
  (b) Few of the students did brilliantly, in fact none did.

13.4.5 Discuss the difference between (a) and (b) (see Allan 1987b, Rusiecki 1985).
  (a) ??How good was your son's accident?
  (b) How bad was your son's accident?

13.5 Compositional quantification

37 We bought *vegetables* and *fruit* and *milk*.
38 *Cherries* are delicious.
39 *Salmon* is very tasty.

When there is no surface quantifier or determiner and the head noun is plural, as in 37–38, the NP is countable. In 39, the NP has no surface quantifier or determiner, the head noun is in the N_0 (bare noun or citation) form, so the NP is uncountable. In 38–39, but not in 37, the NPs are generic. The generic is an inference based not on the semantics of the NP, but on the fact that the proposition is "law-like" (D2.15). The superficial zero quantifier indicated by the N_0 form is semantically consistent with both generic and nongeneric interpretations. The difference between them can be ignored in the semantic specifications for NPs.

Definition 13.16 Quantification of the MORPHOLOGICALLY PLURAL NOUN is semantically $[PL_Q \; x: Fx]$, 40.

40 $[PL_Q \; x: Fx](Gx)$ (i)
    $[PL_Q \; x: Fx] \blacktriangleright |x| > 1 \wedge x \subseteq f$ (ii)
    $[PL_Q \; x: Fx](Gx) \rightarrow |x| > 1 \wedge x \subseteq f \cap g$ (iii)
    $[PL_Q \; x: Fx](Gx) \longleftrightarrow |f \cap g| > 1$ (iv)

Because x is quantified by PL_Q, line (ii) says that the NP denotes more than one (thing that is) F in $M^{w,t}$ – a consequence of the plural quantifier.[6] Therefore, ensemble x denotes a countable NP. The existential presupposition carries through to 40(iv). 40(iii) $x \subseteq f \cap g$ "x is a subensemble of the overlap of f and g" follows from lines (i–ii), cf. 28(ii–iv): $(x \subseteq f \wedge x \subseteq g) \rightarrow (x \subseteq f \cap g)$. 40(iv) sums up, saying that in $M^{w,t}$ "things which are F are G": cf. 38, "things which are cherries are delicious".

Definition 13.17 Quantification of the N_0 form is semantically $[\emptyset_Q \; x: Fx]$, 41.

41 $[\emptyset_Q \; x: Fx](Gx)$ (i)
    $[\emptyset_Q \; x: Fx] \blacktriangleright |x| \neq 0 \wedge x \subseteq f$ (ii)
    $[\emptyset_Q \; x: Fx](Gx) \rightarrow |x| \neq 0 \wedge x \subseteq f \cap g$ (iii)
    $[\emptyset_Q \; x: Fx](Gx) \longleftrightarrow |f \cap g| \neq 0$ (iv)

41(ii) says that there is an existential presupposition: in $M^{w,t}$, x is non-null. The existential presupposition carries forward to line (iv). There is nothing in 41 to tell us that the overlap of f and g, $f \cap g$, denotes countables so the default interpretation is that the NP is uncountable, cf. 39.

Definition 13.18 LEFT QUANTIFIER CONTROL. Leftmost quantifiers impose interpretations that may significantly modify the interpretations otherwise appropriate to quantifiers in their scope (indicated by the "[" to the left of Q and the paired "]" to the right). The controlled quantifiers are c-commanded by the left-quantifier.

The left quantifier control condition is what makes collectivized NP such as *three giraffe* semantically plural (§13.2). It also yields the preferred interpretation for an ungrammatical NP such as *one men* singular. In processing spoken or written English, the leftmost quantifier is encountered before the elements in its scope, but there are many languages where this is not the case e.g. Swahili *ki-boko m-moja* S.CL-hippopotamus S.CL-one "one hippopotamus".

41 is the proper representation for the N_0 form which is found not only in uncountables but also in singular countables. Compare 42 with 28, which it revises.

42 $[a(n)/one$ y: y⊆[∅$_Q$ x: Fx]](Gy)   (i)
    $[a(n)/one$ y: y⊆[∅$_Q$ x: Fx]] ▸ |y|≥1   (ii)
    $[a(n)/one$ y: y⊆[∅$_Q$ x: Fx]] ▹ |y|=1   (iii)
    y⊆[∅$_Q$ x: Fx] ▸ y⊆x⊆f, ∴ y⊆f   (iv)
    $[a(n)/one$ y: y⊆[∅$_Q$ x: Fx]] ▸ |y|≥1 ∧ y⊆f   (v)
    $[a(n)/one$ y: y⊆[∅$_Q$ x: Fx]](Gy) → (y⊆f ∧ y⊆g), ∴ y⊆f∩g   (vi)
    $[a(n)/one$ y: y⊆[∅$_Q$ x: Fx]](Gy) ⟷ |f∩g|≥1   (vii)
    $[a(n)/one$ y: y⊆[∅$_Q$ x: Fx]](Gy) ▹ |f∩g|=1   (viii)

Line (i) of 42 is a revision of 28(i), with F in place of C and G in place of S. 42(ii) shows
that *a(n)* and *one* determine a countable NP: y is a discrete ensemble consisting of at least
one atomic subensemble; y is a subensemble of x which is a subensemble of f, so y is a
subensemble of f (logical transitivity, D6.9). Because y is denumerable (|y|≥1), so are f
and g. 28(ii) is now seen to collapse lines (ii), (iv) and (v) of 42. The conventional
implicature of 42(ii) gives rise to the conversational implicature in 42(iii) which carries
through to line (viii). In 42(iv), transitivity validates the inference from y⊆x⊆f to y⊆f.
Also, the existential import of zero quantification over x (cf. 41(ii)) is omitted as
redundant, given 42(ii). 42(v) summarizes (ii) and (iv). 42(vi) brings in the semantics of
clause predicate G, cf. 28(iv), 40(iii), 41(iii). 42(vii) follows from (ii) and (vi): (|y|≥1 ∧
y⊆f∩g) → |f∩g|≥1. By inspection, line (viii) is validated by (iii), (vi), and (vii).
    Now consider a plural NP with a numerical quantifier. Let m=⌈x:x is man in this room⌉
and p=⌈x:x is secret policeman⌉.

43 *[three* y: y⊆[PL$_Q$ x: Mx]](Py)   (i)
    [three y: y⊆[PL$_Q$ x: Mx]] ▸ |y|≥3   (ii)
    [three y: y⊆[PL$_Q$ x: Mx]] ▹ |y|=3   (iii)
    y⊆[PL$_Q$ x: Mx] ▸ y⊆x⊆m, ∴ y⊆m   (iv)
    [three y: y⊆[PL$_Q$ x: Mx]] ▸ |y|≥3 ∧ y⊆m   (v)
    [three y: y⊆[PL$_Q$ x: Mx]](Py) → |y|≥3 ∧ y⊆m∩p   (vi)
    [three y: y⊆[PL$_Q$ x: Mx]](Py) ⟷ |m∩p|≥3   (vii)
    [three y: y⊆[PL$_Q$ x: Mx]](Py) ▹ |m∩p|=3   (viii)

43 is very similar to 42. In line (vi), y in the formula y⊆m∩p is quantified by *three*, this
is indicated by the preceding |y|≥3.
    Turning to universal quantifiers: whereas *all* ranges over an ensemble that may be
countable or uncountable, *each* and *every* identify the NP as countable. (*Each* differs from
every in that *each N* can be roughly glossed "distributed among every N", see Allan 1986
II:74ff for further discussion). [all x: Fx] identifies ensemble f as the merge of all its
subensembles such that ∃!f[∪x:x⊆f=f], from which it follows that |f| is the quantity of all
f's subensembles (D13.11).

44 All gold is valuable.

$[all \; y: y \subseteq [\emptyset_Q \; x: Gx]](Vy)$ (i)

$[all \; y: y \subseteq [\emptyset_Q \; x: Gx]] \; \blacktriangleright \; \bigcup y: y \subseteq [\emptyset_Q \; x: Gx] = [\emptyset_Q \; x: Gx]$ (ii)

$[\emptyset_Q \; x: Gx] \; \blacktriangleright \; |x| \neq 0 \wedge x \subseteq g, \; \therefore \; |g| \neq 0$ (iii)

$y \subseteq [\emptyset_Q \; x: Gx] \; \blacktriangleright \; y \subseteq x \subseteq g, \; \therefore \; y \subseteq g \wedge |g| \neq 0$ (iv)

$[all \; y: y \subseteq [\emptyset_Q \; x: Gx]] \; \blacktriangleright \; \exists! g [\bigcup y: y \subseteq g = g] \wedge |g| \neq 0$ (v)

$[all \; y: y \subseteq [\emptyset_Q \; x: Gx]](Vy) \to \exists! g [g = \bigcup y: y \subseteq g] \wedge y \subseteq v, \; \therefore \; \exists! g [\bigcup y: y \subseteq g \cap v = g]$ (vi)

$[all \; y: y \subseteq [\emptyset_Q \; x: Gx]](Vy) \longmapsto \exists! g [\bigcup y: y \subseteq g \cap v = g] \wedge |g| \neq 0$ (vii)

44(ii) establishes that the quantified NP *all gold* conventionally implicates the merge of all subensembles of gold. 44(iii) establishes the ensemble g and quantifies it; in effect, it translates *gold*. 44(iv) identifies y as a subensemble of g. 44(v) brings together lines (ii), (iv) and (iii). Formula $\exists! g [\bigcup y: y \subseteq g = g]$ in line (v) means "there is exactly one ensemble g such that the merge of all subensembles of g is identical to g." In other words, everything that is y is G or, alternatively, $[all \; y: y \subseteq [\emptyset_Q \; x: Gx]]$ denotes $[\![g]\!]$. This is why 44 is virtually synonymous with the generic *Gold is valuable*; the difference being that the latter refers to the ensemble of gold whereas 44 focuses on the quantity by referring to all the subensembles whose merge is this ensemble. In 44(vi) the conclusion $\exists! g [\bigcup y: y \subseteq g \cap v = g]$ is justified by the fact that y in the subformula Vy (line (i)) is quantified by *all*. In other words "everything that is y is V." Line (v) established that $[all \; y: y \subseteq [\emptyset_Q \; x: Gx]]$ denotes $[\![g]\!]$; so it follows that g ("everything that is y") is a subensemble of v. There is nothing in the semantics of 44 to show that the NP is countable, therefore by default it is uncountable.

Next consider *all* quantifying a countable NP.

45 All men in this room are secret policemen.

$[all \; y: y \subseteq [PL_Q \; x: Mx]](Py)$ (i)

$[all \; y: y \subseteq [PL_Q \; x: Mx]] \; \blacktriangleright \; \bigcup y: y \subseteq [PL_Q \; x: Mx] = [PL_Q \; x: Mx]$ (ii)

$[PL_Q \; x: Mx] \; \blacktriangleright \; |x| > 1 \wedge x \subseteq m, \; \therefore \; |m| > 1$ (iii)

$y \subseteq [PL_Q \; x: Mx] \; \blacktriangleright \; y \subseteq x \subseteq m, \; \therefore \; y \subseteq m \wedge |m| > 1$ (iv)

$[all \; y: y \subseteq [PL_Q \; x: Mx]] \; \blacktriangleright \; \exists! m [\bigcup y: y \subseteq m = m] \wedge |m| > 1$ (v)

$[all \; y: y \subseteq [PL_Q \; x: Mx]](Py) \longmapsto \exists! m [\bigcup y: y \subseteq m \cap p = m] \wedge |m| > 1$ (vi)

45(iii) establishes the ensemble m and quantifies it; in effect, it translates *men*. 45(iv) identifies y as a subensemble of m. 45(v) brings together lines (ii), (iv) and (iii). 45(vi) simplifies on lines (vi) and (vii) of 44. Like most universal quantifiers, *all* ignores countability. Countability is determined in 45 by the plural quantifier. Hence 45(vi) identifies all subensembles of a discrete ensemble m and only by inference is this equivalent to all members of a set M.

Definition 13.19. EVERY:

$[every \; x: Fx] \; \blacktriangleright \; \forall x [Fx \longleftrightarrow \forall y, z [(y \subseteq x \wedge z \subseteq x) \to |y| \geq 1 \wedge |y| \approx |z|]]$

Every differs from *all* in two ways:

(a)   *Every* identifies the NP as countable. Sentences like *Take a pill every four hours* suggest it quantifies over discrete ensembles (sets) rather than individuals.

(b)   *Every* selects objects of roughly identical quantity (in *Every few days, every now and then*, recurrence at similar intervals seems to be the critical factor).

All and *every* are interchangeable only when these two conditions obtain. What they have in common in [Qx:Fx](Gx) is that both imply $|f| = |f \cap g| \neq 0$.

46 Every man in this room is a secret policeman.

$[every\ y: y \subseteq [\varnothing_Q\ x: Mx]](Py)$ (i)

$\quad [every\ y: y \subseteq [\varnothing_Q\ x: Mx]] \blacktriangleright \forall y,w,z[|y| \geq 1 \land (w \subseteq y \land z \subseteq y) \to |w| \approx |z|]$ (ii)

$\quad y \subseteq [\varnothing_Q\ x: Mx] \blacktriangleright y \subseteq m$ (iii)

$\quad [every\ y: y \subseteq [\varnothing_Q\ x: Mx]] \blacktriangleright |y| \geq 1 \land$

$\qquad\qquad\qquad \forall y[y \subseteq m \longleftrightarrow \forall w,z[(w \subseteq y \land z \subseteq y) \to |w| \approx |z|]]$ (iv)

$\quad [every\ y: y \subseteq [\varnothing_Q\ x: Mx]](Py) \to y \subseteq m \cap p$ (v)

$\quad [every\ y: y \subseteq [\varnothing_Q\ x: Mx]](Py) \longleftrightarrow |m| = |m \cap p| \geq 1 \land$

$\qquad\qquad\qquad \forall y[y \subseteq m \longleftrightarrow \forall w,z[(w \subseteq y \land z \subseteq y) \to |w| \approx |z|]]$ (vi)

46(iv) follows from lines (ii) and (iii). In lines (iv) and (vi), m is a constant.
  Turning to *no*:

47 $[no\ y: y \subseteq [\varnothing_Q\ x: Fx]](Gy)$ (i)

$\quad [no\ y: y \subseteq [\varnothing_Q\ x: Fx]] \blacktriangleright \neg(y \subseteq [\varnothing_Q\ x: Fx])$ (ii)

$\quad y \subseteq [\varnothing_Q\ x: Fx] \blacktriangleright |x| \neq 0 \land y \subseteq x \subseteq f, \therefore y \subseteq f \land |y| \neq 0$ (iii)

$\quad [no\ y: y \subseteq [\varnothing_Q\ x: Fx]] \blacktriangleright |y| = 0 \lor y \not\subseteq f$ (iv)

$\quad [no\ y: y \subseteq [\varnothing_Q\ x: Fx]](Gy) \to |y| = 0 \lor y \not\subseteq f \cap g$ (v)

$\quad [no\ y: y \subseteq [\varnothing_Q\ x: Fx]](Gy) \longleftrightarrow |f \cap g| = 0$ (vi)

47(ii) says that the quantifier *no* of line (i), in effect, negates $y \subseteq f \land |y| \neq 0$ of line (iii). This is spelled out as the conventional implicature in 47(iv): y is either null (there is nothing that is F) and/or, whether or not y is null, it is no part of ensemble f. Line (v) follows logically: if there is nothing that is F, then there is nothing that is both F and G. The latter is the crucial disjunct, which motivates 47(vi). Like *all*, *no* ignores countability.
  Compare 47 with 48, *not an/one F is G*.

48 $[not\ z: z \subseteq [a(n)/one\ y: y \subseteq [\varnothing_Q\ x: Fx]]](Gz)$ (i)

$\quad [not\ z: z \subseteq [a(n)/one\ y: y \subseteq [\varnothing_Q\ x: Fx]]] \blacktriangleright \neg(z \subseteq [a(n)/one\ y: y \subseteq [\varnothing_Q\ x: Fx]])$ (ii)

$\quad [a(n)/one\ y: y \subseteq [\varnothing_Q\ x: Fx]] \blacktriangleright |y| \geq 1 \land y \subseteq f$ (iii)

$\quad [not\ z: z \subseteq [a(n)/one\ y: y \subseteq [\varnothing_Q\ x: Fx]]] \blacktriangleright \neg(z \subseteq (|y| \geq 1 \land y \subseteq f)), \therefore |z| \not\geq 1 \lor z \not\subseteq f$ (iv)

$\quad [not\ z: z \subseteq [a(n)/one\ y: y \subseteq [\varnothing_Q\ x: Fx]]](Gz) \to |z| \not\geq 1 \lor z \not\subseteq f \cap g$ (v)

$\quad [not\ z: z \subseteq [a(n)/one\ y: y \subseteq [\varnothing_Q\ x: Fx]]](Gz) \longleftrightarrow |f \cap g| \not\geq 1$ (vi)

$\quad [not\ z: z \subseteq [a(n)/one\ y: y \subseteq [\varnothing_Q\ x: Fx]]](Gz) \rhd |f \cap g| = 0$ (vii)

48(ii–iv) may be compared with 47(ii–iv). In 48(iv) $|z| \not\geq 1$ means that the quantity of z is either not equal to 1 or it is less than one; $z \not\subseteq f$ means "there are no z's that are F". 48(vi) $|f \cap g| \not\geq 1$ entails that $|f \cap g| < 1 \lor |f \cap g| \neq 1$. *Not* has narrow scope: it negates the concatenated quantifier *a(n)/one*. The preferred sense is $|f \cap g| < 1$ and this gives rise to the implicature in (vii) which is identical to the semantics of *no*. The dispreferred sense surfaces in *Not **ONE** but **TWO** Fs are G* which, in its intonation and in the presence of the adversative *but*, has the hallmarks of presupposition negation (§6.5): what is being denied is the implicature of *One F is G*: $|f \cap g|=1$.

When *all* ranges over a numeral quantifier Q_n, it limits the quantity from "at least Q_n" to "exactly Q_n".

49 All three men in this room are secret policemen.

$[all\ z: z \subseteq [three\ y: y \subseteq [PL_Q\ x: Mx]]](Pz)$ (i)

$[all\ z: z \subseteq [three\ y: y \subseteq [PL_Q\ x: Mx]]] \blacktriangleright \bigcup z:z \subseteq [three\ y: y \subseteq [PL_Q\ x: Mx]]=$

$[three\ y: y \subseteq [PL_Q\ x: Mx]]$ (ii)

$[three\ y: y \subseteq [PL_Q\ x: Mx]] \blacktriangleright |y| \geq 3 \wedge y \subseteq m, \therefore |m| \geq 3$ (iii)

$z \subseteq [three\ y: y \subseteq [PL_Q\ x: Mx]] \blacktriangleright |m| \geq 3 \wedge z \subseteq m$ (iv)

$[all\ z: z \subseteq [three\ y: y \subseteq [PL_Q\ x: Mx]]] \blacktriangleright \exists!m[\bigcup z:z \subseteq m=m] \wedge |m|=3$ (v)

$[all\ z: z \subseteq [three\ y: y \subseteq [PL_Q\ x: Mx]]](Pz) \longleftrightarrow \exists!m[\bigcup z:z \subseteq m \cap p = m] \wedge |m|=3$ (vi)

49(v) recognizes that if *all three men* is the merge of all subensembles of three men, there is no possibility that there are more than three. Consequently, the relation $\geq$ "greater than or equal to" is reduced to the stronger relation $=$ "(exactly) equals". This is a function of all universal quantifiers, and correlates with their structural location as leftmost quantifiers, thus c-commanding and controlling the quantifiers within their scope (D13.18).

§13.5 has provided semantic specifications for a number of quantifiers, but concentrated upon the means for computing the semantic interpretation when a NP has more than one quantifier.

Exercises

13.5.1 Using the templates provided in §13.5, suggest semantic analyses for the quantified NPs in (a–d).
(a) All wildfire is dangerous.
(b) Two cars crashed.
(c) Not a creature stirred.
(d) No two are identical.

13.5.2 What is the difference in meaning (if any) between (a), (b) and (c)?

(a$_1$) Harry invited us all back to his place.
(a$_2$) Suzie blew us all a kiss.

(b$_1$) Harry invited everyone back to his place.
(b$_2$) Suzie blew us, every one, a kiss.

(c$_1$) Harry invited each of us back to his place.
(c$_2$) Suzie blew each of us a kiss.

13.6 *The* as a universal quantifier

> *The train* went on up *the track* out of sight, around one of *the hills* of burnt timber. *Nick* sat
> down on *the bundle* of canvas and bedding *the baggage man* had pitched out of *the door* of
> *the baggage car.*
> > (Opening sentences of Hemingway 1987:163, quoted in
> > Chafe 1994:250. Italics added to definite NPs)

Every English NP is either countable or uncountable (A13.1) and definite or indefinite
(A13.2).

> Definition 13.20 The INDEFINITE requires Hearer to create an ensemble x
> from an ensemble y such that x⊂y.

If Sue wants a couple of trout from the fishmonger, she might say 50.

50 Give me two trout, please.

50 instructs Hearer to select a discrete ensemble of two from the ensemble of trout on the
counter. A definite NP identifies a recognized or recognizable ensemble of denotata
uniquely (we shall see how).

> Definition 13.21 The DEFINITE picks out the ensemble x for Hearer by
> equating it with ensemble y such that x=y (which is what universals do), or
> naming it, for example [h/x]Φ where [h=Harry] and x is a variable in formula
> Φ. Loosely speaking, a definite indicates readily identifiable reference.

Indicating two trout, Sue can say 51.

51 Give me those two trout, please.

In uttering 51, Sue identifies exactly the ensemble of trout that she wants. Like *all* and
other universals, the definite article determines an improper subensemble, suggesting that
Russell 1905 was right: *the* is a kind of universal quantifier.
    It is generally agreed that a definite serves to pick out the particular ensemble Speaker
refers to, i.e. a definite NP has 'unique reference'.[7] But what is the force of the word
'unique' here? Proper names may seem to refer uniquely, but if Speaker were to say *I had
a letter from Anna, yesterday* s/he could be referring to one of several people s/he happens
to know, and to use this sentence unambiguously s/he needs to ensure that Hearer has
enough contextual information to give the name unique reference within $M^{w,t}$ (Chapter 3).
Furthermore the so-called 'unique reference' may be to a set of individuals in a plural
countable NP such as *the cats* or to an ensemble denoted by an uncountable NP such as *the
lightning* or *the gold in my wedding ring*. Provided we interpret 'unique reference' broadly
enough to encompass all these things, the description is satisfactory.
    Like definite articles in many other languages, English *the* derived historically from a
demonstrative. D13.21 refers to the property which makes definites such as *Harry* or *the*

loo or *the son of one of my students* pick out the contextually appropriate ('accessible' in Ariel 1990) referent in M^{w,t}. The words 'picks out' link definites to demonstratives.

Definition 13.22 A DEMONSTRATIVE serves to pick out a particular referent or set of referents.

Demonstratives are a deictic category rooted in common ground (D1.19). So are all definites.

Assumption 13.10 THE is the prototypical marker of definiteness in English.

Typical definite pronouns and determiners can readily be glossed using *the* as a semantic component. Table 13.3. shows how *the* can be used as the common foundation element among definite NPs (the glosses in Table 13.3 do not give their definitive semantic content; see Recanati 1993).

---

here	"the location near S[peaker] or indicated as the first or starting point by S"
there	"the location away from S or from the first or starting point"
this N$_\varnothing$	"the N located near S or indicated as the first or starting point by S"
that N$_\varnothing$	"the N located away from S or from the first or starting point"
these N.PL	"the Ns located near S or indicated as the first or starting point by S"
those N.PL	"the Ns located away from S or from the first or starting point"
my N$_\varnothing$	"the N which is mine"
your N.PL	"the Ns which are yours", etc.
I	"the person who is speaking or writing"
you	"the person(s) being addressed"
he	"the male one", etc.
PN	"the person, thing, or place called PN" ['PN' is a proper name]

Table 13.3 *The* as the prototypical definite

Because the definite marks unique reference, it is the favoured choice for SUPERLATIVES. There can be only one man who is the tallest man in the world at any one time, therefore the definite is natural in 52. The indefinite in 53 is decidedly peculiar because it implies that there are other tallest men as well, and the only felicitous way to express this is 54.

52 The tallest man in the world today is 2.94m.

53   ??A tallest man in the world today is 2.94m.[2]
54   One of the tallest men in the world today is 2.94m.

54 identifies a set of tallest men (say, all those over 2.5m) and this set is superlative in height by comparison with other men.

One clue that definites indicate readily identifiable reference is that countability marking is presumed retrievable and therefore is not marked in singulars like *the lightning* (uncountable), *the cat* (countable), or the pronoun *it* – which can stand for either of them. 55 reveals that whether a definite or an indefinite NP is used depends on the characteristics of the NP's referent in $M^{w,t}$. The only two indefinites are in bold type, but we shall be discussing the italicized definites.

55 **One morning** *Tom* found *his Jaguar* wouldn't start. He phoned Ed and asked him to come and look at it. Ed didn't really want to, but he came anyway. He saw that *the plugs* were worn, and advised Tom to fit **some new ones**. Tom did so. After that *the car* worked perfectly.

The proper name 'Tom' introduces a person as if he is known to Hearer. If this story were an anecdote about a real person, more information would be expected to be known to both Speaker and Hearer, or would need to be made known to Hearer by saying something like *There's this guy I know called Tom*, or *My brother Tom*. In a fiction such as 55, nothing more is needed beyond knowing that *Tom* is the name for a male. This common narrative convention (see the Hemingway quote at the head of this section) is intended to draw the reader into the action by pretending that s/he shares common ground with the narrator. In 55, the common ground is awareness of this narrative ploy. '[H]is Jaguar' refers indirectly to Tom, the only male so far mentioned in the story; and, although a jaguar is a big cat, the initial capital J and the predicate 'wouldn't start' clearly indicate that the NP refers to some kind of motor vehicle. Even if Hearer did not know at this stage that 'Jaguar' is an automobile marque, the assumption can immediately be inferred from the predicate and confirmed by the remainder of the story. '[His] Jaguar' indicates that Tom has only one Jaguar, otherwise Speaker should have said *one of his Jaguars*; the entire set of Tom's Jaguars is therefore identified by the definite NP. (Even though I have two daughters I can say 56 without risk of misleading anybody.

56   My daughter was mugged yesterday.
57   One of my daughters was mugged yesterday.

Were I to say 57 it implicates that more than one of them was a potential victim, which is not the case with 56.) Going back to 55, a car frame has been invoked which accounts for the definites 'the plugs' and 'the car'. What a frame or script does is identify certain necessary and/or possible attributes (Chapter 8) for which values may or may not be explicitly assigned. In 55 a value is assigned for the plugs in Tom's Jaguar, but none for its steering wheel, brakes, etc. Note that if the text read *he saw some plugs were worn*, the

---

2. There is a paper entitled 'A simplest systematics for turn-taking for conversation' (Sacks et al. 1974), but the indefiniteness of the title is puzzling: no other 'systematics' can also be 'simplest'.

indefinite 'some plugs' would mean "some of the plugs", whereas in 55 'the plugs' refers to the set of all the spark-plugs in the Jaguar's engine because *the* is a universal quantifier. However minimal your knowledge of car mechanics, it is likely that you infer that there is a problem with the engine; so you know that *the car won't start* is a synecdoche (Chapter 5) for *the car's engine won't start*. (Incidentally, when Tom asked Ed 'to come and have a look at it', the implication was that Ed should check out the engine, not, say, the paintwork or the tyres.) Even if you did not know prior to reading this text that at least some car engines have [spark-]plugs, you would learn it by inference from reading 55. It follows that the set of plugs referred to using 'the plugs' is the set uniquely restricted to the Jaguar's engine.

Semantic frames and common ground also explain the definite NPs italicized in 58–59.

58   A fishing boat rammed us. *The captain* was drunk.
59   *The moon* was bright last night.

A boat has only one captain attributed in its frame, so the atomic ensemble of relevant captains is easy to identify and is referred to using a definite NP. Many planets have moons, but if no other planet is under discussion, there is an assumption that Speaker is referring to the most salient (accessible in Ariel 1990) moon for human beings (Chapter 9): the one that orbits the Earth.

Assumption 13.11 That which is not common ground, and is out of the ordinary, is newsworthy.

Newsworthiness can give rise to newspaper headlines like 60:

60   [A] Woman shoots *her friend* in *the foot*.

Despite her act, it is likely that the shooter has more friends than the one she has injured; and it is most improbable that the friend has only one foot – otherwise the headline would have read *Woman shoots one-legged friend in the foot*. A sensational story is expected to be careless with the finer points of the truth: the headline to this one is not concerned with any other of the shooter's friends, they are irrelevant. Similarly with the victim's other foot; if nothing happened to it, there is no reason for it to feature in the headline. 'Woman', however, has to be indefinite; she has to be selected as a unit subset of all possible women that the newspaper might refer to. Once selected, the newsworthy things pertaining to her (the shooting of her friend in the foot) can be uniquely identified with her.

The italicized definite NPs in 61–62 ordinarily do not, or do not necessarily, refer to a specific location but rather seem to be semantically incorporated with the verb to identify a particular kind of activity in which the italicized noun plays an essential role.

61   I need to go to *the* $\left\{ \begin{array}{l} \textit{lavatory.} \\ \textit{bathroom.} \\ \textit{loo.} \end{array} \right.$

62 Let's go to *the* $\begin{cases} \textit{theatre.} \\ \textit{cinema.} \\ \textit{movies.} \\ \textit{opera.} \end{cases}$

This is particularly noticeable with 61 because many speakers can talk about 'going to the bathroom' behind a hedge, or in the sea, or even in the kitchen. The form of words used here is euphemistic (Chapter 5) and alternative verbs (*pee, urinate,* etc.) exist. But with 62 there are no suitable alternative verbs at all. Note that it is possible to ask *Where shall we go to the cinema?* in place of *What film shall we see?* or *Which cinema shall we go to?* Somewhat similar are 63.

63 I have to go to *the* $\begin{cases} \textit{dentist.} \\ \textit{doctor's.} \end{cases}$

It is not necessary for Speaker to have in mind any particular individual dentist or doctor in order to use 63, and certainly not necessary that Hearer be able to identify a particular dentist or doctor. All of 61–63 are consistent with the semantics of the definite as identifying a particular ensemble without partitioning a larger ensemble of similar denotata.

D13.23 shows that *the* is a species of universal quantifier and the identificational property is associated with the entire restricted quantifier.

Definition 13.23 [*the* x: Fx] conventionally implicates $\exists!x[x{\subseteq}f \rightarrow x{=}f]$, to be read "there is exactly one ensemble x and if it is a subsemble of f, then x is identical with f" which can be paraphrased by "there is exactly one ensemble f in $M^{w,t}$."

Russell's 1905 formula translates 64 as 65, where B={x:x is a lamb} and S={x:x is sick}.

64 The lamb is sick.
65 $\exists x[Bx \wedge \forall y[By \rightarrow y{=}x] \wedge Sx]$

Reformalizing 65 into our metalanguage yields 66.

66 [*the* y: y⊆[∅_Q x: Bx]](Sy)   (i)
    [*the* y: y⊆[∅_Q x: Bx]] ▶ $\exists!y[y{\subseteq}[\emptyset_Q$ x: Bx] → y=[∅_Q x: Bx]]   (ii)
      [∅_Q x: Bx] ▶ |x|≠0 ∧ x⊆b, ∴ |b|≠0   (iii)
    y⊆[∅_Q x: Bx] ▶ y⊆x⊆b, ∴ y⊆b ∧ |b|≠0   (iv)
    [*the* y: y⊆[∅_Q x: Bx]] ▶ $\exists!y[y{\subseteq}b$ → y=b] ∧ |b|≠0   (v)
  [*the* y: y⊆[∅_Q x: Bx]](Sy) → $\exists!y[y{\subseteq}b$ → y=b] ∧ y⊆s, ∴ $\exists!y[y{\subseteq}b{\cap}s$ → y=b]   (vi)
  [*the* y: y⊆[∅_Q x: Bx]](Sy) → $\exists!y[y{\subseteq}b{\cap}s$ → y=b], ∴ b∩s=b   (vii)
  [*the* y: y⊆[∅_Q x: Bx]](Sy) → $\exists!y[y{\subseteq}b{\cap}s$ → y=b] ∧ |b∩s|≠0   (viii)

66(ii) particularizes on the generic translation of [*the* x: Fx] into $\exists!x[x\subseteq f \rightarrow x=f]$. 66(iii) establishes ensemble b as non-null, in effect it translates *lamb*. Line (iv) establishes y as a subensemble of b. 66(v) says that, quantified by *the*, y is an improper subensemble of b, ∴ y=b. This is counterpart to the subformula $\forall y[By \rightarrow y=x]$ in 65 and shows *the* to be one kind of universal quantifier. (v) translates *the lamb* into "there is exactly one ensemble y and it is identical with b, which is non-null" which can be paraphrased by "there is exactly one non-null ensemble of lamb in $M^{w,t}$". 66(vi) brings in the clause predicate. 66(vii) says that if 64 is true, then the identifiable ensemble of lambs in $M^{w,t}$ is identical with the ensemble of sick lambs in that world. 66(viii) brings down the information that the ensemble of sick lambs is non-null.

Present in 65, but missing in 66 is the information that $|b\cap s|=1$. This information is not directly available from the morphosyntax of 64. The N_0 form 'lamb' is compatible both with a countable singular interpretation and also with an uncountable interpretation – compare 64 with 67.

67 The lamb is delicious.

In 67 the uncountable NP "the lamb" most probably refers to meat, and in 64 the countable singular to an individual animal. The distinguishing factor for 64 and 67 is, of course, the predication. A related matter is what we know about things, based on the encyclopedia entry for the noun (Chapter 3, Allan 1981). For instance, we know that cats are not normally a source of meat but lambs are. However, the question of whether the lamb referred to in 64 is or is not meat is decided by the predicate. The strands in arguing that "the lamb" in 64 is countable are the following meaning postulates:

68 $\qquad\qquad\qquad \forall x[\textbf{lamb}'(x) \rightarrow \textbf{animal}'(x)]$ $\qquad\qquad$ (i)

$\qquad\qquad\qquad \forall x[\textbf{animal}'(x) \rightarrow \textbf{living}'(x) \vee \textbf{food\_source}'(x)]$ $\qquad$ (ii)

$\forall y[\lambda x[\textbf{animal}'(x) \wedge \textbf{living}'(x)](y) \rightarrow |y|\geq 1]$ $\qquad\qquad\qquad\qquad$ (iii)

$\qquad\qquad\qquad \forall x[\textbf{be\_sick}'(x) \rightarrow \textbf{living}'(x)]$ $\qquad\qquad\qquad$ (iv)

$\forall y[\lambda x[\textbf{lamb}'(x) \wedge \textbf{be\_sick}'(x)](y) \rightarrow |y|\geq 1]$ $\qquad\qquad\qquad\qquad$ (v)

68 grossly oversimplifies, but provides grounds for replacing 66(viii) with:

66 [*the* y: y⊆[∅$_Q$ x: Bx]](Sy) → $\exists!y[y\subseteq b\cap s \rightarrow y=b]$, ∴ b∩s=b $\wedge$ $|b\cap s|=1$ $\qquad$ (ix)

[*the* y: y=[∅$_Q$ x: Bx]](Sy) $\longleftrightarrow \exists!y[y\subseteq b\cap s \rightarrow y=b] \wedge |b\cap s|=1$ $\qquad\qquad$ (x)

In 66(ix) the clause predicate is instrumental in determining reference to a sick and therefore living animal; consequently the NP is countable. By default the N_0 form in a countable NP indicates a single referent as shown by $|b\cap s|=1$; it is "exactly one" and not "at least one" because *the* is a universal quantifier. 66(x) says *the lamb is sick* is true in $M^{w,t}$ if and only if there is exactly one ensemble of lambs that is identical with the ensemble of sick lambs and it is an atomic ensemble. This is what is meant by saying the definite makes unique reference.

Although 66 is correct for a singular definite countable NP that refers to an individual, it is not appropriate for a definite generic, which typically refers to a genus or kind. The definite generic applies only to countable NPs for the reason that it identifies the ensemble and not the set of individuals that are countable. The ensemble of an uncountable NP is denoted by N_0, **Gold is valuable**. To dissimilate the ensemble denoting a genus of countable entities from the stuff of which those entities are constituted we get *the N_0*: compare **Rabbit** *is delicious* referring to the flesh and **The rabbit** *is a pest in Australia* referring to the genus.

Let's turn to a more complex example, and one that involves a plural definite:

69   All (of) the men in this room are secret policemen.

$[all\ z: z{\subseteq}[_\Phi the\ y: y{\subseteq}[_\Psi PL_Q\ x: Mx_\Psi]_\Phi]](Pz)$ (i)

$[all\ z: z{\subseteq}[_\Phi the\ y: y{\subseteq}[_\Psi PL_Q\ x: Mx_\Psi]_\Phi]] \blacktriangleright \bigcup z{:}z{\subseteq}\Phi{=}\Phi$ (ii)

$[the\ y: y{\subseteq}[_\Psi PL_Q\ x: Mx_\Psi]] \blacktriangleright \exists! y[y{\subseteq}\Psi \rightarrow y{=}\Psi]$ (iii)

$[_\Psi PL_Q\ x: Mx_\Psi] \blacktriangleright |x|{>}1 \wedge x{\subseteq}m, \therefore |m|{>}1$ (iv)

$[_\Phi the\ y: y{\subseteq}[PL_Q\ x: Mx]_\Phi] \blacktriangleright \exists! y[y{\subseteq}x{\subseteq}m \rightarrow y{=}m] \wedge |m|{>}1,$

$\therefore \exists! y[y{\subseteq}m \rightarrow y{=}m] \wedge |m|{>}1$ (v)

$[all\ z: z{\subseteq}[_\Phi the\ y: y{\subseteq}[PL_Q\ x: Mx]_\Phi]] \blacktriangleright \exists! m[\exists! y[\bigcup z{:}z{\subseteq}(y{\subseteq}m \rightarrow y{=}m) =$

$(y{\subseteq}m \rightarrow y{=}m)]] \wedge |m|{>}1$ (vi)

$[all\ z: z{\subseteq}[_\Phi the\ y: y{\subseteq}[PL_Q\ x: Mx]_\Phi]] \blacktriangleright \exists! m[\exists! y[\bigcup z{:}z{\subseteq}m{=}m \wedge$

$(y{\subseteq}m \rightarrow y{=}m)]] \wedge |m|{>}1$ (vii)

$[all\ z: z{\subseteq}[the\ y: y{\subseteq}[PL_Q\ x: Mx]]](Pz) \longleftrightarrow \exists! m[\exists! y[\bigcup z{:}z{\subseteq}m{\cap}p{=}m \wedge$

$(y{\subseteq}m \rightarrow y{=}m)]] \wedge |m{\cap}p|{>}1$ (viii)

69(iv) identifies the semantics for Ψ, *men*. 69(v) substitutes Ψ in the conventional implicature of line (iii) with its interpretation from line (iv) and in doing so conflates 66(iii–v) to give the semantics for Φ, *the men*. It follows from $\exists! y[y{\subseteq}x{\subseteq}m \rightarrow y{=}m]$ that $y{=}x$ and $x{=}m$. 69(vi) substitutes Φ in line (ii) with the interpretation given for it in line (v), providing an interpretation for *all the men*. 69(vii) reduces both instances of $(y{\subseteq}m \rightarrow y{=}m)$ from line (vi) to m and restates the crucial identificational information as a conjunct. 69(viii) incorporates the semantics of the clause predicate. 69 differs from 45, *All men in this room are secret policemen*, only in the identificational property contributed by *the*.

70   Three of the men in this room are secret policemen.

$[three\ z: z{\subseteq}[the\ y: y{\subseteq}[PL_Q\ x: Mx]]](Pz)$ (i)

$[the\ y: y{\subseteq}[PL_Q\ x: Mx]] \blacktriangleright \exists! y[y{\subseteq}m \rightarrow y{=}m] \wedge |m|{>}1$ (ii)

$z{\subseteq}[the\ y: y{\subseteq}[PL_Q\ x: Mx]] \blacktriangleright \exists z[\exists! y[z{\subseteq}(y{\subseteq}m \rightarrow y{=}m)] \rightarrow z{\subseteq}m]$ (iii)

$[three\ z: z{\subseteq}[the\ y: y{\subseteq}[PL_Q\ x: Mx]]] \blacktriangleright \exists z[\exists! y[z{\subseteq}(y{\subseteq}m \rightarrow y{=}m)] \wedge$

$|z{\subseteq}m|{\geq}3], \therefore |m|{\geq}3$ (iv)

$[three\ z: z{\subseteq}[the\ y: y{\subseteq}[PL_Q\ x: Mx]]] \triangleright \exists z[z{\subseteq}m \wedge |z{\subseteq}m|{=}3]$ (v)

$[three\ z: z{\subseteq}[the\ y: y{\subseteq}[PL_Q\ x: Mx]]](Pz) \rightarrow \exists z[z{\subseteq}m \wedge |z{\subseteq}m{\cap}p|{\geq}3],$

$\therefore |m{\cap}p|{\geq}3$ (vi)

$[three\ z: z{\subseteq}[the\ y: y{\subseteq}[PL_Q\ x: Mx]]](Pz) \longleftrightarrow \exists z[\exists! y[z{\subseteq}(y{\subseteq}m \rightarrow y{=}m){\cap}p \wedge$

$|z{\subseteq}m{\cap}p|{\geq}3]]$ (vii)

$[three\ z: z{\subseteq}[the\ y: y{\subseteq}[PL_Q\ x: Mx]]](Pz) \triangleright |m{\cap}p|{=}3$ (viii)

The semantics for 70 must be compatible with *Three of the five men in this room are secret policemen* and also for occasions when the cooperative principle is ignored and there are only three men in the room. These are explicitly allowed for in lines (iii), (iv), and (vii).

The facts presented in lines (vi) and (viii) show why 70 is virtually synonymous with 43, *Three men in this room are secret policemen*; 70(vii) shows the difference.

In 71, universal quantifier *the* ranges over *three*. Whereas *three men* means "at least three men", *the three men* and *all three men* both mean "exactly three men". As before, this is the precision effect of a universal quantifier.

71 The three men in this room are secret policemen.

$$[the\ z:\ z{\subseteq}[_{\Phi}three\ y:\ y{\subseteq}[PL_Q\ x:\ Mx]_{\Phi}]](Pz) \tag{i}$$

$$[the\ z:\ z{\subseteq}[three\ y:\ y{\subseteq}[PL_Q\ x:\ Mx]] \blacktriangleright \exists!z[z{\subseteq}\Phi \to z{=}\Phi] \tag{ii}$$

$$[three\ y:\ y{\subseteq}[PL_Q\ x:\ Mx]] \blacktriangleright |m|{\geq}3 \tag{iii}$$

$$[the\ z:\ z{\subseteq}[three\ y:\ y{\subseteq}[PL_Q\ x:\ Mx]] \blacktriangleright \exists!z[z{\subseteq}y{\subseteq}m \to z{=}m] \land |m|{=}3 \tag{iv}$$

$$[the\ z:\ z{\subseteq}[three\ y:\ y{\subseteq}[PL_Q\ x:\ Mx]]](Pz) \longmapsto \exists!z[z{\subseteq}m{\cap}p \to z{=}m] \land$$
$$|m|{=}|m{\cap}p|{=}3 \tag{v}$$

72 All three of the men in this room are secret policemen.

$$[all\ w:\ w{\subseteq}[three\ z:\ z{\subseteq}[the\ y:\ y{\subseteq}[PL_Q\ x:\ Mx]]]](Pw) \tag{i}$$

$$[all\ w:\ w{\subseteq}[_{\Phi}three\ z:\ z{\subseteq}[the\ y:\ y{\subseteq}[PL_Q\ x:\ Mx]]_{\Phi}]] \blacktriangleright \cup w{:}w{\subseteq}\Phi{=}\Phi \tag{ii}$$

$$[three\ z:\ z{\subseteq}[the\ y:\ y{\subseteq}[PL_Q\ x:\ Mx]]] \blacktriangleright \exists z[\exists!y[z{\subseteq}(y{\subseteq}m \to y{=}m)] \land$$
$$|z{\subseteq}m|{\geq}3], \therefore |m|{\geq}3 \tag{iii}$$

$$[all\ w:\ w{\subseteq}[_{\Phi}three\ z:\ z{\subseteq}[the\ y:\ y{\subseteq}[PL_Q\ x:\ Mx]]_{\Phi}]] \blacktriangleright$$
$$\exists!m[\exists z[\exists!y[\cup w{:}w{\subseteq}(z{\subseteq}(y{\subseteq}m \to y{=}m)) = (z{\subseteq}(y{\subseteq}m \to y{=}m))]]] \land |m|{=}3 \tag{iv}$$

$$[all\ w:\ w{\subseteq}[_{\Phi}three\ z:\ z{\subseteq}[the\ y:\ y{\subseteq}[PL_Q\ x:\ Mx]]_{\Phi}]] \blacktriangleright$$
$$\exists!m[\exists!y[\cup w{:}w{\subseteq}m{=}m \land (y{\subseteq}m \to y{=}m)]] \land |m|{=}3 \tag{v}$$

$$[all\ w:\ w{\subseteq}[three\ z:\ z{\subseteq}[the\ y:\ y{\subseteq}[PL_Q\ x:\ Mx]]]](Pw) \longmapsto$$
$$\exists!m[\exists!y[\cup w{:}w{\subseteq}m{=}m{\cap}p \land (y{\subseteq}m \to y{=}m)]] \land |m|{=}|m{\cap}p|{=}3 \tag{vi}$$

72(iv) substitutes the Φ of line (ii) with its interpretation from line (iii), but because *all* is a universal quantifier it constrains $|m|{\geq}3$ to $|m|{=}3$. 72(v) makes the same kind of substitution as we saw in 69(vii).

The is a universal quantifier such that in $[the\ x:\ Fx](Gx)$, $f{=}f{\cap}g$. The universal quantifiers differ from one another as shown in Table 13.4.

$[the\ x:\ Fx](Gx)$	$\to \exists!x[x{\subseteq}f{\cap}g \to x{=}f] \land |f{\cap}g|{\neq}0$
$[all\ x:\ Fx](Gx)$	$\to \exists!f[\cup x{:}x{\subseteq}f{=}f] \land |f|{\neq}0$
$[every\ x:\ Fx](Gx)$	$\to |f|{=}|f{\cap}g|{\geq}1 \land \forall x[x{\subseteq}f \longleftrightarrow \forall y,z[(y{\subseteq}x \land z{\subseteq}x) \to |y|{\approx}|z|]]$
$[no\ x:\ Fx](Gx)$	$\to |f{\cap}g|{=}0$

Table 13.4. The differences among the universal quantifiers

When using *the* and *all*, Speaker purportedly commits to a belief in the existence of some F which is G. It is semantically irrelevant (even though pragmatically consequential) whether or not (a) Speaker actually holds such a belief, and (b) the belief is correct.

Universal quantifiers always occur as the leftmost quantifiers within the structure of simple NPs in English. Notably *all the N* and *both the N* consist of two NPs as revealed by the synonymous *all of the N* and *both of the N*. Other combinations of quantifiers in which the second is universal must occur in the NP⌢*of*⌢NP construction: *any of the N, every one of the Ns, two of the Ns*, etc. Why is *all the men* acceptable but not **the all men*? Although *the* is a universal quantifier it does not focus on quantity, its function is to mark the identifiability of the referent (Du Bois 1980), and quantification is incidental. Thus, although *the men* means "all of the men referred to" referring to the set as a whole, *all the men* focuses on the merge of the subsets.

Is quantification also incidental to the indefinite article? The Quantity2 implicatures of 73–74 are revealing: they show that the indefinite conversationally implicates that a definite is not applicable.

73 I ran over a dog at the weekend ▷ The dog was not mine or yours
74 Sally went out with a man last night ▷ The man was not her partner

Languages display lots of evidence for a 'familiarity hierarchy' which ranks the familiar higher than the unfamiliar (Allan 1987a). A consequence of the familiarity hierarchy is

> **Assumption 13.12** A definite is preferred to an indefinite.

We can now define the functions of the articles.

> **Definition 13.24** Although articles *the, a(n)* and *some* are quantifiers, quantification is incidental to their primary functions. The FUNCTION OF DEFINITE ARTICLE *THE* is to mark the identifiability of the referent. The FUNCTION OF INDEFINITE ARTICLES is to indicate that the definite is not applicable.

As seen in 42, the semantics of indefinite *a(n)* is identical with that for *one*. But the implicature is not, because being an article, *a(n)* is in contrast with *the* – this is its differential value (D8.5). The semantics of *one* is given in 75, that for *a(n)* in 76 (which revises 28(vi)).

75 [*one* y: y⊆[∅$_Q$ x: Fx]](Gy) ⟼ |f∩g|≥1
    [*one* y: y⊆[∅$_Q$ x: Fx]](Gy) ▷ |f∩g|=1

76 [*a(n)* y: y⊆[∅$_Q$ x: Fx]](Gy) ⟼ |f∩g|≥1
    [*a(n)* y: y⊆[∅$_Q$ x: Fx]](Gy) ▷ |f∩g|=1 ∧ ¬∃!y[y⊆f → y=f]

The second conjunct of the implicature in 76, ¬∃!y[y⊆f → y=f], says that it is not the case that there is exactly one ensemble y which, if it is a subensemble of f, is identical with f. This contrasts with a definite – as graphically demonstrated by comparing Fig. 13.5 with Fig. 13.6 (no sketch is definitive).

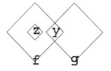

Figure 13.5 Sketches of indefinites such as 75–76

Figure 13.6 Sketch of [*the* x: Fx](Gx)

When applied to the particular contexts of 73–74, the second conjunct of the implicature in 76 gives rise to the Quantity2 implicatures. The implicature given in each of 73–74 is just one of several possible lexicalizations of $\neg\exists!y[y\subseteq f \rightarrow y=f]$ in the context of the implicating sentence.

Generalizing on the complex quantification we have examined:

Definition 13.25 For any pair of concatenated quantifiers $Q_i \cap Q_j$ within the structure of a NP, the relation is that the leftmost quantifier, Q_i, is a subensemble of Q_j – which it c-commands: $[Q_i\, y:\, y\subseteq[Q_j\, x:\, \Phi]]$

We saw that a numeral quantifier is semantically interpreted "at least Q", and has a standard implicature "exactly Q"; however, when it concatenates to the right of a universal quantifier, the numeral quantifier is interpreted "exactly Q". E.g

77 (a)   All five men [in $M^{w,t}$] are bald. ⊩

                   Exactly five [and not six] of the men [in $M^{w,t}$] are bald.

   (b)   The five men are [in $M^{w,t}$] bald. ⊩

                   Exactly five [and not six] of the men [in $M^{w,t}$] are bald.

   (c)   Any five men [in $M^{w,t}$] will do. ⊩

                   Exactly five men [and not six] [in $M^{w,t}$] are required.

It may be this precision effect that constrains the concatenation of the universal quantifiers with fuzzy quantifiers such as *most, many, much, some, a few/little*. If the concatenation is grammatical at all, there needs to be a restrictive relative clause for the concatenation to be good whereas this is not necessary with a numeral quantifier.

78 (a)   *All (of) some men were Russians.

   (b)   All of some men I met were Russians. ⊪ I met some men; they were Russians.

79 (a)   ?The many sailors were all charming.   [OK when elliptical]

   (b)   The many sailors I met were all charming ⊪

                   I met many sailors; they were all charming.

80(b) is superlative, "most" is not functioning like, for instance, the quantifier *five*.

80 (a)   *The most models were in New York.

   (b)   The most models I ever saw was in New York. ⊩

                   I saw more models in New York than anywhere else.

An indefinite NP instructs Hearer to construct an ensemble x of denotata by partitioning some recognized or recognizable ensemble f denoted by the head noun of the NP such that $x \subseteq f$; a subsequent reference to the same entity will be made using a definite NP (81). Reference to like entities uses the indefinite (82).

81   Harry was smoking $[$a cigarette$_{c_1}]$ and had to take $[$it$_{c_1}]$ out of his mouth to cough.
82   Harry lit up $[$a cigarette$_{c_1}]$ and I asked him for $[$one$_{c_2}]$.

Both types occur in 83, which differs from 82 in that 82 entails $c_1 \neq c_2$ whereas 83 allows that possibly $p_2 = p_1$.

83   $[$A prisoner$_{p_1}]$ has written an obscenity on the wall and unless $[$he$_{p_1}]$ owns up $[$a prisoner$_{p_2}]$ will be flogged every hour until $[$he$_{p_1}]$ does.

A definite NP is a universal quantifier in that it uniquely refers to an ensemble by exhausting the range of a clause predicate on the NP. A proper name (used as a rigid designator, cf. Chapter 3) is, perhaps, the quintessential definite NP because of its identificational function. Notably, some proper names, e.g. river names, take the definite article as a matter of course. A definite description is a temporarily-rigid designator within a subset of contextually related worlds and times in M. We saw that newsworthy topics can be treated almost like proper names. The identificational function of the definite is what allows a definite NP to be used in making initial reference to an entity that is unique in $M^{w,t}$ in the sense that there are no competitors matching the denotation of the NP (e.g. *the moon* refers unambiguously if there is one moon and no other moons to compete as possible referents for the NP). An indefinite NP is only used when a definite is inapplicable.

Exercises

13.6.1 In informal style colloquial language *this* may be used to introduce an entity that plays some major function within the reported anecdote, e.g.
    (a)   There was this guy in a pub offered me tickets to the Floyd concert below face value. ...
What evidence could you adduce that 'this' in (a) is indefinite rather than definite?

13.6.2   What is the difference in meaning between (a) and (b)? Try to explain the difference.
    (a)   A first baby born in Australia in the year 2000.
    (b)   The first baby born in Australia in the year 2000.

13.6.3 Comment on the use of definite and indefinite NPs in (a–c).
    (a)   A truck went by and the fumes were nauseating.
    (b)   Max had a cholera shot and the pain was excruciating.
    (c)   The daughter of one of my students has been killed in a car accident.

13.6.4 Explain the indefinite NPs containing superlatives in (a–b).
    (a) A most enjoyable party   (b) A personal best

13.6.5 How do you think the semantics for *The lamb is delicious* would look? Assume that
line (iv) of 68 is replaced by $\forall x[\textbf{be\_delicious}'(x) \rightarrow \textbf{food\_source}'(x)]$ and line (v) by
$\forall y[\lambda x[\textbf{be\_delicious}'(x) \wedge \textbf{lamb}'(x) \wedge \textbf{food\_source}'(x)](y) \rightarrow |y| \neq 0]$.

13.6.6 Show that if it is true at an index that *The mice are happy* then there are no mice
which are not also happy (at that index).

13.6.7 Comment on the following possibilities, offering some kind of explanation for the
options:

Take $\begin{Bmatrix} a \\ the \end{Bmatrix} \begin{Bmatrix} bus \\ train \end{Bmatrix}$ from $\begin{Bmatrix} *an \\ the \end{Bmatrix}$ airport to Woking and $\begin{Bmatrix} the \\ a \end{Bmatrix}$ taxi from there to here.

13.7 Relationships among quantifiers

This section introduces monotonicity and then tables the relationships it reveals among
quantifiers.

> *Definition 13.26*   MONOTONICITY is an entailment relation between
> propositions containing quantifiers. One kind is NP MONOTONE, the other is
> PRED MONOTONE. Each of these can be **upward** or **increasing**, symbolized
> ↑, or **downward/decreasing**, symbolized ↓, and sometimes neither.[8]

Consider some examples to see the mnemonic value of ↑ and ↓. In 84 the second
proposition is a valid inference from the first; this is not so in 85.

84 (a) All linguists are Chomskyites. ⊩ All bald linguists are Chomskyites.   NP↓
    (b) Herod killed all the newborn babies. ⊩
                            Herod killed all the blind newborn babies. NP↓
    (c) All women and children are at risk. ⊩ All children are at risk.   NP↓

85 (a) All bald linguists are Chomskyites. ⊮ All linguists are Chomskyites.
    (b) Herod killed all the blind newborn babies. ⊮
                            Herod killed all the newborn babies.
    (c) All children are at risk. ⊮ All women and children are at risk.

Note that in 84(a)–85(a) the denotation of 'bald linguists' is a subset of the denotation of
'linguists'; 'blind newborn babies' is a subset of 'newborn babies'; and 'children' is a
subset of 'women and children'. In 84 the entailment goes from the superset to the subset,

that is, downward, ↓; and 85 shows it cannot go in the other direction. *All* is therefore NP↓ monotonic (or simply, NP↓). The Venn diagrams below picture 84(a) and 85(a).

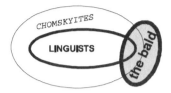

All linguists are Chomskyites, 84(a)   All bald linguists are Chomskyites, 85(a)

Now consider

86 All magpies sing ⊮ All magpies sing sweetly.
87 All magpies sing sweetly ⊩ All magpies sing.   Pred↑

Those things that sing sweetly (S in the diagrams below) are a subset of the things that sing. In 87 the entailment goes from subset to superset, so we say that *all* is Pred↑ monotonic.

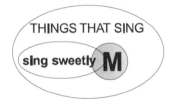

All magpies sing (86)   All magpies sing sweetly (87)

Every and *each* have the same monotonic properties as *all*, NP↓ Pred↑; but *no* is NP↓ and also Pred↓.

88 (a)   No linguists are elephant poachers. ⊩
                              No bearded linguists are elephant poachers   NP↓
          No bearded linguists are elephant poachers. ⊮
                              No linguists are elephant poachers.

    (b)   No magpie snores. ⊩ No magpie snores loudly.   Pred↓
          No magpie snores loudly. ⊮ No magpie snores.

Only presupposition negation of *no* and *each* is possible, for example *Not NO but THREE students failed the course!* and *Not EACH but only TWO students got a test paper.* However, *no* and *each* do have contradictories (D6.6): *all* and *not all* are contradictories; the contradictory of *no* is *at least some* and, for countables only, *at least one*. *All* and *no* are contraries (D6.5). Q¬ negation on *no* (italicized in 89) is NP↓ Pred↑ like its contrary *all/every*.

89 *No* club member does*n't* smoke cigars. ⊩

$\qquad$ *No* female club member does*n't* smoke. NP↓ Pred↑

Negating *each* negates distribution to every N to yield *not every* (or *not all* when this is synonymous with *not every*):

90 ¬[Each child] has an apple. ⫤⊩ Not every child has an apple.

$\quad$ ¬[Each participant] stood up in turn. ⫤⊩ Not all participants stood up in turn.

91 [*not all/every* x: Fx](Gx) ⟷ |f| ≠ |f∩g| ∨ |f|=0

$\quad$ [*not all/every* x: Fx](Gx) ▷ |f∩g| ≠ 0 ∧ |f| > |f∩g|

[*not all/every* x: Fx](Gx) means "some F(s) is(are) G or else no F(s) is(are) G". Note the asymmetry of [*no* x: Fx](Gx) → [*not all/every* x: Fx](Gx). As a statement of nonexistence, [*no* x: Fx](Gx) is preferred under the cooperative principle because it is stronger and more explicit. Consequently, there is an existential implicature in 91. The rest of the implicature accounts for the fact that *not all/every* is closer to *most* than to lesser quantities (cf. Fig. 13.4).

$\quad$ The fact that [*not all/every* x: Fx](Gx) ▷ |f∩g| ≠ 0 (91) is exactly why [*some* x: Fx](Gx) can be inferred from it. The quantifier *some* is nonspecific as to quantity between all and nothing:

92 [*some* x: Fx](Gx) $\hfill$ (i)

$\quad$ [*some* x: Fx] ▸ |x| ≠ 0 ∧ x⊆f, ∴ |f| ≠ 0 $\hfill$ (ii)

$\quad$ [*some* x: Fx](Gx) ⟷ |f∩g| ≠ 0 $\hfill$ (iii)

$\quad$ [*some* x: Fx](Gx) ▷ |f∩g| < |f−f∩g| $\hfill$ (iv)

We interpret *some man* as countable and *some gold* as uncountable, on grounds similar to those appealed to in establishing the countability of lamb in 64–68. 92(ii) represents the existential presupposition in the NP, which carries through to line (iii). |f−f∩g| in lines (iii) and (iv) is "the quantity of F which is not G"; in countable NPs this is interpreted "the number of Fs that don't G". There is a difference in monotonicity between *not all/every* and *some*: *not all/every* are NP↑ Pred↓, whereas *some* is NP↑ Pred↑.

93 Not all (the) boys drive carelessly ⊮ Not all (the) boys drive

$\quad$ Some boys drove carelessly ⊩ Some boys drove $\hfill$ Pred↑

¬Q negation is not possible on *some* – presumably being blocked by its contradictory, *no*.

$\quad$ The subformula |f| ≠ 0 in the semantics for *some* really means "Speaker has reason to believe it is the case that the referent exists." The truth of this can be modified by various predications that hedge or otherwise vary the evidential status (cf. Table 11.4):

94 **I think** there is someone at the door.

95 There **might** be some eggs in the fridge.

96 **Possibly** there are some eggs in the fridge.

Any is often said to be the irrealis counterpart of realis *some* in the scope of negation (97), request (98), and subjunctive (99):

97 I can't see **any**body there.
98 Can you see **any**body there?
99 (a) If **any**one calls, get their number.
      (b) Compare **any** two lemons, ...   ["no matter which two"]

Thus when Speaker has reason to believe that the referent does not exist or might not exist or might exist at some hypothetical index, then – under certain syntactic conditions – *any* is used.

> *Assumption 13.13*   Inability to guarantee existentiality for the reference
> characterizes the use of any.

Quine 1960:138ff argued on the basis of examples comparable with 100–01 that the universal quantifiers *all* and *every* are captured by $\forall$ with narrow scope, and *any* by $\forall$ with wide scope.

100 Ed didn't kiss everyone → $\neg[\forall x[\textbf{kiss}'(e,x)]]$
101 Ed didn't kiss anyone → $\forall x[\neg[\textbf{kiss}'(e,x)]]$

Many scholars agree, though Horn 1972 has an alternative proposal using the existential quantifier $\exists$ for *any* on the basis of its relationship with *some*. The link between *any* and the universal seems to be intuitively correct for some contexts, and the link with *some* in others. For instance, 102 is synonymous with one interpretation of 103, when Speaker does not know that there is an extension for 'traitors'.

102 Any traitors will be shot.
103 All traitors will be shot.

However, 103 with *all* can be used when the extension of 'traitors' is known, whereas 102 with *any* cannot. Quine's analysis is correct for negative contexts,

104 $\neg([any\ x: Fx](Gx))$ → $|f|=|f \cap g|=0$

but for interrogative and hypothetical contexts the meaning is more like 105 – the interrogative mood operator is **?** (D11.2) and the subjunctive operator is **¡** (D11.5). $\Diamond\Phi$ means "it is possible that Φ".

105 $\left.\begin{array}{l} \textbf{?}([any\ x: Fx](Gx)) \\ \textbf{¡}([any\ x: Fx](Gx)) \end{array}\right\}$ → $\Diamond|f \cap g| \neq 0$

The semantics of *any*, $\Diamond|f \cap g| \neq 0$, indicates that Speaker purportedly entertains the possibility that the overlap of f and g is non-null – whether or not Speaker actually has such a belief is another matter. Examples like 99 invoke a world, w_h, accessible from the current world, w_i, where (loosely speaking) Speaker imagines that $|f \cap g| \neq 0$ – traitors are shot or two lemons are compared. *Any* is not used in a positive clause when the NP is known to have extension: *all, every*, and *some* are used instead. Nor is *any* used in an NP that is known to have no extension, because *no* or *not one* are the appropriate quantifiers in such a case. In the scope of a negative, *any* is, appropriately, NP↓ Pred↓ like *no*, but there are problems with NP monotonicity in negated conditionals with *if any*. In fact, for all quantifiers discussed hereafter we shall ignore NP monotonicity because it is, by and large, problematic and unsystematic.

A question *Is/Does any F G?* SEEKS extension for f∩g, whereas the questions *How much F Gs?* or *How many Fs G?* PRESUPPOSE extension for f∩g. The semantics of *much* and *many* are similar to the semantics for *some*, but the standard implicatures are different. 106 refers to some quantity |**APPRO**| which is a nonstandard abbreviation for "quantity judged appropriate or that might reasonably be expected" for the reference ensemble (D13.15). ⪊ means "not much-greater than".

106 [*many/much* x: Fx](Gx) ⟷ |f∩g| > |**APPRO**|
    [*many/much* x: Fx](Gx) ⊳ |f∩g| ⪊ |f−f∩g|

The formula |f∩g| ⪊ |f−f∩g| can be glossed "the quantity of F which is G is not much-greater than the quantity of F which is not G." *Many* and *much* are Pred↑ monotonic as are *a little/few* and *some*. *Many/much* are complements of *a few/little* compare 106 with 107–08 (where |f∩g| ⪉ |f−f∩g| means "the quantity of F which is G is not very-much-less-than the quantity of F which is not G").

107 [*a few/little* x: Fx](Gx) ⟷ |f∩g| < |f−f∩g| ∧ |f∩g| ⪉ |f−f∩g|
    [*a few/little* x: Fx](Gx) ⊳ |f∩g| ⪉ |f−f∩g|

There is something strange about *a little/few*: the monotonicity of their apparent negations, *not a little/few* is Pred↑, identical to the positives.

108 [*not a little/few* x: Fx](Gx) ⟷ ¬(|f∩g| < |f−f∩g| ∧ |f∩g| ⪉ |f−f∩g|)
    [*not a little/few* x: Fx](Gx) ⊳ |f∩g| > |**APPRO**|

The semantics (top line) of the negative 108 is ambiguous. The upscale implicature is not ambiguous and is moreover identical to the semantics of *many/much* in 106. Monotonicities are upward in 109 and downward in the Q¬ sentences of 110.

109 Much of the hour (40 minutes, in fact) was taken up with a dispute over procedure.
    ⊣⊢ Not a little of the hour (40 minutes, in fact) was taken up with a dispute over
        procedure.   Pred↑

110 Not a few women don't smoke cigars.
    ⊣⊢ Many women don't smoke cigars.   Pred↓

Few/little (Pred↓) are the converses of *most* (Pred↑) as is obvious from the comparison of 111 and 112.

111 $[most$ x: Fx$](Gx) \longleftrightarrow |f{\cap}g| {\gg} |f{-}f{\cap}g|$
$\quad [most$ x: Fx$](Gx) \triangleright |f{\cap}g| {\not\gg} |f{-}f{\cap}g|$

112 $[little/few$ x: Fx$](Gx) \longleftrightarrow |f{\cap}g| {\ll} |f{-}f{\cap}g|$
$\quad [little/few$ x: Fx$](Gx) \triangleright |f{\cap}g| {\not\ll} |f{-}f{\cap}g|$

It has often been assumed that *few/little* are the converses of *many/much*. There are three points against this:

(a)   Their meanings.
(b)   The symmetry of the quantity scale (Fig. 13.4), which pairs as converses *most* with *few/little* and *many/much* with **a** *few/little*.
(c)   The fact that ¬Q negation of *most* and *few/little* is not possible in the forms **not most/few/little*; whereas ¬Q negation of *many/much* and *a few/little* is normal.

On the other hand, there is a good deal of overlap between *most* and *much/many* upscale and between *a few/little* and *few/little* downscale. In fact *much/many* range way downscale from *most*. Conversely, *few/little* are restricted to the lower end of the range quantified by *a few/little*. In consequence there is a converse relation between *most/much/many* upscale and *(a) few/little* downscale as evidenced in 113. The (Pred) monotonicity of the quantifiers is given.

113 (a) *Most/many* ↑ of my friends are professionals, **but**/?and *a few* ↑ have blue-collar jobs.
   (b) *A few* ↑ of my friends are professionals, **but**/??and *most/many* ↑ have blue-collar jobs.
   (c) *Most/many* ↑ of my friends are professionals **and**/*but *few* ↓ have blue-collar jobs.
   (d) *Few* ↓ of my friends are professionals, **and**/*but *most/many* ↑ have blue-collar jobs.

The differences in conjunction in 113 result from the fact that when partitioning the ensemble of friends into non-overlapping subensembles, a conjunction of quantifiers of different monotonicity requires *and* (113(c–d), 114), whereas identical Pred monotonicity prefers *but*, though *and* is possible when going downscale; check (113(a–b), 115).

114 *Not all* ↓ of my friends are professionals **and**/*but *a few* ↑ have blue-collar jobs.
   Some ↑ of my friends are professionals **and**/*but *not all* ↓ have blue-collar jobs.
   All ↑ of my friends are professionals **and**/*but *none* ↓ have blue-collar jobs.

115 *Not all* ↓ my friends are professionals **but/and** *few/none* ↓ have blue-collar jobs.
   Not many ↓ of my friends are professionals **but/and** *few/none* ↓ have blue-collar jobs.
   Some ↑ of my friends are professionals **but**/??and *many/most* ↑ have blue-collar jobs.

In 116 the subensembles of friends overlap.

116 *Some* ↑ of my friends are professionals **and**/*but *many* ↑ are women.

Let's now summarize the findings on monotonicity and see what relations they reveal between quantifiers. NP monotonicity is a quagmire as can be seen from Table 13.5.

NP↑	*the, some/a(n)/one/two, some/a(n)/one/two...not, not all/every, all/every...not, a few/little, (not) a few/little...not,* counterfactual *if not any / if any...not.* Doubtful: *?many/much, ?not a few/little*
NP↓	*no, not a(n)/one/two, all/every, no...not, any.* Noncounterfactual *if not any / if any...not.* Doubtful: *?not many/much, ?few/little, ?few/little...not*

NP nonmonotonic	*most...not, much/many...not, not a few/little...not*

Table 13.5 NP monotonicity

Before concluding that NP monotonicity is of no great interest to systematic semantic inquiry, there are some interesting points worth noting. First of all though, consider the traditional 'square of opposition'.[9] The vertices are named from vowels in the Latin *AffIrmo* "I affirm" and *nEgO* "I deny". (Duals are defined and discussed below, D13.27.)

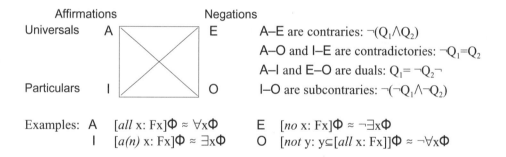

	Affirmations	Negations	
Universals	A	E	A–E are contraries: $\neg(Q_1 \wedge Q_2)$
			A–O and I–E are contradictories: $\neg Q_1 = Q_2$
			A–I and E–O are duals: $Q_1 = \neg Q_2 \neg$
Particulars	I	O	I–O are subcontraries: $\neg(\neg Q_1 \wedge \neg Q_2)$

Examples: A $[all\ x: Fx]\Phi \approx \forall x\Phi$ E $[no\ x: Fx]\Phi \approx \neg\exists x\Phi$
            I $[a(n)\ x: Fx]\Phi \approx \exists x\Phi$ O $[not\ y: y\subseteq[all\ x: Fx]]\Phi \approx \neg\forall x\Phi$

Figure 13.7 The traditional square of opposition

Doubtful cases of NP monotonicity are eliminated from Table 13.6. The top and bottom lines of each box are contradictories, vertices A–O and I–E from Fig. 13.7.

A	NP↓ Pred↑	all/every, no...not
O	NP↑ Pred↓	not all/every, all/every...not, some/a(n)/one/two...not, a few/little...not

I	NP↑ Pred↑	the, some/a(n)/one/two, a few/little
E	NP↓ Pred↓	no, not a(n)/one/two, ?any

Table 13.6 Contradictories among quantifiers

Pred monotonicity is comparatively systematic.

Pred↑	the, all/every, no...not, few/little...not, most, many/much, (not) a few/little, some/a(n)/one/two, if not any, if any...not
Pred↓	not all/every, all/every...not, no, any, most...not, not much/many, much/many...not, not a few...not, few/little, not a(n)/one/two, some/a(n)/one/two...not

Table 13.7 Pred monotonicity

A comparison of the top and bottom lines in Table 13.7 shows that Pred↑ are all affirmative (despite a couple of negative forms); check the A–I vertices of Fig. 13.7. In contrast, the Pred↓ line is negative, corresponding to the E–O axis of the traditional square of opposition. These vertices identify DUALS, something quite different from dual number (§13.2).

> *Definition 13.27* If the dual of Q is Q*, then Q=¬Q*¬

If Q is ↑ (we are no longer concerned with NP monotonicity, so ↑=Pred↑ and ↓=Pred↓ hereafter) then Q* is ↑, if Q is ↓ then Q* is ↓. Some examples in which the italicized quantifiers are duals of one another:

117 Not *all* cats are not sick ⫤⊢ *Some/a(n)/one/two* cat(s) is/are sick
$\quad$ $\neg\forall x\neg\Phi \leftrightarrow \exists x\Phi$
$\quad$ Not *every*one doesn't know Harry ⫤⊢ *Some*one knows Harry

$\quad$ $\neg\forall x\neg\Phi \leftrightarrow \exists x\Phi$
$\quad$ Not *any*one [=¬(someone)] doesn't know Harry ⫤⊢ *Every*one knows Harry

$\quad$ $\neg\exists x\neg\Phi \leftrightarrow \forall x\Phi$
$\quad$ It is not the case that *not all* cats are not sick

$\quad$ ⫤⊢ *No* cat is sick ⫤⊢ All cats are not sick
$\quad$ $\neg\neg\forall x\neg\Phi \leftrightarrow \neg\exists x\Phi$

It is not the case that *no* cat is not sick

⫤ *Not all* cats are sick ⫤ Some cat is not sick
¬¬∃x¬Φ ⟷ ¬∀xΦ
Not *a few* people don't smoke ⫤ *A few* people smoke

Summarizing, with monotonicity indicated on the right:

some/a(n)/one/two	= ¬ all/every ¬	↑
all/every	= ¬ some/any/a(n)/one/two ¬	↑
no	= ¬ not all/every ¬	↓
not all/every	= ¬ no ¬	↓
a few/little	= ¬ a few/little ¬	↑ (*a few/little* is its own dual)

NP conjunctions of different Pred monotonicity prefer *but* to *and* for the most part, in contrast to the facts concerning clause conjunction exemplified in 113–16.

118 ?*Every* ↑ child and *no* ↓ adult died.
✓Every child **but** no adult died.

119 ?We tested *all* ↑ the cats and *not all* ↓ the dogs for rabies.
✓We tested all the cats **but** not all the dogs for rabies.

120 ?*Not a few* ↑ men and *few* ↓ women play rugby.
✓Not a few men **but** few women play rugby   [Stylistically awkward]

121 *Many* ↑ men and *few* ↓ women play rugby.
✓Many men **but** few women play rugby.

122 I'll have *some* ↑ anchovies and *not much* ↓ lettuce, thanks.
✓I'll have some anchovies **but** not much lettuce, thanks.

123 ✓A few ↑ olives **and** *no* ↓ garlic, thanks.

For no obvious reason (listed items? colloquial style?), 123 is completely acceptable.
  And-conjunctions of NPs with identical Pred monotonicity are the only possibility – *but*-conjunctions are ungrammatical.

124 (a) *Every* ↑ child **and**/*but *a few* ↑ women were vaccinated.
    (b) *Some/many* ↑ women **and**/*but *all* ↑ children were inoculated.
    (c) *Not any* ↓ women **and**/*but *not all* ↓ children escaped unharmed.
    (d) *No* ↓ women **and**/*but *few* ↓ men play Russian roulette.
    (e) *Not many* ↓ anchovies **and**/*but *not much* ↓ lettuce, thanks.

In addition to specifying the semantics for some more quantifiers, this section marshalled entailment relations to categorize the semantic relations that exist across English quantifiers and show some of the syntactico-semantic effects that result from the interactions of quantifiers in conjoined sentences.

Exercises

13.7.1 Draw a Venn diagram to demonstrate that *some* is NP↑ Pred↑.

13.7.2 Examine the claim that the monotonicity of the definite is NP↑ Pred↑ (base your discussion on either *his mother* or *John*).

13.7.3 Some quantifiers, such as *exactly half, exactly one, exactly 10,000*, are NON-MONOTONIC. Demonstrate this for at least one of them.

13.7.4 (a) Show that *all* and *no* are contraries and not contradictories.

(b) Identify f−f∩g in the Venn diagram where ☐ is g and ◯ is f:

13.7.5 On most accounts, entailments cannot be determined for interrogative environments because they don't have truth values. However from a_1 and b_1 we can apparently deduce a_2 and b_2. What grounds do you think might justify this view?

a_1. Do/don't you have any crayons?
a_2. Do/don't you have any red crayons?

b_1. Did/didn't you break any plates?
b_2. Did/didn't you cause something to happen to any plates?

13.7.6 Which of the following pairs, A or B, logically implies the other, and what kind of monotonicity is indicated?

		A	B	
(i)	A:	Harry ate some red beans	B:	Harry ate some beans
(ii)	A:	Every rocking horse has a painted face	B:	Every toy is painted
(iii)	A:	Not all foreign students got high grades	B:	Not all students got A's
(iv)	A:	Fred doesn't like any creepy-crawlies	B:	Fred doesn't like any spiders
(v)	A:	There are no Persian carpets in this house	B:	There are no carpets in this place

13.7.7 Discuss the possibility that coordinated propositions like *Many of my friends are heterosexual, but many aren't* capture a change in point of view – e.g. from friends who are heterosexual to friends who are homosexual, given the different proportions of heterosexuals and homosexuals within a population.

13.7.8 Discuss the fact that *all* and *few* do not occur in coordinated propositions like (a–b).
  (a) *Not all people **LIKE** visiting the dentist, and all people **DON'T** like it at all.
  (b) *Few of my friends are heterosexual, and/but few aren't.

13.7.9 Review the evidence that *some* is associated with extension and *any* with the lack of extension.

13.8 Scope relations between quantifiers

Hitherto we have discussed quantification only in one-place clause predicates, G in [Qx:Fx](Gx). The same principles apply to multiplace predicates, e.g. the two-place predicate H in 125.

125 [Qx:Fx]([Qy:Gy](Hxy))

In 125, restricted quantifiers [Qx:Fx] and [Qy:Gy] respectively bind the x and y of (Hxy), and correspond to quantified NPs. This section looks at the relation between quantifiers in sentences like 125. In 126 'some-' has wide scope, it c-commands (D2.13) 'every-', which has narrow scope.

126 Someone loves everyone
  [*some* x: **person′**(x)]([*every* y: **person′**(y)](**love′**(x,y))   Cf. ∃x[∀y[Lxy]]

Tree 126

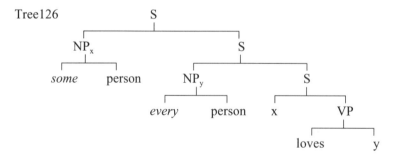

Scope relations are not always evident from surface structure, as we see from the two meanings (a–b) attributable to 127. In (a) 'every-' has wide scope; in (b) it has narrow scope.

127 Everyone loves someone
  (a) [*every* x: **person′**(x)]([*some* y: **person′**(y)](**love′**(x,y)))   Cf. ∀x[∃y[Lxy]]
  (b) [*some* y: **person′**(y)]([*every* x: **person′**(x)](**love′**(x,y)))   Cf. ∃y[∀x[Lxy]]

In (a) 'some-' is in the scope of 'every-' and this means that "everyone has someone whom they love, but they do not all love the same person." In (b) 'every-' is in the scope of 'some-' (as in 126, but the quantifiers bind different variables) and (b) means "there is one person that everyone loves." Compare the trees.

Tree127(a)

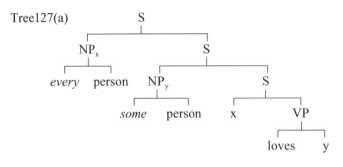

Tree127(b)

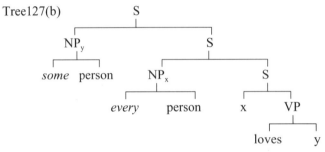

It has often been said that 128 is ambiguous, whereas 129 is not.

128 Every girl [G] danced [D] with *a* bearded [B] sailor [S].
129 Every girl danced with *the* bearded sailor.

In fact, they are both ambiguous (Neale 1990). The well known ambiguity of 128 is between the distribution of one sailor per girl, as in 130 and the same sailor for every girl, as in 131 (cf. 127(a–b)).

130 *[every* x: Gx]([*a(n)* y: Sy ∧ By](Dxy))
        "For every girl, x, there was a bearded sailor, y, and x danced with y."

131 *[a(n)* y: Sy ∧ By]([*every* x: Gx](Dxy))
        "For some bearded sailor, y, every girl, x, danced with y."

132 gives a similar semantics for 129.

132 *[every* x: Gx]([*the* y: Sy ∧ By](Dxy))
        "For every girl, x, there was the bearded sailor, y, such that x danced with y."

132 implies a distribution: if a party of sailors were grouped into pairs, one of whom is bearded and the other isn't, then 132 states that only the bearded sailors got to dance on the occasion referred to.

133 [*the* y: Sy ∧ By]([*every* x: Gx](Dxy))

"For the bearded sailor, y, every girl, x, danced with y."

133, in which every girl danced with the same bearded sailor, is usually given as the only interpretation of 129.

Exercises

13.8.1 Negation and quantifiers. In the Pred₂ clause [Qx:Fx]([Qy:Gy](Hxy)) there are five points of negation logically possible: ¬[Qx:¬Fx](¬[Qy:¬Gy]¬(Hxy)). However a sentence with more than three becomes almost impossible to interpret in any normal context of use; compare (i) and (ii):

  (i)   ¬[*every* x: Px](¬[*some* y: Py]¬(Lxy)) "Not everyone doesn't love noone"
  (ii)   ¬[*every* x: ¬Px](¬[*some* y: Py]¬(Lxy))   "Not everything not a person doesn't love noone"

Notice that ¬[Qx:Fx] = [¬Qx:Fx] e.g. ¬[*some* y: Py] = [¬*some* y: Py] = [*no* y: Py]. This is because the whole NP is in the scope of negation:

  (iii) NP_y[¬ N'[Q[*some*] N[*person*]_N']_NP_y] "noone"

Only the rightmost Q is negated in ¬[Qx:Fx], cf. *not all of some men* but **all of no men*. In surface structure (iii) is the only possibility so that the logically possible ¬[Qx:¬Fx] must be expressed through circumlocution, cf. (ii) where ¬[*every* x: ¬Px] must be expressed using two NPs "not everything not a person". Also, because of the constraint in (iii), negation of the restrictor (corresponding to the head noun of the NP) as in [*many* x: ¬Ax] sometimes allows for the scope of the negative to be indicated by heavy stress on the head noun provided it is within the scope of a negative:

  (iv)   [*many* x: ¬Ax]([*the* y: Ty](Hxy)) "Not many ARROws hit the target" = "Many things that were not arrows hit the target"
  (v)   [*some* y: ¬Py]([*every* x: Px](Lxy)) "There is something not a person which everyone loves" = "It is not a PERson which everyone loves"

Radical negation (presupposition denial) is found in instances like (vi–viii).

  (vi)   [*every* x: Px](¬[*some* y: Py]¬(Lxy)) "Everyone doesn't love noone"
  (vii) [*every* x: Px]([*some* y: ¬Py]¬(Lxy)) "Everyone doesn't love something other than a person"
  (viii) [*some* y: Py]([*every* x: ¬Px]¬(Lxy)) "There is someone whom everything not a person doesn't love"

Now try to match up sentences (a–j) below with the semantic descriptions (r–z).

(a) Not many arrows didn't hit the target.
(b) Many arrows didn't hit the TARget [but something else].
(c) Many arrows didn't hit the target [they missed].
(d) The target wasn't hit by MAny arrows [only a few].
(e) The target, not many arrows didn't hit.
(f) Many arrows hit the thing that wasn't a target.
(g) Many things that weren't arrows hit the target.
(h) The target was hit by many things that weren't arrows.
(j) The target wasn't HIT by many arrows [most of them missed].

(z) ¬[*many* x: Ax]([*the* y: Ty]¬(Hxy))
(y) [*many* x: Ax]([*the* y: ¬Ty](Hxy))
(x) [*many* x: Ax]([*the* y: Ty]¬(Hxy))
(w) [*many* x: Ax](¬[*the* y: Ty](Hxy))
(v) [*many* x: ¬Ax]([*the* y: Ty](Hxy))
(u) [*the* y: Ty](¬[*many* x: Ax]¬(Hxy))
(t) [*the* y: Ty]([*many* x: Ax]¬(Hxy))
(s) [*the* y: Ty](¬[*many* x: Ax](Hxy))
(r) [*the* y: Ty]([*many* x: ¬Ax](Hxy))

13.9 From *a* to *the*

In 134 we understand not that some strawberries were mushy, but that all the strawberries that Harry bought were mushy. In other words, 'they' is not bound by 'some', i.e. the semantics in 135 is wrong (Evans 1985).

134 Harry bought [B] some strawberries [S] and they were mushy [M].
135 [*some* x: Sx]([h=Harry](Bhx ∧ Mx))

135 means "Harry bought some strawberries and some were mushy". Neale 1990:180 proposes a formula like 136.

136 [*some* x: Sx]([h=Harry](Bhx)) ∧ [*the* y: Sy ∧ ([h=Harry](Bhy)](My))

However, 136 fails to capture the identificational property implicit in the definite pronoun 'they'; i.e. that the strawberries 'Sy' that were mushy are the very same ones 'Sx' which Harry bought 'Bhx'. 136 could be true for two occasions on which Harry bought strawberries, one batch being mushy, the other not. 137 rectifies this.

137 [*some* x: Sx]([h=Harry](Bhx ∧ [*the* y: Sy → y=x](My)))

137 seems to mention strawberries too often; a rough gloss is "Harry bought some strawberries and the strawberries were mushy". We can reduce the restrictive quantifier [*the* y: Sy → y=x] in 137 to [*the* y: y=x] "the y such that y is identical with x" because x

is still restricted by Sx in the c-commanding restricted quantification [*some* x: Sx]. Thus in 138, [*the* y: y=x](My) can be glossed "they [the strawberries which Harry bought, [*some* x: Sx]([h=Harry](Bhx)] are mushy."

138 [*some* x: Sx]([h=Harry](Bhx $\wedge$ [*the* y: y=x](My)))

139 adds in the plural.

139 [*some* y: y⊆[PL$_Q$ x: Sx]]([h=Harry](Bhy $\wedge$ [*the* z: z⊆[PL$_Q$ w: w=y]](Mz)))

We have just seen how definites can be linked to antecedent indefinite coreferential NPs. The crucial point of this section is the definition of a definite successor.

Definition 13.28 For any restrictor F and clause predicates G and H, the definite successor to a NP coreferential with the antecedent indefinite is the second conjunct of the formula [Q$_{indef}$ x: Fx](Gx $\wedge$ [*the* y: Fy $\rightarrow$ y=x](Hy)).

137–39 showed file updating (§2.7) on the strawberries (their being bought by Harry and turning out to be mushy). The same kind of incremental interpretation can be put on any sequence involving a particular entity, e.g. the rabbit in 140:[3]

140 Tom caught a rabbit, killed it, skinned it, and cooked it ‖ (a–d):
    (a)   Tom caught a rabbit.
    (b)   Tom killed the rabbit which he'd caught.
    (c)   Tom skinned the rabbit which he had caught and then killed.
    (d)   Tom [t] cooked [C] the rabbit [R] which he had caught [G] and then killed [K] and skinned [S].

The semantics of 140 is 141, in which **P** represents the past tense and where $\Phi < \Psi$ symbolizes "Φ precedes Ψ chronologically".

141 [t=Tom]([*a(n)* y: y⊆[∅$_Q$ x: Rx]]**P**(Gty $\wedge$ [*the* z: z⊆[∅$_Q$ w: w=y]](Ktz $\wedge$ Stz $\wedge$ Ctz)))
    → Gty < (Ktz $\wedge$ Stz $\wedge$ Ctz)
    ▷ Gty < Ktz < Stz < Ctz

141 captures the fact that the rabbit Tom caught underwent some radical changes: the rabbit that Tom cooked was the same individual, but hardly the same rabbit that Tom originally caught. It is exactly such information increment that goes to building up a file on a referent. This process is at the root of world creation, and is the means by which knowledge about the real world is developed and through which story worlds are created. It is crucial to normal understanding in natural language.

---

3. If you are an animal lover horrified by the brutality of this sentence, recast it as *Tom dug up a turnip, peeled it, cut it up, and cooked it* – and make appropriate substitutions.

Exercise

13.9.1 Create a semantic description for (a) using the template provided in §13.9.
  (a) Bert caught two fish, scaled them, gutted them, cooked them, and ate them.

13.10 The semantics and pragmatics of simple classificatory sentences

Suppose that in 142 the hand represents the gesture of pointing at the picture there to its left.

142  [☞ That] is a cow.

> *Definition 13.29* Demonstrative *that* has the semantics [*the* y: y⊆[∅$_Q$ x: **there'**(x)]] (Table 13.3).

> *Definition 13.30* In classificatory and identity statements **be'** is a relation between ensembles and superensembles such that **be'**(x_U,y) → x⊆y

D13.29 applies in generics like *A cow$_x$ is a mammal$_y$* where x⊂y, and to identity statements like *Cicero$_x$ is Tully$_y$* where x=y. The semantics of the predicate NP in 142 is 143.

143 [*a* w: w⊆[∅$_Q$ z: **cow'**(z)]] ∧ |w|≥1

Putting together the parts discussed so far and adding present tense, N, (D11.9):

144 [*the* y: y⊆[∅$_Q$ x: **there'**(x)]](N(**be'**$(y_U,$[*a* w: w⊆[∅$_Q$ z: **cow'**(z)]]))) ∧ y⊆w
    ∧ |w|≥1, ∴ |y|=1

The justification for the conclusion that |y|=1 is that y⊆w, ∴ |w|≥1 → |y|≥1; |y|=1 results from y being in the scope of the universal quantifier *the* (§13.6).
    144 is constructed on the basis of the semantics of the decontextualized sentence *That is a cow* (i.e. without the picture or any other normal context). From the data in 144, someone who knows the meaning of *cow* but is unable to see the picture in 142 can make the following inferences. (The term **bozine* was defined in D8.13.)

145 That is a cow ⟼ That is a female *bozine
146 *That is a cow* ⟼ [*the* y: y⊆[∅$_Q$ x: **there'**(x)]](N(**be'**$(y_U,$[*a* w: w⊆[∅$_Q$ z:
                    λu[**cow'**(u) ∧ **female'**(u) ∧ ***bozine'**(u)](z)]))) ∧ y⊆w ∧ |y|=1

The properties predicated of decontextualized z in 146 are transferable to x, because the referent of 'That' is (said to be) a cow. To be more precise, y, the referent of 'That' is a subensemble of the overlap of cows, females, and *bozines.

Building on work done in Chapters 8–9, it should be evident that:

(a)   Bovines form the core subcategory of *bozines, and the large animals to which the terms *bull, cow,* and *calf* have been extended in radial categories.
(b)   Domestic cattle are at the core of the bovine category: none of a North American bison, cape buffalo, nor eland is a typical bovine in a context such as this book.

Thus, 146 motivates the Quantity2 implicature in 147.

147 *That is a cow* $\hookrightarrow$ [*the* y: y$\subseteq$[$\varnothing_Q$ x: **there′**(x)]](N(**be′**(y$_U$,[*a* w: w$\subseteq$[$\varnothing_Q$ z:
λu[**cow′**(u) $\wedge$ **female′**(u) $\wedge$ ***bozine′**(u)](z)]))) $\wedge$ y$\subseteq$w $\wedge$ |y|=1

     $\triangleright$ λu[**bovine′**(u) $\wedge$ **adult′**(u)](y)

The implicature in 147 gives rise to further inferences because female adult bovines are animals that typically have horns and udders – this is encyclopedic, not lexical, knowledge. Thus, even when decontextualized, the proposition in 142 gives rise to 148.

148 *That is a cow* $\hookrightarrow$ [*the* y: y$\subseteq$[$\varnothing_Q$ x: **there′**(x)]](N(**be′**(y$_U$,[*a* w: w$\subseteq$[$\varnothing_Q$ z:
λu[**cow′**(u) $\wedge$ **female′**(u) $\wedge$ ***bozine′**(u)](z)]))) $\wedge$ y$\subseteq$w $\wedge$ |y|=1

     $\triangleright$ λu[**bovine′**(u) $\wedge$ **adult′**(u) $\wedge$ **horned′**(u) $\wedge$ **uddered′**(u)](y)

Contextual interpretation of 142 in which 'That' is used demonstratively (Kaplan's 1978 'dthat') calls on pragmatics. Let us assume as common ground that 142 refers to the CONTENT of the picture, and that the picture is recognized to depict an animal with horns and udder – a characteristic of female bovines. In 149, instead of being merely implicated as in 148, this is indicated as fact that supersedes the implicature.

149   [☞ That] is a cow $\hookrightarrow$ [*the* y: y$\subseteq$[$\varnothing_Q$ x: λu[**there′**(u) $\wedge$
bovine′(u) $\wedge$ **adult′**(u) $\wedge$ **horned′**(u) $\wedge$ **uddered′**(u) $\wedge$
female′](x)]](N(**be′**(y$_U$,[*a* w: w$\subseteq$[$\varnothing_Q$ z: **cow′**(z)]]))) $\wedge$
y$\subseteq$w $\wedge$ |y|=1

Suppose that 150 occurs.

150   [☞ That] is a cow.

The referent of 'dthat' has none of the characteristics necessary in a *bozine; the incompatibility of what is apparently referred to by 'That' and its being classified as a cow renders the utterance anomalous. We would guess that the anomaly results from a slip of tongue, or inattention to what is pictured and/or pointed to, from a misunderstanding of the word *cow*, or it is a cruel attempt to mislead. 150 is just as anomalous as 151.

151 *That dog is a cow* $\hookleftarrow$ [*the* y: y$\subseteq$[$\varnothing_Q$ x: **dog$'$**(x) $\wedge$ **there$'$**(x)]](**N**(**be$'$**(y$_U$,[*a* w:
w$\subseteq$[$\varnothing_Q$ z: **cow$'$**(z)]]))) $\wedge$ y$\subseteq$w $\wedge$ |y|=1

Except where y has mean mislabelled (Chapter 6, ex.98), y cannot at the same time be a dog and a cow because, being hyponyms of *animal*, these two predicates are contraries.

That concludes the discussion. This section has painstakingly examined the semantic complexity of a very simple classificatory sentence under two conditions:

(a)   decontextualized (without the picture); and
(b)   in the context of the picture.

The aim has been to throw light upon the semantics of such sentences; to show the difference between the sense of a sentence containing *that*, and the same sentence in which *that* is used demonstratively as 'dthat'. It drew on aspects of semantics discussed in Chapters 1, 6, 7, 8, 9, 11, 12, and earlier in this chapter, 13.

Exercises

13.10.1 Create a semantics for (a–b).

(a)      [Those] are two cows.

(b)   Paolo was a happy man.

13.11 Summary

The chapter began with discussion of number and countability. It was shown that countability is a property of NPs and that number marking on NPs and predicates can be exploited in the creation of meaning. The main purpose of the chapter was to propose a comprehensive, internally consistent account of number, countability, and quantification in English that links meaning with morphological form. The interesting question is whether it applies to other languages. Some of the observations do:

(a)   Quantifiers exhibit scope relations.
(b)   Quantifiers are 'conservative' (*Not many women smoke cigars* ⫢ *Not many women are women who smoke cigars.*)[10]

(c)   Quantifiers demonstrate Pred and sometimes NP monotonicity.
(d)   Most quantifiers have contradictories.
(e)   It is likely that all languages have a counterpart to *all* and *no* and *some*. It would be surprising if more than a handful of languages had an exact counterpart to *any*.
(f)   It is probable that all languages have some counterpart to the quantity scale, much less probable that the scale is divided up in a way exactly parallel to English.

Ensemble theory was introduced to capture the properties of both countable and uncountable NPs. There is a category of quantifiers, symbolized Q, which includes articles and denumerators. Formula $[Qx:Fx](Gx)$, with which we began, is equivalent to the labelled bracketing $[_S[_{NP}Q\,N]_i\,[_S e_i\,VP]]$ at the level of LF in GB theory. The more complex compositional semantics involving a series of concatenated quantifiers that include the ⊘ quantifier N_0 and the morphological plural quantifier PL_Q does not match standard accounts of GB theory. The principal function of quantifiers is to determine a measure function on ensembles and their overlaps. The standard implicatures of quantifiers are an essential part of their semantic specification. Indefinites and definites were defined and discussed. The properties of uniqueness and identifiability associated with *the* were shown to derive from its semantic specifications, which show it to be a universal quantifier. Nevertheless, quantification is not the primary function of articles. We identified the entailment relations of quantifiers in terms of monotonicity and defined classes of relationships among them on the basis of their monotonicity. The compositionality of quantification was focused upon throughout the discussion. There is a left-quantifier condition (D13.18), an effect of c-command, which has the leftmost quantifier constraining and even contradicting the implications of other quantifiers within its domain. We reviewed the effects of quantifier scope and finally identified a semantic formula for relating an indefinite NP to its definite successor.

As a finale, §13.10 exhaustively expounded the semantics of a full clause using tools and procedures discussed in earlier sections of *Natural Language Semantics*. Although this is the last chapter, you should read the short Epilogue that follows; it. looks back on what has been achieved and forward to the future of linguistic semantics. It also answers the question whether or not the semantics for quantification in English presented in this chapter is believed to have psychological reality.

● Key words and phrases:

∃!xΦ "there is exactly one x such that ..."
accessibility
all (D13.11)
anomaly
any (A13.13)
|APPRO| (106)
articles (D13.24)
artificial units
atomicity (D13.9)
be (D13.30)
*bozine (D8.13)
c-command (D2.13, D13.18)

classificatory sentence
(English) classifiers
collectivizing (A13.6)
comparative scale (Table 13.2)
compositional quantification
(number) concord
contradictories (Table 13.6, Fig. 13.7)
contraries (Fig. 13.7)
conventional implicature
conversational implicature
converses
countability (D13.14, A13.3, A13.5, A13.8)

● English NPs are countable or uncountable and definite or indefinite (A13.1–2).
● Countability is determined by the internal or external number registration of NPs, and many nouns can occur within either countable or uncountable NPs, though a given noun often prefers one to the other. Thus, countability is a characteristic of NPs, and we ought to refer to a noun as countable or uncountable only within the context of a particular NP (A13.3–4).

● The motivation for countability is individuation (A13.5) into units of a similar kind (A13.8).

● NP-internal number registration is normally concordant. Grammatical number is prototypically registered by the presence or absence of plural inflexion on the NP head – respectively $[PL_Q \, x: Fx]$ and $[\emptyset_Q \, x: Fx]$ (D13.16–17).

● NP-external number registration is typically concordant but may be discordant with semantic and/or pragmatic consequences.

● Semantic effects result from exploitation of number registration. (a) There is prototypical opposition of "one" versus "more than one". (b) Number registration is used with singular NPs headed by collective and institutional nouns to focus on the collection or institution as a single entity, or the members of the collection or institution. (c) Speaker can exploit the external number registration of a quantified plural NP with certain quantifying predicates in order to focus either on the quantity of entities denoted by the NP, or on the entities themselves. (d) A similar manipulation of focus is possible for certain kinds of classified NPs.

● Most mass nouns can occur within countable NPs. Whereas the uncountable NP invariably corresponds with the principle of N_0 usage (D13.2), in a countable NP Speaker refers to significant artificial units or to natural kinds, varieties, or species of whatever the mass noun denotes. Thus, there is a clear semantic difference between the uncountable and countable NP headed by the same lexeme. The principle of least effort (D8.12) plays a part in this.

● 'Collectivizing' occurs in hunting, conservation, and farming jargon when in-groupers use the N_0 form where a plural would usually be used by out-groupers (A13.6). The absence of a plural inflexion functions as a jargon indicator and has a connotative (not denotative) effect.

● A noun has the same lexical and semantic properties in both countable and uncountable NPs (A13.9). This requires that the listeme is in the N_0 form (D13.12). It follows that the semantics of both countables and uncountables should be captured in a common metalanguage. Ensemble theory (D13.3–11) provides such a metalanguage.

● Countable NPs denote atomic ensembles or a merge of atomic ensembles into a discrete ensemble or set (D13.9, D13.14).

● Uncountable NPs denote ensembles that have no atomic ensembles as parts.

● Countability is determined: (a) by a quantifier; (b) from the semantic properties of the head noun (via meaning postulates); and/or (c) from co-text or encyclopedic knowledge.

● In the formula $[Qx:Fx](Gx)$, $[Qx:Fx]$ is a restricted quantifier: the domain of Q is restricted to those x's which satisfy the subformula Fx (loosely speaking, Q quantifies those x's which are F). The restricted quantifier binds x within (Gx). The predicates F and G denote ensembles f and g respectively, and x is a part of their overlap, i.e. $x \subseteq f \cap g$. Q determines a measure function $|f|$ (D13.13) on ensemble f: in other words f's quantity. In a countable, $|f|$ is a number ≥ 1 of Fs.

● Quantification between *many* and *few* on the quantity scale (Fig. 13.4) is usually made in respect of a reference set (D13.15).

● Leftmost quantifiers may significantly modify the interpretation of a quantifier in its scope. The relation between concatenated quantifiers $Q_i \, \hat{} \, Q_j$ is $[Q_i \, y: y \subseteq [Q_j \, x: \Phi]]$.

● A numeral quantifier Q_n is semantically interpreted "at least Q" and has a standard implicature "exactly Q". However, when Q_n concatenates to the right of a universal quantifier, such as *all, the, any,* Q_n is interpreted "exactly Q".

● Indefinite NPs partition ensembles (D13.20). Definite articles derive from demonstratives, and demonstratives serve to pick out a particular referent or set of referents (D13.22); it is this ancestral link that gives *the* – the prototypical definite (A13.10, Table 113.3) – its character. Because *the* is semantically a universal quantifier (D13.23), a definite NP uniquely identifies the referent by exhausting the range of a predicate on the NP.

● Common ground, frames, and scripts enable reference to necessary and/or possible attributes that may be assigned explicit values in what is said. Where there is only one ensemble identified as the value for the attribute, it will normally be referred to using a definite NP. Some definite NPs seem to be semantically incorporated into verbs when the head noun identifies an essential attribute in the act denoted.

● In the articles *the, a(n)*, and *some*, quantification is incidental. Other quantifiers focus on quantity. The definite article focuses on identifiability and the indefinite articles implicate that no definite is applicable (D13.24).

● Entailment relations of quantifiers indicate their monotonicity (D13.26). There are two kinds of monotone, NP and Pred; and two directions: upward entailing ↑, when the inference goes from subensemble to superensemble, and downward entailing, ↓, when the inference goes the other way. NP monotonicity is problematic and mostly unsystematic (Table 13.5). Pred monotonicity is systematic (Table 13.7). Pred↑ quantifiers are positive and Pred↓ quantifiers are negative.

● Confirmed NP↑ Pred↑ (positive) quantifiers are contradictories of (negative) NP↓ Pred↓ quantifiers. Confirmed NP↓ Pred↑ (positive universal) quantifiers are contradictories of (negative) NP↑ Pred↓ quantifiers.

● Conjoined NPs containing quantifiers of different Pred monotonicity prefer *but* to *and*, those with identical Pred monotonicity require *and*.

● Conjoined clauses $[Q_1x:Fx](Gx)$ and $[Q_2x:Fx](Hx)$ where g and h partition f (i.e. $(f \cap g) \cup (f \cap h) = f$) prefer *but* if Q_1 and Q_2 have the same Pred monotonicity, and prefer *and* if the monotonicity is different.

● The formula for a two-place clause predicate H, and any F and G, is: $[Qx:Fx]([Qy:Gy](Hxy))$. A three-place predicate B would have the form: $[Q_ix:Fx]([Q_jy:Gy]([Q_kz:Hz](Bxyz)))$. In the Pred$_3$ formula, Q_k is in the scope both Q_j and Q_i, and Q_j is in the scope of Q_i. These scope relations affect the interpretation of the lower quantifiers.

● D13.28 specifies the semantic relationship between an antecedent indefinite NP and its coreferential definite successor.

● In copular classificatory sentences knowledge of the meaning of the predicate NP gives significant information about the referent of the trajector NP even in decontextualized sentences. In a normal context of use, the properties of the referent give important clues about the properties of the predicate NP. That is why one can use ostension to teach names, e.g. by holding up a pen and saying *This is a pen*.

13.12 Notes on further reading

[1] On countability, see Quine 1960:90ff, Pelletier (ed.) 1979, Allan 1980, Wierzbicka 1988, Ojeda 1991.

[2] There is a large body of opinion that set theory can cope with mass terms without the need to postulate ensembles. See Link 1983, Landman 1989, Lønning 1997, Chierchia 1998.

[3] On mereology, see Leśniewski 1988, Moravscik 1973, Ojeda 1991, Schein 1993.

[4] On generalized quantifiers, see Barwise and Cooper 1981, Benthem and Meulen (eds) 1984, Keenan and Westerstahl 1997. The particular representation used here is based on May 1985, Neale 1990, Schein 1993.

[5] The formula in [*a(n)* x: Cx](Sx) an equivalent in government binding theory at the level of LF (logical form) as shown in abbreviated form below. The variable x in the formula [*a(n)* x: Cx](Sx) corresponds to the index $_i$ in the tree below. At LF, the NP is indexed and moved by Quantifier Raising, and Chomsky-adjoined as sister to S_1 under S_2, leaving behind an indexed trace e_i as shown. Cf. Hornstein 1984, May 1985, Chierchia and McConnell-Ginet 1990, Neale 1990, Diesing 1992.

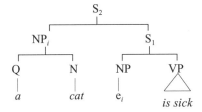

[6] For a different approach to plurals, see Landman 1996, Lasersohn 1995.

[7] On aspects of (in)definiteness, see Russell 1905, Hawkins 1978, Lewis 1979, Givón 1984, May 1985, Heim 1983, 1988, 1990, Neale 1990, Gamut 1991, Kamp and Reyle 1993, Lambrecht 1994, Lyons 1999.

[8] On monotonicity see Chierchia and McConnell-Ginet 1990, Gamut 1991, Cann 1993. NP monotone is also called 'left monotone' and 'subject monotone' . Pred monotone is also called 'right monotone'.

[9] On the traditional square of opposition, see Aristotle *On Interpretation*, L. Apuleius 2ndC. 1968:261ff, Martianus Capella 5thC., 1969:193ff, Boethius 6thC. 1894:319ff, 468ff, 775ff, Gamut 1991, II:238).

[10] On conservativity, see Barwise and Cooper 1981, Gamut 1991, Cann 1993.

Epilogue

> In every work regard the writer's end,
> Since none can compass more than they intend.
>
> (Pope *Essay on Criticism*, 255f)

Natural Language Semantics has been a general introduction to methods for describing and theorizing about meaning in human languages. Throughout, the book has stressed that meanings are cognitively and functionally motivated. The cognitive view is that the categories and structure of language reflect the way that we humans perceive and conceive of worlds. It is consistent with the functional view that language categories and language structure are motivated by the uses to which language is put. Cognitivists and functionalists identify what a formal theory of language, such as that constructed in model theoretic or dynamic semantics, needs to be a model of. Cognitivists and functionalists can benefit from the rigour of mathematically abstract formalists because well-formed formulae help make statements about meaning precise.

The end of Chapter 13 promised an answer to the question: is it credible that the semantics for quantification in English has psychological reality? Do we really compute meanings using the formulae and procedures described in Chapter 13? The answer is surely 'No'. The metalanguage employed offers a reasoned account for the kinds of processes and meaning relations of which we do (or can be made to) have cognitive awareness. The relationships and semantic structures captured in the formulae do plausibly have psychological reality, but it is implausible that our 'wetware' represents them using the formulae employed in this chapter. This scepticism extends to semantic formulae used elsewhere in this book, and indeed to all semantic metalanguages of whatever kind. All theories are abstractions from reality (Chapter 1): to borrow Einstein's simile, the relation between semantic metalanguage and the natural language being described, and that of the cognitive processes involved in using a natural language, is that of 'check number to overcoat' rather than 'soup to beef'.

We have seen that expressing meaning through language is deeply influenced by the social-interactive functions of language. This explains the pervasive importance of the cooperative principle, common ground, and implicature in the story of linguistic meaning. Language is not a code through which Speaker converts cognitive structures into auditory or visual signals on a one-to-one basis that Hearer then decodes. Used normally, language provides a set of underspecified clues that need to be expanded by semantic and pragmatic inferences based on knowledge of the lexicon and grammar, but heavily reliant upon encyclopedic knowledge and awareness of the conventions for language use.

Language as a medium of communication about things outside of language was the focus of Chapter 2. All through, this book laid emphasis on the need to demonstrate the relation of language expressions to models of the worlds and times spoken of. It sought to reveal the nature of human language by establishing semantic categories and constructions, and exhibiting their properties, interrelations, and motivations. Chapter 3 separated lexical semantics from encyclopedic information about the denotatum by examining conditions on naming. Sources for listemes and the relation of form to meaning were topics of Chapters 4–5. Chapter 4 specialized in the semantics of morphology and sound symbolism. The importance of connotation, often downplayed in books on semantics, was the focus of Chapter 5.

Chapter 1 had emphasized the importance of inference; Chapter 6 looked to propositional logic as reliable calculus of valid inference within truth-conditional semantics. It led to the non-truth-conditional relations of conventional and conversational implicature. Conversational implicature is pragmatic inference, essential in the interpretation of utterance meaning. The chapter concluded by showing how Speaker's presupposition is indicated in conversational implicatures of the utterance. Having discussed the externals of sentential semantics in Chapter 6, Chapter 7 established formal tools to tackle the compositionality of clause constituents – tools used throughout the rest of the book.

Chapter 8 examined decomposition in terms of semantic components or primitives, semantic frames, and scripts. They obviously depend on human cognitive awareness, a conclusion that was explored and confirmed beyond doubt in Chapter 9 and subsequent chapters. Chapter 2 had referred to 'a typical denotatum', Chapter 10 defined it in the light of cognitive (and functional) criteria and sought to explain how reference is achieved.

Chapters 11–13 demonstrated the application of formal methods of semantic analysis to an extensive corpus of English data, revealing the cognitive and functional motivations for semantic composition. Chapters 11–12 tackled aspects of clause semantics, beginning with the secondary grammatical categories of mood, tense, and modality. Mood was shown to be a first clue to the illocutionary forces in an utterance, the initial step in determining Speaker's illocutionary point (message). An account of thematic relations linked Chapter 11 directly to Chapter 12, which elaborated upon the internal semantics of predicates in terms of two theories. Chapter 13, on quantifiers, turned to the most significant feature of the internal semantics of NPs.

Thus has *Natural Language Semantics* combined theoretical exegesis with detailed and practical semantic analysis. But no book of this length includes everything worthy of investigation. Comparatives received short shrift, voice and event structures none; and the list of omissions can be vastly expanded. The most regrettable weakness has been to neglect semantics in languages other than English (Frawley 1992 makes up for this). A glaring omission from most books on semantics is proper discussion of prosodic meaning (see Allan 1986, Bolinger 1965, 1989, Cruttenden 1986, 1994, Gussenhoven 1984, Ladd 1980, 1996). It is plain that different interpretations arise from differences in tone of voice. Imagine *Clever boy* uttered in a congratulatory tone to a child versus a sarcastic tone to a man; and note the semantic effects of different stress in 1, disjuncture in 2, and dynamic pitch levels in 3.

1 (a) **MAI**sie didn't shoot her husband   →   It was someone else who shot him.
   (b) Maisie didn't **SHOOT** her husband   →   She did something else to him.
   (c) Maisie didn't shoot her **HUS**band   →   She shot someone/something else.

2 (a) Thanks for phoning, John.   [Expresses gratitude to John]
   (b) Thanks for phoning John.   [Expresses gratitude to someone for phoning John]

3 (a) simple fall   Yès!   Assertive.
       rise-fall   Yês.   Confirmatory, advisive, patronizing.
       fall-rise-fall   Yĕs.   You've got it absolutely right.

   (b) simple rise   Yés?   Inquiring, deferential.
       fall-rise   Yĕs, but X   Dubiousness, tentative agreement.
       rise-fall-rise   Yĕs [but] ...   Very dubious, very tentative.

   (c) level   Yēs ...   There's more to say.

If *Natural Language Semantics* has seemed unnecessarily long, my excuse is that a monograph has been or could be written on almost every topic dealt with. Nevertheless, semantics remains an underdeveloped field of linguistic inquiry. If semanticists with different theoretical and procedural preferences are open-minded enough to benefit from the insights of other approaches, the prospects are good. There is much research to do in formal, cognitive, and functional approaches to meaning, in lexical semantics, the semantics of grammar, and the semantics of texts.

References with selective annotations

Abbey, Edward. 1968. *Desert Solitaire*. New York: Ballantine.

Adams, Douglas. 1992. *The Hitchhiker's Guide to the Galaxy: A Trilogy in Four Parts*. London: Pan Books.

Adams, Robert M. 1985. Soft Soap and Nitty Gritty. In *Fair of Speech: The Uses of Euphemism* ed. D.J. Enright, Oxford: Oxford University Press, pp.44–55.

Adams, Valerie. 1973. *An Introduction to Modern English Word-Formation*. London: Longman.

Aikhenvald, Alexandra Y. 2000. *Classifiers: A Typology of Noun Categorization Devices*. Oxford: Oxford University Press. [A comprehensive survey of classifiers]

Alford, Richard D. 1988. *Naming and Identity: A Cross-cultural Study of Personal Naming Practices*. New Haven: HRAF Press.

Algeo, John. 1973. *On Defining the Proper Name*. Gainesville: University of Florida Press.

Allan, Keith. 1976. Collectivizing. *Archivum Linguisticum* 7:99–117.

Allan, Keith. 1977. Classifiers. *Language* 53:285–311. [A superseded classic]

Allan, Keith. 1980. Nouns and countability. *Language* 56:541–67.

Allan, Keith. 1981. Interpreting from context. *Lingua* 53:151–73.

Allan, Keith. 1986. *Linguistic Meaning*. 2 vols. London: Routledge and Kegan Paul.

Allan, Keith. 1987a. Hierarchies and the choice of left conjuncts (with particular attention to English). *Journal of Linguistics* 23:51–77.

Allan, Keith. 1987b. Interpreting English comparatives. *Journal of Semantics* 5:1–50

Allan, Keith. 1994a. Felicity conditions on speech acts. In *Encyclopedia of Language and Linguistics*, ed. Ron Asher. Oxford: Pergamon Press, vol.3, pp. 1210–13.

Allan, Keith. 1994b. Indirect speech acts (and off-record utterances). In *Encyclopedia of Language and Linguistics*, ed. Ron Asher. Oxford: Pergamon Press, vol.3, pp. 1653–6.

Allan, Keith. 1994c. Performative clauses. In *Encyclopedia of Language and Linguistics*, ed. Ron Asher. Oxford: Pergamon Press, vol.6, pp. 3001–3.

Allan, Keith. 1994d. Speech act classification and definition. In *Encyclopedia of Language and Linguistics*, ed. by Ron Asher. Vol.8, pp. 4124–7. Oxford: Pergamon Press.

Allan, Keith. 1994e. Speech act theory – An overview. In *Encyclopedia of Language and Linguistics*, ed. Ron Asher. Vol.8, pp. 4127–38.

Allan, Keith. 1994f. Speech act hierarchy, Locutions, illocutions and perlocutions. In *Encyclopedia of Language and Linguistics*, ed. Ron Asher. Vol.8, pp. 4141–2.

Allan, Keith. 1994g. Moods, clause types, and speech acts. In *Encyclopedia of Language and Linguistics*, ed. Ron Asher. Vol.5, pp. 2540–2.

Allan, Keith. 1994h. Speech acts and grammar. In *Encyclopedia of Language and Linguistics*, ed. Ron Asher. Vol.8, pp. 4140–1.

Allan, Keith. 1995a. The anthropocentricity of the English word(s) *back*. *Cognitive Linguistics* 6:11–31.

Allan, Keith. 1995b. What names tell about the lexicon and the enyclopedia. *Lexicology* 1:280–325.

Allan, Keith. 1998. On the semantic frames of *be* and 'possessive' *have*. In *Case, Typology and Grammar*, ed. Anna Siewierska and Jae Jung Song. Amsterdam: John Benjamins, pp. 1–18.

Allan, Keith. 2000. Quantity implicatures and the lexicon. *The Lexicon-Encyclopedia Interface* ed. by Bert Peeters. Oxford: Elsevier Science, pp. 169-218.

Allan, Keith and Kate Burridge. 1991. *Euphemism and Dysphemism: Language Used as Shield and Weapon*. New York: Oxford University Press.

Allwood, Jens, Lars-Gunnar Andersson and Östen Dahl. 1977. *Logic in Linguistics*. Cambridge: Cambridge University Press. [An excellent introduction that has stood the test of time]

Alpher, Barry. 1994. Yir-Yoront ideophones. In *Sound Symbolism* ed. Leanne Hinton, Johanna Nichols and John J. Ohala. Cambridge: Cambridge University Press, pp. 161–77.

Anderson, Elaine S. 1978. Lexical universals of body-part terminology. In *Universals of Human Language, Volume 3: Word Structure*, ed. Joseph H. Greenberg. Stanford: Stanford University Press, pp. 335–68.

Anderson, John M. 1971. *A Grammar of Case: Towards a Localistic Theory*. Cambridge: Cambridge University Press.

Anderson, Stephen R. 1971. *On the Linguistic Status of the Performative/Constative Distinction*. Bloomington: Indiana University Linguistics Club.

Anglin, Jeremy M. 1977. *Word, Object, and Conceptual Development*. New York: W.W. Norton

Aoun, Joseph. 1985. *A Grammar of Anaphora*. Cambridge, MA: MIT Press.

Apuleius, L. 1968. De philosophia rationali sive περι ερμηνειας. In *Opera Omnia II*, ed. G.F. Hildebrand. Hildesheim: Georg Olms, pp. 261–78. [Said to be wrongly attributed to Apuleius]

Argyle, Michael. 1988. *Bodily Communication*. 2nd edn. London: Methuen.

Ariel, Mira. 1990. *Accessing Noun-Phrase Antecedents*. London: Croom Helm. [Source book on accessibility theory]

Aristotle. 1938. *The Categories and On Interpretation,* trans. Harold P. Cooke. Loeb Classical Library. London: Heineman. [Every semantics student should read at least these works by Aristotle]

Armstrong, Sharon, Lila Gleitman and Henry Gleitman. 1983. What some concepts might not be. *Cognition* 13:263–308.

Arnauld, Antoine. 1662. *La Logique, ou l'art de penser*. Paris.

Arnott, David W. 1967. Some reflections on the content of individual classes in Fula and Tiv. *La Classification nominale dans les langues négro-africaines*. Paris: C.N.R.S., 45–74.

Aronoff, Mark. 1976. *Word Formation in Generative Grammar*. Cambridge, MA: MIT Press.

Athanasiadou, Angeliki and René Dirven (eds). 1997. *On Conditionals Again*. Amsterdam: John Benjamins.

Atkinson, Martin, David Kilby and Iggy Roca. 1988. *Foundations of General Linguistics*. 2nd edn. London: Unwin Hyman.

Atlas, Jay. 1984. Comparative adjectives and adverbials of degree: an introduction to radically radical pragmatics. *Linguistics and Philosophy* 7:347–77.

Atlas, Jay and Stephen Levinson. 1981. 'It-clefts, informativeness, and logical form. *Radical Pragmatics*, ed. by Peter Cole. New York: Academic Press, pp. 1–62.

Austin, John L. 1975 [1962]. *How To Do Things With Words*. 2nd edn ed. J.O. Urmson and
    Marina Sbisà. Oxford: Oxford University Press. [A readable book that kickstarted interest
    in speech act theory]

Austin, John L. 1963. Performative-Constative. In *Philosophy and Ordinary Language* ed.
    Charles E. Caton. Urbana: University of Illinois Press, 22–54. Reprinted in *The Philosophy
    of Language* ed. John Searle. London: Oxford University Press, 1971:1–12. [Should be read
    in addition to Austin 1975]

Bach, Emmon. 1987. *Informal Lectures on Formal Semantics*. Albany: State University of New
    York. [An easy to read introduction.]

Bach, Emmon and Robert T. Harms (eds). 1968. *Universals in Linguistic Theory*. New York:
    Holt, Rinehart and Winston.

Bach, Kent. 1975. Performatives are statements too. *Philosophical Studies* 28:229–36.
    Reprinted, slightly amended, in Bach and Harnish 1979, pp.203–08.

Bach, Kent. 1987. *Thought and Reference*. Oxford: Clarendon Press.

Bach, Kent and Robert M. Harnish. 1979. *Linguistic Communication and Speech Acts*.
    Cambridge, MA: MIT Press. [A very good introduction to speech act theory in the
    Searle tradition]

Backhouse, Anthony E. 1992. Connotation. *International Encyclopaedia of Linguistics*, ed.
    William Bright. New York: Oxford University Press, vol.1, pp. 297f.

Backhouse, Anthony E. 1994. *The Lexical Field of Taste: A Semantic Study of Japanese Taste
    Terms*. Cambridge: Cambridge University Press. [Very few books are devoted to
    semantic fields]

Barsalou, Lawrence W. 1992. Frames, concepts, and conceptual fields. In Lehrer and Kittay
    (eds), pp. 21–74.

Barsalou, Lawrence W. and Christopher R. Hale. 1993. Components of conceptual
    representation: from feature lists to recursive frames. In *Categories and Concepts:
    Theoretical Views and Inductive Data Analysis*, ed. I. Van Mechelin et al. London:
    Academic Press, pp. 97–144.

Barwise, Jon and Robin Cooper. 1981. Generalized quantifiers and natural language. *Linguistics
    and Philosophy* 4:159–219. [The original text on this topic]

Barwise, Jon and John Perry. 1983. *Situations and Attitudes*. Cambridge, MA: MIT Press. [A
    classic text on situation semantics]

Basso, Keith. 1967. Semantic aspects of linguistic acculturation. *American Anthropologist*
    69:471–7.

Basso, Keith. 1968. The Western Apache classificatory verb system: a formal analysis.
    Southwestern Journal of Anthropology 24:252–66.

Battig, William F. and William E. Montague. 1969. Category norms for verbal items in 56
    categories. *Journal of Experimental Psychology Monograph* 80.

Bauer, Laurie. 1983. *English Word-Formation*. Cambridge: Cambridge University Press.

Bauer, Laurie. 1992 [1988]. *Introducing Linguistic Morphology*. Edinburgh: Edinburgh
    University Press.

Bauer, Laurie. 1993. Un-bloody-likely words. In *Of Pavlova, Poetry and Paradigms: Essays in
    Honour of Harry Orsman* ed. Laurie Bauer and C. Franzen. Wellington: Victoria University
    Press.

Bäuerle, Rainer, Urs Egli and Arnim von Stechow (eds). 1979. *Semantics from Different Points
    of View*. Berlin: Springer-Verlag.

Bäuerle, Rainer, Christoph Schwarze, and Arnim von Stechow (eds). 1983. *Meaning, Use, and Interpretation of language.* Berlin: De Gruyter.

Bealer, George. 1982. *Quality and Concept.* Oxford: Clarendon Press.

Beaugrande, Robert de. 1994. Function and form in language theory and research: the tide is turning. *Functions of Language* 1:163–200.

Beaver, David I. 1997. Presupposition. In *Handbook of Logic and Language*, ed. by Johan F.A.K. van Benthem and Alice ter Meulen. Amsterdam: Elsevier; Cambridge, MA: MIT Press, pp. 939–1008.

Beaver, David I. 1999. *What Comes First in Dynamic Semantics: A Critical Review of Linguistic Theories of Presupposition and a Dynamic Alternative.* Stanford University: CSLI Publications.

Becker, Alton L. 1975. A linguistic image of nature: the Burmese numerative classifier system. *Linguistics* 165:109 21.

Bendix, Edward H. 1966. *Componential Analysis of General Vocabulary.* Bloomington: Indiana University Press. [An analysis of verbs related to have. In this book the term generative semantics first appeared]

Benson, Robert W. 1985. The end of legalese: the game is over. *Review of Law and Social Change* 13:519–73.

Benthem, Johan F.A.K. van. 1988. *A Manual of Intensional Logic.* Chicago: Chicago University Press.

Benthem, Johan F.A.K. van and Alice ter Meulen (eds). 1984. *Generalized Quantifiers in Natural Language.* Dordrecht: Foris.

Benthem, Johan F.A.K. van and Alice ter Meulen (eds). 1997. *Handbook of Logic and Language.* Amsterdam: Elsevier; Cambridge, MA: MIT Press. [A valuable collection of papers on formal semantics]

Berlin, Brent. 1968. *Tzeltal Numeral Classifiers: A Study in Ethnographic Semantics.* The Hague: Mouton.

Berlin, Brent and Elois A. Berlin. 1975. Aguaruna color categories. *American Ethnologist* 2:61–87.

Berlin, Brent and Paul Kay. 1969. *Basic Color Terms: Their Universality and Evolution.* Berkeley and Los Angeles: University of California Press. [The classic work on colour terms]

Bierce, Ambrose. 1971. *The Enlarged Devil's Dictionary*, ed. Ernest J. Hopkins. Harmondsworth: Penguin. [Jocular]

Bierwisch, Manfred. 1967. Some semantic universals of German adjectivals. *Foundations of Language* 3:1–36.

Bierwisch, Manfred. 1969. On certain problems of semantic representation. *Foundations of Language* 5:153–84.

Bierwisch, Manfred. 1970. Semantics. In *New Horizons in Linguistics,* ed. John Lyons. Harmondsworth: Penguin, pp. 166–84.

Blake, Barry J. 1977. *Case Marking in Australian Languages.* Canberra: Australian Institute of Aboriginal Studies.

Blommaert, Jan (ed.). 1995. *Handbook of Pragmatics.* Amsterdam and Philadelphia: John Benjamins. [Comprehensive]

Bloomfield, Leonard. 1926. A set of postulates for the science of language. *Language* 2:153–64. Reprinted in Joos (ed.) 1957/1971, pp. 26–31.

Blum-Kulka Shoshana, J. House, and Gabriele Kasper. 1989. Investigating cross-cultural pragmatics: an introductory overview. In *Cross-Cultural Pragmatics: Requests and Apologies*, ed. Blum-Kulka, House, and Kasper. Norwood NJ: Ablex, pp. 1–34. [An empirical study]

Boas, Franz. 1911. *Handbook of American Indian Languages. Volume 1.* Washington, DC: Smithsonian Institution. [The 'Introduction' is a linguistic classic]

Boër, Steven and William Lycan. 1976. *The Myth of Semantic Presupposition*. Bloomington: Indiana University Linguistics Club. [An exposé of semantic presupposition]

Boethius, Manlius S. 1894. *Opera Omnia*, ed. J.-P. Migne. Patrologiae Latinae Tomus LXIV. Paris: J.-P. Migne.

Boguraev, Branimir and Ted Briscoe. 1989a. Introduction. In *Computational Lexicography for Natural Language Processing*, ed. Branimir Boguraev and Ted Briscoe. London: Longman, pp. 1–40.

Boguraev, Branimir and Ted Briscoe (eds). 1989b. *Computational Lexicography for Natural Language Processing*. London: Longman.

Bolinger, Dwight. 1950. Rime, assonance, and morpheme analysis. *Word* 6:117–36.

Bolinger, Dwight. 1965. *Forms of English: Accent, Morpheme, Order,* ed. I. Abe and T. Kanekiyo. Cambridge, MA: Harvard University Press.

Bolinger, Dwight. 1965. The atomization of meaning. *Language* 41:555–73.

Bolinger, Dwight. 1971. *The Phrasal Verb in English*. Cambridge, MA: Harvard University Press.

Bolinger, Dwight. 1972. Accent is predictable (if you're a mind-reader). *Language* 48:633–44.

Bolinger, Dwight. 1980. *Language: The Loaded Weapon*. London: Longman.

Bolinger, Dwight. 1989. *Intonation and Its Uses*. Stanford: Stanford University Press.

Bolinger, Dwight. 1992. Sound symbolism. *International Encyclopedia of Linguistics* 4:28–30.

Bolinger, Dwight and Louis J. Gerstman. 1957. Disjuncture as a cue to constructs. *Word* 13:246–55.

Bonomi, A. 1987. *Le immagini dei nomi*. Milan: Garzanti.

Boucher, Jerry and Charles E. Osgood. 1969. The pollyanna hypothesis. *Journal of Verbal Learning and Verbal Behavior* 8:1–8.

Bowe, Heather, Lois Peeler and Sharon Atkinson. 1997. *Yorta Yorta Language Heritage*. Clayton: Monash University Linguistics Department.

Bradley, Raymond and Norman Swartz. 1979. *Possible Worlds: an Introduction to Logic and Its Philosophy*. Oxford: Basil Blackwell.

Bransford, John D. and Marcia K. Johnson. 1972. Contextual prerequisites for understanding: some investigations of comprehension and recall. *Journal of Verbal Learning and Verbal Bahavior* 11:717–26.

Bronowski, Jacob. 1978. *The Origins of Knowledge and Imagination*. New Haven: Yale University Press.

Brown, Cecil H. 1990. A survey of category types in natural language. In *Meanings and Prototypes: Studies in Linguistic Categorization*, ed. Savas L. Tsohatzidis. London: Routledge, pp. 17–47.

Brown, Cecil H. and Stanley R. Witkowski. 1983. Polysemy, lexical change and cultural importance. *Man* 18:72–89.

Brown, Gillian, Karen L. Currie, and Joanne Kenworthy. 1980. *Questions of Intonation*. London: Croom Helm.

Brown, Gillian and George Yule. 1983. *Discourse Analysis*. Cambridge: Cambridge University Press. [Remains a useful introduction]

Brown, Penelope and Stephen Levinson. 1987. *Politeness: Some Universals in Language Usage*. Cambridge: Cambridge University Press. [The classic work on politeness and face]

Brown, Roger W. and Albert Gilman. 1960. The pronouns of power and solidarity. In *Style in Language* ed. Thomas A. Sebeok. Cambridge, MA: MIT Press, pp. 253–76. Reprinted in Pier P. Giglioli (ed.) *Language and Social Context*. Harmondsworth: Penguin, pp. 252–82. [A classic paper]

Brown, Roger W. and Albert Gilman. 1989. Politeness theory and Shakespeare's four major tragedies. *Language in Society* 18:159–212.

Brown, Roger W. and M. Ford. 1961. Address in American English. *Journal of Abnormal and Social Psychology* 62:375–85.

Brugman, Claudia M. 1983a. *The Story of Over*. Bloomington: Indiana University Linguistics Club. [The original cognitive account]

Brugman, Claudia M. 1983b. The use of body-part terms as locatives in Chalcatongo Mixtec. In *Studies in Meso-American Linguistics: Reports from the survey of California and other Indian languages*. Report #4, ed. Alice Schlichter et al. Department of Linguistics, University of California, Berkeley, pp. 235–90.

Bryson, Bill. 1984. *The Penguin Dictionary of Troublesome Words*. London: Allen Lane.

Bunt, Harry C. 1976. The formal semantics of mass terms. *Papers from the Third Scandinavian Conference on Linguistics*, ed. F. Karlsson. Turku: Academy of Finland, pp. 81–94.

Bunt, Harry C. 1979. Ensembles and the formal semantic properties of mass terms. In *Mass Terms: Some Philosophical Problems*, ed. Francis J. Pelletier. Dordrecht: D. Reidel, pp. 249–77.

Bunt, Harry C. 1985. *Mass Terms and Model-Theoretic Semantics*. Cambridge: Cambridge University Press. [The classic work on ensemble theory]

Bunte, Pamela A. and Robert J. Franklin. 1988. San Juan Southern Paiute numerals and mathematics. In *In Honor of Mary Haas*, ed. Willam Shipley. Berlin: Mouton de Gruyter, pp. 15–36.

Burling, Robbins. 1965. How to choose a Burmese numeral classifier. *Context and Meaning in Cultural Anthropology*, ed. Melford Spiro. Glencoe IL: Free Press, pp. 243–65.

Bybee, Joan L. 1985. *Morphology: A Study of the Relation Between Meaning and Form*. Amsterdam: John Benjamins.

Bybee, Joan L., Revere Perkins, and William Pagliuca. 1994. *The Evolution of Grammar: Tense, Aspect, and Modality in the Languages of the World*. Chicago: Chicago University Press. [A standard work on these topics]

Bybee, Joan L. and Suzanne Fleischman (eds). 1995. *Modality in Grammar and Discourse*. Amsterdam and Philadelphia: John Benjamins. [A useful compendium]

Cann, Ronnie. 1993. *Formal Semantics*. Cambridge: Cambridge University Press. [An introduction that relates formal semantics with syntactic categories]

Capella, Martianus. *Martianus Capella*, ed. Adolfus Dick. (Bibliotheca Scriptorum Graecorum et Romanorum Teubneriana). Stuttgart: B.G. Teubner, 1969.

Carlson, Gregory N. and Francis J. Pelletier (eds) 1995. *The Generic Book*. Chicago: University of Chicago Press. [A very comprehensive compendium on generics]

Carlson, Robert and Doris Payne. 1989. Genitive classifiers. In *Proceedings of the 4th Pacific Linguistics Conference*. Eugene: University of Oregon, pp. 89–119.

Carnap, Rudolph. 1937. *Logical Syntax of Language*. London: Routledge and Kegan Paul.

Carnap, Rudolph. 1956 [1947]. *Meaning and Necessity*. 2nd edn. Chicago: Chicago University Press.

Carpenter, Kathie. 1991. Later rather than sooner: children's use of extralinguistic information in the acquisition of Thai classifiers. *Journal of Child Language* 18:93–113.

Carroll, Lewis. 1965. *The Works of Lewis Carroll*, ed. Roger L. Green. Feltham: Hamlyn (Spring Books).

Carstairs-McCarthy, Andrew. 1992. *Current Morphology*. London: Routledge.

Caton, Charles E. (ed.) 1963. *Philosophy and Ordinary Language*. Urbana: University of Illinois Press.

Chafe, Wallace. 1994. *Discourse, Consciousness, and Time: The Flow and Dislacement of Conscious Experience in Speaking and Writing*. Chicago: University of Chicago Press.

Chafe, Wallace and Johanna Nichols (eds). 1986. *Evidentiality: The Linguistic Coding of Epistemology*. Norwood: Ablex. [To date, the best compendium on the topic]

Chaffin, Roger. 1992. The concept of a semantic relation. In Lehrer and Kittay (eds), pp. 253–88.

Charniak, Eugene. 1976. Inference and knowledge I and II. In *Computational Semantics: An Introduction to Artificial Intelligence and Natural Language Comprehension*, ed. Eugene Charniak and Yorick Wilks. Amsterdam: North Holland, pp. 1–21, 129–54.

Charniak, Eugene 1977. Inferences in comprehension. In *Basic Processes in Reading: Perception and Comprehension*, ed. David LaBerge and S. Jay Samuels. Hillsdale: Lawrence Erlbaum, pp. 243–63.

Chierchia, Gennaro. 1989. Structured meanings. In *Properties, Types, and Meaning: Volume I Foundational Issues*, ed. Gennaro Chierchia, Barbara H. Partee and Robin Turner. Doredrecht: Reidel, pp. 131–66.

Chierchia, Gennaro. 1998. Plurality of mass nouns and the notion of "semantic parameter". In *Events in Grammar*, ed. Susan Rothstein. Dordrecht: Kluwer, pp. 53–103.

Chierchia, Gennaro and Sally McConnell-Ginet. 1990. *Meaning and Grammar: An Introduction to Semantics*. Cambridge, MA: MIT Press. [An introduction that relates formal semantics to Chomskian syntax]

Childs, G. Tucker. 1994. African ideophones. In *Sound Symbolism* ed. Leanne Hinton, Johanna Nichols and John J. Ohala. Cambridge: Cambridge University Press, pp. 178–204.

Chomsky, Noam. 1957. *Syntactic Structures*. The Hague: Mouton.

Chomsky, Noam. 1965. *Aspects of the Theory of Syntax*. Cambridge, MA: MIT Press.

Chomsky, Noam. 1975. *Reflections on Language.* New York: Pantheon.

Chomsky, Noam. 1981. *Lectures on Government and Binding*. Dordrecht: Foris.

Chomsky, Noam. 1986. *Knowledge of Language: Its Nature, Origin, and Use*. New York: Praeger.

Chomsky, Noam. 1995. Language and nature. *Mind* 104:1–61.

Church, Alonzo. 1940. A formulation of a simple theory of types. *Journal of Symbolic Logic* 5:56–68.

Church, Alonzo. 1941. *The Calculi of Lambda Conversion*. Princeton: Princeton University Press.

Church, Alonzo. 1956. *Introduction to Mathematical Logic*. Princeton: Princeton University Press.

Cicero. *Letters to His Friends (Epistulae ad Familiares*, trans. W. Glynn Williams. London: Heinemann. 1959.

Clark, Eve V. 1973. What's in a word? On the child's acquisition of semantics in his first language. In *Cognitive Development and the Acquisition of Language*, ed. Timothy E. Moore. New York: Academic Press, pp. 65–110.

Clark, Herbert H. 1973. Space, time, semantics, and the child. In *Cognitive Development and the Acquisition of Language*, ed. Timothy E. Moore. New York: Academic Press, pp. 27–63.

Clark, Herbert H. 1977. Inferences in comprehension. In *Basic Processes in Reading: Perception and Comprehension*, ed. David LaBerge and S. Jay Samuels. Hillsdale: Lawrence Erlbaum, pp. 243–63.

Clark, Herbert H. 1996. *Using Language*. Cambridge: Cambridge University Press. [A useful introduction to pragmatics]

Clark, Herbert H. and Thomas B. Carlson. 1982. Hearers and speech acts. *Language* 58:332–73.

Clark, Herbert H. and Eve V. Clark. 1977. *Psychology and Language: An Introduction to Psycholinguistics*. New York: Harcourt Brace.

Coates, Jennifer. 1983. *The Semantics of Modal Auxiliaries*. London: Croom Helm. [A classic]

Coates, Jennifer. 1997. The construction of a collaborative floor in women's friendly talk. In *Conversation: Cognitive, Communicative, and Social Perspectives*, ed Talmy Givón. Amsterdam: John Benjamins, pp. 55–89.

Cohen, L. Jonathon. 1964. Do illocutionary forces exist? *Philosophical Quarterly* XIV No. 55:118–37. Reprinted in *Readings in the Philosophy of Language*, ed. Jay Rosenberg and Charles Travis. Englewood Cliffs: Prentice-Hall, pp 580–99.

Cohen, Philip R., Jerry Morgan, and Martha E. Pollack (eds). 1990. *Intentions in Communication*. Cambridge, MA: MIT Press.

Cole, Peter (ed.). 1978. *Syntax and Semantics 9: Pragmatics*. New York: Academic Press.

Cole, Peter (ed.). 1981. *Radical Pragmatics*. New York: Academic Press. [Many useful papers]

Cole, Peter and Jerry L. Morgan (eds). 1975. *Syntax and Semantics 3: Speech Acts*. New York: Academic Press. [A wonderful compendium of papers that includes Grice 1975]

Coleman, Linda and Paul Kay. 1981. Prototype semantics: the English word *Lie*. *Language* 57:26–44.

Comrie, Bernard. 1976. *Aspect: An Introduction to the Study of Verbal Aspect and Related Problems*. Cambridge: Cambridge University Press.

Comrie, Bernard. 1985. *Tense*. Cambridge: Cambridge University Press.

Cooper, David E. 1986. *Metaphor*. Oxford: Basil Blackwell.

Corbett, Greville G. 1991. *Gender*. Cambridge: Cambridge University Press. [Includes noun classes, classifiers, etc.]

Corbett, Greville G. and Marianne Mithun. 1996. Associative forms in a typology of number systems: evidence from Yup'ik. *Journal of Linguistics* 32:1–17.

Craig, Colette (ed.) 1986. *Noun Classes and Categorization*. Amsterdam and Philadelphia: John Benjamins. [A variety of approaches to the topic]

Craig, Colette. 1994. Classifier languages. In *Encyclopedia of Language and Linguistics*, ed. Ron Asher. Oxford: Pergamon Press, vol.2, pp. 565–9.

Cresswell, Max J. 1973. *Logics and Languages*. London: Methuen.

Cresswell, Max J. 1985. *Structured Meanings: The Semantics of Propositional Attitudes*. Cambridge, MA: MIT Press.

Semantical Essays: Possible Worlds and Their Rivals. Dordrecht:

me thoughts on agentivity. *Journal of Linguistics* 9:11–23.
ical Semantics. Cambridge: Cambridge University Press. [The classic
emantics]
ototype theory and lexical semantics. In *Meanings and Prototypes:
Categorization*, ed. Savas L. Tsohatzidis. London: Routledge, pp.

tonymy revisited: some thoughts on the relationship between words and
nd Kittay (eds), pp. 289–306.
ntonation. Cambridge: Cambridge University Press.
Rises in English. In *Studies in General and English Phonetics: Essays
or J.D. O'Connor*, ed. J. Windsor Lewis. London: Routledge, pp.

Jackendoff. 1994. *Something Else for the Binding Theory*. Cognitive
ports #9. Ohio State University Center for Cognitive Science.
Cutler, Anne (ed.) 1982. *Slips of the Tongue and Language Production*. Berlin: Mouton.
Cutts, Martin and Chrissie Maher. 1984. *Gobbledygook*. London: George Allen and Unwin.
Dahl, Östen. 1975. On generics. In *Cambridge Colloquium on Formal Semantics of Natural
Language*, ed. Edward L. Keenan. London: Cambridge University Press, pp. 99–111.
Dalrymple, Mary. 1993. *The Syntax of Anaphoric Binding*. Stanford, CA: Center for the Study of
Language and Information.
Danat, Brenda. 1980. Language in the legal process. *Law and Society Review* 14:445–564.
Davidoff, Jules. 1997. The neuropsychology of color. In Hardin and Maffi (eds), pp. 118–34.
Davidson, Donald. 1971. Truth and meaning. Reprinted in *Readings in the Philosophy of
Language*, ed. Jay Rosenberg and Charles Travis. Englewood Cliffs: Prentice-Hall, pp
450–65. First published in *Synthese* 17, 1967:304–23.
Davidson, Donald and Gilbert Harman (eds). 1972. *Semantics of Natural Language*. Dordrecht:
Reidel.
Davidson, W., L.W. Elford and Harry Hoijer. 1963. Athapaskan classificatory verbs. In *Studies
in Athapaskan Languages*, ed. Harry Hoijer et al. (UCPL 29). Berkeley and Los Angeles:
University of California , pp. 30–41.
Dawkins, Richard. 1988 [1986]. *The Blind Watchmaker*. Harmondsworth: Penguin. [Read this if
you are interested in evolution]
Deane, Paul. 1996. On Jackendoff's conceptual semantics. *Cognitive Linguistics* 7:35–92.
Declerck, Renaat. 1991. *Tense in English: its structure and use in discourse*. London: Routledge.
De León, Lourdes. 1992. *Body parts and location in Tzotzil: ongoing grammaticalization*.
Working Paper #16. Nijmegen: Cognitive Anthropology Research Group.
De Silva, Clarence W. 1995. *Intelligent Control: Fuzzy Logic Applications*. Boca Raton: CRC
Press.
Devlin, Keith. 1993. *The Joy of Sets: Fundamentals of Contemporary Set Theory*. 2nd edn. New
York: Springer-Verlag.
Dewell, Robert B. 1994. *Over* again: image-schema transformations in semantic analysis.
Cognitive Linguistics 5:351–80.
Diesing, Molly. 1992. *Indefinites*. Cambridge, MA: MIT Press.

Diffloth, Gérard. 1994. *i:* big, *a:* small. In *Sound Symbolism* ed. Leanne Hinton, Johanna Nichols and John J. Ohala. Cambridge: Cambridge University Press, pp. 107–14.

Dijk, Teun A. van and Walter Kintsch. 1983. *Strategies of Discourse Comprehension.* New York: Academic Press.

Dillon, George. 1977. *Introduction to Contemporary Linguistic Semantics.* Englewood Cliffs: Prentice-Hall.

The Dinkum Dictionary: A Ripper Guide to Aussie English (Lenie Johansen). 1988. Ringwood: Viking O'Neil.

Di Sciullo, Anna-Maria and Edwin Williams. 1987. *On the Definition of Word.* Cambridge, MA: MIT Press.

Diogenes Laertius. 1925. *Lives of Eminent Philosophers*, vol.2, trans. R.D. Hicks. Loeb Classical Library. London:Heinemann.

Dixon, Robert M.W. 1968. Noun classes. *Lingua* 21:104–25.

Dixon, Robert M.W. 1971. A method of semantic description. In Steinberg and Jakobovits (eds), pp. 436–71. Revised version in Dixon 1982, pp.65–115.

Dixon, Robert M.W. 1972. *The Dyirbal Language of North Queensland.* Cambridge: Cambridge University Press.

Dixon, Robert M.W. 1982. *Where Have All the Adjectives Gone? and Other Essays in Semantics and Syntax.* Berlin: Mouton.

Doke C.M. 1935. *Bantu Linguistics Terminology.* London: Longman, Green.

Donnellan, Keith S. 1966. Reference and definite descriptions. *Philosophical Review* 75:281–304. Reprinted in *Semantics: an Interdisciplinary Reader in Philosophy, Linguistics, and Psychology*, ed. Danny D. Steinberg and Leon A. Jakobovits. London: Cambridge University Press, pp. 100–14. [Distinguishes 'referential' from 'attributive' NPs]

Donnellan 1974. Speaking of nothing. *Philosophical Review* 83:3–32. Reprinted in Schwartz (ed.) 1977.

Downing, Pamela. 1977. On the creation and use of English compound nouns. *Language* 53:810–42.

Dowty, David R. 1979. *Word Meaning and Montague Grammar: The Semantics of Verbs and Times in Generative Semantics and in Montague's PTQ.* Dordrecht: Reidel.

Dowty, David R. 1991. Thematic proto-roles and argument selection. *Language* 67:547–619.

Dowty, David R., Robert E. Wall, and Stanley Peters. 1981. *Introduction to Montague Semantics.* Dordrecht: Reidel. [The classic introduction to Montague's intensional model theoretic semantics]

Dryer, Matthew. 1986. Primary objects, secondary objects, and antidative. *Language* 62:808–45.

DuBois, John W. 1980. Beyond definiteness: the trace of identity in discourse. In *The Pear Stories*, ed. Wallace Chafe. Norwood NJ:Ablex, pp. 203–74.

Dummett, Michael. 1981. *Frege. Philosophy of Language.* 2nd edn. Cambridge, MA: Harvard University Press.

Dummett, Michael. 1991. *The Logical Basis of Metaphysics.* London: Duckworth.

Eco, Umberto. 1976. *A Theory of Semiotics.* Bloomington: Indiana University Press.

Eco, Umberto. 1984. *Semiotics and the Philosophy of Language.* Bloomington: Indiana University Press.

Edmondson, Willis. 1981. *Spoken Discourse: A Model for Analysis.* New York: Longman.

Einstein, Albert. 1973. *Ideas and Opinions.* London: Souvenir Press.

Embleton, Sheila. 1992. Mathematical concepts. In *International Encyclopaedia of Linguistics*. New York: Oxford University Press, vol 2, pp. 131–4.

Enç, Mürvet. 1991. The semantics of specificity. *Linguistic Inquiry* 22:1–25.

Encyclopedia of Languages and Linguistics. 1994. 10 vols, ed. Ron Asher. Oxford: Pergamon Press. [Contains information on everything linguistic]

Eppen, Garry D. and F.J.Gould. 1979. *Quantitative Concepts for Management: Decision Making Without Algorithms*. Englewood Cliffs: Prentice-Hall

Ertel, Suitbert. 1977. Where do the subjects of sentences come from? In *Sentence Production: Developments in Research and Theory*, ed. Sheldon Rosenberg. Hillsdale: Lawrence Earlbaum, 141–68.

Ervin, Susan and Harry Landar. 1963. Navajo word associations. *American Journal of Psychology* 76:49–57.

Ervin-Tripp, Susan M. 1972. Sociolinguistic rules of address. In Pride and Holmes (eds), pp. 225–40.

Ervin-Tripp, Susan M. et al. 1984. Language and power in the family. In *Language and Power*, ed. Cheris Kramarae, Muriel Schulz, and William M. O'Barr. Beverly Hills: Sage, pp. 116–35.

Evans, Gareth. 1982. *Varieties of Reference*. Oxford: Oxford University Press. [View of an ordinary-language philosopher]

Evans, Gareth. 1985 [1977]. Pronouns, quantifiers, and relative clauses (I) and (II). In *The Collected Papers*. Oxford: Clarendon Press, pp. 76–175.

Fauconnier, Gilles. 1985. *Mental Spaces: Aspects of Meaning Construction in Natural Language*. Cambridge, MA: MIT Press. [The classic work on mental spaces]

Fauconnier, Gilles and Eve Sweetser (eds). 1996. *Spaces, Worlds, and Grammars*. Chicago: University of Chicago Press. [Mostly on mental spaces]

Fillmore, Charles J. 1968. The case for case. In Bach and Harms (eds), pp. 1–88. [A precursor to theta theory]

Fillmore, Charles J. 1971. Verbs of judging. In Fillmore and Langendoen (eds), pp. 273–89.

Fillmore, Charles J. 1975. An alternative to checklist theories of meaning. *Proceedings of the First Annual Meeting of the Berkeley Linguistics Society*, ed. Cathy Cogen et al., pp. 123–31.

Fillmore, Charles J. 1977. The case for case reopened. In *Syntax and Semantics 8: Grammatical Relations*, ed. Peter Cole and Jerry Sadock. New York: Academic Press, pp. 59–82.

Fillmore, Charles J. 1978. On the organization of semantic information in the lexicon. In *Papers from the Parasession on the Lexicon*, ed. Donka Farkas et al. Chicago: Chicago Linguistics Societ, pp. 148–73.

Fillmore, Charles J. 1982a. Frame semantics. In *Linguistics in the Morning Calm*, ed. Linguistic Society of Korea. Seoul: Hanshin, pp. 111–38.

Fillmore, Charles J. 1982b. Towards a descriptive framework for spatial deixis. In *Speech, Place, and Action: Studies in Deixis and Related Topics*, ed. Robert J. Jarvella and Wolfgang Klein. Chichester: John Wiley, pp. 31–59.

Fillmore, Charles J. and Beryl T. Atkins. 1992. Toward a frame-based lexicon: the semantics of RISK and its neighbors. In Lehrer and Kittay (eds), pp. 75–102.

Fillmore, Charles J. and Terence D. Langendoen (eds). 1971. *Studies in Linguistic Semantics*. New York: Holt, Rinehart and Winston. [Influential papers from the late 1960s]

Firth, John R. 1968. Descriptive linguistics and the study of English [1956]. In *Selected Papers of J.R. Firth, 1952–59*, ed. Frank R. Palmer. Bloomington: Indiana University Press, pp. 96–113.

Fodor, Janet D. 1977. *Semantics: Theories of Meaning in Generative Grammar*. New York: Thomas Crowell.

Fodor, Janet D. and Ivan A. Sag. 1982. Referential and quantificational indefinites. *Linguistics and Philosophy* 5:355–98.

Fodor, Jerry A. 1987. *Psychosemantics: the Problem of Meaning in the Philosophy of Mind*. Cambridge, MA: MIT Press.

Fodor, Jerry A. and Ernest Lepore. 1996. The red herring and the pet fish: why concepts still can't be protoypes. *Cognition* 58:253–70

Folb, Edith. 1980. *Runnin' Down Some Lines: The Language and Culture of Black Teenagers*. Cambridge, MA: Harvard University Press.

Foley, William A. and Robert D. Van Valin Jr. 1984. *Functional Syntax and Universal Grammar*. Cambridge: Cambridge University Press. [The earliest book on RRG]

Fox, Barbara. 1987. *Discourse Structure and Anaphora*. Cambridge: Cambridge University Press.

Frank, Francine W. and Paula A. Treichler (eds). 1989. *Theoretical Approaches and Guidelines for Nonsexist Usage*. New York: Modern Language Association of America.

Frawley, William. 1992. *Linguistic Semantics*. Hillsdale: Lawrence Erlbaum. [Investigates the semantic properties of entities, acts, states, causes, motion, transference, thematic roles, space and deixis, aspect, tense, modality, and modification. Many examples from languages other than English]

Frazer, Sir James G. 1911. *The Golden Bough. Part II: Taboo and The Perils of the Soul*. 3rd edn. London: Macmillan.

Frege, Gottlob. 1892. Über Sinn und Bedeutung *Zeitschrift für Philosophie und philosophische Kritik* 100:25–50. English version: On sense and reference. In *Translations from the Philosophical Writings of Gottlob Frege*, ed. Peter Geach and Max Black. Oxford: Blackwell, 56–78. [No student of semantics should fail to read this]

Fromkin, Victoria (ed.) 1980. *Errors in Linguistic Performance: Slips of the Tongue, Ear, Pen and Hand*. New York: Academic Press.

Gamut, L.T.F. 1991. *Language Logic and Meaning*. Vol. 1. *Introduction to Logic*. Vol. 2. *Intensional Logic and Logical Grammar*. Chicago: Chicago University Press. [One of the best introductions to formal semantics]

Gandour, Jack, S.H. Petty, R. Dardaranda, S. Dechongkit, and S. Mukngoen. 1984. The acquisition of numeral classifiers in Thai. *Linguistics* 22:455–79.

Gandour, Jack, Hugh Buckingham Jr, and Rochana Dardarananda. 1985. The dissolution of numeral classifiers in Thai. *Linguistics* 23:547–66.

Gazdar, Gerald. 1979. *Pragmatics: Implicature, Presupposition, and Logical Form*. New York: Academic Press. [Remains a very useful text]

Gazdar, Gerald. 1981. Speech act assignment. In Joshi, Webber, Sag (eds), pp. 64–83.

Geach, Peter T. 1968. *Reference and Generality*. Emended edn. Ithaca: Cornell University Press.

Geckeler, Horst. 1971. *Strukturelle Semantik und Wortfeldtheorie*. München: Fink

Geertz, Clifford. 1972. Linguistic etiquette. In Pride and Holmes (eds), pp. 167–79.

Gernsbacher, Morton Ann. 1990. *Language Comprehension as Structure Building*. Hillsdale, NJ: Lawrence Erlbaum. [A psycholinguistic approach]

Gernsbacher, Morton Ann and Talmy Givón (eds). 1995. *Coherence in Spontaneous Texts*. Amsterdam: John Benjamins.

Gibbs, Raymond W. 1990. Psycholinguistic studies on the conceptual basis of idiomaticity. *Cognitive Linguistics* 1:417–51.

Givón, Talmy. 1970. The resolution of gender conflicts in Bantu conjunction: when syntax and semantics clash. *Papers from the Sixth Regional Meeting of the Chicago Linguistics Society*, pp. 250–61.

Givón, Talmy (ed.). 1979b. *Syntax and Semantics 12: Discourse and Syntax*. New York: Academic Press.

Givón, Talmy (ed.). 1983. *Topic Continuity in Discourse: A Quantitative Cross-Language Study*. Amsterdam and Philadelphia: John Benjamins. [A classic text on referent tracking]

Givón, Talmy. 1984. *Syntax: A Functional-Typological Perspective*. Vol. 1. Amsterdam: John Benjamins.

Givón, Talmy (ed.). 1997. *Conversation: Cognitive, Communicative, and Social Perspectives*. Amsterdam: John Benjamins.

Goddard, Cliff. 1994. Semantic theory and semantic universals. In Goddard and Wierzbicka (eds), pp. 7–29.

Goddard, Cliff. 1998. *Semantic Analysis: A Practical Introduction*. Oxford: Oxford University Press. [Semantics from the NSM point of view]

Goddard, Cliff and Anna Wierzbicka. 1994. Introducing lexical primitives. In Goddard and Wierzbicka (eds), pp. 31–54

Goddard, Cliff and Anna Wierzbicka (eds). 1994. *Semantic and Lexical Universals: Theory and Empirical Findings*. Amsterdam: John Benjamins. [A comprehensive review of NSM applied to many languages other than English]

Goffman, Erving. 1981. *Forms of Talk*. Philadelphia: University of Pennsylvania Press.

Goldberg, Adele E. 1995. *Constructions: A Construction Grammar Approach to Argument Structure*. Chicago: University of Chicago Press.

Goodenough, Ward H. 1956. Componential analysis and the study of meaning. *Language* 32:195–216.

Graesser, Arthur C. and Leslie F. Clark. 1985. *Structures and Procedures of Implicit Knowledge*. Norwood, NJ: Ablex.

Grice, H. Paul. 1957. Meaning. *Philosophical Review* 66:377–88. Reprinted: (1) In *Readings in the Philosophy of Language*, ed. Rosenberg and Travis 1971, pp. 436–44. (2) In *Semantics: an Interdisciplinary Reader in Philosophy, Linguistics, and Psychology*, ed. Steinberg and Jakobovits 1971, pp. 53–59. (3) In Grice 1986.

Grice, H. Paul. 1968. Utterer's meaning, sentence meaning, and word-meaning. *Foundations of Language* 4:225–42. Reprinted in Grice 1986.

Grice, H. Paul. 1969. Utterer's meaning and intentions. *Philosophical Review* 78:147–77. Reprinted in Grice 1986.

Grice, H. Paul. 1975. Logic and conversation. In *Syntax and Semantics 3: Speech Acts*, ed. Peter Cole and Jerry L. Morgan. New York: Academic Press, pp. 41–58. Reprinted in Grice 1986.

Grice, H. Paul. 1986. *Studies in the Way of Words*. Cambridge, MA: Harvard University Press. [Essential reading. Contains all the Grice papers you need]

Grose, (Captain) Francis. 1811 [1783]. *Dictionary of the Vulgar Tongue*. London.

Gruber, Jeffrey S. 1965. *Studies in Lexical Relations*. Ph.D. Thesis, Massachusetts Institute of Technology. Published by the Indiana University Linguistics Club (Bloomington) in 1970.

Revised version in *Lexical Structures in Syntax and Semantics,* 1976. Amsterdam: North Holland. [One of the original works in generative semantics]

Gruber, Jeffrey S. 1967. 'Look' and 'see'. *Language* 43:937–47.

Gumperz, John J. and Stephen G. Levinson (eds). 1996. *Rethinking Linguistic Relativity.* London: Croom Helm.

Gussenhoven, Carlos. 1984. *On the Grammar and Semantics of Sentence Accents.* Dordrecht: Foris.

Habermas, Jürgen. 1979. *Communication and the Evolution of Society,* trans. T. McCarthy. Boston: Beacon Press.

Hailperin, T. 1957. A theory of restricted quantification. *Journal of Symbolic Logic* 22:19–35, 113–29.

Haiman, John. 1980a. The iconicity of grammar: isomorphism and motivation. *Language* 56:515–40.

Haiman, John. 1980b. Dictionaries and encyclopedias. *Lingua* 50:329–57.

Haiman, John. 1985. *Natural Syntax: Iconicity and Erosion.* Cambridge: Cambridge University Press.

Haiman, John (ed.). 1985. *Iconicity in Syntax.* Amsterdam and Philadelphia: John Benjamins. [A classic compendium]

Halliday, Michael A.K. 1970. *A Course in Spoken English: Intonation.* Oxford: Oxford University Press.

Halliday, Michael A.K. and Ruqaiya Hasan. 1976. *Cohesion in English.* London: Longman.

Hamano, Shoko. 1994. Palatalization in Japanese sound symbolism. In *Sound Symbolism* ed. Leanne Hinton, Johanna Nichols and John J. Ohala. Cambridge: Cambridge University Press, pp. 148–57.

Hankamer, Jorge. 1973. Why there are two thans in English. *Papers from the Ninth Regional Meeting of the Chicago Linguistic Society,* 179–88.

Hankamer, Jorge. 1989. Morphological parsing and the lexicon. In Marslen-Wilson (ed.) 1989a:393–408.

Harder, Peter. 1996. *Functional Semantics: A Theory of Meaning, Structure and Tense in English.* Berlin: Mouton de Gruyter.

Hardin, Clyde L. and Luisa Maffi (eds). 1997. *Color Categories in Thought and Language.* Cambridge: Cambridge University Press.

Hare, Richard M. 1971. *Practical Inferences.* London: Macmillan.

Harris, Randy A. 1993. *The Linguistics Wars.* New York: Oxford University Press.

Harris, Zellig S. 1948. Componential analysis of a Hebrew paradigm. *Language* 24:87–91.

Harris, Zellig S. 1951. *Methods in Structural Linguistics.* Chicago: University of Chicago Press.

Hawkins, John A. 1978. *Definiteness and Indefiniteness.* London: Croom Helm. [Remains a useful work]

Hawkinson, Annie K. and Larry M. Hyman. 1974. Hierarchies of natural topic in Shona. *Studies in African Linguistics* 5:147–70.

Heim, Irene. 1983. File change semantics and the familiarity theory of definiteness. *Meaning, Use, and Interpretation of language,* ed. Rainer Bäuerle, Christoph Schwarze, and Arnim von Stechow. Berlin: De Gruyter, pp. 164–89.

Heim, Irene. 1988. *The Semantics of Definite and Indefinite Noun Phrases.* New York: Garland.

Heim, Irene. 1990. E-type pronouns and donkey anaphora. *Linguistics and Philosophy* 13:137–77.

Heim, Irene and Angelika Kratzer. 1998. *Semantics In Generative Grammar*. Oxford: Blackwell. [An introduction to argument structure, quantification, and binding theory]

Heinämäki, Orvokki. 1972. Before. In *Papers from the 8th Regional Meeting of the Chicago Linguistic Society*, ed. Paul M. Peranteau et al. Chicago: Chicago Linguistic Society, pp. 139–51.

Heine, Bernd. 1989. Adpositions in African languages. *Linguistique Africaine* 2:77–127.

Heine, Bernd, Ulrike Claudi and Friederike Hünnemeyer. 1991. From cognition to grammar – evidence from African languages. In *Approaches to Grammaticalization*. Vol. I. *Focus on Theoretical and Methodological Issues*, ed. Elizabeth C. Traugott and Bernd Heine. Amsterdam and Philadelphia: John Benjamins, pp. 149–87.

Hemingway, Ernest. 1987. *The Complete Short Stories of Ernest Hemingway: The Finca Vigia Edition*. New York: Scribners.

Henderson, Leslie. 1989. On mental representation of morphology and its diagnosis measures of visual access speed. In *Lexical Representation and Processing*, ed. William Marslen-Wilson. Cambridge, MA: MIT Press, pp. 357–91.

Hepworth, James and Gregory McNamee (eds). 1989, *Resist Much, Obey Little: Some notes on Edward Abbey*. Tucson: Harbinger House.

Herder, Johann G. 1953 [1772]. Abhandlung über den Ursprung der Sprache. *Werke in Zwei Bänden, Erste Band*. München: Carl Hanser Verlag, pp. 733–830.

Herskovits, Annette. 1986. *Language and Spatial Cognition: An Interdisciplinary Study of Prepositions in English*. Cambridge: Cambridge University Press.

Hill, Clifford A. 1975. Variation in the use of 'front' and 'back' bilingual speakers. In *Proceedings of the First Annual Meeting of the Berkeley Linguistics Society*, ed. Cathy Cogen et al. University of California, Berkeley, pp. 196–206.

Hill, Clifford A. 1982. Up/down, front/back, left/right: a contrastive study of Hausa and English. In *Here and There: Cross-linguistic Studies on Deixis and Demonstration*, ed. Jürgen Weissenborn and Wolfgang Klein. Amsterdam: Benjamins, pp. 13–42.

Hinton, Leanne, Johanna Nichols and John J. Ohala (eds). 1994a. *Sound Symbolism*. Cambridge: Cambridge University Press. [The most comprehensive and useful work available on the topic]

Hinton, Leanne, Johanna Nichols and John J. Ohala. 1994b. Introduction: sound symbolic processes. In Hinton et al. (eds) 1994a, pp. 1–14.

Hirschman, Lynette and Naomi Sager. 1982. Automatic information formatting of a medical sublanguage. In Kittredge and Lehrberger (eds), pp. 27–80.

Hirst, Graeme. 1991. Existence assumptions in knowledge representation. *Artificial Intelligence* 49: 199–242.

Hjelmslev, Louis. 1943. *Omkring Sprogteoriens Grundlaeggelse*. Copenhagen. English version: *Prolegemona to a Theory of Language,* trans. Francis J. Whitfield. 1961. Madison: University of Wisconsin.

Hockett, Charles F. 1958. *A Course in Modern Linguistics*. New York: MacMillan.

Hodge, Robert and Gunther Kress. 1988. *Social Semiotics*. Cambridge: Polity Press.

Hodges, Wilfrid. 1977. *Logic*. Harmondsworth: Penguin. [An excellent easy-to-read introduction to predicate logic]

Holisky, Dee A. 1987. The case of the intransitive subject in Tsova-Tush (Batsbi). *Lingua* 71:103–32.

Hollenbach, Barbara. 1990. Semantic and syntactic extensions of Copala Trique body part nouns. In *Homenaje a Jorge Suarez*, ed. Paulette Levy and Beatriz Garza. Mexico: Colegio de Mexico.

Hopkins, Gerard Manley. 1953. *Poems and Prose of Gerard Manley Hopkins.* Harmondsworth: Penguin Books.

Horn, Laurence R. 1972. *On the Semantic Properties of the Logical Operators in English.* Bloomington: Indiana University Linguistics Club.

Horn, Laurence R. 1984. Toward a new taxonomy for pragmatic inference: Q-based and R-based implicature. In *Meaning, Form, and Use in Context: Linguistic Applications* (Georgetown University Round Table on Languages and Linguistics) ed. Deborah Schriffin. Washington DC: Georgetown University Press, pp. 11–42.

Horn, Laurence R. 1989. *A Natural History of Negation.* Chicago: University of Chicago Press. [The classic work on negation]

Hornstein, Norbert. 1984. *Logic as Grammar.* Cambridge, MA: MIT Press.

Householder, Fred W. (ed.). 1981. *The Syntax of Apollonius Dyscolus.* Amsterdam: John Benjamins.

Huddleston, Rodney. 1995. The English perfect as a secondary past tense. In *The Verb in Contemporary English: theory and Description*, ed. Bas Aarts and Charles F. Meyer. Cambridge: Cambridge University Press, pp. 102–22.

Huddleston, Rodney and Geoffrey K. Pullum. 1997. *The Cambridge Grammar of English.* Cambridge: Cambridge University Press.

Hudson, Keith. 1978. *The Jargon of the Professions.* London: Macmillan.

Hüllen, Werner and Rainer Schulze (eds). 1988. *Understanding the Lexicon: Meaning, Sense, and World Knowledge in Lexical Semantics.* Tübingen: Max Niemeyer Verlag.

Humboldt, Wilhelm von. 1836. *Über die Verschiedenheit des Menschlichen Sprachbaues.* Berlin

Hussey, Edward. 1972. *The Pre-Socratics.* London: Duckworth.

Hymes, Dell. 1972. On communicative competence. In Pride and Holmes (eds), pp. 269–93.

International Encyclopedia of Linguistics, ed. William Bright. 4 Vols. New York: Oxford University Press. 1992. [A comprehensive review of topics in linguistics, including many articles on semantics]

Irving, John. 1979. *The World According to Garp.* London: Corgi.

Jackendoff, Ray S. 1972. *Semantic Interpretation in Generative Grammar.* Cambridge, MA: MIT Press.

Jackendoff, Ray. 1975. Morphological and semantic regularities in the lexicon. *Language* 51:639–71.

Jackendoff, Ray. 1976. Toward and explanatory semantic representation. *Linguistic Inquiry* 7:89–150.

Jackendoff, Ray. 1983. *Semantics and Cognition.* Cambridge, MA: MIT Press. [An early account of conceptual semantics]

Jackendoff, Ray. 1985. Multiple subcategorization and the θ-criterion: the case of *climb*. *Natural Language and Linguistic Theory* 3:271–95.

Jackendoff, Ray. 1987a. *Consciousness and the Computational Mind.* Cambridge, MA: MIT Press.

Jackendoff, Ray. 1987b. The status of thematic relations in linguistic theory. *Linguistic Inquiry* 18:369–411.

Jackendoff, Ray. 1990. *Semantic Structures.* Cambridge, MA: MIT Press.

Jackendoff, Ray. 1992a. *Languages of the Mind: Essays on Mental Representation*. Cambridge, MA: MIT Press.

Jackendoff, Ray. 1992b. Mme Tussaud meets the binding theory. *Natural Language and Linguistic Theory* 10:1–31.

Jackendoff, Ray. 1995. The boundaries of the lexicon. In *Idioms: Structural and Psychological Perspectives*, ed. Martin Everaert, Erik-Jan van der Linden, André Schenk, and Ron Schreuder. Hillsdale: Erlbaum, pp. 133–65.

Jackendoff, Ray S. 1996. Conceptual semantics and cognitive linguistics. *Cognitive Linguistics* 7:93–129.

Jackendoff, Ray. 1997. *Architecture of the Language Faculty*. Cambridge, MA: MIT Press.

Jakobson, Roman. 1936. Beitrag zur allgemeinen Kasuslehre. *Travaux du Cercle Linguistique de Prague* 6:240–88.

Jensen, John. 1990. *Morphology*. Amsterdam: John Benjamins.

Johnson, Mark. 1987. *The Body in the Mind*. Chicago: University of Chicago Press.

Johnson-Laird, Philip N. 1981. Mental models of meaning. In *Elements of Discourse Understanding*, ed. Aravind K. Joshi, Bonnie L. Webber, and Ivan A. Sag. Cambridge: Cambridge University Press, pp. 106–26.

Johnson-Laird, Philip N. 1983. *Mental Models: Towards a Cognitive Science of Language, Inference, and Consciousness*. Cambridge: Cambridge University Press.

Jolly, Julia A. 1993. Preposition assignment in English. In Van Valin (ed.), 1993b, pp. 275–310.

Jones, Daniel. 1960. *An Outline of English Phonetics*. 9th edn. Cambridge: Heffer.

Joos, Martin (ed.). 1957. *Readings in Linguistics*. Washington DC: American Council of Learned Societies. Reissued as *Readings in Linguistics I* 1971. Chicago: Chicago University Press. [A compendium of classic works on American structural linguistics]

Joos, Martin. 1961. *The Five Clocks*. New York: Harcourt, Brace and World. [A classic work on style]

Joshi, Aravind K., Bonnie L. Webber, and Ivan A. Sag (eds). 1981. *Elements of Discourse Understanding*. Cambridge: Cambridge University Press.

Jowett, Benjamin. 1953. *The Dialogues of Plato*. 4 Vols. 4th edn. Oxford: Clarendon Press.

Kahn, Charles H. 1979. *The Art and Thought of Heraclitus: an Edition of the Fragments with Translation and Commentary*. Cambridge: Cambridge University Press.

Kamp, Hans. 1981. A theory of truth and semantic representation. In *Formal Methods in the Study of Language*, ed. Jereon A.G. Groenendijk, Theo M.V. Janseen, and Martin B.J. Stokhof. Mathematical Centre Tracts 135. Amsterdam: Mathematisch Centrum, pp. 277–322.

Kamp, Hans and Barbara H. Partee. 1995. Prototype theory and compositionality. *Cognition* 57:129–91.

Kamp, Hans and Uwe Reyle. 1993. *From Discourse to Logic*. 2 vols. Dordrecht: Kluwer. [A comprehensive review of discourse representation theory (dynamic semantics). Not for the faint-hearted]

Kaplan, David. 1978. Dthat. In *Syntax and Semantics 9: Pragmatics*, ed. Peter Cole. New York: Academic Press, pp. 221–43.

Karttunen, Lauri. 1969. Pronouns and variables. In *Papers from the Fifth Regional Meeting of the Chicago Linguistics Society*, ed. Robert I. Binnick et al. Chicago: Chicago Linguistics Society, pp. 108–16.

Karttunen, Lauri. 1973. Presuppositions of compound sentences. *Linguistic Inquiry* 4:169–93.

Karttunen, Lauri and Stanley F. Peters. 1979. Conventional implicature. In *Syntax and Semantics 11: Presupposition*, ed. Choon-Kyu Oh and David A. Dinneen. New York: Academic Press, 1–56.

Katamba, Francis. 1993. *Morphology*. London: Macmillan.

Katz, Jerrold J. 1964b. Semantic theory and the meaning of "good". *Journal of Philosophy* 61:739–66.

Katz, Jerrold J. 1966. *The Philosophy of Language*. New York: Harper and Row.

Katz, Jerrold J. 1967. Recent issues in semantic theory. *Foundations of Language* 3:124–94.

Katz, Jerrold J. 1972. *Semantic Theory*. New York: Harper and Row. [The definitive book on Katz's semantic markerese]

Katz, Jerrold J. 1973. On defining 'Presupposition'. *Linguistic Inquiry* 4:256–60.

Katz, Jerrold J. 1977a. *Propositional Structure and Illocutionary Force*. New York: Thomas Crowell. Reprinted 1980. Cambridge, MA: Harvard University Press.

Katz, Jerrold J. 1977b. A proper theory of names. *Philosophical Studies* 31:1–80.

Katz, Jerrold J. 1981. *Language and Other Abstract Objects*. Totowa, NJ: Rowman and Littlefield.

Katz, Jerrold J. 1990. Has the description theory of names been refuted? In *Meaning and Method: Essays in Honor of Hilary Putnam*, ed. George Boolos. Cambridge: Cambridge University Press, pp. 31–61.

Katz, Jerrold J. and Paul M. Postal. 1964. *An Integrated Theory of Linguistic Descriptions*. Cambridge, MA: MIT Press.

Katz, Jerrold J. and Paul M. Postal. 1991. Realism vs conceptualism in linguistics. *Linguistics and Philosophy* 14:515–54.

Kay, Paul and Chad McDaniel. 1978. The linguistic significance of the meanings of basic color terms. *Language* 54:610–46.

Keenan, Edward L. and Dag Westerstahl. 1997. Generalized quantifiers in linguistics and logic. In Benthem and Meulen (eds), pp. 837–93.

Keesing, Roger M. and Jonathan Fifiʔi. 1969. Kwaio word tabooing in its cultural context. *Journal of the Polynesian Society* 78:154–77.

Keil, F.C. 1986. The acquisition of natural kind and artifact terms. In *Language Learning and Concept Acquisition*, ed. W. Demopoulos and A. Marras. Norwood NJ: Ablex, pp. 133–53.

Keyser, Samuel J. and Thomas Roeper. 1992. Re: the abstract clitic hypothesis. *Linguistic Inquiry* 23:89–125.

Kintsch, Walter, Theodore S. Mandel and Ely Kozminsky. 1977. Summarizing scrambled stories. *Memory and Cognition* 5:547–52.

Kipury, Naomi. 1983. *Oral Literature of the Maasai*. Nairobi: Heinemann Educational Books.

Kittay, Eva F. 1987. *Metaphor: Its Cognitive Force and Linguistic Structure*. New York: Oxford University Press.

Kittredge, Richard and John Lehrberger (eds). 1982. *Sublanguage: Studies of Language in Restricted Semantic Domains*. Berlin: De Gruyter.

Klir, George and Bo Yuan. 1995. *Fuzzy Sets and Fuzzy Logic: Theory and Applications*. Upper Sadle River NJ: Prentice-Hall.

Kneale, W. 1962. Modality, de dicto, and de re. In *Logic, Methodology, and Philosophy of Science*, ed. Eugene Nagel, Patrick Suppes, and Alfred Tarski. Stanford: Stanford University Press, pp. 622–33.

Kniffka, Hannes. 1994. Hearsay vs autoptic evidence in linguistics. In *Zeitschrift der Deutschen Morgenländischen Gesellschaft*, ed. Tilman Nagel et al. Stuttgart: Franz Steiner, pp. 345–76.

Kosko, Bart. 1991. *Neural Networks and Fuzzy Systems*. Englewood Cliffs, NJ: Prentice-Hall.

Kozminsky, Ely. 1977. Altering comprehension: the effect of biasing titles on text comprehension. *Memory and Cognition* 5:482–90.

Krifka, Manfred (ed.). 1988. *Genericity in Natural Language: Proceedings of the 1988 Tübingen Conference*. SNS-Bericht 88–42. Seminar für natürlich-sprachliche Systeme, Universität Tübingen.

Kripke, Saul. 1963. Semantical considerations on model logic. In *Proceedings of a Colloquium on Modal and Many-Valued Logics. Helsinki, 23–26 August, 1962.* Acta Philsophica Fennica: Helsinki.

Kripke, Saul. 1972. Naming and necessity. In *Semantics of Natural Language*, ed. Donald Davidson and Gilbert Harman. Dordrecht: Reidel, pp. 253–355. Republished separately as *Naming and Necessity*, Oxford: Blackwell, 1980. [A classic work on the semantics of proper names; essential reading]

Kroeber, Alfred L. 1909. Classificatory systems of relationship. *Journal of the Royal Anthropological Institute* 39:77–84.

Kruisinga, E. 1932. *A Handbook of Present Day English*. Groningen: Nordhoff.

Kuhn, Thomas S. 1970. *The Structure of Scientific Revolutions.* International Encyclopaedia of Unified Science. 2nd edn. Chicago: Chicago University Press.

Kuno, Susumu. 1976a. Subject, theme, and the speaker's empathy – re-examination of relativization phenomena. In Li (ed.), pp. 417–44.

Kuno, Susumu. 1979. On the interaction between syntactic rules and discourse principles. In *Explorations in Linguistics: Papers in Honor of Kazuko Inoue*, ed. George Bedell, Eichi Kobayashi, and Masatake Muraki. Tokyo: Kenkyusha, 279–304.

Kuno, Susumu and Etsuko Kaburaki. 1977. Empathy and syntax. *Linguistic Inquiry* 8:627–72.

Labov, William. 1973. The boundaries of words and their meanings. In *New Ways of Analyzing Variation in English*, ed. Charles-J. Bailey and Roger Shuy. Washington, DC: Georgetown University Press, pp. 340–73.

Labov, William. 1978. Denotational structure. In *Papers from the Parasession on the Lexicon* ed. Donka Farkas, Wesley M. Jacobsen, and Karol W. Todrys. Chicago: Chicago Linguistics Society, pp. 220–60.

Labov, William and David Fanshel. 1977. *Therapeutic Discourse: Psychotherapy as Conversation.* New York: Academic Press.

Ladd, D. Robert. 1980. *The Structure of Intonational Meaning.* Bloomington: Indiana University Press.

Ladefoged, Peter. 1982. *A Course in Phonetics.* 2nd edn. New York: Harcourt, Brace, Jovanovich.

Lakoff, George. 1965. *On the Nature of Syntactic Irregularity.* Report NSF-16, The Computation Laboratory of Harvard University. Reprinted as Lakoff 1970. [One of the original works in generative semantics]

Lakoff, George. 1970. *Irregularity in Syntax.* (Reprint of Lakoff 1965). New York: Holt, Rinehart and Winston.

Lakoff, George. 1971. The role of deduction in grammar. In Fillmore and Langendoen (eds), pp. 63–70.

Lakoff, George. 1972. Hedges: a study of meaning criteria and the logic of fuzzy concepts. In *Papers from the Eighth Regional Meeting of the Chicago Linguistics Society*, pp. 183–228. Revised version in *Contemporary Research in Philosophical Logic and Linguistic Semantics* ed. D. Hockney, W. Harper, and B. Freed. Dordrecht: Reidel, 221–71. [Introduced fuzzy logic into linguistics]

Lakoff, George. 1987. *Women, Fire, and Dangerous Things*. Chicago: Chicago University Press. [Foundational work on cognitive linguistics]

Lakoff, George and Mark Johnson. 1980. *Metaphors We Live By*. Chicago: University of Chicago Press. [This classic work showed metaphor to be pervasive in everyday language]

Lakoff, George and Henry Thompson. 1975. Introducing Cognitive Grammar. In *Proceedings of the First Annual Meeting of the Berkeley Linguistics Society*, ed. Cathy Cogen et al. University of California, Berkeley, pp. 295–313.

Lamb, Sydney M. 1965. Kinship terminology and linguistic structure. In *Formal Semantic Analysis*, ed. Eugene A. Hammel. Menasha, WI: American Anthropological Association, pp. 37–64.

Lambrecht, Knud. 1994. *Information Structure and Sentence Form: Topic, Focus, and the Mental Representations of Discourse Referents*. Cambridge: Cambridge University Press.

Lancelot, Claude. 1644. *Nouvelle méthode pour comprendre, facilement et en peu de temps, la langue latine*. Paris.

Landau, Barbara and Ray Jackendoff. 1993. "What" and "where" in spatial language and spatial cognition. *Behavioral and Brain Sciences* 16:217–65.

Landman, Fred. 1989. Groups I. Groups II. *Linguistics and Philosophy* 12:559–605, 723–44.

Landman, Fred. 1996. Plurality. In *Handbook of Contemporary Semantics* ed. Shalom Lappin. Oxford: Blackwell.

Lane, A. 1700. *A Key to the Art of Letters*. London. Facsimile, 1969. Menston: Scolar Press.

Langacker, Ronald W. 1987. *Foundations of Cognitive Grammar*. Vol. 1, *Theoretical Prerequisites*. Stanford: Stanford University Press. [Foundational work on cognitive linguistics]

Langacker, Ronald W. 1990. *Concept, Image and Symbol: The Cognitive Basis of Grammar*. Cambridge: Cambridge University Press.

Langacker, Ronald W. 1991. *Foundations of Cognitive Grammar*. Vol. 2. Stanford: Stanford University Press.

Lasersohn, Peter. 1995. *Plurality, Conjunction, and Events*. Dordrecht: Kluwer.

Lee, Penny. 1996. *The Whorf Theory Complex: A Critical Reconstruction*. Amsterdam: John Benjamins. [A useful supplement to Whorf 1956]

Lee-Wong, Song Mei. 2000. *Politeness and Face in Chinese Culture*. Frankfurt-am-Main: Peter Lang.

Leech, Geoffrey. 1981. *Semantics: A Study of Meaning*. 2nd edn. Harmondsworth: Penguin.

Leech, Geoffrey. 1983. *Principles of Pragmatics*. London: Longman.

Lehrer, Adrienne. 1974. *Semantic Fields and Lexical Structure*. Amsterdam: North Holland. [A classic work on semantic fields and componential analysis]

Lehrer, Adrienne. 1983. *Wine and Conversation*. Bloomington: Indiana University Press.

Lehrer, Adrienne. 1985. Markedness and antonymy. *Journal of Linguistics* 21:397–429.

Lehrer, Adrienne. 1986. English classifier constructions. *Lingua* 68:109–48.

Lehrer, Adrienne. 1990. Polysemy, conventionality, and the structure of the lexicon. *Cognitive Linguistics* 1:207–46.

Lehrer, Adrienne. 1992a. Names and naming: why we need fields and frames. In Lehrer and Kittay (eds), pp. 123–42.

Lehrer, Adrienne. 1992b. Blocking and the principle of conventionality. *Proceedings of the Western Conference on Linguistics WECOL 92*. Fresno: Dept of Linguistics, California State University, vol. 5, pp. 183–94.

Lehrer, Adrienne. 1992c. Componential semantics. In *International Encyclopaedia of Linguistics*, ed. William Bright. New York: Oxford University Press, vol. 1, pp. 284–86.

Lehrer, Adrienne. 1995. Prefixes in English word formation. *Folia Linguistica* 29:133–48.

Lehrer, Adrienne. 1996. Identifying and interpreting blends: an experimental approach. *Cognitive Linguistics* 7:359–90.

Lehrer, Adrienne and Eva F. Kittay (eds). 1992. *Frames, Fields, and Contrasts*. Hillsdale: Lawrence Erlbaum. [A valuable compendium of papers on these topics]

Lehrer, Adrienne and Keith Lehrer (eds). 1970. *Theory of Meaning*. Englewood Cliffs: Prentice-Hall.

Lehrer, Adrienne and Keith Lehrer. 1982. Antonymy. *Linguistics and Philosophy* 5:483–501.

Lerdahl, Fred and Ray Jackendoff. 1982. *A Generative Theory of Tonal Music*. Cambridge, MA: MIT Press.

Leśniewski, Stanislaw. 1988. *Collected Works*, ed. Jan Srzednicki et al. Dordrecht: Kluwer.

Levi, Judith. 1978. *The Syntax and Semantics of Complex Nominals*. New York: Academic Press.

Levinson, Stephen. 1983. *Pragmatics*. Cambridge: Cambridge University Press. [For well over a decade the best and most comprehensive introduction to pragmatics]

Levinson, Stephen. 1992. *Vision, shape and linguistic description: Tzeltal body-part terminology and object description*. Working Paper #12. Nijmegen: Cognitive Anthropology Research Group.

Levinson, Stephen. 1995. Three levels of meaning. In *Grammar and Meaning: Essays in Honour of Sir John Lyons*, ed. Frank R. Palmer. Cambridge: Cambridge University Press, pp. 90–115.

Levinson, Stephen. Forthcoming. *Generalized Conversational Implicature*. Cambridge: Cambridge University Press.

Lewis, David. 1969. *Convention*. Cambridge, MA: Harvard University Press.

Lewis, David. 1970. General semantics. *Synthese* 22:18–67. Reprinted in *Semantics of Natural Language*, ed. Donald Davidson and Gilbert Harman. Dordrecht: Reidel, pp. 169–218.

Lewis, David. 1973. *Counterfactuals*. Oxford: Basil Blackwell. [Classic]

Lewis, David. 1979. Scorekeeping in a language game. *Journal of Philosophical Logic* 8:339–59.

Lewis, David. 1986. *On the Plurality of Worlds*. Oxford: Basil Blackwell.

Li, Charles N. (ed.). 1976. *Subject and Topic*. New York: Academic Press.

Lichtenberk, Frantisek. 1983. Relational classifiers. *Lingua* 60:147–76.

Lieberson, Stanley and Eleanor O. Bell. 1992. Children's first names: an empirical study of social taste. *American Journal of Sociology* 98:511–54.

Lieberson, Stanley and Kelly S. Mikelson. 1995. Distinctive African-American names: an experimental, historical, and linguistic analysis of innovation. *American Sociological Review* 60:928–46.

Linell, Per and Natascha Korolija. 1997. Coherence and multi-party conversation: episodes and contexts in interaction. In Givón (ed.), pp. 167–205.

Link, Godehard. 1983. The logical analysis of plurals and mass terms: a lattice theoretic approach. In *Meaning, Use, and Interpretation of language*, ed. Rainer Bäuerle, Christoph Schwarze, and Arnim von Stechow. Berlin: De Gruyter, pp. 303–23.

Linsky, Leonard (ed.). 1971. *Reference and Modality*. London: Oxford University Press.

Loar, Brian. 1976. The semantics of singular terms. *Philosophical Studies* 30:353–77.

Loar, Brian. 1980. Names and descriptions: A reply to Michael Devitt. *Philosophical Studies* 38:85–9.

Loftus, Elizabeth F. 1979. *Eyewitness Testimony*. Cambridge, MA: Harvard University Press.

Lønning, Jan T. 1997. Plurals and collectivity. In Benthem and Meulen (eds), pp. 1009–53.

Lounsbury, Floyd G. 1956. A semantic analysis of the Pawnee kinship usage. *Language* 32:158–94.

Loveday, Leo. 1981. Pitch, politeness, and sexual role: an exploratory investigation into the pitch correlates of English and Japanese politeness formulae. *Language and Speech* 24:71–89.

Lucy John A. 1992. *Language Diversity and Thought: A reformulation of the linguistic relativity hypothesis*. Cambridge: University Press.

Lutz, William. 1989. *Doublespeak: From "Revenue Enhancement" to "Terminal Living". How Government, Business, Advertisers, and Others Use Language to Deceive You*. New York: Harper and Row.

Lutzeier, Peter R. (ed.). 1993. *Studien zur Wortfeldtheorie*. Tübingen: Max Niemeyer.

Lynn, Jonathan and Anthony Jay. 1989. *The Complete Yes Prime Minister*. London: BBC Books

Lyons, Christopher. 1999. *Definiteness*. Cambridge: Cambridge University Press.

Lyons, John. 1963. *Structural Semantics: An Analysis of Part of the Vocabulary of Plato*. Oxford: Blackwell.

Lyons, John. 1967. A note on possessive, existential and locative sentences. *Foundations of Language* 3:390–96.

Lyons, John. 1968. *Introduction to Theoretical Linguistics*. London: Cambridge University Press.

Lyons, John. 1977. *Semantics*. 2 Vols. Cambridge: Cambridge University Press. [Still the classic reference work on semantics]

Lyons, John. 1995. *Linguistic Semantics: An Introduction*. Cambridge: Cambridge University Press.

MacIver, A.M. 1938. Some questions about "know" and "think". *Analysis* 5:43–50.

MacLaury, Robert E. 1986. *Color in Mesoamerica*. Vol.1 (PhD dissertation in anthropology, University of California Berkeley.) Ann Arbor: UMI University Microfilms, No.8718073.

MacLaury, Robert E. 1987. Coextensive semantic ranges: different names for distinct vantages of one category. In *Papers from the Twenty-Third Annual Meeting of the Chicago Linguistics Society*, ed. Barbara Need, Eve Schiller, and Anna Bosch. Chicago: Chicago Linguistics Society, pp. 268–82.

MacLaury, Robert E. 1989. Zapotec body-part locatives: prototypes and metaphoric extensions. *International Journal of American Linguistics* 55:119–54.

MacLaury, Robert E. 1991. Social and cognitive motivations of change: measuring variability in color semantics. *Language* 67:34–62.

MacLaury, Robert E. 1995. Vantage theory. In *Language and the Cognitive Construal of the World* ed. John R. Taylor and Robert E. MacLaury. Berlin: Mouton de Gruyter, pp. 231–76.

MacLaury, Robert E. 1997. *Color and Cognition in Mesoamerica: Constructing Categories as Vantages*. Austin: University of Texas Press.

MacLaury, Robert E. 1998. Linguistic relativity and the plasticity of categorization: universalism in a new key. Paper read to the LAUD Symposium on Linguistic Relativity. University of Duisburg, April 1–4, 1998 and to appear in LAUD Working Papers.

Macmillan, James B. 1980. Infixing and interposing in English, *American Speech* 55: 163–83.

Macquarie Dictionary. 1991. 2nd edn, revised. McMahons Point: Macquarie Library.

MacWhinney, Brian, Janice M. Keenan and Peter Reinke. 1982. The role of arousal in memory for conversation. *Memory and Cognition* 10:308–17.

Maffi, Luisa and Clyde L. Hardin. 1997. Closing thoughts. In Hardin and Maffi (eds), pp. 347–72.

Malkiel, Yakov. 1968. Studies in irreversible binomials. *Essays on Linguistic Themes*, 311–55. Oxford: Basil Blackwell.

Malotki, Ekkehart. 1983. *Hopi Time*. Berlin: Mouton.

Marantz, Alec. 1984. *On the Nature of Grammatical Relations*. Cambridge, MA: MIT Press.

Marchand, Hans. 1969. *The Categories and Types of Present-Day English Word-Formation*. 2nd edn. Munchen: C.H. Beck'sche.

Marconi, Diego. 1997. *Lexical Competence*. Cambridge, MA: MIT Press.

Marr, David. 1982. *Vision*. San Francisco: W.H. Freeman.

Marslen-Wilson, William. 1985. Speech shadowing and speech comprehension. *Speech Communication* 4:55–73.

Marslen-Wilson, William (ed.) 1989a. *Lexical Representation and Processing*. Cambridge, MA: MIT Press.

Marslen-Wilson, William. 1989b. Access and integration: projecting sound onto meaning. In Marslen-Wilson (ed.) 1989a:3–24.

Matisoff, James A. 1994. Tone, intonation, and sound symbolism in Lahu: loading the syllable canon. In Hinton, Nichols, and John J. Ohala, pp. 115–29.

Matthews, Peter H. 1974. *Morphology: An Introduction to the Theory of Word Structure*. Cambridge: Cambridge University Press.

Matthews, Richard. 1991. *Words and Worlds: on the Linguistics of Modality*. Frankfurt: Peter Lang.

May, Robert. 1985. *Logical Form: Its Structure and Derivation*. Cambridge, MA: MIT Press.

McCarthy, John J. 1982. Prosodic structure and expletive infixation. *Language* 58:574–90

McCawley, James D. 1968a. Concerning the base component of a transformational grammar. *Foundations of Language* 4:243–69. Reprinted in McCawley 1973, pp. 35–58.

McCawley, James D. 1968b. The role of semantics in a grammar. In Bach and Harms (eds) 1968, pp. 124–69. Reprinted in McCawley 1973, pp. 59–98.

McCawley, James D. 1968c. Lexical insertion in a transformational grammar without deep structure. In *Papers from the Fourth Regional Meeting of the Chicago Linguistic Society,* pp. 71–80. Reprinted in McCawley 1973, pp. 155–66.

McCawley, James D. 1971. Prelexical syntax. In *Monograph Series on Languages and Linguistics No.24. Report of the Twenty-Second Round Table Meeting on Linguistics and Language Studies*, ed. Richard J. O'Brien. Washington, DC: Georgetown University Press, pp. 19–33. Reprinted in McCawley 1973, pp. 343–56.

McCawley, James D. 1973. *Grammar and Meaning.* Tokyo: Taikushan. [A valuable collection of McCawley's foundational papers in generative semantics]

McCawley, James D. 1993 [1981]. *Everything that Linguists have Always Wanted to Know about Logic, but were ashamed to ask.* 2nd edn. Chicago: University of Chicago Press. [An excellent and interesting review of logic for linguists]

McCulloch, Gregory. 1989. *The Game of the Name.* Oxford: Clarendon Press.

Meillet, Antoine. 1924. Le développement du verbe "avoir". *Antidoron: Festschrift Jacob Wackernagel.* Göttingen, pp. 9–13.

Mel'cuk, Igor A. 1992. Lexicon: An Overview. In *International Encyclopedia of Linguistics.* New York: Oxford University Press, vol. 2, pp. 332–4.

Mel'cuk, Igor A. and Alexander Kolkovsky. 1984. *Explanatory Combinatorial Dictionary of Modern Russian: Semantico-Syntactic Study of Russian Vocabulary.* Vienna: Wiener Slawisrischer Almanach.

Mel'cuk, Igor A. et al. 1984–1991. *Dictionaire explicatif et combinatoire du français contemporain.* 3 Vols. Montréal: Les Presses de l'Université de Montréal.

Mill, John S. 1881. *A System of Logic.* London.

Miller, Casey and Kate Swift. 1991. *Words and Women Updated.* New York: HarperCollins.

Miller, Casey and Kate Swift. 1995. *The Handbook of Nonsexist Writing for Writers, Editors and Speakers.* 3rd edn. London: Women's Press.

Miller, George and Philip N. Johnson-Laird. 1976. *Language and Perception.* Cambridge, MA: Harvard University Press.

Minsky, Marvin. 1977. Frame-system theory. In *Thinking: Readings in Cognitive Science* ed. Philip N. Johnson-Laird and Peter C. Wason. Cambridge: Cambridge University Press, 355–76.

Mithun, Marianne. 1986. The convergence of noun classification systems. *Noun Classes and Categorization*, ed. Colette Craig. Amsterdam and Philadelphia: John Benjamins, pp. 379–98.

Moedjanto, G. 1986. *The Concept of Power in Javanese Culture.* Yogyakarta: Gadjah Madu University Press.

Mohanan, Karuvannur P. 1986. *The Theory of Lexical Phonology.* Dordrecht: Reidel.

Montague, Richard. 1974. *Formal Philosophy,* ed. Richmond Thomason. New Haven: Yale University Press. [The book to read for Montague's semantics]

Moore, George E. 1952. A reply to my critics. *The Philosophy of G.E. Moore*, ed. Paul A. Schilpp. 2nd edn. New York: Tudor, pp. 533–687.

Moore, Judy et al. 1980. *The Complete Australian Gardener.* Sydney: Bay Books.

Moore, Timothy E. (ed.). 1973. *Cognitive Development and the Acquisition of Language.* New York: Academic Press.

Moravscik, Julius M.E. 1973. Mass terms in English. In *Approaches to Natural Language*, ed. Jaako Hintikka, Julius Moravscik and Patrick Suppes. Dordrecht: Reidel, pp. 263–85.

Morolong Malillo and Larry H. Hyman. 1977. Animacy, objects and clitics in Sesotho. *Studies in African Languages* 8:199–218.

Morton, Eugene S. 1994. Sound symbolism and its role in non-human vertebrate communication. In Hinton, Nichols, and Ohala, pp. 348–65.

Moses, Peter. 1993. Non-consent in rape: a critique of the 'no means yes' controversy. *Alternative Law Journal* 18/6:290–92.

Nash, Walter. 1993. *Jargon: Its Uses and Abuses.* Oxford: Blackwell.

Neale, Stephen. 1990. *Descriptions*. Cambridge, MA: MIT Press. [As the title suggests, Neale is a Russellian]

Neisser, U. (ed.) 1987a. *Concepts and Conceptual Developments: Ecological and Intellectual Factors in Categorization*. Cambridge: Cambridge University Press.

Neisser, U. 1987b. From direct perception to conceptual structure. In Neisser (ed), pp. 11–23.

The New Grove Dictionary of Jazz, ed. Barry Kernfeld. London: Macmillan. 1994.

Newmeyer, Frederick J. 1980. *Linguistic Theory in America: The First Quarter Century of Transformational Generative Grammar*. New York: Academic Press.

Nida, Eugene A. 1951. A system for the description of semantic elements. *Word* 7:1–14.

Nida, Eugene A. 1975. *Componential Analysis of Meaning: An Introduction to Semantic Structures*. The Hague: Mouton.

Ng, Bee Chin and Kate Burridge. 1993. The female radical: portrayal of women in the Chinese script. In *Language and Gender in the Australian Context*, ed. Joanne Winter and Gillian Wigglesworth. Canberra: Australian Review of Applied Linguistics, pp. 54–85.

Noppen, Jean-Pierre van and Edith Hols. 1990. *Metaphor II: A Classified Bibliography of Publications 1985 to 1990*. Amsterdam: Benjamins.

Nunberg, Geoffrey, Ivan A. Sag and Thomas Wasow. 1994. Idioms. *Language* 70:491–538.

OED = Oxford English Dictionary. 2nd edn. Oxford: Clarendon Press. 1989. Also available on Compact Disc.

Ogden, Charles K. and Ivor A. Richards. 1949. *The Meaning of Meaning*. 10th edn. London: Routledge and Kegan Paul.

Ohala, John J. 1994. The frequency code underlies the sound-symbolic use of voice pitch. In Hinton, Nichols, and Ohala, pp. 325–47.

Ojeda, Almerindo. 1993. *Linguistic Individuals*. CSLI Lecture Notes #31. Stanford: Center for the Study of Language and Information.

Osgood, Charles E., George J. Suci and Percy H. Tannenbaum. 1957. *The Measurement of Meaning*. Urbana: University of Illinois Press.

Osherson, Dan N. and Edward E. Smith. 1981. On the adequacy of prototype theory as a theory of concepts. *Cognition* 9:35–58.

Oswalt, Robert L. 1994. Inanimate imitatives in English. In Hinton, Nichols, and Ohala, pp. 293–306.

Palmer, Frank R. 1986. *Mood and Modality*. Cambridge: Cambridge University Press.

Pannick, David. 1985. The law. In Enright (ed.), pp. 135–50.

Parsons, Terence. 1980. *Nonexistent Objects*. New Haven: Yale University Press.

Partee, Barbara H. 1972. Opacity, coreference, and pronouns. In *Semantics of Natural Language*, ed. Donald Davidson and Gilbert Harman. Dordrecht: Reidel, pp. 415–41.

Partee, Barbara H. 1979. Semantics – mathematics or psychology. In *Semantics from Different Points of View*, ed. Rainer Bäuerle, Urs Egli and Arnim von Stechow. Berlin: Springer-Verlag, pp. 1–14.

Partee, Barbara H., Alice ter Meulen, and Robert E. Wall. 1990. *Mathematical Methods in Linguistics*. Dordrecht: Kluwer.

Partridge, Eric. 1952. Introduction to *Chamber of Horrors: A glossary of official Jargon both English and American*, ed. 'Vigilans'. London: Andre Deutsch.

Partridge, Eric. 1970. *A Dictionary of Slang and Unconventional English*. 2 Vols. 7th edn. London: Routledge and Kegan Paul.

Pauwels, Anne. 1991. *Non-Discriminatory Language*. Canberra: Australian Government
    Publishing Service.
Peeters, Bert. 1991. More about axiological fields. *Canadian Journal of Linguistics* 36:113–36.
Peeters, Bert. 1994. L'axiologie conceptuelle: presentation d'une recherche en cours. *Cahiers de
    l'Institut de Linguistique de Louvain* 20/3,4:89–118.
Peirce, Charles S. 1940. *The Philosophy of Peirce: Selected Writings*, ed. Justus Buchler.
    London: Routledge and Kegan Paul.
Pelletier, Francis J. (ed.). 1979. *Mass Terms: Some Philosophical Problems*. Dordrecht: D.
    Reidel.
Peralta, Jesus T. 1980. Perception and color categories: a view from the I'wak. *Philippine
    Sociological Review* 28:51–59.
Pike, Kenneth L. 1945. *The Intonation of American English*. Ann Arbor: University of Michigan
    Press.
Pinker, Steven. 1989. *Learnability and Cognition: The Acquisition of Argument Structure*.
    Cambridge, MA: MIT Press.
Pirsig, Robert M. 1976. *Zen and the Art of Motorcycle Maintenance*. London: Corgi Books.
Plato. 1956. *Protagoras and Meno,* trans. W.K.C. Guthrie. Harmondsworth: Penguin.
Poincaré, Henri. 1946. *The Foundations of Science: Science and Hypothesis, The Value of
    Science, Science and Method*, trans. George B. Halstead. Lancaster, PA: The Science Press.
Pollard, Carl and Ivan Sag. 1994. *Head Driven Phrase Structure Grammar*. Chicago: University
    of Chicago Press.
Pope, Alexander. 1924. *Collected Poems* ed. Ernest Rhys. Everyman's Library No 760. London:
    Dent.
Porzig, Walter. 1950. *Das Wunder der Sprache*. Bern: Francke.
Pride, John B. and Janet Holmes (eds). 1972. *Sociolinguistics*. Harmondsworth: Penguin.
Pulman, Stephen G. 1983. *Word Meaning and Belief*. London: Croom Helm. [A useful
    introduction to semantics]
Pustejovsky, James. 1995. *The Generative Lexicon*. Cambridge, MA: MIT Press.
Putnam, Hilary. 1962. It ain't necessarily so. *Journal of Philosophy* 59:658–71. Reprinted in
    Mathematics, Matter and Method: Philosophical Papers. 1975. Cambridge: Cambridge
    University Press, vol. 1, pp. 237–49.
Putnam, Hilary. 1975. The meaning of 'meaning'. In Gunderson, pp. 131–93.
Pütz, Martin and Marjolijn Verspoor (eds). 2000. *Explorations in Linguistic Relativity*.
    Amsterdam: John Benjamins.
Quine, Willard V.O. 1956. Quantifiers and propositional attitudes. *Journal of Philosophy*
    53:177–87. Reprinted in Linsky 1971 pp. 101–11.
Quine, Willard V.O. 1960. *Word and Object*. Cambridge, MA: MIT Press.
Quine, Willard V.O. 1961 [1953]. *From a Logical Point of View: 9 Logico-Philosophical
    Essays*. Cambridge, MA: Harvard University Press.
Ransom, Evelyn N. 1977. Definiteness, animacy and NP ordering. In *Proceedings of the Third
    Annual Meeting of the Berkeley Linguistics Society*. University of California, Berkeley, pp.
    418–29.
Read, Allen W. 1977. *Classic American Graffiti: Lexical Evidence from Folk Epigraphy in
    Western North America*. Waukesha, WI: Maledicta Press. (First published in Paris, 1935)
Recanati, François. 1987. *Meaning and Force: The Pragmatics of Performative Utterances*.
    Cambridge: Cambridge University Press.

Recanati, François. 1993. *Direct Reference: From Language to Thought*. Oxford: Blackwell.

Reinhart, Tanya. 1976. *The Syntactic Domain of Anaphora*. PhD Dissertation, MIT.

Reinhart, Tanya. 1980. Conditions of coherence. *Poetics Today* 1:61–180.

Reinhart, Tanya. 1983. *Anaphora and Semantic Interpretation*. London: Croom Helm.

Reinhart, Tanya. 1986. On the interpretation of 'donkey' sentences. In Traugott, et al. (eds), pp. 103–22.

Rhodes, Richard. 1994. Aural images. In Hinton, Nichols, and Ohala, pp. 276–92.

Rosch, Eleanor. 1973. On the internal structure of perceptual and semantic categories. In Moore (ed.), pp. 111–44.

Rosch, Eleanor. 1978. Principles of categorization. In *Cognition and Categorization*, ed. Eleanor Rosch and L.L. Lloyd. Hillsdale: Erlbaum, pp. 27–48.

Rosch, Eleanor, C.B. Mervis, W.D. Gray, D.M. Johnson, and P. Boyes-Brame. 1976. Basic objects in natural categories. *Cognitive Psychology* 8:382–439.

Rosenberg, Jay and Charles Travis (eds). 1971. *Readings in the Philosophy of Language*. Englewood Cliffs: Prentice-Hall.

Ross, John R. 1967. *Constraints on Variables in Syntax*. PhD Dissertation, MIT.

Ross, John R. 1972. Act. In Davidson and Gilbert Harman, pp. 70–126.

Rusiecki, Jan. 1985. *Adjectives and Comparison in English: a Semantic Study*. London: Longman.

Russell, Bertrand. 1905. On denoting. *Mind*. Reprinted in *Logic and Knowledge*. 1956. London: Allen and Unwin. [Should be read by every student of semantics]

Russell, Bertrand. 1918. Knowledge acquaintance and knowledge description. In *Mysticism and Logic and Other Essays*. London: Allen and Unwin, pp. 209–32.

Sacks, Harvey, Emmanuel Schegloff and Gail Jefferson. 1974. A simplest systematics for the organization of turn-taking for conversation. *Language* 50:696–735.

Sadock, Jerrold M. 1974. *Toward a Linguistic Theory of Speech Acts*. New York: Academic Press.

Sadock, Jerry M. and Arnold Zwicky. 1985. Speech act distinctions in syntax. In *Language Typology and Syntactic Description*. Vol. I. *Clause Structure*, ed Timothy Shopen. Cambridge University Press, Cambridge, pp. 155–96.

Sanada, Shinji. 1993. The dynamics of honorific behavior in a rural community in Japan. *Multilingua* 12:81–94.

Sanctius, F. 1585. *Minerva, seu de Causis Lingue*. Madrid.

Sapir, Edward. 1921. *Language*. New York: Harcourt, Brace.

Sapir, Edward. 1929. The status of linguistics as a science *Language* 5:207–14. Reprinted in *Culture, Language and Society: Selected Essays*, ed. D.G. Mandelbaum, Berkeley: U of Cal. Press, 1956, pp. 65–77. Also in *Selected Writings of Edward Sapir in Language, Culture and Personality*, ed. D.G. Mandelbaum, Berkeley: University of California Press, 1949.

Saussure, Ferdinand de. 1974 [1915]. *A Course in General Linguistics* ed. Charles Bally and Albert Sechehaye, trans. Wade Baskin. Glasgow: Fontana/Collins.

Scalise, Sergio. 1986. *Generative Morphology*. 2nd edn. Dordrecht: Foris.

Schank, Roger C. 1982. *Dynamic Memory: a Theory of Reminding and Learning in Computers and People*. Cambridge: Cambridge University Press.

Schank, Roger C. 1984. *The Cognitive Computer*. Reading, MA: Addison-Wesley.

Schank, Roger C. 1986. *Explanation Patterns*. Hillsdale, NJ: Lawrence Erlbaum.

Schank, Roger C. and Robert C. Abelson. 1977. *Scripts, Plans, Goals and Understanding: An Inquiry into Human Knowledge Structures.* Hillsdale, NJ: Lawrence Erlbaum. [The classic work on scripts]

Schein, Barry. 1993. *Plurals and Events.* Cambridge, MA: MIT Press.

Schiffrin, Deborah. 1994. *Approaches to Discourse.* Oxford: Blackwell.

Schmidt, Annette. 1985. *Young People's Dyirbal: an example of language death from Australia.* Cambridge: Cambridge University Press.

Schreiber, Peter A. 1972. Style disjuncts and the performative analysis. *Linguistic Inquiry* 3:321–47.

Schwartz, Linda. 1993. On the syntactic and semantic alignment of attributive and identificational constructions. In Van Valin (ed.), 1993b, pp. 433–63.

Schwartz, Stephen P. (ed.). 1977. *Naming, Necessity, and Natural Kinds.* Ithaca, NY: Cornell University Press.

Schwartz, Stephen P. 1980. Natural kinds and nominal kinds. *Mind* 89:182–95.

Scollon, Ronald and Suzanne Wong Scollon. 1995. *Intercultural Communication: A Discourse Approach.* Oxford and Malden, MA: Blackwell

Scott, Sir Walter. 1907 [1816]. *The Antiquary.* London: Dent.

Searle, John R. 1958. Proper names. *Mind* 67:166–73. Reprinted in Caton (ed.), 1963, pp. 154–61.

Searle, John R. 1969. *Speech Acts.* London: Cambridge University Press. [A classic]

Searle, John R. 1975a. A taxonomy of illocutionary acts. In Gunderson (ed.), pp. 344–69. Reprinted in *Language in Society* 5, 1976:1–23 and Searle 1979.

Searle, John R. 1975b. Indirect speech acts. In Cole and Morgan (eds) 1975, pp. 59–82. Reprinted in Searle 1979.

Searle, John R. 1979. *Expression and Meaning: Studies in the Theory of Speech Acts.* Cambridge: Cambridge University Press. [A valuable collection of Searle's papers]

Sebeok, Thomas A. 1994. *An Introduction to Semiotics.* London: Pinter.

Selkirk, Elizabeth O. 1982. *The Syntax of Words.* Cambridge, MA: MIT Press.

Seuren, Pieter A.M. 1973. The comparative. *Generative Grammar in Europe*, ed. Ferenc Kiefer and Nicolas Ruwet. Dordrecht: Reidel, pp. 528–64.

Seuren, Pieter A.M. 1984. The comparative revisited. *Journal of Semantics* 3:109–42.

Seuren, Peter A.M. 1985. *Discourse Semantics.* Oxford: Basil Blackwell. [A valuable monograph on the topic]

Seuren, Peter A.M. 1994. Donkey sentences. In *Encyclopedia of Language and Linguistics*, ed. Ron Asher. Oxford: Pergamon Press, vol. 2, pp.1059f.

Shakespeare, William. 1951. *The Complete Works,* ed. Peter Alexander. London and Glasgow: Collins.

Shapin, Steven. 1994. *A Social History of Truth: Civility and Science in Seventeenth-Century England.* Chicago: Chicago University Press.

Shibatani, Masayoshi (ed.). 1988. *Passive and Voice.* Amsterdam and Philadelphia: John Benjamins

Shibatani, Masayoshi. 1994. Honorifics. In *Encyclopedia of Language and Linguistics*, ed. Ron Asher. Oxford: Pergamon Press, vol. 3, pp. 1600–8.

Shipley, Joseph T. 1977. The origin of our strongest taboo-word. *Maledicta* 1:23–29.

Siewierska, Anna M. 1984. *The Passive: A Comparative Linguistic Analysis.* London: Croom Helm.

Simons, Gary F. 1982. Word taboo and comparative austronesian linguistics. In *Papers from the Third International Conference on Austronesian Linguistics*. Vol 3. *Accent on Variety*, ed. Amran Halim, Lois Carrington and Stephen A. Wurm. Canberra: Pacific Linguistics, pp. 157–226.

Simpson, Ken and Nicolas Day. 1993. *Field Guide to the Birds of Australia*. 4th edn. Melbourne: Viking O'Neil

Small, Steven I, Garrison W. Cottrell, and Michael K. Tanenhaus (eds). 1988. *Lexical Ambiguity Resolution*. San Mateo: Morgan Kaufman Publishers.

Smith, Philip M. 1985. *Language, The Sexes, and Society*. Oxford: Basil Blackwell.

Sperber, Dan and Deirdre Wilson. 1995. *Relevance*. (2nd edn) Oxford: Blackwell. [The classic work on relevance theory, put forward as a cognitive alternative to Grice's cooperative principle]

Stalnaker, Robert C. 1973. Presupposition. *Journal of Philosophical Logic* 2:77–96.

Stalnaker, Robert C. 1974. Pragmatic presupposition. In *Semantics and Philosophy*, ed. M.K. Munitz and P.K. Unger. New York: New York University Press.

Stalnaker, Robert C. 1978. Assertion. In *Syntax and Semantics 9: Pragmatics*, ed. Peter Cole. New York: Academic Press, pp. 315–32.

Steedman, Mark. 1997. Temporality. In Benthem and Meulen (eds), pp. 895–938.

Steinberg, Danny D. and Leon A. Jakobovits (eds). 1971. *Semantics: An Interdisciplinary Reader in Philosophy, Linguistics, and Psychology*. London: Cambridge University Press.

Stern, Gustaf. 1965 [1931]. *Meaning and Change of Meaning (with Special Reference to the English Language)*. Bloomington: Indiana University Press.

Strawson, Peter F. 1950. On referring. *Mind* 59:320–44. Reprinted in Rosenberg and Travis (eds), 1971, pp 175–95.

Strawson, Peter F. 1952. *Introduction to Logical Theory*. London: Methuen.

Strawson, Peter F. 1959. *Individuals: an essay in descriptive metaphysics*. London: Methuen.

Svorou, Soteria. 1994. *The Grammar of Space*. Amsterdam: Benjamins.

Swadesh, Morris. 1955. Towards greater accuracy in lexico-statistic dating. *International Journal of American Linguistics* 21/2:121–37.

Sweetser, Eve. 1987. The definition of *lie*. In *Cultural Models in Language and Thought*, ed. Dorothy Holland and Naomi Quinn. Cambridge: Cambridge University Press, pp. 43–66.

Sweetser, Eve. 1990. *From Etymology to Pragmatics: Metaphorical and Cultural Aspects of Semantic Structure*. Cambridge: Cambridge University Press.

Swift, Jonathan. 1958 [1735]. *Gulliver's Travels and Other Writings Jonathan Swift*, ed. Ricardo Quintana. New York: Random House.

Talmy, Leonard. 1978. The relation of grammar to cognition. In *Proceedings of TINLAP-2: Theoretical Issues in Natural Language Processing*. Urbana: University of Illinois.

Tannen, Deborah. 1990. *You Just Don't Understand: Women and Men in Conversation*. New York: William Morrow and Milsons Point N.S.W.: Random House

Tarski, Alfred. 1956. The concept of truth in formalized languages. In *Logic, Semantics, Metamathematics*. Oxford: Clarendon Press, pp. 152–278.

Taylor, John R. 1996. On running and jogging. *Cognitive Linguistics* 7:21–34.

Tesnière, Louis. 1959. *Éléments de syntaxe structurale*. Paris: Klincksieck.

Thorndyke, Perry W. 1976. The role of inferences in discourse comprehension. *Journal of Verbal Learning and Verbal Behavior* 15:437–46.

Thorndyke, Perry W. 1977. Cognitive structures in comprehension and memory of narrative discourse. *Cognitive Psychology* 9:77–110.

Thornton, Agathe. 1987. *Maori Oral Literature as Seen a Classicist.* Dunedin: University of Otago Press.

Thun, Nils. 1963. *Reduplicative Words in English: A Study of the Types 'Tick-tick', 'Hurly-burly' and 'Shilly-shally'.* Uppsala.

Traugott, Elizabeth C., Alice ter Meulen, Judy S. Reilly, and Charles A. Ferguson (eds). 1986. *On Conditionals.* Cambridge: Cambridge University Press. [A valuable collection of papers]

Trier, Jost. 1931. *Der Deutsche Wortschatz im Sinnbezirk des Verstandes: die Geschichte eines Sprachlichen Feldes.* Heidelberg.

Trubetzkoy, Nikolaj S. 1939. *Grundzüge der Phonologie. Travaux du Cercle Linguistique de Prague* 7. Republished as *Principles of Phonology,* trans. Christiane A.M. Baltaxe. 1969. Berkeley and Los Angeles: University of California Press.

Tsohatzidis, Savas L. (ed.). 1990. *Meanings and Prototypes: Studies in Linguistic Categorization.* London: Routledge. [A useful compendium]

Tversky, Barbara. 1990. Where partonomies and taxonomies meet. In Tsohatzidis (ed.), pp. 334–44.

Tyler, Stephen A. (ed.). 1969. *Cognitive Anthropology.* New York: Holt, Rinehart and Winston.

Ullmann, Stephen. 1962. *Semantics: An Introduction to the Science of Meaning.* Oxford: Blackwell.

Ultan, Russell. 1978. On the development of the definite article. In *Language Universals* ed. Hansjakob Seiler. Tübingen: Gunter Narr, pp. 249–65.

Uyl, Martijn den and Herre van Oostendorp 1980. *Macrostructures: an Interdisciplinary Study of Global Structures in Discourse, Interaction and Cognition.* Hillsdale: Lawrence Erlbaum.

Valenstein, Edward and Kenneth M. Heilman. 1979. Emotional disorders resulting from lesions of the central nervous system. In *Clinical Neuropsychology,* ed. Heilman and Valenstein. New York: Oxford University Press, pp. 413–38.

Vandeloise, Claude. 1990. Representation, prototypes, and centrality. In Tsohatzidis (ed.), pp. 403–37.

Vandeloise, Claude. 1991. *Spatial Prepositions: A Case Study from French,* trans. Anna R.K. Bosch. Chicago: Chicago University Press.

Vaught, Robert L. 1995. *Set Theory: An Introduction.* 2nd edn. Boston: Birkhauser.

Van Valin, Robert D. Jr. 1990. Semantic parameters of split intransitivity. *Language* 66:221–60.

Van Valin, Robert D. Jr. 1993a. A synopsis of role and reference grammar. In Van Valin (ed.) 1993b, pp. 1–164.

Van Valin, Robert D. Jr (ed.) 1993b. *Advances in Role and Reference Grammar.* Amsterdam: John Benjamins.

Van Valin, Robert D. Jr and Randy LaPolla. 1997. *Syntax: Structure, Meaning, and Function.* Cambridge: Cambridge University Press. [The most recent and comprehensive account of RRG]

Van Valin, Robert D. Jr and David P. Wilkins. 1993. Predicting syntactic structure from semantic representations: *remember* in English and its equivalents in Mparntwe Arrernte. In Van Valin (ed.) 1993b, pp. 499–534.

Varro, Marcus T. 1938. *De Lingua Latina – On the Latin Language*, trans. Roland G. Kent. Loeb Classical Library 333–4. London: Heinemann.

Veltman, Frank. 1994. Counterfactuals. In *Encyclopedia of Language and Linguistics*, ed. Ron Asher. Oxford: Pergamon Press, vol 3, pp.782f.

Vendler, Zeno. 1967. *Linguistics in Philosophy*. Ithaca, NY: Cornell University Press.

Vendler, Zeno. 1972. *Res Cogitans*. Ithaca, NY: Cornell University Press.

Wardhaugh, Ronald. 1986. *An Introduction to Sociolinguistics*. Oxford: Basil Blackwell.

Watts, Richard J., Sachiko Ide, and Konrad Ehlich (eds). 1992. *Politeness in Language: Studies in its History, Theory, and Practice*. Berlin: Mouton de Gruyter.

Webster's New Collegiate Dictionary. 1977. Springfield, MA: G and C Merriam.

Weinreich, Uriel. 1966. Explorations in semantic theory. In *Current Trends in Linguistics 3*, ed. Thomas A. Sebeok. The Hague: Mouton, pp. 395–477. Reprinted in Weinreich 1980, pp. 99–201.

Weinreich, Uriel. 1980. *Weinreich on Semantics,* ed. William Labov and Beatrice S. Weinreich. Philadelphia: University of Pennsylvania Press. [All Weinreich's papers on lexicography and semantics]

Welman, J.B. 1948. *Preliminary Survey of the Freshwater Fishes of Nigeria*. Lagos: Government Printer.

Wertheimer, Max. 1959. *Productive Thinking*. New York: Harper.

Weisgerber, Leo. 1950. *Vom Weltbild der Deutschen Sprache*. Düsseldorf: Schwann.

White, John S. 1992. Lexical and world knowledge: theoretical and applied viewpoints. In *Lexical Semantics and Knowledge Representation*, ed. James Pustejovsky and S. Bergler. Berlin: Springer, pp. 171–83.

Whitney, William D. 1888. *A Compendious German Grammar*. 6th edn. New York: Holt, Rinehart and Winston.

Whorf, Benjamin L. 1956. *Language, Thought, and Reality: Selected Writings*, ed. John B. Carroll. Cambridge, MA: MIT Press. [All the classic papers, but see also Lee 1996]

Wierzbicka, Anna. 1972. *Semantic Primitives*. Berlin: Athenaum.

Wierzbicka, Anna. 1980. *Lingua Mentalis: the Semantics of Natural Language*. Sydney: Academic Press.

Wierzbicka, Anna. 1984. Cups and mugs: lexicography and conceptual analysis. *Australian Journal of Linguistics* 4:205–56.

Wierzbicka, Anna. 1985. *Lexicography and Conceptual Analysis*. Ann Arbor, MI: Karoma.

Wierzbicka, Anna. 1987. *English Speech Act Verbs: A Semantic Dictionary*. Sydney: Academic Press.

Wierzbicka, Anna. 1988. *The Semantics of Grammar*. Amsterdam: John Benjamins.

Wierzbicka, Anna. 1990a. Russian personal names: the semantics of expressive derivation. *International Journal of Slavic Linguistics and Poetics*. Special issue ed. C. Chvany.

Wierzbicka, Anna. 1990b. The semantics of color terms: semantics, culture, and cognition. *Cognitive Linguistics* 1:99–150.

Wierzbicka, Anna. 1991. *Cross-Cultural Pragmatics: The Semantics of Human Interaction*. Berlin: Mouton de Gruyter.

Wierzbicka, Anna. 1992a. Semantic primitives and semantic fields. In Lehrer and Kittay (eds), pp. 209–27.

Wierzbicka, Anna. 1992b. Personal names and expressive derivation. In Wierzbicka 1992c, pp. 225–307.

Wierzbicka, Anna. 1992c. *Semantics, Culture, and Cognition: Universal Human Concepts in Culture-specific Configurations*. New York: Oxford University Press.

Wierzbicka, Anna. 1992d. The search for semantic primitives. In *Thirty Years of Linguistic Evolution: Studies in Honor of René Dirven on the Occasion of his Sixtieth Birthday*, ed. Martin Putz. Amsterdam: John Benjamins.

Wierzbicka, Anna. 1994. Semantic primitives across languages. In Goddard and Wierzbicka (eds), pp. 445–500.

Wierzbicka, Anna. 1996. *Semantics: Primes and Universals*. Oxford: Oxford University Press.

Wilkins, David P. and Robert D. Van Valin Jr. 1993. *The Case for Case Reopened: Agents and Agency Revisited*. Technical Report 93–2. Buffalo: Center for Cognitive Science. Abbreviated version 'The case for "effector": Case roles, agents, and agency revisited' in *Grammatical Constructions*, ed. Masayoshi Shibatani and Sandra A. Thompson. Oxford: Oxford University Press. 1996, pp. 289–322.

Wilkins, John. 1668. *Essay toward a Real Character and a Philosophical Language*. London: Royal Society. Facsimile, 1968. Menston: Scolar Press.

Wilkins, Wendy. 1988a. Thematic structure and reflexivization. In Wilkins (ed.), 1988b, pp. 191–214.

Wilkins, Wendy (ed.). 1988b. *Syntax and Semantics 21: Thematic Relations*. New York: Academic Press.

Williams, Edwin. 1981. On the notions "lexically related" and "head of a word". *Linguistic Inquiry* 12:245–74.

Wittgenstein, Ludwig. 1953. *Philosophical Investigations*. Oxford: Blackwell.

Wright, Walter D. 1978 [1956]. *A First English Companion*. Digswell Place, Welwyn: James Nisbet.

Zadeh, Lotfi A. 1965. Fuzzy sets. *Information and Control* 8:338–53.

Zadeh, Lotfi A. 1971. Quantitative fuzzy semantics. *Information Sciences* 3:159–76.

Zadeh, Lotfi A. 1972. A fuzzy-set-theoretic interpretation of linguistic hedges. *Journal of Cybernetics* 2:4–34.

Zipf, George K. 1948. *Human Behavior and the Principle of Least Effort*. Cambridge, MA: Addison-Wesley.

Zubin, David A. 1979. Discourse function of morphology: the focus system in German. In Givón (ed.) 1979b, pp. 469–504.

Zubin, David A. and Klaus M. Köpcke. 1986. Gender and folk-taxonomy: the indexical relation between grammatical and lexical categorization. In Craig (ed.), pp. 139–80. [Shows semantic systems within German gender assignment]

Zwicky, Arnold and Ann Zwicky. 1982. Register as a dimension of linguistic variation. In Kittredge and Lehrberger (eds), pp. 213–18.

Index

Items in lists of keywords and phrases are not indexed. Entries in **bold type** indicate greater significance, e.g. the location of definitions. Sometimes the index identifies only the first few occurrences of those items which occur very frequently throughout the subsequent text.